Armistice!

Mini Book Series

VOLUME XXXII

By

Ronald Pattinson

Mini Book Series volume XXXII: Armistice!

Copyright © 2018 Ronald Pattinson

The right of Ronald Pattinson to be identified as the author of his work has been asserted by him in accordance with the

COPYRIGHT, DESIGNS AND PATENTS ACT OF 1988

All rights reserved. No part of this publication may be reproduced, stored in a retrieval system, or transmitted, in any form or by any means without the prior written permission of the publisher, nor be otherwise circulated in any form other than that in which it is published and without a similar condition being imposed upon the subsequent purchaser.

1st edition

Published in November 2018 by

Kilderkin
171 hs Warmondstraat, Amsterdam, Noord- Holland

ISBN 978-94-90270-35-3

Contents

Armistice!...1
Copyright © 2018 Ronald Pattinson...2
Foreword...13
I Brewing...14
    Introduction...15
    Ingredients..15
        Malt..16
        Hops...18
        Sugar..19
        Adjuncts...22
        Yeast...22
    Restrictions on the drinks trade..23
        Beer output...24
        Timeline of restrictions...25
        Government Ale...28
        Sticking to the rules..29
        Malting...30
        Styles by decree..32
    Tax...35
    Wages and Prices..36
        Wages...36
        Prices..37
        Publicans' profits..38
        Brewery profits...39
    Pubs...41
        Opening hours..42
        Women in pubs..43
        The Carlisle State Management Scheme..44
    Beer Supply..46
    Brewing outside the UK..48
        Beer production during WW I...48
        Belgium..49
        France...49
        Germany...49
        Austria..54
        Denmark...56
        Holland...62
    The aftermath of WW I...64
        World beer production 1912 - 1922..64
        Hop production by country 1900 - 1921..66
II Beer styles...68
    Introduction..69
        Beers:..70
    Mild Ale...72
        Before WW I...72
        During WW I..73
        After WW I...83
    Brown Ale..88
        Before WW I...88

During WW I	88
After WW I	89
Pale Ale	90
Before WW I	90
During WW I	93
After WW I	99
IPA	105
Before WW I	105
During WW I	105
After WW I	113
Porter	116
Before WW I	116
During WW I	116
After WW I	118
Stout	120
Before WW I	120
During WW I	122
After WW I	128
Strong Ales	138
Burton Ale	138
Old Ale	141
Barley Wine	144
Scotch Ale	147
Before WW I	147
During WW I	147
After WW I	149
Lager	151
III Let's Brew	155
Introduction to recipes	156
Adnams	157
1914 Adnams X Ale	158
1914 Adnams XX Ale	159
1915 Adnams XXXX Ale	160
1914 Adnams BLB	161
1914 Adnams BS	162
1914 Adnams Double Stout	163
1914 Adnams Tally Ho	165
1915 Adnams PA	166
1916 Adnams XX Ale	167
1916 Adnams BLB	168
1916 Adnams Double Stout	169
1916 Adnams Tally Ho	170
1917 Adnams XX	171
1917 Adnams PA	172
1917 Adnams Double Stout	173
1917 Adnams Tally Ho	174
1918 Adnams XX	175
1918 Adnams PA	176
1919 Adnams Double Stout	177
1921 Adnams XX	178

1921 Adnams PA 179
1921 Adnams XXXX 180
Barclay Perkins 181
  1914 Barclay Perkins X Ale 184
  1914 Barclay Perkins XLK (trade) 185
  1914 Barclay Perkins XLK (bottling) 186
  1914 Barclay Perkins PA 187
  1914 Barclay Perkins KK 188
  1915 Barclay Perkins Dark Lager 189
  1916 Barclay Perkins X Ale 190
  1916 Barclay Perkins XLK (trade) 191
  1916 Barclay Perkins XLK (bottling) 192
  1916 Barclay Perkins XLK (Watney) 193
  1916 Barclay Perkins PA 194
  1916 Barclay Perkins KK 195
  1917 Barclay Perkins X 196
  1917 Barclay Perkins GA 197
  1917 Barclay Perkins XLK (trade) 198
  1917 Barclay Perkins XLK (crate) 199
  1918 Barclay Perkins Ale 4d 200
  1918 Barclay Perkins XLK (trade) 201
  1918 Barclay Perkins XLK (crate) 202
  1919 Barclay Perkins X Ale 203
  1919 Barclay Perkins Ale 4d 204
  1919 Barclay Perkins XLK (trade) 205
  1919 Barclay Perkins XLK (bottling) 206
  1919 Barclay Perkins XLK (crate) 207
  1919 Barclay Perkins KK 208
  1921 Barclay Perkins X Ale 209
  1921 Barclay Perkins Ale 5d 210
  1921 Barclay Perkins XLK (trade) 211
  1921 Barclay Perkins XLK (bottling) 212
  1921 Barclay Perkins XLK (crate) 213
  1921 Barclay Perkins PA 214
  1921 Barclay Perkins KK 215
  1921 Barclay Perkins KK (bottling) 216
  1921 Barclay Perkins BS Exp 217
  1921 Barclay Perkins IBS 219
  1922 Barclay Perkins BS 220
  1922 Barclay Perkins RNS 221
  1921 Barclay Perkins BS S 222
  1922 Barclay Perkins BBS Export 223
Boddington 224
  1913 Boddington XXX 225
  1914 Boddington B 227
  1914 Boddington BB 228
  1914 Boddington Stout 229
  1914 Boddington AK 231
  1914 Boddington PA 232
  1914 Boddington IP 233

1914 Boddington CC 234
1915 Boddington XXX 235
1915 Boddington B 236
1915 Boddington BB 237
1915 Boddington Stout 238
1915 Boddington AK 239
1915 Boddington IP 240
1915 Boddington CC 241
1917 Boddington AK 242
1917 Boddington CC 243
1917 Boddington XX (24th April) 244
1917 Boddington Stout (25th April) 245
1917 Boddington XXX (1st May) 246
1917 Boddington IP (7th May) 247
1917 Boddington Bitter (3rd Oct) 248
1918 Boddington B 249
1918 Boddington XX 250
1918 Boddington Bitter 251
1918 Boddington IP 252
1918 Boddington Stout 253
1918 Boddington CC 254
1919 Boddington B 255
1919 Boddington XX 256
1919 Boddington Bitter 257
1919 Boddington IP 258
1919 Boddington Stout 259
1921 Boddington XX 260
1921 Boddington IP 261
1921 Boddington CC 262
1921 Boddington Stout 263
Courage 264
1914 Courage X Ale 270
1914 Courage XX 271
1914 Courage Porter 272
1914 Courage Double Stout 273
1914 Courage Imperial Stout 274
1916 Courage X Ale 275
1916 Courage Porter 276
1916 Courage Double Stout 277
1916 Courage KK 278
1917 Courage X Ale 279
1917 Courage Porter 280
1917 Courage Double Stout 281
1917 Courage KK 282
1918 Courage X Ale (January) 283
1918 Courage Stout 284
1918 Courage Double Stout 285
1918 Courage Porter 286
1918 Courage X Ale (November) 287
1919 Courage Stout 288

1919 Courage X Ale 289
1920 Courage X Ale 290
1920 Courage Porter 291
1920 Courage Double Stout 292
1920 Courage SA 293
Crowley 294
1914 Crowley AK 295
1914 Crowley L 296
1914 Crowley B 297
1914 Crowley BB 298
1914 Crowley BBB 299
1914 Crowley Porter 300
1914 Crowley Stout 301
1916 Crowley AK 302
1916 Crowley AK F 303
1916 Crowley L 304
1916 Crowley B 305
1916 Crowley BB 306
1916 Crowley BBB 307
1916 Crowley Porter 308
1916 Crowley Stout 309
1917 Crowley L 310
1917 Crowley AK 311
1917 Crowley BB 312
1917 Crowley Porter 313
1917 Crowley Stout 314
1918 Crowley AK 315
1918 Crowley BBB 316
1918 Crowley Stout 317
1919 Crowley AK 318
1919 Crowley BBB 319
1919 Crowley Stout 320
Drybrough 321
1913 Drybrough PI 323
1913 Drybrough PI 60/- 324
1913 Drybrough PI 48/- 325
1913 Drybrough PI 42/- 326
1913 Drybrough XP 327
1915 Drybrough 100/- Mild 328
1915 Drybrough XXX Stout 329
1917 Drybrough PI 330
1917 Drybrough PI 60/- 331
1917 Drybrough PI 42/- 332
1917 Drybrough PI 48/- 333
1917 Drybrough 80/- Mild 334
1917 Drybrough 60/- Mild 335
1917 Drybrough XXX Stout 336
1918 Drybrough PI 337
1918 Drybrough PI 48/- 338
1918 Drybrough PI X 339

1918 Drybrough XX Stout	340
1919 Drybrough PI 48/-	341
1919 Drybrough PI	342
1919 Drybrough PI 54/-	343
1919 Drybrough PI 60/-	344
1919 Drybrough PI 60/- X	345
1919 Drybrough XX Stout	346
1920 Drybrough PI 48/-	347
1920 Drybrough PI 54/-	348
1920 Drybrough PI 60/-	349
1920 Drybrough Special 8d PA	350
1920 Drybrough BS XXX	351
Fullers	352
1914 Fullers X Ale	353
1914 Fullers PA	354
1914 Fullers AK	355
1914 Fullers Porter	356
1914 Fullers BS	357
1914 Fullers BO	358
1916 Fullers X Ale	359
1916 Fullers AK	360
1916 Fullers PA	361
1916 Fullers Porter	362
1916 Fullers BS	363
1917 Fullers X Ale	364
1917 Fullers AK	365
1917 Fullers PA	366
1917 Fullers Porter	367
1918 Fullers X Ale	368
1918 Fullers AK	369
1918 Fullers PA	370
1918 Fullers Porter	371
1919 Fullers X Ale	372
1919 Fullers XX Ale	373
1919 Fullers BS	374
1919 Fullers Porter	375
1919 Fullers AK	376
1919 Fullers XK	377
1919 Fullers PA	378
1925 Fullers X Ale	379
1925 Fullers BO	380
1925 Fullers XX Ale	381
1925 Fullers XK	382
1925 Fullers AK	383
1925 Fullers PA	384
1925 Fullers Porter	385
1925 Fullers BS	386
Kidd	387
1917 Kidd BB	388
1917 Kidd X	389

1917 Kidd SXXX 390
1917 Kidd XXXX 391
1917 Kidd Porter 392
1917 Kidd Stout 393
1917 Kidd GA X (13th July) 394
1917 Kidd LPA (24th August) 395
1917 Kidd Porter (24th July) 396
1918 Kidd DA 397
1918 Kidd XXXX (16th Jan) 399
1918 Kidd GA (12th April) 400
1918 Kidd Porter (17th April) 401
1918 Kidd Stout 402
1918 Kidd PB (16th April) 403
1918 Kidd XX PB (30th April) 404
1918 Kidd LPA 405
1919 Kidd X 406
1919 Kidd XXX 407
1919 Kidd Stout 408
1919 Kidd PA 409
1920 Kidd X 410
1920 Kidd XXX 411
1920 Kidd Stout 412
1920 Kidd Stock PA 413
Noakes 414
1915 Noakes LBA 415
1915 Noakes Porter 416
1915 Noakes Double Stout 417
1915 Noakes XXX 418
Tetley 419
1916 Tetley X 421
1916 Tetley X1 422
1916 Tetley X2 423
1916 Tetley X3 424
1916 Tetley XX 425
1916 Tetley PA 426
1916 Tetley K 427
1916 Tetley Porter 428
1916 Tetley Stout 429
1919 Tetley X 430
1919 Tetley F 431
1919 Tetley X1 432
1919 Tetley X2 433
1919 Tetley K 434
Truman (Burton) 435
1914 Truman P2 438
1914 Truman P3 439
1914 Truman A 440
1914 Truman No. 8K 441
1914 Truman No. 8 442
1914 Truman No. 7 443

1914 Truman No. 6 444
1914 Truman No. 5 445
1914 Truman No. 3 446
1915 Truman No. 4 447
1915 Truman P1 448
1916 Truman No. 1 Barley Wine 449
1917 Truman P2 450
1917 Truman P3 451
1917 Truman A 452
1917 Truman No. 8 453
1917 Truman No. 7 454
1917 Truman No. 5 455
1917 Truman No. 4 456
1917 Truman No. 1 Barley Wine 457
1917 Truman Stock No. 1 Barley Wine 458
1917 Truman X 459
1917 Truman XX 460
1917 Truman XXX 461
1918 Truman X 462
1918 Truman XXX W 463
1918 Truman XXX 464
1918 Truman XXX S 465
1918 Truman S4 466
1919 Truman P1 467
1919 Truman S4 468
1919 Truman XXX S 469
1919 Truman XXX W 470
1919 Truman XXX 471
1919 Truman XX 472
1919 Truman 6d 473
1919 Truman X 474
Truman (London) 475
1916 Truman (London) X 476
1916 Truman (London) LK 477
1917 Truman (London) X 478
1917 Truman (London) LK (May) 479
1917 Truman Government Ale 480
1917 Truman (London) LK (August) 481
1918 Truman (London) LK 482
1918 Truman (London) Government Ale 483
1918 Truman (London) X 484
Whitbread 485
1914 Whitbread P 488
1914 Whitbread LS 489
1914 Whitbread ES 490
1914 Whitbread Export Stout 491
1914 Whitbread SS 492
1914 Whitbread SSS 493
1914 Whitbread X 494
1914 Whitbread IPA 495

1914 Whitbread Family Ale..496
1914 Whitbread 2PA..497
1914 Whitbread PA..498
1914 Whitbread KK...499
1914 Whitbread 2KKK...500
1914 Whitbread KKK..501
1916 Whitbread X..502
1916 Whitbread IPA..503
1916 Whitbread PA..504
1916 Whitbread KKK..505
1917 Whitbread P..506
1917 Whitbread X..507
1917 Whitbread GA...508
1918 Whitbread MA (strong)...510
1918 Whitbread MA (straight)...511
1918 Whitbread MA (weak)...512
1918 Whitbread IPA..513
1918 Whitbread PA..514
1918 Whitbread P..515
1918 Whitbread Imperial Stout..516
1918 Whitbread LS..517
1919 Whitbread MA..518
1919 Whitbread X..519
1919 Whitbread IPA..520
1919 Whitbread PA..521
1919 Whitbread P..522
1919 Whitbread S..523
1921 Whitbread P..524
1921 Whitbread LS..525
1921 Whitbread KK...526
William Younger..527
  1913 William Younger XXP..529
  1913 William Younger XP...530
  1913 William Younger P..531
  1913 William Younger MM...532
  1914 William Younger Export...533
  1914 William Younger LAE..534
  1914 William Younger SLE...535
  1913 William Younger LDA..536
  1913 William Younger H 60/-..537
  1913 William Younger 60/-..538
  1913 William Younger 80/-..539
  1913 William Younger 100/-..540
  1914 William Younger 160/-..541
  1913 William Younger XX K...542
  1913 William Younger XXXX...543
  1913 William Younger No. 1...544
  1914 William Younger No. 2 Sc..545
  1913 William Younger No. 3...546
  1913 William Younger S1..547

- 1913 William Younger S2 548
- 1913 William Younger MBS 549
- 1913 William Younger DBS 550
- 1917 William Younger P 551
- 1917 William Younger XP 552
- 1917 William Younger XXP 553
- 1917 William Younger LAE 554
- 1917 William Younger Export 555
- 1917 William Younger H 60/- 556
- 1917 William Younger 60/- 557
- 1917 William Younger Mild 558
- 1917 William Younger S1 559
- 1917 William Younger S3 560
- 1917 William Younger No. 1 561
- 1918 William Younger 5B 562
- 1918 William Younger XXP 563
- 1918 William Younger Export 564
- 1918 William Younger S1 565
- 1918 William Younger 5S 566
- 1918 William Younger 5M 567

IV Appendix 568
- Food Control Orders 569
  - Beer 569
  - Malt 585
  - Hops 593
  - Sugar 594
- LICENSING ACT 1921 597
- Licensing Act 1988 598
- Weights and measures 600
  - Weight 600
  - Volume 600
  - Liquid 600
  - Money 600
  - Temperature 601

Foreword

I've been obsessed with WWI ever since I realised how much impact it had on British beer culture. And how even when I started drinking 60 years later, how much had shaped the beer and pub culture I experienced.

Looking back, it's bizarre how readily I accepted that pubs closed for a couple of hours in the afternoon. And that you'd get chucked out at eleven o' clock every evening.

WWI cast a very long shadow on British drinking culture. I can remember my amazement when reading in What's Brewing that the average OG in 1914 was over 1050°. What? Everyone was drinking looney juice like Fuller's ESB?

Ron Pattinson,

Amsterdam 3rd November 2018.

Mini Book Series volume XXXII: Armistice!

I Brewing

Introduction

UK brewing entered WW I in a troubled state. The decade before 1914 had been a difficult one for the industry.

Increased licence duties for breweries and pubs had seriously disrupted the industry. Specifically through a fall in the price of public houses, which left many breweries with nominal share values far in excess of their real assets. Many breweries were forced to reduce their share values. Others went into liquidation, including big names like Allsopp.

Brewers must have been anxious about what the war would mean for them. Most would have expected one thing: an increase in tax. Successive UK governments had used beer as a source of extra revenue.

Here's what happened with beer output and strength across the war years:

UK beer production and average OG 1912 - 1922								
	England		Scotland		Ireland		United Kingdom	
Year	bulk barrels	average OG	bulk barrels	average OG	bulk barrels	average OG	bulk barrels	average OG
1912	30,991,776	1051.76	2,153,569	1048.11	3,330,174	1065.43	36,475,519	1052.72
1913	30,758,800	1051.52	2,119,666	1047.85	3,417,851	1065.73	36,296,317	1052.64
1914	31,737,384	1051.69	2,288,481	1047.67	3,532,902	1065.93	37,558,767	1052.80
1915	29,310,783	1051.16	2,042,477	1046.85	3,412,520	1065.93	34,765,780	1052.35
1916	26,914,428	1050.49	1,917,148	1046.45	3,279,032	1066.43	32,110,608	1051.88
1917	25,497,825	1047.01	1,816,003	1043.16	2,850,170	1065.69	30,163,998	1048.54
1918	16,340,250	1038.25	1,141,114	1036.74	1,603,679	1057.89	19,085,043	1039.81
1919	20,133,048	1029.35	1,325,439	1029.77	1,806,046	1044.43	23,264,533	1030.55
1920	29,891,845	1038.57	2,186,604	1038.83	2,969,498	1043.35	35,047,947	1039.41
1921	28,927,178	1041.72	2,096,080	1042.31	3,481,312	1050.18	34,504,570	1042.61
1922	25,468,663	1042.21	1,770,175	1041.68	2,939,893	1049.44	30,178,731	1042.88
Sources:								
Brewers' Journal 1921, page 246.								
Brewers' Almanack 1928, page 110.								

It's striking how much higher the average OG was in Ireland. And how it got ever more out of sync up to 1916 as it increased while it was falling elsewhere.

Ingredients

Before the war, UK brewers sourced their ingredients from all over the world. This would become a big problem as German U-boat activity seriously disrupted world trade. And brewing ingredients, quite sensibly, didn't receive the highest priority when it came to assigning scarce shipping resources.

The following table shows how the use of different ingredients changed during the war:

UK malt, sugar and adjunct usage 1910 - 1923 (1,000 cwt)								
	Malt		malt adjuncts		unmalted corn		sugar		
year	cwt	%	cwt	%	cwt	%	cwt	%	total (cwts)
1910	18,777	80.20%	1725	7.37%	0	0.00%	2910	12.43%	23,412
1911	19,410	80.20%	1782	7.36%	0	0.00%	3011	12.44%	24,203
1912	19,368	79.63%	1887	7.76%	0	0.00%	3068	12.61%	24,323
1913	19,647	78.39%	2136	8.52%	0	0.00%	3280	13.09%	25,063
1914	19,698	78.58%	2091	8.34%	0	0.00%	3280	13.08%	25,069
1915	16,662	80.86%	1236	6.00%	30	0.15%	2679	13.00%	20,607
1916	15,633	80.56%	1344	6.93%	29	0.15%	2400	12.37%	19,406
1917	10,749	81.55%	801	6.08%	17	0.13%	1614	12.24%	13,181
1918	8,349	90.37%	0	0.00%	0	0.00%	890	9.63%	9,239
1919	11,172	85.26%	351	2.68%	48	0.37%	1532	11.69%	13,103
1920	15,759	83.14%	1023	5.40%	36	0.19%	2136	11.27%	18,954
1921	14,751	83.67%	980	5.56%	26	0.15%	1874	10.63%	17,631
1922	12,420	83.49%	810	5.45%	24	0.16%	1622	10.90%	14,876
1923	10,743	81.56%	804	6.10%	26	0.20%	1599	12.14%	13,172

Source:
The British malting industry since 1830 by Christine Clark, 1998, pages 247-248
Note:
I assume 1 quarter of malt = 3 cwt

Brewers were forced to make changes in the ingredients that they used, mostly through problems with their supply. This applied mostly to imported ingredients, but also to sugar which was both imported and produced locally.

The changes in ingredient use forced by the war were mostly temporary. As soon as supplies of imported ingredients improved, brewer went back to their pre-war habits.

Malt

Though malting was always performed in the UK, before the war barley was imported from every corner of the globe. The most important sources were California, Chile and the Middle East.

Brewers, especially those using a large proportion of adjuncts, liked malt made from Californian six-row barley because of its high diastatic power. In a typical grist, between a quarter and a third of the pale malt was made from foreign six-row barley, the rest being UK 2-row.

Most beers were brewed from a pale malt base with no coloured malts at all. The only exceptions to this were Porter and Stout, which could contain brown, black and Amber malt, and Mild Ale, which often contained crystal malt. The use of crystal malt in Pale Ales was pretty much unknown before WW I.

Supplies of foreign barley gradually dried up during the war, forcing brewers to use all malt from UK barley. Fortunately, as the availability of adjuncts was also reduced, this didn't have as much impact as it might have.

I've seen wild claims that the roasting of malt was forbidden during WW I. This is totally untrue. Not only were there no restrictions on roasting in the Food Control Manual, brewers continued to use brown malt, black malt and roasted barley right through the war years.

There was a big increase in the price of mat during the war. Not surprising, really, given that it was in short supply.

When war broke out, pale malt cost around 40s. a quarter. By 1920, it was around triple that price. What's also fascinating is that the specialist types of pale malt – PA malt, SA malt (Strong Ale) malt and mild malt all disappeared for a while towards the end of the war. It looks like maltsters were trimming their range of products just as brewers did.

Price of malt used by Barclay Perkins 1914 - 1917 (in shillings per quarter)

	1914		1915		1916			1917	
	Mar	Oct	Jun	Oct	Jan	Apr	Oct	Jan	Apr
English pale malt	41.67	39.50	40.10	51.80	61.00	63.20	63.67	70.50	79.00
English PA malt	42.00	42.50	42.00	41.50	67.00	67.00	70.00	79.00	83.25
American pale malt	39.00	38.67	41.88	42.38	50.00	52.67	61.63	64.00	64.00
Indian pale malt	35.50			50.00	53.50		67.25	67.38	
Spanish pale malt					53.50		59.50	69.00	75.50
English mild malt	39.00	40.00	41.00	41.00	60.00	60.00	60.00	60.00	60.00
English SA malt	42.50	43.00	43.00	43.00	67.00			90.00	
Crystal malt	31.00	31.50	32.50	46.00	46.00	46.00		58.00	
Amber malt	37.50	38.50	39.75	44.00	48.00	48.00	70.00	70.00	67.00
Brown malt				30					63
Roasted malt									

Source:
Barclay Perkins brewing records held at the London Metropolitan Archives.

Price of malt used by Barclay Perkins 1917 - 1920 (in shillings per quarter)

	1917	1918			1919			1920	
	Oct	Jan	Apr	Oct	Jan	Apr	Oct	Jan	Apr
English pale malt	81.00	85.50	89.30	91.83	95.25	97.40	93.65	90.25	127.00
English PA malt	84.25	89.00						132.00	132.00
American pale malt	64.00	64.00	80.75	101.17	108.00	108.00	99.50	92.00	117.50
English mild malt									132.00
English SA malt								132.00	132.00
Crystal malt		75.00	85.00	86.00	89.00	89.00	87.50	85.50	125.50
Amber malt	67.00	86.00	89.00	95.00	98.00	98.00	96.00	94.00	132.00
Brown malt	60	60	62	66	68	68	87.5		
Roasted malt				80	84	84	84		

Source:
Barclay Perkins brewing records held at the London Metropolitan Archives

In February 1917 the government enacted a total ban on the malting of barley and the selling of malt. Which must have had huge financial impact on the industry.

After the war's end, brewers were delighted to have Californian barley again to malt and again used a mixture of UK two-row and US six-row pale malt in their grists.

Presumably in attempt to compensate for the drop in gravity, crystal malt occasionally started to feature in Pale Ale grists. Though this was the exception rather than the rule.

Hops

The UK started struggling to grow enough hops to satisfy demand from brewers in the 1850s. As the century progressed, more and more foreign hops were imported.

The principal source was the USA, initially from New York State, later California and Oregon. But hops were imported from every region in the world. Large quantities of European hops were imported, too. Bavarian and Bohemian hops were considered equal to quality UK hops. Lower quality hops from Belgium and France were also used, despite brewers not much caring for them. They did have the big advantage of being cheap.

Despite the UK being one of the world's biggest producers of hops, it was enough to meet the needs of brewing. The industry was dependent on importing large quantities of hops.

There was an enormous fall in the quantity of hops being imported, down to just a few hundred cwts. In 1918. Oddly, one country from which supplies continued to be imported was Belgium, despite most of the country being occupied by the Germans. The one corner still in Belgian hands just happened to include Poperinge, home to the Belgian hop industry.

You can see from the table below that hop imports came to an almost complete stop in the final two years of the war:

Hop production and imports (cwt)								
year	Acreage	UK production	yield per acre	Average price of English hops			net imports of foreign hops	exports of British hops
				£	s.	d.		
1910	32,886	302,675	9.20	5	6	6	172,032	8,927
1915	34,744	254,101	7.31	6	7	0	199,347	8,288
1917	16,946	225,763	13.32	8	15	0	8,530	12,796
1918	15,666	138,491	8.84	18	15	0	259	6,928
1919	16,745	187,795	11.21	20	5	0	154,091	2,606
1920	21,002	258,042	12.29	19	10	0	455,799	3,672
1921	25,133	236,172	9.40	19	10	0	216,571	2,200
Source: 1928 Brewers' Almanack, page 119								

The price of hops also increased dramatically to around three times the pre-war level.

Hop Control

The Hop Control Board was established in 1917 after the government had forced hop growers to grub up half their hop bines and grow food instead. The Board bought the whole of the crop and then sold it on to brewers. During the war the idea was to protect what was left of the hop industry. After it, to help it rebuild and get the acreage back to pre-war levels.

The Hop Controller also fixed the price of English hops. By keeping the price relatively high and not allowing any foreign hops to be purchased by brewers until the whole of the UK crop had been sold, they hoped to prevent a flood of cheap imported hops. The higher the price, the greater the acreage that would be planted, was the reasoning.

It worked to a certain extent, but not completely. Interwar hope acreage peaked at 26,452 in 1922. It remained at 23,000-25,000 acres for the rest of the 1920's, but fell to around 18,000 acres for most of the 1930s. Or about half the pre-WW I level.[1]

After the war the UK hop industry was in a very fragile position. The UK acreage had been reduced and there were plenty of foreign hops available because of the collapse in beer production in particular in Central Europe. Despite the restriction on disposing of the whole UK crop first, large quantities of hops were imported. Up from near zero in 1917 and 1918 to 450,000 cwt. in 1920, the equivalent of a whole year's consumption.

Total quantity of Hops available for consumption in the United Kingdom, and the averages for ten years.						
Year.	Area. Acres.	Estimated Production Cwts.	Imports less Exports. Cwts.	Available for Consumption. Cwts.	Consumption (See Table 2).	% imports
1905	48,967	695,943	83,278	779,221	656,792	12.68%
1908	38,916	470,761	257,792	728,463	562,247	45.85%
1909	32,539	214,484	118,568	333,052	548,445	21.62%
1910	32,886	302,675	163,105	465,780	551,248	29.59%
1911	33,056	328,023	102,167	430,190	574,260	17.79%
1912	34,829	373,438	223,566	596,994	549,507	40.68%
1913	35,676	265,641	234,837	490,478	561,708	41.81%
1914	36,661	507,258	73,778	581,031	559,423	13.19%
average 1905-14	**38,518**	**376,803**	**166,008**	**542,802**	**560,549**	**29.62%**
1915	34,744	254,101	191,059	495,160	467,142	40.90%
1916	31,352	307,856	135,385	443,241	450,257	30.07%
1917	16,626	226,763	4,446	230,209	329,334	1.35%
1918	15,626	138,491	6,664	145,155	263,392	2.53%
1919	16,762	187,795	151,485	339,280	400,000	37.87%
1920	21,685	258,042	452,124	710,166	450,000	100.47%
1921	25,186	236,172	214,364	450,536	425,000	50.44%
Source: 1922 Brewers' Almanack, page 119.						

The Hop Control Board continued to operate until 1924.

Sugar

After the Free Mash Tun Act of 1880, sugar became an important ingredient. The use of sugar had been legal since 1847, but a special duty had to be paid on it which seems to have put brewers off.

After 1880, the use of sugar became increasingly sophisticated. First, through the use of

---
[1] Brewers' Almanack 1955, page 63.

different grades of invert sugar, Nos. 1, 2, 3 and 4, with 1 being the palest and 4 the darkest. Nos. 1 and 2 were mostly used in Pales, no. 3 in Mild Ales and Nos. 3 and 4 in Porter and Stout.

Later, proprietary sugars gained in popularity. These were mixtures of invert sugars and caramel, often formulated for specific styles of beer, such as Mild Ale or Oatmeal Stout.

In 1914, on average 13% of a beer grist consisted of sugar. That included both sugar added during the boil and priming sugars added at racking time.

The biggest problem with sugar, was that it was readily usable in food products. Whereas barley had limited use as a human food and hops none at all. Which meant that brewers were competing with other food industries for the limited supplies of sugar.

Brewers became obsessed with prices during the war, which is handy because it means that the price of every ingredient is listed in the brewing logs. People often assume that sugar was only used in brewing because it was cheaper than malt. During the war, this wasn't necessarily true. And, of course, there were other reasons for brewers to employ sugar. For colour and flavour in Mild, for example.

Here's are examples where the sugar was more expensive than the malt. This is a PA brewed by Whitbread on February 2nd 1917:

> 72 quarters malt total cost 4,574/-, cost per quarter 65.34/-
> 20 quarters No. 1 invert sugar cost 1,496/-, cost per quarter[2] 68/-

This Mild brewed June 7th 1918 is more extreme:

> 140 quarters malt total cost 12,250/-, cost per quarter 87.5/-
> 33 quarters No. 3 invert sugar cost 4,059/-, cost per quarter 123/-

As with malt, there were large increases in the price of sugar during the war. In fact, they were even more extreme than in the case of malt, rising from 25s a quarter in 1914 to around 130s, in 1920.

Price of sugar used by Barclay Perkins 1914 - 1917 (in shillings per quarter)									
	1914		1915		1916			1917	
	Mar	Oct	Jun	Oct	Jan	Apr	Oct	Jan	Apr
Garton No.2	26.5	26	28	42	49	55	67	67	82
Garton No.3	24.5	24	26	40	40	50	65	65	80
Martineau No.3	23.5	23.5			46.5	52.5			65
Glucose	25						58	64	
Source: Barclay Perkins brewing records held at the London Metropolitan Archives									

---

[2] I'm taking 224 pounds of sugar as being the equivalent of a quarter of malt.

Price of sugar used by Barclay Perkins 1917 - 1920 (in shillings per quarter)									
	1917	1918			1919			1920	
	Oct	Jan	Apr	Oct	Jan	Apr	Oct	Jan	Apr
Garton No.2	86						125	130	140
Garton No.3	84	94	98	151	151	113	123	128	
Martineau No.3				151	151	120	123	128	138
Glucose					151	151			
Source: Barclay Perkins brewing records held at the London Metropolitan Archives									

Brewers Sugar Orders

In February 1917 an Order came into force pretty much totally banning the use of brewers' sugar. All brewers' sugar in transit was to be placed in warehouses. The only exception to these rules were the following types of sugar:

>British West India Grocery Crystallised Sugar
>British West India Muscovado Sugar
>British West India Grocery Syrup Sugar

The impact of the Order is clearly visible in brewing records. The numbered invert sugars disappear and in their place ones with descriptions like "Barbados" or "Mauritius" appear. Though Mauritius is in the Indian Ocean, not the West Indies.

A second Order in November tightened the restrictions even more. Only these types of sugar were allowed to be used in brewing:

>(a) Solid Glucose;

>(b) Invert of Low Grade Cane Sugar of a polarisation not exceeding 89 from which not less than 40 per cent, of its weight in the form of Crystal Sugar or Grocery Syrup or Grocery Honey Sugar has been extracted ;

>(c) Any caramelised products of Solid Glucose or of such Invert of Low Grade Cane Sugar as is hereinbefore described ; and

>(d) Mixtures of Solid Glucose and the Invert and caramelized products hereinbefore mentioned or of any of them. But, except that a brewer for sale may use in the brewing of beer any sugar which at the date of this Order he had in stock or which was in course of transit to his brewery from any manufacturer in the United Kingdom, he shall not use any sugar other than sugar of the kinds hereinbefore specifically mentioned.

I'd wondered why glucose suddenly appeared in so many brewing records towards the end of the war.

In addition to the types of sugar, the quantity of sugar that could be used in brewing was also restricted.

Adjuncts

Unmalted grains were first made legal to use in 1880. Initially brewers experimented with flaked rice and flaked maize, before mostly plumping for the latter. Maize grits were used to a lesser extent, mostly in Scotland.

There were big problems with the supply of maize during the later war years. At the time. No maize was grown in the UK and it all had to be imported, principally from the USA. With transatlantic transport severely disrupted by German U-boats, supplies for brewing dried up. Having the odd effect that wartime beers often contained a larger percentage of malt than those from before the war.

Unlike in WW II, where brewers were forced to use flaked barley and oats, flaked maize was not replaced by other unmalted grains.

As soon as supplies were available again, brewers returned to their pre-war adjunct usage. The vast majority of brewers had 10-15% adjuncts in their grists. As before the war, this was mostly in the form of flaked maize.

Yeast

Falling gravities caused a problem that you might not have expected. Brewers struggled with the health of their yeast due to the massively reduced gravities. Their solution was to occasionally brew beers at a gravity close to pre-war levels to produce a crop of healthy yeast.

There's another practice I've noticed in some brewing records that I think was all about yeast health. In Truman's Burton brewery, they parti-gyle two Milds, X and XXX. It started the usual way, with a blend of the worts before fermentation. But then the beers are blended again post-fermentation. XXX, which at the start of fermentation was 1055°, was blended with the weaker X to leave a beer with an effective OG of 1044°.

At William Younger they used an even simpler technique: liquoring back. For example, in 1921 they brewed 141 barrels of XX Mild at 1044° then added water at racking time to bring the effective OG down to 1035°.

Watering beer after fermentation was illegal before the war. A clause in the Beer Orders rescinded this rule, under certain circumstances:

> (b) Where provision has been made to the satisfaction of the Commissioners of Customs and Excise for the dilution with water of beer after brewing, and the dilution is carried out under conditions approved by the Commissioners, the diluted beer shall for the purpose of the foregoing sub-clause be deemed to have been brewed at such original gravity as the Commissioners may determine."
> "Food Supply Manual April 1918", HM Stationary Office, 1918, page 172.

Under normal conditions, the Excise wouldn't have liked anything, such a s dilution, being performed after fermentation for fear of some sort of tax fiddle.

As well as aiding yeast health, when some of the beer was fermented at a higher gravity it drank fuller.

Restrictions on the drinks trade

At the start of the war, there was a predictable call from the temperance lobby for total prohibition. This was particularly true in Scotland when, in the early months of the war the Glasgow School Board and the Corporation of Glasgow called on the government to ban all alcohol for the duration of the war.[3]

They couldn't manage to persuade the government to take quite such drastic action, but neither were they prepared to leave the trade alone. Lloyd George, who was Chancellor at the time, really threw the cat amongst the pigeons in a speech in Bangor in February 1915:

> "Most of our workmen are putting every ounce of strength into this urgent work for their country, loyally and patriotically. But that is not true of all. There are some, I am sorry to say, who shirk their duty in this great emergency. I hear of workmen in armament Works who refuse to work a full week's work for the nation's need. What is the reason? They are a minority. But, you must remember, a small minority of workmen can throw a whole works out of gear. What is the reason? Sometimes it is one thing, sometimes it is another, but let us be perfectly candid. It is mostly the lure of the drink. They refuse to work full time, and, when they return, their strength and efficiency arc impaired by the way in which they have spent their leisure. Drink is doing us more damage in the War than all the German submarines put together.
>
> "What has Russia done? Russia, knowing her deficiency, knowing how unprepared she was, said, 'I must pull myself together. I am not going to be trampled upon, unready as I am. I will use all my resources.' What is the first thing she does? She stops the drink. I was talking to M. Barck, the Russian Minister of Finance, a singularly able man, and I asked, 'What has been the result?' lie said, 'The productivity of labour, the amount of work which is put out by the workmen, has gone up between 30 and 50 per cent.' I said, 'How do they stand it without their liquor?' and he replied, 'Stand it? I have lost revenue over it up to £65,000,000 a year, and we certainly cannot afford it, but if I proposed to put it back there would be a revolution in Russia.' That is what the Minister of Finance told me. He told me that it is entirely attributable to the act of the Czar himself. It was a bold and courageous step— one of the most heroic things in the War. One afternoon we had to postpone our conference in Paris, and the French Minister of Finance said, 'I have got to go to .the Chamber of Deputies, because I am proposing a Bull to abolish absinthe.' Absinthe plays the same part in France that whisky plays in this country. It is really the worst form of drink used, not only among workmen, but among other classes as well. Its ravages are terrible, and they abolished it by a majority of something like ten to one that afternoon.
>
> "That is how these great countries are facing their responsibilities. We do not propose anything so drastic as that—we are essentially moderate men. But we are armed with full powers for the Defence of the Realm. We are approaching it, I do not mind telling you, for the moment, not from the point of view of people who have been considering this as a social problem—we are approaching it purely from the point of view of these works. We have got great powers to deal with drink, and we mean to

---

[3] "The Control of the Drink Trade" by Longmans, Green & Co., London, 1919, page 46.

use them. We shall use them in a spirit of moderation, we shall use them discreetly, we shall use them wisely, but we shall use them fearlessly, and I have no doubt that, as the country's needs demand it, the country will support our action, and will allow no indulgence of that kind to interfere with its prospects in this terrible war which has been thrust upon us"
"The Control of the Drink Trade" by Longmans, Green & Co., London, 1919, pages 47 - 48.

It must have delighted the temperance lobby, who would have seen it as a green light to attack the drink trade even more. Note the emotive phrases Lloyd George employed, such as "the lure of the drink". He was, of course, a teetotaller himself. Though he did hold back from advocating full prohibition. I suspect that was what he personally wanted, but realised that it wouldn't fly with the working classes. But were the problems in supply of munitions really due to lazy, drunken workers?

In industry, there were differing responses, depending on which side of the class divide you stood. The Shipbuilding Employers' Federation, which represented the big shipbuilders in Scotland and the North of England, urged for total prohibition.[4]

Labour unions accepted the need for some sort of control, but that fell far short of prohibition. The Executive of the Transport Workers' Federation wrote to the Chancellor saying:

"We are convinced that, although excessive drinking is indulged in by only a small minority, so interdependent is modern labour that the diminished efficiency of this minority has a marked influence upon the output of the total number of men engaged in any set of operations.

"This being so, and in the interests of national well-being, we would urge the Government to take immediate and decisive action to reduce the results of intemperance to a minimum."

"Where work is conducted during the night in shipyards, docks, and other places of production, some canteen provision should be set up to fulfil the requirements of the men for necessary refreshment."
"The Control of the Drink Trade" by Longmans, Green & Co., London, 1919, pages 49 - 50.

Beer output
As the war progressed, the restrictions on brewing became ever tighter. Initially, just the amount of beer that could be produced was limited. But later in the war there were controls on beer gravity and also price.

Initially, the only government control was on the amount of beer that breweries were allowed to brew. There were no limits on its gravity

---

[4] "The Control of the Drink Trade" by Longmans, Green & Co., London, 1919, page 50.

Mini Book Series volume XXXII: Armistice!

Beer output and limits			
date	year	standard barrels	note
30th Sep	1914	36,165,000	Output for year ending at that date
31st Mar	1916	30,292,977	Output for year ending at that date
31st Mar	1917	26,626,039	Output for year ending at that date
1st Apr	1917	11,470,000	limit set by the Food Controller
1st Jul	1917	15,043,000	limit set by the Food Controller
1st Apr	1918	11,470,000	limit set by the Food Controller
1st Jan	1919	13,260,000	limit set by the Food Controller
23rd May	1919	26,000,000	limit set by the Food Controller
Source: "The Brewers' Almanack 1928" pages 100 – 101			

In 1916, beer output was limited to about 85% of the pre-war total. Nothing too drastic. And by dropping the gravity a little of the more popular beers such as Mild and, in London, Porter, a brewer could continue to brew stronger beers much as before. And still produce about the same number of bulk barrels.

Timeline of restrictions

The 1926 Brewers' Almanack summarised the restrictions to brewing around the war years well. There were certainly plenty of them, sometimes only a few months apart.

"**Overview of changes 1914 to 1924**
The following is a chronological statement of beer duty changes and restrictions since 1914:

Year ended Sept. 30 1914: Output 36,165,000 standard barrels, which may be described as the pre-war rate.

Nov. 15 1914: Duty raised from 7s. 9d. to 23s. per standard barrel.

Year ended March 31 1916: Output 30,292,977 standard barrels.

April 1 1916: Duty raised to 24s.

Year ended March 31 1917: Output 26,626,039 standard barrels, the reduction being due to the Output of Beer (Restriction) Act, 1916.

April 1 1917: Output for quarter reduced by Food Controller to rate of 11,470,000 standard barrels a year, including beer for the Navy and Army. Duty raised to 25s. per barrel.

July 1 1917: Statutory output for quarter increased by 33 1/3 per cent. To rate of 15,043,000 standard barrels, half the beer to be brewed at a gravity not exceeding 1036°, 20 per cent. Offered to all brewers on those terms, the balance of 13 ½ per cent. Being brewed under special licence for consumption in munition areas.

Oct. 1 1917: Rate and conditions of previous quarter continued but gravity for one-half of the output raised to 1042°. Prices also fixed at 4d. per pint under 1036°, 5d. per pint under 1042°.

Jan. 1 1918: Rate and conditions of previous quarter again continued.

April 1 1918: Output for quarter reduced to rate of 11,470,000 standard barrels. The extra 20 per cent. Offer withdrawn and 33 1/3 per cent. For munition areas reduced to 10.4 per cent., equal to 1,120,000 barrels, leaving total output at rate of 12,590,000 a year. Conditions changed by provision that average gravity of all beer brewed shall not exceed 1030° for Great Britain and 1045° for Ireland, and that no beer shall be brewed below 1010°: and prices fixed at 4d. per pint below 1030°, and 5d. per pint for 1030° to 1034°. Food Controller imposed a special charge of 25s. per standard barrel for a munition beer brewed under his licence.

April 23 1918: Duty increased to 50s.

Jan. 1 1919: Statutory barrelage increased by 25 per cent., making annual rate of total output 13,260,000 standard barrels. Gravities raised 2° both for Great Britain and Ireland.

Feb. 20 1919: Food Controller stated that "it is being constantly represented to us from Labour and other organisations that the shortage of beer and spirits is a cause contributing to the unrest in the country. I hope very shortly to be in a position to allow a considerably larger additional output of beer, and of better quality, than that recently sanctioned."

April 1 1919: Beer duty raised to 70s. Statutory barrelage increased by 50 per cent., and gravity raised to 1040° in Great Britain. Special charge of 25s. per barrel for munition beer abolished as from April 30 1919.

May 23 1919: Statutory barrelage further increased by 45 per cent., bringing total output up to rate of 26,000,000 standard barrels a Year. July 1 1919: All restriction on volume of output removed, and average permitted gravity increased in Great Britain to 1044°, and in Ireland to 1051°.

Aug. 1 1919: In lieu of proposed increase of beer duty to 80s. on freedom of output being established, the gravities at which the different priced beers might be sold retail were revised in a new Order by the Food Controller. The range of gravities was raised 4° all round, beer under 1020' being fixed at the maximum price of 2d. per pint in a public-bar.

April 20 1920: Duty raised to 100s., which is practically 13 times as great as the pre-war rate and represents an increase of 1,190%. Food –Controller's maximum retail prices raised by ld. Per pint. See schedules next page.

June 30 1921: Restriction as to Average Permitted Gravities ended.

Aug. 31 1921: All control of prices abolished.

April 1 1923: Rebate of 20s. per bulk barrel made from duty of £5 per standard barrel with arrangement that the Trade should bear the balance of 4s. by reducing as from

April 17 1923: the price of beer by 1d. per pint, equal to 24s. per bulk barrel.

The Beer Prices Order, as it existed up to the time of its revocation, is set out in full in the Brewers' Almanack 1921, pp. 74-83. For purposes of reference the First and Second Schedules to the Order are reprinted as follows:-

First Schedule.- Sales of Beer by Retail in a Public Bar or for Consumption off the Premises.

Beer by gravity	Non-bottled price per pint	Bottled Price per		
		half pint	pint	quart
Under 1020°	3d.	3d.	6d.	10d.
> 1020° < 1027°	4d.	3 ½d.	7d.	11d.
> 1027° < 1033°	5d.	4d.	7 l/2d.	1/1
> 1033° < 1039°	6d.	4 ½d.	8d.	1/3
> 1039° < 1046°	7d.	5 ½d.	9d.	1/5
> 1046° < 1054°	8d.	6 ½d.	11d.	1/7
> 1054°	9d.	7d.	1/1	1/9

Second Schedule.-Sales of Beer by Retail for Consumption on the Premises Elsewhere than in a Public Bar

Beer by gravity	Non-bottled price per pint	Bottled Price per		
		half pint	pint	quart
Under 1020°	4d.	4d.	8d	1/-
> 1020° < 1027°	5d.	4 ½d.	9d.	1/1
> 1027° < 1033°	6d.	5d.	9 ½d.	1/3
> 1033° < 1039°	7d.	5 ½d.	10d.	1/5
> 1039° < 1046°	8d.	6 ½d.	11d.	1/7
> 1046° < 1054°	9d.	7 ½d.	1/1	1/9
> 1054°	10d.	8 ½d.	1/3	1/11

Where bottled beer is sold in a bottle containing less than an imperial quart but containing a quantity not specified in Column 3 above, the maximum price shall be a price at the rate applicable to bottled beer of a like original gravity sold in a bottle containing the next greater quantity specified in Column 3.

Where bottled beer is sold in a bottle containing more than one imperial quart, the maximum price shall be a price at tile rate applicable to bottled beer of a like original gravity sold in a bottle containing one imperial quart.

In either case, in estimating the maximum price a broken halfpenny shall he reckoned as a halfpenny."
Taken from "The Brewers' Almanack 1928" pages 100 – 101.

These regulations had a very long-lasting effect. The last government-imposed average OG of 1044° is very similar to the average OG between the wars, which hovered around 1042-1043°.

The 20 shilling reduction per bulk barrel was another disincentive to brew strong beer. As the 100 shilling tax was per **standard** barrel (36 gallons at 1055°). A barrel of beer of 1100° would pay 200 shillings tax minus 20 shillings: 180 shillings, a 10% discount. While a barrel at 1055° would pay 100-20 = 80 shillings, a 20% discount.

Government Ale

In April 1917, when the stipulation came into force that half a brewery's output had to be at a gravity of under 1036°, brewers started calling this class of beer Government Ale. GA crops up regularly in brewing records of the period.

Government Ale was brewed within specified gravity bands (pretty low) and sold at a controlled price. The intention was to ensure more beer was brewed from the same quantity of raw materials and keep down the price to stop unrest amongst the working class. It doesn't seem to have quite worked out as planned, due to resistance from brewers and publicans.

Oct. 1 1917: Prices fixed at 4d. per pint under 1036°, 5d. per pint under 1042°.
April 1 1918: Prices fixed at 4d. per pint below 1030°, and 5d. per pint for 1030° to 1034°.

But the government itself wasn't keen on the term and in the next set of regulations calling a beer "Government Ale" was expressly forbidden.

> "8. A person shall not on the occasion of a sale of any beer of an original gravity less than 1036° or in any advertisement, circular or placard relating to any such beer describe the same as "Government Ale" or "Government Beer" or use any other form of words calculated to lead to the belief that such beer is brewed under the authority, or pursuant to the directions of His Majesty's Government, or any Government Department."

"Food Supply Manual October 1917", HM Stationary Office, 1917, page 82.

The official reaction was no doubt connected with the poor reputation of Government Ale. An indication of how annoyed the population was with Government Ale are the number of jokes about it. Here are some examples from Punch.

> "How much water," asks a technical journal, "does it take to make a gallon of Government ale?" We do not profess to be expert, but we should say about a gallon.
> January 1st, 1919

"Government ale, says a trade paper, will shortly be on sale in some parts of Ireland. This certainly ought to be a lesson to them."
May 28th, 1919.

"A Pittsburg inventor is reported by Mr. MARCONI to have discovered a method of bottling light. If he can bottle anything lighter than the new Government ale his claim to be a wizard is established."
July 25th, 1917.

A notice exhibited in the window of a Bermondsey public-house bears the words, "There is nothing like Government Ale." Agreed.
Dec. 5th, 1917.

"We understand that the Foreign Office takes a serious view of the large number of public-houses which have been burgled during the last few weeks. It is feared that it may be the work of a foreign spy who is endeavouring to secure the recipe of British Government ale."
March 10th, 1920.

"The Vicar of South Acton suggests that a huge prize should be offered for the invention of a good temperance drink. We regret to say that this is not the first studied insult that has been offered to Government ale."
June 18th, 1919.

"It appears that a Wallasey licensee, in order to satisfy his customers, sent a sample of Government ale to be analysed. We understand that the analyst reported that there was nothing in it."
May 21, 1919.

Sticking to the rules

Brewers had to be very careful to adhere to the rules on average gravity and output allowed. This was assessed on a quarter by quarter basis. If a brewer produced beer of a higher average gravity or more standard barrels than their allocated allowance, they faced fines.

The concern of brewers about making sure they stuck to the rules can be read in Boddington's brewing records. In 1918 they wrote the average gravity of each week's brews into their brewing records. This is an example from April 1918:

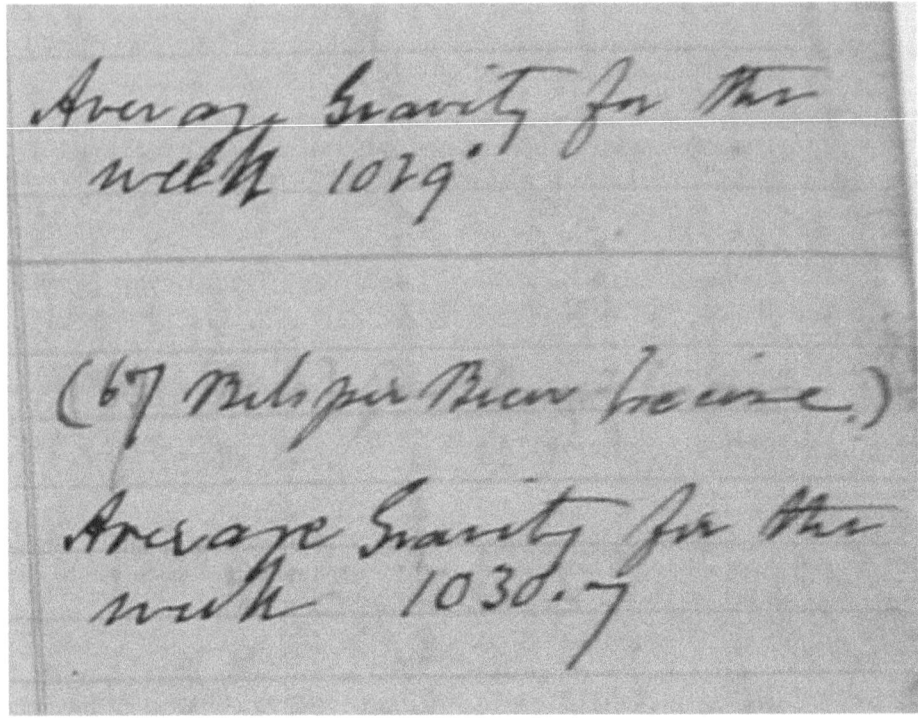

Malting

The Food Control Manuals include information on the restrictions imposed on maltsters during the war. Which in the first couple of years were none at all. Only when the German U-boat campaign began to bite in 1917 did things get tougher for the malting industry.

The first Malt Order was draconian. It prohibited maltsters from delivering, buying or making malt. It makes you wonder what maltsters could do, other than twiddle their thumbs, as they weren't allowed to carry on any part of their business.

The Brewers (Malt Purchases) Order, 1917. Dated February 3rd 1917. Order 1917 no. 132.
Prohibited maltsters from selling malt without the permission of the Food Controller. Brewers were prohibited from buying or making malt.

> "1. Except under the authority of the Food Controller no maltster or dealer in malt shall on or after the 10th February, 1917, agree to sell any malt to any brewer for sale or make delivery to any brewer for sale of any malt other than deliverable under contracts made before that date.
>
> 2. Except under the authority of the Food Controller, no brewer for sale shall on or

after the 10th February, 1917, agree to buy any malt or take delivery of any malt other than deliverable under contracts made before that date.

3. Except under the authority of the Food Controller, no brewer for sale shall manufacture any malt from barley agreed to be bought on or after the 10th February, 1917."

The Malt (Restriction) Order, 1917. Dated February 20, 1917. Order 1917 no. 159.
Prohibited maltsters from making malt from any grains without the permission of the Food Controller.

The Malt (Restriction on Shipping) Order, 1917. Dated March 21, 1917. Order 1917 no. 259.
Prohibited exporting malt from Ireland to Great Britain or from Great Britain to Ireland without permission of the Food Controller.

The Malt (Restriction) No. 2 Order, 1917. Dated April 12, 1917. Order 1917 no. 345.
Prohibited maltsters from making malt from any grains without the permission of the Food Controller.
Prohibited maltsters from selling malt without the permission of the Food Controller.
Prohibited the use of malt for any purpose without the permission of the Food Controller, except for brewers making their permitted barrelage.

The Malt (Restriction) Order, 1917. Dated February 26, 1918. Order 1918 no. 225.
Prohibited maltsters from making malt or malt extract without the permission of the Food Controller.
Prohibited maltsters from selling malt without the permission of the Food Controller.
Prohibited the use of malt or malt extract for any purpose without the permission of the Food Controller, except for brewers making their permitted barrelage.

Order, Dated the 30th December, 1918, revoking the The Malt (Restriction on Shipping) Order, 1917. Order 1918 no. 1755.
Revoked Order 1917 no. 259.

No sign of any rules forbidding the manufacture of dark malt. Where could they be hiding?

UK barley acreage, produce, price and imports 1857 – 1927

Year ended Dec. 31.	Acreage.	Estimated Product Quarters (400 lbs.).	Estimated Product cwts.	Average Price per Quarter.	Average Price per cwt.	Barley. Imports.
				s. d.	s. d.	Cwts.
1857	--	--		42 1	11 9	6,076,679
1860	--	--		36 7	10 3	7,545,932
1870	2,371,739	--		34 7	9 8	7,217,369
1880	2,695,000	5,408,376	19,315,629	33 1	9 3	11,705,290
1890	2,300,994	10,099,190	36,068,536	28 8	8 0	16,677,988
1900	2,172,129	8,568,286	30,601,021	24 11	7 0	17,189,358
1910	1,899,130	7,880,562	28,144,864	23 3	6 6	18,281,500
1913	1,980,046	8,204,066	29,300,236			
1914	1,871,166	8,066,678	28,809,564			
1915	1,624,816	5,862,244	20,936,586	37 2	10 5	12,291,685
1915	1,522,646	6,802,244	24,293,729			
1916	1,651,874	6,612,660	23,616,643			
1920	2,049,306	8,212,000	29,328,571	89 3	25 0	12,667,700
1922	1,691,007	6,664,350	23,801,250	39 11	11 2	12,703,275
1923a	1,485,604	6,154,400	21,980,000	33 8	9 5	18,129,280
1924a	1,465,660	6,400,800	22,860,000	46 9	13 1	21,656,359
1925a	1,470,731	6,456,800	23,060,000	42 0	11 9	15,779,162
1926a	1,269,959	5,740,000	20,500,000	36 11	10 4	11,550,617
1927a	1,166,295	5,353,600	19,120,000	42 0	11 9	16,502,710

Note:
a Great Britain only.
Sources:
Journal of the Institute of Brewing, Volume 23, Issue 3, May-June 1917, page 182.
1928 Brewers' Almanack, page 119.

Styles by decree

I'm a bit slow sometimes. You'll have to excuse me. I've been really thick. This is a pattern I should have noticed long ago.

You must have noticed my thing about WW I. It's hard to miss. I keep going on about it. As part of my continuing research, I've been looking up all the beer-related Orders from the Food Controller. Some of the most interesting are from just after the war's end, in 1919 and 1920. These are the ones that regulate the price of beer according to the original gravity. This is a summary:

Mini Book Series volume XXXII: Armistice!

Price control 1917-1921					
Price	Oct 1917	Apr 1918	Feb 1919	Jul 1919	Apr 1920
2d				<1019	
3d			<1022	1020-1026	<1019
4d	<1036	<1030	1023-1028	1027-1032	1020-1026
5d	1036-1042	1030-1034	1029-1034	1033-1038	1027-1032
6d			1035-1041	1039-1045	1033-1038
7d			1042-1049	1045-1053	1039-1045
8d			>1050	>1054	1045-1053
9d					>1054

Sources:
The Brewers' Almanack 1928 pages 100 – 101.
"The British Brewing Industry 1830-1980" by T.R. Gourvish and R.G Wilson, 1994, Cambridge University Press, page 323.

Fascinating stuff, eh? I've had some of these numbers for quite a long. The very last column. They are quoted in The Brewers' Almanack 1928. These were the last controlled prices that were in effect until August 1921.

I've a mass of data for the 1920's and 1030's. Courtesy of the Whitbread and Truman Gravity Books. So much that I still haven't got through it all. Funnily enough, the first entries in the Whitbread Gravity Book are for late 1921. Just when all the restrictions on gravity and prices were removed.

It isn't a coincidence. There was a reason for Whitbread's sudden interest in the gravity of their competitors' beer. To see what they were up to now government control had been removed.

Where does the me being thick part come in? I'd never thought to compare the price control table with the details gleaned from the Gravity Books. Why don't you give it a go? Look at the table below. Spot any similarities with the other table?

Beer prices and gravity 1921-1939								
	1921-1923		1924-1929		1931-1933		1933-1939	
Beer	Price	OG	Price	OG	Price	OG	Price	OG
Mild			4d	1030.2	5d	1030.41	4d	1029.91
Mild	6d	1034.25	5d	1033.49	6d	1036.92	5d	1036.31
Mild	7d	1040.47	6d	1042.08			6d	1040.54
PA	8d	1046.54	7d	1045.24	8d	1045.14	7d	1047.06
PA	9d	1053.87	8d	1052.73			8d	1052.12
Porter	6d	1036.03	5d	1037.62			5d	1037.77
Stout	8d	1046.09	7d	1049.45	8d	1044.92	7d	1047.47
Stout	9d	1052.83	8d	1054.01	9d	1048.16	8d	1054.58
Strong Ale					8d	1048.24	7d	1048.21
Strong Ale	9d	1053.27	8d	1053.69	9d	1050.69	8d	1052.49

Sources:
Truman Gravity Book
Whitbread Gravity Book

I've arrived at the gravities by averaging out dozens of examples from different breweries. I can see a clear pattern. Brewers were making beers that fitted into the old price control gravity bands. And charging the same price. So although there was, officially, no price control in 1922 and 1923, there may as well have been.

Why do I have four columns in my second table? It's to match the changes in tax. Here's an overview:

Tax per standard barrel	
Year	tax
1919	50s
1920	70s
1921-23	100s
1924-30	80s
1931-33	114s
1934-39	80s
Source: Brewers' Almanack 1928, p. 110 Brewers' Almanack 1955, p. 50	

Ignoring the blips caused by adjustments in the beer tax, the strength and price of beer brewed right up until the outbreak of WW II was effectively determined by the price control regulations at the end of WW I. Styles between the wars were, to a great extent, determined by government decree. Even though for the vast majority of the period brewers were theoretically free to brew any strength beer and to sell it for whatever price they pleased.

Tax

After 1880, beer was taxed according to its original gravity before fermentation. It was all based around something called a standard barrel.

A standard barrel was 36 gallons at an OG of 1055°. For beer that was stronger or weaker than 1055°, the tax was charged proportionately. For example, in 1914 the tax per standard barrel was 7s 4d. A beer of 1027.5° would pay half that tax, 3s 8d. A beer of 1100° would pay 14s 8d. Though in 1914, 1055° was very close to the average gravity of beer.

There were only three adjustments to the tax between 1880 and 1914. In 1889 the gravity of a standard barrel was lowered from 1057° to 1055°, effectively raising the tax. In 1895 the duty was raised from 6s 3d to 6s 9d, and again in 1901 to 7s 9d. The latter was to help pay for the Boer War. But that was nothing compared to the changes that would take place after 1914.

Taxing beer to pay for war was a great tradition in the UK. The very first beer tax was introduced in 1643, during the English Civil War.[5] The Napoleonic Wars were similarly funded by taxes on beer, malt and hops.

The tax had remained at 7s 9d since 1901. Within a few months of the outbreak of war, in November 1914, it was nearly trebled to 23s.[6] This had the effect of raising the price of beer by 1d per pint.[7] That might not sound like much, but a pint of Mild was only 2d. a pint, so that's a 50% increase.

In the following years the tax increased a little, but the biggest increases came in the final year of war and the first couple of peace, when it hit 100s. That's a massive 1109% rise.

As you can see in the table below, beer tax brought in considerable sums. The average price is slightly deceptive, because beer fell so much in strength between 1914 and 1920. A beer that sold for 3d in 1914 would have cost 9d or 10d in 1921.

UK beer tax before, during and after WW I						
Year	Total Tax £	Tax/Bulk Brl.	Tax/Std. Brl	price pint	tax pint	Tax (% retail price)
1914	13,622,971	7s 4d	7s 9d	3d	0.30d	10.08
1915	15,856,412	9s 1d	23s	3d	0.38d	12.67
1916	33,747,269	21s	23s	3d	0.88d	29.19
1917	31,567,940	20s 11d	24s	4d	0.87d	21.80
1918	19,108,663	20s	25s	4.5d	0.83d	18.54
1919	25,423,393	21s 10d	50s	5d	0.91d	18.21
1920	71,276,230	40s 8d	70s	6d	1.69d	28.25
1921	123,406,257	71s 6d	100s	7d	2.98d	42.58
Source: 1928 Brewers' Almanack pages 100 – 103, 111.						

The main purpose of the tax increase in 1914 wasn't to curtail drinking, but to raise revenue.

---

[5] A History of Beer and Brewing by Ian S. Hornsey, p.378.
[6] "The Brewers' Almanack 1928" page 100.
[7] "The Control of the Drink Trade" by Longmans, Green & Co., London, 1919, page 45.

However, it was expected that a reduction in consumption would be a happy side effect. Lloyd George estimated that the combined effect of the price increase, the absence of large numbers of men on military service and the shortened opening hours would be to reduce beer consumption by 35%.[8]

The increased tax did have an immediate effect on beer consumption, though longer term it was far less than the 35% Lloyd George had hoped for:

Barrels of Beer, at Standard Gravity Charged with Duty (War-tax on beer imposed on November 18, 1914.)			
	The 12 months preceding the Tax.	The 12 months following the Tax.	Percentage of decrease.
	1913	1914	
December	3,068,000	1,922,000	37.4
	1914	1915	
January	2,736,000	2,131,000	22.1
February	2,532,000	1,975,000	21.9
March	2,938,000	2,450,000	16.6
April	3,000,000	2,255,000	24.8
X May	3,181,000	2,595,000	18.4
Juno	3,065,000	2,709,000	11.6
July	3,560,000	2,887,000	18.9
August	2,955,000	2,716,000	8.0
September	3,111,000	2,834,000	8.9
October	3,121,000	2,490,000	20.2
November	2,629,000	2,288,000	12.9
Source: "The Control of the Drink Trade" by Longmans, Green & Co., London, 1919, page 45.			

After an initial large drop of 37%, it levelled out at a 10%-20% fall.

Wages and Prices

WW I was a huge surprise to a population unused to inflation. Prices had scarcely increased since the 1850's, in some cases actually having fallen. In four years of war, they doubled. But it wasn't all bad news for workers, as wages also shot up during the war.

Wages

Scarcity of labour, caused both by the absence of young men in the military and the increased demand from munitions factories, caused considerable wage inflation. Manual workers earned wages far in excess of anything seen before. It helped soften the blow of price increases, especially of items like beer, which became more expensive than ever.

Pre-war: "the average weekly wage varied from 26s. 4d. per week to 34s. 4d. Half the

---

[8] "The Control of the Drink Trade" by Longmans, Green & Co., London, 1919, page 45.

women employed were paid from 10s. to 15s. per week."[9]

1917: London bus drivers were earning 60s. per week, even the cleaners were getting 40s.[10]

1918: Even agricultural labourers, the lowest paid manual workers, were earning 60s. to 70s. a week.[11]

Munitions workers earned considerably more – from £6 (120s.) to as much as £10 (200s.) or £20 (400s.) per week.[12]

Prices

It's hard for us to imagine what a shock WW I must have been when it came to prices. There hadn't really been any inflation in the preceding decades. Even though wages were higher during the war, the sharp rise in the cost of food must have been a worry.

To put into context the prices, the average price of a pint had been 3d. in 1914. By 1920, the average price had doubled to 6d per pint, while average OG had dropped by 25%. Beers at strengths that would have been considered normal before the war were considerably more expensive.

You'll note that back then, just as now, beer was more expensive in London than elsewhere. For purposes of comparison, here are UK pub beer prices today.

Here's a concrete example of the changes in gravities during the war period. These are the draught beers (and their prices) of the Mellersh & Neale brewery of Reigate.

Price of beers to the publican and their OG's						
Date	X (Mild)		Pale Ale		Stout	
	OG	Price	OG	Price	OG	Price
to November 1914	1045°	36 s.	1054°	52 s.	1065°	52 s.
from November 1914	1043°	55 s.	1052°	71 s.	1064°	71 s.
from January 1917	1039°	61 s.	1050°	77 s.	1060°	77 s.
from April 1917	1039°	90 s.	1049°	77 s.	1060°	108 s.
from June 1917	1039°	80 s.	1049°	109 s.	1060°	108 s.
from April 1918	1025°	66 s.	1040°	120 s.	1040°	120 s.
from May 1918	1025°	68 s.	1040°	120 s.	1040°	120 s.
from March 1918	1025°	68 s.	1040°	108 s.	1040°	108 s.
from May 1919	1025°	72 s.	1040°	108 s.	1040°	108 s.
from June 1919	1025°	72 s.	1040°	130 s.	1040°	130 s.
from January 1920	1033°	120 s.	1046°	158 s.	1040°	158 s.
%age change 1914 – 1920*	-27%	+233%	-15%	+204%	-38%	+204%
Source: "A Brewing Heritage: The Story of Brewing in Reigate and Redhill", by Richard Paul Symonds, 2001, p . 55 **Notes:** Prices in shillings per barrel. * my calculation						

---

[9] Weekly Dispatch, Dec 30 1917.
[10] Weekly Dispatch, May 13 1917.
[11] Daily News, Aug 7th 1918.
[12] Daily News, Aug 3 1918.

You can clearly see the effect of the ruling in April 1918, which specified that the average gravity of all beer brewed should not exceed 1030°. Assuming Mellersh & Neale were sticking to this average, the ratio Mild to Pale Ale to Stout was 4:1:1. At the same ratio, the average OG a month earlier was about 1044°. Using the same 4:1:1 ratio, in 1920 the average gravity of the three beers was about 1036° (the average gravity of beer brewed in England and Wales that year was 1038.57°)

It's interesting to note that Pale Ale suffered a far smaller drop in gravity than either Mild or Stout. The latter two must have changed considerably in character. With Stout weaker than pre-war Porter, the latter found itself elbowed out of the last available strength slot. Little wonder it all but disappeared.

Publicans' profits

One of the oddities of the control of beer prices at the end of WW I was that it only dealt with retail prices. There was no control of the wholesale prices brewers charged publicans. Which, in theory, could have left a landlord with no profit margin whatsoever.

It's possible to see what the mark-up was for some publicans by comparing the wholesale prices with the controlled retail prices. A letter from the Wigan and District Brewers' Association, dated 31st July 1919, lays out the agreed wholesale price for beers of various price categories. It's a bit of simple mathematics to calculate what the landlord made per pint sold.

Wigan and District Brewers' Association wholesale prices				
retail price per pint (pence)	wholesale price per barrel (shillings)	retail price per barrel (shillings)	profit per pint (pence)	% profit
4	72	96	1	25.00%
5	90	120	1.25	25.00%
6	100	144	1.83	30.56%
7	120	168	2	28.57%
Source: A letter dated 31st July 1919.				

Interestingly, the profit on the stronger classes was greater. Though, obviously, due to the restrictions on average OG (which was 1048° as of 1st August 1919), the quantity of stronger beer available was limited.

In the early stages of the war there were accusations of profiteering by publicans. Which is one of the reasons price controls were introduced. But looking at the numbers, it doesn't look like that was the case in 1919. In 1914, London "Four Ale" (X Ale) retailed for 2d. per pint and cost 36 shillings a barrel. Which also comes out to a gross profit of around 25%.

Brewery profits

The decade before WW I had been a difficult one. The Liberal government had used increased licence duties for pubs and breweries to partially finance social programmes, such as an old age pension.

The increased licence fees suppressed pub prices, which left many breweries overcapitalised as the value of their assets shrank dramatically. Several brewery companies revalued their shares at 10% of their original value.

Massively increased licence fees for breweries, who were charged according to the size of their output, decreased margins at a time when it was difficult to raise the price of beer. Few breweries were doing well in 1914. But the war helped turn that around.

Whitbread is a good example. Despite doing relatively well compared to many of their peers, they weren't exactly raking money in.

Whitbread Brewery profits and dividends 1912 - 1925						
Year	net profit	brought in	carried forward	dividend Ordinary shares	barrels brewed	net profit per barrel
1912	£17,491	£15,828	£12,054	0.5%	988,981	£0.02
1913	£125,792	£12,054	£46,653	1%	901,807	£0.14
1914	£51,256	£46,653	£46,419	0.5%	900,636	£0.06
1915	£72,997	£46,420	£53,649	2%	762,438	£0.10
1916	£45,078	£53,649	£79,379	2%	777,127	£0.06
1917	£198,349	£79,379	£92,404	7%	578,502	£0.34
1918	£204,806	£92,404	£123,057	7%	413,112	£0.50
1919	£232,866	£123,057	£165,136	7%	565,624	£0.41
1920	£242,432	£160,138	£213,124	10%		
1921	£209,520	£213,125	£257,639	7%	675,647	£0.31
1922	£226,270	£257,639	£289,580	10%	576,118	£0.39
1923	£222,749	£289,580	£319,531	10%	505,097	£0.44
1924	£217,277	£319,532	£342,489	10%	551,616	£0.39
1925	£246,499	£342,489	£394,076	10%	527,977	£0.47

Sources:
Yorkshire Post and Leeds Intelligencer - Monday 05 August 1912, page 10.
Manchester Courier and Lancashire General Advertiser - Friday 01 August 1913, page 5.
Manchester Courier and Lancashire General Advertiser - Friday 31 July 1914, page 4.
Dundee Courier - Friday 06 August 1915, page 2.
Birmingham Daily Post - Friday 04 August 1916, page 7.
Birmingham Daily Post - Saturday 04 August 1917, page 6.
Yorkshire Post and Leeds Intelligencer - Tuesday 06 August 1918, page 7.
Yorkshire Post and Leeds Intelligencer - Monday 11 August 1919, page 11.
Yorkshire Post and Leeds Intelligencer - Saturday 07 August 1920, page 17.
Yorkshire Post and Leeds Intelligencer - Saturday 06 August 1921, page 15.
Yorkshire Post and Leeds Intelligencer - Saturday 05 August 1922, page 15.
Yorkshire Post and Leeds Intelligencer - Saturday 04 August 1923, page 15.
Yorkshire Post and Leeds Intelligencer - Thursday 07 August 1924, page 13.
Yorkshire Post and Leeds Intelligencer - Friday 07 August 1925, page 15.

In 1912, Whitbread made a mere £17,491 net profit. Given that they brewed just shy of a million barrels that year, it works out to a feeble 4.5d per barrel. Ironically, when their output shrank considerably in 1917, their profits increased considerably from under £50,000 to around £200,000. The profit per barrel shot up even more, to 82d per barrel. Whitbread brewed only around half of their 1914 output in 1917 and 1918, but made for times as much net profit.

At the same time, the dividend paid out on Ordinary shares increased from 2% to 7%. Clearly Whitbread was doing well. It's ironic that, exactly when restrictions on brewing started to be ever more severe, breweries started making much more money.

The profits brewers were making led to them being denounced as profiteers in some quarters, notably temperance campaigners.

Pubs

In this period, pubs had a multi-room layout. The different bars each had their own character, type of customer and pricing structure. It wasn't unusual for a pub to have 3, 4 or 5 different rooms. All except the Public Bar charged the higher Saloon Bar prices. British pubs maintained this arrangement until the 1960's, when dividing walls were demolished to create a single drinking space.

Public bar – the most basic room and the exclusive domain of the working-class male. Also called Tap Room or Four Ale Bar. This was the only part of the pub where the first government price controls applied.

Saloon Bar – had better furnishings than the Public Bar, a more prosperous clientele, higher prices and often waiter service. Landlords were initially free to charge whatever prices they pleased in the saloon and took full advantage of this freedom. By the end of the war a second set of controlled prices had been introduced to cover this part of the pub. Also called the Lounge Bar.

Other bars – many pubs had four or five different rooms, each designed for a specific type of customer. For example, only certain rooms usually admitted. The names and character of these other rooms varied according to location. For example in the Northwest there would likely be a snug and a tap room in addition to the standard public bar and lounge.

Beerhouse – a pub with a license to sell only beer, not wine or spirits. They were the smallest and most basic type of pub. During the course of the 20th century beerhouses mostly either closed or obtained full licences. I can remember drinking in pubs with beer-only licences as late as the 1980's (The Roscoe in Leeds) and there may still be a couple left.

While beer wasn't officially rationed, it was in short supply, especially during the later years. Which meant it was effectively rationed by breweries. They would limit the amount supplied to each public house. Pubs often ran out of beer.

Not a great situation either for drinkers or publicans. This passage makes that very clear:

> **"WHAT, NO BEER!**
> The little bye-path inns on the outskirts of London, where prior to the war the casual pedestrian from the metropolis found solace and refreshment, are having a very bad time in these days when beer is hard to buy, and most of the wayfarers are foot-slogging elsewhere in khaki. To-day, in a well-inned area within easy tramp of a bus route terminus, I found a state of things that must bring sorrow to the heart of every lover of the quiet countryside round London. Some my favourite hostelries had put their shutters up for good, and not one of those that remained but had on the door of the parlour bar, where of old the good brown ale used to be found, a pathetic little notice with the legend "No beer." Mine hostess of a favourite inn declared that she had been allowed a scrimpy 18 gallons in month, "and how far do they think that will go, sir," she exclaimed indignantly, "with a sun that would melt you to a greasedrop, and the second hay making season its height?" After a pause she added, "Not that haymaking makes so much difference — it's all being done by German prisoners. Perhaps you have seen them, sir?" I had, and very lazy and un-British lot of men they seemed to be."[13]

Even in in a quiet pub, 18 gallons would only be enough for a couple of days. For a month, it works out to slightly less than five pints a day. Enough for a boozy lunch for one customer.

Opening hours

One of the biggest changes to pubs during WW I was the restriction of pub opening hours. The change was prompted by a fear that munitions workers would get too drunk to work. The high wages being paid meant that workers had plenty of spare cash. The limited hours were part of the Defence of the Realm Act, commonly referred to as D.O.R.A.

Although before the war there had been fixed closing times (first introduced by *The Intoxicating Liquor (Licensing) Bill* of 1872), pubs opened at dawn. In London, pubs could open between 05:00 and 00:30 on weekdays, 13:00 – 15:00 and 18:00 – 23:00 on Sundays. Elsewhere, pubs could open 16 or 17 hours a day (06:00 – 22:00 weekdays, 13:00 – 15:00 and 18:00 – 23:00 on Sundays). As the war progressed opening times were progressively reduced. Evening closing moved to 11:00 PM, then 10 PM and by the middle of 1915 was as early as 09:00 or 09:30. At the same time afternoon closing was introduced, and outside London, pubs were only opening for 5.5 hours on weekdays, 5 hours on Sunday. [14]

> 'The greatest change introduced was a drastic reduction in the hours of sale. Previously these had been on week-days - in London 19½ hours, namely from 5 A. M. to 12.30 midnight (Saturdays 12 midnight); in other English towns 17 hours, namely from 6 A. M. to 11 P. M.; in country districts 16 hours, namely from 6 A.M. to 10 P.M.' - 'The Board reduced these hours at one stroke to 5½ in all districts, namely 2½ hours at midday (12 to 2.30 P. M.) And 3 in the evening (6 P.M. to 9 P.M., or 6.30 P.M. to 9.30 P.M.). Except during these hours the sale of alcoholic liquor for consumption on the premises was prohibited, and this applied to clubs as well as to licensed houses of all kinds.' Three main changes effected by this. 1 - 'Public-house drinking in the forenoon was completely stopped', 2 - 'drinking in the evening ceased much earlier'; 3 - 'an interval of several hours was interposed in the afternoon between the morning and the evening periods of sale, so that the consumption of liquor coincided broadly with meal-times, and ceased in the intervening period.' [15]

The *1921 Licensing Act* allowed pubs to open 8 hours (9 in London) on weekdays, starting no earlier than 11:00 and ending no later than 22:00 (23:00 in London), with a minimum 2-hour break in the afternoon. On Sundays, pubs were only allowed to open for 5 hours. These rules remained little changed until afternoon closing was ended in the 1980's. Only in 2006 were the rules relaxed to allow pubs to open as long as they had in Edwardian times.

From anecdotal evidence (Harry's grandad) it seems the British workman didn't surrender his morning pint quite so easily. In the 1920's some Manchester pubs would open illegally at 6 AM to cater for the going to work trade. I'm sometimes tempted to continue this great tradition, as the pub next to my kids' school is open when I drop them off.

---

[13] Western Daily Press - Tuesday 13 August 1918, page 3.
[14] 1911 Ecyclopaedia Brittanica: Liquor Licensing, Beer.
[15] Shadwell, Drink, pp.37-8.

The shorter hours weren't necessarily a bad thing for publicans as in concentrated trading into a shorter time. It seems like some were earning good money, despite all the problems.

> "The high price of beer and stout, which springs in the main from their scarcity, is apparently proving a blessing in disguise to certain elements of the community. The brewers are increasing their profits and publicans, particularly in munition areas, are growing rich, in sharp contrast to their circumstances before the war.
>
> In the Woolwich area the fortunate landlords of good houses openly boast that they are going to retire after the war on the wealth they have accumulated. One host is known to have saved £8,000 since August 1914. Public-houses where it was always a difficulty to make ends meet are now gold mines, and free houses change hands at such prices as £8,000.
>
> The publican's expenses are much lower owing to the reduced labour and lighting which the modified hours of opening permit. His business, instead of being distributed over a long day, is now concentrated in a short space of time, and it is a quick, profitable trade."[16]

Women in pubs

The war brought about changes in social behaviour that had an impact on the brewing industry. Women, often doing men's jobs and earning higher wages than before, wanted to drink beer, too. It came as a great shock to some.

> "I remember, too, that we had a visit from some Chief Constables from towns in the North of England, including Newcastle and Durham, who had come to tell the Control Board of a serious increase in drinking among women in their towns, which was, they emphasised, a growing evil, one non-existent before the war. D'Abvernon sent for figures of convictions for drunkenness in the town concerned, and remarked that from the figures it did not appear that there had been any marked increase in drunkenness among women in these areas - on the contrary, there was an improvement. The Chief Constables replied that there was little actual drunkenness among women, but that their present purpose was to draw their attention to the large increase in the number of women who now drank. In the old days few decent women would go into a public house at all, and now they were walking in 'bold as brass', putting down their money and calling for beer. The Chief Constables assured Lord D'Abernon that this state of affairs had been practically unheard-of in peace time; they feared that it might continue after the war. I had, of course, known that women in ordinary times used public houses much less up north than in the London district, but I was not aware until then how wide was the difference. It seemed to me strange that leading police officials should be so troubled at what in the south was quite a normal custom.
>
> I have always regretted that it should have been regarded as proper for a man to enter a public house but unsuitable for a woman; however, that view was strongly held, particularly in the north - perhaps one reason was the low standard of public houses in the northern industrial districts - or perhaps one result!"

---

[16] Weekly Dispatch, September 9th 1917.

"Seventy Rolling Years" by Sydney Nevile, page 108.

The Carlisle State Management Scheme
The government didn't just regulate the brewery industry. It also got directly involved by taking over breweries a pubs in munitions manufacturing areas.

In late 1915 construction was begun of a giant munitions plant, the National Factory, just outside Gretna. Thousands of labourers flooded into the Carlisle and Gretna district to work on the factory's construction. Well-paid and with little in the form of entertainment available, they flooded Carlisle's pubs.

The number of convictions for drunkenness rocketed:

Convictions for drunkenness		
date	Annan	Carlisle
Jan-Jun 1915	6	72
Jan-Jun 1916	146	564
Source: "The Control of the Drink Trade" by Longmans, Green & Co., London, 1919, page 202.		

It sounds like the Wild West:

> The Rev. G. Bramwell Evens, who was resident in Carlisle throughout the period, thus describes the position in the city: "October, 1915-June, 1916 witnessed the coming of a new population. Into this quiet city of 50,000 inhabitants . . . there poured 10,000 to 12,000 of the navvy class whose hard-drinking propensity is proverbial. In addition to these, 2000 to 4000 more took up their abode in the Gretna hutments and neighbouring hamlets, making Carlisle, especially on Saturday nights, their drinking rendezvous. . . . The housing problem at once became acute. Small houses were simply stacked with men. Every available room was commandeered for sleeping purposes. Hundreds were compelled to board out. At night these men were practically turned out into the street until bed-time. Their landladies did not want them inside the house; their money was wanted but not their company. . . . The cafes and places of entertainment were crowded, and after these there only remained the public-house as a place of refuge.
>
> "Here, then, were thousands of men wandering aimlessly about, with no home ties, with plenty of money and with public-houses at every few yards inviting them to conviviality and seeming comfort. It is not to be wondered at that scenes of the most nauseating and degrading character became a common occurrence. Men fought like beasts; fierce fights raged round the doors of the public-houses. The diminished police force was unable to cope with the situation. Almost every alley was littered with prostrate drunken men. The main thoroughfare of Carlisle was Bedlam."
> The Truth about Direct Control in Carlisle, p. 4 (P. S. King).

Action was swift. On 22nd November 1915, draconian restrictions were introduced in the area around Carlisle on both sides of the border:

- Opening hours for the on trade reduced to 5.5 per day.
- Opening hours for the off trade reduced to 4.5 per day.
- Off sales of spirits limited to 2.5 hours per day.
- Off sales of spirits limited to Monday to Friday.
- Off sales of spirits forbidden in railway refreshment rooms.
- Off sales of spirits in quantities smaller than a reputed quart (about 1.33 pints) forbidden.
- Treating (buying alcohol for someone else), selling alcohol on credit and the "long pull" (serving a greater quantity than the supposed measure) all prohibited.
- Total closure on Sundays.
- Bona fide traveller no longer allowed to buy alcohol outside the permitted hours.[17]

But this wasn't enough to quell the disorder.

> "The Central Control Board, for which the ministry of Munitions is responsible, has acquired permanently 175 licensed houses, and in 50 cases it has acquired the licence without taking over the property.
>
> Some of the houses acquired have been shut up as unnecessary; but the Board is now carrying on business under the Defence of the Realm (Liquor Control) Regulations in 156 houses, including eight occupied under lease or tenancy and three constructed on its own initiative.
>
> The Board has made its greatest experiment in Carlisle and the surrounding district, and there, out of 201 licensed houses, 72 have been closed. Two breweries have also been shut down. The trade is being strictly regulated to meet local requirements, and it is becoming increasingly apparent that where private interest in public-houses is extinguished, and food and recreation as well as liquor are provided, the temptation to excessive drinking is being steadily reduced."
> Weekly Dispatch, May 13 1917.

There were some who would have liked to have nationalised the whole brewing trade. They had a couple of arguments. First, was the removal of the profit incentive for selling alcohol. Second, was efficiency, by concentrating production in a small number of breweries. Some of the people proposing this saw it as an initial step towards the complete suppression of the industry.

In reality, all but the Carlisle Old Brewery were closed. The other plant, the Carlisle New Brewery, was only used for bottling.

As the first set of restrictions didn't appear to be working, every more restrictions were introduced:

> "1. Redundant and undesirable licences were suppressed; this included the suppression of all "grocers' licences."
> 2. Further restrictions were placed on the sale of spirits, viz.—

---

[17] "The Control of the Drink Trade" by Longmans, Green & Co., London, 1919, pages 201 - 202.

(1) Temporary Prohibition of the sale of spirits in houses near the National Factory.
(2) Institution of the "spirit-less Saturday."
(3) Reduction of the number of houses selling spirits for "off" consumption.
(4) Mixed drinking—i.e., the custom of drinking beer and spirits mixed — was checked.
3. The "on" sale of liquor to young persons under eighteen was forbidden, excepting the sale of beer served with a meal.
4. The display of liquor-advertisements on the fronts of licensed premises ceased.
5. Complete Sunday Closing was extended with each extension of the State Purchase area in Cumberland."
"The Control of the Drink Trade" by Longmans, Green & Co., London, 1919, page 208.

Grocers' licences were for shops that sold both food and alcohol. There were ten such licenses in Carlisle. Seven discontinued selling alcohol, the other three dropped food. Of the seven in Gretna, only one, which stopped selling food, remained licensed.[18]

Fifty licenses were rescinded by the Control Board, mostly small pubs in the narrow lanes of the old part of the city. These were, by dint of their location, intrinsically difficult to police.[19] In addition many of the pubs which remained open were not allowed to sell spirits for consumption off the premises any longer.[20]

The thinking behind "spirit-less Saturday" was to remove temptation from workers who had just received their week's wages.[21] It sounds a bit miserable to me. I'd have got legless on Monday evening, just out of spite.

The ban on liquor advertisements had a massive impact on the appearance of Carlisle pubs. Until the introduction of state control, pubs had massive boards advertising all types of alcoholic drinks and displays of bottles in their windows. All of this disappeared, replaced by just the name of the pub and the name of the licensee over the door.[22]

Along with all these restrictive actions, there were also some constructive ones:

1. selling meals in pubs
2. improving the structure of licensed promises
3. offering attractions other than alcoholic drinks
4. providing other locations at which to hold gatherings such as trade union meetings.[23]

Beer Supply

Beer production was drastically reduced in April 1 1917, when output was set at a rate equivalent to 11,470,000 standard barrels a year. This was less than one-third of the pre-war level.

---

[18] "The Control of the Drink Trade" by Longmans, Green & Co., London, 1919, page 209.
[19] "The Control of the Drink Trade" by Longmans, Green & Co., London, 1919, page 209.
[20] "The Control of the Drink Trade" by Longmans, Green & Co., London, 1919, page 209.
[21] "The Control of the Drink Trade" by Longmans, Green & Co., London, 1919, page 210.
[22] The Control of the Drink Trade" by Longmans, Green & Co., London, 1919, page 213.
[23] "The Control of the Drink Trade" by Longmans, Green & Co., London, 1919, page 214.

1914: 36,165,000 standard barrels
1916: 30,292,977 standard barrels.
Year ended March 31 1917: 26,626,039 standard barrels

But note that these are standard barrels, a convenience for revenue purposes, not the actually volume of beer brewed. The number of bulk barrels (the volume actually produced) was much more, as this table shows:

	Duty		Standard barrels	Bulk barrels	Average OG England & Wales	Average price per pint
	s.	d.				
1914	7	9	36,057,913	37,558,767	1051.69	3d.
1915	23	0	33,099,000	34,736,000	1051.16	3d.
1916	23	0	30,292,000	32,110,000	1050.49	3d.
1917	24	0	26,626,000	30,163,000	1047.01	4d
1918	25	0	13,816,000	19,085,000	1038.25	4.5d
1919	50	0	12,925,000	23,264,000	1029.35	5d.
1920	79	0	25,115,000	35,047,000	1038.57	6d.

(Duty is for a standard barrel.)

In the final year of the war, beer production was at about 50% of its pre-war level.[24]

---

[24] "The Brewers' Almanack 1928", pages 73-74, 100-101.

Brewing outside the UK

Britain wasn't the only Country where the war had an enormous impact. The disruption it caused to world trade had a serious effect on brewing in every country in Europe, whether they were engaged in fighting the war or not.

Shortages of raw materials caused governments to restrict brewing in one way or another across the continent. The worst affected where countries belonging to the Central Powers, where foodstuffs of every type were in short supply.

Beer production during WW I

The war had an impact on the production of beer everywhere in Europe. And not just in those countries involved in the conflict.

Beer production 1913 - 1921 (hl)							
Year	Austria	Belgium	Czecho-slovakia	Denmark	France	Germany	UK
1913	21,082,000	16,727,000		2,466,000	12,844,000	69,200,000	56,960,947
1914	20,076,000	-		2,527,000	9,056,000	59,373,000	61,467,176
1915	16,040,000	8,139,000		2,425,000	5,824,000	45,820,000	56,896,285
1916	11,910,000	7,086,000		2,581,000	7,705,000	36,835,000	52,550,937
1917	-	5,391,000		2,306,000	7,115,000	23,837,000	49,365,176
1918	1,179,000	4,930,000		1,669,000	6,375,000	24,825,000	31,233,818
1919	-	9,488,000	4,420,000	2,374,000	10,785,000	29,458,000	38,073,804
1920	3,049,000	10,408,000	5,889,000	2,662,000	11,548,000	23,438,000	57,358,068
1921	3,040,000	12,536,000	6,554,000	2,471,000	12,254,000	33,993,000	56,468,799
Sources: European Statistics 1750-1970 by B. R. Mitchell, 1978, page 285. Brewers' Almanack 1928, p. 110 Note: 1913 – 1918 Austria = all Austria-Hungary, 1920 – 1921 just Austria.							

In most countries it wasn't until the early 1920's that some degree of normality returned.

I'm surprised that even 5 million hl were produced in Belgium in the later war years. This must include German-occupied Belgium as the area outside their control was tiny. A large proportion of the beer brewed in the occupied portion of Belgium was intended for German troops.

Belgium

Almost all of Belgium was occupied by the Germans. Only a tiny corner in the extreme northwest was spared.

It's not such a great surprise to discover that Belgium was stuffed full of breweries back then. The peak number of breweries (3,349 in 1910[25]) in the country was achieved just before WW I. To put that number into context, there were only slightly more in the UK, 3,647. A number which included 2,357 pub breweries[26].

The Belgian hop industry

Despite being close to the front line, hop-growing around Poperinge continued throughout the war. Belgian hops continued to be imported into the UK right through the war. It's not surprising that they exported their hops. The vast majority of Belgian breweries were in German-occupied territory. Plus they had exported large quantities of hops to the UK before the war.

France

It was unfortunate that the largest concentration of breweries were in the northeast of France, exactly the part of France where most of the fighting took place.

1,000 brewers were in the territory occupied by the Germans. All had their breweries stripped of copper and many of the buildings were damaged. But some had been able to re-equip with iron equipment and brewed a low-quality beer called "tiszane" from a little grain and some sugar.

After the war, worried about the damage to their brewing industry, the French government took measures to help it rebuild. The principal one being to provide standard brewhouses of various sizes to enable breweries to quickly replace the equipment stripped out by the Germans.

Germany

While their U-boat campaign might have severely impacted British imports from 1917 onwards, Germany had had to endure shortages much earlier. Hemmed in on all sides by hostile powers and blockaded at sea by the Royal Navy, Germany had difficulties in obtaining raw materials of any kind.

If WW I was unkind to British beer, it was downright malevolent to German beer. Beer production ground to a virtual stop in the final year of the war. And when peace came things didn't get much better.

Raw materials were so scarce that they even suspended the Reinheitsgebot:

> "Use of Raw Grain in German Brewing. - In consequence of the scarcity of barley and malt in Germany, the prohibition of raw grain for brewing is to be relaxed in so

---

[25] "Het Brouwersblad" June 2004, pages 6-7
[26] 1928 Brewers' Almanack, page 118.

far that husked and de-germed maize and rice screenings unsuitable for food are to be permitted as malt adjuncts. With a view to informing the German brewer of the character and treatment of these unfamiliar substances, Windisch, Grohn and Coblitz have contributed to the Wochenschrift fur Brauerei lengthy articles emphasising the necessity for investigating the method of using these grains with different qualities of: malt, the means of preventing yeast degeneration, etc., subjects which, as Petit observes, in Brasserie et Malterie, have been well known to brewers in other countries for many years."
Brewers' Journal 1921, Page 114.

While German U-boats might have sunk a considerable amount of Allied shipping in 1917 and briefly threatened Britain's food supply, the situation for Germany was far, far worse. By 1915 its merchant fleet had disappeared from the seas completely.

The supply of beer and its constituent raw materials might have been bad in Britain in 1917 and 1918, but the situation was much worse, and sooner, in Germany.

> **"BEER CRISIS IN PRUSSIA.**
> All the North German associations of hotelkeepers, licensed victuallers, owners of concert and dancing rooms, and so on, have addressed to the Food Dictator, Herr von Batocki, an urgent appeal against further restrictions, which are now imminent, of the production of beer. It is understood that the authorised supply of barley to the breweries, which has already been reduced one-half, is now to reduced to one-fourth of the peace figures.
>
> The petitioners make the interesting statement that the Prussian Army takes 11 per cent of the peace-time consumption, so that there would remain for the Prussian public only 14 per cent of the peace-time consumption. It is complained that in Bavaria beer is privileged as "an article of food," and that such differentiation will cause great bitterness in North Germany. It is declared that the petitioners have suffered more than any other class owing partly to the various restrictions on amusements, but still more to the fact that "meat, eggs, butter, fats, coffee, milk, tea and now spirits can hardly be obtained."
>
> The "Berliner Tageblatt" observes that there are 16,000 restaurants Berlin alone, and that a great part of them are already hardly able to exist. It is expected that the supply of Munich beer for North Germany will cease and Pilsen beer is very scarce."
> Manchester Evening News - Friday 17 November 1916, page 4.

That's a massive drop in beer output. Though it's safe to assume that the decline in the amount of beer brewed was smaller because, as in Britain, gravities were lowered. Meaning a greater quantity of beer was brewed from the same amount of materials.

I'll recap an earlier table for comparison purposes:

Drop in UK beer output		
period	standard barrels	bulk barrels
1914 to 1916	15.99%	14.51%
1914 to 1917	26.16%	19.69%
1914 to 1918	67.20%	53.18%
1914 to 1919	76.37%	44.52%
Source: The Brewers' Almanack 1928 pages 100 and 110.		

Standard barrels is what you need to look at as that relates directly to the quantity of materials being used. Even by 1917, that had fallen by just over 25%, compared to a 75% drop in Germany by 1916.

As you can see, the reduction in raw materials did eventually hit German levels, but not until 1919. Though drastic gravity cuts meant that bulk beer production only fell to a little under 50% of the pre-war level.

Food Dictator sounds like a pretty crazy office, though effectively the Food Controller filled the same role. His Thomas the Tank Engine name is somehow less frightening.

I can understand why the publicans were complaining in Berlin. Their livelihoods were under direct threat. In Britain the situation was more complex. On the one hand, they had less beer to sell. On the other, price increases meant that by keeping the same margin of profit, their income could increase. And restrictions on pub opening hours drastically reduced their working day and the amount they paid bar staff. Only in areas where the men had all been called away by the war did publicans really suffer.

The brewing industry in Bavaria 1910 – 1915

A Bavarian brewing journal, Bayerisches Brauer-Journal, published some handy statistics about the industry in Bavaria. They give an impression of the impact of the war on brewing in Bavaria. And they didn't even have the worst of it. As beer was officially recognised as a food in Bavaria, supplies of beer were greater than elsewhere in Germany.

Sadly this magazine didn't publish any of these numbers after 1915. They were probably too depressing. The effect of the war is already clear in the 1915 figures. Malt usage is down 25%, but beer production only 18%. That can only mean one thing: a drop in beer gravity.

The brewing industry in Bavaria 1910 - 1915

	1910	1911	1912	1913	1914	1915
malt usage (D -Ztr)	3,515,466	3,719,250	3,585,684	3,531,458	3,089,019	2,327,042
beer production total	18,119,473	19,641,640	19,300,262	19,088,071	17,020,404	14,191,893
bottom-fermenting	17,943,345	19,462,625	19,121,839	18,908,908	16,865,399	14,086,697
top-fermenting	167,128	179,015	178,423	179,163	155,005	105,196
beer exports	2,576,364	2,670,577	2,748,336	2,759,218	2,306,601	2,497,779
beer imports (Zollgebiet)	71,498	76,617	74,982	73,723	72,737	58,334
beer imports (abroad)	4,080	4,354	1,775	1,948		
bottom-fermenting breweries			3,582	3,485	3,396	3,031
Aktienbrauereien			86	84	80	81
Other breweries				2,911	2,807	2,482
Kommunbrauereien				490		
Braunbierbrauer			11,937	11,931	12,083	10,580
Kommunbrauer				8,936		
home-use Kommunbrauer			6,735	6,843		6,523
commercial Kommunbrauer			2,128	2,093	2,015	1,480
Weisbierbrauer			4,832	4,741	4,825	4,385
Munich breweries						
malt usage (D -Ztr)		956,941	905,632	889,952	742,603	642,840
beer production total		4,853,994	4,638,063	4,528,741	3,854,735	3,749,708
Weissbier production					43,728	32,795
beer exports		1,283,544	1,325,700	1,325,262	1,048,012	1,253,442

Sources:
1910 - 1913: Bayerisches Brauer-Journal 1914, pages 375-376
1914 - 1915: Bayerisches Brauer-Journal 1916, pages 241-242

I'm not totally sure what is meant by beer exports in this table. It could include shipments to other parts of Germany. Given that the amount exported increased in 1915, that's probably the case. Whatever the exact details, you can see that, although they were only responsible for about 25% of beer production, around 50% of Bavarian exports came from Munich breweries.

What's also obvious is that the huge number of Weissbier breweries produced bugger all beer. Before the war only 40-odd hectolitres each.

I was pleasantly surprised to see the number of Kommunbrauers making beer for personal use increased between 1912 and 1913. Though it did start dropping once war started. These Kommunbrauer were almost all in two regions: around Bamberg and Schweinfurt. On the eve of war there were a very respectable 490 communal breweries. I doubt there are 20 left today.

The organisation of the majority of bottom-fermenting breweries was still pretty old-fashioned, as only 80-odd out of 3,000 plus were limited companies. I'd bet a good percentage of those 80 were located in Munich and Nuremberg.

The proportion of top-fermented beer was tiny, under 1% for all of these years. I'm sure that's very different now, given the huge surge in popularity of Weissbier since the 1970's.

Let's look at Britain first. You can see from this table that beer was still almost at its pre-war strength in 1916. Gravity only started to be slashed in 1917, when Germany's U-boat campaign began to bite.

Average UK gravity 1916 - 1919			
1916	1917	1918	1919
1051.88	1048.54	1039.81	1030.55
Source: Brewers' Almanack 1928, p. 110			

In Bavaria, average beer gravity was far lower by 1916, as you can see from the next two tables. 8.56° Plato is about 1034°, and 8.35° Plato about 1033°. Only half way through the war Bavarian beer gravity was already almost as low as British beer gravity would get.

Urban Bavarian breweries 1916 (767 samples)			
	highest	lowest	average
Extract	6.56	0.4	3.95
Alcohol (ABW)	3.6	0.42	2.35
OG	13.48	1.24	8.56
attenuation	69.96	34.73	54.1
Source: Bayerisches Brauer-Journal 1919, page 249.			

Rural Bavarian breweries 1916 (138 samples)			
	highest	lowest	average
Extract	5.6	2.3	3.74
Alcohol (ABW)	3.93	1.49	2.33
OG	12.06	5.87	8.35
attenuation	66.03	40.45	55.08
Source: Bayerisches Brauer-Journal 1919, page 249.			

Look at the lowest gravities: 5.87 and 1.24. 1.24° Plato? That's just 1005°. Even in the darkest times, beer had to have a minimum gravity of 1010° in Britain.

You can see that, while some proper-strength beer was still brewing brewed in Bavaria in 1916, it was still on average pretty thin stuff. In 1917 and 1918 things were much, much worse as the supply of raw materials totally dried up.

When the war was over

But in one way German drinkers did fare better. As this article demonstrated. And I don't just mean they got free beer. German beer eventually returned to its pre-war strength, something that we're still waiting for in Britain:

> "Pre-war Beer in Germany.—The return to the beer drinkers status quo, by which Munich citizens are enabled after a suspension of more than six years again to indulge in beer of pre-war strength, was joyously celebrated in the chief Lion Brew beer hall, says the Munich correspondent of the Daily Express, the mouth of a gigantic statue of Gambrinus, the beer-god, which had been connected with the cellars beneath, poured forth a continuous stream of beer for an hour, during which no charge was made for the refreshment. Numbers of well-dressed men and women,

and even boys and girls, provided with mugs and vessels of all kinds, filed in and out of the building, and filling their vessels with the foaming liquor, drank to the god Gambrinus while they danced round in their joy."
Brewers Journal 1921, page 332.

Why should that be? Why did German beer get back all its strength when British beer didn't? I think it's connected with the German way of classifying and labelling beer. Schenkbier, Vollbier, Export, Bock and Märzen were defined in law as being in specific gravity bands. Whereas in Britain it was a free for all.

And then there's the taxation element. Not only were the UK wartime tax increases not repealed, beer duty was raised even more. I suspect that wasn't the case in Germany, though I don't have any figures.

That sounds like quite a party at Löwenbräu. Wish I could have been there.

Austria

You can tell when things are getting bad when governments start cutting beer production. And putting up the price. Why? Because it's a great way of pissing the public off. Something governments rarely do deliberately.

The more observant among you might have noticed that I've started writing about Germany and Austria in WW I. There's a good reason for that. One that I'm not going to tell you quite yet. It is very revealing, though, to look at the war from the other side. The food and booze situation at home for the Central Powers made Britain look like the promised land, overflowing with milk and honey, Or at least bread and beer.

Of course, the German U-boat campaign against British shipping didn't really kick off until 1917. Which is when Britain began to experience grain shortages, though at never anything like the same level as Germany or Austria.

> **"Beer Scarcity in Austria**
> Berne, September 1.
> Owing to the poorness of the barley harvest in Austria the production of beer will be reduced from October by fully 50 per cent. The brewers, who hitherto had old stocks of barley, have now received from the Government only 30 per cent. of the habitual quantity. This will entail a heavy loss of revenue to both the Government and the municipalities of Austria, where the taxes on beer formerly yielded 220 million kronen annually. A further rise in the price of beer is therefore announced for October. Austrian beer prices have already risen six kronen per hectolitre, Hungarian fourteen kronen, and German ten marks per hectolitre since the beginning of the war.
>
> Owing to the limited quantity of beer allowed in Germany the beer halls are often obliged to close at 8 p.m., all their beer having been already consumed."
> Western Times - Saturday 04 September 1915, page 4.

Output to be reduced 50% but only 30% of the normal amount of barley available. That means there must have been a gravity cut as well. I make that a 40% reduction in gravity. So if average gravity had been 1048°, it would have dropped to 1028°. Austrian beer had been quite strong before the war, so my guess is that average gravity was higher, probably in the low 1050's. Which would still have meant it dropping to about 1030°. The sort the depth not reached until 1918 in Britain.

"PERSONAL SACRIFICES.
Fewer Cigarettes and Weaker Beer for the Enemy.
Zurich, Monday.—The recent medical examinations of recruits have shown that the growing habit of cigarette smoking is exercising the most deleterious effect on the health of the future Bavarian soldiers. The authorities have imposed rigid restrictions with a view to preventing cigarette smoking among boys and youths.

In Austria a Ministerial decree has just been issued restricting the production of beer from December to next March inclusive to 55 per of the normal quality. This measure is taken to protect the stocks of barley in the country. Not a single transaction was reported the Buda Pest Corn Exchange on Saturday.

The grain trade in Hungary entirely a standstill. A large number flour mills are being shut down unable to obtain supplies wheat. The millers' only hope is in the Government requisitioning large stocks which are being kept back by landowners and farmers in the hope obtaining still higher prices. - Reuter."
Manchester Evening News - Tuesday 07 December 1915, page 4.

This appears to contradict the first report, allowing 55% of the normal level of beer output as opposed to 50%. Did they permit slightly more beer to be produced or was that 55% of the 50%?

"VIENNA BEER RIOTS.
RISE IN PRICE INFURIATES THE MOB.
According to a telegram from Rotterdam says an Exchange Amsterdam telegram today, it is reported that serious riots have taken place in cafes in Vienna owing to the announcement of an increase of five kroner per hectolitre of beer.

A number of cafes have been attacked by an infuriated mob, who destroyed everything inside.

The police have ordered the closing of all cafes after 8 p.m., unless under special licence. The inhabitants of Vienna are very excited about the raising of the price of beer, and trouble is expected over the whole of Austria."
Liverpool Echo - Tuesday 18 January 1916, page 8.

I can't condone smashing up pubs, but drinkers must have been pretty upset to go on the rampage like that. There were angry reactions in Britain to beer price rises, too, but they don't seem to have ever spilled over into violence.

Pilsner Urquell sort of continued to brew throughout the war. Initially, it did get some barley to brew with: in 1915 the brewery it received just 1.2% of the peacetime volume, considerably less than the 8% it was supposed to get. By 1917 it was reduced using chestnuts, potatoes and beets as a source of starch to brew a pseudo-beer called Pivolín.

Denmark

Just because Denmark was neutral in WW I, doesn't mean the war had no impact on the country's brewing industry. It did. And in some ways developments parallel what happened in Britain.

The main cause was the disruption caused to world trade by the war. Some of this was direct, as in the destruction of shipping and difficulties in sourcing goods from abroad. Some was indirect, such as increased prices. These factors also influenced British brewing, but you'll see that the effect in Denmark was less extreme.

> "The great expansion of the bottled beer trade in Denmark during the last year is very remarkable in view of the enormous handicap imposed in almost every direction by high prices and war conditions. High prices are world-wide and affect neutral countries equally and in special cases even more than belligerents. Such a special case occurred in Denmark in respect of coal. Imports were practically brought to a standstill and prices soared from their pre-war level of Kr. 20 per 1,000 kilos, to Kr. 150 in 1918, since when the increase has gone steadily on till they now stand at Kr. 230 per 1,000 kilos. (£1 per ton to £11 10s. per ton at normal exchange Kr. 20 = £I). The price of bottles may be given as another example of the constantly increasing burden of expenses borne by the trade during the period under review. Bottles of 330 c.cm. capacity (about 14 oz.) bought before the war at 5.5 ore (about 0.5.) now cost 30 ore (about 3d.).
>
> Wages also have increased from Kr. 26 (26s.) per week in 1914 to an average now of Kr. 89.24 (£4 10s.), while working hours have fallen from 9.5 to 8 per day."
> Journal of the Institute of Brewing, Volume 27, Issue 1, January 1921, pages 25 - 26.

I can understand why coal would have become more expensive, as Denmark would have imported it. But I don't quite see why wages should have increased so much. There was a simple reason why wages had risen in Britain during the war: shortage of manpower. With so many men serving in the armed forces, employers struggled to find anyone to work for them. Why did wages almost quadruple in Denmark? Was it just inflation or was there an underlying structural change?

As in Britain, shortages in food supplies prompted the Danish government to intervene in the brewing industry:

> "Restrictions on brewing were also imposed as national necessity demanded, the following regulations being successively brought into force:—
>
> April 3rd. 1917.— Restriction of brewing material to not more than 80 per cent, of the normal consumption.
>
> Nov. 9th, 1917.— Prohibition of the use of Danish barley for malting.
>
> Nov. 24th, 1917.— Prohibition of export of beers and yeast. This regulation is not yet withdrawn, but it is possible to obtain permits for export. the restrictions on the

use of brewing materials and on the employment of Danish barley for malting have, on the other hand, been recently withdrawn, but economies are still enforced by the prohibition since Feb. 6th, 1920, of the sale in Denmark of beer containing more than 3 per cent, by weight of absolute alcohol."
Journal of the Institute of Brewing, Volume 27, Issue 1, January 1921, page 26.

This is freaky. April 1917 is exactly when the first big restrictions on beer output were introduced, reducing the number of standard barrels brewed to about a third of its pre-war level. It's not really a coincidence. In February 1917 German U-boats began unrestricted attacks on merchant shipping and it initially had a huge impact. Large numbers of merchant ships were sunk in the spring of 1917 and food supplies began to dwindle in Britain.

Before the war, Danish breweries like Carlsberg had been big exporters. It's only logical that exports should be restricted at a time when raw materials were in short supply. A ban on the export of yeast is stranger. Though, again through Carlsberg and its yeast labs, Denmark exported lots of yeast, too.

In yet another parallel with Britain, new restrictions continued after the war's end. 3% ABW is about 3.75% ABV. The strictest restrictions on beer strength in Britain were in 1918, when the average of all beer brewed was capped at 1030°. Though by 1920 the situation in Britain had improved and the limit on average gravity had been raised to 1044°.

Just as in Britain, restrictions caused the range of beers brewed to be drastically reduced:

Average Original Gravities of Danish Beers 1914 - 1920						
October 1st	1914	1915	1916	1917	1918	1919
September 30th	1915	1916	1917	1916	1919	1920
Lager beer	1052	1051	1048	1045	0	0
Pilsener beer	1044	1044	1041.5	1032	1038	1038
Stout, tax class I	1076	1076	1072	0	0	0
Stout, tax class II	1068	1068	1065	1058	1055	1056
Munich beer	1056	1056	1055	0	0	0
Export beer	1052	1050	1049.5	0	0	0
New Pilsener, tax class II	1032	1032	1032	1030	1031	1031
Source: Journal of the Institute of Brewing, Volume 27, Issue 1, January 1921, page 27.						

For comparison purposed, here's what happened to Whitbread's beers during the war:

Whitbread beers 1914 - 1920								
beer	style	1914	1915	1916	1917	1918	1919	1920
FA	Pale Ale	1048.5		1045.3	1035.2	1032.6	1032.4	
IPA	IPA	1049.9		1046.8	1038.8	1033	1036	1034
PA	Pale Ale	1061.1		1056.5	1044.3	1035.1	1047.4	1047.5
KK	Stock Ale	1072.7		-	-	-	-	-
KKK	Stock Ale	1082		1069.6	-	-	-	-
X	Mild	1055.1		1047.9	-	-	1040	1043
MA	Mild	-	-	-	-	1022.7	1028.4	1027.8
ES	Stout	1066.8	-	-	-	-	1055	1055.3
LS	Stout	1055.7	1054.7	1050.4		1041.7	1042.9	1047.8
P	Porter	1052.4	1052.4	1050.4	1049	1036.1	1042.6	1041.4
SS	Stout	1081.7	1075	1074.9	-	-	-	-
SSS	Stout	1096.1	1094.5	1091.2	-	-	-	-
Source: Whitbread brewing records held at the London Metropolitan Archives, document numbers LMA/4453/D/09/109, LMA/4453/D/09/111, LMA/4453/D/09/112, LMA/4453/D/09/113, LMA/4453/D/01/080, LMA/4453/D/01/081, LMA/4453/D/01/082, LMA/4453/D/01/083, LMA/4453/D/01/084 and LMA/4453/D/01/085.								

Just as in Britain, the tax on beer shot up in Denmark during the war:

> "In addition to these restrictions the taxes on beer have been greatly increased. Up till Nov. 10th, 1917, beers containing less than 2.25 per cent, by weight of absolute alcohol were duty free. Those with over 2.25 per cent, being taxed at Kr. 9.50 per hectolitre (equivalent to about 15s. 6d. per barrel). But now all beers are taxed, being divided into "Skatteklasse I" and "Skatteklasse II" (Tax classes I and II), the former containing more than 2.25 percent, by weight of absolute alcohol bearing a tax of Kr. 18 per hectolitre (about 29s. 6d. per barrel) and the latter so-called temperance beers with less than 2.25 per cent, alcohol at Kr. 5.70 per hectolitre (9s. 4d. per barrel)."
> Journal of the Institute of Brewing, Volume 27, Issue 1, January 1921, page 26.

Seems like a good time for some contextualisation. Let's take a look at the tax in the UK during WW I:

UK tax and average OG 1914 - 1921			
	Tax/Bulk Barrel	Tax/Std. Barrel	Average OG
1914	7s 4d	7s 9d	1052.8
1915	21s 11d	23s	1052.35
1916	21s	23s	1051.88
1917	20s 11d	24s	1048.54
1918	20s	25s	1039.81
1919	21s 10d	50s	1030.55
1920	40s 8d	70s	1039.41
1921	71s 6d	100s	1042.61
Source: 1928 Brewers' Almanack			

That's creepy. The pre-war Danish tax of 15s. 6d. per barrel was exactly double the UK rate of 7s. 9d. You may have noticed that I've included both the tax per standard barrel (36 gallons with an OG of 1055°) and per bulk barrel of a beer with an average OG. You can see that the two were almost the same in 1914, when average gravity was close to 1055° but diverged as the war progressed.

Repeated tax increases in Britain left the rate considerably higher than in Denmark. Surprisingly, the largest increases came after war's end. I can understand why there was less pressing need to boost tax revenue in Denmark, which didn't need to buy all those expensive guns and shells, but it seems perverse that the tax rocketed in Britain once war expenses were done with.

Now we come to the price of beer. A direct comparison is a bit tricky, as the types, strengths and packaging of beer were so different in the two countries. But I'm going to make an attempt anyway. First the Danish numbers:

> "These and greatly increased expenses in every other direction have raised the prices of "Pilsener" beer from 11 ore (about 1d.) to 26 ore (2.5d.) per bottle of 330 c.cm. and in cask from Kr. 26 to Kr. 72 per hectolitre (about 42s. 6d. to 117s. 6d. per barrel). The beers with less than 2.25 per cent alcohol show an even greater increase. The new Pilsener for instance increasing from Kr. 7.5 to 24.25 ore per bottle (about 0.75d. to 2.5d.) and from Kr. 16 to Kr. 60 per hectolitre in cask (or 26s. 3d. to 98s. 6d. per barrel)."
> Journal of the Institute of Brewing, Volume 27, Issue 1, January 1921, pages 26 - 27.

1d for 33cl of Pilsner is the equivalent of about 1.7d per pint. It's stupid to compare it with the price of Pilsner in Britain, because that was an expensive niche product. It makes most sense to compare it with Britain's favourite, Mild Ale, which cost 2d per pint in 1914. But we also need to take into account the different gravities: Danish Pilsner was 1044°, Mild Ale about 1050°. Taking that into account, the Danish Pilsner was about 2d per pint. remarkably close to the British price.

Beer was price-controlled in Britain in the later war years. Which is handy, since, as it was based on gravity, I know exactly what beers of a specific strength cost in Britain. We know that in 1920 Danish Pilsner had an OG of 1038°, which puts it firmly in the 1033° to 1039° band. Which cost 6d. for draught beer, 8d. for bottled[27]. How much did the Danish Pilsner cost? The equivalent of about 4.3d. per pint. A good bit cheaper than the British price.

I've also done the maths for draught Pilsner, which works out to 1.77d. per pint in 1914. After taking into account the difference in gravity, it comes out to exactly 2d. per pint. Or the same as Mild Ale. And the same price as bottled beer. It's no wonder bottled beer was popular in Denmark if draught beer was no cheaper.

The 1920 price of draught Danish Pilsner is the equivalent of 4.9d. per pint. More expensive than the bottled version, but still a good bit cheaper than the 6d. you'd have paid for a pint of British beer of a similar gravity.

I've been promising you something about Danish beer styles and here you are. First the sad

---

[27] "The Brewers' Almanack 1928" pages 100 - 101.

tale of a discontinued style:

> "The brewing of the stronger "Lager beer" was stopped in Feb., 1918, and export trade brought to a complete standstill, and despite the renewed freedom of the seas, freights still prevent more than a partial resumption."
> Journal of the Institute of Brewing, Volume 27, Issue 1, January 1921, page 27.

What was that lost Lager beer like? According to the table we saw earlier, it had a gravity of 1052° in 1914, while Pilsner was 1044°. Here's a little more description of the style:

> "Bottled beers during recent years have been mainly of two types "Pilsener," a pale beer, and "Lager," a darker and rather stronger beer. The Lager is no longer brewed on account of the restrictions on gravity, and alcohol, and with the exception of old stocks which at the time of writing are approaching exhaustion, the only bottled beer in consumption in Denmark is of a gravity of 1038 or less. At the Carlsberg and Tuborg breweries the 1038 beers are of the Pilsener type, sparkling and palatable light beers, but not equal in point of flavour or character to their pre-war prototypes of 11° Balling or 1044°. At the smaller breweries at other places darker beers of the same maximum gravity are brewed. The old top fermentation beers peculiar to the country are being gradually displaced by these finer bottom fermentation beers, and of late the national beverage Schnapps is also being ousted by bottled Pilsener on account of its greatly enhanced price."
> Journal of the Institute of Brewing, Volume 27, Issue 1, January 1921, page 27.

How dark was "rather darker"? Probably not properly dark, as there was also Munich beer at 1056°. That would have been properly dark. As in most countries where Lager took off early, the first bottom-fermenting brews were in the dark Munich style. When I first visited Copenhagen in the 1980's, both Tuborg and Carlsberg had beers sort of in the Munich style. I suspect this Lager beer was still pale, but a rather more golden shade than the Pilsner.

The author clearly views the 1038° Pilsener as inferior to the stronger version. Though the drop in gravity is tiny compared to that in Britain. Mild had its gravity halved between 1914 and 1919. And never got back to its pre-war level. Whitbread's for example, that had been 1055° in 1914, was only 1042° in the 1920's. Whereas in Denmark Pilsner went back to its pre-war strength:

Danish Pilsener in the 1930's

Year	Brewer	Beer	package	Acidity	OG	FG	colour	ABV	App. Atten-uation
1936	Carlsberg	Pilsner	bottled	0.06	1044.8	1011.1		4.38	75.22%
1939	Carlsberg	Pilsner	bottled	0.04	1044.5	1009.9	9	4.50	77.75%
1934	Tuborg	Pilsner	bottled	0.06	1044.7	1013.4		4.05	70.02%
1939	Tuborg	Pilsner	bottled	0.04	1044.6	1011.5	8	4.30	74.22%

Source:
Whitbread Gravity book held at the London Metropolitan Archives, document number LMA/4453/D/02/001

Interesting that the smaller breweries made a dark beer at the maximum gravity of 1038°. Was that a sort of Munich Lager? According to the table we saw earlier, proper Munich beer disappeared in 1917.

Unsurprisingly, top-fermenting beers were under pressure from the fancy new, industrially-brewed Lagers. I guess he means low-gravity things like Hvidtøl and Skibsøl. The tradition never totally died out and Refsvindinge still brews a top-fermenting Hvidtøl. It's a shame the author didn't write a little more about these.

I've just noticed something that doesn't tally. The author says that a maximum gravity of 1038° was introduced in 1918, but the table of beer gravities shows Stout at 1055° in 1918 and 1056° in 1919. Bit of a mystery, that one.

The proportion of bottled to draught beer was a big difference between the British and Danish brewing industries.

> "Despite all these difficulties, increased prices, and lower gravities, the trade has recently gone ahead until the breweries are entirely unable to cope with the demands. Table II shows the strides made at the Carlsberg Brewery alone, and the increases are paralleled by those at the Tuborg Brewery.
>
> Table II.
>
> | Beer Sales (Carlsberg Brewery) in Barrels. | | | |
> |---|---|---|---|
> | | Bottled. | Cask. | Total. |
> | 1914-15 | 250,300 | 19,200 | 269,500 |
> | 1915-16 | 270,100 | 19,200 | 289,800 |
> | 1916-17 | 281,300 | 40,000* | 321,300 |
> | 1917-18 | 182,000 | 13,900 | 195,900 |
> | 1918-19 | 254,800 | 17,600 | 272,400 |
> | 1919-20 | 406,400 | 21,400 | 427,800 |
>
> * Including 25,000 hectl. Pilsener at 18 Balling exported to Germany.
>
> It will be noticed that whereas before the war the proportion of bottled beer to cask was as 14 to 1, it is now 20 to 1, a most remarkable development."

Journal of the Institute of Brewing, Volume 27, Issue 1, January 1921, pages 27 - 28.

25,000 hl of Pilsner at 18 Balling sent to Germany? A beer of that strength isn't a Pilsner, it's a Doppelbock with an ABV north of 7%. It seems really odd to have exported a beer that strong to Germany in the middle of the war. By that time the stuff brewed in Germany was pretty watery. In 1916, gravities were typically in the range 8-8.5° Balling[28].

During the war bottled beer, already wildly popular, strengthened its hold on the market. By the end of the war it accounted for 95% of sales. I'd be failing my duty if I didn't come up with similar figures for a British brewery. And guess what? I have just the numbers:

---

[28] Bayerisches Brauer-Journal 1919, page 249.

Whitbread Draught and Bottled sales 1901 – 1919							
	total draught		Bottling		Burton		
Year	barrels	%	barrels	%	barrels	%	Total
1914	418,402	49.38%	427,455	50.45%	1,415	0.17%	847,272
1915	374,682	51.79%	347,489	48.03%	1,253	0.17%	723,424
1916	359,215	48.44%	381,397	51.43%	980	0.13%	741,592
1917	281,549	50.15%	278,976	49.69%	924	0.16%	561,449
1918	246,665	63.10%	143,902	36.81%	367	0.09%	390,934
1919	369,845	69.08%	165,000	30.82%	527	0.10%	535,372
1920	400,605	57.14%	298,873	42.63%	1,660	0.24%	701,138
Source:							
Whitbread archive document number LMA/4453/D/02/16							
Note:							
Year ending July							

I'm not sure what the Burton column refers to but, as it concerns tiny amounts of beer, I don't think we need to worry about that.

I'm truly staggered that just over half of Whitbread's sales were in bottled format in 1914. I'd have guessed a much lower percentage. But the fall in the share of bottled during the war is exactly what I'd expect. Bottled beer takes more resources and energy to produce compared to draught beer. Which makes the increase at Carlsberg even more striking.

Holland

WW I, and in particular the German submarine campaign didn't just affect the British brewing industry. Dutch breweries suffered, too. Possibly even more than British ones.

This is a passage from a glossy new history of Amstel.

> "'War Beer'
> The problems facing the Amstel and other Dutch brewers caused by the war seemed at first to be manageable. The year 1917 brought a tax increase and problems with raw materials which had far reaching effects for the Dutch beer industry. The huge tax increase on beer which Minister Treub introduced, meant that all breweries had to increase dramatically their retail prices in March 1917. In addition, stocks of malting barley and malt further declined, because of which Dutch breweries, in consultation with each other, decided to reduce the strength of their beer. From July 1917, Amstel made only two types of weak 'war beer': light-coloured Pilsner and dark Lager. The higher prices combined with the deterioration in quality of the 'war beer' were not conducive to the domestic beer consumption. The export of bottled beer, which in previous years had caused an increase in sales, also collapsed.
>
> The scarcity was a direct result of the unrestricted submarine warfare declared by Germany on February 1, 1917. The risk of being torpedoed was great and ships were therefore not given permission by the Dutch government to fetch malt from the United States. Together with Heineken and Oranjeboom, Amstel then decided to

charter a Danish ship. This Danish ship, the Maersk Olaf did successfully make the risky passage three times. The third load of malt to reach the Netherlands in this way, in June 1917, was seized by the Dutch government, which forced the large breweries to give a portion to the small breweries. This ended immediately the risky trans-Atlantic malt charters. All Dutch brewers worked from mid-1917 through stocks in their malt. As the war dragged on, a collective decision to further dilute Dutch beer was inevitable. That decision was in April 1918. Following this decision, the quality of Amstel Pilsener and Amstel Lager declined even further. The recipes of these war beers differed significantly from those of pre-war times. In addition to malt, now rice, maize, tapioca and sugar were also used in the grist.

In the course of 1918 had many Dutch brewers had to stop beer production due to lack of raw materials."
"Amstel, het Verhaal van ons Bier 1870 - Heden" by Peter Zwaal, 2010, pages 59 and 66.

I like the bit about them having to use sugar and maize because of shortages. Later, of course, these adjuncts were totally standard ingredients in Dutch beer. The war was probably when brewers learnt about their use.

Note that, just as in the UK and Denmark, restrictions on brewing in Holland started in spring 1917, just after Germany started its U-boat campaign. This had an impact on all maritime trade in the North Atlantic and North Sea, for both combatant and neutral nations.

Mini Book Series volume XXXII: Armistice!

The aftermath of WW I

World beer production 1912 - 1922

These numbers from just before and just after WW I demonstrate the enormous impact of the war on the brewing industry not just in Europe but across the world.

I used to think that British beer took a hammering in WW I. Now I've looked into it more, I realise that Britain got off lightly compared to most of the rest of Europe. Even those countries which weren't directly involved, such as Switzerland and Denmark, saw beer production shrink. The only exception was the Southern European countries (Spain, Portugal and Italy).

It's a bit tricky making direct comparisons for the two major powers on the losing side, Germany and Austria-Hungary because of border changes. Especially in the case of Austria-Hungary, which was split among several new countries. Germany also lost a considerable amount of territory to Poland in the East and France in the West. But still nowhere like enough to account for a fall in production of 39 million hectolitres.

World hop consumption and beer production 1912 - 1922						
	1912/13			1921/22		
Counrtry	Probable beer production (hl)	hops (pfund) per hl beer	hop consumption (1,000 Zentner)	Probable beer production (hl)	hops (pfund) per hl beer	hop consumption (1,000 Zentner)
Germany	69,000,000	0.38	262	30,000,000	0.38	114
Austria	26,000,000	0.55	143			
German Austria and Hungary				2,000,000	0.55	11
Czechoslovakia and eastern states				6,000,000	0.55	33
Yugoslavia and the Balkans				1,300,000	0.6	7.8
France	17,000,000	0.5	85	8,000,000	0.5	40
Belgium and the Netherlands	19,000,000	0.5	95	8,000,000	0.5	40
Russia	11,000,000	0.8	88			
Scandinavia and Denmark	5,700,000	0.5	28	5,500,000	0.4	22
Switzerland	3,000,000	0.5	15	1,500,000	0.5	7.5
Spain, Portugal and Italy	800,000	0.5	4	1,600,000	0.5	8
Continental Europe	**151,500,000**	**0.48**	**720**	**63,900,000**	**0.44**	**283.3**
UK	58,000,000	1.0	580	42,000,000	1.2	504
Europe	**209,500,000**	**0.62**	**1300**	**105,900,000**	**0.74**	**787.3**
USA	74,000,000	0.5	370	Prohibition	-	110
Canada	1,900,000	0.6	11	1,200,000	0.6	7.2
Central America	600,000	0.6	3.5	600,000	0.6	3.6
South America	2,800,000	0.6	16	3,100,000	0.6	18.6
Americas	**79,300,000**	**0.51**	**400.5**	**4,900,000**	**0.60**	**29.4**
East Asia	400,000	0.6	2.5	1,400,000	0.6	8.4
Australia and New Zealand	2,800,000	0.75-1.0	23	3,200,000	0.9	28.8
Africa and India	300,000	0.6	2	800,000	0.7	5.6
Asia and Africa	**3,500,000**	**0.79**	**27.5**	**5,400,000**	**0.79**	**42.8**
World	**293,200,000**	**0.59**	**1734**	**116,200,000**	**0.83**	**969.5**
Source: Barth Hop Report 1911-1912, Barth Hop Report 1914-1915 to 1920-1921						

One other handy feature of this table is the quantity of hops used. In 1912/13 the UK used almost a third of total world consumption. By 1921/22 that was up to more than 50%. That can be partly accounted for by the much heavier hopping of British beer, around treble the rate in Germany. The British really did love their hops in the past.

Just to emphasise how big the drop in beer production was, here is the fall in percentage terms:

World beer production	
Country	% change
Germany	-56.52%
France	-52.94%
Belgium and the Netherlands	-57.89%
Scandinavia and Denmark	-3.51%
Switzerland	-50.00%
Spain, Portugal and Italy	100.00%
Continental Europe	*-57.82%*
UK	-27.59%
Europe	*-49.45%*
Canada	-36.84%
Central America	0.00%
South America	10.71%
Americas	*-93.82%*
East Asia	250.00%
Australia and New Zealand	14.29%
Africa and India	166.67%
Asia and Africa	*54.29%*
World	*-60.37%*
Source (derived from): Barth Hop Report 1911-1912 Barth Hop Report 1914-1915 to 1920-1921	

The only region of the world to see an increase in beer production was Asia, which was mostly untouched by the war.

Note also that the fall in beer production was greater in victorious France than defeated Germany. The explanation is pretty simple: a high percentage of French breweries were in the area occupied by the Germans. All lost their copper, many had their buildings damaged or destroyed as well.

I'd argue that Prohibition, which was responsible for the massive decline in beer output in the Americas, was also a result of the war. It was pushed through during the war, partly based on fear of the Germans who dominated American brewing.

Put in a nutshell, WW I more than halved world beer production. An unprecedented disaster.

Hop production by country 1900 - 1921

We're back with hops today. With another sexy little table to seduce us, fluttering its eyelids and waggling its arse. Aren't we lucky?

Why am I bothering you with this particular table? Because it straddles WW I and shows the effect of the war on the hop trade. Or lack of effect, in some cases.

The four countries with the biggest share of hop production - Germany, USA, UK and Czechoslovakia - remained at the top of the pile for most of the 20th century. With the exception of Britain, whose hop industry collapsed in the 1980's.

It's a great irony that the country to profit most from the effects of the war, the USA, wasn't brewing any beer at all by the time of the last figures. Presumably it was exports that kept hop growing alive in the US. I can't think of many uses for hops other than in making beer.

Share of world hop production by country						
Country	1900/01	1905/06	1910/11	1914/15	1919/20	1920/21
Germany	27.97%	24.56%	25.14%	24.50%	11.94%	13.56%
UK	22.80%	28.60%	18.88%	26.51%	25.47%	25.92%
USA	21.25%	20.39%	25.52%	26.20%	35.27%	32.08%
Czechoslovakia formerly Bohemia	10.01%	11.85%	14.43%	14.41%	11.67%	11.63%
Russia	5.17%	4.05%	3.70%	war zone	-	-
France	4.65%	2.87%	3.45%	2.83%	7.98%	8.69%
Belgium	3.36%	4.33%	3.70%	war zone	1.99%	3.38%
Australia	1.04%	0.60%	0.65%	0.82%	2.90%	2.28%
Other countries	3.75%	2.75%	4.53%	4.73%	2.78%	2.46%
Source: Barth Hop Report 1914-1915 to 1920-1921						

In Britain and Belgium (more surprisingly) Belgium the war appears from this table to have had little effect. But if you look at the acreage under hops and the quantity of hops produced, you can see that this wasn't the case.

Hop production and acreage				
	1913	1921	1912	1922
Country	ha	ha	zentners	zentners
Germany	27,048	11,279	460,000	173,000
UK	14,449	10,179	375,000	325,000
USA	21,790	11,300	499,000	275,000
Czechoslovakia	15,878	8,640	334,000	109,000
France	2,861	4,214	60,000	86,000
Alsace-Lorraine	4,185	2,665	95,000	61,000
Belgium	2,283	1,500	70,000	27,000
World	101,078	52,955	1,975,000	1,074,000
Sources: Barth Hop Report 1913-1914, Barth Hop Report 1922-1923				

(I've used different years for the production because 1913 and 1921 were both years with a particularly bad harvest.)

In absolute terms, production fell everywhere except France. And the only reason it increased there was because of the transfer of Alsace-Lorraine back to France. Globally hop production was approximately cut in half as a result of WW I.

II Beer styles

Mini Book Series volume XXXII: Armistice!

Introduction

The war caused big changes in beer styles. The most obvious one being their strength. But there were also more subtle changes, for example to the ingredients employed in their production. Principally due to the problem of maintaining supplies of imported items, for example maize. Sugar became harder to obtain, too, partially because of available supplies being diverted to food production.

Most breweries of any size produced a wide range of styles with a wide variety of strengths. Though there were also clear geographical differences. Every brewery reduced the range of beers they produced during the war. Less popular and very stronger beers were dropped, often never to return.

In the 19th century big London breweries competed on strength rather than price. They were able to use their economies of scale to brew stronger beer that cost the same as weaker beer from their smaller rivals. Prices for the same type of beer were remarkably consistent across the country, whatever their strength.

You'll see in the sections that follow that, in general, London beers were stronger than those from elsewhere. The first image that comes into my head is of unknowing provincials visiting London and getting totally plastered after drinking X Ale that was 5.5% ABV rather than the 3.5% - 4% they were used to.

The war levelled out regional differences in price and strength. For one simple reason. Tax became such a large proportion of the price of beer that economies in production became less important.

A corollary of this effect is that beers from outside London suffered smaller falls in gravity than the beers from the capital.

British beer strengths 1900 – 1922								
	1900		1911		1913		1922	
	OG	ABV	OG	ABV	OG	ABV	OG	ABV
Light Ale (bottle)	1050	5%	1045°	4.5%	1045°	4.5%	1035°	3.5%
London pale bitter ale	1060°	6%	1055°	5. 5%	1055°	5. 5%	1045-50°	5.5%
London four-ale (mild)	1052-56°	5.5%	1055°	5.5%	1052°	5%	1035-40°	3.5-4%
Burton strong ale (KK)	1075°	7.5%	1072°	7.1%	1072°	7.1%	1054°	5.5%
Burton Pale Ale	1065°	6.5%	1059°	6.1%	1059°	6.1%	1050°	5%
London porter	1052-60°	5.5%	1054°	5.5%	1052°	5.25%	1035-40°	3.5%
Single stout	1064-72°	6.5%	1054°	6%	1055°	6%	1045°	4.5%
Double stout	1072-80°	7.5%	1082°	7.6%	1080°	7.5%	1054°	5.5%
Imperial stout	1110°	10%	1110°	10%	1095°	10%	1095°	10%
Guinness Porter	1063°	6%	1058°	5.5%	1058°	5.5%	1036°	3.5%
Guinness Extra Stout	1074°	7%	1074°	7%	1074°	7%	1054°	5.5%

The war changed British beer styles forever. Just about every style of beer was considerably weaker after the war than they had been before it.

Stock Ales, which had already been rapidly going out of fashion before the war, all but disappeared. A few specialist strong beers survived, such as Imperial Stout, but few beers over 8% ABV were brewed.

The categories defined by the last set of fixed government prices had a weirdly long life, lasting until WW II.

Beers:

Burton was a type of strong brown ale, one of the standard draught beers in a 1917 London pub. Wahl & Henius, describing the beer in 1902, defined it as being 1064-1069° OG and hopped at a rate of 2 to 3 pounds per American barrel. As a comparison, Burton Pale Ale is also 1064-1069° OG, with a hopping rate of 2.5 to 3 pounds per American barrel. Burton Mild Ale was 1053-1058° OG hopped at 1.25 to 1.5 pounds per American barrel. As Burton's price was the highest per barrel in 1917, we can infer it was the strongest draught beer.

Burton had a long history, being mentioned by Combrune in "Theory and Practice of Brewing" in 1762. Its journey from ubiquity to obscurity is a lesson in the fickle nature of public taste. It finally died out in the 1970's, when Fuller's was replaced by ESB and Youngs renamed theirs Winter Warmer. Though, Youngs did recently brew a seasonal beer called Burton.

Ballantine - the USA's largest ale brewery for decades – also produced a beer called Burton Ale.

Bitter was, as today, part of the standard pub draught range. Wahl & Henius describe London Pale Bitter Ale in 1902 as having an OG of 1055-1058° hopped at a rate of 1.5 to 2 pounds per American barrel. By 1914 the gravity had aleady dropped to around 1050°.

Mild was one of the most popular draught beers. Always cheaper than Bitter, it wasn't necessarily weaker before 1914. Wahl & Henius describe London Four Ale (Mild) in 1902 as having an OG of 1053-1058° hopped at a rate of 1 to 1.25 pounds per American barrel. It dropped from an average OG of 1048° in 1914 to 1032° (about the same as today) in 1919. It bore the brunt of the cuts needed to get the average gravity for all beer down to 1030°. At the height of the wartime restrictions in 1918 it sank to 1024°, 1027° or lower and barely counted as intoxicating. Mild has remained a low-alcohol drink ever since.

Porter long a London favourite, was stumbling uncertainly, even before 1914. The war gave it a final kick in the bollocks when it was already lying in a pool of its own wee. The weakest of the Porter/Stout style beers, it was elbowed out of its strength slot by Stout. Wahl & Henius describe Porter as having an OG of 1050-1061° hopped at a rate of 0.75 to 1.5 pounds per American barrel.

Stout remained a popular draught beer. It was the second-strongest draught, after Burton. Wahl & Henius describe Single Stout as 1064-1075° OG, hopped at a rate of 1.5 to 2 pounds per American barrel. Bottled stouts were stronger, with gravities as high as 1110° pre-war.

Lager is a surprising inclusion in the price fixing agreements. Finding someone who knew how to make it was a major headache for Britain's few lager breweries.

Lager has a surprisingly long history in Britain. The first to try bottom-fermentation was John Muir of Edinburgh in 1835. The legendary Munich brewer Gabriel Sedlmayr had visited Muir's brewery whilst on a study trip to Britain in the early 1830's. Sedlmayr sent some Bavarian yeast to Scotland on Muir's request. Despite being impressed with the results, Muir abandonned his attempts when he was unable to propagate the yeast successfully.

The **Wrexham Lager Beer Company** was founded in 1878 and, despite a takeover by Ind Coope in 1949, only closed in 2000.

Tennent's of Glasgow first brewed lager in 1885 and built a new dedicated brewhouse for its production in 1891.

Guinness was one of the strongest beers on sale in pubs. On April 1st 1917 Guinness Extra Stout was still 1074° OG (its pre-war strength), dropping in July the same year to 1062°. Guinness did not drop in strength as much as its English rivals because different rules applied in Ireland. By April 1st Guinness Extra Stout was down to 1049° (still higher than today – bottled Extra Stout is currently 1042°), but the average gravity in England by then was just 1030°.

Bass, like Guinness, was widely sold in bottled form, also in pubs tied to other brewers. It's gravity averaged 1062° in the 1800's. By 1919, it had dropped to 1044°. It later recovered a little in strength, getting up to 1046° in the 1950's.

British beer strengths 1900 – 1922								
	1900		1911		1913		1922	
	OG	ABV	OG	ABV	OG	ABV	OG	ABV
Light Ale (bottle)	1050	5%	1045°	4.5%	1045°	4.5%	1035°	3.5%
London pale bitter ale	1060°	6%	1055°	5.5%	1055°	5.5%	1045-50°	5.5%
London four-ale (mild)	1052-56°	5.5%	1055°	5.5%	1052°	5%	1035-40°	3.5-4%
Burton strong ale (KK)	1075°	7.5%	1072°	7.1%	1072°	7.1%	1054°	5.5%
Burton Pale Ale	1065°	6.5%	1059°	6.1%	1059°	6.1%	1050°	5%
London porter	1052-60°	5.5%	1054°	5.5%	1052°	5.25%	1035-40°	3.5%
Single stout	1064-72°	6.5%	1054°	6%	1055°	6%	1045°	4.5%
Double stout	1072-80°	7.5%	1082°	7.6%	1080°	7.5%	1054°	5.5%
Imperial stout	1110°	10%	1110°	10%	1095°	10%	1095°	10%
Guinness Porter	1063°	6%	1058°	5.5%	1058°	5.5%	1036°	3.5%
Guinness Extra Stout	1074°	7%	1074°	7%	1074°	7%	1054°	5.5%

Mild Ale

Before WW I

Mild Ale had been the most popular style of beer since the mid-19th century. For most breweries, Mild Ale accounted for more than 50% of output.

In the second half of the 19th century, it was typical for a brewery to produce four Mild Ales, usually called X, XX, XXX, XXXXX. By 1914, many breweries had reduced their range of Mild Ales to just two or three. Most extreme was London, where the large breweries often brewed just a single Mild, called X Ale.

The number of Milds brewed wasn't the only difference between London and the provinces. While a London X Ale had a gravity or at least 1050°, provincial versions could be as weak as 1040°. An XXX or XXXX Ale from the provinces was around the same strength as a London X.

Provincial Mild Ale before WW I								
Year	Brewer	Beer	OG	FG	ABV	App. Atten-uation	lbs hops/ qtr	hops lb/brl
1914	Boddington	B	1037.0	1010.0	3.57	72.97%	2.86	0.51
1914	Boddington	BB	1047.0	1014.0	4.37	70.21%	3.62	0.85
1914	Boddington	XXX	1051.0	1015.0	4.76	70.59%	3.67	0.99
1914	Adnams	X	1033.0	1005.5	3.64	83.33%	4.38	0.58
1914	Adnams	XX	1042.0	1007.0	4.63	83.33%	4.20	0.73
1910	Warwicks	X	1043.2	1013.9	3.88	67.95%	5.00	0.85
1910	Warwicks	XX	1048.5	1014.7	4.47	69.71%	4.95	0.95
1910	Warwicks	XXX	1055.4	1017.7	4.98	68.00%	4.95	1.14
1911	Lees	U	1034.0	1007.0	3.57	79.41%	4.74	0.66
1911	Lees	K	1049.0	1010.0	5.16	79.59%	5.82	1.12
Sources: Boddington brewing record held at Manchester Central Library, document number M693/405/126. Adnams brewing record Book 2 held at the brewery. Warwicks & Richardsons brewing record held at the Nottinghamshire Archives, document number DD/NM/8/4/1.								

While the provincial Milds are mostly hopped at a similar rate to London Milds – around 5 lbs per quarter of malt, those from Boddington are extremely lightly hopped.

London Mild Ale before WW I								
Year	Brewer	Beer	OG	FG	ABV	App. Atten- uation	lbs hops/ qtr	hops lb/brl
1914	Whitbread	X	1052.1	1010.0	5.57	80.80%	6.04	1.29
1914	Barclay Perkins	X	1051.3	1013.6	4.99	73.54%	5.49	1.15
1914	Fullers	X	1049.6	1011.1	5.09	77.65%	5.15	1.15
1910	Truman	X	1052.6				5.42	1.22
1914	Courage	X	1054.6	1019.4	4.65	64.47%	4.96	1.05

Sources:
Whitbread brewing record held at the London Metropolitan Archives, document number LMA/4453/D/01/079.
Barclay Perkins brewing record held at the London Metropolitan Archives, document number ACC/2305/1/603.
Truman brewing record held at the London Metropolitan Archives, document number B/THB/C/190.
Courage brewing record held at the London Metropolitan Archives, document number ACC/2305/08/247.

Scottish Mild Ales follow a similar pattern to provincial English versions, with the strongest examples about the same strength as a London X Ale. This was the last hurrah of Mild Ale in Scotland. After the war, very little of it was brewed.

Scottish Mild Ale before WW I								
Year	Brewer	Beer	OG	FG	ABV	App. Atten- uation	lbs hops/ qtr	hops lb/brl
1914	Thomas Usher	60/- MA	1038	1015	3.04	60.53%	5.00	0.79
1914	Thomas Usher	X	1045	1013	4.23	71.11%	7.25	1.35
1914	Thomas Usher	80/- MA	1046	1016.5	3.90	64.13%	5.00	0.96
1914	Thomas Usher	X 60/-	1051	1013.5	4.96	73.53%	7.25	1.52
1909	Maclay	Mild 42/-	1034	1013	2.78	61.76%	6.31	0.91
1909	Maclay	Mild 56/-	1061	1025	4.76	59.02%	6.31	1.63
1913	Younger, Wm.	XX	1055	1018	4.89	67.27%	4.07	0.87
1913	Younger, Wm.	XXK	1056	1016	5.29	71.43%	4.07	0.81
1913	Younger, Wm.	XXX	1065	1021.5	5.75	66.92%	4.55	1.15

Sources:
Thomas Usher brewing record held at the Scottish Brewing Archive, document number TU/6/1/5.
William Younger brewing record held at the Scottish Brewing Archive, document number WY/6/1/2/58.
Maclay brewing record held at the Scottish Brewing Archive, document number M/6/1/1/2.

As with provincial English Milds, the weakest examples are under 1040°. No London beer was as weak as that before the war.

During WW I

As the most popular style, Mild Ale bore the brunt of gravity reductions. At most breweries Government Ale was a version of Mild Ale. Though there were some surprisingly strong Milds brewed up until early 1917.

In Scotland, where Mild Ale was already becoming rare, the war seems to have pretty much finished it off. Low-gravity, lightly-hopped Pale Ale served as a replacement. This type of beer eventually became post-WW II 60/-.

London

Courage's X Ale went through quite a few changes during the war:

Courage X Ale 1914 - 1920							
Date	Year	OG	FG	ABV	App. Atten-uation	lbs hops/ qtr	hops lb/brl
17th Oct	1914	1054.6	1019.4	4.65	64.47%	4.96	1.05
8th Mar	1915	1049.9	1018.3	4.18	63.33%	4.00	0.78
23rd Sep	1915	1048.2	1011.1	4.91	77.01%	4.96	0.96
11th Oct	1916	1048.2	1007.2	5.42	85.06%	5.00	0.97
9th May	1916	1044.9	1006.9	5.02	84.57%	6.51	1.18
2nd Jan	1917	1045.7	1010.0	4.73	78.18%	3.88	0.76
8th Jun	1917	1041.6	1007.2	4.54	82.67%	8.72	1.16
19th Oct	1917	1034.6	1006.4	3.74	81.60%	7.57	1.13
18th Jan	1918	1034.6	1006.9	3.66	80.00%	7.38	1.13
20th Apr	1918	1023.8	1004.4	2.57	81.40%	9.41	1.01
19th Nov	1918	1021.1	1003.9	2.27	81.58%	10.89	1.01
30th Jun	1919	1023.5	1003.6	2.64	84.71%	6.78	0.75
7th Jul	1919	1027.4	1004.4	3.04	83.84%	8.17	0.99
29th Dec	1919	1037.7	1007.2	4.03	80.88%	5.98	1.00
22nd Apr	1920	1037.7	1007.5	3.99	80.15%	5.91	0.98
Sources: Courage brewing records held at the London Metropolitan Archives, document numbers ACC/2305/08/247, ACC/2305/08/248, ACC/2305/08/249, ACC/2305/08/250 and ACC/2305/08/251.							

There was quite a change in the rate of attenuation. My guess is that they were trying to compensate for the fall in gravity. In 1918, with gravities under 1025°, they were really pushing the limits of what you could call beer. Because of the rules about average gravity, every barrel they brewed at 1021° meant they could brew one at 1039°, or a half barrel at 1047°. It was very tempting to slash the gravity of a big seller like Mild to maximise the amount of stronger, more profitable beer you could brew.

It's interesting to note that the hopping rate per barrel remaining fairly constant at around 1 pound per barrel when the gravity was more than halved. That's reflected by the increase in the hopping rate per quarter, which rose from 4-5 lbs to over 10 lbs. Again, I assume that to compensate for the fall in gravity and boost flavour.

The grist was tweaked several times during the war years:

Courage X Ale grists 1914 - 1920									
Date	Year	OG	pale malt	black malt	crystal malt	no. 3 sugar	caramel	glucose	black invert
17th Oct	1914	1054.6	82.1%	0.8%	6.1%	11.0%			
8th Mar	1915	1049.9	82.8%		6.1%	11.1%			
23rd Sep	1915	1048.2	82.4%		6.3%	11.3%			
11th Oct	1915	1048.2	82.8%		6.1%	11.1%			
9th May	1916	1044.9	80.5%		6.0%	13.4%			
2nd Jan	1917	1045.7	75.0%		9.1%	15.9%			
8th Jun	1917	1041.6	73.6%		11.3%	15.1%			
19th Oct	1917	1034.6	76.2%	1.7%	13.3%	6.6%			2.2%
18th Jan	1918	1034.6	76.1%	1.7%	13.0%	9.2%			
20th Apr	1918	1023.8	70.9%	2.9%	18.4%	7.8%			
19th Nov	1918	1021.1	64.5%	5.4%	19.4%			10.8%	
30th Jun	1919	1023.5	66.3%	2.0%	15.3%	13.6%	2.7%		
7th Jul	1919	1027.4	67.6%	2.0%	15.4%	13.7%	1.4%		
29th Dec	1919	1037.7	64.4%		19.8%	15.8%			
22nd Apr	1920	1037.7	69.1%		16.7%	13.2%	1.0%		

Sources:
Courage brewing records held at the London Metropolitan Archives, document numbers ACC/2305/08/247, ACC/2305/08/248, ACC/2305/08/249, ACC/2305/08/250 and ACC/2305/08/251.

The big increase in the proportion of crystal malt from 1917 on is intriguing. As it seems to correlate with the fall in gravity. It looks like another attempt to compensate for the falling strength of X Ale. While the appearance of black malt corresponds to a fall in the percentage of No. 3 invert sugar. So it's surely a colour correction.

The 1920 recipe is quite different from the 1914 one: far less base malt, slightly more No. 3 invert, almost three times as much crystal malt.

The modifications made to the hopping scheme of Courage X are equally fascinating. Apart from a period in 1915, there were always some foreign hops.

Courage X hops 1914 - 1921			
date	year	OG	hops
17th Oct	1914	1054.6	Hallertau (1912), English (1912, 1914)
8th Mar	1915	1049.9	English (1913, 1914)
23rd Sep	1915	1048.2	English (1913, 1914), Californian (1914)
11th Oct	1916	1048.2	English (1913, 1914), Californian (1914)
9th May	1916	1044.9	Poperinge (1915), English (1914)
2nd Jan	1917	1045.7	Poperinge (1914), English (1915)
8th Jun	1917	1041.6	Poperinge (1914), English (1914, 1916)
19th Oct	1917	1034.6	Poperinge (1914), English (1914)
18th Jan	1918	1034.6	Poperinge (1914), English (1914)
20th Apr	1918	1023.8	Poperinge (1914), English (1916)
19th Jul	1918	1022.2	English (1914, 1916), Californian (1915)
19th Nov	1918	1021.1	Poperinge (1914), English (1915)
30th Jun	1919	1023.5	English (1915), Californian (1915)
7th Jul	1919	1027.4	English (1915), Californian (1915)
29th Dec	1919	1037.7	English (1917), Californian (1915), Poperinge (1915)
22nd Apr	1920	1037.7	English (1917), Californian (1916)
20th Jul	1920	1032.7	Saaz (1917), English (1918)
1st Jul	1920	1032.7	Saaz (1917), English (1917), Californian (1916)
13th Aug	1920	1032.7	Bohemian (1917), English (1917), Californian (1916)
21st Sep	1920	1032.7	Saaz (1919), English (1917), Californian (1916)
8th Oct	1920	1032.7	Alsace (1917), English (1917), Californian (1916)
2nd Mar	1921	1032.7	English (1917), Californian (1915)

Sources:
Courage brewing records held at the London Metropolitan Archives, document numbers ACC/2305/08/247, ACC/2305/08/248, ACC/2305/08/249, ACC/2305/08/250 and ACC/2305/08/251.

In 1914 and early 1915 they were using hops from the most recent crop, 1914. Which wasn't true again apart from briefly in 1917 when some of the 1916 harvest turn up. I think the reason for this is that there was a glut of English hops in the middle of the war. In 1917, 1918 and 1919 it looks like they were using up old stocks of hops as most were two or three seasons old.

Between 1916 and 1918, there are loads of Poperinge hops in Courage X, from the 1914 and 1915 crop. Bothe of these would have been harvested after Germany had occupied most of the country

Californian hops were used intermittently right through the war. Until after the war ended the freshest were from the 1915 harvest. That's easy to explain: hop imports almost totally dried up in the last couple of years of the war.

Most intriguing are the hops sourced from what was the wartime enemy. At the start of the war Hallertau hops, after it was over, from Bohemia and Alsace. Interestingly, these were mostly from the 1917 harvest, when the war was still raging. There were probably lots of Bohemian hops knocking about because brewing came to a near total halt in Austria in the last two years of the war.

Provincial England

XX Ale was Adnams biggest-selling Mild Ale. And one they brewed right through the war. Since it started off with a far lower gravity than standard London Milds, the relative drop in gravity was much smaller. In the later stages of the war it formed the vast majority of the beer Adnams brewed.

Adnams XX Ale 1914 - 1920							
Date	Year	OG	FG	ABV	App. Attenuation	lbs hops/ qtr	hops lb/brl
10th Aug	1914	1042	1007.0	4.63	83.33%	4.20	0.73
30th Apr	1915	1042	1008.9	4.38	78.90%	4.33	0.76
18th Aug	1915	1041	1004.4	4.84	89.19%	4.46	0.76
18th Nov	1915	1040	1006.4	4.45	84.07%	4.46	0.76
31st Mar	1916	1038	1005.5	4.29	85.42%	4.59	0.75
2nd Oct	1916	1035	1005.5	3.90	84.17%	4.91	0.73
1st Jan	1917	1035	1006.1	3.82	82.59%	4.91	0.79
19th Mar	1917	1034	1005.0	3.84	85.34%	4.91	0.72
14th May	1917	1027	1003.3	3.13	87.69%	5.33	0.62
29th May	1917	1024	1003.3	2.74	86.15%	5.10	0.53
4th Apr	1918	1024	1004.2	2.63	82.69%	5.82	0.59
10th May	1918	1022	1003.9	2.40	82.37%	6.14	0.58
30th July	1918	1022	1002.8	2.54	87.41%	6.16	0.60
27th Nov	1918	1022	1002.8	2.54	87.41%	6.14	0.59
11th Apr	1919	1022	1002.8	2.54	87.41%	6.14	0.60
2nd Sep	1919	1027	1005.0	2.91	81.53%	7.53	0.86
19th Jan	1920	1027	1003.3	3.13	87.69%	5.23	0.71
Source: Adnams brewing records held at the brewery.							

In 1918 it had the same OG as Courage X Ale, even though that it had started the war with a gravity more than 12 points lower, 1042° as opposed to 1054.6°. It's a good example of the war levelling out strength differences across the UK.

The Adnams XX recipe was amended several times during WW I:

Adnams XX Ale grists 1914 - 1920											
Date	Year	OG	pale malt	crystal malt	medium malt	flaked maize	no. 2 sugar	no. 3 sugar	glucose	cane blocks	tintose
10th Aug	1914	1042	31.1%	6.2%	43.5%	6.2%				12.4%	0.6%
30th Apr	1915	1042		6.4%	73.7%	6.4%			4.3%	8.5%	0.6%
18th Aug	1915	1041		6.6%	72.9%	6.6%	4.4%			8.8%	0.6%
18th Nov	1915	1040	39.7%	6.6%	33.1%	6.6%		4.4%		8.8%	0.6%
31st Mar	1916	1038	41.1%	6.8%	30.8%	6.8%	4.6%			9.1%	0.7%
2nd Oct	1916	1035	33.1%	7.3%	36.7%	7.3%	4.9%			9.8%	0.8%
1st Jan	1917	1035	33.1%	7.3%	36.7%	7.3%	4.9%			9.8%	0.8%
19th Mar	1917	1034	14.7%	7.3%	55.1%	7.3%	4.9%			9.8%	0.8%
14th May	1917	1027	10.6%	5.3%	63.7%	5.3%	7.1%			7.1%	0.9%
29th May	1917	1024	12.4%	6.2%	61.9%	6.2%	4.1%			8.2%	1.0%
4th Apr	1918	1024	22.0%	5.5%	55.0%	5.5%	7.3%			3.7%	0.9%
10th May	1918	1022	22.9%	5.7%	57.1%	5.7%				7.6%	1.0%
30th July	1918	1022	11.7%	5.8%	64.2%	5.8%	7.8%			3.9%	0.8%
27th Nov	1918	1022	35.0%	5.8%	46.6%		7.8%			3.9%	1.0%
11th Apr	1919	1022	11.7%	5.8%	69.9%			7.8%	3.9%		1.0%
2nd Sep	1919	1027		5.0%	80.7%					13.4%	0.8%
19th Jan	1920	1027	16.8%	4.2%	67.1%					11.2%	0.7%
Source: Adnams brewing records held at the brewery,											

The most obvious change is the disappearance of flaked maize in 1918. It's something that's seen at every brewery. Obviously, it simply wasn't available. Either because maize wasn't being imported or it was being diverted for food use. The proportion of maize when it was used is fairly low. 10-15% of the grist was common.

The occasional use of glucose and No. 3 invert was almost certainly due to supply problems. Glucose pops up quite often in wartime recipes while before the war it was quite rare.

Up in Manchester, Boddington started the war with three Milds: B (1037°), BB (1047°) and XXX (1051°). Only the strongest came anywhere close to the strength of a London X Ale. By the end of the war they were down to a single Mild, one which hadn't even existed in 1914, XX. B was discontinued in the middle of 1916 (it returned in 1918). BB seems to have morphed into XX, though they were both brewed for a while at the end of 1916 and beginning of 1917. Surprisingly, XXX managed to hang on until April 1917.

Boddington Mild Ale 1914 - 1921

Date	Year	Beer	OG	FG	ABV	App. Attenuation	lbs hops/qtr	hops lb/brl
7th Jul	1914	BB	1047.0	1014.0	4.37	70.21%	3.62	0.85
4th May	1915	BB	1046.0	1015.0	4.10	67.39%	3.79	0.96
14th Oct	1915	BB	1047.0	1016.0	4.10	65.96%	3.87	0.98
15th May	1916	BB	1047.0	1014.0	4.37	70.21%	3.17	0.82
18th Dec	1916	BB	1046.0	1015.0	4.10	67.39%	3.87	0.97
1st Feb	1917	BB	1043.0	1018.0	3.31	58.14%	3.97	1.32
18th Dec	1916	XX	1041.0	1012.0	3.84	70.73%	3.40	0.71
30th Jan	1917	XX	1038.0	1015.0	3.04	60.53%	3.92	0.92
13th Apr	1917	XX	1037.0	1011.0	3.44	70.27%	5.11	1.02
2nd Jul	1917	XX	1035.0	1012.0	3.04	65.71%	5.22	0.97
4th Oct	1917	XX	1034.0	1014.0	2.65	58.82%	4.59	1.11
25th Apr	1918	XX	1030.0	1011.0	2.51	63.33%	6.84	1.06
7th May	1918	XX	1028.0	1010.0	2.38	64.29%	7.12	1.04
23rd Dec	1918	XX	1029.0	1010.0	2.51	65.52%	7.22	1.10
7th Jan	1919	XX	1029.0	1011.0	2.38	62.07%	7.22	1.07
25th Mar	1919	XX	1030.0	1012.0	2.38	60.00%	7.22	1.36
12th Jun	1919	XX	1033.0	1011.0	2.91	66.67%	6.84	1.15
13th Oct	1919	XX	1036.0	1012.0	3.18	66.67%	6.05	1.12
7th Oct	1920	XX	1034.0	1012.0	2.91	64.71%	5.58	1.02
4th Oct	1921	XX	1033.0	1010.0	3.04	69.70%	6.51	1.12

Sources:
Boddington brewing records held at Manchester Central Library, document numbers M693/405/126 and M693/405/126.

Like Adnams XX, Boddington XX ended up with exactly the same gravity as Courage X in 1921. While the resurrected B filled the sub-1030° slot.

Compared to Adnams XX, Boddington's Mild had a very simple grist:

Boddington Mild Ale grists 1914 - 1921						
Date	Year	Beer	OG	pale malt	flaked maize	sugar
7th Jul	1914	BB	1047.0	90.36%		9.64%
4th May	1915	BB	1046.0	97.67%		2.33%
14th Oct	1915	BB	1047.0	97.83%		2.17%
15th May	1916	BB	1047.0	100.00%		
18th Dec	1916	BB	1046.0	97.83%		2.17%
1st Feb	1917	BB	1043.0	93.59%	4.18%	2.23%
18th Dec	1916	XX	1041.0	97.30%		2.70%
30th Jan	1917	XX	1038.0	92.38%	4.97%	2.65%
13th Apr	1917	XX	1037.0	86.33%	10.79%	2.88%
2nd Jul	1917	XX	1035.0	97.06%		2.94%
4th Oct	1917	XX	1034.0	85.71%	11.28%	3.01%
25th Apr	1918	XX	1030.0	96.43%		3.57%
7th May	1918	XX	1028.0	96.28%		3.72%
23rd Dec	1918	XX	1029.0	92.31%		7.69%
7th Jan	1919	XX	1029.0	92.31%		7.69%
25th Mar	1919	XX	1030.0	92.31%		7.69%
12th Jun	1919	XX	1033.0	92.73%		7.27%
13th Oct	1919	XX	1036.0	78.05%	12.20%	9.76%
7th Oct	1920	XX	1034.0	78.05%	12.20%	9.76%
4th Oct	1921	XX	1033.0	78.05%	12.20%	9.76%

Sources:
Boddington brewing records held at Manchester Central Library, document numbers M693/405/126 and M693/405/126.

Mostly it's pale malt and sugar, with sometimes some flaked maize. The proportion of sugar declined during the war, but after its end went back up to its pre-war level of just under 10%.

Scotland

Mild had already been losing popularity in Scotland in the decades before WW I. The war seems to have just about finished it off, with Pale Ales of various strengths becoming totally dominant.

Thomas Usher of Edinburgh did, however, brew quite a wide range of Mild Ales during the war. As in Provincial England, some of these beers were far weaker than anything found in London:

Thomas Usher 60/- Mild 1914 - 1918

Date	Year	OG	FG	ABV	App. Attenuation	lbs hops/qtr	hops lb/brl
19th Aug	1914	1038	1015	3.04	60.53%	5.00	0.79
24th Dec	1914	1039	1016	3.04	58.97%	5.00	0.84
29th Feb	1916	1039	1016	3.04	58.97%	5.00	0.78
14th Mar	1916	1037	1015	2.91	59.46%	5.00	0.51
3rd Jul	1917	1031	1014	2.25	54.84%	5.00	0.50
13th Feb	1918	1031	1015	2.12	51.61%	5.00	0.65

Source: Thomas Usher brewing record held at the Scottish Brewing Archive, document number TU/6/1/5.

Being already pretty weak, their 60/- didn't fall in gravity much during the war, losing just 8 gravity points. The hopping rate of 5 lbs. per quarter of malt is very similar to that of Adnams XX, though less than a London Mild. The rate remained incredibly stable throughout the war years. The rate of attenuation was very poor, which was typical of Scottish beers.

Usher's three main Mild Ales, 60/-, 80/- and 100/- were usually parti-gyled together, hence the identical hopping rates.

Thomas Usher 80/- Mild 1914 - 1918

Date	Year	OG	FG	ABV	App. Attenuation	lbs hops/qtr	hops lb/brl
19th Aug	1914	1046	1016.5	3.90	64.13%	5.00	0.96
26th Aug	1914	1046	1017	3.84	63.04%	5.00	0.99
24th Dec	1914	1047	1018	3.84	61.70%	5.00	1.01
29th Feb	1916	1047	1017	3.97	63.83%	5.00	0.94
14th Mar	1916	1047	1014	4.37	70.21%	5.00	0.65
3rd Jul	1917	1038	1015	3.04	60.53%	5.00	0.61
13th Feb	1918	1038	1017	2.78	55.26%	5.00	0.79

Source: Thomas Usher brewing record held at the Scottish Brewing Archive, document number TU/6/1/5.

As with 60/-, the fall in gravity wasn't huge. Even their strongest Mild Ale held up surprisingly well during the war. Possibly because they didn't brew very much of it.

Thomas Usher 100/- Mild 1914 - 1918

Date	Year	OG	FG	ABV	App. Atten-uation	lbs hops/ qtr	hops lb/brl
26th Aug	1914	1065	1027	5.03	58.46%	5.00	1.40
24th Dec	1914	1063	1027	4.76	57.14%	5.00	1.35
29th Feb	1916	1065	1027	5.03	58.46%	5.00	1.29
14th Mar	1916	1064	1026.5	4.96	58.59%	5.00	0.89
3rd Jul	1917	1056	1025	4.10	55.36%	5.00	0.90
13th Feb	1918	1055	1026	3.84	52.73%	5.00	1.15

Source: Thomas Usher brewing record held at the Scottish Brewing Archive, document number TU/6/1/5.

The FG in 1917 and 1918 is close to what the OG was of many English Mild Ales in the same period. As they were all parti-gyled together, I'll just show one set of the grists:

Thomas Usher Mild grists 1914 1918

Date	Year	OG	pale malt	crystal malt	flaked maize	DL sugar	cane sugar	Vertose
19th Aug	1914	1046	75.00%	5.36%	5.36%	7.14%	7.14%	
26th Aug	1914	1046	67.35%	6.12%	6.12%	8.16%	12.24%	
24th Dec	1914	1047	70.91%	5.45%	5.45%	7.27%	10.91%	
29th Feb	1916	1047	73.47%		6.12%	6.80%	13.61%	
14th Mar	1916	1047	70.87%	4.72%	7.09%	3.94%	13.39%	
3rd Jul	1917	1038	78.05%	4.88%		4.07%	13.01%	
13th Feb	1918	1038	85.07%	4.48%		3.73%		6.72%

Source: Thomas Usher brewing record held at the Scottish Brewing Archive, document number TU/6/1/5.

Like Adnams XX, the basic recipe was pale malt, crystal malt and various sugars. It was common to find crystal malt in Mild recipes. Which shouldn't be a surprise as it's that type of beer that it was developed for. I assume some sort of supply problem is the reason for its absence in the one 1916 example.

Drybrough Mild Ale 1915 - 1920

Date	Year	Beer	OG	FG	ABV	App. Atten-uation	lbs hops/ qtr	hops lb/brl
8th Jan	1915	100/- m	1060	1020	5.29	66.67%	4.59	1.14
25th Jan	1915	100/- m	1060	1018	5.56	70.00%	4.65	1.09
16th Nov	1917	60/- m	1029	1010	2.51	65.52%	3.98	0.41
16th Nov	1917	80/- m	1040	1014	3.44	65.00%	3.98	0.56
9th Jan	1920	60/- Mild	1040	1013	3.57	67.50%	5.85	1.00

Sources: Drybrough brewing record held at the Scottish Brewing Archive, document number D/6/1/1/3.

Similarly, the disappearance of flaked maize in 1917 I'm sure was because it simple wasn't available. Brewers were forced to work with what they could get hold of. Which also applies to sugar, the use of which in brewing was severely after February 1917.

Drybrough occasionally brewed Mild Ales during the war and immediately after it.

After WW I

As a very popular and cheap beer, Mild Ale was amongst the most strongly affected by the war. Government Ale lived on in the form of 4d Ale. These were very low gravity, in the range 1027°-1030°, and were obviously there to provide a cheap alternative for poorer drinkers.

London

Stronger Milds were brewed and in London an X Ale had a gravity of 1040°-1043° in the early 1920s. Milds of over 1050° were a thing of the past. Though some Southern breweries did produce a seasonal draught Old Ale which was essentially a strong Mild. Harvey's Old Ale is an example of such a type of beer that still exists today.

Oddly, London brewers that had brewed just one Mild Ale in the run-up to WW I, began to brew multiple versions in the 1920s.

London Mild Ale after WW I								
Year	Brewer	Beer	OG	FG	ABV	App. Attenuation	lbs hops/ qtr	hops lb/brl
1922	Barclay Perkins	Ale	1028.4	1006.5	2.90	77.11%	7.50	0.92
1922	Barclay Perkins	X	1040.3	1010.0	4.01	75.19%	7.50	1.27
1924	Camden	XX	1029.9	1006.1	3.15	79.63%	7.42	0.89
1924	Camden	XXX	1036.6	1008.9	3.66	75.76%	7.42	1.08
1923	Courage	X	1032.7	1006.1	3.52	81.36%	6.94	0.92
1926	Courage	MC	1042.7				7.35	1.26
1925	Fullers	X	1034.8	1009.1	3.39	73.71%	7.17	1.05
1925	Fullers	XX	1045.5	1014.4	4.11	68.31%	7.17	1.37
1923	Whitbread	MA	1027.1	1006.0	2.80	77.90%	7.41	0.81
1923	Whitbread	X	1042.1	1008.0	4.51	80.99%	7.41	1.26

Sources:
Barclay Perkins brewing record held at the London Metropolitan Archives, document number ACC/2305/01/609.
Camden brewing record held at the London Metropolitan Archives, document number ACC/2305/9/5.
Courage brewing records held at the London Metropolitan Archives, document numbers ACC/2305/08/253 and ACC/2305/08/255.
Fullers brewing record held at the brewery.
Whitbread brewing record held at the London Metropolitan Archives, document number LMA/4453/D/01/088.

The Milds around 1030° are the successors to wartime Government Ale. The watery wartime stuff seems to have created a market for cheap and not very cheersome Mild that brewers were happy to cater to. It wasn't a huge volume market, but by parti-gyling with the stronger Milds it was one that was easy to satisfy.

What did a pint of Mild cost? Well, that depended on the strength.

Draught London Mild Ale after WW I							
Year	Brewer	Beer	Price	OG	FG	ABV	App. Attenuation
1923	Barclay Perkins	X	6d	1041.1	1010.6	3.96	74.21%
1923	Barclay Perkins	X	7d	1044.7	1013.2	4.08	70.47%
1923	Cannon	X	6d	1034.8	1007.8	3.50	77.59%
1923	Charrington	X	7d	1042.6	1009.6	4.29	77.46%
1923	City of London	X	5d	1031	1007	3.11	77.42%
1923	City of London	X	6d	1035.2	1006.2	3.77	82.39%
1923	Courage	X	6d	1034.3	1006.8	3.57	80.17%
1923	Hoare	X	6d	1034.3	1011.8	2.91	65.60%
1923	Huggins	X	5d	1035.5	1008	3.57	77.46%
1923	Huggins	X	6d	1037.6	1007.6	3.90	79.79%
1923	Lion	X	7d	1042.1	1007.6	4.49	81.95%
1923	Mann	X	7d	1042.5	1010	4.22	76.47%
1923	Meux	MA	5d	1028	1005	2.99	82.14%
1923	Meux	X	7d	1042	1008.5	4.36	79.76%
1923	Truman	MA	5d	1030.8	1007.8	2.98	74.68%
1923	Truman	X	7d	1041.7	1010.2	4.09	75.54%
1923	Watney	X	6d	1041.1	1007.6	4.36	81.51%
1923	Watney	X	7d	1045	1009	4.68	80.00%
1923	Wenlock	X	5d	1033.7	1005.7	3.64	83.09%
1923	Wenlock	X	6d	1037.3	1006.8	3.97	81.77%
Source: Whitbread Gravity book held at the London Metropolitan Archives, document number LMA/4453/D/02/001.							

There were three classes of draught Mild in London: 5d., 6d. and 7d. With gravities of approximately 1032°, 1037° and 1042°. That's quite a change from before the start of the war, when a standard London X Ale had a gravity in the low 1050's. Even the strongest Milds were 20% or so lower in gravity.

Provincial England

Before WW I, provincial Milds tended to be weaker than those brewed in London, but not always necessarily cheaper. After the war, probably because of the effect of price controls, they continued to be weaker, but were the same price as a Mild of equivalent strength in London.

Breweries choosing to brew a single Mild often chose one in one of the weaker classes:

Mini Book Series volume XXXII: Armistice!

Provincial Mild Ale after WW I

Year	Brewer	Beer	OG	FG	ABV	App. Atten-uation	lbs hops/qtr	hops lb/brl
1923	Boddington	XX	1034.0	1010.0	3.18	70.59%	5.92	1.19
1923	Adnams	XX	1029.0	1004.2	3.29	85.67%	4.99	0.59
1920	Lees	U	1032.0				2.86	0.85
1920	Lees	K	1038.0				2.69	0.95
1921	Truman (Burton)	XX	1033.8	1006.1	3.66	81.97%	6.74	0.90
1921	Truman (Burton)	XXX	1047.4	1009.4	5.02	80.12%	6.74	1.26

Sources:
Boddington brewing record held at Manchester Central Library, document number M693/405/127.
Adnams brewing record Book 9
Lees brewing record held at the brewery
Truman brewing record held at the London Metropolitan Archives, document number B/THB/C/335.

Only Truman in the above set produced a Mild close to the strength of standard London Mild.

The grists of these beers aren't very exciting, with almost nothing in the way of coloured malts, even crystal.

Provincial Mild Ale grists after WW I

Year	Brewer	Beer	OG	pale malt	high dried malt	amber malt	crystal malt	flaked maize	cara-mel	other sugar
1923	Boddington	XX	1034.0	67.61%				25.35%		7.04%
1923	Adnams	XX	1029.0	77.86%		4.58%	4.58%		0.76%	12.21%
1920	Lees	U	1032.0	92.59%						7.41%
1920	Lees	K	1038.0	89.19%						10.81%
1921	Truman (Burton)	XX	1033.8	79.55%	9.09%			9.09%		2.27%
1921	Truman (Burton)	XXX	1047.4	79.55%	9.09%			9.09%		2.27%

Sources:
Boddington brewing record held at Manchester Central Library, document number M693/405/127.
Adnams brewing record Book 9
Lees brewing record held at the brewery
Truman brewing record held at the London Metropolitan Archives, document number B/THB/C/335.

Most provincial breweries seem to have chosen the 4d per pint class for their standard Mild. I'm guessing for economic reasons. The 1920s weren't the happiest of times in Britain's industrial regions, where Mild was the drink of the working man.

Draught Provincial Mild after WW I							
Year	Brewer	Beer	Price per pint (d)	OG	FG	ABV	App. Atten- uation
1926	Ashby Brewery	L.A.	4	1029.9			
1926	Buddon Bigg	Ale	4	1030			
1925	Hancock	XPA		1032			
1925	Hancock	Dark Malt		1042			
1925	Hancock	XXXX		1051			
1926	Kemp Town	L.A.	4	1031	1006.6	3.17	78.71%
1926	Kidd & Hotblack	L.A.	3	1024.8	1004.1	2.69	83.47%
1927	Leney	X	4	1027.2	1004.2	2.99	84.56%
1926	Mason	Ale	4	1030.6			
1927	Meux	Ale	4	1028.7			
1925	Pentre Brewery	XX		1044.6			
1926	Rock Brewery	L.A.		1030.6	1003.7	3.50	87.91%
1926	Shepherd Neame	Ale	4	1030.1			
1926	Smithers	L.A.	4	1032.6	1009.6	2.98	70.55%
1926	Style & Winch	Ale	4	1027.4			
1926	Tamplin	L.A.	4	1030.1	1009.9	2.61	67.11%
1926	Tilney	X	6	1039.6			
1927	Young & Co	Ale	4	1029.6			
Sources: Truman Gravity Book held at the London Metropolitan Archives, document number B/THB/C/252. "Cardiff Pubs and Breweries" by Brian Glover, 2005. pages 97-101 Whitbread Gravity book held at the London Metropolitan Archives, document number LMA/4453/D/02/001.							

These analyses are a little later in date than the London ones. The 3d, 4d and 6d classes are the equivalent of 4d, 5d and 7d in the London table. Weaker 4d Milds were brewed in London, but in quite small quantities compared to the two stronger categories.

Scotland

WW I all but killed off genuine Mild in Scotland. Its place being taken instead by low-gravity Pale Ales. The few that did continue to brew Mild Ales I suspect only did so to supply the English market, where Mild was still extremely popular.

The Scottish practice of colouring Pale Ales at racking time, sometimes very dark, helped blur the distinction between Mild Ale and weaker Bitters. I always assumed that post-WW II 60/- was just the Scottish version of Dark Mild. I didn't realise it was just a weak Bitter coloured with caramel.

Based on this small sample, it looks like post-war, as in provincial England, most brewers opted for quite weak versions as standard.

Draught Scottish Mild after WW I								
Year	Brewer	Beer	Price per pint (d)	OG	FG	ABV	App. Attenuation	colour
1922	Younger, Geo.	Mild	6	1034.5	1005.9	3.73	83.04%	95
1923	Mackay	Mild	5	1033	1008	3.24	75.76%	
1926	Mackay	60/- MA		1041	1017	3.09	58.54%	
1923	Murray	Mild		1037	1006	4.03	83.78%	

Sources:
Thomas Usher Gravity Book held at the Scottish Brewing Archive, document number TU/6/11.
Younger, Wm. & Co Gravity Book document WY/6/1/1/19 held at the Scottish Brewing Archive

A colour of 95 is very dark for a mild in this period. Few were darker than around 50.

Mini Book Series volume XXXII: Armistice!

Brown Ale

Before WW I

A very new style, Brown Ale had only been brewed since around 1900, when London brewer Mann introduced one. It only really took off as a popular style in the 1920's. Before then, only a handful of breweries made one.

During WW I

Brown Ale wasn't a very common style at the time. None of the breweries for which I have records brewed one. Hence I have little information on the style.

An advertisement for Simonds Brown Ale from October 1914 shows that it retailed for 1s 11d per dozen for half pints and 3s 3d for pints. [29] Implying a beer of around standard strength, i.e. 1050°.

This advertisement from 1917 also gives some indication of Brown Ale's strength:

HAMPSTEAD BREWERY,
HIGH STREET, HAMPSTEAD.

TELEPHONE No. 435   POST OFFICE, HAMPSTEAD

LIST OF PRICES NET.

		Per Firkin 9 Gallons	Per Pin 4½ Galls		Jars	Crates
Bitter Ale	AK	14/3	7/3	Fine Tonic Ale	2/2	2,2
Do. Superior	AKA	15/3	7/9	Brown Ale		
Do. Extra	XK	17/3	8/9	Nourishing Stout		
India Pale Ale	IPA	19,3	9/9			
Mild Ale	X	14/3	7/3	Extra Bitter Ale		
Do.	XX	15/3	7/9	Mild Burton		
Do.	XXX	19/3	9,9	Extra Stout	2/4	2'5
Stout		5/3	7/9	(Oatmeal)		
Extra Stout		17/3	8/9			
Double Stout		19/3	9/9	I.P.A.		
GINGER BEER		12/9	6/6	Double Stout	2,7	2/8
GINGER BEER { In Screw-Stopped Jars		1/4 per gallon		OYDER.		Net
In Crate of 4 Flagons		1/6		1/10 and 2/- per gallon		
BOTTLED BEERS { Tonic Ale				3/9 per dozen Imperial pints		
Brown Ale			3/9	" "		
India Pale Ale			4/6	" "		Net
Nourishing Stout			3/9	" "		
Oatmeal Stout			4/3	" "		
Double Stout			4/6	" "		

(½-dozen Bottled Beer supplied if required).

Our Gallon Jars are filled and measured by Patent Machinery stamped by the L.C.C.

PRICE LISTS OF WINES ON APPLICATION

Hendon & Finchley Times. Friday 23 March 1917, page 1

It's the same price as Tonic Ale and Nourishing Stout, which would have been the brewery's two weakest beers, a Light Bitter and Stout of Porter strength. My guess is that it was about 1045° at this point. But not for much longer. It's just before the 1st April 1917 apocalypse.

---

[29] Reading Mercury - Saturday 24 October 1914, page 2.

After WW I

Problems with draught beer quality because of reduced gravities prompted many drinkers to either switch to bottled beer of the more economically choice of mixed draught and bottled. This was a huge boost for Brown Ale which was mixed with draught Mild. It's hard to believe now, but Brown Ale was a trendy, modern style in the 1920s.

While few breweries had produced a Brown Ale before the war, by the nmid-1920's it had become a standard part of most London breweries' range.

London Brown Ale after WW I						
Year	Brewer	Price	OG	FG	ABV	App. Atten- uation
1927	Barclay Perkins	7.5d	1045.1			
1927	Beasley	8d	1047.2	1010.1	4.83	78.60%
1926	Charrington	8d	1039.9			
1926	City of London	9d	1035.6			
1926	Combe	7d	1043.6			
1921	Mann	9d	1040.6	1004.5	4.71	88.92%
1926	Mann	8d	1042.8			
1926	Truman	8d	1044			
1926	Watney	6.5d	1044.8	1013	4.12	70.98%
1926	Whitbread		1053.7			
Sources: Truman Gravity Book held at the London Metropolitan Archives, document number B/THB/C/252. Whitbread Gravity book held at the London Metropolitan Archives, document number LMA/4453/D/02/001.						

There was quite a bit of variation in terms of strength, from 1037° to 1054°. Eventually, most breweries settled on brewing their Brown Ale at about averages gravity, which was 1042°-1043° for most of the interwar period. Which was about the same strength as Best Mild.

Brown Ales are often invisible in brewery logs because they weren't being brewed per se. Many breweries just tweaked a Mild with different primings and bottled it.

Pale Ale

Before WW I

Before 1850, Pale Ale was mostly brewed by specialist brewers, either in Burton or in Scotland. After the middle of the century, the style went mainstream.

The biggest boost to the style was given by the introduction of Light Pale Ales around 1850. The original Pale Ales were all brewed as Stock Ales, being aged for 6 to 12 months before sale, always in trade casks rather than vats. The new running versions were aged for no more than a few weeks and were much lower in gravity. While a typical Stock Pale Ale had an OG around 1060-1065°, AK, a common name for a Light Pale Ale, was in the range 1045°-1050°.

London Pale Ale before WW I								
Year	Brewer	Beer	OG	FG	ABV	App. Attenuation	lbs hops/ qtr	hops lb/brl
1911	Barclay Perkins	PA	1060.0	1014.5	6.02	75.83%	6.00	2.97
1914	Barclay Perkins	XLK (trade)	1049.9	1012.2	4.99	75.58%	7.51	1.52
1914	Barclay Perkins	XLK (bottling)	1045.0	1009.4	4.71	79.07%	7.51	1.35
1914	Whitbread	FA	1047.1	1013.0	4.51	72.39%	10.97	2.22
1914	Whitbread	IPA	1049.3	1013.0	4.80	73.63%	11.96	2.53
1914	Whitbread	2PA	1053.0	1016.0	4.89	69.81%	8.94	2.05
1914	Whitbread	PA	1060.2	1021.0	5.18	65.11%	8.94	2.33
1914	Fuller	AK	1044.3	1009.1	4.65	79.38%	7.33	1.34
1914	Fuller	PA	1054.2	1012.2	5.56	77.52%	8.14	1.98
Sources: Whitbread brewing record held at the London Metropolitan Archives, document number LMA/4453/D/01/079. Barclay Perkins brewing record held at the London Metropolitan Archives, document number ACC/2305/1/602 and ACC/2305/1/603. Fullers brewing record held at the brewery.								

Provincial Pale Ales follow a similar pattern to those from London: a weaker one at about 1045° and a stronger one around 1060°. The exceptions being the two Manchester breweries, Boddington and Lees, whose strongest version was only around 1055°. Truman, unsurprisingly, as they were in Burton, had the strongest Pale Ale.

Provincial Pale Ale before WW I

Year	Brewer	Beer	OG	FG	ABV	App. Attenuation	lbs hops/qtr	hops lb/brl
1914	Adnams	BLB	1044.0	1007.0	4.89	84.09%	7.00	1.34
1904	Tetley	PA	1059.3	1007.8	6.82	86.92%	12.55	2.94
1914	Boddington	AK	1044.0	1013.0	4.10	70.45%	2.92	0.57
1914	Boddington	PA	1046.0	1014.0	4.23	69.57%	3.33	0.97
1914	Boddington	IP	1053.0	1016.0	4.89	69.81%	4.00	1.35
1911	Lees	B	1054.0	1015.0	5.16	72.22%	7.30	1.61
1915	Truman (Burton)	P1	1063.7	1020.5	5.72	67.83%	9.71	2.48
1914	Truman (Burton)	P2	1056.8	1009.4	6.27	83.41%	8.79	2.01
1914	Truman (Burton)	P3	1049.9	1008.3	5.50	83.33%	8.79	1.77
1910	Warwicks	LBB	1042.7	1012.5	3.99	70.78%	3.68	0.62
1910	Warwicks	XXX B	1049.9	1015.5	4.54	68.89%	6.58	1.31
1910	Warwicks	BB	1052.6	1015.8	4.87	70.00%	6.58	1.38
1910	Warwicks	IPA	1058.4	1018.3	5.31	68.72%	7.40	1.76

Sources:
Boddington brewing record held at Manchester Central Library, document number M693/405/126.
Adnams brewing record Book 2 held at the brewery.
Lees brewing record held at the brewery.
Truman's brewing record held at the London Metropolitan Archives, document number B/THB/C/329.
Tetley's brewing record held at the West Yorkshire Archives, document number WYL756/51/ACC1903.
Warwicks & Richardsons brewing record held at the Nottinghamshire Archives, document number DD/NM/8/4/1.

There a big variation in the hopping rates between different breweries: only around 3 lbs per quarter at Boddington to over 12 lbs at Tetley. Though generally the hopping rates are a little lower than in London.

Scottish hopping rates, at 4.5 lbs to 7.5 lbs per quarter, aren't very different from provincial English breweries, but are lower than in London. What does stand out is how weak some versions were. One is even below 1030°, a gravity unknown in England. Even the strongest only has a gravity of 1056°. Odd, given that Scotland was once famous for brewing very strong beer.

The lower gravities were general.

Scottish Pale Ale before WW I

Year	Brewer	Beer	OG	FG	ABV	App. Attenuation	lbs hops/ qtr	hops lb/brl
1914	Drybrough	Pl 48/-	1040	1014	3.44	65.00%	5.07	0.83
1914	Drybrough	Pl	1044	1015	3.84	65.91%	4.97	0.91
1914	Drybrough	Pl 60/-	1054	1018	4.76	66.67%	5.07	1.12
1909	Maclay	Pl 42/-	1033	1010	3.04	69.70%	6.44	0.93
1909	Maclay	Pl 54/-	1042	1013	3.84	69.05%	6.67	1.27
1909	Maclay	Pl 60/-	1051	1013	5.03	74.51%	6.67	1.54
1914	Thomas Usher	40/- PA	1029	1009	2.65	68.97%	7.25	0.87
1914	Thomas Usher	IP	1042	1013	3.84	69.05%	6.00	1.04
1914	Thomas Usher	PA	1048	1014	4.50	70.83%	7.25	1.44
1914	Thomas Usher	PA 60/-	1054	1014.5	5.23	73.15%	7.25	1.62
1913	Wm Younger (Holyrood)	XP	1048	1014	4.50	70.83%	4.57	0.85
1913	Wm Younger (Holyrood)	XXP	1056	1017	5.16	69.64%	5.85	1.25

Sources:
Drybrough brewing record held at the Scottish Brewing Archive, document number D/6/1/1/3.
Maclay brewing record held at the Scottish Brewing Archive, document number M/6/1/1/2.
Thomas Usher brewing record held at the Scottish Brewing Archive, document number TU/6/1/5.
William Younger brewing record held at the Scottish Brewing Archive, document number WY/6/1/3/46.

The lower gravities were general, as you can see from this table:

UK beer production and average OG by country

	England		Scotland		Ireland	
Year	bulk barrels	average OG	bulk barrels	average OG	bulk barrels	average OG
1900	32,146,769	-	2,289,048	-	2,669,225	-
1905	30,594,189	1052.54	2,021,374	1049.6	2,799,960	1063.49
1910	29,284,045	1052.30	1,956,659	1048.48	3,059,210	1064.78
1911	29,679,204	1052.03	2,028,710	1048.18	3,215,374	1065.22
1912	30,991,776	1051.76	2,153,569	1048.11	3,330,174	1065.43
1913	30,758,800	1051.52	2,119,666	1047.85	3,417,851	1065.73
1914	31,737,384	1051.69	2,288,481	1047.67	3,532,902	1065.93
1915	29,310,783	1051.16	2,042,477	1046.85	3,412,520	1065.93
1916	26,914,428	1050.49	1,917,148	1046.45	3,279,032	1066.43
1917	25,497,825	1047.01	1,816,003	1043.16	2,850,170	1065.69
1918	16,340,250	1038.25	1,141,114	1036.74	1,603,679	1057.89
1919	20,133,048	1029.35	1,325,439	1029.77	1,806,046	1044.43
1920	29,891,845	1038.57	2,186,604	1038.83	2,969,498	1043.35
1921	28,927,178	1041.72	2,096,080	1042.31	3,481,312	1050.18
1922	25,468,663	1042.21	1,770,175	1041.68	2,939,893	1049.44
1923	22,334,328	1042.82	1,598,339	1041.36	15,984	1037.5

Sources:
Brewers' Journal 1921, page 246.
Brewers' Almanack 1928, page 110.

In the years running up to the war, average OG was about four points lower in Scotland than in England. The average was so much higher in Ireland basically because of Guinness. The classic OG of Guinness Extra Stout was 1074° and it made up a large percentage of the beer brewed in Ireland.

During WW I

Pale Ale, in the form of draught Bitter, was an extremely popular style. As such, it was inevitable that its gravity would be cut considerably.

London

As well as cuts in gravities, there was often a reduction in the number of different Pales Ales being brewed. Whitbread, for example, began the war brewing four Pale Ales: PA. 2PA, FA and IPA. Only two survived, PA and IPA.

Whitbread Pale Ale production 1914 - 1922 (bulk barrels)						
Year	PA	2PA	FA	IPA	Exp PA	Total
1914	6,311	36,234	65,367	123,509		231,421
1915	4,287	26,926	58,982	106,630		196,825
1916	8,308	19,620	51,069	97,101		176,098
1917	19,829		26,495	71,807		118,131
1918	17,489		28,353	66,534		112,376
1919	40,660			103,545		144,205
1921	84,368			137,633	668	222,669
1922	79,885			131,116	1,962	212,963
Sources: Whitbread brewing records held at the London Metropolitan Archives, document numbers LMA/4453/D/01/079, LMA/4453/D/01/080, LMA/4453/D/01/081, LMA/4453/D/01/082, LMA/4453/D/01/083, LMA/4453/D/01/084 and LMA/4453/D/01/086.						

Output of PA increased considerably during the war years. What was this? My guess is that 2PA had been Whitbread's standard draught Bitter at the start of the war. When it was dropped in 1917, PA took on that role. It's a common occurrence during both wars. Weaker versions are discontinued and the gravity of the stronger version is reduced. Often to a level below that of the discontinued beer. The Export Pale Ale was presumably introduced for export markets, where they still expected beers of pre-war strength.

Whitbread's Pale Ale was one of the few beers that they brewed right through the war years. Its gravity suffered, though it never fell below 3.5% ABV.

Whitbread Pale Ale 1914 - 1921							
Date	Year	OG	FG	ABV	App. Atten-uation	lbs hops/ qtr	hops lb/brl
24th Jun	1914	1061.0	1021.0	5.29	65.59%	9.00	2.36
28th Jan	1916	1056.5	1020.0	4.83	64.62%	8.87	2.23
14th Jul	1916	1051.8	1015.0	4.87	71.04%	10.00	2.23
2nd Feb	1917	1049.6	1011.0	5.10	77.81%	9.97	2.21
22nd May	1917	1045.2	1007.0	5.05	84.50%	12.02	2.42
17th Oct	1917	1044.3	1009.0	4.67	79.67%	10.61	1.96
6th Jun	1918	1035.1	1007.0	3.71	80.04%	10.03	1.53
14th Jul	1918	1036.9	1008.0	3.83	78.33%	9.89	1.59
31st Oct	1918	1035.2	1008.0	3.60	77.26%	9.99	1.62
6th Feb	1919	1041.0	1009.0	4.24	78.06%	9.38	1.63
20th Mar	1919	1036.0	1008.0	3.71	77.78%	9.97	1.53
6th Nov	1919	1047.7	1013.0	4.59	72.73%	8.50	1.76
4th Mar	1920	1047.5	1012.0	4.69	74.71%	7.46	1.52
26th Jan	1921	1048.2	1013.0	4.66	73.03%	8.97	1.81

Sources:
Whitbread brewing records held at the London Metropolitan Archives, document numbers LMA/4453/D/01/079, LMA/4453/D/01/080, LMA/4453/D/01/081, LMA/4453/D/01/082, LMA/4453/D/01/083, LMA/4453/D/01/084, LMA/4453/D/01/085 and LMA/4453/D/01/086.

In this case the hopping rate per barrel declined in parallel with the gravity. Which meant that the hopping rate per quarter of malt remained fairly constant at around 9 lbs.

It wasn't just the strength of PA that changed during the war. The ingredients used weren't constant, either.

Mini Book Series volume XXXII: Armistice!

Whitbread Pale Ale grists 1914 - 1921							
Date	Year	OG	pale malt	PA malt	no. 1 sugar	no. 3 sugar	glucose
24th Jun	1914	1061.0	23.60%	56.12%	20.28%		
28th Jan	1916	1056.5	19.15%	63.83%	17.02%		
14th Jul	1916	1051.8	22.61%	60.30%	17.09%		
2nd Feb	1917	1049.6	17.72%	64.96%	17.32%		
22nd May	1917	1045.2	21.77%	58.87%	19.35%		
17th Oct	1917	1044.3	26.16%	64.53%	9.30%		
6th Jun	1918	1035.1	27.44%	67.68%	4.88%		
14th Jul	1918	1036.9	26.95%	68.26%	4.79%		
31st Oct	1918	1035.2	31.91%	55.32%			12.77%
6th Feb	1919	1041.0	24.46%	63.59%			11.96%
20th Mar	1919	1036.0	27.95%	59.63%		12.42%	
6th Nov	1919	1047.7	67.63%	20.86%		11.51%	
4th Mar	1920	1047.5	31.19%	56.14%		12.67%	
26th Jan	1921	1048.2	53.31%	34.24%		12.45%	
Sources: Whitbread brewing records held at the London Metropolitan Archives, document numbers LMA/4453/D/01/079, LMA/4453/D/01/080, LMA/4453/D/01/081, LMA/4453/D/01/082, LMA/4453/D/01/083, LMA/4453/D/01/084, LMA/4453/D/01/085 and LMA/4453/D/01/086.							

The proportion of sugar used fell continuously 1914 to 1918 and only picked up again when the war was just about over, in October 1918. This would have been a forced change because of problems with the supply of sugar, with much being diverted to food production.

20% sugar was not unusual for top-class Pale Ales before WW I, where the aim was to keep the colour and body as light as possible. Cheaper beers like Mild Ale and Porter usually contained a smaller proportion of sugar.

Most interesting is the switch from No. 1 invert sugar to No. 3. There's a big difference in the colour of the two: No. 1 is 25-25 EBC, No. 3 is 120-140 EBC. The most obvious reason for the switch would be to compensate for the smaller amount of malt used a reduced gravity entailed and maintain the same colour.

Provincial England

Out in the wilds of Suffolk, Adnams produced two Pale Ales at the start of the war. Their standard Bitter, BLB, had a modest gravity of 1044° in 1914. The stronger PA was only brewed very occasionally before the war.

But, as brewing restrictions really began to bite in 1917, BLB was dropped and PA brewed on a regular basis. Albeit at a massively reduced gravity:

Mini Book Series volume XXXII: Armistice!

Adnams PA 1915 - 1920							
Date	Year	OG	FG	ABV	App. Attenuation	lbs hops/ qtr	hops lb/brl
16th Sep	1915	1060	1013.9	6.11	76.92%	9.00	2.36
26th Aug	1917	1032	1007.2	3.28	77.49%	10.00	1.39
8th May	1918	1033	1008.6	3.23	73.98%	10.55	1.49
5th Dec	1918	1034	1005.0	3.84	85.34%	9.55	1.37
17th Apr	1919	1035	1006.1	3.82	82.59%	9.54	1.39
1st Sep	1919	1039	1005.5	4.43	85.79%	9.87	1.61
24th Feb	1920	1039	1011.1	3.69	71.59%	9.17	1.44
3rd Nov	1920	1039	1007.2	4.21	81.53%	9.17	1.44
Source: Adnams brewing records held at the brewery.							

The hopping rate per quarter – which effectively takes the gravity of the beer out of the equation – increased slightly when the gravity tumbled.

This is what the grist looked like:

Adnams PA grists 1915 - 1920									
Date	Year	OG	pale malt	mild malt	no. 1 sugar	no. 2 sugar	no. 3 sugar	glucose	tintose
16th Sep	1915	1060	86.67%			13.33%			
26th Aug	1917	1032	48.39%	38.71%		12.90%			
8th May	1918	1033	46.88%	46.88%		6.25%			
5th Dec	1918	1034	90.81%			6.05%		3.03%	0.11%
17th Apr	1919	1035	89.19%				10.81%		
1st Sep	1919	1039	90.70%		9.30%				
24th Feb	1920	1039	90.51%		9.28%				0.21%
3rd Nov	1920	1039	90.47%		9.28%				0.25%
Source: Adnams brewing records held at the brewery.									

There were considerable changes in the type of sugar used. Interestingly, the percentage of sugar fell. Strong Pale Ales often contained a high percentage of sugar to lighten the body and colour. Obviously, when the gravity fell so much there was less need for such a large amount of sugar in the grist.

Before the war many breweries produced brewed beers called AK. These were classic Light Bitters, with an OG somewhere around 1045°, which was quite low for a Pale Ale. Many AKs fell victim to the war, being elbowed into obscurity as the gravity of stronger Pale Ales tumbled.

Boddington AK is a good example of such a beer, being dropped 1917 when the gravity of IP, their stronger Pale Ale, dropped to a similar level.

Boddington AK 1914 - 1917							
Date	Year	OG	FG	ABV	App. Attenuation	lbs hops/ qtr	hops lb/brl
9th Jul	1914	1044	1013	4.10	70.45%	2.92	0.57
3rd May	1915	1040	1012	3.70	70.00%	4.07	0.86
5th May	1915	1039	1010	3.84	74.36%	4.07	0.90
6th May	1915	1041	1014	3.57	65.85%	4.07	0.89
11th Oct	1915	1043	1013	3.97	69.77%	4.07	0.89
13th Oct	1915	1040	1011	3.84	72.50%	4.07	0.88
25th Oct	1915	1040	1011	3.84	72.50%	4.00	0.85
28th Oct	1915	1040	1013	3.57	67.50%	3.33	0.71
16th May	1916	1040	1010	3.97	75.00%	3.79	0.90
17th May	1916	1040	1013	3.57	67.50%	4.07	0.91
18th May	1916	1041	1012	3.84	70.73%	4.07	0.89
18th May	1916	1039	1013	3.44	66.67%	3.33	0.68
19th May	1916	1040	1010	3.97	75.00%	4.07	0.90
20th Dec	1916	1039	1010	3.84	74.36%	3.40	0.68
22nd Dec	1916	1039	1012	3.57	69.23%	4.00	0.84
1st Feb	1917	1039	1017	2.91	56.41%	3.33	0.81

Sources:
Boddington brewing records held at Manchester Central Library, document numbers M693/405/126 and M693/405/126.

Scotland

In Scotland, Pale Ales were already king, and breweries generally made several at different strengths. Drybrough, for example, had three in 1914: Pl 48/-, Pl and Pl 60/-, at 1040°, 1044° and 1054°, respectively.

Let's take a look at Drybrough's Pale Ales as an example. A sure sign that this was one of Drybrough's biggest-selling beers is just how deeply the gravity was cut. Starting with the modest, by pre-WW I standards, OG of 1040°, at its worst this was halved to a pathetic 1020°.

Mini Book Series volume XXXII: Armistice!

Drybrough Pl 48/- 1914 - 1921							
Date	Year	OG	FG	ABV	App. Atten-uation	lbs hops/qtr	hops lb/brl
31st Dec	1914	1040.0	1014.0	3.44	65.00%	5.07	0.83
8th Jan	1915	1040.0	1016.0	3.18	60.00%	4.59	0.76
7th Jan	1916	1038.0	1013.0	3.31	65.79%	5.02	0.79
19th Jul	1916	1037.0	1011.0	3.44	70.27%	3.99	0.62
16th Jan	1917	1037.0	1011.0	3.44	70.27%	3.95	0.61
14th Aug	1917	1031.0	1009.0	2.91	70.97%	4.04	0.50
20th Aug	1917	1027.0	1010.0	2.25	62.96%	4.04	0.46
19th Oct	1917	1030.0	1008.0	2.91	73.33%	3.98	0.50
15th Jan	1918	1023.4	1007.6	2.09	67.52%	4.91	0.48
27th Aug	1918	1023.0	1007.0	2.12	69.57%	4.93	0.44
1st Nov	1918	1020.0	1009.0	1.46	55.00%	4.93	0.41
24th Jan	1919	1024.0	1006.0	2.38	75.00%	4.93	0.50
4th Feb	1919	1021.0	1007.0	1.85	66.67%	4.37	0.39
25th Feb	1919	1023.0	1007.0	2.12	69.57%	5.00	0.50
22nd Jan	1920	1027.0	1008.0	2.51	70.37%	4.95	0.59

Sources:
Drybrough brewing record held at the Scottish Brewing Archive, document number D/6/1/1/3.

There were also considerable changes to the recipe during the war years:

Drybrough Pl 48/- grists 1914 - 1921										
Date	Year	OG	pale malt	no. 1 sugar	no. 2 sugar	no. 3 sugar	caramel	glucose	other sugar	flaked maize
31st Dec	1914	1040.0	84.21%	4.21%	5.61%				0.35%	5.61%
8th Jan	1915	1040.0	76.85%	2.96%	5.91%	5.91%			0.49%	7.88%
7th Jan	1916	1038.0	83.93%	3.78%	6.05%		0.19%			6.05%
19th Jul	1916	1037.0	84.57%	3.81%	5.33%		0.19%			6.10%
16th Jan	1917	1037.0	83.17%	3.96%	6.34%		0.20%			6.34%
14th Aug	1917	1031.0	86.78%	1.00%	7.98%		0.25%			3.99%
20th Aug	1917	1027.0	84.63%	1.01%	6.05%		0.25%		2.02%	6.05%
19th Oct	1917	1030.0	92.01%	1.28%	3.83%		0.32%			2.56%
15th Jan	1918	1023.4	87.54%		3.65%		0.30%		3.65%	4.86%
27th Aug	1918	1023.0	90.91%		5.05%				4.04%	
1st Nov	1918	1020.0	86.17%		11.70%				2.13%	
24th Jan	1919	1024.0	89.61%		10.39%					
4th Feb	1919	1021.0	89.61%		5.19%			5.19%		
25th Feb	1919	1023.0	87.88%		6.06%			6.06%		
22nd Jan	1920	1027.0	87.61%			7.96%			0.88%	3.54%

Sources:
Drybrough brewing record held at the Scottish Brewing Archive, document number D/6/1/1/3.

The most obvious change is the disappearance of the flaked maize in 1918 and 1919. Presumably because of supply problems.

The malt situation was more complicated than it appears. There were usually five different types of pale malt, made from English, Scottish, Californian and Smyrna barley. No more than 20% was from locally-grown barley. In 1915, that had changed to Tunisian, Californian, Norfolk and Scottish. In 1916, Tunisian, Californian, Indian and Scottish. In 1917, Californian, Indian and Scottish. And finally, in 1919, Tunisian, Californian and Scottish. Doubtless the changes in the source of barley were purely due to what was available.

Initially, there was an increase in the percentage of sugar, from 10% to 15% of the grist. From January 1916 to August 1917 it remained at around the 1914 level of 10%, then dropped to 5-7%. When the war ended in 1918 it jumped to almost 14%, before dropping back again to about the pre-war level.

The types of sugar used also flipped around a lot: No. 1 disappeared after 1917, No. 2, however, was almost always present. No. 3 and caramel were used occasionally, as was glucose and various proprietary sugars.

After WW I

In some parts of the UK Pale Ale was starting to rival Mild in terms of popularity. In Scotland, it was just about the only style that was brewed. Some Scottish breweries had a single recipe that they parti-gyled into a range of Pale Ales and Scotch Ale.

Obviously, gravities were lower after the war. But the top-level beers, usually called Pale Ale, remained powerful beers compared to modern versions. A Bitter with a gravity between 1055° and 1059°, which these PAs have, would be considered extremely strong today.

London

There were also Pale Ales that were much weaker than anything brewed in London before the war. The weakest in the set below, Fullers AK, isn't much over 3% ABV. The two versions of Barclay Perkins XLK, bottling and trade, were the bottled and draught versions, respectively. It was common after WW I for the bottled version of a beer to be weaker than the draught version.

London Pale Ale after WW I

Year	Brewer	Beer	OG	FG	ABV	App. Atten-uation	lbs hops/ qtr	hops lb/brl
1922	Barclay Perkins	XLK (bottling)	1040.2	1008.0	4.26	80.10%	8.00	1.27
1922	Barclay Perkins	XLK (trade)	1047.3	1013.0	4.54	72.52%	7.56	1.44
1921	Barclay Perkins	PA	1059.3	1018.0	5.46	69.65%	9.00	2.29
1922	Camden	DA	1036.6	1009.4	3.59	74.24%	10.95	1.61
1923	Camden	PA	1054.3	1014.1	5.31	73.98%	10.12	2.15
1925	Fullers	AK	1032.2	1006.9	3.35	78.52%	10.46	1.20
1925	Fullers	XK	1040.5	1010.8	3.93	73.34%	10.46	1.51
1925	Fullers	PA	1054.3	1015.5	5.13	71.44%	16.57	2.19
1922	Whitbread	IPA	1035.7	1007.0	3.80	80.40%	12.99	1.94
1922	Whitbread	PA	1046.7	1013.0	4.46	72.16%	12.99	2.54

Sources:
Barclay Perkins brewing records held at the London Metropolitan Archives, document numbers ACC/2305/1/608 and ACC/2305/1/609.
Camden brewing record held at the London Metropolitan Archives, document number ACC/2305/9/5.
Fullers brewing record held at the brewery.
Whitbread brewing record held at the London Metropolitan Archives, document number LMA/4453/D/01/088.

This table shows the relationship between OG and price. It also gives some idea of the types of Bitter sold on draught in London.

Draught London Pale Ale after WW I

Year	Brewer	Beer	Price	OG	FG	ABV	App. Atten-uation
1923	Barclay Perkins	Pale Ale	8d	1045.4	1008.4	4.82	81.50%
1923	Cannon	PA	8d	1045.1	1009.6	4.62	78.71%
1923	Charrington	PA	8d	1049.5	1008	5.42	83.84%
1923	City of London	PA	7d	1046.9	1009.4	4.88	79.96%
1923	Courage	PA	8d	1048.7	1007.2	5.42	85.22%
1923	Courage	PA	9d	1054.6	1011.6	5.60	78.75%
1923	Hoare	PA	8d	1046.3	1010.8	4.61	76.67%
1923	Huggins	PA	8d	1046.9	1009.4	4.88	79.96%
1923	Lion	PA	8d	1046.3	1010.8	4.61	76.67%
1923	Mann	PA	9d	1054.3	1006.8	6.22	87.48%
1923	Meux	PA	7d	1041.5	1008	4.36	80.72%
1923	Meux	PA	8d	1047.3	1007.8	5.15	83.51%
1923	Truman	PA	8d	1048.1	1007.6	5.28	84.20%
1923	Watney	Pale Ale	9d	1055.5	1012	5.67	78.38%
1923	Wenlock	Pale Ale	8d	1047.2	1007.2	5.22	84.75%
1923	Whitbread	PA		1046.4	1014	4.20	69.83%

Source:
Whitbread Gravity book held at the London Metropolitan Archives, document number LMA/4453/D/02/001.

There were three classes of draught Bitter: 7d. a pint and 1042°, 8d. a pint and 1048°, 9d. a pint and 1055°. This fits in very neatly with the last set of price controls, which were abolished in 1921:

price	OG range
7d	1039-1045
8d	1045-1053
9d	>1054
Sources: "The British Brewing Industry 1830-1980" by T.R. Gourvish and R.G Wilson, 1994, Cambridge University Press, page 323.	

Provincial England

The war had the effect of levelling out the differences in gravities between different parts of the country. There was a very simple reason: price control. Plus the high rate of tax, which left breweries little room to compete on price or strength. Which in reality meant that London beers dropped down to something like the strength of provincial beers.

Though, as you can see in this table, provincial brewers still produced Pale Ales weaker than those usually found in London. Many were under 1040° and some barely above 1030°.

Bottled Provincial Pale Ales after WW I								
Year	Brewer	Beer	Price per pint	OG	FG	ABV	App. Atten-uation	
1923	Brandon	Rustic Ale		1048	1010.5	4.88	78.13%
1925	Carr, Exeter	Family Ale	4	1030.5	1007.1	3.03	76.72%
1926	Carters Knottingly Brewery	Prize Ale	6.5	1040.7			
1926	Cowell	Cowell's Ale	6.5	1046.9			
1926	Flower	Light Bitter Ale	6.5	1041.2	1011.1	3.90	73.06%
1923	Fremlin	Elephant Brand Ale	8.5	1042.9	1008.5	4.48	80.19%
1923	Fremlin	Light Dinner Ale	7	1034	1006.7	3.55	80.29%
1926	Kemp Town	Dolphin Pale Ale	7	1032.8	1005.1	3.60	84.45%
1926	Kidd & Hotblack	Pale Ale	7	1044.5	1006.2	5.00	86.07%
1925	Manchester Brewery	Hardy's Crown Ale	6	1035.6	1005.6	3.90	84.27%
1925	Newcastle Breweries	Pale Ale	6.5	1038.5	1006.4	4.18	83.38%
1926	Powell & Co.	Palace Pale Ale	7	1036.2			
1926	Rock Brewery	Rock Pale Ale	8	1036.2	1002.8	4.36	92.27%
1925	Russells	Dinner Ale	6	1043.2	1003.3	5.22	92.36%
1925	Simonds	SB Pale Ale	7	1049.7			
1926	Skinner & Rook	Dinner Ale	7	1039.9	1007	4.28	82.46%
1926	Smithers	Light Bitter Ale	5	1033.8	1007.8	3.37	76.92%
1926	Tamplin	Dinner Ale	6.5	1036.6	1008.8	3.61	75.96%
1926	Tollemache	Light Bitter	7	1044.6			
1926	W Riding Bottling	White Rose Ale No. 5	8	1047.8			
1926	Whitaker	Shire Ale	8	1044.7			
Source: Whitbread Gravity book held at the London Metropolitan Archives, document number LMA/4453/D/02/001.								

Unfortunately my sample of draught versions is quite small. Though you can see that the price and OG correlation was much the same as in London, just that more beers were brewed in the 6d category.

Year	Brewer	Beer	Price per pint	OG	FG	ABV	App. Attenuation
Bottled Provincial Pale Ales after WW I							
1926	Ashby Brewery	Bitter	7	1044.9			
1925	Benskin	PA	9	1053.3	1010.8	5.54	79.74%
1926	Commercial Brewery	Bitter	6	1040.7	1008.1	4.24	80.10%
1925	Hancock	HB		1048			
1922	Northern Clubs Federation	PA		1036	1007	3.77	80.56%
1926	Yates Castle Brewery	Bitter	6	1039.6			

Sources:
"Cardiff Pubs and Breweries" by Brian Glover, 2005. pages 97-101
Thomas Usher Gravity Book held at the Scottish Brewing Archive, document number TU/6/11.
Whitbread Gravity book held at the London Metropolitan Archives, document number LMA/4453/D/02/001.

Scotland

By the time the dust had settled on WW I, Scotland was a land of Pale Ales. Very little else was brewed and when it was, it was often parti-gyled with Pale Ale. For example many Strong Ales were just super-strength versions of a brewery's Pale Ale.

A typical range had a 5d Pale Ale at 1033-1034°, a 6d at 1039-1040°, a 7d at 1044-45° and an 8d at 1054-1055°. Sometimes there was also a 4d Pale Ale at around 1030°. With the exception of William Younger, which brewed mostly single-gyle, all a brewery's Pale Ales were parti-gyled in various combinations. Those are all prices per pint on draught in a public bar.

Here are some examples:

Draught Scottish Pale Ales after WW I								
Year	Brewer	Beer	Price per pint	OG	FG	ABV	App. Attenuation	colour
1922	J Deucher	Lochside Beer	7	1039.5	1011	3.69	72.15%	
1924	Gordon & Blair	Pale Ale		1038.1				
1922	Hamilton	PA		1036	1010.2	3.34	71.67%	
1922	McEwan	Pale Ale		1039.8	1007.6	4.18	80.83%	30
1922	McEwan	Pale Ale	7	1038.7	1010	3.72	74.16%	35
1922	McEwan	PA	7	1039	1007	4.16	82.05%	
1924	McEwan	Pale Ale		1041.6				
1922	Murray	PA		1037	1005	4.17	86.49%	
1924	Murray	Pale Ale		1037.2				
1922	Steel Coulson	PA		1040	1012	3.63	70.00%	
1923	Tennent	Beer		1038	1006	4.17	84.21%	45
1924	Bernard	60/-		1040	1014	3.36	65.00%	42
1924	McEwan	Pale Ale	6	1038.7	1009.4	3.80	75.71%	52
Sources: Thomas Usher Gravity Book held at the Scottish Brewing Archive, document number TU/6/11. Younger, Wm. & Co Gravity Book document WY/6/1/1/19 held at the Scottish Brewing Archive Whitbread Gravity book held at the London Metropolitan Archives, document number LMA/4453/D/02/001.								

At least within breweries, shilling designations were used logically:

Thomas Usher Pale Ales in 1028	
beer	OG
PA	1035
PA 60/-	1041
PA 70/-	1048
PA 80/-	1055
Source: Thomas Usher brewing record held at the Scottish Brewing Archive, document number TU/6/1/6.	

Shilling designations were used pretty randomly for bottled beers. 90/-, for example, was usually a low-gravity Pale Ale.

Bottled Scottish Pale Ales after WW I

Year	Brewer	Beer	Price per pint	OG	FG	ABV	App. Attenuation	colour
1925	Aitchison	PA		1059.5	1009	6.61	84.87%	25
1926	Aitken	Sparkling Ale		1034	1005	3.77	85.29%	40
1925	Ballingall	Pale Ale carbonated		1046	1011.5	4.48	75.00%	40
1923	Bernard	Carbonated Beer	8	1037.6	1012.4	3.26	67.02%	45
1925	Bernard	Pale Ale	8	1038	1010	3.63	73.68%	39
1924	Bernard	Pale Ale	8	1040.2	1013.2	3.49	67.16%	35
1926	Dryborough	Pale Ale	8	1032	1009	2.98	71.88%	50
1926	Dryborough	Pale Ale		1038	1008	3.90	78.95%	
1924	J. Deuchar	Pale Ale		1038.9	1005.3	4.37	86.29%	35
1926	Jeffrey	Pale Ale		1032	1006	3.38	81.25%	35
1926	Jeffrey	PA		1032	1007	3.24	78.13%	20
1926	Mackay	PA		1035	1008	3.50	77.14%	35
1926	McEwan	Pale Ale	8	1034	1006	3.64	82.35%	40
1926	McLennan & Urquhart	PA		1040	1008	4.16	80.00%	40
1924	Murray	Pale Ale	8	1036.3	1011.1	3.26	69.42%	25
1925	Murray	Pale Ale	8	1039.5	1010.5	3.76	73.42%	25
1925	Murray	Strong PA	12	1060	1015	5.86	75.00%	
1926	Tennent	90/-		1035	1005	3.91	85.71%	40
1924	Tennent	Pale Ale	8	1037.3	1009.8	3.57	73.73%	48
1925	Usher	PA 60/-		1038	1006	4.17	84.21%	
1926	Younger, Geo.	PA		1033	1009	3.11	72.73%	30
1923	Younger, Geo.	No. 1 Pale Ale		1040.9	1008.2	4.26	80.07%	31
1925	Younger, Wm.	Pale Ale	8	1039	1007.5	4.10	80.77%	28
1926	Younger, Wm.	PA		1044	1010	4.42	77.27%	30

Sources:
Thomas Usher Gravity Book held at the Scottish Brewing Archive, document number TU/6/11.
Younger, Wm. & Co Gravity Book document WY/6/1/1/19 held at the Scottish Brewing Archive

Murray Strong Pale Ale with an OG of 1060° was unusually hefty. Other than for export, Pale Ales were rarely much more than 1055°, even classy ones like Bass.

IPA

Splitting apart Pale Ale and IPA is tricky, if not impossible. There was little consistency in how brewers used the two terms. At some breweries IPA was the stronger beer. But at others, especially in London, the Pale Ale was the stronger of the two.

Before WW I

The classic Burton IPAs, from brewers like Bass and Allsopp, had OGs of around 1065° and were brewed as Stock Ales. Bass, for example, was aged for as much as 12 months in trade casks just stacked in the brewery yard, completely open to the elements.

In the first decade of the 20th-century, a new style of IPA was evolving in London and the Southeast. This was a very pale, heavily hopped beer of a fairly modest gravity, 1045° to 1050°.

Burton IPA before WW I								
Year	Brewer	Beer	package	OG	FG	ABV	App. Atten- uation	Acidity
1901	Bass	Dog's Head	bottled	1065.63	1003.34	8.06	94.59%	0.171
1901	Bass	White Label	bottled	1063.77	1007.41	7.25	87.73%	0.171
1901	Bass	Pale Ale	draught	1063.99	1013.40	6.48	78.03%	0.144
Source: Wahl & Henius, pages 823-830								

Several of the beers in the Pale Ale tables above are sort of IPAs. A couple are actually called IPA by name. Others, like Younger's XXP and XP I know were marketed as IPAs in the 19th century. And Truman P1 is a classic Burton IPA. It just seemed simpler to lump the Pale Ales and IPAs together in tables rather than try to work out which really count as IPAs.

During WW I

London

The effect of the war on Whitbread's IPA was to transform it into a low-gravity beer. It started the war a couple of gravity points below average OG, but finished around 10 points below.

Whitbread IPA 1914 - 1921

Date	Year	OG	FG	ABV	App. Attenuation	lbs hops/ qtr	hops lb/brl
5th Jun	1914	1049.3	1013.0	4.80	73.63%	11.96	2.53
6th Oct	1914	1049.9	1015.0	4.61	69.92%	10.97	2.39
31st Jan	1916	1047.1	1015.0	4.25	68.15%	10.94	2.26
3rd Jul	1917	1047.1	1012.0	4.64	74.52%	11.90	2.46
10th Oct	1917	1047.4	1012.0	4.68	74.67%	11.87	2.49
16th Oct	1917	1038.8	1007.0	4.20	81.95%	11.41	1.91
17th Oct	1917	1040.9	1008.0	4.35	80.43%	10.61	1.81
11th Jun	1918	1033.0	1008.0	3.30	75.73%	11.68	1.69
30th Oct	1918	1032.4	1005.0	3.63	84.57%	11.97	1.70
19th Mar	1919	1032.4	1007.0	3.36	78.40%	11.85	1.67
11th Nov	1919	1036.0	1009.0	3.57	74.97%	12.95	1.98
5th Mar	1920	1034.0	1007.0	3.58	79.44%	12.99	1.90
8th Mar	1921	1035.5	1007.0	3.76	80.26%	12.94	1.81
21st Jan	1921	1034.2	1006.0	3.73	82.46%	12.88	1.80

Sources:
Whitbread brewing records held at the London Metropolitan Archives, document numbers LMA/4453/D/01/079, LMA/4453/D/01/081, LMA/4453/D/01/082, LMA/4453/D/01/083, LMA/4453/D/01/084, LMA/4453/D/01/085 and LMA/4453/D/01/086.

IPA's gravity didn't bounce back the way that Whitbread's PA's did. In June 1918, there was little between the two beers, PA was 1035.1° and IPA just a couple of points lower at 1033°. But while PA jumped back to 1048.2° in 1912, an increase of 13 gravity points, IPA only increased by two.

Though IPA remained significantly more heavily hopped than PA. Something that might please style Nazis.

Whitbread IPA had a very simple recipe. And one that changed very little during the war.

Whitbread IPA grists 1914 - 1921					
Date	Year	OG	pale malt	PA malt	no. 1 sugar
5th Jun	1914	1049.3	22.0%	58.5%	19.5%
6th Oct	1914	1049.9	22.0%	58.5%	19.5%
31st Jan	1916	1047.1	23.3%	56.0%	20.7%
3rd Jul	1917	1047.1	22.8%	60.9%	16.2%
10th Oct	1917	1047.4	22.8%	60.9%	16.2%
16th Oct	1917	1038.8	22.7%	68.2%	9.1%
17th Oct	1917	1040.9	26.2%	64.5%	9.3%
11th Jun	1918	1033.0	29.2%	64.3%	6.5%
30th Oct	1918	1032.4	21.3%	59.7%	19.0%
19th Mar	1919	1032.4	22.0%	58.5%	19.5%
11th Nov	1919	1036.0	52.3%	31.1%	16.6%
5th Mar	1920	1034.0	23.5%	64.2%	12.2%
8th Mar	1921	1035.5	35.9%	51.4%	12.7%
21st Jan	1921	1034.2	34.7%	52.1%	13.1%

Sources:
Whitbread brewing records held at the London Metropolitan Archives, document numbers LMA/4453/D/01/079, LMA/4453/D/01/081, LMA/4453/D/01/082, LMA/4453/D/01/083, LMA/4453/D/01/084, LMA/4453/D/01/085 and LMA/4453/D/01/086.

The only really significant change was a drop in the sugar percentage in 1917 and 1918. After which it rose back to its old level. The recipe in March 1919 was identical to the one in 1914. Even though the beer itself was far weaker. Whitbread clearly thought the old recipe was a winner.

A look at the hops used in brewing Whitbread IPA gives a fascinating insight to what was happening with the hop industry during the war.

Whitbread IPA hops 1914 - 1921			
Date	Year	OG	hops
5th Jun	1914	1049.3	EK (1912 CS, 1913)
6th Oct	1914	1049.9	EK (1912 CS, 1913 CS, 1913)
31st Jan	1916	1047.1	EK (1914 CS, 1914)
3rd Jul	1917	1047.1	EK (1914 CS, 1914)
10th Oct	1917	1047.4	EK (1915 CS, 1916)
16th Oct	1917	1038.8	EK (1915 CS, 1916)
17th Oct	1917	1040.9	EK (1915 CS, 1916)
11th Jun	1918	1033.0	EK (1915 CS, 1916 CS)
30th Oct	1918	1032.4	EK (1916 CS)
19th Mar	1919	1032.4	EK (1917), EK (1917 CS)
11th Nov	1919	1036.0	EK (1918), MK (1918), Oregon (1917)
5th Mar	1920	1034.0	EK (1918 CS), MK (1918), MK (1919), Pacific (1917)
8th Mar	1921	1035.5	EK (1919), MK (1919), Oregon (1917), Bohemian (1919)
21st Jan	1921	1034.2	EK (1919), MK (1918, 1919), Oregon (1917), Bohemian (1919)
Sources: Whitbread brewing records held at the London Metropolitan Archives, document numbers LMA/4453/D/01/079, LMA/4453/D/01/081, LMA/4453/D/01/082, LMA/4453/D/01/083, LMA/4453/D/01/084, LMA/4453/D/01/085 and LMA/4453/D/01/086.			

Until 1919, Whitbread only used Kent hops in their IPA. Even more specific than that, they only used East Kent hops. Which means Goldings or something similar. Though they are becoming increasingly old. For example, the 1916 crop only turns up in the records about a year after harvest.

Using older hops was nothing new. But usually a Pale Ale would always contain some hops of the most recent season. That wasn't the case during WW I.

After the end of hostilities, several foreign hops appear. Pacific and Oregon from the US and Bohemians, from what had been enemy territory. Given the minimal amounts of hops imported in into the UK in 1917 and 1919, the US from the 1917 crop must have been imported later.

Provincial England

In different parts of the UK, IPA meant different things. For example, a Burton-brewed IPA was very different from a Manchester-brewed one. There's one example from Manchester that went on to national fame. Though not under the name IPA: Boddington's Bitter. Whose Brewhouse name was always IP.

Boddington IP 1914 - 1921							
Date	Year	OG	FG	ABV	App. Attenuation	lbs hops/ qtr	hops lb/brl
10th Jul	1914	1053	1016	4.89	69.81%	4.00	1.35
6th May	1915	1047	1016	4.10	65.96%	4.52	1.18
14th Oct	1915	1050	1016	4.50	68.00%	4.52	1.23
15th May	1916	1053	1015	5.03	71.70%	4.52	1.42
15th May	1917	1044	1015	3.84	65.91%	4.75	1.16
6th Jul	1917	1046	1016	3.97	65.22%	3.78	1.18
9th Oct	1917	1045	1017	3.70	62.22%	4.75	1.15
26th Apr	1918	1038	1012	3.44	68.42%	5.38	1.11
2nd Aug	1918	1038	1014	3.18	63.16%	5.38	1.16
4th Oct	1918	1038	1012	3.44	68.42%	5.38	1.11
20th Dec	1918	1037	1014	3.04	62.16%	5.38	1.08
8th Jan	1919	1039	1015	3.18	61.54%	5.38	1.07
12th Jun	1919	1042	1013	3.84	69.05%	5.00	1.15
14th Oct	1919	1046	1015	4.10	67.39%	4.44	1.21
8th Oct	1920	1046	1015	4.10	67.39%	4.59	1.16
4th Oct	1921	1048	1015	4.37	68.75%	3.93	1.01
Sources: Boddington brewing records held at Manchester Central Library, document numbers M693/405/126 and M693/405/126.							

IP came through the war in a better state than many beers, losing just 13% of its gravity between 1914 and 1921. The average was 23%. The nadir in its gravity, 1037° in 1918, wasn't bad at all. At least it remained intoxicating. Though they were only able to keep OP's gravity at a reasonable level by brewing some very watery Mild.

The hopping rate per quarter of malt increased as the gravity fell, getting up to almost 5.5 lbs in 1918. After the war, when the gravity rose, the hopping rate returned to its pre-war level. But if you look back a couple of pages you'll see that's a far lower rate than that of Whitbread's IPA, which received 12-13 lbs per quarter.

The grist of IP wasn't very exciting, never consisting of more than three elements:

Boddington IP grists 1914 - 1921					
Date	Year	OG	pale malt	flaked maize	sugar
10th Jul	1914	1053	87.38%	8.74%	3.88%
6th May	1915	1047	97.83%		2.17%
14th Oct	1915	1050	97.83%		2.17%
15th May	1916	1053	97.83%		2.17%
15th May	1917	1044	89.14%	8.57%	2.29%
6th Jul	1917	1046	97.67%		2.33%
9th Oct	1917	1045	89.14%	8.57%	2.29%
26th Apr	1918	1038	97.40%		2.60%
2nd Aug	1918	1038	97.40%		2.60%
4th Oct	1918	1038	97.40%		2.60%
20th Dec	1918	1037	97.40%		2.60%
8th Jan	1919	1039	97.40%		2.60%
12th Jun	1919	1042	97.59%		2.41%
14th Oct	1919	1046	85.25%	8.20%	6.56%
8th Oct	1920	1046	87.15%	8.38%	4.47%
4th Oct	1921	1048	87.15%	8.38%	4.47%

Sources:
Boddington brewing records held at Manchester Central Library, document numbers M693/405/126 and M693/405/126.

The patchy use of flaked maize I assume is the result of difficulty in obtaining supplies. It might well be that the type of sugar changed during the course of the war. Unfortunately, Boddington's records give no clue as to what sort of sugar they were using.

Boddington were quite consistent in the hops that they used during the war: English, Belgian (Poperinge) and Californian.

Boddington IP hops 1914 - 1921

Date	Year	OG	Hops
10th Jul	1914	1053	English (1910, 1911, 1912, 1913), Californian (1913); English (1913) & Californian (1913) dry hops
6th May	1915	1047	English (1911, 1912, 1913, 1914), Californian (1913); English (1914) & Californian (1913) dry hops
14th Oct	1915	1050	English (1911, 1912, 1913, 1914), Californian (1914); English (1914) & Californian (1914) dry hops
15th May	1916	1053	English (1912, 1915), Californian (1914); English (1915) & Californian (1914) dry hops
15th May	1917	1044	English (1914, 1915, 1916), Californian (1915), Poperinge (1914); English (1916) & Californian (1915) dry hops
6th Jul	1917	1046	English (1914, 1915, 1916), Californian (1915), Poperinge (1914); English (1916) & Californian (1915) dry hops
9th Oct	1917	1045	English (1914, 1915, 1916), Californian (1915), Poperinge (1915); English (1916) & Californian (1915) dry hops
26th Apr	1918	1038	English (1914, 1915, 1916, 1917), Poperinge (1916), Californian (1915); English (1916, 1917) dry hops
2nd Aug	1918	1038	English (1914, 1916, 1917), Californian (1913, 1915); English (1917) dry hops
4th Oct	1918	1038	English (1914, 1916, 1917), Poperinge (1916), Californian (1913, 1916); English (1917) dry hops
20th Dec	1918	1037	English (1914, 1915, 1917), Poperinge (1915), Californian (1915); English (1917) dry hops
8th Jan	1919	1039	English (1916, 1917), Poperinge (1915), Californian (1915); English (1917) dry hops
12th Jun	1919	1042	English (1916, 1917, 1918), Poperinge (1915), Californian (1915); English dry hops
14th Oct	1919	1046	English (1916, 1918), Poperinge (1914, 1915), Oregon (1917); English (1918), Oregon (1917) dry hops
8th Oct	1920	1046	English (1919), Oregon (1916, 1917), Alsace (1916), Pacific (1919); English (1919), Pacific (1919), Alost (1919) dry hops
4th Oct	1921	1048	Saaz (1918), English (1919, 1920), Alost (1920), Pacific (1920); Pacific (1920), English (1920) dry hops

Sources:
Boddington brewing records held at Manchester Central Library, document numbers M693/405/126 and M693/405/126.

Interestingly, they frequently used ones from California for dry hopping. As British brewers weren't keen on the aroma of American, they usually employed them as early kettle hops.

After the end of hostilities, more foreign hops turn up, from Oregon, Alsace, Pacific, Belgium (Alost or Aalst) and Saaz. Some of them – like the 1916 Alsace and Saaz 1918 – from crops during the war years.

I can understand that. With the collapse in brewing in Austria and Germany in the final years of the war, there must have been lots of hops that went unused. When brewing was slow to recover in Central Europe after the Armistice, those old hops must have been pretty cheap.

Scotland

Trying to pick apart IPA and Pale Ale in Scotland is even trickier than in London. Judging by the brew house names, some brewers considered all their Pale Ales IPAs. And William Younger, confusingly, while not calling any of their beers IPA in the brew house, did market some of its beers as such.

That's just a warning to not take as gospel that the following beers are IPAs. They might have been. Or maybe not. The distinction was probably lost on most drinkers, anyway.

PI 60/- was Drybrough's strongest Pale Ale/IPA at the start of the war. Though it's weaker than a top-class London Pale Ale would have been.

Drybrough Pl 60/- 1914 - 1920

Date	Year	OG	FG	ABV	App. Attenuation	lbs hops/ qtr	hops lb/brl
31st Dec	1914	1054	1018	4.76	66.67%	5.07	1.12
12th Jan	1915	1053	1018	4.63	66.04%	6.01	1.29
7th Jan	1916	1053	1017	4.76	67.92%	5.02	1.10
28th Jul	1916	1050	1015	4.63	70.00%	3.95	0.85
16th Jan	1917	1048	1016	4.23	66.67%	3.95	0.80
13th Feb	1917	1044	1017	3.57	61.36%	4.04	0.74
10th Jul	1919	1036	1009	3.57	75.00%	4.93	0.73
15th Oct	1919	1039	1012	3.57	69.23%	4.34	0.83
29th Jul	1920	1039	1012	3.57	69.23%	5.20	0.86

Sources:
Drybrough brewing record held at the Scottish Brewing Archive, document number D/6/1/1/3.

In the first couple of years of the war, it didn't change a great deal, losing just four gravity points. It was dropped in 1917, probably in April. This was the time when gravity restrictions kicked in. Unlike some breweries, which slashed gravities but kept the name of the strongest beer, Drybrough discontinued the strongest.

It reappears in the records in the middle of 1919, with its gravity even further reduced. Its gravity then stabilised just under 1040° for the rest of the 1920's. However, in 1920 they introduced a new beer, PI 80/- with an OG of 1054° - exactly the same as PI 60/- had been before the war. Confusing, isn't it?

Drybrough Pl 60/- 1914 - 1920

Date	Year	OG	pale malt	flaked maize	invert sugar			caramel	malt extract	dxt	BSC
					no. 1	no. 2	no. 3				
31st Dec	1914	1054	81.91%	8.19%	4.10%	5.46%				0.34%	
12th Jan	1915	1053	82.66%	8.55%	3.80%	4.75%				0.24%	
7th Jan	1916	1053	81.47%	8.81%	3.67%	5.87%		0.18%			
28th Jul	1916	1050	85.87%	4.40%	3.67%	5.87%		0.18%			
16th Jan	1917	1048	80.61%	9.21%	3.84%	6.14%		0.19%			
13th Feb	1917	1044	80.50%	10.06%	3.35%	5.87%		0.21%			
10th Jul	1919	1036	91.18%				8.82%				
15th Oct	1919	1039	78.83%	4.38%			6.57%	10.22%			
29th Jul	1920	1039	70.45%	19.43%			1.62%	1.21%			7.29%

Sources:
Drybrough brewing record held at the Scottish Brewing Archive, document number D/6/1/1/3.

Like the gravity, there's not much change in the early war years. It's not the most fascinating of recipes, just pale malt, flaked maize and some sugar. With all the changes being in the type of sugar used. Though we don't see that in action as PI 60/- had already been discontinued by the time the restrictions on sugar use began in 1917.

After WW I

Burton

Stock Pale Ales, such as Burton-style IPAs, were pretty much wiped out by the war. Only a few Burton breweries, like Bass and Worthington, continued to make beers of this type.

As some was still exported, notably to Belgium, there were versions that weren't that much weaker than those from before the war.

Burton IPA after WW I

Year	Brewer	Beer	Price	package	OG	FG	ABV	App. Attenuation	colour
1921	Allsopp	IPA	17d	bottled	1054.4	1004.4	6.56	91.91%	
1921	Worthington	IPA	13d	bottled	1054.9	1007.4	6.22	86.52%	
1922	Worthington	IPA (Belgian sample)		bottled	1055	1004.7	6.60	91.45%	
1922	Bass	Pale Ale		bottled	1054.7	1011	5.70	79.90%	20
1927	Bass	Pale Ale		draught	1055.5				
1928	Bass	Pale Ale		bottled	1059	1013	6.00	77.97%	19
1929	Bass	Pale Ale		bottled	1056	1008	6.28	85.71%	

Sources:
Whitbread Gravity book held at the London Metropolitan Archives, document number LMA/4453/D/02/001.
Younger, Wm. & Co Gravity Book document WY/6/1/1/19 held at the Scottish Brewing Archive
Thomas Usher Gravity Book document TU/6/11

The colours of 19 and 20 are pretty pale for that gravity. They're in the old Lovibond scale, so are around 5 SRM. Most Pale Ales with gravities in the 1040°'s were 24-28 in that Lovibond scale.

England other than Burton

In different parts of the country, the term IPA meant different things. In parts of the Southeast especially, it was usually a low-gravity bottled beer, much different from the beers brewed in Burton. Though the odd stronger version did still exist elsewhere:

Bottled English IPA after WW I

Year	Brewer	Beer	Price per pint (d)	OG	FG	ABV	App. Attenuation	colour
1928	Barclay Perkins	IPA		1045.8	1012.0	4.47	73.80%	15
1923	Cannon	IPA		1040	1007.7	4.20	80.75%	
1929	Fussell	IPA	7	1047	1013.1	4.40	72.13%	
1926	Smithers	IPA	7	1048.1	1008.9	5.11	81.50%	
1926	Tamplin	IPA	12	1057.9	1004.8	6.97	91.71%	
1925	Vaux	IPA	7	1036.6	1007.8	3.74	78.69%	
1923	Whitbread	IPA		1036	1008	3.64	77.78%	24

Sources:
Whitbread brewing record held at the London Metropolitan Archives, document number LMA/4453/D/01/089.
Whitbread Gravity book held at the London Metropolitan Archives, document number LMA/4453/D/02/001.

Only the Tamplin beer resembles a classic Burton IPA. The others look like either Ordinary or Best Bitter.

Scotland

In the 19th century, Scotland had been a big exporter of IPA to India. In particular, brewers in Edinburgh and Alloa had been quick to enter the trade. The beers they initially brewed were very similar in character to those from Burton. Which made sense, as they were competing in the same market.

But as the export trade top India shrank in importance, Scottish IPA was mostly brewed for the home market, at which point it began to diverge from the Burton version, becoming weak and less heavily hopped.

In the early 20th century, many beers, at least internally in breweries, were reclassed PA rather than IPA. Even when the beers themselves had remained essentially the same. It makes deciding what's a Pale and what's an IPA particularly tricky. For the table below I've chosen only beers specifically branded as IPA.

Mini Book Series volume XXXII: Armistice!

Bottled Scottish IPA after WW I								
Brewer	Beer		Price per pint (d)	FG	OG	ABV	App. Attenuation	colour
1924	Bernard	90/- IPA		1013	1041	3.62	68.29%	
1928	Bernard	90/- IPA		1005	1039	4.43	87.18%	
1929	Bernard	90/- IPA		1009	1039.5	3.96	77.22%	
1929	Bernard	90/- IPA		1009.8	1040	3.93	75.63%	
1929	Bernard	90/- IPA		1009	1040	4.03	77.50%	58
1928	McEwan	Export IPA	12	1009.5	1055.1	5.95	82.76%	
1929	McEwan	Export IPA		1011.8	1055.3	5.67	78.73%	
1929	McEwan	Export IPA		1012	1054.5	5.53	77.98%	

Sources:
Thomas Usher Gravity Book held at the Scottish Brewing Archive, document number TU/6/11. Younger, Wm. & Co Gravity Book document WY/6/1/1/19 held at the Scottish Brewing Archive Whitbread Gravity book held at the London Metropolitan Archives, document number LMA/4453/D/02/001.

The Bernard's and McEwan's IPAs are clearly quite different types of beer, with very different gravities. The McEwan's beer might well have been truly intended for Export. It looks very similar to post-war Burton-brewed versions.

Porter

Before WW I

In the last couple of decades in the 19th century, Porter declined considerably in popularity. In many parts of the country, brewers had dropped Porter, which was principally a draught beer, and concentrated on Stout. In London and parts of the Southeast, however, Porter had retained its popularity. In London it remained one of the standard draught beers, available in every pub.

The war would not be kind to the style. Though, it probably just hastened the inevitable.

London Porter before WW I								
Year	Brewer	Beer	OG	FG	ABV	App. Atten-uation	lbs hops/ qtr	hops lb/brl
1914	Whitbread	P	1052.3	1017.0	4.67	67.49%	4.94	1.09
1906	Barclay Perkins	TT	1052.1	1016.5	4.71	68.33%	4.67	1.11
1910	Fuller	P	1049.2	1010.5	5.11	78.59%	6.31	1.58
1909	Truman	Runner	1058.2				8.2	2.31
1914	Courage	Porter	1051.2	1018.3	4.36	64.32%	7.20	1.51
Sources: Whitbread brewing record held at the London Metropolitan Archives, document number LMA/4453/D/09/108. Barclay Perkins brewing record held at the London Metropolitan Archives, document number ACC/2305/1/605. Truman brewing record held at the London Metropolitan Archives, document number B/THB/C/112. Courage brewing record held at the London Metropolitan Archives, document number ACC/2305/08/247.								

I'd love to give you the details of provincial English Porter, but it was as dead as London Mild is today. Well, I do have one example. From Tetley's, in Yorkshire. I'm sure that they were still brewing it in 1914, as I have brewing records from during the war.

Provincial Porter before WW I								
Year	Brewer	Beer	OG	FG	ABV	App. Atten-uation	lbs hops/ qtr	hops lb/brl
1904	Tetley	P	1050.4	1017.2	4.40	65.93%	4.91	1.03
Sources: Tetley's brewing record held at the West Yorkshire Archives, document number WYL756/51/ACC1903.								

It fits in well with the London versions in terms of strength and hopping. In fact it's almost as strong as many provincial Stouts.

During WW I

The distinction between Porter and Stout was eroded by the war. There are stories of breweries selling the same beer as both Porter and Stout. Having looked at brewing records, I can believe that. Kidd seem to have discontinued their Stout in 1917, while at the same time adding oats to their Porter grist. There could only be one reason for that: they were selling some of it as Oatmeal Stout.

Here's what happened to Courage Porter during the war:

Courage Porter 1914 - 1920							
Date	Year	OG	FG	ABV	App. Attenu-ation	lbs hops/ qtr	hops lb/brl
21st Oct	1914	1051.25	1018.28	4.36	64.32%	7.20	1.51
10th Mar	1915	1050.41	1018.28	4.25	63.74%	7.23	1.52
22nd Sep	1915	1046.26	1011.36	4.62	75.45%	8.09	1.60
17th May	1916	1042.94	1011.91	4.10	72.26%	7.31	1.27
3rd Jan	1917	1044.04	1012.19	4.21	72.33%	6.11	1.33
30th May	1917	1038.78	1008.86	3.96	77.14%	5.82	1.17
24th Oct	1917	1032.69	1009.70	3.04	70.34%	5.98	0.96
16th Jan	1918	1032.69	1009.42	3.08	71.19%	5.85	0.94
21st Jan	1920	1029.64	1009.42	2.68	68.22%	5.51	0.87

Sources:
Courage brewing records held at the London Metropolitan Archives, document numbers ACC/2305/08/247, ACC/2305/08/248 and ACC/2305/08/251.

Courage discontinued its Porter in early 1918 when they dropped the gravity of Stout to just 1035°.

There were several alterations to the recipe of Courage Porter during the war:

Courage Porter grists 1914 - 1920								
Date	Year	OG	pale malt	brown malt	black malt	no. 3 sugar	caramel	black invert
21st Oct	1914	1051.25	60.22%	19.59%	10.52%			9.67%
10th Mar	1915	1050.41	58.43%	20.22%	10.11%			11.24%
22nd Sep	1915	1046.26	61.48%	20.23%	10.51%			7.78%
17th May	1916	1042.94	60.43%	19.79%	9.09%		0.71%	9.98%
3rd Jan	1917	1044.04	64.41%	10.17%	8.47%	7.53%	1.88%	7.53%
30th May	1917	1038.78	64.19%	10.48%	7.86%	6.99%	1.75%	8.73%
24th Oct	1917	1032.69	68.69%	9.81%	8.41%	5.61%	1.87%	5.61%
16th Jan	1918	1032.69	69.79%	8.82%	11.23%		1.60%	8.56%
21st Jan	1920	1029.64	67.30%	9.24%	13.64%		2.79%	7.04%

Sources:
Courage brewing records held at the London Metropolitan Archives, document numbers ACC/2305/08/247, ACC/2305/08/248, ACC/2305/08/249 and ACC/2305/08/251.

Courage Porter started the war with a typical London grist of pale, brown and black malt, plus sugar. There was a big fall in the proportion of brown malt in 1917, which seems to have compensated for by an increase in the percentage of sugar. The proportion of black malt was more stable, mostly hovering around 10%, except in 1917, when it was a little lower.

The combination of large quantities of coloured malts, as well as dark invert sugars and caramel, resulted in a beer that was pretty black.

As their Porter was parti-gyled with their Stouts, the above comments on the grist apply to those beers, too.

After WW I

Of all British styles, Porter was the one most damaged by WW I. Even in London, where it had been a popular draught beer in 1914, sales declined dramatically. With its gravity slashed because it was expected to be cheap, it looks as if many of its drinkers moved over to draught Stout, which in the 1920's was very similar to pre-war Porter.

London Porter after WW I								
Year	Brewer	Beer	OG	FG	ABV	App. Attenuation	lbs hops/ qtr	hops lb/brl
1922	Whitbread	P	1028.0	1007.0	2.78	75.00%	7.42	0.93
1928	Barclay Perkins	TT	1027.0	1009.0	2.38	66.67%	14.19	0.64
1925	Fuller	P	1041.5	1015.5	3.44	62.62%	8.00	1.55
1922	Courage	Porter	1032.7	1008.3	3.22	74.58%	8.56	1.17
Sources: Whitbread brewing record held at the London Metropolitan Archives, document number LMA/4453/D/09/116. Barclay Perkins brewing record held at the London Metropolitan Archives, document number ACC/2305/1/614. Fullers brewing record held at the brewery. Courage brewing record held at the London Metropolitan Archives, document number ACC/2305/08/253.								

What was almost certainly caused Porter's long-term downfall was the decision to brew it as a 6d. beer after the war. That doomed it to being no stronger than about 1038°, which was about 27% weaker than the 1052° it had been before the war. It was just too watery a beer to really appeal.

Draught London Porter after WW I							
Year	Brewer	Beer	Price	OG	FG	ABV	App. Attenuation
1923	Barclay Perkins	Porter	6d	1038	1012.5	3.30	67.11%
1923	Cannon	Porter	6d	1036	1009	3.50	75.00%
1923	City of London	Porter	6d	1037.6	1009.6	3.63	74.47%
1923	Courage	Porter	6d	1043.2	1013.2	3.89	69.44%
1923	Hoare	Porter	6d	1034.2	1010.2	3.11	70.18%
1923	Lion	Porter	6d	1038.3	1009.8	3.70	74.41%
1923	Mann	Porter	6d	1039.3	1009.3	3.89	76.34%
1923	Truman	Porter	6d	1036.8	1010.8	3.37	70.65%
1923	Watney	Porter	6d	1038.8	1009.8	3.76	74.74%
1923	Wenlock	Porter	6d	1034.8	1011.8	2.97	66.09%
Source: Whitbread Gravity book held at the London Metropolitan Archives, document number LMA/4453/D/02/001.							

Sales of Porter fell sharply in the 1920's and by the end of the decade was a marginal product, not available of draught in every pub as it had been before the war.

Whitbread Porter and Stout production 1914 - 1929						
Year	P	S	CS	LS	ES	Total Port
1914	123,085	190		198,806		**382,984**
1915	65,216			208,733	282	**314,169**
1916	80,298			244,889		**369,130**
1917	8,493			241,280		**286,163**
1918	7,136			95,882		**110,695**
1919	21,602	4,797		89,165		**117,284**
1920	24,910	47,789		137,533		**234,413**
1921	15,688	58,452		133,563	30,920	**238,623**
1922	16,562	47,530	84,703	15,340	28,582	**192,717**
1923	14,165	39,960	68,326	20,866	26,660	**169,977**
1924	15,948	37,834	74,258	23,442	26,710	**178,192**
1925	14,943	35,396	62,357	22,262	28,974	**163,932**
1926	13,511	34,567	20,721	69,724	29,990	**168,513**
1927	10,708	30,087		86,569	22,361	**149,725**
1928	10,105	30,017		85,992	16,039	**142,153**
1929	5,558	17,284		51,624	11,313	**85,779**

Sources:
Whitbread brewing records held at the London Metropolitan Archives, document numbers LMA/4453/D/01/079, LMA/4453/D/01/080, LMA/4453/D/01/081, LMA/4453/D/01/082, LMA/4453/D/01/083, LMA/4453/D/01/084, LMA/4453/D/01/085, LMA/4453/D/01/086, LMA/4453/D/01/087, LMA/4453/D/01/088, LMA/4453/D/01/089, LMA/4453/D/01/090, LMA/4453/D/01/091, LMA/4453/D/01/092, LMA/4453/D/01/093 and LMA/4453/D/01/094.

Stout

Before WW I

Despite the decline of Porter, Stout remained very popular. Most breweries produced more than one at different strengths. London brewers often brewed three, four or even more Stouts.

There was a wide variation in the strength of Stouts. Provincial versions could be as weak as 1050°, very similar in strength to a London Porter. The strongest Imperial Stouts were over 1100°.

Milk Stout was an innovation that made an appearance just a few years before the start of the war. It was first brewed on the Kent coast by Mackeson, who acquired a patent for it and allowed other brewers to brew a version under licence.

Another variation was Oatmeal Stout. This was developed by Maclay of Alloa in the 1890s. They also tried to patent their invention, but with rather less success. Their Beer was called Oat Malt Stout and, as the name implies, used malted oats. Other brewers got around this by using oat flakes and calling their beers Oatmeal Stout.

London Stout before WW I								
Year	Brewer	Beer	OG	FG	ABV	App. Atten- uation	lbs hops/ qtr	hops lb/brl
1910	Barclay Perkins	OMS	1053.2	1016.5	4.86	68.98%	7.50	1.82
1910	Barclay Perkins	BS	1074.2	1025.0	6.51	66.31%	8.00	2.75
1910	Barclay Perkins	BS Ex	1076.0	1022.5	7.08	70.39%	12.00	4.12
1914	Courage	Double Stout	1078.9	1033.2	6.05	57.89%	7.20	2.33
1914	Courage	Imperial	1094.2	1038.8	7.33	58.82%	7.20	2.78
1914	Fuller	BS	1066.4	1020.8	6.03	68.70%	6.745	2.01
1914	Whitbread	LS	1054.0	1014.0	5.29	74.05%	5.99	1.37
1914	Whitbread	Exp S	1070.9	1013.0	7.66	81.67%	13.03	4.25
1914	Whitbread	SS	1079.7	1024.0	7.37	69.88%	8.56	3.03
1914	Whitbread	SSS	1095.0	1036.0	7.81	62.11%	8.56	3.62
Sources:								
Barclay Perkins brewing record held at the London Metropolitan Archives, document number ACC/2305/1/602.								
Courage brewing record held at the London Metropolitan Archives, document number ACC/2305/08/247.								
Fullers brewing record held at the brewery.								
Whitbread brewing record held at the London Metropolitan Archives, document number LMA/4453/D/09/108.								

Provincial Stouts were, in general, a good bit weaker than their London cousins. And, while London brewers made multiple Stouts, outside the capital they tended to stick to just one.

Provincial Stout before WW I

Year	Brewer	Beer	OG	FG	ABV	App. Atten-uation	lbs hops/ qtr	hops lb/brl
1914	Adnams	BS	1055.0	1013.5	5.49	75.45%	5.86	1.43
1914	Boddington	Stout	1054.0	1018.0	4.76	66.67%	3.10	0.94
1911	Lees	XXXP	1059.0	1017.0	5.56	71.19%	4.05	0.98
1911	Murphy	XXX	1088.0	1028.5	7.87	67.61%	15.21	5.87
1911	Russell	DS	1074.2				8.37	2.86
1904	Tetley	S	1066.8	1020.5	6.12	69.29%	4.91	1.36
1910	Warwicks	SS	1053.7	1022.2	4.18	58.76%	4.83	1.12

Sources:
Adnams brewing record Book 2 held at the brewery.
Boddington brewing record held at Manchester Central Library, document number M693/405/126.
Lees brewing record held at the brewery.
Tetley's brewing record held at the West Yorkshire Archives, document number WYL756/51/ACC1903.
Warwicks & Richardsons brewing record held at the Nottinghamshire Archives, document number DD/NM/8/4/1.

The exception, in terms of strength, is from Murphy, which was based in Cork, Ireland. The Stouts with gravities in the 1050s look rather like London Porters in terms of strength. The hopping rates are all over the place, but generally lower than in London, with Murphy again being an exception.

Scottish Stout before WW I

Year	Brewer	Beer	OG	FG	ABV	App. Atten-uation	lbs hops/ qtr	hops lb/brl
1915	Drybrough	XXX	1083	1026	7.54	68.67%	4.79	1.34
1909	Maclay	DBS 54/-	1044	1013	4.10	70.45%	7.56	1.53
1909	Maclay	OMS 63/-	1062	1024	5.03	61.29%	7.56	2.16
1914	Thomas Usher	48/-	1046	1021	3.31	54.35%	5.00	1.04
1914	Thomas Usher	54/-	1056	1025	4.10	55.36%	5.00	1.27
1913	Younger, Wm.	S2	1059	1029	3.97	50.85%	1.88	0.45
1913	Younger, Wm.	S1	1065	1031	4.50	52.31%	1.88	0.50
1913	Younger, Wm.	DBS	1065	1022	5.69	66.15%	10.65	2.63
1913	Younger, Wm.	MBS	1065	1020	5.95	69.23%	3.50	0.74

Sources:
Drybrough brewing record held at the Scottish Brewing Archive, document number D/6/1/1/3.
Maclay brewing record held at the Scottish Brewing Archive, document number M/6/1/1/2.
Thomas Usher brewing record held at the Scottish Brewing Archive, document number TU/6/1/5.
William Younger brewing record held at the Scottish Brewing Archive, document number WY/6/1/2/58.

Scottish started going weird in the late 19th century. Especially at William Younger, who combined minimal hopping (including some spent hops) with very poor attenuation. The forerunners of Sweet Stout, which would later become a Scottish speciality.

During WW I

The popularity of Stout was undiminished by the war, though after 1917 few stronger versions were brewed and Imperial Stouts disappeared completely for a few years. One exception was Ireland, where the rules were different. Presumably taking into account the much higher average OG in Ireland in 1914, the gravity restrictions were looser.

This is what happened to Courage Double Stout during the war:

Courage Double Stout 1914 - 1920							
Date	Year	OG	FG	ABV	App. Atten-uation	lbs hops/ qtr	hops lb/brl
21st Oct	1914	1078.9	1033.2	6.05	57.89%	7.20	2.33
10th Mar	1915	1078.9	1033.2	6.05	57.89%	7.23	2.37
22nd Sep	1915	1075.9	1032.1	5.79	57.66%	8.09	2.62
10th May	1916	1068.7	1024.9	5.79	63.71%	7.26	2.24
3rd Jan	1917	1071.7	1028.8	5.68	59.85%	6.11	2.16
10th Jan	1917	1071.7	1029.6	5.57	58.69%	6.16	2.17
24th Oct	1917	1063.7	1023.3	5.35	63.48%	5.98	1.87
16th Jan	1918	1063.7	1021.1	5.64	66.96%	5.85	1.82
29th Dec	1920	1043.8	1011.6	4.25	73.42%	7.37	1.62
Sources: Courage brewing records held at the London Metropolitan Archives, document numbers ACC/2305/08/247, ACC/2305/08/248, ACC/2305/08/249, and ACC/2305/08/251.							

If you're wondering why there's nothing between January 1918 and December 1920, it's because Double Stout was discontinued, replaced by a new beer called simply Stout.

Courage Stout 1917 - 1920							
Date	Year	OG	FG	ABV	App. Atten-uation	lbs hops/ qtr	hops lb/brl
2nd May	1918	1035.5	1008.0	3.63	77.34%	5.52	1.00
2nd Jul	1919	1048.5	1011.1	4.95	77.14%	5.34	1.22
1st Oct	1919	1053.7	1014.7	5.17	72.68%	5.95	1.50
21st Jan	1920	1043.8	1013.3	4.03	69.62%	5.51	1.28
11th Nov	1920	1043.8	1011.1	4.32	74.68%	7.12	1.57
Sources: Courage brewing records held at the London Metropolitan Archives, document numbers ACC/2305/08/249, ACC/2305/08/250 and ACC/2305/08/251.							

Though it looks very much as if rather than bringing back Double Stout, they just renamed Stout in late 1920.

Provincial England

There was quite a difference between London and the provinces when it came to Stout.

Versions from the capital tended to be both more numerous and stronger. The war levelled out the gravity differences to some extent.

Adnams brewed two Stouts at the start of hostilities, BS (Brown Stout, I'd guess) and the stronger DS (Double Stout).

Adnams BS Stout 1914 - 1917							
Date	Year	OG	FG	ABV	App. Atten-uation	lbs hops/ qtr	hops lb/brl
11th Aug	1914	1055.0	1013.5	5.49	75.45%	5.86	1.43
30th Dec	1914	1050.0	1006.6	5.74	86.70%	7.00	1.14
27th Apr	1915	1049.7	1015.0	4.60	69.90%	0.69	1.48
19th Aug	1915	1048.0	1007.2	5.40	85.00%	6.00	1.29
24th Aug	1915	1048.0	1010.0	5.03	79.23%	6.00	1.25
30th Mar	1916	1045.0	1009.4	4.71	79.07%	6.67	1.31
21st Jun	1916	1045.0	1005.8	5.18	87.07%	6.90	1.30
2nd Jan	1917	1042.0	1009.1	4.35	78.24%	6.67	1.18
Source: Adnams brewing records held at the brewery,							

The gravity of DS was slowly whittled down from 1055° (which would have been considered a Porter strength in London) to just 1042° in early 1917, before it disappeared. The quantity of hops per barrel declined a little as the hopping rate per quarter of malt remained fairly constant.

Taking a look at Adnams other Stout, DS, it's obvious why BS was discontinued:

Adnams DS Stout 1914 - 1920							
Date	Year	OG	FG	ABV	App. Atten-uation	lbs hops/ qtr	hops lb/brl
22nd Dec	1914	1065	1016.6	6.40	74.43%	6.97	2.11
27th Aug	1915	1064	1014.7	6.52	77.06%	6.97	2.05
8th Sep	1915	1065	1017.7	6.25	72.73%	6.97	2.01
23rd Nov	1915	1062	1014.1	6.33	77.21%	6.97	1.89
8th Dec	1916	1052	1011.9	5.30	77.09%	7.57	1.68
1st Jun	1917	1040	1007.5	4.30	81.30%	7.00	1.22
10th Aug	1917	1039	1008.3	4.06	78.69%	7.00	1.25
28th Aug	1917	1039	1010.8	3.73	72.30%	7.47	1.25
15th Apr	1919	1041	1008.3	4.32	79.73%	6.97	1.27
3rd Sep	1919	1045	1010.0	4.63	77.84%	6.96	1.35
20th Jan	1920	1045	1013.6	4.16	69.84%	6.87	1.43
Source: Adnams brewing records held at the brewery,							

In 1917, the gravity of DS was reduced to about the same level as BS. Adnams did what most other breweries did in this situation: they dropped the weaker beer and kept the posher one.

As with BS, the hopping rate per quarter of malt remained quite stable leading to a reduction in the amount of hops per barrel. Which fell from around 2 lbs to 1.25 lbs.

Adnams Double Stout started the war with a far lower OG than the 1079° of Courage DS Stout. But in 1920 the gravity of the Courage beer was actually 1° lower than Adnams DS. It's a good demonstration of how the war levelled out regional differences in strength.

I've had to split the ingredients into two tables because there are so many different sugars.

Adnams DS Stout grists 1914 - 1920

Date	Year	OG	pale malt	brown malt	amber malt	choc. Malt	medium malt	sugar
22nd Dec	1914	1065	45.7%	6.5%	13.0%	13.0%	6.5%	15.2%
27th Aug	1915	1064	10.9%		16.4%	10.9%	49.1%	12.7%
8th Sep	1915	1065	10.9%		16.4%	10.9%	49.1%	12.7%
23rd Nov	1915	1062	37.5%		18.8%	12.5%	31.3%	
8th Dec	1916	1052	30.5%		15.3%	10.2%	25.4%	18.6%
1st Jun	1917	1040	34.2%		11.4%	11.4%	30.4%	12.7%
10th Aug	1917	1039	41.8%		11.4%	11.4%	22.8%	12.7%
28th Aug	1917	1039	15.9%		11.9%	11.9%	51.7%	8.6%
15th Apr	1919	1041	13.5%		13.5%	6.7%	53.8%	12.5%
3rd Sep	1919	1045	12.4%		12.4%	6.2%	55.7%	13.4%
20th Jan	1920	1045	24.0%		12.0%	6.0%	41.9%	16.1%

Source:
Adnams brewing records held at the brewery,

Medium malt might be something like mild malt. Or not. I've never come across the term before. It's no surprise that the sugar percentage dropped in 1917, given the restrictions that were introduced that year on the use of sugar in brewing (see appendix Food Control Orders for more details).

Adnams DS Stout sugar 1914 - 1920

Date	Year	OG	invert no. 1	invert no. 2	no. 3	cane blocks	refined cane	CDM	Mauri-tius	Barba-dos	Ille-gible	tintose
22nd Dec	1914	1065		4.3%		8.7%		2.2%				
27th Aug	1915	1064		3.6%		7.3%		1.8%				
8th Sep	1915	1065		3.6%		7.3%		1.8%				
23rd Nov	1915	1062										
8th Dec	1916	1052		10.2%		6.8%		1.7%				
1st Jun	1917	1040						2.5%	10.1%			
10th Aug	1917	1039						2.5%	10.1%			
28th Aug	1917	1039		2.6%		5.3%						0.7%
15th Apr	1919	1041			4.3%					8.6%		3.4%
3rd Sep	1919	1045								10.3%		3.1%
20th Jan	1920	1045	8.0%				8.0%					0.2%

Source:
Adnams brewing records held at the brewery,

Adnams seem to have used pretty much every form of sugar they could get their hands on. The switch To "Mauritius" was surely a result of the restrictions on the types of sugar that could be used in brewing.

Up North in Manchester, Boddington entered the war brewing a single Stout, with the rather imaginative name of Stout.

Boddington Stout 1914 - 1921							
Date	Year	OG	FG	ABV	App. Attenuation	lbs hops/ qtr	hops lb/brl
8th Jul	1914	1054.0	1018	4.76	66.67%	3.10	0.94
19th May	1916	1050.0	1015	4.63	70.00%	3.46	0.95
29th Jan	1917	1052.0	1011	5.42	78.85%	2.91	0.69
14th Apr	1917	1048.0	1016	4.23	66.67%	4.16	1.08
5th Oct	1917	1047.0	1020	3.57	57.45%	4.79	1.22
20th May	1918	1039.0	1015	3.18	61.54%	4.95	0.95
8th Aug	1918	1036.0	1015	2.78	58.33%	4.95	0.90
19th Sep	1918	1038.0	1016	2.91	57.89%	4.95	0.95
9th Jan	1919	1037.0	1016	2.78	56.76%	7.38	0.91
20th Mar	1919	1040.0	1017	3.04	57.50%	4.95	1.02
16th Jun	1919	1043.0	1017	3.44	60.47%	4.53	1.03
14th Oct	1919	1050.0	1023	3.57	54.00%	4.53	1.25
29th Mar	1920	1050.0	1012	5.03	76.00%	4.91	1.29
12th Oct	1921	1051.5	1015	4.83	70.87%	4.56	1.24
Sources: Boddington brewing records held at Manchester Central Library, document numbers M693/405/126 and M693/405/126.							

Boddington Stout started the war at a strength similar to Adnams BS or a London Porter, with an OG in the mid 1050°'s. As would be expected, that gravity fell considerably from 1917, hitting a low of 1036° in the middle of 1918. But it bounced right back up again in 1915 and in 1921 was only a couple of gravity points below its 1914 level.

In terms of grist, there were surprisingly few changes to Boddington Stout during the war years:

Boddington Stout grists 1914 - 1921

Date	Year	OG	pale malt	high dried malt	black malt	amber malt	caramel	other sugar
8th Jul	1914	1054.0	32.39%	29.15%	0.40%	29.15%	2.43%	6.48%
19th May	1916	1050.0	35.77%	28.61%	0.45%	28.61%	1.79%	4.77%
29th Jan	1917	1052.0	35.29%	28.24%	1.76%	28.24%	1.76%	4.71%
14th Apr	1917	1048.0	35.77%	28.61%	0.45%	28.61%	1.79%	4.77%
5th Oct	1917	1047.0	35.29%	28.24%	1.76%	28.24%	1.76%	4.71%
20th May	1918	1039.0	25.35%	33.80%	2.11%	33.80%	2.11%	2.82%
8th Aug	1918	1036.0	25.35%	33.80%	2.11%	33.80%	2.11%	2.82%
19th Sep	1918	1038.0	25.35%	33.80%	2.11%	33.80%	2.11%	2.82%
9th Jan	1919	1037.0	17.39%	34.78%	2.17%	34.78%	2.17%	8.70%
20th Mar	1919	1040.0	17.39%	34.78%	2.17%	34.78%	2.17%	8.70%
16th Jun	1919	1043.0	23.84%	31.79%	1.99%	31.79%	2.65%	7.95%
14th Oct	1919	1050.0	23.84%	31.79%	1.99%	31.79%	2.65%	7.95%
29th Mar	1920	1050.0	55.63%	31.79%	1.99%		2.65%	7.95%
12th Oct	1921	1051.5	51.53%	36.81%	1.84%		2.45%	7.36%

Sources:
Boddington brewing records held at Manchester Central Library, document numbers M693/405/126 and M693/405/126.

The basic recipe of pale, high-dried, amber and black malt plus caramel and some other sugar remained the same until 1920. Though the percentages of the three main malts shifted around a bit. The amount of amber malt is very, mostly around a third of the grist. Which has me wondering if it was a diastatic form.

When the amber malt was dropped in 1920 there doesn't seem to have been any attempt to compensate, especially in terms of colour. It must have come as quite a shock to regular Stout drinkers.

Scotland

Scottish Stout had already diverged from English versions long before WW I. But they always kept some weirdness going on. Particularly when it came to attenuation. It's clear that Scots liked their Stout full and sweet.

Drybrough were particularly weird when it came to brewing Stout. The rubbish attenuation of their XX Stout isn't its strangest feature.

| Drybrough XX Stout 1914 - 1921 ||||||||
Date	Year	OG	FG	ABV	App. Atten-uation	lbs hops/ qtr	hops lb/brl
21st Jul	1916	1055	1026	3.84	52.73%	4.17	0.96
19th Jan	1917	1054	1023	4.13	57.56%	4.00	0.79
8th Feb	1918	1045	1020	3.31	55.56%	5.00	1.35
8th Mar	1918	1045	1021	3.18	53.33%	5.00	1.03
13th Aug	1918	1039	1018	2.78	53.85%	5.02	0.87
29th Oct	1918	1040	1020	2.65	50.00%	5.02	0.82
7th Feb	1919	1040	1020	2.65	50.00%	5.00	0.96
8th Jul	1919	1042	1019	3.04	54.76%	5.11	0.96
16th Jan	1920	1045	1014	4.10	68.89%	5.00	0.97
Source: Drybrough brewing record held at the Scottish Brewing Archive, document number D/6/1/1/3.							

The FG isn't moving in sync as the OG falls. Leading to just 50% apparent attenuation in 1918 and 1919. I don't have a huge number of examples because they rarely brewed Stout, concentrating mainly on endless Pale Ale parti-gyles.

Ireland

The situation wasn't exactly the same in Ireland as it was in the rest of the UK. This was because different rules applied with regard to average gravity. This was always higher in Ireland, never falling below 1045°. I've read claims that this was for fear of unrest in Ireland if beer became too weak.

But there's a fair simpler reason: average gravity was much higher in Ireland in 1914 than elsewhere in the UK. When the war started, average OG in England was 1052° and in Ireland 1066°. The explanation for this disparity is obvious, really. The vast majority of beer brewed in Ireland was Guinness Extra Stout, which had an OG of 1074° in 1914.

| Guinness Extra Stout and Foreign Extra Stout 1901 - 1926 ||||||
Year	Beer	FG	OG	ABV	App. Atten-uation
1901	Extra Foreign Stout	1013.2	1075.0	7.86	81.34%
1914	Extra Stout		1074		
1917	Extra Stout		1067		
1918	Extra Stout		1049		
1919	Extra Stout		1054		
1921	Extra Stout	1015.8	1054.8	5.06	71.17%
1922	Extra Stout	1021.5	1054.7	4.28	60.69%
1923	Extra Stout	1016.2	1054.2	4.93	70.11%
1926	Foreign Extra Stout		1073.6		
Sources: American Handy Book of the Brewing, Malting, and Auxiliary Trades by Robert Wahl and Max Henius, Chicago, pages 823-830 Whitbread Gravity book held at the London Metropolitan Archives, document number LMA/4453/D/02/001.					

It may come as a surprise that when war began Extra Stout and Foreign Extra Stout had the same gravity. After WW I export versions of a beer were usually stronger than domestic versions, but this hadn't been true before. Export beers in earlier times had sometimes even been weaker. But after the war export beers tended to retain their pre-war strength while the gravity of versions for home consumption had declined significantly.

The drop in strength of the domestic version was considerable, 19 points or about 25%, which is a bit above the average.

After WW I
Despite the travails of Porter, its stronger brother remained very popular between the wars. Though outside London it was increasingly rare as a draught beer.

London
Before the war, standard London Stouts had gravities between 1070° and 1080°. The war knocked around 10 points off that gravity. Interestingly, the gravities at the different breweries are much closer to each other. That's probably because they were much more aware of each others' gravities.

But also from the price controls at the end of the war and the tax. Brewers tended to stick with the price/gravity bands of the last set of controls. The Stouts in the mid-1050's all retailed at 9d per pint on draught. And the last controls set the price of beer over 1054° at 9d. per pint. The Courage and Camden Stout would have retailed for 8d., being one gravity class lower.

London Stout after WW I

Date	Year	Brewer	OG	FG	ABV	App. Attenuation	lbs hops/ qtr	hops lb/brl
1925	Barclay Perkins	OMS for bottling	1050.9	1017.5	4.41	65.59%	7.64	1.71
1929	Barclay Perkins	BS	1053.3	1018.0	4.67	66.22%	6.00	1.43
1924	Barclay Perkins	RNS	1055.1	1019	4.78	65.52%	7.49	1.75
1924	Barclay Perkins	IBS	1061	1020	5.42	67.21%	8.50	2.21
1924	Barclay Perkins	BSc	1066	1020.5	6.02	68.94%	8.00	2.44
1924	Barclay Perkins	BS Ex	1072.5	1024	6.42	66.90%	14.00	4.62
1925	Barclay Perkins	BBS Ex	1079.7	1029.5	6.64	62.99%	15.00	5.38
1924	Barclay Perkins	IBS Ex	1103.4	1040	8.39	61.32%	16.00	6.97
1924	Camden	S	1045.4	1012.2	4.40	73.17%	6.70	1.29
1923	Courage	Stout	1043.8	1011.4	4.29	74.05%	7.54	1.58
1925	Fullers	BS	1056.6	1022.2	4.55	60.84%	7.95	2.11
1924	Whitbread	LS	1053.7	1017	4.86	68.37%	7.81	1.82
1924	Whitbread	S	1053.7	1017	4.86	68.37%	7.81	1.82
1924	Whitbread	ES	1053.7	1017	4.86	68.37%	7.81	1.82

Sources:
Barclay Perkins brewing records held at the London Metropolitan Archives, document numbers ACC/2305/01/611 and ACC/2305/01/614.
Camden brewing record held at the London Metropolitan Archives, document number ACC/2305/9/5.
Courage brewing record held at the London Metropolitan Archives, document number ACC/2305/08/253.
Fullers brewing record held at the brewery.
Whitbread brewing record held at the London Metropolitan Archives, document number LMA/4453/D/09/117.

The price and gravity correlation is more obvious in this set:

Draught London Stout after WW I

Year	Brewer	Beer	Price per pint	OG	FG	ABV	App. Attenuation
1923	Barclay Perkins	Stout	9d	1058.1	1016	5.52	73.15%
1922	Beasley	Stout	8d	1054	1017	4.74	67.78%
1923	Charrington	Stout	9d	1053.6	1014	5.20	74.63%
1923	Courage	Stout	8d	1046	1010	4.68	78.26%
1923	Hoare	Stout	9d	1055.4	1020	4.52	63.18%
1923	Huggins	Stout	9d	1063.4	1018	5.85	70.98%
1923	Mann	Stout	8d	1054.8	1013	5.47	76.64%
1923	Meux	Stout	8d	1049.7	1014	4.67	72.43%
1923	Meux	Stout	9d	1056.7	1016	5.26	71.43%
1922	Truman	Stout	8d	1048.2	1014	4.41	70.54%
1923	Watney	Stout	9d	1056.1	1014	5.53	75.76%
1923	Wenlock	Stout	8d	1045.7	1018	3.55	60.18%
1922	Whitbread	Stout	9d	1055.2	1014	5.33	74.28%

Source: Whitbread Gravity Book held at the London Metropolitan Archives, document number LMA/4453/D/02/001.

The fact that these analyses exist is proof that brewers were keeping a close eye on each other. The Whitbread Gravity book contains thousands of analyses of rival brewers' beers.

Provincial England

Stout was still popular, though increasingly only available in bottled form outside London. Provincial breweries brewed Stouts at a range of strengths, no doubt depending on the particular circumstances of the location. Later in the interwar period increasingly weedy Stouts would become the norm.

These are some examples:

Year	Brewer	Beer	OG	FG	ABV	App. Attenuation	lbs hops/ qtr	hops lb/brl
1923	Adnams	DS	1044	1010	4.50	77.34%	6.59	1.19
1923	Boddington	Stout	1050.3	1014	4.80	72.14%	5.63	1.52
1930	Lees	S	1052	1012	5.29	76.92%	4.44	1.16
1920	Kidd	Stout	1047.6	1013.9	4.47	70.93%	8.22	1.71
1929	Russell	Stout	1059.3				7.45	1.88

Provincial Stout after WW I

Sources:
Adnams brewing record Book 9
Boddington brewing record held at Manchester Central Library, document number M693/405/127.
Lees brewing record held at the brewery
Kidd brewing record held at the London Metropolitan Archives, document number ACC/305/16/013.
Russell brewing record held at the London Metropolitan Archives, document number B/THB/RUS/10.

And the grists that go with them:

Year	Brewer	Beer	pale malt	high dried malt	brown malt	black malt	amber malt	choc. malt	crystal malt	mild malt
1923	Adnams	DS	50.00%				12.50%	6.25%		18.75%
1923	Boddington	Stout	43.80%	43.80%		2.19%				
1930	Lees	S	88.89%			11.11%				
1920	Kidd	Stout	66.00%		3.00%	6.00%			3.00%	
1929	Russell	Stout	68.39%		11.06%	5.36%				

Provincial Stout grists after WW I - malts

Sources:
Adnams brewing record Book 9
Boddington brewing record held at Manchester Central Library, document number M693/405/127.
Lees brewing record held at the brewery
Kidd brewing record held at the London Metropolitan Archives, document number ACC/305/16/013.
Russell brewing record held at the London Metropolitan Archives, document number B/THB/RUS/10.

There's just one malt that they all have in common: pale malt. Four out of five contain black malt, as you would expect, but Adnams instead went for a combination of amber and chocolate malt. The two breweries that include brown malt – Kidd and Russell – were both located in Kent, not that far from London. That could have played a role as London brewers were very loyal to brown malt.

Provincial Stout grists after WW I - sugars							
Year	Brewer	Beer	caramel	glucose	cane	invert	other sugar
1923	Adnams	DS	2.08%		10.42%		
1923	Boddington	Stout	2.92%				7.30%
1930	Lees	S					
1920	Kidd	Stout	6.00%				16.00%
1929	Russell	Stout	0.73%	3.58%	3.58%	5.36%	1.94%
Sources:							
Adnams brewing record Book 9							
Boddington brewing record held at Manchester Central Library, document number M693/405/127.							
Lees brewing record held at the brewery							
Kidd brewing record held at the London Metropolitan Archives, document number ACC/305/16/013.							
Russell brewing record held at the London Metropolitan Archives, document number B/THB/RUS/10.							

The sugars are even more diverse than the malts. Lees used none at all in their Stout. All the other examples contain caramel, plus a variety of other sugars.

For reference, here's a collection of post-WW I Stouts from around provincial England, starting with the Midlands:

Provincial Stout after WW I - the Midlands							
Year	Brewer	Beer	Price per pint (d)	OG	FG	ABV	App. Attenuation
1926	Allsopp	Stout	8	1048.4			
1926	Bass	Export Stout (Gibraltar sample)	6	1054.9	1011.2	5.70	79.60%
1926	Flower	Extra Stout	6.5	1047.4	1012.3	4.56	74.05%
1927	James Rose	Oatmeal Stout		1056.6			
1925	Mackie & Gladstone	Extra Stout	8	1054.8	1014.3	5.26	73.91%
1922	Manning	Stout	9	1049.2	1010.6	5.02	78.46%
1926	Mitchell & Butler	Nourishing Stout	8	1048.7			
1925	Morgans, Tamworth	Stout	15	1053.7	1013	5.29	75.79%
1922	Northampton Brewery	Double Stout	9	1048.5	1015.8	4.23	67.42%
1922	Phipps	Ratcliffe Stout	9	1049.6	1020.9	3.70	57.86%
1926	Stretton	Stretton's Stout	8	1050.1			
1922	Worthington	Double Imperial Stout (Belgian)		1070.7	1014	7.42	80.20%
Sources:							
Truman Gravity Book held at the London Metropolitan Archives, document number B/THB/C/252. Whitbread Gravity book held at the London Metropolitan Archives, document number LMA/4453/D/02/001.							

All the examples are of a decent strength and would have been in the top or next to top price control band. Except for Worthington's Stout brewed for the Belgian market, which is significantly stronger.

James Rose was a small Lincolnshire brewer that made one of the first Oatmeal Stouts. It was clearly still a speciality of theirs.

The set for the North is quite small:

Provincial Stout after WW I - the North							
Year	Brewer	Beer	Price per pint (d)	OG	FG	ABV	App. Atten-uation
1927	Cornbrook	Barley Stout		1049.3			
1922	Vaux	Stout	8	1038.5	1013	3.30	66.23%
1925	Vaux	Oatmeal Stout	7	1039.7	1012.6	3.51	68.26%
1925	Vaux	Invalid Stout	9	1052.5	1017.6	4.52	66.48%
1926	Whitaker	Standard Stout	8	1044.3			
Sources: Thomas Usher Gravity Book held at the Scottish Brewing Archive, document number TU/6/11. Whitbread Gravity book held at the London Metropolitan Archives, document number LMA/4453/D/02/001.							

Only one of this set, Vaux Invalid Stout would have been in the top price control bracket. Though Vaux's other two Stouts were under 1040°. Their Stout and Oatmeal Stout were probably identical beers, just with different labels slapped on the bottle. London brewers usually threw a few token oats into their Porter/Stout parti-gyles so they legally sell some as Oatmeal Stout.

The Southern Stouts are all over the place in terms of gravity:

Mini Book Series volume XXXII: Armistice!

Year	Brewer	Beer	Price per pint (d)	OG	FG	ABV	App. Attenuation
\multicolumn{8}{l}{**Provincial Stout after WW I - the South**}
1925	Beer & Rigden	Nourishing Stout	5.5	1031.3	1011.2	2.60	64.22%
1927	Budden & Biggs	Stout	7	1044.8			
1923	Fremlin	Light Dinner Stout	7	1032.4	1007.7	3.20	76.23%
1923	Fremlin	Oatmeal Stout	8.5	1040.6	1011.3	3.80	72.17%
1926	Fremlin	Stout	7.5	1045.6			
1926	Kemp Town	Double Stout	10	1055.3	1014.1	5.36	74.50%
1926	Kemp Town	Dolphin Stout	5	1037.9	1008.4	3.83	77.84%
1926	Kidd & Hotblack	Nourishing Stout	8	1048	1008.7	5.12	81.87%
1927	Leney	Stout	7	1054.7			
1927	Nicholls, Hertford	Nourishing Stout	7	1048.3	1010.2	4.96	78.88%
1927	Noakes	Stout	8	1041.3			
1925	Russells, Gravesend	Stout	7	1056.4	1012	5.79	78.72%
1922	Simonds	Double Stout (Belgian sample)		1073.3	1029.7	5.63	59.48%
1925	Simonds	Milk Stout	11	1062.1			
1925	Simonds	Luncheon Stout	7	1040.9			
1925	Simonds	Oatmeal Stout	8.5	1043.5	1005.7	4.93	86.90%
1926	Smithers	Old Malt Stout	5.5	1037.7	1012.2	3.30	67.64%
1927	Sprake, Chale I of W	Special Stout		1043.2	1010	4.31	76.85%
1926	Style & Winch	Stout	8	1041.02			
1926	Tamplin	Oatmeal Stout		1043.7	1011.3	4.20	74.14%
1926	Tamplin	No.1 Cheerio Stout	14	1074.1	1015.6	7.65	78.95%
1926	Tamplin	Double Stout	5	1044.2	1009	4.58	79.64%
1926	Tollemache	Double Stout	8	1045.5			
1926	Wethered	Oatmeal Stout	8	1049.5			

Sources:
Truman Gravity Book held at the London Metropolitan Archives, document number B/THB/C/252.
Whitbread Gravity book held at the London Metropolitan Archives, document number LMA/4453/D/02/001.

1031° to 1074° is quite a range. And there's pretty much everything inbetween. Yet only three have the classic post-war Stout gravity of around 1055°. Somewhere in the range 1040°-1045° seems to have been the most popular.

While I'm not surprised at the Simonds Belgian-bound sample being quite strong, I didn't expect to see a domestic Stout from Tamplin that was even stronger.

Have you noticed how many Oatmeal Stouts there are? Obviously a popular type.

Finally, the Southwest of England:

Provincial Stout after WW I - the Southwest

Year	Brewer	Beer	Price per pint (d)	OG	FG	ABV	App. Atten-uation
1927	Ashton Gate Brewery	Milk Stout	9	1052.4	1015.7	4.76	70.04%
1927	Georges	Bristol Stout	10	1059.8	1018.1	5.41	69.73%
1927	Oakhill Brewery	Invalid Stout	10	1054.8	1018.5	4.70	66.24%
1927	Rogers	Monarch Stout	7	1044.9	1008.5	4.74	81.07%
1927	Ushers Wiltshire Brewery	Stout	9	1046.2			

Sources:
Truman Gravity Book held at the London Metropolitan Archives, document number B/THB/C/252.
Whitbread Gravity book held at the London Metropolitan Archives, document number LMA/4453/D/02/001.

Most of these are in the around 1055° category, with a couple of weaker examples. The attenuation of most of the beers above is quite reasonable. As Sweet Stout gained popularity after the war, especially Milk Stout, the rate of attenuation for some beers fell to under 50%.

Scotland

Though not as popular as in England, Stout still had a firm foothold in Scotland. They had already started to become sweeter than English versions and this would be carried to ridiculous extremes between the wars. Some versions were as little as 40% attenuated. And also barely alcoholic.

As Scottish breweries started to go over to having a single recipe, single-gyle Stouts mostly disappeared, replaced by ones parti-gyled with Pale Ales. This was achieved through throwing black malt and a load of caramel into one of the coppers and using that exclusively for the Stout.

William Younger was highly unusual for a Scottish brewer in that it brewed more than one Stout.

Scottish Stout after WW I

Year	Brewer	Beer	OG	FG	ABV	App. Atten-uation	lbs hops/ qtr	hops lb/brl
1921	Younger, Wm.	XXS	1050	1020	3.97	60.00%	3.89	0.77
1921	Younger, Wm.	DBS	1060	1025	4.63	58.33%	3.89	0.92
1921	Younger, Wm.	Btg DBS	1060	1019	5.42	68.33%	10.65	2.63
1920	Drybrough	BS	1074	1025	6.48	66.22%	3.82	1.16
1928	Thomas Usher	Stout	1045	1021.5	3.11	52.22%	7.00	1.27

Sources:
William Younger brewing record held at the Scottish Brewing Archive, document number WY/6/1/2/63.
Drybrough brewing record held at the Scottish Brewing Archive, document number D/6/1/1/3.
Thomas Usher brewing record held at the Scottish Brewing Archive, document number TU/6/1/6.

Most of beers are quite strong – only one is below 1050°. And Drybrough's Stout is an impressive 1074°. Not sure how they could afford a beer that strong in 1920, unless it was destined for export.

The bottling version of Younger's DBS is far more heavily hopped than the standard version – roughly 3 times as heavily. Which makes me think that it was being vatted for an extended period before packaging.

Here are the grists:

Scottish Stout grists after WW I - malts							
Year	Brewer	Beer	OG	pale malt	black malt	amber malt	crystal malt
1921	Younger, Wm.	XXS	1050	50.94%	5.66%	5.66%	
1921	Younger, Wm.	DBS	1060	50.94%	5.66%	5.66%	
1921	Younger, Wm.	Btg DBS	1060	47.80%	3.30%	6.59%	
1920	Drybrough	BS	1074	58.70%	6.52%		
1928	Thomas Usher	Stout	1045	57.97%	1.45%		5.80%
Sources: William Younger brewing record held at the Scottish Brewing Archive, document number WY/6/1/2/63. Drybrough brewing record held at the Scottish Brewing Archive, document number D/6/1/1/3. Thomas Usher brewing record held at the Scottish Brewing Archive, document number TU/6/1/6.							

Not one of the examples includes any brown malt, in contrast to London practice. And all have at least some black malt. Unusually, William Younger was still including amber malt in its Stout grists. Amber malt had been the fourth optional malt in London Stout in the 19th century, along with pale, brow and black malt. But even in London it had mostly fallen out of favour by the 20th century.

Scottish Stout grists after WW I - adjuncts and sugars								
Year	Brewer	Beer	OG	flaked maize	grits	caramel	malt extract	other sugar
1921	Younger, Wm.	XXS	1050		33.96%	3.77%		
1921	Younger, Wm.	DBS	1060		33.96%	3.77%		
1921	Younger, Wm.	Btg DBS	1060		37.91%	4.40%		
1920	Drybrough	BS	1074	16.30%		2.17%	1.09%	15.22%
1928	Thomas Usher	Stout	1045	5.80%				28.99%
Sources: William Younger brewing record held at the Scottish Brewing Archive, document number WY/6/1/2/63. Drybrough brewing record held at the Scottish Brewing Archive, document number D/6/1/1/3. Thomas Usher brewing record held at the Scottish Brewing Archive, document number TU/6/1/6.								

With the war over, brewers could return to using adjuncts as they would like. Which, in the case of William Younger, meant throwing in a crazy amount of grits. The other brewers, like their English counterparts, went for flaked maize instead. In slightly more sensible quantities.

All but Usher included caramel, a pretty ingredient in Stout both sides of the border. Drybrough and Usher both used an array of proprietary sugars, which would have made the table too cumbersome, had I included them. This is what they are:

Drybrough: 6 cwt BSC, 6 cwt Durax and 2 cwt Ferlose.
Usher: 8 cwt cane, 4 cwt Penang, 1 cwt Oatine, 1 cwt CDM, 1 cwt maltosan

I've no idea what most of those are.

Here's a random selection of other Scottish Stouts from the 1920s:

Scottish Stout after WW I						
Year	Brewer	Beer	OG	FG	ABV	App. Atten-uation
1922	Calder	Stout (draught)	1053.0	1011	5.47	79.24%
1922	Ushers	Extra Stout (Belgian sample)	1069.2	1021.8	6.15	68.50%
1923	Bernard	Imperial Stout	1057.6	1023.5	4.40	59.21%
1923	Henderson	Stout	1040	1008	4.16	80.00%
1923	Wright	Crown Stout	1050	1017	4.27	66.00%
1924	Ballingall	Imperial Stout Special Quality	1038.7	1016.4	2.87	57.62%
1924	McEwan	Double Imperial Stout	1056.5	1021.7	4.49	61.59%
1924	McEwan	Double Imperial Stout	1078	1020	7.57	74.36%
1924	Tennent	Nourishing Stout	1038.3	1010.8	3.56	71.80%
Sources: Thomas Usher Gravity Book held at the Scottish Brewing Archive, document number TU/6/11. Younger, Wm. & Co Gravity Book document WY/6/1/1/19 held at the Scottish Brewing Archive Whitbread Gravity book held at the London Metropolitan Archives, document number LMA/4453/D/02/001.						

Ireland

There's one name that springs to mind when thinking of Ireland and Stout: Guinness. Though there were other Stout brewers in Ireland – for example, the two Cork breweries Murphy and Beamish & Crawford – Guinness was by far the largest. In fact, it was the largest brewery in the UK until 1922, when most of Ireland gained independence.

Which was a bit of a problem for Guinness, as after the war around 50% of their sales were in the UK:

Mini Book Series volume XXXII: Armistice!

Guinness sales 1914 - 1925						
	Extra Stout					
Year	Britain	Ireland	total	Porter	Other	total
1914	1,070,814	731,511	1,802,325	897,571	141,844	2,642,740
1915	1,122,784	641,346	1,764,130	729,012	109,204	2,602,346
1916	1,135,902	581,577	1,717,479	650,826	116,526	2,484,831
1917	621,374	369,201	990,575	380,145	86,412	1,457,132
1918	613,295	347,753	961,048	395,554	62,010	1,418,612
1919	1,029,235	565,870	1,595,105	610,828	49,617	2,255,550
1920	1,732,881	798,493	2,531,374	583,343	80,074	3,194,791
1921	1,591,908	786,688	2,378,595	484,214	33,940	2,896,750
1922	1,254,920	724,894	1,979,614	416,594	47,438	2,443,644
1923	1,205,468	696,582	1,902,050	378,085	50,940	2,331,075
1924	1,315,325	640,974	1,956,302	367,708	46,501	2,370,511
1925	1,347,174	583,730	1,930,904	351,040	52,504	2,334,548
Source: "A Bottle of Guinness please" by David Hughes, pages 276-279						

After trade tensions between the Republic of Ireland and the UK in the 1920s, Guinness built a new brewery in London in the 1930s as an insurance.

Despite being in a separate country, Guinness, too, was influenced by the last set of price controls, which only ended in 1921, a year before Irish independence. That's clear to see in the OG of Guinness, which was 1055°, just putting it in the highest price control slot.

Guinness Stout 1922 - 1927						
Year	Beer	Price per pint (d)	OG	FG	ABV	App. Atten- uation
1922	Extra Stout		1055			
1922	Extra Stout		1055			
1922	Extra Stout		1054.7	1021.5	4.28	60.69%
1922	Extra Stout	9	1052.2			
1923	Extra Stout		1054.2	1016.2	4.93	70.11%
1926	Foreign Extra Stout		1073.6			
1927	Extra Stout		1055.4			
Sources: Whitbread Gravity book held at the London Metropolitan Archives, document number LMA/4453/D/02/001.						

The example above that was 9d per pint is the only draught beer in the set.

Foreign Extra Stout, a beer only sold in export markets, remained at its pre-war strength. Standard Extra Stout had shared the same gravity until 1917.

Guinness remained at this strength through the interwar period, until WW II came along.

Strong Ales

Stronger beers were some of the most affected by the war. People just couldn't afford such beers with the level of post-war taxation. A few famous beer, such as Bass No. 1 Ale, emerged pretty much unscathed, but such examples were the exception.

I've grouped under Strong Ales several types of beer, some of which were quite loosely defined. The difference between Old Ale and Barley Wine isn't very clear and some beers have been called both over the years. How I've classified beers is, to some extent, arbitrary. Unless the name makes the brewery's intention obvious.

Burton Ale

Before WW I

There were two types of beer known as Burton Ale. The first were Strong Ales actually brewed in Burton on Trent. These came in a variety of strengths, often designated by numbers, with No. 2 being the strongest and No. 4 the weakest. The stronger versions were usually bottled beers.

The second type was local to London. These were usually designated by K's, going from KK to KKKK. KK was the commonest type, being a standard draught beer. Brewed as Stock Ales, Burtons were aged for several months before sale. The ageing mostly took place in trade casks, though the strongest versions were sometime vatted.

They were hopped to buggery, as you can see in the table below. At Barclay Perkins and Whitbread, K Ales had their own specific gyles. Which were similar to their Mild Ale recipes, just with a shitload more hops.

London Burton Ale before WW I								
Date	Year	Brewer	Beer	FG	ABV	App. Atten-uation	lbs hops/ qtr	hops lb/brl
1910	Barclay Perkins	KKK	1087.3	1026.3	8.07	69.86%	14.00	5.33
1909	Barclay Perkins	KK	1073.0	1021.1	6.87	71.16%	14.00	4.25
1914	Whitbread	KK	1071.6	1028.0	5.77	60.91%	11.48	3.47
1914	Whitbread	2KKK	1077.0	1028.0	6.48	63.64%	11.48	3.73
1914	Whitbread	KKK	1081.3	1029.0	6.92	64.32%	11.48	3.93
1910	Fuller	BO	1074.9	1024.4	6.68	67.44%	9.84	3.05
1914	Courage	XX	1079.2	1033.2	6.08	58.04%	9.90	3.07

Sources:
Whitbread brewing record held at the London Metropolitan Archives, document number LMA/4453/D/01/079.
Barclay Perkins brewing record held at the London Metropolitan Archives, document number ACC/2305/1/601.
Fullers brewing record held at the brewery.
Courage brewing record held at the London Metropolitan Archives, document number ACC/2305/08/247.

During WW I

After April 1918, when the average gravity of the beer a brewery produced was restricted to

1030°, it became virtually impossible to brew a beer of any strength. To brew a single barrel of beer with a gravity of 1070°. You'd need to brew four barrels at just 1020°. Unsurprisingly, this regulation led to the disappearance of almost all strong beers for a couple of years.

Which is exactly at Courage, where no Burton Ale was brewed in 1919 or 1920. Up until then, it had fared reasonably well, only falling a few gravity points from 1079° to 1073°.

Courage Burton Ale 1914 - 1920							
Date	Year	OG	FG	ABV	App. Attenuation	lbs hops/ qtr	hops lb/brl
22nd Oct	1914	1079.2	1033.2	6.08	58.04%	9.90	3.07
4th Mar	1915	1079.2	1033.2	6.08	58.04%	11.00	3.53
19th Oct	1915	1076.2	1016.6	7.88	78.18%	10.00	3.10
5th Jul	1916	1076.2	1027.7	6.41	63.64%	11.00	3.42
4th Jan	1917	1075.3	1027.4	6.34	63.60%	11.51	3.54
18th Oct	1917	1072.6	1023.8	6.45	67.18%	12.66	3.63
15th Jan	1920	1054.6	1016.9	4.98	69.04%	6.29	1.37
1st Jul	1920	1053.5	1016.3	4.91	69.43%	8.01	8.68
16th Feb	1921	1053.5	1014.4	5.17	73.06%	5.25	1.21
Sources: Courage brewing records held at the London Metropolitan Archives, document numbers ACC/2305/08/247, ACC/2305/08/248, ACC/2305/08/249 and ACC/2305/08/251.							

When it returned in 1920, however, it was at a much reduced gravity, barely two-thirds of its pre-war figure.

There weren't that many changes to the grist of Courage Burton during the war. Mostly because it was discontinued in 1917, just when difficulties really started.

Courage Burton Ale grists 1914 - 1920							
Date	Year	OG	pale malt	black malt	crystal malt	no. 3 sugar	caramel	flaked maize
22nd Oct	1914	1079.2	80.7%	1.3%		17.9%		
4th Mar	1915	1079.2	85.1%			14.9%		
19th Oct	1915	1076.2	85.1%			14.9%		
5th Jul	1916	1076.2	85.1%			14.9%		
4th Jan	1917	1075.3	83.9%	1.3%		14.7%		
18th Oct	1917	1072.6	83.6%	1.8%		14.7%		
15th Jan	1920	1054.6	84.6%	2.2%		12.7%	0.5%	
1st Jul	1920	1053.5	67.9%		18.4%	9.4%		4.2%
16th Feb	1921	1053.5	68.4%		18.4%	8.8%		4.4%
Sources: Courage brewing records held at the London Metropolitan Archives, document numbers ACC/2305/08/247, ACC/2305/08/248, ACC/2305/08/249 and ACC/2305/08/251.							

After the war the recipe was quite different. There's a good reason for that. Up until 1917, it was brewed single-gyle. From 1920 onwards, it was parti-gyled with X Ale.

After WW I

Though much reduced in gravity, Burton remained a popular style in London and was still a standard draught beer.

It was generally brewed as a 9d. draught beer, that is with a gravity of around 1055°. There were stronger versions, but these were mostly sold in bottled form or on draught or as a winter seasonal.

One exception was Fullers Old Burton Extra (OBE), which was a draught beer that wasn't limited to a specific season. But it was brewed in tiny quantities: at most 40 barrels, often fewer than ten barrels at a time, when Fuller's brew length was 400-500 barrels. That's the glory of parti-gyling, being able to efficiently brew a low-volume beer on a large kit.

London Burton Ale after WW I								
Year	Brewer	Beer	OG	FG	ABV	App. Attenuation	lbs hops/ qtr	hops lb/brl
1921	Barclay Perkins	KK	1055.2	1015.0	5.32	72.83%	9.60	2.12
1924	Barclay Perkins	KK (bottling)	1070.3	1023.5	6.19	66.57%	14.00	4.24
1924	Barclay Perkins	KKK	1082.1	1028.0	7.16	65.90%	14.00	4.75
1924	Camden	SA	1055.1	1013.9	5.46	74.87%	10.42	2.31
1923	Courage	XXX	1053.5	1015.2	5.06	71.50%	7.26	1.73
1923	Courage	KKK	1073.4	1025.5	6.34	65.28%	11.00	3.28
1925	Fullers	BO	1061.5	1018.8	5.65	69.40%	7.308	1.83
1925	Fullers	OBE	1072.2	1021.1	6.77	70.85%	7.214	2.15
1923	Whitbread	KK	1055.4	1017.0	5.08	69.31%	9.07	2.08
Sources: Barclay Perkins brewing records held at the London Metropolitan Archives, document numbers ACC/2305/01/609 and ACC/2305/01/611. Camden brewing record held at the London Metropolitan Archives, document number ACC/2305/9/5. Courage brewing record held at the London Metropolitan Archives, document number ACC/2305/08/253. Fullers brewing record held at the brewery. Whitbread brewing record held at the London Metropolitan Archives, document number LMA/4453/D/01/088.								

The fall in gravity, as with Stout was about 20 points. Like Stout, draught Burton Ale was a 9d. per pint beer. Fullers OBE, Barclay Perkins KKK and Courage KK are very similar to pre-war draught KK. Clearly there was still a demand for strong Burton Ales, despite the price.

The draught Burton Ales available in London after WW I all looked pretty similar.

| Draught London Burton Ale after WW I ||||||||
Year	Brewer	Beer	Price	OG	FG	ABV	App. Atten-uation
1923	Barclay Perkins	KK	9d	1051.9	1010.4	5.41	79.96%
1923	Cannon	KK	9d	1054.9	1011	5.72	79.96%
1923	Charrington	KK	9d	1055.9	1014.4	5.39	74.24%
1923	City of London	KK	9d	1052.1	1012.6	5.14	75.82%
1923	Courage	KK	9d	1052.8	1012.8	5.20	75.76%
1923	Hoare	KK	9d	1054.9	1019.4	4.59	64.66%
1923	Huggins	KK	9d	1054.5	1013	5.40	76.15%
1923	Lion	KK	9d	1054.1	1013.6	5.27	74.86%
1923	Mann	KK	9d	1058.7	1013.2	5.93	77.51%
1923	Meux	KK	9d	1054.6	1009.6	5.87	82.42%
1923	Truman	KK	9d	1056	1012	5.73	78.57%
1923	Watney	KK	9d	1059.4	1012.9	6.06	78.28%
1923	Wenlock	KK	9d	1053.7	1010.2	5.67	81.01%
Source: Whitbread Gravity book held at the London Metropolitan Archives, document number LMA/4453/D/02/001.							

Assuming an average OG for KK of around 1072° before the war and about 1054° after it, that's a fall of 25%, which is slightly more than the average 23% drop.

Old Ale

Before WW I

Most provincial breweries produced an Old Ale. This was basically an aged version of a strong Mild Ale recipe. How the ageing occurred varied, with some breweries vatting and others using trade casks. As the aged flavour went out of fashion towards the end of the 19th century, beers called Old Ale weren't necessarily aged.

Though, even if they weren't vatted and aged for years, Old Ales were likely to be kept in the brewery in trade casks for at least a few weeks before sent out to pubs.

During WW I

I've one really good example of an Old Ale brewed during WW I. A beer you may have drunk yourself, as it still exists: Adnam's Tally Ho.

Mini Book Series volume XXXII: Armistice!

Adnams Tally Ho 1914 - 1917

Date	Year	Beer	OG	FG	ABV	App. Attenuation	lbs hops/qtr	hops lb/brl
5th Aug	1914	Tally Ho	1082.0	1029.5	6.95	64.02%	5.92	2.21
13th Aug	1914	Tally Ho	1081.0	1027.0	7.14	66.67%	6.13	2.24
29th Apr	1915	Tally Ho	1082.0	1026.6	7.33	67.57%	7.40	2.68
21st Aug	1915	Tally Ho	1082.0	1023.3	7.77	71.62%	7.40	2.71
25th Sep	1915	Tally Ho	1081.0	1027.7	7.05	65.80%	7.40	2.69
24th Nov	1915	Tally Ho	1079.0	1024.4	7.23	69.14%	7.44	2.73
28th Mar	1916	Tally Ho	1073.7	1023.3	6.67	68.43%	8.47	2.76
20h Mar	1917	Tally Ho	1082.0	1032.1	6.60	60.81%	8.45	3.01
21st Mar	1917	Tally Ho	1082.0	1013.9	9.02	83.11%	9.05	3.10
Source: Adnams brewing records held at the brewery.								

It's surprising how well its gravity stood up until 1917. When it would have become uneconomic to brew. The modern version isn't much weaker. An example of a beer that manged to retain most of its strength right across the 20th century.

The grist wasn't modified that much during the war, probably because it was discontinued before the supply situation became dire.

Adnams Tally Ho grists 1914 - 1917

Date	Year	OG	pale malt	medium malt	crystal malt	flaked maize	no. 2 sugar	glucose	Tintose
5th Aug	1914	1082.0	46.93%	29.86%	4.27%	4.27%	14.22%		0.46%
13th Aug	1914	1081.0	48.30%	30.74%	4.39%	4.39%	8.78%		3.40%
29th Apr	1915	1082.0	57.77%	19.26%	4.81%	4.81%	6.42%	6.42%	0.52%
21st Aug	1915	1082.0	28.88%	48.14%	4.81%	4.81%	12.84%		0.52%
25th Sep	1915	1081.0	25.29%	55.63%	5.06%		13.49%		0.54%
24th Nov	1915	1079.0	72.34%		4.52%	4.52%	18.08%		0.54%
28th Mar	1916	1073.7	48.08%	28.85%	4.81%	4.81%	12.82%		0.63%
20h Mar	1917	1082.0	28.80%	48.00%	4.80%	4.80%	12.80%		0.80%
21st Mar	1917	1082.0	24.79%	49.58%	4.13%	4.13%	16.53%		0.84%
Source: Adnams brewing records held at the brewery.									

I've no idea what medium malt is. Perhaps something similar to mild malt. I assume it's replacement by pale malt in November 1915 was due to problems acquiring it. Similarly the replacement of some No. 2 invert sugar by glucose in April 1915.

Categorising British Strong Ales can be a real nightmare. Boddington CC being a case in point. The brewery just called it a Strong Ale. But elsewhere it might well have been called an Old Ale. Or a Burton Ale. There's little in the way of consistency. The name of Boddington's Strong Ale doesn't help. What does CC stands for?

Boddington CC 1914 - 1921

Date	Year	OG	FG	ABV	App. Attenuation	lbs hops/qtr	hops lb/brl
9th Jul	1914	1062	1020	5.56	67.74%	3.53	1.18
7th May	1915	1059	1019	5.29	67.80%	3.75	1.20
27th Oct	1915	1058	1018	5.29	68.97%	3.64	1.17
18th May	1916	1062	1017	5.95	72.58%	3.87	1.33
20th Dec	1916	1062	1017	5.95	72.58%	3.53	1.23
31st Jan	1917	1059	1018	5.42	69.49%	3.53	1.46
11th Oct	1917	1056	1018	5.03	67.86%	4.41	1.32
12th Nov	1918	1058	1020	5.03	65.52%	3.97	1.27
24th Dec	1918	1061	1021	5.29	65.57%	3.97	1.31
10th Feb	1919	1059	1020	5.16	66.10%	3.97	1.26
24th Mar	1919	1060	1020	5.29	66.67%	3.97	1.29
17th Jun	1919	1061	1019	5.56	68.85%	4.22	1.35
13th Oct	1919	1060	1020	5.29	66.67%	3.82	1.29
30th Mar	1920	1058	1016	5.56	72.41%	4.06	1.18
7th Oct	1920	1057	1020	4.89	64.91%	3.82	1.20
5th Oct	1921	1059.5	1019	5.36	68.07%	3.53	1.16

Sources:
Boddington brewing records held at Manchester Central Library, document numbers M693/405/126 and M693/405/126.

The biggest surprise is that CC was only briefly dropped during WW I, for about a year between October 1917 and November 1918. Brewing strong beers became virtually impossible after April 1st 1918, when the average gravity of all the beer a brewery produced couldn't be more than 1030°. Pretty difficult to brew a beer of 1060° and stick to that rule.

Like all of Boddington's beers, CC wasn't very heavily hopped in comparison to London beers. A London-brewed Burton Ale was hopped at around 12 lbs per quarter of malt - about treble the rate of CC.

It's surprising how well the OG bounced back after the war. The average drop in gravity between 1914 and the early 1920's when things stabilised again was about 19%. CC's fall was just 4%. Barely even significant. Its gravity did fall a little more between the wars, but in 1939 was still a very respectable 1056°.

After WW I

Before WW I, Old Ales had already started to become just strong Mild Ales, without any ageing process. This became almost universal in the interwar period, with only the occasional example that was still aged. Beer of the strong Mild type still exist today, brewed by established family breweries in the South of England such as Adnams and Harveys.

Two types are clearly visible in this table: one in the low 1050°s and another 1070-1090°. This first type approximates to London draught Burton Ale, though most of the beers in the table were bottled.

Old Ale after WW I							
Year	Brewer	Beer	Price per pint (d)	OG	FG	ABV	App. Atten-uation
1928	Gilmour	Balaclava	9	1052.9	1010.4	5.54	80.34%
1927	Tetley	Dark Ale		1057.1	1017.6	5.12	69.18%
1927	Tollemache	Dark Tolly		1052.9			
1926	Kemp Town	Dolphin No. 1	11	1059	1015.4	5.67	73.90%
1928	Georges	Home Brewed	8.5	1055.3	1010.4	5.86	81.19%
1928	Tetley	Imperial Ale	21	1089.6	1034.8	7.10	61.16%
1928	John Smith	Magnet Old Ale	15	1077.6	1019.6	7.57	74.74%
1936	John Smith	Magnet Old Ale	15	1068	1019.9	6.25	70.74%
1938	Walsall & District Clubs	Old	11	1059.6	1017.5	5.46	70.64%
1927	Telney	Ruddy Ale XXXX	7	1053.6			
1926	Northampton Brewery	Stingo Strong Ale	14	1083.3			
1927	Budden & Biggs	Strong Ale	8	1053.3			
1927	Davenport	Strong Ale	12	1073.9			
1927	Style & Winch	Strong Ale	8	1052.2			
1934	Woodhead	Strong Old Ale	9.5	1044	1011.7	4.19	73.41%

Sources:
Truman Gravity Book held at the London Metropolitan Archives, document number B/THB/C/252.
Whitbread Gravity book held at the London Metropolitan Archives, document number LMA/4453/D/02/001.

Barley Wine

Before WW I

The style had its origins in Burton. The first beer to be marketed as Barley Wine was Bass No. 1 Burton Ale, sometime around 1870. The name was gradually adopted by other brewers for their strongest beer. Though the distinction between Barley Wine and Old Ale is a vague one.

They were very high gravity beers, considered dangerously strong at a time when British beer averaged over 5% ABV. Usually they had a gravity of at least 1090°, but quite often over 1100°.

As with Pale Ale and IPA, the distinction between Barley Wine was often pretty arbitrary. Though there was some differentiation by strength. While a beer called Old Ale might have an OG anywhere between 1065° and 1100°, Barley Wine was limited to the top half of that range.

During WW I

The strict gravity restrictions introduced in April 1918 killed off really strong beers for a couple of years. When all your output had to average 1030°, how could you brew a beer of 1090°? The sacrifice in barrelage was too high.

Especially after February 1919, when maximum prices were introduced for all gravities. The maximum price for a draught beer of an OG over 1050° was 8d a pint. Whether it was 1050.5° or 1100°. Brewing anything much over 1050° made no economic sense. The price controls effectively put an upper limit on gravity.

Truman, in their Burton brewery, did manage to keep on brewing their Barley wine right up until March 19117.

Truman Barley Wine during WW I							
Year	Beer	OG	FG	ABV	App. Attenuation	lbs hops/ qtr	hops lb/brl
1916	1	1097.0	1033.2	8.43	65.71%	7.86	3.02
1917	1	1088.6	1034.3	7.18	61.25%	6.76	2.74
1917	S1	1099.7	1029.4	9.31	70.56%	11.68	6.00
1917	1	1087.3	1028.3	7.81	67.62%	9.43	2.92
Sources: Truman brewing records held at the London Metropolitan Archives, document numbers B/THB/C/332 and B/THB/C/331.							

The table actually contains two different beers: S1, the stock version and 1, the running version. S1 was aged for a year or two in wood, then blended with the running version before packaging. As you can see, the stock version was far more heavily hopped. Which makes sense, as it needed to survive extended secondary conditioning.

Truman's Barley Wine grists aren't that exciting:

Truman Barley Wine grists during WW I							
Year	Beer	OG	pale malt	high dried malt	black malt	flaked maize	glucose	invert sugar
1916	1	1097.0	64.29%	23.81%		11.90%		
1917	1	1088.6	42.94%	38.42%	0.56%	13.56%	4.52%	
1917	S1	1099.7	59.67%	35.36%	0.55%		2.95%	1.47%
1917	1	1087.3	42.94%	38.42%	0.56%	13.56%	4.52%	
Sources: Truman brewing records held at the London Metropolitan Archives, document numbers B/THB/C/332 and B/THB/C/331.								

Mostly just the two base malts – pale and high dried – plus flaked maize, a tiny amount of black malt and sugar. I'd be reluctant to guess what colour the finished beer was as there might have been an addition of caramel at some point.

After WW I

Certain Burton breweries – Bass and Truman, for example – continued to brew full-strength Barley Wines.

Barley Wine 1879 - 1938

Year	Brewer	Beer	OG	FG	ABV	App. Atten-uation
1879	Bass	No. 1	1104	1029	9.83	72.12%
1921	Bass	No. 1	1094	1032	8.06	65.96%
1927	Bass	No. 1 Barley Wine	1105	1035	9.13	66.67%
1934	Bass	Prince's Ale	1112.8	1029.2	11.00	74.11%
1935	Bass	Barley Wine	1109	1023.3	11.32	78.62%
1932	Mann	Barley Wine	1096	1011.9	11.15	87.60%
1933	Mann	Barley Wine	1094.8	1006.9	11.71	92.72%
1938	Mann	Barley Wine	1092.9	1026	8.74	72.01%
1932	Truman	No.1 Burton Barley Wine	1097.3	1017.8	10.49	81.71%

Sources:
Thomas Usher Gravity Book document TU/6/11
Younger, Wm. & Co Gravity Book document WY/6/1/1/19 held at the Scottish Brewing Archive
Whitbread Gravity book held at the London Metropolitan Archives, document number LMA/4453/D/02/001.

Bass No. 1 was one of a very elite club of beers that were still brewed to a 19th-century gravity.

Such beers were never brewed in very large quantities. No-one would drink Barley Wine all night, though they might finish off an evening in the pub with a nip of it. Surprisingly, the style managed to survive both World Wars and even managed to increase its popularity in the 1950s and 1960s though beers such as Gold Label

Scotch Ale

Before WW I

In the 19th century the Scots had a reputation for brewing powerful Ales, beers with enormous gravities and an elegant pale colour. These beers – which I refer to as Shilling Ales because they were usually given shilling designations – were in decline before the start of the war and were mostly killed off by it.

It wasn't the end of Scotch Ale, but what was sold under that name after the war was a very different beast.

Scottish Strong and Shilling Ales before WW I								
Year	Brewer	Beer	OG	FG	ABV	App. Attenuation	lbs hops/ qtr	hops lb/brl
1909	Maclay	Strong Ale	1096	1031	8.60	67.71%	7.6	4.00
1912	Thomas Usher	44/-	1034	1013	2.78	61.76%	5.00	0.71
1912	Thomas Usher	60/-	1039	1015	3.18	61.54%	5.00	0.81
1912	Thomas Usher	80/-	1049	1018	4.10	63.27%	5.00	1.02
1912	Thomas Usher	100/-	1064	1029	4.63	54.69%	5.00	1.34
1913	Younger, Wm.	60/-	1047	1023	3.18	51.06%	3.04	0.28
1913	Younger, Wm.	80/-	1056	1027	3.84	51.79%	3.60	0.75
1913	Younger, Wm.	100/-	1066	1032	4.50	51.52%	3.60	0.89
1913	Younger, Wm.	160/-	1097	1038	7.81	60.82%	5.33	2.83
Sources: Maclay brewing record held at the Scottish Brewing Archive, document number M/6/1/1/2. Thomas Usher brewing record held at the Scottish Brewing Archive, document number TU/6/1/5. William Younger brewing record held at the Scottish Brewing Archive, document number WY/6/1/2/58.								

During WW I

I'll be honest with you. I've very little information about Scotch Ale during the war. Laughably little, considering how diligently I've collected everything connected with Scottish brewing.

What I do have, all relates to one brewery, William Younger, who had another range of Strong Ales in addition to the Shilling Ales above. These were numbered, in the manner of Burton brewers.

William Younger Scotch Ale in and around WW I

Year	Beer	OG	FG	ABV	App. Attenuation	lbs hops/ qtr	hops lb/brl
1913	1	1097	1037	7.94	61.86%	10.28	7.40
1917	1	1081	1023.5	7.61	70.99%	10.00	3.28
1921	1	1082	1028	7.14	65.85%	7.37	2.52
1914	2 Sc	1076	1025	6.75	67.11%	9.35	2.86
1922	2 Btg	1072	1022	6.61	69.44%	8.53	2.75
1913	3	1065	1021.5	5.75	66.92%	4.55	1.15
1913	3a	1072	1025	6.22	65.28%	5.48	1.22
1913	3 btg	1070	1022	6.35	68.57%	5.48	1.78
1914	3 Sc	1065	1022	5.69	66.15%	4.55	1.20
1921	3	1060	1015	5.95	75.00%	5.00	1.20
1921	3	1053.4	1013.3	5.30	75.00%	4.55	1.06

Sources:
Younger, Wm. & Co brewing record held at the Scottish Brewing Archive, document numbers WY/6/1/2/58, WY/6/1/3/50 and WY/6/1/2/63.

No. 1 had already taken a gravity hit by 1917. I can't imagine it made it past April of that year. Restrictions made a beer of that impractical until the 1920s. A gap of around four years.

No. 2 disappeared sometime in the 1920s, leaving Younger with an illogical set of No. 1 and No. 3. Which both continued on well past WW II. No. 3 appeared in several variations that very closely resemble each other, if not differ in name only.

If you're wondering why there are two 1921 examples of No. 3 with different gravities, it's because they watered it down at racking. They're the gravity before and after watering.

The grists are very simple:

William Younger Scotch Ale grists in and around WW I

Year	Beer	OG	pale malt	grits	glucose	DM sugar
1913	1	1097	55.19%	41.04%	1.89%	1.89%
1917	1	1081	73.33%	26.67%		
1921	1	1082	60.53%	39.47%		
1914	2 Sc	1076	54.40%	41.21%	2.20%	2.20%
1922	2 Btg	1072	60.29%	39.71%		
1913	3	1065	57.07%	40.98%		1.95%
1913	3a	1072	53.80%	44.02%	2.17%	
1913	3 btg	1070	57.07%	40.76%	2.17%	
1914	3 Sc	1065	55.10%	42.86%	2.04%	
1921	3	1060	60.71%	39.29%		
1921	3	1053.4	60.71%	39.29%		

Sources:
Younger, Wm. & Co brewing record held at the Scottish Brewing Archive, document numbers WY/6/1/2/58, WY/6/1/3/50 and WY/6/1/2/63.

Just pale malt, loads of grits and a little sugar. Yet they were dark brown in colour. How does that work? Caramel, at racking. Scottish brewers almost never used coloured malts, except when brewing Stout.

After WW I

Sometime around 1921, Strong Scotch Ales returned, but never quite at the strength they had been. Unlike in Burton, where Barley Wines returned to their pre-war gravity. With the notable exceptions of a couple of things like Fowler's 12 Guinea Ale, which were as strong as British beer got.

Scotland was rather schizophrenic when it came to beer strength. The bulk of what was brewed and consumed in Scotland was rather weak, even in comparison to England. The most popular beers were Pale Ales in the 1035-1038° range. But at the same time some very strong beers indeed were brewed.

The strong beers were schizophrenic themselves as what they were called depended on which side of the border you were. North of it, they were usually known as Strong Ale, South of it the y were called Scotch Ale.

I've split the Scotch Ales into two groups, based on their OG. The first is those below 1070°.

Weaker Scotch Ale after WW I								
Date	Year	Beer	Price per pint (d)	OG	FG	ABV	App. Atten-uation	colour
1929	Jeffrey	No. 1 Strong Ale		1062	1015	6.12	75.81%	110
1928	McEwan	Scotch Ale		1069.6	1017.2	6.83	75.29%	
1929	McEwan	Strong Ale		1065	1021	5.71	67.69%	
1924	Murray	Strong Ale		1060.3	1011.5	6.37	80.93%	25
1924	Tennent	Strong Ale		1063.3	1022	5.35	65.24%	74
1929	Younger, Geo	Strong Ale		1066.5	1018.5	6.24	72.18%	
1925	Younger, Wm.	No.3 Scotch Ale	15	1053.8	1009.5	5.81	82.71%	
Sources:								
Thomas Usher Gravity Book held at the Scottish Brewing Archive, document number TU/6/11. Younger, Wm. & Co Gravity Book document WY/6/1/1/19 held at the Scottish Brewing Archive Whitbread Gravity book held at the London Metropolitan Archives, document number LMA/4453/D/02/001.								

The weak outlier, Youngers No. 3, is a strange beast. A weaker type of Scotch Ale that during the 20th century was often available on draught. Especially in London, where it served as a substitute for Burton Ale. It's had a patch existence since the 1970s, being killed and resurrected several times.

The stronger set includes some extremely powerful beers:

Stronger Scotch Ale after WW I

Date	Year	Beer	Price per pint (d)	OG	FG	ABV	App. Attenuation	colour
1926	Bernard	Strong Ale		1080	1020	7.84	75.00%	10C
1929	Dalkeith	Strong Ale		1087	1062	3.16	28.74%	14C
1927	Disher	10 Guinea Ale		1114	1029	11.20	74.56%	13C
1926	Fowler	Twelve Guinea Ale		1117	1031	11.33	73.50%	14C
1928	Jeffrey	Strong Ale		1083	1025	7.55	69.88%	10C
1928	Maclachlan	Strong Ale		1080	1016	8.39	80.00%	8C
1928	Martin	Strong Ale		1078	1019	7.71	75.64%	8C
1928	McEwan	Strong Ale		1089	1026	8.22	70.79%	7C
1928	Murray	Strong Ale		1085	1027	7.55	68.24%	8C
1923	Usher	Old Scotch Ale (ex Brussels)		1082	1016	8.66	80.49%	
1923	Ushers	10 Guinea Ale		1120	1033	11.45	72.49%	72
1928	Younger, Robert	Strong Ale		1080	1030	6.47	62.50%	105
1925	Younger, Wm.	No.1 Strong Scotch Ale	18	1084.7	1013.8	9.34	83.71%	
1928	Younger, Wm.	Strong Ale		1085	1026	7.68	69.41%	7C

Sources:
Thomas Usher Gravity Book held at the Scottish Brewing Archive, document number TU/6/11.
Younger, Wm. & Co Gravity Book document WY/6/1/1/19 held at the Scottish Brewing Archive
Whitbread Gravity book held at the London Metropolitan Archives, document number LMA/4453/D/02/001.

Fowler's 12 Guinea Ale was the original Wee Heavy, the latter simply being slang for a "small strong", referring to the fact that it usually came in nip bottles. Just as well, given how crazily strong it is. Though Disher's 10 Guinea Ale was, unbelievably, also sold on draught.

You can see the name schizophrenia in the two William Younger entries, which are the same beer, just labelled differently for England and Scotland.

Lager

Surprisingly, there was a reasonable amount of Lager around in WW I. Finding someone who knew how to make it was a major headache for Britain's few Lager breweries during the War.

Lager has a surprisingly long history in Britain. The first to try bottom-fermentation was John Muir of Edinburgh in 1835. The legendary Munich brewer Gabriel Sedlmayr had visited Muir's brewery whilst on a study trip to Britain in the early 1830's. Sedlmayr sent some Bavarian yeast to Scotland on Muir's request. Despite being impressed with the results, Muir abandoned his attempts when he was unable to propagate the yeast successfully.

The **Wrexham Lager Beer Company** was founded in 1878 and, despite a takeover by Ind Coope in 1949, only closed in 2000. They had a German-born head brewer called Justus Wilhelm Kolb at the start of the war. Initially they were able to argue that he was irreplaceable due to his specialist knowledge and he was exempted from conscription. But in February 1917 it was ruled that a substitute could be trained and he was conscripted. Despite his having served in the German army.[30]

Tennent's of Glasgow first brewed lager in 1885 and built a new dedicated brewhouse for its production in 1891.

During the war, Barclay Perkins experimented with brewing Lager and decocting on their small kit. Presumably their motivation was the difficulty in obtaining supplies of Lager. Before the war the main sources of imported Lager were Germany and Austria.

Lager turns up in the price-fixing agreements of publicans. This is an example from Scotland:

> **"ARBROATH LICENSE-HOLDERS AND "OFF" PRICES OF BEERS.**
> At a largely-attended meeting of Arbroath license-holders held in the Masonic Hall, Hill Street, yesterday —Mr D. Darroch presiding— the following "off" prices were fixed in regard to beers: —Draught beer, 4d per pint; table beer, 3s per dozen; Burton ales and lager beers, 3s 6d per dozen; small lagers, 2s 9d per dozen; No. 1 Bass, 4s 6d per dozen; London stouts — No. 3 3s 6d and imperial 4s per dozen; Whitbread's large 3s 6d and small 2s 6d per dozen; Ballingall's imperial pints 3s, small 2s 6d, and Ballingall's double stout 3s per dozen. Increased prices to take effect immediately.
>
> A committee of grocers and publicans was appointed to investigate cases of underselling, and to take whatever steps might be considered necessary to have the practice discontinued."
> Dundee Courier - Wednesday 25 November 1914, page 2.

Here's one from London, showing that not only was Lager available, but that it came in two different colours:

---

[30] Weekly Dispatch, Feb 11 1917.

"The new scale of prices as fixed by the Licensed Victuallers' Central Protection Society of London is:

	half pint	Glass
Mild ale	3.5d.	-
Bitter	5d.	4d.
Stout	5d.	5d.
Burton	6d.	5d.
Mild and Bitter	4.5d.	3.5d.
Stout and Mild	5d.	4d.
Mild and Burton	5d.	4d.

Other prices: Small Bass 7d.; Guinness 8d.; London stout (screws) 5d.; pale ale (screws) 5d.; barley wine nips 6d.; lager, light or dark, 8d."
Weekly Dispatch, April 8th 1917.

Lager both being brewed in Britain and imported. The foreign supplies came from neutral countries: Holland, Denmark and Sweden. British-brewed Lagers came mostly from the country's pioneers of bottom-fermenting: Allsopp, Tennant and the Wrexham Lager Brewery.

As you'll see in the table below, the British Lagers were much higher in gravity than later versions would be and were pretty similar to beers brewed on the Continent.

Lager in the UK in WW I

Year	Brewer	country	Beer	Style	FG	OG	ABV	Atten-uation
1915	Allsopp	UK	Pilsener	Pilsener	1010	1049	5.08	79.59%
1915	Peter Walker	UK	Pilsener	Münchner	1010.3	1044.4	4.43	76.80%
1915	J & R Tennent	UK	Munich	Münchner	1015.3	1049.2	4.39	68.90%
1915	Salomon	UK	Nonalcoholic Lager	Lager	1027.5	1038.5	1.40	28.57%
1915	Haantje	Holland	Munich	Münchner	1011.6	1043.8	4.18	73.52%
1915	Haantje	Holland	Pilsener	Pilsener	1014.4	1044.8	3.93	67.86%
1915	Wrexham	UK	Pilsener	Pilsener	1013.9	1051.3	4.86	72.90%
1915	Jeffreys	UK	Pilsener	Pilsener	1009.8	1039.9	3.91	75.44%
1915	Jeffreys	UK	Munich	Münchner	1012.1	1041.3	3.78	70.70%
1915	Barclay Perkins	UK	Pilsener experimental	Pilsener	1008.4	1050.8	5.53	83.46%
1915	Barclay Perkins	UK	Munich experimental	Münchner	1020.2	1051.6	4.05	60.85%
1915	J & R Tennent	UK	Pilsener	Pilsener	1010.3	1047	4.77	78.09%
1915	J & R Tennent	UK	Munich	Münchner	1015.6	1050.4	4.51	69.05%
1915	Peter Walker	UK	Munich	Münchner	1013.2	1048.7	4.61	72.90%
1915	Carlsberg	Denmark	Light	Lager	1014	1053.6	5.15	73.88%
1915	Barclay Perkins	UK	Dark (Pasteurised)	Münchner	1019.9	1051.9	4.13	61.66%
1915	Barclay Perkins	UK	Dark (not Pasteurised)	Münchner	1019.8	1051.6	4.11	61.63%
1915	Barclay Perkins	UK	Light (Pasteurised)	Pilsener	1011.8	1051.1	5.11	76.91%
1915	Barclay Perkins	UK	Light (not Pasteurised)	Pilsener	1010.5	1051.2	5.30	79.49%
1915	Lyckholm, Gothenburg	Sweden	Lager	Lager	1009.4	1047.5	4.96	80.21%
1915	Lyckholm, Gothenburg	Sweden	Lager	Lager	1012.6	1050.5	4.92	75.05%
1915	Budweiser, St Louis	USA	Busek's Lager	Lager	1015.9	1050.5	4.48	68.51%
1915	Tuborg	Denmark	Lager	Lager	1011.3	1045.1	4.39	74.94%
1919	Allsopp	UK	Lager	Lager	1007.9	1043.9	4.69	82.00%

Source:
Document ACC/2305/1/712 in the Barclay Perkins archive held in the London Metropolitan Archives

The experimental dark lager Barclay Perkins brewed on March 10th 1915 was an odd beast. For a start there are the malts: 83% mild malt, 8.5% amber malt, 8.5% Californian pale malt. I guess they were using mild malt instead of Munich malt. The hops were at least partly continental.: 50% Worcester, 50% Burgundy.

The log form wasn't designed to record a decoction mash and there are several lines of comments in an empty part describing the process. It doesn't seem to gave gone quite to plan:

"Mashed 5.5 qtrs @ 7.5 a.m. Underlet at 7.35 - set taps & ran off 6.5 barrels @ 8.5. Raised to boiling point with boiling liq. & steam by 9 am. & boiled 0.5 hour. Brought back to 165° by 2.15 p.m. (should have been 150° - tun nearly full - could not add any more cold) Mashed in 0.5 quarter Calif. very stiff at 2.30 & raked well, conversion complete & taps set @ 3.20 p.m. - Goods would not drain at all - wort only got off by repeated underletting & raking & by siphoning. No reliable tap heats or gravities obtainable. First wort drawn from M.T. kept at about 190° all the time.

Goods were not sparged at all"

That definitely sounds experimental to me.

The fermentation was more like you would expect - comparatively long and cold. Lager yeast was pitched at 46° F and the beer was racked into an aluminium tank in the cold store after 7 days.

The OG was 1052° and the racking gravity 1023°.

Mini Book Series volume XXXII: Armistice!

III Let's Brew

Introduction to recipes

A couple of remarks before you dive into the recipes.

These recipes have been written using original brewing records as the source. The level of detail on old brewing logs varies greatly. Some, especially the older ones, are a bit vague. Many miss out completely vital pieces of information.

How have I coped with missing information? I'll be honest: I've guessed. Not just random guesses, but ones based on other sources, such as brewing manuals. Or later brewing records from the same brewery. It's not perfect, but it's the best that can be done.

Virtually no logs have any record of the hop additions. With the exception of some Barclay Perkins logs. All the other hop additions listed in these recipes are a guesstimate. Feel free to tinker with them as suits you.

The ingredients, mashing details, OG and FG are always taken from the original brewing records.

I assume all quarters of grain to be 336 pounds and a quarter of sugar as 224 pounds.

Care should be taken with the quantity of hops used. I've reduced the original quantities, to take into account the age of the hops. But it's all very much guesswork. When the hops were kept in a cold store, I've not reduced the quantities by as much.

Sugars are a bit of a problem. Brewers used a whole range of different sugars, many of them proprietary brands. I'm not sure if exact equivalents are available at all today, let alone to home brewers.

Hops are rather simpler. Where it says EK or MK, you can't go far wrong with either Fuggles or Goldings. Cluster is best for anything called American, Oregon, Californian or Pacific.

The mash temperature I give is the initial heat after the water and grains have been mixed. Whereas the sparge is the temperature of the water.

Adnams

Based in Southwold on the Suffolk coast, Adnams was very different from the other breweries in this recipe section. The others all come from urban areas, whereas Adnams were in quite a rural location.

This is reflected in their beers which are, in general, weaker than those from more urban settings, especially London beers.

The brewery, which was originally established in the middle of the 17th century in the Swan Hotel, was acquired by George and Ernest Adnams around 1870.

At the outbreak of war, Adnams brewed quite a wide range of beers:

Adnams beers in 1914							
Beer	Style	OG	FG	ABV	App. Atten-uation	lbs hops/ qtr	hops lb/brl
X	Mild Ale	1033	1005.5	3.64	83.33%	4.38	0.58
XX	Mild Ale	1042	1007	4.63	83.33%	4.20	0.73
Tally Ho	Old Ale	1082	1029.5	6.95	64.02%	5.92	2.21
BLB	Pale Ale	1044	1007	4.89	84.09%	7.00	1.34
PA	Pale Ale	1056	1011	5.95	80.36%	6.53	1.30
BS	Stout	1055	1013.5	5.49	75.45%	5.86	1.43
DS	Stout	1065	1016.6	6.40	74.43%	6.97	2.11
Source: Adnams brewing record Book 2 held at the brewery.							

By the time affairs had returned to relative normality in the 1920s, they brewed far fewer beers:

Adnams beers in 1923							
Beer	Style	OG	FG	ABV	App. Atten-uation	lbs hops/ qtr	hops lb/brl
XX	Mild Ale	1029	1004.2	3.29	85.67%	4.99	0.59
XXXX	Old Ale	1057	1016.6	5.34	70.84%	6.70	1.53
PA	Pale Ale	1038	1007.2	4.07	81.05%	8.52	1.29
DS	Stout	1044	1010	4.50	77.34%	6.59	1.19
Source: Adnams brewing record Book 9 held at the brewery.							

The gravities of the beers which have survived have fallen considerably.

1914 Adnams X Ale

The further you got out into the countryside, the weaker beer would often become. Especially Mild Ale.

Adnams X Ale is a good example. In London, an X Ale was at least 1050°. Beer under 1040° were totally unknown in the capital. If you were a naïve yokel, used to beers like this, you'd have got pissed out of your head drinking London X Ale the same way you did the stuff back home. This beer is so weak, it could pass for a modern Mild.

This isn't a particularly complex beer in terms of the recipe. Just base malt, sugar and caramel. What I've listed as mild malt was something called "medium" malt in the original brewing record. No idea what that was and mild malt is just a guess at an approximate substitute. The sugar is described as cane blocks. Which could mean some sort of lightly-refined West Indian sugar, or pure sucrose.

I've interpreted Oregon and East Kent hops to be Cluster and Goldings, respectively. Though in a cheaper beer like this it's possible that they were Fuggles rather than Goldings.

The final beer is quite dark, but the colour all comes from the caramel, which is called "Tintose" in the log. 5000 SRM is just a guess. But from the small quantities used, it must have been very highly coloured. If it were less than 5000 SRM, obviously the final colour would be much paler.

1914 Adnams X Ale		
mild malt	4.25 lb	58.06%
pale malt	2.50 lb	34.15%
cane sugar	0.50 lb	6.83%
caramel 5000 SRM	0.07 lb	0.96%
Cluster 105 mins	0.33 oz	
Goldings 60 mins	0.33 oz	
Goldings 30 mins	0.33 oz	
OG	1033	
FG	1005.5	
ABV	3.64	
Apparent attenuation	83.33%	
IBU	17	
SRM	23	
Mash at	153° F	
Sparge at	170° F	
Boil time	105 minutes	
pitching temp	60° F	
Yeast	WLP025 Southwold	

1914 Adnams XX Ale

Normally I'd expect XX Ale to be just a scaled-up version of X Ale, possibly parti-gyled with it. But Adnams XX Ale has a completely different recipe to their X Ale.

The grist is more complex, containing two extra ingredients, crystal malt and flaked maize. I'm sort of surprised that the cheaper X Ale had no maize in its grist. Perhaps they were afraid of the beer being too thin.

The hopping is very similar to X Ale, consisting of a combination of Oregon and East Kent hops. Which says Cluster and Goldings to me.

The gravity is still pretty feeble for a pre-WW I Mild, but, a high degree of attenuation leaves it with a fairly respectable 4.5% ABV. A 1042° is pretty typical of an interwar Best Mild.

1914 Adnams XX		
pale malt	2.75 lb	30.32%
mild malt	4.00 lb	44.10%
crystal malt 80 L	0.50 lb	5.51%
flaked maize	0.50 lb	5.51%
cane sugar	1.25 lb	13.78%
caramel 5000 SRM	0.07 lb	0.77%
Cluster 105 mins	0.50 oz	
Goldings 60 mins	0.50 oz	
Goldings 30 mins	0.50 oz	
OG	1042	
FG	1008	
ABV	4.50	
Apparent attenuation	80.95%	
IBU	23	
SRM	25	
Mash at	152° F	
Sparge at	170° F	
Boil time	105 minutes	
pitching temp	60° F	

1915 Adnams XXXX Ale

This is a beer I initially missed in Adnams brewing records. An understandable mistake, as they never actually brewed it.

Rather, it was assembled, as it was a blend of XX Ale and Tally Ho. Usually, I would have expected a brewery to simply parti-gyle XX and XXXX together. It's not particularly complicated. But Adnams didn't indulge in parti-gyling.

The recipe is simple: 4 gallons of XX and half a gallon of Tally Ho. And there you have it, instant Strong Mild. Though not all that strong.

Why did Adnams produce it this way? Probably because of limited demand. It was usually only 2.25 barrels that they blended up. They had brewed a beer called XXXX in the 1890's, but I guess sales had fallen too low to warrant brewing it by the time WW I rolled around.

1915 Adnams XXXX	
OG	1046
FG	1009
ABV	4.89
Apparent attenuation	80.43%
IBU	27
SRM	24

1914 Adnams BLB

I'm fascinated by the fact that at the start of WW I Adnams brewed two Stouts yet only produced a single Pale Ale, BLB.

I'm not sure what that stands for exactly, but I'm betting that the LB bit stands for "Light Bitter". Whether it does or not, this certainly looks like a Light Bitter, with its OG in the mid 1040°'s. There's nothing odd about that, but I'd usually expect a brewery to also have a stronger Pale Ale, in the 1055°-1060° range.

The recipe is about as simple as they come: pale malt, invert sugar and flaked maize. The high percentage of No. 2 invert suggests to me that they were trying to keep the body and colour of this beer as light as possible. People often get the wrong idea about sugar, assuming its role was purely one of economy. Yet BLB contains double the proportion of sugar of the cheaper X Ale.

The malt was slightly more complicated than appears in the recipe below. About half was made from Oregon-grown barley. It was fairly standard to have up to half of the malt to have been made from foreign barley.

The hops were a fairly even three-way split between Oregon, East Kent and Kent, all from the 1913 harvest. Which was the most recent crop when this was brewed in August 1914.

1914 Adnams BLB		
pale malt	7.50 lb	78.95%
flaked maize	0.50 lb	5.26%
No. 2 invert sugar	1.50 lb	15.79%
Cluster 90 mins	1.00 oz	
Fuggles 60 mins	1.00 oz	
Goldings 30 mins	1.00 oz	
Fuggles dry hops	1.50 oz	
OG	1044	
FG	1007	
ABV	4.89	
Apparent attenuation	84.09%	
IBU	45	
SRM	8	
Mash at	155° F	
Sparge at	170° F	
Boil time	90 minutes	
pitching temp	60° F	
Yeast	WLP025 Southwold	

1914 Adnams BS

It wasn't just rural Mild Ales that were lower in gravity than their London counterparts. Their Stouts weren't always that Stout, either.

Adnams Brown Stout (I'm pretty sure that's what BS stands for) looks very like a London Porter in terms of strength. Porter, as such started, disappearing outside London in the last couple of decades of the 19th century. By WW I, there were few beers called Porter outside London and the Southeast of England.

There are a couple of points of note in the grist of BS. Brown malt is very traditional in English Stouts, but by 1914 it had been dropped by many breweries outside London. So its presence here is a nod to the past. While chocolate malt rather than black malt is very much a glimpse into the future. Whitbread, for example, dropped black malt in favour of chocolate malt in the 1920's. Its use here by Adnams is surprisingly modern.

As usual, there's a fair bit of interpretation in the recipe below. No. 4 invert is my substitute for CDM - Caramelised Dextro-Maltose. The No. 2 invert, on the other hand, is exactly as noted in the brewing record.

1914 Adnams BS		
pale malt	4.50 lb	37.50%
mild malt	3.50 lb	29.17%
brown malt	1.25 lb	10.42%
chocolate malt	1.25 lb	10.42%
No. 2 invert sugar	1.25 lb	10.42%
No. 4 invert sugar	0.25 lb	2.08%
Cluster 120 mins	1.00 oz	
Goldings 60 mins	1.00 oz	
Goldings 30 mins	1.00 oz	
OG	1055	
FG	1013.5	
ABV	5.49	
Apparent attenuation	75.45%	
IBU	44	
SRM	38	
Mash at	156° F	
Sparge at	170° F	
Boil time	120 minutes	
pitching temp	60° F	
Yeast	WLP025 Southwold	

1914 Adnams Double Stout

Adnams were unusual with their recipes. Not only did they have two Mild ales with different recipes, their two Stouts had dissimilar grists.

That wasn't how most breweries operated. Even if they weren't parti-gyling them together, beers of the same style usually had the same basic recipe. But not at Adnams. Not only are there two extra ingredients in Double Stout – amber malt and cane blocks – the proportions of the malts are different.

The percentage of coloured malts is much higher in Double Stout: about 33% as opposed to 20% in Brown Stout. There's also more pale malt compared to medium malt (interpreted as mild malt below). In London, the presence of amber malt usually indicated a posh beer. It was absent in Porter and the cheaper Stouts.

The hops are an interesting mix of American (Oregon), Bohemian and English. The latter being from Mid-Kent and Kent. I've reduced the quantities because they were from the 1912 and 1913, except for some of the Oregons which were 1908. And, unlike BS, Double Stout was dry-hopped.

The original was brewed on the 22nd December, a few months after the outbreak of war. But Adnams was still happy to use hops grown on enemy soil. And why not? No point in wasting something you'd already bought. But, with all the sentiment against the Central Powers, what would drinkers have thought about Austrian hops in their pint?

Given all the dark malts, it's no surprise that it comes out pretty damn black.

1914 Adnams Double Stout		
pale malt	6.00 lb	43.64%
brown malt	1.00 lb	7.27%
amber malt	1.75 lb	12.73%
chocolate malt	1.75 lb	12.73%
mild malt	1.00 lb	7.27%
No. 2 invert sugar	0.75 lb	5.45%
cane sugar	1.25 lb	9.09%
No. 4 invert sugar	0.25 lb	1.82%
Cluster 120 mins	0.75 oz	
Fuggles 90 mins	1.00 oz	
Fuggles 60 mins	1.00 oz	
Saaz 30 mins	1.00 oz	
Goldings dry hops	0.50 oz	
OG	1065	
FG	1017	
ABV	6.35	
Apparent attenuation	73.85%	
IBU	46	
SRM	45	
Mash at	154° F	
Sparge at	170° F	
Boil time	120 minutes	
pitching temp	60° F	
Yeast	WLP025 Southwold	

1914 Adnams Tally Ho

Named beer – ones called something other than Joe Bloggs X Ale – were rare before WWI. Yet Adnams Tally Ho is much older than that. The earliest brewing record for it I've seen is from 1879.

I class Tally Ho as an Old Ale. Though I know they now market it as a Barley Wine. It's very arbitrary. And I'm sure they weren't that arsed about such fine distinctions 100 years ago.

As with all Adnams beers, there are two base malts: pale and "medium". Plus a little bit of crystal malt, flaked maize and sugar. What's in the recipe as No. 3 was listed as "X Primings" in the brewing record. How dark the "Tintose" – caramel below – is anyone's guess. It could well have been darker, as I've interpreted it in some other recipes.

The hops are described as Oregon and East Ken, with Worcester dry hops. Which I've interpreted as Cluster, Goldings and Fuggles, respectively. All the hops were from the 1913 harvest so, as this beer was brewed 13th August 1914, I've left the hopping rate alone.

1914 Adnams Tally Ho		
pale malt	5.25 lb	29.86%
mild malt	8.75 lb	49.77%
crystal malt 60 L	0.75 lb	4.27%
flaked maize	0.75 lb	4.27%
No. 2 invert sugar	1.50 lb	8.53%
No. 3 invert sugar	0.50 lb	2.84%
caramel 1000 SRM	0.08 lb	0.46%
Cluster 135 mins	1.50 oz	
Goldings 90 mins	1.50 oz	
Goldings 30 mins	1.50 oz	
Fuggles dry hops	1.50 oz	
OG	1081	
FG	1027	
ABV	7.14	
Apparent attenuation	66.67%	
IBU	58	
SRM	18	
Mash at	154° F	
Sparge at	170° F	
Boil time	135 minutes	
pitching temp	60° F	
Yeast	WLP025 Southwold	

1915 Adnams PA

It wasn't quite correct what I said about Adnams only brewing one Pale Ale. They did have a second one called PA. They just didn't brew it very often.

At 1060°, it's a proper, full-strength Pale Ale. Much stronger than their standard Pale Ale, BLB, which was in the mid-1040°'s.

The grist is even simpler than BLB's, as there's no flaked maize, just pale malt and No. 2 invert sugar. To make things slightly more exciting, the pale malt is about half rom English, half from Californian barley.

The hops were a combination of Worcester, Sussex and Kent from the 1914 crop and Oregon from the 1913 harvest. I've reduced the hop quantities a little, since the original was brewed in September 1915. But it still works out to 62 calculated IBUs. If it takes your fancy, you could replace some or all of the Fuggles with Goldings.

It wouldn't surprise me if PA was still being brewed as a Stock Ale, that is aged before sale. Three to six months would be about a minimum ageing period, but a full twelve months is quite possible.

1915 Adnams PA		
pale malt	11.50 lb	86.79%
No. 2 invert sugar	1.75 lb	13.21%
Cluster 120 mins	1.50 oz	
Fuggles 60 mins	1.50 oz	
Fuggles 30 mins	1.50 oz	
Fuggles dry hops	2.00 oz	
OG	1060	
FG	1014	
ABV	6.09	
Apparent attenuation	76.67%	
IBU	62	
SRM	9	
Mash at	155° F	
Sparge at	170° F	
Boil time	120 minutes	
pitching temp	59° F	
Yeast	WLP025 Southwold	

1916 Adnams XX Ale

Adnams appear to have dropped X Ale pretty much right at the start of the war, concentrating instead on XX Ale. Though that didn't remain unchanged.

The grist isn't hugely different form in 1914, save for the addition of No. 2 invert sugar. Which makes the recipe very similar to that of Tally Ho. So you could interpret Tally Ho as a sort of strong Mild Ale.

The biggest change in the hopping is the age of the hops. In 1914, the hops were all from the most recent season. In the 1916 version, only about a third of the hops were from the most recent crop. The rest – Oregon and Worcester – were from 1914. This is a trend I've noticed at several breweries, with the age of hops used becoming older and older as the war progressed.

The OG has dropped about 10%, from 1042° to 1038°. Which wouldn't have impressed London drinkers, even during wartime.

1916 Adnams XX		
pale malt	3.50 lb	41.62%
mild malt	2.75 lb	32.70%
crystal malt 80 L	0.50 lb	5.95%
flaked maize	0.50 lb	5.95%
No. 2 invert sugar	0.33 lb	3.92%
cane sugar	0.75 lb	8.92%
caramel 5000 SRM	0.08 lb	0.95%
Cluster 120 mins	0.50 oz	
Fuggles 60 mins	0.50 oz	
Fuggles 30 mins	0.25 oz	
OG	1038	
FG	1007	
ABV	4.10	
Apparent attenuation	81.58%	
IBU	22	
SRM	27	
Mash at	154° F	
Sparge at	170° F	
Boil time	120 minutes	
pitching temp	60° F	
Yeast	WLP025 Southwold	

1916 Adnams BLB

Brewing was still relatively normal in 1916. Yes, there were limits on how much beer a brewery could produce, but brewers could still brew at any strength they liked.

There were slight falls in gravity, but these were mostly centred on the more popular styles, such as Mild Ale. This seems to be the case at Adnams, where between 1914 and 1916 XX Ale fell from 1042° to 1038°, while BLB only fell from 1044° to 1042°.

The only change to the grist is a slight fall in the proportion of No. 2 invert sugar. It doesn't make it any more complicated.

1916 Adnams BLB		
pale malt	7.75 lb	81.58%
flaked maize	0.50 lb	5.26%
No. 2 invert sugar	1.25 lb	13.16%
Cluster 90 mins	1.00 oz	
Fuggles 60 mins	1.00 oz	
Fuggles 30 mins	0.75 oz	
Fuggles dry hops	2.00 oz	
OG	1042	
FG	1008	
ABV	4.50	
Apparent attenuation	80.95%	
IBU	41	
SRM	7	
Mash at	156° F	
Sparge at	170° F	
Boil time	120 minutes	
pitching temp	60° F	
Yeast	WLP025 Southwold	

1916 Adnams Double Stout

Having said that there was only a little nibbling away at gravities, mostly of the weaker and more popular beers, Adnams Double Stout proves me a liar.

Because it's had a very hefty fall in gravity since 1914: 1065° to 1052°. Don't ask me why it took such a big hit. Perhaps just because they could get away with it. The number of standard barrels Adnams was allowed to brew was limited. By dropping the gravity of their Stout, they'd be able to brew a greater volume of Mild.

The biggest change in the grist is the dropping of brown malt. But it remains pretty damn complicated, with four malts and three sugars.

1916 Adnams Double Stout		
pale malt	3.25 lb	30.23%
amber malt	1.50 lb	13.95%
chocolate malt	1.00 lb	9.30%
mild malt	2.75 lb	25.58%
No. 2 invert sugar	1.25 lb	11.63%
cane sugar	0.75 lb	6.98%
No. 4 invert sugar	0.25 lb	2.33%
Cluster 120 mins	1.00 oz	
Fuggles 60 mins	1.00 oz	
Fuggles 30 mins	1.00 oz	
OG	1052	
FG	1012	
ABV	5.29	
Apparent attenuation	76.92%	
IBU	44	
SRM	32	
Mash at	154° F	
Sparge at	170° F	
Boil time	120 minutes	
pitching temp	61° F	
Yeast	WLP025 Southwold	

1916 Adnams Tally Ho

I'm really intrigued as to what Adnams were doing with Tally Ho. I have a feeling that they were vatting it. Or at least some of it.

Why do I think that? Because sometimes they brewed it twice in a row. With a strong beer such behaviour flags up the possibility that they needed multiple brews to fill a vat. Also the fact that they would blend a quarter or a half barrel of Tally Ho with XX Ale to produce XXXX Ale. It wouldn't be a problem drawing a half barrel off from a vat. Otherwise, where would you be storing such a small quantity of beer?

The recipe hasn't changed much since 1914. The grist is still a combination of pale, mils and crystal malt, plus flaked maize. There has been a change in the sugars, with No. 3 invert being dropped.

Another change is in the hops. They're still a combination of American and Kent hops, but they're older. While in 1914 all the hops were from the previous year, most of those in this brew were two years old. Oregon hops from 1914 and Kent ones from 1914 and 1915. The dry hops are listed as 1916 Kent, which must be a mistake, as this beer was brewed in March 1916.

There's also been a reduction in the gravity, down from 1081° to 1074°.

1916 Adnams Tally Ho		
pale malt	7.75 lb	48.14%
mild malt	4.75 lb	29.50%
crystal malt	0.75 lb	4.66%
flaked maize	0.75 lb	4.66%
No. 2 invert sugar	2.00 lb	12.42%
caramel 5000 SRM	0.10 lb	0.62%
Cluster 120 mins	1.75 oz	
Fuggles 90 mins	1.75 oz	
Fuggles 30 mins	1.75 oz	
Fuggles dry hops	2.00 oz	
OG	1074	
FG	1023	
ABV	6.75	
Apparent attenuation	68.92%	
IBU	70	
SRM	18	
Mash at	153° F	
Sparge at	170° F	
Boil time	120 minutes	
pitching temp	60° F	
Yeast	WLP025 Southwold	

1917 Adnams XX

When this beer was originally brewed, in May 1917, the screws were starting to tighten. Though it was only the start.

That's obvious by the much-reduced gravity, down 1038° in 1916 to just 1024°. But it's slightly more complicated than that. Towards the end of March, just before a new set of restrictions came in, Adnams brewed a couple of batches of Tally Ho. Which they then blended with later brews of XX Ale.

In this case, 6 barrels of Tally Ho at a gravity of 1082° were blended with 43.75 barrels of XX. That would effectively raise the OG to about 1034°. It would also boost the bitterness, as Tally ho was more heavily hopped. If you want to make this beer properly, it means you'll need to brew some Tally Ho, too.

Did Adnams always intend using the Tally Ho for blending or was it just an ad hoc reaction to changed conditions? I can only guess. Though they had been blending XX and Tally Ho to create XXXX for several years.

Other than the gravity drop, recipe is pretty much unchanged and still contains several malts and several sugars. As in 1916, the hops are getting to be on the old side: Oregon from 1915, Kent from 1914, 1915 and, 1916. Accordingly, I've reduced the quantity of hops in the recipe below.

1917 Adnams XX		
pale malt	0.50 lb	8.76%
mild malt	3.50 lb	61.30%
crystal malt 80 L	0.33 lb	5.78%
flaked maize	0.50 lb	8.76%
No. 2 invert sugar	0.33 lb	5.78%
cane sugar	0.50 lb	8.76%
caramel 5000 SRM	0.05 lb	0.88%
Cluster 105 mins	0.50 oz	
Fuggles 60 mins	0.25 oz	
Fuggles 30 mins	0.25 oz	
OG	1027	
FG	1003	
ABV	3.18	
Apparent attenuation	88.89%	
IBU	19	
SRM	20	
Mash at	152° F	
Sparge at	170° F	
Boil time	105 minutes	
pitching temp	61° F	
Yeast	WLP025 Southwold	

1917 Adnams PA

How the mighty have fallen. If you can remember back a few pages, Adnams Pale Ale was a mighty 1060° in 1915. It's gone from Burton IPA strength to just Boy's Bitter in a mere two years. Bet its drinkers enjoyed that.

Adnams other Pale Ale, BLB, had been discontinued by this point. With PA having a gravity of just 1032°, there just wasn't room for a lower-gravity Pale Ale.

The recipe is still very simple: just base malt and No. 2 invert sugar. Though the base malt is now split between pale malt and "medium" malt, which I interpret as mild malt. Not sure how accurate that is. The pale malt was all made from Californian barley.

Some of Adnams beers – PA, BLB and Tally Ho – had a crazy amount of dry hops, 1 pound per barrel. That would be a lot in a high-gravity Stout or Stock Ale. In a beer of this low a gravity it's totally insane. It's almost as much as all the kettle hop combined. Very modern, you could say.

1917 Adnams PA		
pale malt	3.25 lb	48.15%
mild malt	2.50 lb	37.04%
No. 2 invert sugar	1.00 lb	14.81%
Cluster 120 mins	0.75 oz	
Fuggles 90 mins	0.75 oz	
Fuggles 30 mins	0.75 oz	
Fuggles dry hops	2.00 oz	
OG	1032	
FG	1007	
ABV	3.31	
Apparent attenuation	78.13%	
IBU	37	
SRM	6	
Mash at	153° F	
Sparge at	170° F	
Boil time	120 minutes	
pitching temp	60° F	
Yeast	WLP025 Southwold	

1917 Adnams Double Stout

By this phase of the war Adnams was down to a single Stout. BS was discontinued early in 1917 for a pretty obvious reason: Double Stout was forced to drop down to a similar gravity.

This iteration of Double Stout has a gravity two points lower than the final version of BS. The gravity is 12 points lower than it had been a year earlier. At 1040° it's not really "stout" in the original sense of "strong".

In terms of grist, the only real change is a reduction in the proportion of amber malt and a corresponding increase in the base malt. Not sure what the motivation behind that was. Possibly it was connected with the yield from amber malt. Or maybe they just didn't have as much on hand as before. And the No. 2 invert has been dropped.

The hops Oregon and Kent form the 1915 crop, Kent from 1916 and Worcester dry hops from 1916. Other interpretations than mine are possible. For, example, the Worcester dry hops might have been something more like Goldings.

Like most of Adnams beers, Double Stout had quite a high degree of attenuation – over 80%. So I suppose you could call this an early Dry Stout.

1917 Adnams Double Stout		
pale malt	2.50 lb	29.41%
mild malt	2.75 lb	32.35%
amber malt	1.00 lb	11.76%
chocolate Malt	1.00 lb	11.76%
cane sugar	1.00 lb	11.76%
No. 4 invert sugar	0.25 lb	2.94%
Cluster 120 mins	0.75 oz	
Fuggles 90 mins	0.75 oz	
Fuggles 30 mins	0.75 oz	
Fuggles dry hops	0.50 oz	
OG	1040	
FG	1007.5	
ABV	4.30	
Apparent attenuation	81.25%	
IBU	35	
SRM	30	
Mash at	149° F	
Sparge at	170° F	
Boil time	120 minutes	
pitching temp	61° F	
Yeast	WLP025 Southwold	

1917 Adnams Tally Ho

If you're going to brew 1917 Adnams XX authentically, you're also going to need to make this, as the two were blended together.

Oddly, the gravity has increased again to its pre-war level. Though that wasn't to last long as Tally Ho was discontinued later in 1917 when brewing strong beer became practically impossible.

The recipe is little changed from the previous, a little more sugar in this version being the only real difference in the grist. There are several different types of hops, mostly at least a couple of years old: Oregon (1915), Kent (1914, 1915, 1916) and Worcester dry hops (1916). As usual, feel free to interpret these differently to the way I have, which is Cluster and Fuggles.

1917 Adnams Tally Ho		
pale malt	9.00 lb	51.06%
mild malt	4.25 lb	24.11%
crystal malt 60 L	0.75 lb	4.26%
flaked maize	0.75 lb	4.26%
No. 2 invert sugar	2.75 lb	15.60%
caramel 5000 SRM	0.13 lb	0.71%
Cluster 120 mins	1.75 oz	
Fuggles 60 mins	1.75 oz	
Fuggles 30 mins	2.00 oz	
Fuggles dry hops	2.00 oz	
OG	1082	
FG	1014	
ABV	9.00	
Apparent attenuation	82.93%	
IBU	68	
SRM	20	
Mash at	154° F	
Sparge at	170° F	
Boil time	120 minutes	
pitching temp	61° F	
Yeast	WLP025 Southwold	

1918 Adnams XX

When this beer was brewed in May 1918, there were still six months of the war to go. Not that drinkers at the time knew.

It was a particularly disturbing period, as the German spring offensive was in full swing. Equally disheartening for those at home were the ever stricter regulations on brewing and a further slashing of gravities.

By this point Adnams only brewed three different beers: XX, PA and Double Stout. Though I'm not totally sure about the last one. They may only have been brewing a Bitter and Mild. In April 1918, the average gravity of a brewery's beers had been set at 1030°. As Adnams still wanted to brew a reasonable-strength Bitter, that meant dropping XX's gravity well below 1030°. Which explains the pathetic 1022° OG of this version. Even a high degree of attenuation still leaves it basically non-intoxicating.

The recipe, however, is identical to in 1917. In fact, the total weight of the grist, 1,680 lbs., is exactly the same. The only difference being that there was slightly more pale malt and slightly less "medium" malt. Otherwise everything else is exactly the same.

That also includes the hopping rate. If you're wondering why then that the quantities or slightly lower here it's because the hops were older. Oregon and Kent from the 1915 season, Sussex from 1917.

1918 Adnams XX		
pale malt	1.00 lb	22.03%
mild malt	2.25 lb	49.56%
crystal malt 80 L	0.25 lb	5.51%
flaked maize	0.25 lb	5.51%
No. 2 invert sugar	0.50 lb	11.01%
cane sugar	0.25 lb	5.51%
caramel 5000 SRM	0.04 lb	0.88%
Cluster 105 mins	0.25 oz	
Fuggles 90 mins	0.25 oz	
Fuggles 30 mins	0.25 oz	
OG	1022	
FG	1004	
ABV	2.38	
Apparent attenuation	81.82%	
IBU	14	
SRM	17	
Mash at	154° F	
Sparge at	170° F	
Boil time	105 minutes	
pitching temp	61° F	
Yeast	WLP025 Southwold	

1918 Adnams PA

You're only chance of inebriation in an Adnams pub in 1918 was to drink Bitter. Which remained much the same as it had been in 1917.

Almost identical, in fact. The only changes are a little less sugar and a little more base malt. And slightly more hops. Other than that, it's very much the same.

It's interesting to note that not only did PA fare better than XX in terms of strength, it also got better hops. While only a quarter of XX's hops were from the 1917 crop, two-thirds of PA's were. Which is bucking the trend, as, in general, the hops being used got older the longer the war went on.

1918 Adnams PA		
pale malt	3.50 lb	46.67%
mild malt	3.50 lb	46.67%
No. 2 invert sugar	0.50 lb	6.67%
Cluster 120 mins	1.00 oz	
Fuggles 90 mins	1.00 oz	
Fuggles 30 mins	1.00 oz	
Fuggles dry hops	1.75 oz	
OG	1033	
FG	1009	
ABV	3.18	
Apparent attenuation	72.73%	
IBU	50	
SRM	5	
Mash at	154° F	
Sparge at	170° F	
Boil time	120 minutes	
pitching temp	61° F	
Yeast	WLP025 Southwold	

1919 Adnams Double Stout

I'm not 100% sure if Double Stout was discontinued in 1918. Maybe they only brewed it a couple of times and I missed it. But it had definitely returned in April 1919.

It's very similar to the 1917 version, in terms of strength, being just one degree higher. The recipe is similar, too, with the exception of the sugars. Out is CDM, replaced by Mauritius, presumably cane sugar, No. 3 invert and tintose, which I assume is a type of caramel.

The coloured malts have changed a little as well. There's a bit more amber malt and a bit less chocolate malt. Not mind-blowing changes. It looks like they were adapting the recipe to suit the ingredients that were available.

1919 Adnams Double Stout		
pale malt	1.25 lb	13.40%
mild malt	5.00 lb	53.59%
amber malt	1.25 lb	13.40%
chocolate malt	0.50 lb	5.36%
No. 3 invert sugar	0.50 lb	5.36%
cane sugar	0.50 lb	5.36%
caramel 5000 SRM	0.33 lb	3.54%
Cluster 120 mins	0.50 oz	
Fuggles 90 mins	0.75 oz	
Fuggles 30 mins	0.75 oz	
Goldings dry hops	0.50 oz	
OG	1041	
FG	1008	
ABV	4.37	
Apparent attenuation	80.49%	
IBU	29	
SRM	71	
Mash at	150° F	
Sparge at	170° F	
Boil time	120 minutes	
pitching temp	61° F	
Yeast	WLP025 Southwold	

1921 Adnams XX

In 1921 most UK beers took on the form they were to have for the next decade. It's when I consider that the post-war period really began. It's also the year that price controls were abolished.

The war had seen Adnams beer range greatly reduced. It was down do the bare bones: a Bitter, a Mild and a Stout. Some of the discontinued beers made a return, but most disappeared forever. Of the three Milds at the start of the war, X, XX and XXXX, only XX survived. It's the reverse of what happened in London, where before the war only one Mild was brewed and after it there were several.

The 1921 version of XX is about as weak as they could get away with. It's what I'd call a minimum-gravity beer. Because however low the gravity was, you always had to pay the tax as if it were 1027°. Only by having an extremely high degree of attenuation does it scrape over 3% ABV. Which is about the minimum to count as intoxicating.

The grist is simpler than in the war years, with just one type of sugar plus some caramel.

The effect of the war having ended is obvious in the hopping, as not only are there new American hops, there are also some from an area that had been part of Germany until recently, Alsace. It's an even four-way split between Worcester from 1919, Kent from 1920, Oregon from 1918 and 1919 and Alsace from 1919.

1921 Adnams XX		
pale malt	1.00 lb	19.84%
mild malt	2.50 lb	49.60%
crystal malt 80 L	0.25 lb	4.96%
cane sugar	1.25 lb	24.80%
caramel 5000 SRM	0.04 lb	0.79%
Cluster 120 mins	0.25 oz	
Strisselspalt 90 mins	0.25 oz	
Fuggles 60 mins	0.25 oz	
Fuggles 30 mins	0.25 oz	
OG	1026	
FG	1003	
ABV	3.04	
Apparent attenuation	88.46%	
IBU	17	
SRM	17	
Mash at	152° F	
Sparge at	170° F	
Boil time	120 minutes	
pitching temp	59° F	
Yeast	WLP025 Southwold	

1921 Adnams PA

The PA that emerged from the war was basically a totally different beer to the one that entered it. Starting as a full-strength and probably Stock Pale, it ended as a Running Bitter.

It's strength post-war, I'm sure, was determined by what Adnams thought their customers were prepared to pay. Being in a very rural location, that clearly wasn't a huge amount, as what they plumped for was a 6d a pint beer. Whereas most London brewers produced a 7d and an 8d Bitter.

In terms of strength, this iteration of IPA looks very much like the Ordinary Bitters I grew up with.

The grist has changed a little, with No. 2 invert sugar being replaced by No. 1 and the addition of tintose, which is some sort of caramel colouring.

The hops were quite a mix: Worcester (1919), Kent (1920), Oregon (1919), Alsace (1919); Kent (1920) dry hops. As with XX, there are post-war foreign hops. All through the war Adnams had been using Oregon hops from the 1913, 1914 and 1915 crops.

1921 Adnams PA		
pale malt	7.75 lb	90.96%
No. 1 invert sugar	0.75 lb	8.80%
caramel 5000 SRM	0.02 lb	0.23%
Cluster 120 mins	0.75 oz	
Strisselspalt 90 mins	0.50 oz	
Fuggles 60 mins	0.75 oz	
Fuggles 30 mins	0.75 oz	
Goldings dry hops	1.00 oz	
OG	1038	
FG	1007	
ABV	4.10	
Apparent attenuation	81.58%	
IBU	42	
SRM	11	
Mash at	153° F	
Sparge at	170° F	
Boil time	120 minutes	
pitching temp	60° F	
Yeast	WLP025 Southwold	

1921 Adnams XXXX

A sure sign that things were returning to some sort of normality was the reappearance of stronger beers. Adnams XXXX being an example.

Tally Ho, Adnams Strong Ale, disappeared in 1917. Rather than bring that back, they came up with a new Old Ale, XXXX. Which must have confused some drinkers because a few years earlier it had been a strong Mild Ale, created by blending XX Ale and Tally Ho.

Why didn't they just resurrect Tally Ho? It's all to do with the last set of price controls. Anything 1054° and upwards had a maximum price of 9d. It made no economic sense to brew anything much stronger than that. Adnams did eventually bring back Tally Ho, but only after price controls ended in August 1921.

This looks very much like Adnams X Ale on steroids. Which is what many Old Ales from traditional Southern breweries still are. Including Adnams own Old Ale.

As was usual with Adnams, there are two base malts: pale and "medium" which, as usual, I've interpreted as mild malt. Flaked maize has made a return, after being absent at the end of the war. As have standard invert sugars, rather than the weird combinations of cane sugars brewers were forced to use.

An awful lot of Saaz turns up in British beers just after WW I. I think it's because the Central European brewing industry was in such a mess. My guess is that they were quite cheap for the quality.

1921 Adnams XXXX		
pale malt	7.25 lb	60.02%
mild malt	2.50 lb	20.70%
crystal malt	0.50 lb	4.14%
flaked maize	0.50 lb	4.14%
No. 3 invert sugar	1.25 lb	10.35%
caramel 5000 SRM	0.08 lb	0.66%
Cluster 120 mins	0.75 oz	
Fuggles 90 mins	0.75 oz	
Fuggles 60 mins	0.75 oz	
Saaz 30 mins	0.75 oz	
Goldings dry hops	1.00 oz	
OG	1054	
FG	1015	
ABV	5.16	
Apparent attenuation	72.22%	
IBU	42	
SRM	30	
Mash at	152° F	
Sparge at	170° F	
Boil time	120 minutes	
pitching temp	59° F	
Yeast	WLP025 Southwold	

Barclay Perkins

Based on the South bank of the Thames, Barclay Perkins had once been the largest brewery in the world. One of the large Porter brewers of the 18th century, it had diversified into Ales in the middle of the 19th century. Despite that, it had moved down the brewers' league table and had a production well short of giants such as Bass and Guinness.

Barclay Perkins struggled a bit in the 20th century. In 1954, they only brewed 236,166[31] barrels – less than the 235,100 barrels they had in 1810.[32] No surprise, then that in 1955 they "merged" with near neighbours Courage. Barclay's Park Street brewery stopped brewing in 1958. Except for the Lager brewery, which remained open until the early 1970s.

Before WW I Barclay Perkins brewed a huge range of beers. The table below doesn't even include them all – TT (standard Porter) and IBS (Russian Stout) are both missing. And Maybe another Stout or two.

Barclay Perkins beers 1910 - 1914								
Year	Beer	Style	OG	FG	ABV	App. Attenuation	lbs hops/ qtr	hops lb/brl
1914	X	Mild	1051.2	1013.0	5.05	74.57%	5.01	1.04
1910	PA	Pale Ale	1060.2	1014.5	6.05	75.91%	12.80	3.11
1914	XLK (bottling)	Pale Ale	1045.0	1011.6	4.41	74.15%	8.06	1.51
1914	XLK (trade)	Pale Ale	1049.6	1013.3	4.80	73.19%	8.06	1.63
1910	EIP Ex	Porter	1063.5	1020.0	5.75	68.50%	12.00	3.40
1910	RDP	Porter	1068.0	1023.5	5.92	65.81%	8.00	2.54
1914	KK	Stock Ale	1073.1	1023.5	6.59	68.17%	12.00	3.56
1910	KKK	Stock Ale	1087.3	1026.3	8.07	69.86%	14.00	5.33
1910	BS	Stout	1074.1	1027.5	6.16	62.89%	7.73	2.69
1910	BS Ex	Stout	1076.2	1024.0	6.91	68.50%	12.00	4.03
1910	OMS	Stout	1053.2	1016.5	4.86	68.98%	7.50	1.83
Sources: Barclay Perkins brewing record held at the London Metropolitan Archives, document number ACC/2305/1/601, ACC/2305/1/602 and ACC/2305/1/602.								

Unlike most breweries, the number of beers Barclay Perkins brewed doesn't seem to have been reduced by the war:

---

[31] Document ACC/2305/1/711/1 held at the London Metropolitan Archives
[32] "The Brewing Industry in England 1700-1830", Peter Mathias, 1959, pages 551-552.

Barclay Perkins beers 1922 - 1924								
Year	Beer	Style	OG	FG	ABV	App. Atten-uation	lbs hops/qtr	hops lb/brl
1922	Ale	Mild	1028.4	1006.5	2.90	77.11%	7.50	0.92
1924	X	Mild	1043.2	1011.0	4.26	74.54%	5.50	0.96
1924	PA export	Pale Ale	1059.0	1017.0	5.56	71.19%	9.00	2.25
1922	XLK (bottling)	Pale Ale	1040.2	1008.0	4.26	80.10%	8.00	1.27
1922	XLK (trade)	Pale Ale	1047.1	1014.0	4.38	70.28%	8.00	1.52
1924	TT blend	Porter	1026.0	1007.0	2.51	73.08%	16.00	1.11
1924	BS Ex	Stout	1072.5	1024.0	6.42	66.90%	14.00	4.62
1924	BSc	Stout	1066.2	1021.5	5.91	67.52%	8.00	2.43
1924	IBS	Stout	1061.4	1021.0	5.34	65.80%	8.00	2.02
1924	IBS Ex	Stout	1103.4	1040.0	8.39	61.32%	16.00	6.97
1924	RNS	Stout	1055.4	1017.0	5.08	69.31%	7.49	1.77
1923	KK	Strong Ale	1055.2	1016.0	5.19	71.01%	10.00	2.24
1924	KK (bottling)	Strong Ale	1070.0	1019.0	6.75	72.86%	14.00	3.95
1924	KKK	Strong Ale	1082.4	1028.5	7.13	65.41%	14.00	4.71

Sources:
Barclay Perkins brewing record held at the London Metropolitan Archives, document number ACC/2305/1/608, ACC/2305/1/609 and ACC/2305/1/611.

While the war may have reduced gravities, the hopping rates remained very high.

Barclay Perkins beers during WW I								
	X	XLK (trade)	XLK (bottling)	XLK (crate)	KK	PA	GA	4d Ale
Mar 1914	1051.3	1049.9	1045		1073.1	1060.4		
Apr 1915	1050.9	1049.8	1045		1072.9	1060.3		
Apr 1916	1049.6	1049.7	1045					
May 1916	1048.6	1049.7	1045			1058.6		
Oct 1916	1047.8	1049.7	1045			1058.5		
May 1917	1046.7	1049.6	1045	1040				
July 1917	1046.7	1049.6	1045	1036.3			1036.3	
Sep 1917	1046.6	1049.7	1045	1036.2			1036.2	
Oct 1917	1046.6	1049.7	1045	1036	1070.4		1037.9	
Apr 1918		1040.3	1032.5	1025.4				1025.9
Apr 1919		1043.5	1037.4	1030.5				1027.5
June 1919	1039.3	1043.5	1037.4	1030.5				1027.5
July 1919	1040.2	1047.3	1040.4	1034.5				1026.4
Oct 1919	1042.3	1047.4	1040.4	1034.5	1061.3			1028.4
June 1920	1042.4	1047.4	1040.4	1034.4	1055.4			1028.4
Oct 1920	1041.5	1047.4	1040.4	1034.5				1028.4
Feb 1920	1041.5	1047.4	1040.4	1034.5				1028.4

Source:
Brewing logs from the Courage archive in the London Metropolitan Archive.

There's a reason why Barclay Perkins were able to brew so many different beers. In addition to their main brewhouse that was capable of churning out batches of over 1,000 barrels, there was also a smaller one. That had a brew length of between 30 and 150 barrels.

This is what happened to Barclay Perkins two draught Black Beers, TT (Porter) and BS (Brown Stout) during the war years:

Barclay Perkins Porter and Best Stout 1913 - 1922			
month	year	TT	BS
Apr	1913	1046.1	1066.7
Apr	1914	1046.1	1066.7
Oct	1914	1046.1	1071
Apr	1915	1046.1	1066.7
Oct	1915	1046.1	1066.7
Apr	1916	1046.1	1066.7
Oct	1916	1045.1	1064
Apr	1917	1045.1	1066.7
Oct	1917	1045.1	1064
Apr	1918	1036.7	1051.7
Oct	1918	1036.7	1051.7
Apr	1919		1051.7
Oct	1919		1050.8
Apr	1920		1050.8
Oct	1920	1038.5	1050.8
Apr	1921	1037.6	1050.8
Oct	1921	1029.1	1050.8
Apr	1922	1029.1	1050.8
Source: Barclay Perkins brewing records			

Why are there numbers missing for TT? Because it wasn't brewed for almost two years. Its gravity was surprisingly low in 1914. About as weak as London beers got. By the early 1920's it was even weaker, venturing into barely alcoholic territory.

Best Stout, on the other hand, was brewed right through the war and never dropped below 1050. A very respectable gravity for the darkest days of the war. No wonder many switched from Porter to Stout.

1914 Barclay Perkins X Ale

Like most other big London brewers, Barclay Perkins brewed a single Mild Ale at the outbreak of the war.

When they started brewing Ales in the 1830's, they had a full set - X, XX, XXX and XXXX – but the stronger versions were gradually discontinued and by the 1890s only X Ale remained. Though that was their biggest seller.

Barclay Perkins X Ale had evolved a lot since its first appearance in the 1830s. Originally a pale beer, its colour started to darken at the end of the 19th century. At the outbreak of WW I it was about half way through its gradual change to a truly Dark Mild.

The grist is quite unusual in that it includes a dark malt. Most Milds got all their colour from sugar. That's only partially true in this case. Flaked maize features in almost all Barclay Perkins beers of this period.

The hops are a little on the old side: East Kent (1913), Mid-Kent Fuggles (1912 CS), Mid-Kent Goldings (1913), Bavarian Hallertau (1912 CS). Though the oldest ones had been kept in a cold store. Hallertau hops were surprisingly popular in the UK before WW I.

1914 Barclay Perkins X Ale		
pale malt	7.25 lb	68.98%
amber malt	0.75 lb	7.14%
flaked maize	0.50 lb	4.76%
No. 3 invert sugar	2.00 lb	19.03%
caramel 500 SRM	0.01 lb	0.10%
Hallertau 120 mins	0.75 oz	
Fuggles 90 mins	1.00 oz	
Goldings 30 mins	1.00 oz	
OG	1052	
FG	1014	
ABV	5.03	
Apparent attenuation	73.08%	
IBU	34	
SRM	14	
Mash at	152° F	
Sparge at	170° F	
Boil time	120 minutes	
pitching temp	61° F	
Yeast	Wyeast 1099 Whitbread Ale	

1914 Barclay Perkins XLK (trade)

XLK came in two versions, "trade" being the draught version.

This was Barclay Perkins Ordinary Bitter and was produced in considerable quantities. It was first introduced in the 1880's, which was quite late. Initially, only a draught version was brewed.

The grist is typical for the period: around 75% base malt, with the rest made up of flaked maize and brewing sugar. Barclay Perkins started using unmalted adjuncts just about as soon as it was made legal in 1880. Initially, they employed flaked rice, but they swapped to flaked maize in 1899.

The hops are all English: Mid-Kent (1913), East Kent (1913), Worcester (1912 CS) and Mid-Kent Goldings (1912 CS); Worcester (1912 CS) dry hops. Note that all the hops that weren't from the most recent season had been kept in a cold store (that's what the CS means).

1914 Barclay Perkins XLK (trade)		
pale malt	7.50 lb	73.17%
flaked maize	0.75 lb	7.32%
No. 2 invert sugar	1.00 lb	9.76%
glucose	1.00 lb	9.76%
Fuggles 120 mins	1.25 oz	
Fuggles 90 mins	1.00 oz	
Goldings 30 mins	1.00 oz	
Goldings dry hops	0.50 oz	
OG	1050	
FG	1013	
ABV	4.89	
Apparent attenuation	74.00%	
IBU	41	
SRM	6	
Mash at	152° F	
Sparge at	170° F	
Boil time	120 minutes	
pitching temp	59.5° F	
Yeast	Wyeast 1099 Whitbread Ale	

1914 Barclay Perkins XLK (bottling)

Barclay Perkins introduced the bottled version of XLK just before WW I. Presumably to meet the growing demand for bottled beer.

Right from the outset it was always parti-gyled with the draught version and always a few degrees weaker. At first the only real difference with the draught version was that it contained slightly fewer dry hops, 3 ozs. rather than 4 ozs. per barrel.

As this was parti-gyled with the draught version above, all the remarks about that beer's ingredients also apply here.

1914 Barclay Perkins XLK (bottling)		
pale malt	6.75 lb	72.97%
flaked maize	0.75 lb	8.11%
No. 2 invert sugar	0.75 lb	8.11%
glucose	1.00 lb	10.81%
Fuggles 120 mins	1.00 oz	
Fuggles 90 mins	1.00 oz	
Goldings 30 mins	1.00 oz	
Goldings dry hops	0.50 oz	
OG	1045	
FG	1012	
ABV	4.37	
Apparent attenuation	73.33%	
IBU	39	
SRM	6	
Mash at	152° F	
Sparge at	170° F	
Boil time	120 minutes	
pitching temp	59.5° F	
Yeast	Wyeast 1099 Whitbread Ale	

1914 Barclay Perkins PA

Barclay Perkins were relatively late to the Pale Ale game, first brewing one in the 1880s, a couple of decades later than London rivals Whitbread.

Though they did immediately start with two examples, XLK and the stronger PA. The quantities brewed of PA were very modest: around 100 barrels, at a time when they made Mild in batches of 1,000 barrels. Barclay Perkins had more flexibility than other large London brewers because they had a small brew house in addition to their main kit. This is where they brewed PA, a sure indication that it was a low-volume beer. This example was a batch of just 60 barrels.

PA was obviously a posh beer as, unlike its weaker younger brother, XLK, the grist contained no flaked maize. With just pale malt and invert sugar, it's a very simple recipe.

The hops look like they're higher quality than those in XLK. Mid-Kent (1913 CS), East Kent (1913 CS) and Worcester (1913 CS) copper hops plus East Kent (1913 CS) dry hops. It's interesting that all the hops had been kept in a cold store, even though they were from the most recent season.

There was both a draught and bottling version of this brew, the difference being that the latter was much more heavily dry-hopped: the equivalent of 1.24 ozs. for a batch of this size.

1914 Barclay Perkins PA		
pale malt	11.50 lb	85.19%
No. 1 invert sugar	2.00 lb	14.81%
Fuggles 150 mins	2.00 oz	
Fuggles 90 mins	2.00 oz	
Goldings 30 mins	2.00 oz	
Goldings dry hops	0.50 oz	
OG	1062	
FG	1016	
ABV	6.09	
Apparent attenuation	74.19%	
IBU	71	
SRM	7	
Mash at	152° F	
Sparge at	172° F	
Boil time	150 minutes	
pitching temp	58° F	
Yeast	Wyeast 1099 Whitbread Ale	

1914 Barclay Perkins KK

Draught Burton Ale, the type of beer often dubbed KK in the brewhouse, is a weirdly obscure 20th-century beer style.

Why weirdly obscure? Because up until around 1960, it was a ubiquitous sight in London pubs. A couple of decades later and it was almost totally forgotten. It's not uncommon nowadays for it to be confused with Burton Pale, a completely different style of beer.

The original didn't contain mild malt, but SA malt. A type specifically designed with Stock Ale in mind. It produces a less easily fermentable wort, which is what you want in a beer that's going to undergo a long secondary fermentation.

On the other hand, almost 25% of the grist consists of sugar, two types of invert plus a dollop of caramel. The 60 L bit on the crystal malty is a guess. All old records ever say is crystal malt. The exact colour would have depended on which maltster made it.

The hops are Mid-Kent (1914), East Kent (1913 CS), Oregon (1913 CS) and East Kent Goldings (1914) dry hops. All pretty new and lots of them. Which is why the calculated IBUs are so high. Though, as this probably had at least a couple of months conditioning before sale, that bitterness would have mellowed before it hit the glass.

1914 Barclay Perkins KK		
mild malt	6.75 lb	44.73%
pale malt	2.25 lb	14.91%
crystal malt 60 L	1.00 lb	6.63%
flaked maize	1.75 lb	11.60%
No. 2 invert sugar	2.50 lb	16.57%
No. 3 invert sugar	0.75 lb	4.97%
caramel 500 SRM	0.09 lb	0.60%
Cluster 120 mins	0.75 oz	
Fuggles 120 mins	1.75 oz	
Goldings 60 mins	2.50 oz	
Goldings 30 mins	2.50 oz	
Goldings dry hops	1.00 oz	
OG	1073	
FG	1024	
ABV	6.48	
Apparent attenuation	67.12%	
IBU	87	
SRM	19	
Mash at	151° F	
Sparge at	170° F	
Boil time	120 minutes	
pitching temp	59.5° F	
Yeast	Wyeast 1099 Whitbread Ale	

1915 Barclay Perkins Dark Lager

Barclay Perkins had the luxury of owning a small Brewhouse in addition to their main plant. In it they brewed small-batch beers but also experimental brews. This beer falls into the latter category.

Lager was popular enough in London to turn up publicans' price-fixing agreements. But the war presented Lager drinkers with a problem: most of it was imported from Germany or Austria. Some replacement supplies were found in Holland and Denmark, but importing anything became more and more problematic as the war progressed.

Barclay Perkins brewed both a decoction and infusion mash a couple of days apart in March. This is the infusion mash version. I've chosen that for a couple of reasons. One: it's easier for home brewers to do and infusion mash. Also, I don't understand fully what's written in that record. Lastly, it doesn't seem to have gone very well as they didn't get the extract they expected.

The recipe is very simple: two malts and two hops. The latter being Worcester (1914 CS) and Burgundy (1914 CS).

The fermentation was conducted at a proper, cool Lager temperature, never getting above 50° F. After primary fermentation it was racked to an aluminium tank in the cold store, presumably for lagering.

Unusually for Barclay Perkins, the brewing water wasn't treated.

After the war Barclay Perkins built a shiny new Lager brewery and became one of the leading UK brewers of the style.

1915 Barclay Perkins Dark Lager		
pale malt	11.25 lb	91.84%
amber malt	1.00 lb	8.16%
Fuggles 120 mins	1.25 oz	
Strisselspalt 39 mins	1.25 oz	
OG	1053	
FG	1023	
ABV	3.97	
Apparent attenuation	56.60%	
IBU	27	
SRM	6	
Mash at	157° F	
Sparge at	160° F	
Boil time	120 minutes	
pitching temp	45.5° F	
Yeast	Wyeast 2042 Danish lager	

1916 Barclay Perkins X Ale

A couple of years into the war, not much had changed with Barclay Perkins X Ale. Other than a slight fall in gravity.

The grist is much the same as in 1914, though the proportion of invert sugar has declined.

While the hops are starting to get a little on the old side: Mid-Kent (1914, 1915), Kent (1914 CS).

1916 Barclay Perkins X Ale		
pale malt	7.25 lb	68.92%
amber malt	0.75 lb	7.13%
flaked maize	1.00 lb	9.51%
No. 3 invert sugar	1.50 lb	14.26%
caramel 500 SRM	0.02 lb	0.19%
Fuggles 120 mins	0.75 oz	
Fuggles 90 mins	0.50 oz	
Fuggles 30 mins	0.50 oz	
OG	1050.5	
FG	1015	
ABV	4.70	
Apparent attenuation	70.30%	
IBU	22	
SRM	13	
Mash at	152° F	
Sparge at	170° F	
Boil time	120 minutes	
pitching temp	61° F	
Yeast	Wyeast 1099 Whitbread Ale	

1916 Barclay Perkins XLK (trade)

It's still a little early in the war for any dramatic changes, though there have been what look like a few forced changes to the recipe.

For a start, some of the base is now mild malt. Not a huge change, but before the war you'd never see mild malt in a Pale Ale. My guess is that they used it just because they had it. The sugar content has also been modified, No. 3 invert replacing glucose.

The hops look like they were all in good condition, either being fresh or having been kept in a cold store: Mid-Kent (1914 CS, 1915); East Kent (1915 CS) dry hops.

1916 Barclay Perkins XLK (trade)		
pale malt	6.00 lb	55.81%
mild malt	1.75 lb	16.28%
flaked maize	1.00 lb	9.30%
No. 2 invert sugar	1.50 lb	13.95%
No. 3 invert sugar	0.50 lb	4.65%
Fuggles 120 mins	1.00 oz	
Fuggles 60 mins	0.75 oz	
Fuggles 30 mins	0.75 oz	
Goldings dry hops	0.50 oz	
OG	1050	
FG	1012	
ABV	5.03	
Apparent attenuation	76.00%	
IBU	30	
SRM	10	
Mash at	152° F	
Sparge at	170° F	
Boil time	120 minutes	
pitching temp	59.5° F	
Yeast	Wyeast 1099 Whitbread Ale	

1916 Barclay Perkins XLK (bottling)

A couple of years of war have only prompted a few minor changes to XLK.

It was still the same gravity and still parti-gyled with the draught version. The one significant difference is that the bottling versions was no longer dry-hopped. Otherwise the recipe is identical to the draught version above, with which this was parti-gyled.

1916 Barclay Perkins XLK (bottling)		
pale malt	5.25 lb	56.27%
mild malt	1.50 lb	16.08%
flaked maize	0.75 lb	8.04%
No. 2 invert sugar	1.50 lb	16.08%
No. 3 invert sugar	0.33 lb	3.54%
Fuggles 120 mins	0.75 oz	
Fuggles 60 mins	0.75 oz	
Fuggles 30 mins	0.75 oz	
OG	1045	
FG	1008	
ABV	4.89	
Apparent attenuation	82.22%	
IBU	28	
SRM	9	
Mash at	152° F	
Sparge at	170° F	
Boil time	120 minutes	
pitching temp	59.5° F	
Yeast	Wyeast 1099 Whitbread Ale	

1916 Barclay Perkins XLK (Watney)

One of the weirder appearances in the Barclay Perkins records are what appear to be brews for Watney.

It has the same name as one of their own beers – XLK. But that name wasn't unique to Barclay Perkins. Truman also had a beer with the same name. The cheap and cheerful Bitter that, unlike their other Pale Ales, was brewed in London rather than Burton.

As it's different in grist and gravity from either of Barclay Perkins own XLKs, I can only assume that this was being brewed for Watney. Maybe Barclay Perkins had spare capacity. As breweries had were pegged as a percentage of their 1914 output, I'm not sure why they would waste some of that brewing for someone else.

The recipe is quite similar to Barclay's own XLK. That's not a surprise, seeing as they were both brewed for the same London market. Its gravity falls about exactly between those of Barclay's draught and bottled versions.

The hopping is a bit different from Barclay's, though the hops are all still English: Kent (1914 CS, 1915 CS, 1916 and; Worcester (1915 CS) dry hops.

1916 Barclay Perkins XLK (Watney)		
pale malt	6.75 lb	69.80%
flaked maize	1.25 lb	12.93%
No. 2 invert sugar	0.67 lb	6.93%
glucose	1.00 lb	10.34%
Fuggles 120 mins	1.00 oz	
Fuggles 90 mins	0.75 oz	
Goldings 30 mins	0.75 oz	
Goldings dry hops	0.25 oz	
OG	1047	
FG	1012	
ABV	4.63	
Apparent attenuation	74.47%	
IBU	32	
SRM	5	
Mash at	152° F	
Sparge at	170° F	
Boil time	120 minutes	
pitching temp	59.5° F	
Yeast	Wyeast 1099 Whitbread Ale	

1916 Barclay Perkins PA

Drinkers were unaware at the time, but Barclay's Best Bitter wasn't going to be around much longer.

When restrictions started to bite in spring 1917, it was one of the beers to be sacrificed. It didn't reappear until December 1921.

There are three base malts: pale malt, PA malt and mild malt. I was so surprised to see the latter that I had to check to see I wasn't substituting it for something else. It's not an ingredient you see often in Pale Ales, especially top class ones like this.

The hops are all English: East Kent (1915 CS), Kent (1914 CS) and Worcester (1915 CS) dry hops. It leaves quite a bitter beer.

1916 Barclay Perkins PA		
pale malt	7.25 lb	58.00%
mild malt	2.00 lb	16.00%
flaked maize	1.50 lb	12.00%
No. 1 invert sugar	0.75 lb	6.00%
glucose	1.00 lb	8.00%
Fuggles 120 min	2.50 oz	
Goldings 30 mins	2.50 oz	
Goldings dry hops	1.00 oz	
OG	1059	
FG	1018	
ABV	5.42	
Apparent attenuation	69.49%	
IBU	57	
SRM	5	
Mash at	153° F	
Sparge at	170° F	
Boil time	120 minutes	
pitching temp	58° F	
Yeast	Wyeast 1099 Whitbread Ale	

1916 Barclay Perkins KK

KK, Barclay Perkins draught Burton Ale, was left pretty much alone during the war. At least until April 1917, when it was dropped.

The grist is little different from in 1914. There's still over 20% sugar and around 10% flaked maize. Which leaves quite a low percentage of malt. As in 1914, the mild malt is a substitute for SA malt.

The hops are mostly from Kent, with some US West Coast ones. East Kent (1916, 1915 CS), Mid-Kent (1914 CS), Oregon (1915 CS); East Kent (1915 CS) dry hops. All are relatively recent or had been stored cold.

1916 Barclay Perkins KK		
mild malt	2.50 lb	16.04%
pale malt	7.25 lb	46.50%
crystal malt 60 L	0.75 lb	4.81%
flaked maize	1.75 lb	11.23%
No. 2 invert sugar	2.00 lb	12.83%
No. 3 invert sugar	1.25 lb	8.02%
caramel 500 SRM	0.09 lb	0.58%
Cluster 120 mins	1.50 oz	
Fuggles 120 mins	2.00 oz	
Goldings 60 mins	4.00 oz	
Goldings dry hops	0.75 oz	
OG	1076	
FG	1026	
ABV	6.61	
Apparent attenuation	65.79%	
IBU	97	
SRM	19	
Mash at	152° F	
Sparge at	170° F	
Boil time	120 minutes	
pitching temp	59° F	
Yeast	Wyeast 1099 Whitbread Ale	

1917 Barclay Perkins X

When they introduced their gravity-restricted GA, Barclay Perkins didn't immediately drop X Ale. They continued to brew it, parti-gyled with GA for another year.

Though in far smaller quantities than GA. A typical parti-gyle was 1,000 barrels of GA and 200 barrels of X Ale. X continued to have a gravity of 1047° right until it was discontinued.

The biggest difference with the 1916 version above are the dropping of flaked maize and the addition of crystal malt. A change which must have boosted the body. The proportion of invert sugar has also been reduced by around a third.

The hops are all Mid-Kent: 1914 CS, 1915 and 1916. The use of older and older hops is a recurring theme in the later war years.

1917 Barclay Perkins X		
pale malt	7.75 lb	76.84%
amber malt	1.00 lb	9.91%
crystal malt 60 L	0.33 lb	3.27%
No. 3 invert sugar	1.00 lb	9.91%
caramel 500 SRM	0.006 lb	0.06%
Fuggles 120 mins	0.75 oz	
Fuggles 90 mins	0.75 oz	
Fuggles 30 mins	0.75 oz	
OG	1047	
FG	1013	
ABV	4.50	
Apparent attenuation	72.34%	
IBU	28	
SRM	12	
Mash at	152° F	
Sparge at	170° F	
Boil time	120 minutes	
pitching temp	61° F	
Yeast	Wyeast 1099 Whitbread Ale	

1917 Barclay Perkins GA

First ever brew of Barclay Perkins Government Ale. Parti-gyled with the X Ale above.

Government Ale could be viewed as the start of modern Mild Ale. Which it is, really. I see it as the death of pre-war X Ale. The watery shit that replaced it and ultimately brought about its destruction.

1917 Barclay Perkins GA		
pale malt	5.75 lb	74.16%
amber malt	1.00 lb	12.90%
crystal malt 60 L	0.25 lb	3.22%
No. 3 invert sugar	0.75 lb	9.67%
caramel 500 SRM	0.004 lb	0.05%
Fuggles 120 mins	0.75 oz	
Fuggles 90 mins	0.50 oz	
Fuggles 30 mins	0.50 oz	
OG	1036	
FG	1008	
ABV	3.70	
Apparent attenuation	77.78%	
IBU	24	
SRM	10	
Mash at	152° F	
Sparge at	170° F	
Boil time	120 minutes	
pitching temp	61° F	
Yeast	Wyeast 1099 Whitbread Ale	

1917 Barclay Perkins XLK (trade)

It's interesting that even after the first gravity restrictions in April 1917, the draught version of XLK continued to be brewed at its 1914 strength.

Though there have been changes to the grist. Since the 1916 version, the flaked maize has been dropped and there's no longer any mild malt.

The hops are: Mid-Kent (1914 CS, 1915 CS, 1916) and East Kent (1916) dry hops. As you can see, the hops are starting to get older. Though at least all the ones older than the most recent season have been in a cold store.

1917 Barclay Perkins XLK (trade)		
pale malt	10.00 lb	90.91%
No. 2 invert sugar	0.50 lb	4.55%
No. 3 invert sugar	0.50 lb	4.55%
Fuggles 120 mins	1.25 oz	
Fuggles 60 mins	1.25 oz	
Goldings dry hops	0.50 oz	
OG	1050	
FG	1012	
ABV	5.03	
Apparent attenuation	76.00%	
IBU	33	
SRM	8	
Mash at	152° F	
Sparge at	170° F	
Boil time	120 minutes	
pitching temp	58° F	
Yeast	Wyeast 1099 Whitbread Ale	

1917 Barclay Perkins XLK (crate)

In April 1917 Barclay Perkins dropped their bottling version of XLK and replaced it with "crate".

At first I wondered what the hell they meant with crate. Surely all bottled beer was delivered in crates? Then I remembered some old adverts. Where they show a four-quart crate. It's always cheap and cheerful beer being marketed that way. It looks to me like a transitional thing, when having a cask was going out of fashion, but people still wanted to buy in relative bulk.

Which explains a fairly low OG. Weirdly, the type of quart screw-topped bottles they used for crate beer were still around when I lived in Leeds in the later 1970s. I can remember buying Whitbread beer in bottles like that from Mr. Fisher, the bloke who ran the open all hours grocery and offie opposite 97 Brudenell Road. A house I lived in several times.

A forerunner of Light Ale is how I'd describe this. Light Ale being the low-gravity bottled Pale Ale that was all the rage between 1930 and 1970.

This beer was parti-gyled with the "trade" version above, hence all that's recipe notes apply here, too.

1917 Barclay Perkins XLK (crate)		
pale malt	7.25 lb	91.66%
No. 2 invert sugar	0.33 lb	4.17%
No. 3 invert sugar	0.33 lb	4.17%
Fuggles 120 mins	1.00 oz	
Fuggles 60 mins	0.75 oz	
OG	1036	
FG	1008	
ABV	3.70	
Apparent attenuation	77.78%	
IBU	25	
SRM	6	
Mash at	152° F	
Sparge at	170° F	
Boil time	120 minutes	
pitching temp	60.5° F	
Yeast	Wyeast 1099 Whitbread Ale	

1918 Barclay Perkins Ale 4d

April 1918 wasn't a happy time for drinkers. On the first of the month, average OG was pegged at 1030°. And on the 23rd the tax per standard barrel was doubled from 25s to 50s.

This prompted an immediate change in Barclay Perkins Milds. X Ale was discontinued and the gravity of GA slashed from 1036° to 1027°. Its name was changed, too, becoming Ale 4d. This might be connected with the government forbidding the use of the term "Government Ale".

The gravity might have been falling, but the grist looks more interesting. There are no fewer than four malts, including two roasted malts, amber and brown.

The hops are starting to get pretty old: Mid-Kent (1916, 1917) and East Kent (1914 CS). Obviously, that's led me to drop the quantity in the recipe.

1918 Barclay Perkins Ale 4d		
pale malt	3.50 lb	63.18%
amber malt	0.75 lb	13.54%
brown malt	0.25 lb	4.51%
crystal malt 60 L	0.25 lb	4.51%
No. 3 invert sugar	0.75 lb	13.54%
caramel 500 SRM	0.04 lb	0.72%
Fuggles 120 mins	0.25 oz	
Fuggles 60 mins	0.25 oz	
Goldings 30 mins	0.25 oz	
OG	1027	
FG	1006	
ABV	2.78	
Apparent attenuation	77.78%	
IBU	11	
SRM	11	
Mash at	152° F	
Sparge at	170° F	
Boil time	120 minutes	
pitching temp	61° F	
Yeast	Wyeast 1099 Whitbread Ale	

Mini Book Series volume XXXII: Armistice!

1918 Barclay Perkins XLK (trade)

Finally the impact of the war has been felt by Barclay Perkins Ordinary Bitter, XLK.

Though it's not quite as cataclysmic as what happened to their Mild Ale. For a start, XLK still contains enough alcohol to be intoxicating: 4% ABV. Which was a very respectable strength. Remember all a brewery's beer had to average out to 1030°. They had to brew a lot of sub-1030° to maintain that average.

There's been a fair bit of fiddling with the grist, too. The No. 2 invert sugar is gone and there's a rather surprising new addition: amber malt.

The hops aren't as ancient as in Ale 4d, but aren't exactly the freshest, either. Mid-Kent (1915 CS), East Kent (1915 CS, 1917) and East Kent (1917) dry hops.

1918 Barclay Perkins XLK (trade)		
pale malt	7.25 lb	82.86%
amber malt	1.00 lb	11.43%
No. 3 invert sugar	0.50 lb	5.71%
Fuggles 120 mins	1.25 oz	
Fuggles 60 mins	1.25 oz	
Goldings 30 mins	1.25 oz	
Goldings dry hops	0.50 oz	
OG	1040	
FG	1010	
ABV	3.97	
Apparent attenuation	75.00%	
IBU	49	
SRM	9	
Mash at	154° F	
Sparge at	170° F	
Boil time	120 minutes	
pitching temp	60.5° F	
Yeast	Wyeast 1099 Whitbread Ale	

1918 Barclay Perkins XLK (crate)

Here's something new: a sub-1030° Pale Ale.

As you'd expect, it was parti-gyled with the draught version above. Surprisingly, there was more of the stronger version brewed: 473 to 293 barrels. I don't need a calculator to realise that that doesn't average out to 1030°.

Oddly, bottled Pale Ales just a little stronger than this became quite popular between the wars. I guess people had got a taste for them.

1918 Barclay Perkins XLK (crate)		
pale malt	4.50 lb	80.65%
amber malt	0.33 lb	5.91%
No. 3 invert sugar	0.75 lb	13.44%
Fuggles 120 mins	0.50 oz	
Fuggles 60 mins	0.50 oz	
Goldings 30 mins	0.25 oz	
OG	1026	
FG	1007	
ABV	2.51	
Apparent attenuation	73.08%	
IBU	18	
SRM	8	
Mash at	154° F	
Sparge at	170° F	
Boil time	120 minutes	
pitching temp	60.5° F	
Yeast	Wyeast 1099 Whitbread Ale	

Mini Book Series volume XXXII: Armistice!

1919 Barclay Perkins X Ale

The war may have been over, but 1919 wasn't a drinkers' paradise. But at least X Ale had returned.

This is the very first brew, on 26th May, of the resurrected X Ale. A full ten gravity points weaker than the final 1917 version. Barclay Perkins would never brew a Mild Ale as strong as that again.

26th May this beer was brewed. It's no coincidence that X Ale returned at this date. Three days earlier the average OG was raised from 1040° to 1044°. Making stronger beers more feasible. Like X Ale. Surely not coincidentally, average OG between the wars was around 1043°.

One thing that it has retained is its complicated wartime grist. There are five different grains, including two unmalted ones. The roast barley is the most interesting. In particular, the way it was administered: all in the second copper. Meaning that it probably added more colour than my brewing software calculated. It's a typical Barclay Perkins technique. They usually boiled some of the black malt (or roasted barley) when brewing Porter and Stout.

The hops are quite a rarity. Mid Kent from 1917 and 1918. Two seasons when very few hops were grown in the UK.

1919 Barclay Perkins X Ale		
pale malt	4.75 lb	60.36%
amber malt	1.00 lb	12.71%
brown malt	0.33 lb	4.19%
roast barley	0.02 lb	0.25%
flaked maize	0.75 lb	9.53%
No. 3 invert sugar	1.00 lb	12.71%
caramel 500 SRM	0.02 lb	0.25%
Fuggles 75 mins	0.75 oz	
Fuggles 30 mins	0.50 oz	
OG	1037	
FG	1009	
ABV	3.70	
Apparent attenuation	75.68%	
IBU	16	
SRM	13	
Mash at	152° F	
Sparge at	170° F	
Boil time	75 minutes	
pitching temp	61° F	
Yeast	Wyeast 1099 Whitbread Ale	

1919 Barclay Perkins Ale 4d

The return of X Ale didn't doom Ale 4d to oblivion. If only because there was still a cap on the average gravity of the beer a brewery produced.

Fourpenny Ale was surprisingly resilient between the wars. Probably not unconnected from loads of people having bugger all money. 4d Ale was the beer for someone who couldn't afford to drink. Or get drunk. Because, let's face it, you weren't going to get plastered on this. Unless you were a gnat.

See the X Ale above, with which this beer was parti-gyled, for notes on the recipe.

1919 Barclay Perkins Ale 4d		
pale malt	4.00 lb	63.55%
amber malt	0.75 lb	11.92%
brown malt	0.25 lb	3.97%
roast barley	0.03 lb	0.48%
flaked maize	0.50 lb	7.94%
No. 3 invert sugar	0.75 lb	11.92%
caramel 500 SRM	0.014 lb	0.22%
Fuggles 75 mins	0.50 oz	
Fuggles 30 mins	0.50 oz	
OG	1029.5	
FG	1007	
ABV	2.98	
Apparent attenuation	76.27%	
IBU	13	
SRM	10	
Mash at	152° F	
Sparge at	170° F	
Boil time	75 minutes	
pitching temp	61° F	
Yeast	Wyeast 1099 Whitbread Ale	

1919 Barclay Perkins XLK (trade)

As well as the return of X Ale, 1919 saw an increase in the gravity of Barclay Perkins remaining Pale Ales.

Though the recipe does look rather odd. In particular, the 13% No. 3 invert. That's an awful lot for a Pale Ale. Though they have dropped the amber malt that was in the 1918 version. You can see the impact of all that dark sugar in the SRM value of 10. That's very dark for this type of beer. I can only assume that was deliberate. As drinkers tended to identify a darker beer with higher strength.

Then there's the mild malt that makes up 50% of the base. You wouldn't expect to see that in a Bitter, either. Barclay Perkins did this now and again during the war years. Presumably because they had more than they needed to brew their Mild.

The return to normalcy in transatlantic trade is reflected in the reappearance of flaked maize. Barclay Perkins had been big fans of it before the war and returned it to their grists as soon as they could.

The hops are all English: Mid Kent (1915 CS, 1917, 1918) and East Kent (1916 CS) dry hops, so mostly quite old.

1919 Barclay Perkins XLK (trade)		
pale malt	3.75 lb	39.47%
mild malt	3.75 lb	39.47%
flaked maize	0.75 lb	7.89%
No. 3 invert sugar	1.25 lb	13.16%
Fuggles 90 mins	1.00 oz	
Fuggles 30 mins	1.00 oz	
Goldings dry hops	0.50 oz	
OG	1044	
FG	1008	
ABV	4.76	
Apparent attenuation	81.82%	
IBU	23	
SRM	10	
Mash at	153° F	
Sparge at	170° F	
Boil time	90 minutes	
pitching temp	60.5° F	
Yeast	Wyeast 1099 Whitbread Ale	

1919 Barclay Perkins XLK (bottling)

Unlike the draught version, bottling XLK didn't increase in gravity in the spring of 1919. It remained at its 1918 level. Not sure why that might be.

Note the shorter boil time. Barclay reduced the time of their boils in the summer of 1918, from 120 minutes to 75 to 90 minutes. This was in order to reduce coal consumption. In didn't last that long. In 1921 they increased them again to 120 minutes or more.

The degree of attenuation of all three versions of XLK is very high. I suppose the brewery wanted to get as much alcohol into them as it could. Pre-war it had been 75-80%.

1919 Barclay Perkins XLK (bottling)		
pale malt	3.25 lb	39.39%
mild malt	3.25 lb	39.39%
flaked maize	0.75 lb	9.09%
No. 3 invert sugar	1.00 lb	12.12%
Fuggles 90 mins	1.00 oz	
Fuggles 30 mins	0.75 oz	
OG	1037.5	
FG	1006	
ABV	4.17	
Apparent attenuation	84.00%	
IBU	22	
SRM	9	
Mash at	153° F	
Sparge at	170° F	
Boil time	90 minutes	
pitching temp	60.5° F	
Yeast	Wyeast 1099 Whitbread Ale	

1919 Barclay Perkins XLK (crate)

This is confusing. The OG of the draught and crate versions both increased in the spring of 1919, while the bottling version remained unchanged.

At least the crate XLK has now returned to the intoxication fold, weighing in now at a mighty 3.4% ABV. The 1918 version was just 2.5% ABV. What a party that must have been, when the stronger XLK appeared for the first time.

1919 Barclay Perkins XLK (crate)		
pale malt	2.50 lb	38.46%
mild malt	2.50 lb	38.46%
flaked maize	0.50 lb	7.69%
No. 3 invert sugar	1.00 lb	15.38%
Fuggles 90 mins	0.75 oz	
Fuggles 30 mins	0.75 oz	
OG	1030.5	
FG	1005	
ABV	3.37	
Apparent attenuation	83.61%	
IBU	19	
SRM	9	
Mash at	153° F	
Sparge at	170° F	
Boil time	90 minutes	
pitching temp	60.5° F	
Yeast	Wyeast 1099 Whitbread Ale	

1919 Barclay Perkins KK

Towards the end of 1919, Barclay's draught Burton Ale, returned after an absence of around two and a half years. There was, however, quite a large drop in its gravity.

It must have been a testing time for drinkers, when your favourite tipple could disappear overnight. Especially when it was forever. Whitbread, for example never brewed a really strong Stout again.

The word that springs to minds when looking at this grist is "complicated". Though it is very similar to the one from early 1917. There is one substitution: mild malt instead of SA malt. You could also just use more pale malt.

As was typical ion this period, most of the hops are on the old side, with only a quarter from the most recent season. Mid-Kent (1916 CS, 1917 CS, 1918 CS), Oregon (1916 CS) and Mid-Kent (1915 CS) dry hops. There's a reason why not many English hops from 1918 turn up in brewing records: there weren't very many of them.

1919 Barclay Perkins KK		
mild malt	3.75 lb	28.69%
pale malt	5.50 lb	42.08%
crystal malt 60 L	0.50 lb	3.83%
flaked maize	1.25 lb	9.56%
No. 2 invert sugar	1.00 lb	7.65%
No. 3 invert sugar	1.00 lb	7.65%
caramel 500 SRM	0.07 lb	0.54%
Cluster 120 mins	0.25 oz	
Fuggles 120 mins	1.75 oz	
Fuggles 60 mins	2.00 oz	
Fuggles dry hops	0.50 oz	
OG	1061	
FG	1021	
ABV	5.29	
Apparent attenuation	65.57%	
IBU	50	
SRM	15	
Mash at	152° F	
Sparge at	170° F	
Boil time	120 minutes	
pitching temp	59.5° F	
Yeast	Wyeast 1099 Whitbread Ale	

1921 Barclay Perkins X Ale

X Ale was one of the mainstays of Barclay Perkins range. By 1921 it had attained the form it would have for the remainder of the decade. As XX Ale after 1931, it lasted much like this until WW II.

Barclay Perkins were unusual in having Mild Ales with fairly complex malt. In addition to pale and crystal malt, there was also amber malt. Amber malt had been in the recipe since 1909, but the crystal malt was only added in late 1916, around six months before X Ale was discontinued.

This beer was made in the small brew house as a "Special brew with Australian malt". Which explains why there's no SA malt as part of the base, but all pale malt.

The hops were mostly pretty new: Mid Kent 1920 and Pacific 1920, both kept in a cold store. There were also some Alsace hops from 1917. Which means they were grown when the region was still part of Germany.

Unusually for a Barclay Perkins Mild, it doesn't appear to have been primed.

1921 Barclay Perkins X Ale		
pale malt	5.75 lb	64.25%
amber malt	1.00 lb	11.17%
crystal malt 60 L	0.50 lb	5.59%
flaked maize	1.00 lb	11.17%
No. 3 invert sugar	0.67 lb	7.49%
caramel 500 SRM	0.03 lb	0.34%
Alsace 90 mins	0.25 oz	
Cluster 60 mins	1.00 oz	
Fuggles 30 mins	0.75 oz	
OG	1041.5	
FG	1010	
ABV	4.17	
Apparent attenuation	75.90%	
IBU	31	
SRM	11	
Mash at	151° F	
Sparge at	170° F	
Boil time	90 minutes	
pitching temp	60.5° F	
Yeast	Wyeast 1099 Whitbread Ale	

1921 Barclay Perkins Ale 5d

Barclays continued to brew a low-gravity Mild similar to wartime Government Ale. There must have been a market for it, albeit a relatively small one. It was brewed in much smaller quantities than X Ale.

They weren't the only brewery to do so. Whitbread had a similar beer called MA (presumably standing for Mild Ale). These beers struggled on between the wars, with sales slipping every year and eventually petered out early in WW II.

As this was parti-gyled with X Ale, obviously it had the same recipe. Though not the same as the X Ale above, which was a special brew. If you fancy brewing the standard X Ale recipe, just scale this one up to an OG of 1043°.

The hops are exactly the same as in X Ale.

1921 Barclay Perkins Ale 5d		
pale malt	2.50 lb	40.92%
mild malt	1.25 lb	20.46%
amber malt	0.75 lb	12.27%
crystal malt 60 L	0.33 lb	5.40%
flaked maize	1.00 lb	16.37%
brown sugar	0.01 lb	0.16%
No. 3 invert sugar	0.25 lb	4.09%
caramel 500 SRM	0.02 lb	0.33%
Strisselspalt 75 mins	0.25 oz	
Cluster 60 mins	0.50 oz	
Fuggles 30 mins	0.50 oz	
OG	1029.5	
FG	1007	
ABV	2.98	
Apparent attenuation	76.27%	
IBU	16	
SRM	9	
Mash at	152° F	
Sparge at	170° F	
Boil time	75 minutes	
pitching temp	62° F	
Yeast	Wyeast 1099 Whitbread Ale	

1921 Barclay Perkins XLK (trade)

When PA was discontinued in the middle of the war, XLK became Barclay Perkins' only Pale Ale. Though, as it came in a couple of different forms, there were still technically three Pale Ales.

The draught version remained the strongest of the three. At 1047.5°, this beer is only a couple of gravity points weaker than it had been in 1914. Something you could not say about many beers in the early 1920s.

Replacing some of the No. 3 invert with No. 2 invert is the biggest change to the recipe since 1919. That and dropping mild malt.

As with most of their beers of this period, the hops are a combination of Mid Kent and Pacific, mostly from the most recent harvest (1920).

1921 Barclay Perkins XLK (trade)		
pale malt	8.00 lb	76.15%
flaked maize	1.50 lb	14.28%
No. 2 invert sugar	0.67 lb	6.38%
No. 3 invert sugar	0.33 lb	3.14%
caramel 500 SRM	0.005 lb	0.05%
Cluster 90 mins	0.75 oz	
Fuggles 60 mins	1.00 oz	
Fuggles 30 mins	1.00 oz	
Fuggles dry hops	0.50 oz	
OG	1047.5	
FG	1010	
ABV	4.96	
Apparent attenuation	78.95%	
IBU	38	
SRM	7.5	
Mash at	152° F	
Sparge at	170° F	
Boil time	90 minutes	
pitching temp	60.5° F	
Yeast	Wyeast 1099 Whitbread Ale	

1921 Barclay Perkins XLK (bottling)

The bottling version of XLK has also increased in gravity since 1919, this time by three points. Happy days for drinkers.

Otherwise, there's not much to say. Being parti-gyled with the trade version above, the recipe is identical. Except for the dry hopping. I'm pretty sure the bottled beer wasn't dry hopped. It's not totally clear on this particular brewing record.

1921 Barclay Perkins XLK (bottling)		
pale malt	7.00 lb	77.73%
flaked maize	1.25 lb	13.88%
No. 2 invert sugar	0.50 lb	5.55%
No. 3 invert sugar	0.25 lb	2.78%
caramel 500 SRM	0.005 lb	0.06%
Cluster 90 mins	0.50 oz	
Fuggles 60 mins	0.75 oz	
Fuggles 30 mins	0.75 oz	
OG	1040.5	
FG	1009.5	
ABV	4.10	
Apparent attenuation	76.54%	
IBU	28	
SRM	6	
Mash at	152° F	
Sparge at	170° F	
Boil time	90 minutes	
pitching temp	60.5° F	
Yeast	Wyeast 1099 Whitbread Ale	

1921 Barclay Perkins XLK (crate)

Not wanting to be left out, the crate version of XLK has also had its gravity boosted by four points since 1919.

Even though this wasn't included in the parti-gyle for the above draught and bottled versions, this beer did have an identical recipe. Why change things when you don't need to?

Like Ale 5d, crate XLK was brewed in relatively small quantities compared to the other two XLK variants. But it didn't last as long as Ale 5d, being discontinued sometime in the early 1920s.

1921 Barclay Perkins XLK (crate)		
pale malt	5.50 lb	73.31%
flaked maize	1.00 lb	13.33%
No. 2 invert sugar	0.67 lb	8.93%
No. 3 invert sugar	0.33 lb	4.40%
caramel 500 SRM	0.002 lb	0.03%
Cluster 135 mins	0.50 oz	
Fuggles 45 mins	0.75 oz	
Fuggles 30 mins	0.75 oz	
OG	1034.5	
FG	1006.5	
ABV	3.70	
Apparent attenuation	81.16%	
IBU	29	
SRM	7	
Mash at	152° F	
Sparge at	170° F	
Boil time	135 minutes	
pitching temp	60.5° F	
Yeast	Wyeast 1099 Whitbread Ale	

1921 Barclay Perkins PA

PA, Barclay's flagship Pale Ale, disappeared in the middle of the war. And didn't return until 1921. I suspect that, initially at least, it was a beer destined purely for export.

I say that for a couple of reasons. First, it was produced in tiny quantities: this batch was just 27.5 barrels. Secondly, in some of the records from a little later it specifically says "PA export". When a domestic version of PA did return, that had an OG of 1052.6°.

The recipe is extremely simple: pale malt and No. 1 invert sugar. Which is another reason this beer shouts export at me: classy ingredients. The grist is slightly more complicated than it appears from the recipe, part of the base being PA malt, the best-quality type of pale malt.

The hops continue the classy theme: East Kent from the 1921 crop, Mid Kent from 1920 and Saaz, also from 1920. All had been kept in a cold store. The dry hops are East Kent (1921).

It looks very much like the domestic PA from 1914. That too was brewed from just pale malt and No. 1 invert sugar. Though the proportion of malt is higher here, and the hopping a little less heavy.

1921 Barclay Perkins PA		
pale malt	11.75 lb	90.32%
No. 1 invert sugar	1.26 lb	9.68%
Fuggles 150 mins	1.50 oz	
Saaz 90 mins	1.50 oz	
Goldings 60 mins	2.00 oz	
Goldings dry hops	0.50 oz	
OG	1059.5	
FG	1018	
ABV	5.49	
Apparent attenuation	69.75%	
IBU	60	
SRM	6	
Mash at	149° F	
Sparge at	172° F	
Boil time	150 minutes	
pitching temp	58° F	
Yeast	Wyeast 1099 Whitbread Ale	

1921 Barclay Perkins KK

KK fared exceptionally well in the early war years. The OG actually increased a couple of points after 1914. In February 1917 it had the impressive gravity of 1075.7°. But that was just before it was dropped, in reaction to the restrictions on brewing implemented in April 1917.

It didn't reappear until the end of 1919, when it had an OG of 1061°. Quite a bit lower than in 1917, but still a powerful beer. A couple of years later the effect of price control is obvious: it has just over the 1054° minimum OG for a beer retailing for 9d per pint.

The grist isn't a million miles away from the X Ale one, though KK lacks amber malt. Smaller breweries, such as Fuller, for example, often parti-gyled their Burton and Mild Ales. Not Barclay Perkins: their Burtons were always brewed single-gyle. That was the joy of having multiple brew houses. Their less popular beers were brewed in the smaller brew house. Though this particular beer was brewed in the large brewhouse, in a batch just shy of 900 barrels.

The No. 3 invert is a substitute for something called "new mix". I've absolutely no idea what that might be. No. 3 just seemed like a good guess.

The hops much like those for their other beers: Mid Kent from 1919 and 1920, plus Pacific from 1920, all of which had been in a cold store. The dry hops were East Kent from 1921.

1921 Barclay Perkins KK		
pale malt	5.75 lb	48.42%
mild malt	3.25 lb	27.37%
crystal malt 60 L	0.50 lb	4.21%
flaked maize	1.00 lb	8.42%
No. 3 invert sugar	1.25 lb	10.53%
caramel 500 SRM	0.125 lb	1.05%
Cluster 120 mins	1.50 oz	
Fuggles 60 mins	1.50 oz	
Fuggles 30 mins	1.50 oz	
Goldings dry hops	0.50 oz	
OG	1055	
FG	1016	
ABV	5.16	
Apparent attenuation	70.91%	
IBU	87	
SRM	16	
Mash at	152° F	
Sparge at	170° F	
Boil time	120 minutes	
pitching temp	59° F	
Yeast	Wyeast 1099 Whitbread Ale	

1921 Barclay Perkins KK (bottling)

With price controls abolished at the end of the summer, Barclays were able to bring back a rather stronger beer. Which they did, in the form of a bottled Burton Ale. Sold as Southwarke Olde Ale, it was one of their standard products throughout the interwar years.

Pre-war, they brewed two Burton Ales: KK and KKK, at gravities of $1073°$ and $1087°$, respectively. Though it looks as though the latter may have been discontinued before the start of the war as my last sighting of it in the brewing records is in 1910.

The recipe does differ from the draught version of KK, most notably in the use of No. 2 rather than No. 3 invert sugar. Otherwise, there's a bit more crystal malt and a bit less flaked maize, but it's not an enormous difference.

In the original, the base malt was mostly SA malt with about 25% mild malt. I've substituted more mild malt for the SA malt.

The hopping is heavy, both in the copper and in cask. The hops were either very fresh or about a year old and kept in a cold store. Accordingly, I didn't reduce the rate by much.

1921 Barclay Perkins KK (bottling)		
mild malt	11.50 lb	74.92%
crystal malt 50 L	1.00 lb	6.51%
flaked maize	1.25 lb	8.14%
No. 2 invert sugar	1.50 lb	9.77%
caramel 500 SRM	0.10 lb	0.65%
Fuggles 120 mins	4.00 oz	
Saaz 60 mins	2.00 oz	
Goldings 30 mins	2.00 oz	
Saaz dry hops	0.50 oz	
Goldings dry hops	0.50 oz	
OG	1070	
FG	1024.5	
ABV	6.02	
Apparent attenuation	65.00%	
IBU	86	
SRM	15	
Mash at	152° F	
Sparge at	170° F	
Boil time	120 minutes	
pitching temp	58° F	
Yeast	Wyeast 1099 Whitbread Ale	

1921 Barclay Perkins BS Exp

This was definitely an export beer. Written in red at the top of the record it says "For exportation only".

I assume that's because of the strength. It would have been uneconomical to brew this beer for the domestic market due to the price controls that were still in place. You could only charge a maximum of 9d per pint for anything with a gravity over 1054°. The domestic version of BS was 1055°, exactly what you would expect, as that was the most profitable gravity to brew to.

Interestingly, it says "Sterax lined casks", presumably meaning the casks it was racked into for maturation. It's one of the few pieces of evidence I've come across for lined casks being used in the UK.

The grist is pretty complicated, with five malts. Though what's missing caught my eye: flaked maize, which was a standard ingredient in their Ales. There is, however, a small quantity of oats. Presumably so they could sell some of it as Oatmeal Stout. It's not clear from the brewing record what form they were in, malted or flaked. The latter would be my guess.

The mild malt in the recipe is my substitution for SA malt. The pale malt was PA malt in the original. I thought it was odd having PA malt – the highest quality pale malt – in a Stout. But there's a note next to it saying that it was used in error and should have been SA malt.

Some of the roasted malt – 0.25 quarters of the 3.5 quarters in total – was added in the copper. It was usual for Barclay Perkins to throw some of the black malt into the copper for their Stouts. I assume that it's for colour.

There's only one sugar and that's No. 3. Surprisingly, there's no caramel, which turns up in most of their beers.

The real FG would have been lower as I'm sure this beer underwent a long secondary fermentation.

Almost forgot to mention that it's very heavily hopped. The hops were all pretty fresh so I saw no reason to knock down the hopping rate. Though the maturation period that I'm sure this beer underwent would have reduced bitterness levels by the time the beer was consumed.

1921 Barclay Perkins BS Exp		
mild malt	7.25 lb	46.40%
pale malt	1.25 lb	8.00%
brown malt	1.25 lb	8.00%
black malt	1.25 lb	8.00%
amber malt	2.00 lb	12.80%
oats	0.125 lb	0.80%
No. 3 invert sugar	2.50 lb	16.00%
Cluster 120 mins	1.50 oz	
Saaz 120 mins	1.50 oz	
Fuggles 60 mins	3.00 oz	
Fuggles 30 mins	3.00 oz	
Fuggles dry hops	1.00 oz	
OG	1072	
FG	1025	
ABV	6.22	
Apparent attenuation	65.28%	
IBU	105	
SRM	44	
Mash at	148° F	
Sparge at	172° F	
Boil time	120 minutes	
pitching temp	59° F	
Yeast	Wyeast 1099 Whitbread Ale	

1921 Barclay Perkins IBS

The war had an impact on all beers. Even such special ones as Barclay's Imperial Russian Stout, which is the retail name of IBS.

The classic OG of Russian Stout is around 1100°, considerably more than the 1064° of this version. But it has to be borne in mind that when it was brewed, price controls were still in effect. Which, as the top band started at 1054°, there was a huge financial disincentive to brew anything much stronger. Given that constraint, I'm surprised the gravity is as high as 1064

The grist is typical of a strong London Stout, where in addition to brown malt and roast barley, there's also amber malt. You have to look very closely at Barclay Perkins brewing records because sometimes used roast malt – i.e. black malt – and at others roasted barley, as in this case.

The mild malt base is my substitution for SA malt. Unlike BS Exp, IBS does contain flaked maize.

Most of the hops were Mid-Kent and Pacific hops from the 1920 crop. However, as quarter were Mid-Kent from 1915. They must have been some leftover hops they wanted to use up.

1921 Barclay Perkins IBS		
mild malt	7.00 lb	45.16%
brown malt	1.50 lb	9.68%
amber malt	1.75 lb	11.29%
roast barley	1.50 lb	9.68%
flaked maize	1.75 lb	11.29%
No. 3 invert sugar	1.75 lb	11.29%
caramel 500 SRM	0.25 lb	1.61%
Cluster 120 mins	1.50 oz	
Fuggles 60 mins	1.00 oz	
Fuggles 30 mins	1.50 oz	
Fuggles dry hops	0.25 oz	
OG	1064	
FG	1020	
ABV	5.82	
Apparent attenuation	68.75%	
IBU	57	
SRM	41	
Mash at	150° F	
Sparge at	172° F	
Boil time	120 minutes	
pitching temp	58.5° F	
Yeast	Wyeast 1099 Whitbread Ale	

1922 Barclay Perkins BS

The domestic version of BS – I'm not sure if at this point it still stood for Brown Stout or if it had become Best Stout – was, at 1055°, more the gravity that you'd expect from a 1920s London draught Stout.

Most London breweries – especially the ones that had made their name brewing Porter – had similar beers. The gravity obviously being set by the last set of price controls. 1055° puts it at the minimum OG for a beer in the 9d per pint class.

Surprisingly, as Barclay Perkins were enthusiastic users of both, there's neither adjuncts nor sugar in the grist. Well, apart from roast barley. Oh, hang on a minute. On the brewing record it says in red ink "Special all malt brew for yeast". That explains it, then. I wonder if drinkers noticed anything special about this batch?

The hops were a little on the old side, but had all been kept in a cold store: Mid Kent from 1919 and 1920, Pacific from 1920.

1922 Barclay Perkins BS		
mild malt	9.00 lb	69.23%
brown malt	1.00 lb	7.69%
amber malt	1.00 lb	7.69%
crystal malt 60 L	1.00 lb	7.69%
roast barley	1.00 lb	7.69%
Cluster 120 mins	1.75 oz	
Fuggles 60 mins	1.50 oz	
Fuggles 30 mins	1.75 oz	
OG	1055	
FG	1017	
ABV	5.03	
Apparent attenuation	69.09%	
IBU	74	
SRM	27	
Mash at	154° F	
Sparge at	170° F	
Boil time	120 minutes	
pitching temp	60° F	
Yeast	Wyeast 1099 Whitbread Ale	

1922 Barclay Perkins RNS

Barclay Perkins continued to brew a confusingly large range of Stouts. Including RNS, which I assume was brewed for the Royal Navy.

The recipe is very similar to the BS above, the major difference being the presence of No. 3 invert sugar in this recipe. Though, as that BS was a special all-malt brew, this is probably much like the standard BS recipe.

The hops are notable for all being reasonably old. There are none from the most recent season, 1921, the freshest being from 1920. Mid Kent 1919 and 1920 CS, plus Pacific 1920. At least they had all been kept in a cold store. Even reducing the quantities to account for that age, it still comes out at 54 (calculated) IBUs.

1922 Barclay Perkins RNS		
mild malt	6.50 lb	52.00%
brown malt	0.75 lb	6.00%
amber malt	1.00 lb	8.00%
crystal malt 60 L	1.00 lb	8.00%
roast barley	1.25 lb	10.00%
No. 3 invert sugar	2.00 lb	16.00%
Cluster 135 mins	1.25 oz	
Fuggles 60 mins	1.25 oz	
Fuggles 30 mins	1.25 oz	
OG	1057	
FG	1019	
ABV	5.03	
Apparent attenuation	66.67%	
IBU	54	
SRM	34	
Mash at	154° F	
Sparge at	170° F	
Boil time	135 minutes	
pitching temp	60° F	
Yeast	Wyeast 1099 Whitbread Ale	

1921 Barclay Perkins BS S

Here's a very special beer. A special experimental brew of an "Irish Stout type". What makes this beer specifically Irish in style? It's because of the blending.

It's clear from the brewing record that they were making a Stout the Guinness way. All of Guinness's products contained three elements: fresh beer, old beer and headings. The latter was a high-gravity wort 24 hours into fermentation, so effectively a sort of Kräusen.

Exactly the same was happening here. At racking time about 10% old beer was blended in. Half the batch got BBS Ex (1080°) the other half IBS Ex (1102°). Four days after racking half a gallon per 36-gallon barrel of fermenting BS wort (1055°) was added to the casks. The additions would have raised the effective OGs to 1054° and 1056°.

Blending aside, this brew is also notable for being all malt. Well, apart from the roast barley. And I've just spotted the note saying that the water was untreated. That's really unusual. Barclay Perkins normally treated the water for all their beers. They were quite sophisticated, having one treatment regime for Mild Ale, one for Pale Ales, one for Burton Ales and one for Porter and Stout.

At 24%, the proportion of roasted grains is pretty high. Though actually a bit less than in most of their other Stouts.

1921 Barclay Perkins BS S		
pale malt	3.00 lb	25.00%
mild malt	6.00 lb	50.00%
brown malt	1.25 lb	10.42%
amber malt	1.00 lb	8.33%
roast barley	0.75 lb	6.25%
Cluster 120 mins	1.50 oz	
Fuggles 90 mins	1.25 oz	
Fuggles 30 mins	1.25 oz	
Fuggles dry hops	0.50 oz	
OG	1051	
FG	1016	
ABV	4.63	
Apparent attenuation	68.63%	
IBU	63	
SRM	22	
Mash at	150° F	
Sparge at	172° F	
Boil time	120 minutes	
pitching temp	61° F	
Yeast	Wyeast 1099 Whitbread Ale	

1922 Barclay Perkins BBS Export

Strongest of all Barclay's Stouts at this point was BBS Ex, a beer that looks, because of it high gravity, like a genuine export beer.

I'm surprised not just by how many Stouts they produced, but also how varied their grists were. They all contain a couple of common elements: brown and amber malt, also quite often some SA or mild malt. A couple contain crystal malt and the odd one flaked maize. Some contain black malt but other roast barley. All in all, they're quite a diverse bunch.

Here, unusually, the sugar is No. 2 rather than No. 3 invert. It seems an odd choice. There's no caramel, either, meaning most of the colour comes from the dark malts. At almost 30% of the grist, there are certainly plenty of them.

The hopping is extremely heavy: just over 5 lbs per barrel, 14 lbs per quarter of malt. That's about double the hopping rate of their Pale Ales. A third of the hops were East Kent from 1921. The rest were Mid Kent and Saaz, both from 1919. All the hops had been kept in a cold store.

1922 Barclay Perkins BBS Export		
pale malt	5.50 lb	30.56%
mild malt	4.50 lb	25.00%
brown malt	2.00 lb	11.11%
amber malt	1.50 lb	8.33%
black malt	2.00 lb	11.11%
No. 2 invert sugar	2.50 lb	13.89%
Fuggles 150 mins	3.25 oz	
Saaz 90 mins	3.25 oz	
Goldings 30 mins	3.75 oz	
Goldings dry hops	1.00 oz	
OG	1080	
FG	1028	
ABV	6.88	
Apparent attenuation	65.00%	
IBU	104	
SRM	53	
Mash at	148° F	
Sparge at	172° F	
Boil time	150 minutes	
pitching temp	60.5° F	
Yeast	Wyeast 1099 Whitbread Ale	

Boddington

Based in Manchester, Boddington's was a medium-sized provincial brewery. But a successful one that managed to survive until the 1990s.

Before the war they produced a wide range of beers: 3 Milds, 3 Pale Ales, a Porter and a Strong Ale. By 1921 it was down to just four: Mild, Bitter, Stout and Strong Ale. Something similar happened at most breweries in the UK.

This was their range in 1914:

Beer	Style	OG	FG	ABV	App. Attenuation	lbs hops/ qtr	hops lb/brl
IP	IPA	1053	1016	4.89	69.81%	4.00	1.35
B	Mild	1037	1010	3.57	72.97%	2.86	0.51
BB	Mild	1048	1016	4.23	66.67%	3.28	0.88
XXX	Mild	1051	1015	4.76	70.59%	3.67	0.99
AK	Pale Ale	1044	1013	4.10	70.45%	2.92	0.57
PA	Pale Ale	1046	1014	4.23	69.57%	3.33	0.97
Stout	Stout	1054	1018	4.76	66.67%	3.10	0.94
CC	Strong Ale	1062	1020	5.56	67.74%	3.53	1.18
Source: Boddington brewing record held at Manchester Central Library, document number M693/405/126.							

Which by the early 1920s had been whittled down to just this:

Beer	Style	OG	FG	ABV	App. Attenuation	lbs hops/ qtr	hops lb/brl
IP	IPA	1049	1015	4.50	69.39%	5.29	1.54
XX	Mild	1034	1010	3.18	70.59%	6.17	1.19
Stout	Stout	1050.3	1014	4.80	72.14%	5.63	1.52
CC	Strong Ale	1057	1018	5.16	68.42%	5.16	1.64
Source: Boddington brewing record held at Manchester Central Library, document number M693/405/127.							

The drop in gravity in the surviving beers is quite small: 4 points in the case of IPA, 4.7 points for Stout and 5 points for CC. The biggest drop has been for Mild, but that's hard to quantify because none of the three pre-war Milds remained. 1034° is weak for a 1920s standard Mild.

1913 Boddington XXX

This recipe is intended to give you an idea about what Mild was like before the great catastrophe of WW I.

Having first become acquainted with the beers of the big London brewers, I was in for a surprise when I looked into provincial brewers. By the eve of war, they mostly brewed a single Mild in London. But it was a decent strength, somewhere in the low 1050's. Whereas outside the capital multiple Milds were still being brewed, but many of them were comparatively weak.

XXX was Boddington's top-of-the-range Mild. But, despite having the designation XXX, it was only about the same strength as a London X Ale. Though that still makes it far more powerful than any Mild sold after WW I. 1917 was a the last year of 1050° Mild Ale.

The grist is fairly simple, as most were at the time. It's just pale malt, flaked maize and sugar. In the recipe, I have the sugar down as No. 2 invert. In reality I've no idea what type it was. The log just records it as sugar. No. 2 invert is a neutral bet. It could have been No. 3, but I doubt it. Even in the 1980's Boddies Mild wasn't very dark. It only looked dark in comparison to their straw-coloured Bitter.

The original contained no less than six different hops in the copper and another three as dry hops. One of the copper hops and one of the dry hops were Californian, the rest were English. At least as far as I can tell. The handwriting is pretty scrawly. They all look like grower names, so that's what I've assumed. Using American hops for dry hopping is quite unusual. As they didn't like the flavour much, they were mostly used at the start of the boil.

The attenuation is a bit rubbish. Though it should be borne in mind that the FG I've listed was the racking gravity and it was a cask-conditioned beer. The FG by the time it was served would have been lower.

1913 Boddington XXX		
pale malt	10.25 lb	87.23%
flaked maize	1.00 lb	8.51%
No. 2 invert sugar	0.50 lb	4.26%
Cluster 90 mins	0.50 oz	
Fuggles 60 mins	0.50 oz	
Fuggles 30 mins	0.50 oz	
Cluster dry hops	0.25 oz	
OG	1052	
FG	1017	
ABV	4.63	
Apparent attenuation	67.31%	
IBU	21	
SRM	6	
Mash at	152° F	
Sparge at	168° F	
Boil time	90 minutes	
pitching temp	62° F	
Yeast	Wyeast 1318 London ale III (Boddingtons)	

1914 Boddington B

I used to think that low-gravity Milds didn't exist until WW I. But I've now realised that wasn't true.

My perceptions were distorted by only having looked at large London breweries, whose Milds were untypically strong. Outside London there were sub-1040° Milds well before the war. Boddington B being a good example.

This was Boddington's weakest Mild. Looking at it just the recipe, I'd struggle to identify which period it was brewed in. It looks very much like a 1930's Mild in terms of strength. It could even be 1950's Mild at the strong end of the spectrum.

It must have been a bit of a shock for provincial Mild drinkers if they visited London. An X Ale in the capital was usually over 5% ABV and there was no weaker alternative, if you wanted to drink Mild. X Ale was the only Mild they brewed.

There's not a great deal to the grist, just pale malt, flaked maize and sugar. As the type of sugar isn't specified, I've hedged my bets and plumped for No. 2 invert. It really could be anything. Though, as it appears they used the same sugar in all their beers, I doubt it was anything very dark.

Most of Boddington's beers at this time contained Californian hops, but, for some reason, this has Bohemian hops instead. Which I've interpreted as Saaz. Some of the dry hops were Californian, but all the rest were English. I've guessed Fuggles, but some or all Goldings would be fine, too.

1914 Boddington B		
pale malt	6.50 lb	78.79%
flaked maize	1.25 lb	15.15%
No. 2 invert sugar	0.50 lb	6.06%
Fuggles 140 mins	0.50 oz	
Fuggles 60 mins	0.25 oz	
Saaz 30 mins	0.25 oz	
Cluster dry hops	0.13 oz	
Fuggles dry hops	0.13 oz	
OG	1037	
FG	1010	
ABV	3.57	
Apparent attenuation	72.97%	
IBU	13	
SRM	5	
Mash at	153° F	
Sparge at	168° F	
Boil time	140 minutes	
pitching temp	63° F	
Yeast	Wyeast 1318 London ale III (Boddingtons)	

1914 Boddington BB

Boddington still produced a range of Mild Ales on the eve of WW I: B, BB and XXX. How long would that last?

I mention that because of what happened in the later years of the brewery. Their 1980's brewing records are some of the most boring I've come across. They brewed just two beers: Bitter and Mild. What joy it was after the closure of the Oldham Brewery to find two new beers in the records.

Though there may be more beers in the 1914 records, there is a certain residual dullness to them. There's very little difference between the recipes, which are all pale malt, flaked maize and an unspecified type of sugar. Only their Stout contained anything in the way of coloured malt.

BB, as you would expect, is just a slightly amplified version of B. The combination of a higher OG and a relatively low degree of attenuation must have resulted in quite a full beer. Quite different to what Mild Ale became after the war.

The same caveats apply as for B. I've no real idea what the sugar was and all I know about the hops is that they were English and Californian.

1914 Boddington BB		
pale malt	8.00 lb	80.00%
flaked maize	1.00 lb	10.00%
No. 2 invert sugar	1.00 lb	10.00%
Cluster 140 mins	0.50 oz	
Fuggles 60 mins	0.50 oz	
Fuggles 30 mins	0.50 oz	
Cluster dry hops	0.25 oz	
Fuggles dry hops	0.125 oz	
OG	1047	
FG	1015	
ABV	4.23	
Apparent attenuation	68.09%	
IBU	25	
SRM	7	
Mash at	152° F	
Sparge at	168° F	
Boil time	140 minutes	
pitching temp	63° F	
Yeast	Wyeast 1318 London ale III (Boddingtons)	

1914 Boddington Stout

This is going to be a real treat. A Boddington beer with several types of malt. You must be so excited.

In 1903, Boddington still produced two Stouts: SS (Single Stout) and DS (Double Stout) at 1052° and 1069°, respectively. It looks like they dropped the latter and renamed SS simply Stout.

There's no way that you could have called a beer with a gravity of just 1054° a Stout in 1914. Whitbread's Porter, for example, was 1052° in 1914. Which has got me thinking more about Porter and its fate. It's looking more and more as if, rather than disappearing, Porters were just relabelled as Stouts.

Let's crack on with the grist, which is pretty exciting but also includes a big problem. The percentage of base pale malt is pretty low, only a third of the grist. Two other malts make up most of the rest: amber and high-dried. The percentage of amber malt is very high, making me wonder if this might be a diastatic form. Then there's the high-dried.

I really don't know what the best substitute for this malt is. I'm tempted to go with a dark Munich malt, but I'm really not sure how close that is. If you have a better idea, let me know.

The sugar in this beer is something described as "UI". At least UI think that's what it says. The handwriting is pretty bad. I've replaced it with No. 3 invert. Though it might have been something closer to No. 4 invert.

As with all Boddingtons records, the logs only tell me that the hops were English and Californian.

1914 Boddington Stout		
pale malt	4.25 lb	34.55%
black malt	0.05 lb	0.41%
amber malt	3.50 lb	28.46%
high dried malt	3.50 lb	28.46%
No. 3 invert sugar	0.75 lb	6.10%
caramel 2000 SRM	0.25 lb	2.03%
Cluster 185 mins	0.50 oz	
Fuggles 90 mins	0.50 oz	
Fuggles 60 mins	0.50 oz	
Fuggles 30 mins	0.50 oz	
OG	1054	
FG	1018	
ABV	4.76	
Apparent attenuation	66.67%	
IBU	29	
SRM	36	
Mash at	150° F	
Sparge at	168° F	
Boil time	135 minutes	
pitching temp	63° F	
Yeast	Wyeast 1318 London ale III (Boddingtons)	

1914 Boddington AK

At the outbreak of WW I Boddington produced three Pale Ales, of which AK was the weakest.

I have a bit of an obsession with AK, you might recall. It's strange to think now of just how excited I was when I saw my first AK brewing record (Fullers, if you're interested). Even now, after seeing dozens of AKs from several different breweries, it still sends a certain frisson down my spine when I spot one.

The grist is pretty damn simple, just pale malt, flaked maize and a little sugar. Though there were two different types of pale malt, 20 quarters from UK barley, 3 quarters from foreign barley. As you can see, this grist produces a very pale beer.

I've knocked down the hopping by about a fifth because some hops were from the 1910 and 1912 season. Not that there were a great deal of hops to start with. Weirdly, AK is less bitter than most of Boddington's Milds. The hops were a combination of English and Bohemian in the copper and English and Californian in the cask. I've interpreted them as Fuggles, Saaz and Cluster.

Not really much else to say about this very light beer.

1914 Boddington AK		
pale malt	8.50 lb	85.00%
flaked maize	1.25 lb	12.50%
No. 2 invert sugar	0.25 lb	2.50%
Fuggles 185 mins	0.25 oz	
Fuggles 90 mins	0.25 oz	
Fuggles 60 mins	0.25 oz	
Saaz 30 mins	0.25 oz	
Cluster dry hops	0.125 oz	
Fuggles dry hops	0.125 oz	
OG	1044	
FG	1013	
ABV	4.10	
Apparent attenuation	70.45%	
IBU	13	
SRM	5	
Mash at	156° F	
Sparge at	168° F	
Boil time	165 minutes	
pitching temp	63° F	
Yeast	Wyeast 1318 London ale III (Boddingtons)	

1914 Boddington PA

PA was the middle of Boddington's three Pale Ales. But only a couple of gravity points stronger than AK.

What's the point in that? Was my immediate reaction. Until I looked a little more closely. Then I noticed that PA was about twice as heavily hopped as AK. Now that's interesting.

The grist is very similar to AK's. The only difference is that there's a bit more sugar and pale malt and a bit less maize. To be honest, all of Boddington's grists, other than the one for Stout, all look pretty similar. I'm finding it very hard to pin down what makes one beer a Mild and another a Bitter.

The hop varieties are my best guess again. A combination of English and Californian hops is all I know for sure. Feel free to sub out the Fuggles with any English hop that was around at that time.

1914 Boddington PA		
pale malt	8.50 lb	85.00%
flaked maize	1.00 lb	10.00%
No. 2 invert sugar	0.50 lb	5.00%
Cluster 185 mins	0.50 oz	
Fuggles 90 mins	0.50 oz	
Fuggles 60 mins	0.50 oz	
Fuggles 30 mins	0.50 oz	
Cluster dry hops	0.25 oz	
Fuggles dry hops	0.125 oz	
OG	1046	
FG	1014	
ABV	4.23	
Apparent attenuation	69.57%	
IBU	30	
SRM	5	
Mash at	152° F	
Sparge at	168° F	
Boil time	165 minutes	
pitching temp	63° F	
Yeast	Wyeast 1318 London ale III (Boddingtons)	

1914 Boddington IP

The strongest of Boddies Pale Ales was their IPA. And it's a beer that you might well have drunk.

Because IP was the brewhouse name for Boddington's Bitter, right through until the brewery closed. Though, obviously, it's not what a style Nazi would consider an IPA. Then again, they can eff off. Most of them know bugger all about the real history of IPA.

The proportions of pale malt, flaked maize and sugar are very similar to those of PA. Fittingly, it has the highest hopping rate of 4 lbs per quarter of malt. But that's very low. To put that into context, in 1917 Whitbread's IPA contained 12 lbs of hops per quarter[33] and Kidd's BB 14lbs[34]. That's a hell of a difference.

Which confuses the hell out me because in the 1970's Boddington's Bitter was renowned for being very Bitter. Though, glimpsing forward to the late 1930's, I can see that their hopping rates had about doubled.[35] I must run a 1970's recipe through BeerSmith and see how many IBUs it had.

As with all these Boddington recipes, the hops and the sugar type are a guess.

1914 Boddington IP		
pale malt	10.50 lb	87.50%
flaked maize	1.00 lb	8.33%
No. 2 invert sugar	0.50 lb	4.17%
Cluster 185 mins	0.75 oz	
Fuggles 90 mins	0.75 oz	
Fuggles 60 mins	0.75 oz	
Fuggles 30 mins	0.75 oz	
Cluster dry hops	0.25 oz	
Fuggles dry hops	0.50 oz	
OG	1053	
FG	1016	
ABV	4.89	
Apparent attenuation	69.81%	
IBU	43	
SRM	6	
Mash at	152° F	
Sparge at	168° F	
Boil time	205 minutes	
pitching temp	63° F	
Yeast	Wyeast 1318 London ale III (Boddingtons)	

---

[33] Whitbread brewing record held at the London Metropolitan Archives, document number LMA/4453/D/01/082.
[34] Kidd brewing record held at the London Metropolitan Archives, document number ACC/305/16/013.
[35] Boddington brewing record held at Manchester Central Library, document number M693/405/129.

1914 Boddington CC

The strongest beer that Boddington produced was CC. Though it doesn't look super-strong by, say, London standards.

A draught London Strong Ale had an OG in the mid-1070°'s at the start of the war. CC is quite a way short of that. A poor degree of attenuation leaves at just 5.5% ABV.

It's difficult to say very much about Boddington grists as, Stout excepted, they're all pretty much the same: pale malt, sugar and flaked maize. I suppose it made stock management easy, using so few different ingredients.

1914 Boddington CC		
pale malt	12.00 lb	87.27%
flaked maize	1.00 lb	7.27%
No. 2 invert sugar	0.75 lb	5.45%
Cluster 170 mins	0.50 oz	
Fuggles 90 mins	0.50 oz	
Fuggles 60 mins	0.50 oz	
Fuggles 30 mins	0.50 oz	
Cluster dry hops	0.25 oz	
Fuggles dry hops	0.25 oz	
OG	1062	
FG	1020	
ABV	5.56	
Apparent attenuation	67.74%	
IBU	27	
SRM	7	
Mash at	152° F	
Sparge at	168° F	
Boil time	170 minutes	
pitching temp	63° F	
Yeast	Wyeast 1318 London ale III (Boddingtons)	

1915 Boddington XXX

A year into the war and Boddington's top of the range Mild Ale was still a reasonably potent beer. It's only lost three gravity points.

The only change to the recipe is the dropping of flaked maize.

The hopping, as always with Boddington, is pretty complicated. And there are lots of old hops: English (1911, 1912, 1913 and 1914) and Californian (1913) copper hops plus English (1914) & Californian (1913) dry hops. I've reduced the hops to reflect the age of most of them.

1915 Boddington XXX		
pale malt	11.00 lb	97.78%
No. 2 invert sugar	0.25 lb	2.22%
Cluster 150 mins	0.50 oz	
Fuggles 90 mins	0.50 oz	
Fuggles 30 mins	0.50 oz	
Fuggles dry hops	0.125 oz	
Cluster dry hops	0.125 oz	
OG	1049	
FG	1015	
ABV	4.50	
Apparent attenuation	69.39%	
IBU	23	
SRM	5	
Mash at	153° F	
Sparge at	168° F	
Boil time	150 minutes	
pitching temp	63° F	
Yeast	Wyeast 1318 London ale III (Boddingtons)	

1915 Boddington B

Boddie's bargain-basement Mild has dropped three gravity points since 1914. And dropped the flaked maize.

Not much more to say about this run-of-the-mill beer. I'm not insulting it by saying that. It's clearly an everyday drinking beer for the working man. Nothing wrong with that. I'd finish a punishing day sweeping the bus garage floor with several pints if Tetley's Mild, which was about the same strength as B.

I'm rambling, The hops in the original were English (1911, 1912, 1914), Californian (1914), Poperinge (1914); English (1914) & Californian (1914) dry hops.

1915 Boddington B		
pale malt	7.50 lb	96.77%
No. 2 invert sugar	0.25 lb	3.23%
Strisselspalt 155 mins	0.50 oz	
Fuggles 60 mins	0.50 oz	
Fuggles dry hops	0.25 oz	
OG	1034	
FG	1008	
ABV	3.44	
Apparent attenuation	76.47%	
IBU	14	
SRM	4	
Mash at	152° F	
Sparge at	168° F	
Boil time	155 minutes	
pitching temp	62° F	
Yeast	Wyeast 1318 London ale III (Boddingtons)	

1915 Boddington BB

There's been even less change with Boddington's Double Mild. Just 1 degree of gravity.

But the (calculated) bitterness has fallen quite a bit. Partially due to the use of hops of all ages. Some up to four years old. Bit of a recurring theme, that, especially in the later war years. Old hops.

For those as obsessively interested in the minutiae as me, the hops were: English (1911, 1912, 1913, 1914), Californian (1914); English (1914) & Californian (1914) dry hops

1915 Boddington BB		
pale malt	9.25 lb	97.37%
No. 2 invert sugar	0.25 lb	2.63%
Cluster 165 mins	0.50 oz	
Fuggles 60 mins	0.50 oz	
Fuggles 30 mins	0.50 oz	
Fuggles dry hops	0.25 oz	
Cluster dry hops	0.125 oz	
OG	1046	
FG	1015	
ABV	4.10	
Apparent attenuation	67.39%	
IBU	19	
SRM	5	
Mash at	154° F	
Sparge at	168° F	
Boil time	165 minutes	
pitching temp	62.5° F	
Yeast	Wyeast 1318 London ale III (Boddingtons)	

1915 Boddington Stout

It didn't start the war that "stout" at just 1054° - only just above average gravity. The war hasn't made it any stronger.

Not much change with the grist, which remains quite complex with four types of malt. The - as always - calculated IBUs (based on a few assumptions about the effect of ageing) are almost halved. Whatever that might mean. Pretty sure this one was less bitter than the 1914 version.

But probably quite thick might all that dark malt and the fairly low attenuation.[36]

1915 Boddington Stout		
pale malt	3.25 lb	30.09%
black malt	0.05 lb	0.46%
amber malt	3.25 lb	30.09%
high dried malt	3.25 lb	30.09%
No. 3 invert sugar	0.75 lb	6.94%
caramel 2000 SRM	0.25 lb	2.31%
Cluster 130 mins	0.33 oz	
Strisselspalt 90 mins	0.33 oz	
Fuggles 60 mins	0.33 oz	
OG	1046	
FG	1017	
ABV	3.84	
Apparent attenuation	63.04%	
IBU	15	
SRM	36	
Mash at	153° F	
Sparge at	168° F	
Boil time	130 minutes	
pitching temp	63° F	
Yeast	Wyeast 1318 London ale III (Boddingtons)	

---

[36] Thank Stalin. That's the last beer description done. My adjective drawer is empty, my pen dry. My mouth, too. I need a beer. Dolores – where did you put the Amstel Bock?

1915 Boddington AK

One year into the war and its effect was already visible. Not only has the OG fallen, but there have also been changes to the recipe.

It's not a huge modification: just the dropping of the flaked maize. I assume that wasn't voluntary. Otherwise the grist is identical.

The hops are also quite similar to 1914, but mostly old. English from 1911, 1912, 1913 and 1914, Poperinghe and Californian from 1913; English (1914) & Californian (1913) dry hops. It was typical; of the war years that older and older hops were used.

1915 Boddington AK		
pale malt	8.50 lb	97.14%
No. 2 invert sugar	0.25 lb	2.86%
Cluster 165 mins	0.50 oz	
Fuggles 60 mins	0.50 oz	
Fuggles 30 mins	0.50 oz	
Fuggles dry hops	0.125 oz	
Cluster dry hops	0.125 oz	
OG	1039	
FG	1010	
ABV	3.84	
Apparent attenuation	74.36%	
IBU	24	
SRM	4	
Mash at	155° F	
Sparge at	168° F	
Boil time	155 minutes	
pitching temp	63° F	
Yeast	Wyeast 1318 London ale III (Boddingtons)	

1915 Boddington IP

IP was one of a few beers that Boddington brewed right through the war. Although it took a big gravity hit.

Even as early as 1915, it had already shed seven gravity points. Which was narrowing the gap in strength between it and the weaker AK.

1915 Boddington IP		
pale malt	10.25 lb	97.62%
No. 2 invert sugar	0.25 lb	2.38%
Cluster 145 mins	0.50 oz	
Fuggles 60 mins	0.75 oz	
Fuggles 30 mins	0.75 oz	
Fuggles dry hops	0.25 oz	
Cluster dry hops	0.25 oz	
OG	1046	
FG	1017	
ABV	3.84	
Apparent attenuation	63.04%	
IBU	28	
SRM	5	
Mash at	154° F	
Sparge at	168° F	
Boil time	145 minutes	
pitching temp	63° F	
Yeast	Wyeast 1318 London ale III (Boddingtons)	

1915 Boddington CC

During the war years CC remained Boddington's strongest beer. Though by 1915 it had shed a couple of gravity points.

As with all of Boddington's beers, the flaked maize had disappeared from the grist. Leaving it about as simple as it could be: just base malt and sugar.

As is often the case with Boddington, there's a long list of hops: English (1911, 1912, 1913 and 1914) and Californian (1914)copper hops, plus English (1914) and Californian (1914) dry hops.

1915 Boddington CC		
pale malt	12.50 lb	94.34%
No. 2 invert sugar	0.75 lb	5.66%
Cluster 130 mins	0.67 oz	
Fuggles 90 mins	0.67 oz	
Fuggles 30 mins	0.67 oz	
Fuggles dry hops	0.25 oz	
Cluster dry hops	0.25 oz	
OG	1059	
FG	1019	
ABV	5.29	
Apparent attenuation	67.80%	
IBU	28	
SRM	7	
Mash at	156° F	
Sparge at	168° F	
Boil time	130 minutes	
pitching temp	63° F	
Yeast	Wyeast 1318 London ale III (Boddingtons)	

1917 Boddington AK

In February 1917 Boddington was still brewing AK, which was the weakest of their three Pale Ales at the start of the war. But that wouldn't last much longer. It disappeared after April 1917, when the real downward pressure on beer gravity began.

What happened to it? It's a familiar tale. When the gravity of their top-of-the-range Pale Ale, IP was forced down to around the same level as AK, there was no place for the latter to go. Put simply, it was muscled out of its gravity spot by a posher beer.

Up until this point, AK hadn't fared too badly, only having its gravity reduced by about 10%. The grist is much the same as all Boddington's beers: pale malt and sugar. Though flaked maize, which wasn't present in the 1915 version, has reappeared. I've no idea what the sugar was. No. 2 invert is just my best guess.

There are five different types of copper hops in the original: English (1914, 1915, 1916), Californian (1915), Poperinge (1915); plus English (1916) and Californian (1915) dry hops. A mixture of new and older, English and foreign.

1917 Boddington AK		
pale malt	8.00 lb	91.43%
flaked maize	0.50 lb	5.71%
No. 2 invert sugar	0.25 lb	2.86%
Cluster 135 mins	0.25 oz	
Strisselspalt 135 mins	0.25 oz	
Fuggles 90 mins	0.50 oz	
Fuggles 30 mins	0.50 oz	
Goldings dry hops	0.25 oz	
Cluster dry hops	0.125 oz	
OG	1039	
FG	1017	
ABV	2.91	
Apparent attenuation	56.41%	
IBU	22	
SRM	4	
Mash at	152° F	
Sparge at	168° F	
Boil time	135 minutes	
pitching temp	62° F	
Yeast	Wyeast 1318 London ale III (Boddingtons)	

1917 Boddington CC

Another beer taking its final bow in 1917 was Boddington's Strong Ale, CC. Though not forever, in its case, as it only disappeared for around a year between late 1917 and late 1918. While AK was lost forever.

It's still much the same beer as in 1915. Lots of pale malt and a touch of sugar. Just like the rest of their beers. I sometimes struggle to see what separates the different styles in their range as the Pale Ales and Milds have very similar recipes.

CC didn't have quite as many different hops as AK, just four copper hops, English (1914, 1915, 1916) and Californian (1915); then English (1916) and Californian (1915) dry hops.

1917 Boddington CC		
pale malt	12.75 lb	96.23%
No. 2 invert sugar	0.50 lb	3.77%
Cluster 180 mins	0.75 oz	
Fuggles 90 mins	0.75 oz	
Fuggles 30 mins	0.75 oz	
Goldings dry hops	0.125 oz	
Cluster dry hops	0.375 oz	
OG	1059	
FG	1018	
ABV	5.42	
Apparent attenuation	69.49%	
IBU	33	
SRM	6	
Mash at	157° F	
Sparge at	168° F	
Boil time	180 minutes	
pitching temp	64° F	
Yeast	Wyeast 1318 London ale III (Boddingtons)	

1917 Boddington XX (24th April)

XX was a new Mild Ale that Boddington introduced sometime in the second half of 1916. By the middle of 1917, it was the only Mild they were brewing, B, BB and XXX all having been dropped.

And they brewed lots of it. Apart from the occasional brew of IP and Stout it was about all Boddington brewed for a while. The original 1916 version had an OG of 1041°, but by spring 1917 it was down to 1037°. It still had a good bit of falling to do before the war was over.

The recipe is as dull as all of Boddington's: base malt, flaked maize and an undefined type of sugar.

1917 Boddington XX (24th April)		
pale malt	7.25 lb	85.29%
flaked maize	1.00 lb	11.76%
No. 2 invert sugar	0.25 lb	2.94%
Strisselspalt 140 mins	0.50 oz	
Fuggles 90 mins	0.50 oz	
Fuggles 30 mins	0.50 oz	
Fuggles dry hops	0.125 oz	
Cluster dry hops	0.125 oz	
OG	1037	
FG	1011	
ABV	3.44	
Apparent attenuation	70.27%	
IBU	19	
SRM	4	
Mash at	154° F	
Sparge at	168° F	
Boil time	140 minutes	
pitching temp	62.5° F	
Yeast	Wyeast 1318 London ale III (Boddingtons)	

1917 Boddington Stout (25th April)

The quantities of Stout Boddington brewed were quite modest, but at least it still had a reasonable gravity.

And it retained the, for Boddington, ridiculously complicated grist containing four different types of malt. As well as sugar and quite a large amount of caramel. The latter providing a good bit of the colour.

In contrast, the hops were simpler than was usually the case with Boddington: English (1914), Californian (1915) and Poperinge (1914). Though they were all pretty old.

1917 Boddington Stout (25th April)		
pale malt	4.00 lb	35.40%
black malt	0.05 lb	0.44%
amber malt	3.25 lb	28.76%
high dried malt	3.25 lb	28.76%
No. 3 invert sugar	0.50 lb	4.42%
caramel 2000 SRM	0.25 lb	2.21%
Strisselspalt 145 mins	0.50 oz	
Fuggles 90 mins	1.00 oz	
OG	1048	
FG	1016	
ABV	4.23	
Apparent attenuation	66.67%	
IBU	20	
SRM	35	
Mash at	152° F	
Sparge at	168° F	
Boil time	145 minutes	
pitching temp	63° F	
Yeast	Wyeast 1318 London ale III (Boddingtons)	

1917 Boddington XXX (1st May)

By the spring of 1917, things were starting to get difficult with regard to raw materials. Leading to more gravity cuts. XXX has lost six gravity points since 1915.

Though, oddly enough, flaked maize has reappeared in the recipe. I doubt it will be there much longer, now the U-boats are causing havoc in the North Atlantic.

The hopping is as complicated as ever: English (1914, 1915 and 1916), Californian (1915), Poperinge (1914) copper hops, plus English (1916) and Californian (1915) dry hops. Once again, a majority of the hops are quite old. It wasn't going to get any better as UK hop production slumped in 1917 and 1918.

1917 Boddington XXX (1st May)		
pale malt	8.50 lb	89.47%
flaked maize	0.75 lb	7.89%
No. 2 invert sugar	0.25 lb	2.63%
Strisselspalt 145 mins	0.25 oz	
Cluster 145 mins	0.25 oz	
Fuggles 90 mins	0.75 oz	
Fuggles 30 mins	0.75 oz	
Fuggles dry hops	0.250 oz	
Cluster dry hops	0.125 oz	
OG	1043	
FG	1013	
ABV	3.97	
Apparent attenuation	69.77%	
IBU	27	
SRM	5	
Mash at	152° F	
Sparge at	168° F	
Boil time	145 minutes	
pitching temp	64° F	
Yeast	Wyeast 1318 London ale III (Boddingtons)	

1917 Boddington IP (7th May)

By late spring 1917 Boddington was brewing a very narrow range of beers. Mostly, it was just XX Ale. The brews of their stronger beers were getting few and far between.

If you're starting to wonder what the difference is between Boddington XXX, a Mild Ale, and Boddington IP, a Bitter, you're not the only one. The recipes are as near as dammit identical. And the beers had exactly the same hopping rate. The only difference I can see is the slightly more Californian and slightly fewer Poperinge hops. It's minimal.

1917 Boddington IP (7th May)		
pale malt	9.00 lb	90.00%
flaked maize	0.75 lb	7.50%
No. 2 invert sugar	0.25 lb	2.50%
Strisselspalt 145 mins	0.125 oz	
Cluster 145 mins	0.375 oz	
Fuggles 90 mins	0.75 oz	
Fuggles 30 mins	0.75 oz	
Fuggles dry hops	0.25 oz	
Cluster dry hops	0.125 oz	
OG	1044	
FG	1015	
ABV	3.84	
Apparent attenuation	65.91%	
IBU	27	
SRM	5	
Mash at	156° F	
Sparge at	168° F	
Boil time	140 minutes	
pitching temp	63° F	
Yeast	Wyeast 1318 London ale III (Boddingtons)	

1917 Boddington Bitter (3rd Oct)

Towards the end of 1917 Boddington dropped AK and introduced a new low-gravity Pale Ale, called simply Bitter.

It didn't hang around for all that long, having disappeared again by the summer of 1918.

The recipe is, well, like all the Boddington beers: pale malt, flaked maize and an unspecified type of sugar. As with the other recipes, I've guessed No. 2 invert sugar. But remember, that's just my guess.

There are Boddington's standard confusingly large number of different hops: English (1914, 1915 and 1916), Californian (1915), Poperinge (1915) copper hops, plus English (1916) and Californian (1915) dry hops.

1917 Boddington Bitter (3rd Oct)		
pale malt	7.00 lb	87.50%
flaked maize	0.75 lb	9.38%
No. 2 invert sugar	0.25 lb	3.13%
Strisselspalt 130 mins	0.125 oz	
Cluster 130 mins	0.25 oz	
Fuggles 90 mins	0.75 oz	
Fuggles 30 mins	0.75 oz	
Fuggles dry hops	0.125 oz	
Cluster dry hops	0.125 oz	
OG	1035	
FG	1013	
ABV	2.91	
Apparent attenuation	62.86%	
IBU	27	
SRM	4	
Mash at	156° F	
Sparge at	168° F	
Boil time	130 minutes	
pitching temp	63° F	
Yeast	Wyeast 1318 London ale III (Boddingtons)	

1918 Boddington B

In the last two years of the war Boddington kept tinkering with their beer range. Particularly weird was the reappearance of B, which had been discontinued in 1916.

There have been massive changes in the grist department. Well, one change: the dropping of flaked maize. I assume it just wasn't available any more. Leaving a pretty boring recipe of mostly pale malt with a tiny bit of sugar. This is a Mild Ale, by the way. Not that you'd really be able to tell from the recipe. Boddington are confusing like that.

The hops were the usual Boddington mix of ages and nationalities: English (1914, 1915, 1916 and 1917), Poperinghe (1916), Californian (1915) copper hops, plus English (1916 and 1917) dry hops.

1918 Boddington B		
pale malt	5.50 lb	95.65%
No. 2 invert sugar	0.25 lb	4.35%
Strisselspalt 100 mins	0.25 oz	
Cluster 100 mins	0.50 oz	
Fuggles 60 mins	0.50 oz	
Fuggles 30 mins	0.50 oz	
Fuggles dry hops	0.25 oz	
OG	1026	
FG	1009	
ABV	2.25	
Apparent attenuation	65.38%	
IBU	29	
SRM	4	
Mash at	155° F	
Sparge at	168° F	
Boil time	100 minutes	
pitching temp	62° F	
Yeast	Wyeast 1318 London ale III (Boddingtons)	

1918 Boddington XX

XX was one of the beers that was ever-present in Boddington's range throughout WW I.

There's nothing much I can say about the grist. It's the same as all their other beers by this point, just pale malt and sugar.

The attenuation is pretty poor – were they trying the leave some body in the beer to hide the drop in gravity? Possibly. But it does leave it at a mere 2.5% ABV. Not something that was going to get you very merry. Not unless you were 5 years old.

1918 Boddington XX		
pale malt	6.50 lb	96.30%
No. 2 invert sugar	0.25 lb	3.70%
Strisselspalt 100 mins	0.25 oz	
Cluster 100 mins	0.50 oz	
Fuggles 60 mins	0.75 oz	
Fuggles 30 mins	0.50 oz	
Fuggles dry hops	0.25 oz	
OG	1030	
FG	1011	
ABV	2.51	
Apparent attenuation	63.33%	
IBU	32	
SRM	4	
Mash at	157° F	
Sparge at	168° F	
Boil time	120 minutes	
pitching temp	62° F	
Yeast	Wyeast 1318 London ale III (Boddingtons)	

1918 Boddington Bitter

In early 1918, Boddington brewed an array of very similar Milds and Bitters. I sort of wonder what the point was.

The gravity of Bitter has fallen since 1917, it's down by three points. Coupled with a pretty crappy rate of attenuation, it leaves a beer that doesn't quite make 3% ABV.

Overall, the difference with XX is minimal: a tiny bit higher gravity, but a roughly similar level of hopping. The types of hops were exactly the same as in B and XX.

1918 Boddington Bitter		
pale malt	7.00 lb	96.55%
No. 2 invert sugar	0.25 lb	3.45%
Strisselspalt 120 mins	0.25 oz	
Cluster 120 mins	0.50 oz	
Fuggles 60 mins	0.75 oz	
Fuggles 30 mins	0.75 oz	
Fuggles dry hops	0.25 oz	
OG	1032	
FG	1010	
ABV	2.91	
Apparent attenuation	68.75%	
IBU	34	
SRM	4	
Mash at	157° F	
Sparge at	168° F	
Boil time	120 minutes	
pitching temp	62° F	
Yeast	Wyeast 1318 London ale III (Boddingtons)	

1918 Boddington IP

IP, Boddington's strongest Pale Ale, is another beer that was brewed all the way through the war.

Even in the dark days of 1918, it still had a reasonable gravity. At almost 3.5% ABV, it might even have got you a bit tipsy.

The ingredients are exactly the same as in the other beers. Except there are a bit fewer Californian hops. It's nit exactly a huge difference, Weirdly, the hopping rate is slightly lower than for the weaker Bitter.

1918 Boddington IP		
pale malt	8.50 lb	97.14%
No. 2 invert sugar	0.25 lb	2.86%
Strisselspalt 120 mins	0.25 oz	
Cluster 120 mins	0.25 oz	
Fuggles 60 mins	0.75 oz	
Fuggles 30 mins	0.75 oz	
Fuggles dry hops	0.375 oz	
OG	1038	
FG	1012	
ABV	3.44	
Apparent attenuation	68.42%	
IBU	27	
SRM	4	
Mash at	157° F	
Sparge at	168° F	
Boil time	120 minutes	
pitching temp	62° F	
Yeast	Wyeast 1318 London ale III (Boddingtons)	

1918 Boddington Stout

Despite having lost 9 gravity points since the previous year, Stout was Boddington's strongest beer in 1918. Though the poor attenuation means that it just creeps over 3% ABV.

The grist is much the same: pale, amber, high-dried and black malt, plus caramel and sugar. I've no idea what the sugar was exactly, the records being pretty vague on this point. No. 3 invert is just a guess.

Lots of different hops again, quite a few of them pretty old: English (1914, 1915, 1916 and 1917), Poperinghe (1916) and Californian (1913 and 1915).

1918 Boddington Stout		
pale malt	2.50 lb	27.17%
black malt	0.25 lb	2.72%
amber malt	3.00 lb	32.61%
high dried malt	3.00 lb	32.61%
No. 3 invert sugar	0.25 lb	2.72%
caramel 2000 SRM	0.20 lb	2.17%
Strisselspalt 130 mins	0.25 oz	
Cluster 130 mins	0.50 oz	
Fuggles 90 mins	0.50 oz	
Fuggles 30 mins	0.50 oz	
OG	1039	
FG	1015	
ABV	3.18	
Apparent attenuation	61.54%	
IBU	27	
SRM	34	
Mash at	153° F	
Sparge at	168° F	
Boil time	130 minutes	
pitching temp	62° F	
Yeast	Wyeast 1318 London ale III (Boddingtons)	

1918 Boddington CC

After an absence of around a year, CC returned in November 1918. This particular version was brewed just two days after the Armistice.

It's returned to a gravity not far off the pre-war level: 1058° instead of 1062°. Most beers didn't fare as well as that. And that gravity was just about maintained right through until WW II.

1918 Boddington CC		
pale malt	12.50 lb	96.15%
No. 2 invert sugar	0.50 lb	3.85%
Strisselspalt 130 mins	0.33 oz	
Cluster 130 mins	0.25 oz	
Fuggles 90 mins	0.75 oz	
Fuggles 30 mins	0.75 oz	
Fuggles dry hops	0.375 oz	
OG	1058	
FG	1020	
ABV	5.03	
Apparent attenuation	65.52%	
IBU	28	
SRM	5	
Mash at	157° F	
Sparge at	168° F	
Boil time	130 minutes	
pitching temp	64° F	
Yeast	Wyeast 1318 London ale III (Boddingtons)	

1919 Boddington B

While 1919 saw a loosening of gravity restrictions it didn't have an effect on Boddington B. I assume the reason was that the brewery wanted to keep it as a 4d per pint beer.

The gravity has actually fallen by one point which, coupled with the poor rate of attenuation, leaves it just scraping past 2% ABV. Not much stronger than shandy.

The grist remains a rather dull combination of pale malt and sugar. Just like the rest of their recipes, other than Stout.

1919 Boddington B		
pale malt	5.00 lb	90.91%
No. 2 invert sugar	0.50 lb	9.09%
Strisselspalt 85 mins	0.75 oz	
Fuggles 60 mins	0.50 oz	
Fuggles 30 mins	0.50 oz	
Fuggles dry hops	0.125 oz	
OG	1025	
FG	1009	
ABV	2.12	
Apparent attenuation	64.00%	
IBU	23	
SRM	4	
Mash at	157° F	
Sparge at	168° F	
Boil time	85 minutes	
pitching temp	62° F	
Yeast	Wyeast 1318 London ale III (Boddingtons)	

1919 Boddington XX

Unlike B, XX did get a little stronger after hostilities had ended. Not by a huge amount – just 3 gravity points – but enough to get it vaguely intoxicating.

There's nothing very exciting to report about the recipe, which is, surprise, surprise, a combination of pale malt and sugar.

The hops are a mix of old foreign hops and rather younger English ones. English (1916, 1917, 1918), Poperinghe (1914, 1915) and Californian (1915) copper hops; English dry hops.

1919 Boddington XX		
pale malt	6.75 lb	93.10%
No. 2 invert sugar	0.50 lb	6.90%
Strisselspalt 100 mins	0.25 oz	
Cluster 100 mins	0.125 oz	
Fuggles 60 mins	0.75 oz	
Fuggles 30 mins	0.75 oz	
Fuggles dry hops	0.25 oz	
OG	1033	
FG	1011	
ABV	2.91	
Apparent attenuation	66.67%	
IBU	25	
SRM	5	
Mash at	157° F	
Sparge at	168° F	
Boil time	100 minutes	
pitching temp	62° F	
Yeast	Wyeast 1318 London ale III (Boddingtons)	

1919 Boddington Bitter

Introduced in late 1917, Bitter had been up and down in strength in the meantime. By 1919, it was even a little stronger than when it had first appeared.

Though it has a reasonable enough gravity, poor attenuation leaves it only just scraping above 3% ABV.

Just like XX, it used old foreign hops and newish English ones. If you're starting to think that Boddington's beers all look very similar in terms of recipe, colour, etc, you wouldn't be wrong.

1919 Boddington Bitter		
pale malt	7.50 lb	93.75%
No. 2 invert sugar	0.50 lb	6.25%
Strisselspalt 145 mins	0.25 oz	
Cluster 145 mins	0.125 oz	
Fuggles 90 mins	1.00 oz	
Fuggles 30 mins	1.00 oz	
Fuggles dry hops	0.33 oz	
OG	1036	
FG	1013	
ABV	3.04	
Apparent attenuation	63.89%	
IBU	32	
SRM	5	
Mash at	158° F	
Sparge at	168° F	
Boil time	145 minutes	
pitching temp	62° F	
Yeast	Wyeast 1318 London ale III (Boddingtons)	

1919 Boddington IP

Boddington's stronger Bitter had also seen a rise in gravity since the end of the war. By a might four points.

After a couple of years of watery beer with a minimal alcohol content, this version of IP must have been either a shock or a delight to drinkers.

Just for a bit of variation, the hopping is slightly different as there are no Belgian hops. Which I suppose is a sign that this was a classier beer.

1919 Boddington IP		
pale malt	9.25 lb	97.37%
No. 2 invert sugar	0.25 lb	2.63%
Cluster 120 mins	0.50 oz	
Fuggles 90 mins	0.75 oz	
Fuggles 30 mins	0.75 oz	
Fuggles dry hops	0.33 oz	
OG	1042	
FG	1013	
ABV	3.84	
Apparent attenuation	69.05%	
IBU	28	
SRM	5	
Mash at	154° F	
Sparge at	168° F	
Boil time	120 minutes	
pitching temp	62° F	
Yeast	Wyeast 1318 London ale III (Boddingtons)	

1919 Boddington Stout

Stout was one Boddington beer that retained a reasonable strength all through the war. Even during the most difficult period of late 1918 to early 1919 it's gravity never fell lower than 1037°.

By the summer of 1918 when this beer was brewed, the gravity had clambered above 1040° again. But it was still considerably down on the 1054° gravity it had when the war started.

The grist is the same rather unusual combination of pale, black, amber and high-dried malt. The proportions are much the same as in 1918, though there is rather more No.3 invert sugar and a little less of the malts.

The hops were mostly pretty old: English (1916), Poperinghe (1914, 1915) and Californian (1915) copper hops; no dry hops. Stout was the only beer Boddington didn't dry hop.

1919 Boddington Stout		
pale malt	2.50 lb	25.64%
black malt	0.25 lb	2.56%
amber malt	3.00 lb	30.77%
high dried malt	3.00 lb	30.77%
No. 3 invert sugar	0.75 lb	7.69%
caramel 2000 SRM	0.25 lb	2.56%
Strisselspalt 115 mins	0.50 oz	
Fuggles 90 mins	0.75 oz	
Fuggles 30 mins	0.75 oz	
OG	1043	
FG	1017	
ABV	3.44	
Apparent attenuation	60.47%	
IBU	24	
SRM	39	
Mash at	153° F	
Sparge at	168° F	
Boil time	115 minutes	
pitching temp	62° F	
Yeast	Wyeast 1318 London ale III (Boddingtons)	

1921 Boddington XX

By 1921, Boddington was down to a single Mild, XX. The weaker B having been discontinued in the middle of 1919. With XX remaining a fairly modest 1033°, there wasn't much room for a weaker Mild.

The biggest change in the grist is the return of flaked maize. It seems to have returned sometime late in 1919.

Turning to the hops, around a third are now Saaz. The full set is: Saaz (1918), English (1919, 1920), Alost (1920) and Pacific (1920) copper hops, plus Pacific (1920) and, English (1920) dry hops. The Alost don't turn up in my recipe because the quantity was so small.

I assume the presence of Saaz is because of a glut. Brewing came to pretty much a complete stop in Bohemia during the final years of the war. There must have been a lot of surplus hops.

1921 Boddington XX		
pale malt	5.50 lb	75.86%
flaked maize	1.00 lb	13.79%
No. 2 invert sugar	0.75 lb	10.34%
Fuggles 105 mins	0.25 oz	
Cluster 105 mins	0.50 oz	
Fuggles 90 mins	0.75 oz	
Saaz 30 mins	0.75 oz	
Cluster dry hops	0.125 oz	
Goldings dry hops	0.125 oz	
OG	1033	
FG	1010	
ABV	3.04	
Apparent attenuation	69.70%	
IBU	32	
SRM	5	
Mash at	150° F	
Sparge at	168° F	
Boil time	105 minutes	
pitching temp	62° F	
Yeast	Wyeast 1318 London ale III (Boddingtons)	

Mini Book Series volume XXXII: Armistice!

1921 Boddington IP

By the time 1921 rolled around, Boddington's beers were starting to take the form that they would have until the next conflict erupted.

Having dropped from 1053° at the start of the war, IP had lost about 9.5% of its gravity. That's not bad. Considering the average fall in OG between 1914 and 1921 was 19%. It was much worse for most other beers.

Though it wasn't always so easy to calculate. For example, with Boddington Mild. They brewed three of different strength before the war. Which one would you compare 1921 XX with?

1921 Boddington IP		
pale malt	9.25 lb	86.05%
flaked maize	1.00 lb	9.30%
No. 2 invert sugar	0.50 lb	4.65%
Fuggles 125 mins	0.25 oz	
Cluster 125 mins	0.50 oz	
Fuggles 90 mins	0.75 oz	
Saaz 30 mins	0.75 oz	
Cluster dry hops	0.125 oz	
Goldings dry hops	0.25 oz	
OG	1048	
FG	1015	
ABV	4.37	
Apparent attenuation	68.75%	
IBU	40	
SRM	6	
Mash at	152° F	
Sparge at	168° F	
Boil time	125 minutes	
pitching temp	63° F	
Yeast	Wyeast 1318 London ale III (Boddingtons)	

1921 Boddington CC

Another beer that fared fairly well in terms of gravity reduction was Boddington's Strong Ale, CC.

Pre-war it was 1062° and in 1921 it was a mere 2.5 gravity points weaker. That's extremely small: a mere 4%. Why was the drop so small? Probably partly because it hadn't been that strong by pre-war standards. Remember that a standard London Mild was over 1050°.

The recipe is slightly different from XX and IP in that it lacks flaked maize.

1921 Boddington CC		
pale malt	13.00 lb	96.30%
No. 2 invert sugar	0.50 lb	3.70%
Fuggles 125 mins	0.75 oz	
Cluster 125 mins	0.33 oz	
Fuggles 90 mins	0.75 oz	
Saaz 30 mins	0.75 oz	
Cluster dry hops	0.125 oz	
Goldings dry hops	0.25 oz	
OG	1059.5	
FG	1019	
ABV	5.36	
Apparent attenuation	68.07%	
IBU	32	
SRM	6	
Mash at	153° F	
Sparge at	168° F	
Boil time	150 minutes	
pitching temp	63° F	
Yeast	Wyeast 1318 London ale III (Boddingtons)	

1921 Boddington Stout

Boddington Stout fared better than some of their other beers gravity-wise during the war years. Even at its nadir in early 1919, it still had an OG of 1037°. When some of their beers were below 1030°.

By 1921, Stout was almost back to its pre-war level of 1054°, being just 3 gravity points lower. Interestingly, this left it at a similar gravity to London Stouts, while before the war it had been considerably weaker. It's another example of the war erasing regional variations in strength.

There's been quite a substantial change to the grist. In 1920 the amber malt was dropped and replaced by more pale malt. Surprisingly, this hasn't had an impact on the beer's colour. Otherwise, the grist is identical to previous versions.

Surprisingly, the hops are all foreign: Saaz (1918), Alost (1920) and Pacific (1920). And mostly reasonably fresh. Which was a change from the final years of the war, when their hops were becoming increasingly older.

1921 Boddington Stout		
pale malt	5.75 lb	50.00%
black malt	0.25 lb	2.17%
high dried malt	4.25 lb	36.96%
No. 3 invert sugar	1.00 lb	8.70%
caramel 2000 SRM	0.25 lb	2.17%
Cluster 120 mins	0.75 oz	
Strisselspalt 90 mins	0.75 oz	
Saaz 30 mins	0.75 oz	
OG	1051	
FG	1015	
ABV	4.76	
Apparent attenuation	70.59%	
IBU	26	
SRM	38	
Mash at	149° F	
Sparge at	165° F	
Boil time	120 minutes	
pitching temp	61.5° F	
Yeast	Wyeast 1318 London ale III (Boddingtons)	

Courage

While not one of the original large Porter brewers of the 18th century, Courage, which grew quickly in the 19th century, was initially also a Black Beer specialist. They had expanded into Mild and Burton Ales, but still didn't brew any Pale Ales. Those they got from another brewery they owned in Alton, Hampshire.

The Horsleydown Brewery, at the Southeast corner of Tower Bridge, closed in 1981. The building has been converted into flats.

X Ale

As the most popular beer of the day, X Ale is a good barometer of the war's impact on beer and drinkers.

Courage X Ale 1914 - 1918							
Date	Year	OG	FG	ABV	App. Attenuation	lbs hops/ qtr	hops lb/brl
17th Oct	1914	1054.6	1019.4	4.65	64.47%	5	1.05
8th Mar	1915	1049.9	1018.3	4.18	63.33%	4	0.78
23rd Sep	1915	1048.2	1011.1	4.91	77.01%	4.96	0.96
11th Oct	1916	1048.2	1007.2	5.42	85.06%	5	0.97
9th May	1916	1044.9	1006.9	5.02	84.57%	6.51	1.18
2nd Jan	1917	1045.7	1010.0	4.73	78.18%	3.88	0.76
5th Jan	1917	1045.7	1009.4	4.8	79.39%	3.85	0.76
24th Apr	1917	1045.7	1008.0	4.98	82.42%	4.81	0.95
8th Jun	1917	1041.6	1007.2	4.54	82.67%	8.72	1.16
19th Oct	1917	1034.6	1006.4	3.74	81.60%	7.57	1.13
9th Nov	1917	1034.6	1008.0	3.52	76.80%	7.57	1.14
18th Jan	1918	1034.6	1006.9	3.66	80.00%	7.38	1.13
20th Apr	1918	1023.8	1004.4	2.57	81.40%	9.41	1.01
19th Jul	1918	1022.2	1004.4	2.35	80.00%	10.48	1
19th Nov	1918	1021.1	1003.9	2.27	81.58%	10.89	1.01
Sources: Documents held in the Courage Archives at the London Metropolitan Archives: ACC/2305/08/247, ACC/2305/08/248, ACC/2305/08/249, ACC/2305/08/250							

Mini Book Series volume XXXII: Armistice!

Courage X Ale 1914 - 1918										
Date	Year	pale malt	black malt	crystal malt	no. 3 sugar	black invert	Glu-cose	other sugar	flaked maize	Pri-mings
17th Oct	1914	82.78%		6.11%				11.11%		
8th Mar	1915	82.78%		6.11%				11.11%		
23rd Sep	1915	82.39%		6.34%				11.27%		
11th Oct	1916	82.78%		6.11%				11.11%		
9th May	1916	76.92%		5.77%				12.82%	4.49%	
2nd Jan	1917	66.12%		8.03%	14.01%				6.18%	5.66%
5th Jan	1917	66.04%		8.02%	13.84%				6.13%	5.97%
24th Apr	1917	52.92%		6.38%	30.61%				5.10%	4.99%
8th Jun	1917	70.27%		10.81%	14.41%					4.50%
19th Oct	1917	70.59%	1.53%	12.28%	6.14%	2.05%				7.42%
9th Nov	1917	69.17%	1.50%	12.03%	8.02%	2.01%				7.27%
18th Jan	1918	70.59%	1.60%	12.03%	8.56%					7.22%
20th Apr	1918	64.60%	2.65%	16.81%	7.08%					8.85%
19th Jul	1918	67.05%	3.44%	16.33%			7.45%			5.73%
19th Nov	1918	60.20%	5.02%	18.06%			10.03%			6.69%
Sources:										
Documents held in the Courage Archives at the London Metropolitan Archives: ACC/2305/08/247, ACC/2305/08/248, ACC/2305/08/249, ACC/2305/08/250										

You'll see how the gravity dropped rapidly after 1917. Interestingly, the grist also became more complex. Were they trying to compensate for the reduction in gravity? Or were they just using whatever ingredients they could get? Or a combination of the two.

The approach of Courage contrasts with that of Whitbread. Courage stuck with a single type of Mild, one which eventually was pretty weak. Whitbread brewed 3 different strengths of Mild, with OG's of: 1038.1, 1023.7 and 1011.4. Barclay Perkins were more like Courage. By early 1918 they were brewing just one Mild, Ale 4d, with a gravity of 1025.5.

Porter
First a bit of background. In 1914, Courage always parti-gyled Porter and Double Stout. Often a bit of Imperial Stout was brewed, too. Porter was very much the senior partner, with less than half the amount of Double Stout produced in each brew.

Then early in 1918 Porter was discontinued. Stout was still brewed, but at a gravity so low, 1035, that it was considerably weaker than pre-war Porter. When Porter did make a comeback in 1920, it was a shadow of its former self with a gravity just a shade under 1030. Now it was Stout than made up the greatest volume of the parti-gyles. And often Stout was just brewed by itself. Which means that the volume of Porter brewed was far less than before the war, though the total amount of Porter and Stout brewed remained much the same.

There was a similar process at Whitbread. So what had happened? Well, it looks as if many drinkers swapped from Porter to Stout. Or rather, that when Porter wasn't available, drinkers turned to Stout. And when an enfeebled version of Porter did reappear, many stuck with Stout. Which makes sense, as what was sold as Stout in the 1920's was much like 1914 Porter in terms of strength.

The biggest change over the war years, other than the gravity drop, was the reduction in the brown malt content. It was approximately halved, from a respectable 20% of the grist to less than 10%. It appears black invert was used as a replacement for some of the dark malts. Which seems logical enough.

Courage Porter 1914 - 1918											
Date	Year	OG	FG	ABV	App. Atten- uation	lbs hops/ qtr	hops lb/brl	boil time (hours)			Pitch temp
21st Oct	1914	1051.25	1018.28	4.36	64.32%	7.20	1.51	2	2	1	60°
10th Mar	1915	1050.41	1018.28	4.25	63.74%	7.23	1.52	1.5	2	1	64°
17th Feb	1915	1050.41	1018.28	4.25	63.74%	7.20	1.51	1.5	2	1	64°
3rd Feb	1915	1050.41	1018.28	4.25	63.74%	7.23	1.51	1.5	2	1	64°
22nd Sep	1915	1046.26	1011.36	4.62	75.45%	8.09	1.60	2	2	1	64°
29th Sep	1915	1046.26	1017.73	3.77	61.68%	8.14	1.71	2	2	1	64°
6th Oct	1915	1046.26	1012.19	4.51	73.65%	7.23	1.52	2	2	1	64°
1st Dec	1915	1046.26	1011.08	4.65	76.05%	7.13	1.39	2	2	1	64°
10th May	1916	1042.94	1010.80	4.25	74.84%	7.26	1.40	2	2	1	60°
17th May	1916	1042.94	1011.91	4.10	72.26%	7.31	1.27	2	2	1	60°
3rd Jan	1917	1044.04	1012.19	4.21	72.33%	6.11	1.33	2	2	1	60°
10th Jan	1917	1044.04	1011.63	4.29	73.58%	6.16	1.33	2	2	1	60°
26th Apr	1917	1044.04	1009.42	4.58	78.62%	5.96	1.31	2	2	1	60°
30th May	1917	1038.78	1008.86	3.96	77.14%	5.82	1.17	2	2	1	60°
24th Oct	1917	1032.69	1009.70	3.04	70.34%	5.98	0.96	2	2	1	59°
7th Nov	1917	1032.69	1009.97	3.00	69.49%	5.98	0.96	2	2	1	59°
16th Jan	1918	1032.69	1009.42	3.08	71.19%	5.85	0.94	2	2	1	61°

Courage Porter 1914 - 1918									
Date	Year	pale malt	brown malt	black malt	no. 3 sugar	black invert	caramel	other sugar	primings
21st Oct	1914	60.22%	19.59%	10.52%				9.67%	
10th Mar	1915	58.43%	20.22%	10.11%				11.24%	
17th Feb	1915	59.47%	19.47%	10.53%				10.53%	
3rd Feb	1915	58.08%	19.76%	10.18%				11.98%	
22nd Sep	1915	61.48%	20.23%	10.51%				7.78%	
29th Sep	1915	57.78%	19.26%	10.11%				12.84%	
6th Oct	1915	58.43%	20.22%	10.11%				11.24%	
1st Dec	1915	59.20%	20.62%	11.31%				8.87%	
10th May	1916	60.10%	20.03%	10.02%		9.35%	0.50%		
17th May	1916	60.43%	19.79%	9.09%		9.98%	0.71%		
3rd Jan	1917	58.46%	9.23%	7.69%	6.84%	6.84%	1.71%		9.23%
10th Jan	1917	43.92%	12.84%	10.81%	4.50%	13.51%	2.25%		12.16%
26th Apr	1917	59.32%	9.76%	7.51%	7.01%	7.01%	1.50%		7.88%
30th May	1917	56.00%	9.14%	6.86%	6.10%	7.62%	1.52%		12.76%
24th Oct	1917	63.50%	9.07%	7.78%	5.18%	5.18%	1.73%		7.56%
7th Nov	1917	63.50%	9.07%	7.78%	5.18%	5.18%	1.73%		7.56%
16th Jan	1918	63.66%	8.05%	10.24%		7.80%	1.46%		8.78%

Source: Documents held in the Courage Archives and the London Metropolitan Archives: ACC/2305/08/247, ACC/2305/08/248, ACC/2305/08/249, ACC/2305/08/250

You'll notice that there's a similar change to rather less coloured malts as we saw with Porter. As they were parti-gyled, this is no great surprise.

Stout
Let's see what happened to Courage Stout during the war.

Courage Stout 1914 - 1918								
Date	Year	Beer	OG	FG	ABV	App. Atten-uation	lbs hops/ qtr	hops lb/brl
21st Oct	1914	Double Stout	1078.95	1033.24	6.05	57.89%	7.20	2.33
10th Mar	1915	Double Stout	1078.95	1033.24	6.05	57.89%	7.23	2.37
17th Feb	1915	Double Stout	1078.95	1033.24	6.05	57.89%	7.20	2.37
29th Sep	1915	Double Stout	1075.90	1019.39	7.48	74.45%	8.14	2.81
6th Oct	1915	Double Stout	1075.90	1027.70	6.38	63.50%	7.23	2.49
1st Dec	1915	Double Stout	1075.90	1025.48	6.67	66.42%	7.13	2.28
10th May	1916	Double Stout	1068.70	1024.93	5.79	63.71%	7.26	2.24
17th May	1916	Double Stout	1068.70	1025.48	5.72	62.90%	7.31	2.03
3rd Jan	1917	Double Stout	1071.74	1028.81	5.68	59.85%	6.11	2.16
10th Jan	1917	Double Stout	1071.74	1029.64	5.57	58.69%	6.16	2.17
24th Oct	1917	Double Stout	1063.71	1023.27	5.35	63.48%	5.98	1.87
7th Nov	1917	Double Stout	1063.71	1024.10	5.24	62.17%	5.98	1.87
16th Jan	1918	Double Stout	1063.71	1021.05	5.64	66.96%	5.85	1.82
26th Apr	1917	Stout	1071.74	1030.19	5.50	57.92%	5.96	2.14
2nd May	1918	Stout	1035.46	1008.03	3.63	77.34%	5.52	1.00
25th Jul	1918	Stout	1035.46	1008.31	3.59	76.56%	5.55	1.01
14th Nov	1918	Stout	1035.46	1008.31	3.59	76.56%	5.51	1.01
21st Oct	1914	Imperial	1094.18	1038.78	7.33	58.82%	7.20	2.78
10th Mar	1915	Imperial	1094.18	1040.44	7.11	57.06%	7.23	2.83
3rd Feb	1915	Imperial	1094.18	1038.78	7.33	58.82%	7.23	2.83
6th Oct	1915	Imperial	1091.96	1033.24	7.77	63.86%	7.23	3.01
Source: Documents held in the Courage Archives and the London Metropolitan Archives: ACC/2305/08/247, ACC/2305/08/248, ACC/2305/08/249, ACC/2305/08/250								

The name-change mid-war of their Stout seems only fair. After halving the gravity, it would have been a bit of a cheek to keep calling it Double Stout. You can also observe the sort of rationalisation of beers that took place. In 1914 Courage brewed, in ascending order of strength: Porter, Double Stout and Imperial Stout. By 1918 they were only brewing Stout. But that, at 1035, was considerably weaker than pre-war Porter. Imperial Stout, like Whitbread's strong Stouts SS and SSS, never reappeared. (Barclay Perkins, on the other hand, did brew strong Stouts after the war. Several of them, in fact.)

This is what happened to Courage Stout grists during the war:

Courage Stout 1914 - 1918

Date	Year	Beer	pale malt	brown malt	black malt	no. 3 sugar	black invert	Caramel	Glucose	other sugar	Primings
21st Oct	1914	Double Stout	60.22%	19.59%	10.52%					9.67%	
10th Mar	1915	Double Stout	58.43%	20.22%	10.11%					11.24%	
17th Feb	1915	Double Stout	59.47%	19.47%	10.53%					10.53%	
29th Sep	1915	Double Stout	57.78%	19.26%	10.11%					12.84%	
6th Oct	1915	Double Stout	58.43%	20.22%	10.11%					11.24%	
1st Dec	1915	Double Stout	59.20%	20.62%	11.31%					8.87%	
10th May	1916	Double Stout	60.10%	20.03%	10.02%		9.35%	0.50%			
17th May	1916	Double Stout	60.43%	19.79%	9.09%		9.98%	0.71%			
3rd Jan	1917	Double Stout	58.46%	9.23%	7.69%	6.84%	6.84%	1.71%			9.23%
10th Jan	1917	Double Stout	43.92%	12.84%	10.81%	4.50%	13.51%	2.25%			12.16%
24th Oct	1917	Double Stout	66.07%	9.44%	8.09%	5.39%	5.39%	1.80%			3.82%
7th Nov	1917	Double Stout	66.07%	9.44%	8.09%	5.39%	5.39%	1.80%			3.82%
16th Jan	1918	Double Stout	67.44%	8.53%	10.85%	0.00%	8.27%	1.55%			3.36%
26th Apr	1917	Stout	61.88%	10.18%	7.83%	7.31%	7.31%	1.57%			3.92%
2nd May	1918	Stout	58.70%	9.32%	9.32%		6.21%	1.86%			14.60%
25th Jul	1918	Stout	57.47%	8.77%	10.71%			1.95%	6.49%		14.61%
14th Nov	1918	Stout	56.31%	8.74%	10.68%			1.94%	7.77%		14.56%
21st Oct	1914	Imperial	60.22%	19.59%	10.52%					9.67%	
10th Mar	1915	Imperial	58.43%	20.22%	10.11%					11.24%	
3rd Feb	1915	Imperial	58.08%	19.76%	10.18%					11.98%	
6th Oct	1915	Imperial	58.43%	20.22%	10.11%					11.24%	

Source:
Documents held in the Courage Archives and the London Metropolitan Archives: ACC/2305/08/247, ACC/2305/08/248, ACC/2305/08/249, ACC/2305/08/250.

Burton Ale

Finally, the other beer brewed at Hosrleydown, Courage's Burton Ale.

Courage Strong Ale 1914 -1917

Date	Year	Beer	OG	FG	ABV	App. Attenuation	lbs hops/qtr	hops lb/brl	boil time (hours)			Pitch temp
22nd Oct	1914	XX	1079.22	1033.24	6.08	58.04%	10.00	3.07	2	2.5	1	60°
4th Mar	1915	XX	1079.22	1033.24	6.08	58.04%	11.00	3.53	2	2.5	1	60°
5th Oct	1915	KK	1076.18	1017.73	7.73	76.73%	10.00	3.10	2	2.5	1	60°
19th Oct	1915	KK	1076.18	1016.62	7.88	78.18%	10.00	3.10	2	2	1	60°
5th Jul	1916	KK	1076.18	1027.70	6.41	63.64%	11.00	3.42	2	2	1	60°
4th Jan	1917	KK	1075.34	1027.42	6.34	63.60%	11.51	3.54	2	2	1	60°
18th Oct	1917	KK	1072.57	1023.82	6.45	67.18%	12.66	3.63	2	2	1	59°

Wondering why there's not much of a cut in the gravity? That's because they discontinued the beer just as the draconian hacking started.

The grists aren't the most exciting I've ever seen. Pale malt and sugar. With a dash of black malt in 1917. Oh, and I.M. Co (or is it IM C?), whatever that is. Some type of malt, that's for sure. It crops up in Truman's Burton logs, too. Not the foggiest idea what it is. Any suggestions are welcome.

Courage Strong Ale 1914 -1917								
Date	Year	Beer	dry hops (oz / barrel)	pale malt	black malt	no. 3 sugar	other sugar	I.M. Co.	total
22nd Oct	1914	XX	8.00	67.16%			14.93%	17.91%	100.00%
4th Mar	1915	XX	8.00	67.16%			14.93%	17.91%	100.00%
5th Oct	1915	KK		85.07%			14.93%		100.00%
19th Oct	1915	KK		85.07%			14.93%		100.00%
5th Jul	1916	KK		85.07%			14.93%		100.00%
4th Jan	1917	KK	8.05	83.95%	1.33%	14.73%			100.00%
18th Oct	1917	KK	8.44	83.58%	1.76%	14.66%			100.00%

Source:
Documents held in the Courage Archives and the London Metropolitan Archives: ACC/2305/08/247, ACC/2305/08/248, ACC/2305/08/249

1914 Courage X Ale

Here's one of those stronger London X Ales that I've been telling you about. From Courage's Horsleydown brewery right next to Tower Bridge.

Though, in a couple of ways, it's not totally typical of Mild Ales from the capital. The OG is the same as Milds from rival London breweries, but there are some differences in the grist. For a start, there's some black malt included, presumably for colour rather than flavour. Crystal malt was becoming quite common in Mild by this point, so that's not odd. It's what's missing that struck me: no flaked maize.

I've no idea what the sugar was, but No.3 invert seems a reasonable guess. Especially as I know for certain that Courage were using it in their X Ale a couple of years later.

Amusingly, given that this beer was brewed in October, a couple of months after the outbreak of war, it contains some German hops. Though they must have bought them some time before as they were from the 1912 crop. They had been in a cold store so shouldn't have deteriorated much. As usual, all I know about the other hops is that they were English. I've gone for Fuggles as they usually reserved Goldings for classier beers like Pale Ale.

This is what I would call a transitional Mild, with regard to colour. It's not full out dark, but dark enough to be distinguished from Bitter. It's fascinating to see how Mild gradually changed colour. Especially as it didn't happen everywhere at the same time. London seems to have led the way.

1914 Courage X Ale		
pale malt	10.00 lb	81.63%
crystal malt 60 L	0.75 lb	6.12%
black malt	0.25 lb	2.04%
No. 3 invert sugar	1.25 lb	10.20%
Fuggles 120 mins	1.00 oz	
Fuggles 60 mins	0.50 oz	
Hallertau 30 mins	0.50 oz	
OG	1055	
FG	1019	
ABV	4.76	
Apparent attenuation	65.45%	
IBU	21	
SRM	19	
Mash at	152° F	
Sparge at	165° F	
Boil time	120 minutes	
pitching temp	60° F	
Yeast	Wyeast 1099 Whitbread Ale	

1914 Courage XX

I was initially confused by this beer, thinking it was a stronger Mild Ale. But looking at more records I realised what it really was: a Burton Ale.

It's difficult now to imagine, but before WW I Burton Ales of over 7% ABV were standard draught beer in London pubs. I still dream of setting up a pub with an Edwardian range of beers: Mild, Bitter, Burton, Porter and Stout. With perhaps a KKKK or Imperial Stout on for the winter.

There isn't a whole lot to the grist. Pale malt and an unspecified type of sugar, which I've guessed as No. 3 invert. Though it could have been No. 2 invert. Or something else completely. But in 1917 it definitely contained No. 3 invert, so I think my guess is reasonable.

I'm starting to notice another difference between beers from the big London brewers and those made in the provinces: the hopping rate. Many London beers before WW I used lots of hops. Really lots. And this is a good example of that.

This was also the only beer that Courage dry-hopped. Well, the only beer they brewed at Horselydown. Because they has another brewery in Alton that where their Pale Ale was brewed. Their London brewery only produced Porter, Stout, Mild and Burton.

1914 Courage XX		
pale malt	14.25 lb	86.36%
No. 3 invert sugar	2.25 lb	13.64%
Cluster 120 mins	2.75 oz	
Fuggles 60 mins	2.00 oz	
Fuggles 30 mins	2.00 oz	
Fuggles dry hops	1.00 oz	
OG	1079	
FG	1025	
ABV	7.14	
Apparent attenuation	68.35%	
IBU	84	
SRM	15	
Mash at	153° F	
Sparge at	165° F	
Boil time	120 minutes	
pitching temp	60° F	
Yeast	Wyeast 1099 Whitbread Ale	

1914 Courage Porter

At the outbreak of war, Porter was still a big deal in London. While it may have disappeared in many parts of the country, in the capital it was still a popular draught beer.

That was all to change during the course of the war and Porter never really fully recovered. It's undoing was dropping to a feeble OG below 1040°. The reason: drinkers expected Porter to be a cheap beer and if it had been any stronger it would have been too expensive.

The recipe is exactly the same as for the two Stouts. It had to be, as they were all parti-gyled together.

1914 Courage Porter		
pale malt	7.25 lb	61.70%
brown malt	2.25 lb	19.15%
black malt	1.25 lb	10.64%
No. 4 invert sugar	1.00 lb	8.51%
Fuggles 120 mins	1.00 oz	
Fuggles 60 mins	1.00 oz	
Hallertau 30 mins	0.50 oz	
OG	1051	
FG	1018	
ABV	4.37	
Apparent attenuation	64.71%	
IBU	31	
SRM	48	
Mash at	152° F	
Sparge at	165° F	
Boil time	120 minutes	
pitching temp	60° F	
Yeast	Wyeast 1099 Whitbread Ale	

1914 Courage Double Stout

Porter wasn't the only beer parti-gyled with Courage Imperial Stout. Their standard Stout was, too.

No need for a long spiel on this one as, obviously, the recipe is exactly the same as for the Imperial. Just a little less of everything.

Double Stout was almost certainly packaged both as a draught and bottled beer. The draught version would have been on sale in all Courage's tied pubs.

1914 Courage Double Stout		
pale malt	10.75 lb	59.72%
brown malt	3.50 lb	19.44%
black malt	2.00 lb	11.11%
No. 4 invert sugar	1.75 lb	9.72%
Fuggles 120 mins	1.75 oz	
Fuggles 60 mins	1.75 oz	
Hallertau 30 mins	0.75 oz	
OG	1079	
FG	1022	
ABV	7.54	
Apparent attenuation	72.15%	
IBU	40	
SRM	67	
Mash at	152° F	
Sparge at	165° F	
Boil time	120 minutes	
pitching temp	61° F	
Yeast	Wyeast 1099 Whitbread Ale	

1914 Courage Imperial Stout

Before you get all excited, this is not an early version of Courage Russian Imperial Stout. Because that beer was Barclay's Russian Imperial Stout until 1968, when it was rebranded as Courage. This is a completely different and unrelated beer.

Though, obviously, it is an Imperial Stout. The OG is a bit lower than the Barclay's version, which was over 1100°, but it's still a pretty powerful Stout. I think even I would make do with just a couple of pints.

The grist is the classic London combination of pale, brown and black malt. The capital's brewers were faithful to brown malt to the bitter end. Most provincial breweries had ditched before 1900. And to those style Nazis who think that roast barley is the defining feature of Stout, I'll point out that it was almost never used in London. And that is the city where the style was invented.

It's heavily hopped with a combination of English and Hallertau hops. I've knocked the hopping rate down a bit because the hops were from the 1912 and 1913 seasons. You could swap the Fuggles for Goldings. This was an expensive beer, so might well have included posh hops. But, it was also parti-gyled with Porter, which was a cheap beer. Take your pick.

As the original would have had a secondary conditioning before sale, I've dropped the FG down from the racking gravity of 1039. I know from consulting both the brewing records and analyses of the finished beer that the gravity of Barclay's Imperial Stout fell considerably after racking. Like that, Courage's Imperial Stout would also have been vatted and most likely worked on by Brettanomyces.

1914 Courage Imperial Stout		
pale malt	13.00 lb	60.47%
brown malt	4.25 lb	19.77%
black malt	2.25 lb	10.47%
No. 4 invert sugar	2.00 lb	9.30%
Fuggles 120 mins	2.00 oz	
Fuggles 60 mins	2.00 oz	
Hallertau 30 mins	1.00 oz	
OG	1094	
FG	1025	
ABV	9.13	
Apparent attenuation	73.40%	
IBU	42	
SRM	73	
Mash at	152° F	
Sparge at	165° F	
Boil time	120 minutes	
pitching temp	58° F	
Yeast	Wyeast 1099 Whitbread Ale	

1916 Courage X Ale

Jumping forward the middle of the war, there have been a few changes to Courage's Mild.

The most obvious – and rather surprising – is the inclusion of flaked maize. Why surprising? Because it needed to be imported, usually from the USA. And by 1916 the Germans were seriously disrupting transatlantic trade. Otherwise the grist is much the same as in 1914, other than the small quantity of black malt being dropped.

What is really odd is the inclusion of Poperinge hops. Odd, because they're from the 1915 season. The Germans occupied pretty much the whole of Belgium in 1914. Only a tiny corner in the northwest remained in Belgian hands. Coincidentally, that's also where the country's hop-growing district is. With the Germans in charge of most of the country, there can't have been much local demand for hops left.

Other than that, the OG has dropped by 10 points. Though there was a much bigger gravity drop just around the corner. The boil time has also been reduced, probably as a measure to save coal.

1916 Courage X Ale		
pale malt	7.50 lb	76.92%
crystal malt 60 L	0.50 lb	5.13%
flaked maize	0.50 lb	5.13%
No. 3 invert sugar	1.25 lb	12.82%
Strisselspalt 90 mins	0.75 oz	
Fuggles 60 mins	0.75 oz	
Fuggles 30 mins	0.75 oz	
OG	1045	
FG	1007	
ABV	5.03	
Apparent attenuation	84.44%	
IBU	26	
SRM	12	
Mash at	154° F	
Sparge at	165° F	
Boil time	90 minutes	
pitching temp	60° F	
Yeast	Wyeast 1099 Whitbread Ale	

1916 Courage Porter

The first two years of the war didn't see any particularly massive changes. Though there was a down ward pressure on gravities.

It was mostly the weaker more popular beers in a brewery's range that suffered the early gravity cuts. Beers like X Ale and Porter. Courage Porter has lost 8 gravity points since 1914, but otherwise has changed little.

The grist is near identical in terms of percentages: 60% pale malt, 20% brown malt, 10% black malt and 10% black invert. Which produces a pretty black beer.. So it makes you wonder the reasoning behind the one change, the addition of caramel.

The hops have changed a little. Unsurprisingly, the German hops have been dropped. There are still foreign hops, in the form of Poperinge (1915) and Californian (1914) as well as English (1914).

1916 Courage Porter		
pale malt	5.75 lb	58.67%
brown malt	2.00 lb	20.41%
black malt	1.00 lb	10.20%
No. 4 invert sugar	1.00 lb	10.20%
caramel 500 SRM	0.05 lb	0.51%
Strisselspalt 120 mins	0.50 oz	
Cluster 120 mins	0.25 oz	
Fuggles 60 mins	0.75 oz	
Fuggles 30 mins	0.75 oz	
OG	1043	
FG	1011	
ABV	4.23	
Apparent attenuation	74.42%	
IBU	30	
SRM	44	
Mash at	152° F	
Sparge at	159° F	
Boil time	120 minutes	
pitching temp	60° F	
Yeast	Wyeast 1099 Whitbread Ale	

1916 Courage Double Stout

Parti-gyled with the Porter above was Double Stout. A two beer parti-gyle, as Imperial Stout had been discontinued in 1915.

Like the Porter, the gravity of Double Stout has taken a hit. It's now 10 gravity points weaker than in 1914. Though the grist was much the same. As it's just a beefed up version of the Porter above, there's nothing much to say about the recipe.

1916 Courage Double Stout		
pale malt	9.50 lb	60.98%
brown malt	3.00 lb	19.26%
black malt	1.50 lb	9.63%
No. 4 invert sugar	1.50 lb	9.63%
caramel 500 SRM	0.08 lb	0.51%
Strisselspalt 120 mins	0.75 oz	
Cluster 120 mins	0.50 oz	
Fuggles 60 mins	1.25 oz	
Fuggles 30 mins	1.25 oz	
OG	1069	
FG	1025	
ABV	5.82	
Apparent attenuation	63.77%	
IBU	43	
SRM	58	
Mash at	152° F	
Sparge at	159° F	
Boil time	120 minutes	
pitching temp	60° F	
Yeast	Wyeast 1099 Whitbread Ale	

1916 Courage KK

The change that's happened here since 1914 is the brew house name. It's gone from XX to KK. In one very important aspect, it's much the same. The strength.

The grist is the same. Not just the same sort of, but exactly the same. 190 quarters of pale malt and 50 quarters of No. 3 invert sugar. You have to admire the simplicity of it. Some brewers fiddled around with three or four proprietary sugars. One malt and one sugar. Just about. 50 quarters of the pale malt were from Californian barley, the rest from English.

The sugar is only described as "invert". No. 3 is my guess. Though it came from three different manufacturers: Garton, Manbré and S & M.

Around 60% of the hops were Californian from the 1913 crop. Though they had been in a cold store. The rest were English from the 1914 and 1915 seasons, the former also having bee stored cold.

1916 Courage KK		
pale malt	13.25 lb	84.13%
No. 3 invert sugar	2.50 lb	15.87%
Cluster 120 mins	3.00 oz	
Fuggles 60 mins	1.50 oz	
Fuggles 30 mins	1.50 oz	
Fuggles dry hops	1.00 oz	
OG	1076	
FG	1028	
ABV	6.35	
Apparent attenuation	63.16%	
IBU	81	
SRM	16	
Mash at	152° F	
Sparge at	159° F	
Boil time	120 minutes	
pitching temp	60° F	
Yeast	Wyeast 1099 Whitbread Ale	

1917 Courage X Ale

April 1917 is when the bad times started to kick in. And when gravities began to drop in earnest.

As well as the gravity dropping a few points, there have also been quite a few changes to the grist. Flaked maize has gone and the proportion of crystal malt and invert sugar has increased. In combination, they've darkened the colour a little.

The hops are much the same as in 1916, Poperinge from 1914 and English from 1914 and 1916. They were a three-way even split but, given their age, I've reduced the quantity of the Belgian hops.

1917 Courage X Ale		
pale malt	6.50 lb	74.29%
crystal malt 60 L	1.00 lb	11.43%
No. 3 invert sugar	1.25 lb	14.29%
Strisselspalt 90 mins	0.50 oz	
Fuggles 60 mins	0.75 oz	
Fuggles 30 mins	0.75 oz	
OG	1042	
FG	1007	
ABV	4.63	
Apparent attenuation	83.33%	
IBU	23	
SRM	13	
Mash at	148° F	
Sparge at	175° F	
Boil time	90 minutes	
pitching temp	60° F	
Yeast	Wyeast 1099 Whitbread Ale	

1917 Courage Porter

By November 1917, when this Porter was brewed, the rules had recently changed. Again.

As of 1st October 1917, beer under 1036° retailed for a maximum price of 4d per pint. Between 1036° and 1042° for 5d a pint. Courage clearly were positioning their Porter as a 4d beer. For commercial reasons, I'm sure. Drinkers expected Porter to be cheap.

They've switched the grist around quite a bit since 1916. The percentage of brown malt has halved. And No. 3 invert has been added. As well as the caramel being massively increased, presumably to compensate for the drop in gravity and brown malt content.

As for the hops, they were all three seasons old: Poperinge and English from 1914. A consequence of grubbing up half of the hop bines. The 1917 English hop crop was tiny. Hence brewers dipping into their emergency stocks. Especially for as cheap beer like Porter, where hop character wasn't paramount. The more recent hops would have been reserved for posher beers.

1917 Courage Porter		
pale malt	5.00 lb	66.14%
brown malt	0.75 lb	9.92%
black malt	0.67 lb	8.86%
No. 3 invert sugar	0.50 lb	6.61%
No. 4 invert sugar	0.50 lb	6.61%
caramel 500 SRM	0.14 lb	1.85%
Strisselspalt 120 mins	0.50 oz	
Fuggles 60 mins	0.75 oz	
OG	1033	
FG	1010	
ABV	3.04	
Apparent attenuation	69.70%	
IBU	18	
SRM	35	
Mash at	149° F	
Sparge at	175° F	
Boil time	120 minutes	
pitching temp	59° F	
Yeast	Wyeast 1099 Whitbread Ale	

1917 Courage Double Stout

Double is quite appropriate in this case, as it's about exactly double the Porter above it was parti-gyled with.

It's surprising how much of this was brewed: 285 barrels to 555 barrels of the Porter. Late in 1917, there wasn't a huge amount of beer at this s ort of strength. Double Stout didn't stick around much longer, disappearing in the spring of 1918 when average OG was set at 1030°.

It never returned. Its replacement, a lower-gravity beer called simply Stout, continued on after war's end. In the 1920s, it was a fairly feeble 1044°.

1917 Courage Double Stout		
pale malt	10.00 lb	68.97%
brown malt	1.50 lb	10.34%
black malt	1.25 lb	8.62%
No. 3 invert sugar	0.75 lb	5.17%
No. 4 invert sugar	0.75 lb	5.17%
caramel 500 SRM	0.25 lb	1.72%
Strisselspalt 120 mins	1.25 oz	
Fuggles 60 mins	1.50 oz	
OG	1064	
FG	1024	
ABV	5.29	
Apparent attenuation	62.50%	
IBU	32	
SRM	50	
Mash at	149° F	
Sparge at	175° F	
Boil time	120 minutes	
pitching temp	59° F	
Yeast	Wyeast 1099 Whitbread Ale	

1917 Courage KK

This is the Courage's pre-war Burton on its farewell tour. Not quite as energetic as earlier, but still able to rock.

The gravity is still a relatively hefty 1073°. Surprising for a beer brewed in October 1917 and just six points lower than in 1914.

The recipe has been slightly tweaked, with a little black malt replacing some of the pale malt. Presumably to darken the colour, which is now dark brown.

The hops are English from the 1916 harvest and Californian from 1915. In the later war years it's quite common to see no hops from the most recent season. Simply because the 1917 and 1918 crops were so small.

1917 Courage KK		
pale malt	12.75 lb	83.61%
black malt	0.25 lb	1.64%
No. 3 invert sugar	2.25 lb	14.75%
Cluster 120 mins	3.25 oz	
Fuggles 60 mins	3.25 oz	
Goldings dry hops	1.25 oz	
OG	1073	
FG	1024	
ABV	6.48	
Apparent attenuation	67.12%	
IBU	94	
SRM	21	
Mash at	153° F	
Sparge at	175° F	
Boil time	120 minutes	
pitching temp	59° F	
Yeast	Wyeast 1099 Whitbread Ale	

1918 Courage X Ale (January)

Almost at the end of the war, and Courage's Mild has seen more changes. Including another cut in the gravity.

Out has gone the flaked maize and back is the black malt. Probably as a consequence of the fall in strength, in order to keep the colour dark enough. In the early part of the 20th century Mild was changing colour. WW I London X Ales were about half way through their transformation from pale to dark beer. They were already dark enough to be easily distinguished from Bitter, but nowhere near the dark brown of modern Mild.

The hops are a combination of Poperinge and English, all from the 1914 crop. Taking that into account, I've cut the hops from 2.5 ozs. to 1.5 ozs.

The degree of attenuation is far above the 65% level of the 1914 version. Compensating for the gravity drop, undoubtedly. Lots of breweries did exactly the same thing. If they had stuck at the pre-war rates of attenuation, many wartime beers would have been non-intoxicating.

1918 Courage X Ale (January)		
pale malt	5.50 lb	74.58%
black malt	0.13 lb	1.69%
crystal malt 60 L	1.00 lb	13.56%
No. 3 invert sugar	0.75 lb	10.17%
Strisselspalt 90 mins	0.75 oz	
Fuggles 60 mins	0.75 oz	
OG	1035	
FG	1007	
ABV	3.70	
Apparent attenuation	80.00%	
IBU	20	
SRM	15	
Mash at	150° F	
Sparge at	170° F	
Boil time	90 minutes	
pitching temp	61° F	
Yeast	Wyeast 1099 Whitbread Ale	

1918 Courage Stout

At the time, this must have been one of the weakest Stouts ever brewed.

It was parti-gyled with Porter which was only a couple of gravity points weaker. It's clear that the distinction between Porter and Stout was beginning to blur. Doubtless this was caused by the big fall in gravity for all beers.

Note that even at this stage of the war they were still using Belgian hops. British brewers weren't particularly impressed by the quality of Poperinge hops but there was one thing they liked about them: they were cheap.

1918 Courage Stout		
pale malt	5.50 lb	67.69%
brown malt	1.00 lb	12.31%
black malt	1.00 lb	12.31%
No. 4 invert sugar	0.50 lb	6.15%
caramel	0.125 lb	1.54%
Strisselspalt 120 mins	0.50 oz	
Fuggles 60 mins	0.50 oz	
Fuggles 30 mins	0.50 oz	
OG	1035	
FG	1008	
ABV	3.57	
Apparent attenuation	77.14%	
IBU	19	
SRM	40	
Mash at	149° F	
Sparge at	168° F	
Boil time	120 minutes	
pitching temp	60° F	
Yeast	Wyeast 1099 Whitbread Ale	

1918 Courage Double Stout

A surprisingly strong Stout for this phase of the war. Very little beer of this strength was being brewed in 1918.

In May 1918, when this beer was brewed, the average OG of everything made in a brewery could only be 1030°. To brew something of this strength, you'd need to brew a lot of sub-1030° beer. Why did brewers bother, then? Because anything over 1034° didn't fall under government price controls. Brewers could charge what they wanted, making such beers very profitable.

The hops are really ancient. Belgian and English from the 1914 crop. A sure sign that Courage were raiding their emergency hop supplies. In 1918, too few hops were grown in the UK to meet demand and imports had dried up.

I used to think that WW I had been a disaster for British brewing. In fact, despite all the restrictions, the opposite was true. Many breweries had struggled in the years leading up to the war, increased licence duties in the 1909 budget had greatly reduced the value of pubs. Many breweries saw the value of their assets so reduced that they had to reduce the value of their share capital. Few brewers were making much money. The war changed all that. Despite brewing far less beer, brewery profits were up.

1918 Courage Double Stout		
pale malt	10.00 lb	68.97%
brown malt	1.25 lb	8.62%
black malt	1.75 lb	12.07%
No. 4 invert sugar	1.25 lb	8.62%
caramel	0.25 lb	1.72%
Strisselspalt 120 mins	1.00 oz	
Fuggles 60 mins	1.00 oz	
Fuggles 30 mins	0.75 oz	
OG	1064	
FG	1021	
ABV	5.69	
Apparent attenuation	67.19%	
IBU	29	
SRM	62	
Mash at	151° F	
Sparge at	170° F	
Boil time	120 minutes	
pitching temp	61° F	
Yeast	Wyeast 1099 Whitbread Ale	

1918 Courage Porter

A late war Porter that is quite similar to those of the 1930's, when Porter became a low-ABV drink.

You'll note that this has an OG only two points lower than their Stout. Which must have helped blurred the distinction between the two styles in drinkers' eyes. This particular example was parti-gyled with the Double Stout above. Rather more of this was brewed: 567 to 208 barrels.

This being parti-gyled with the Double Stout above, there's no need for further recipe discussion.

1918 Courage Porter			
pale malt	5.25 lb	68.85%
brown malt	0.75 lb	9.84%
black malt	1.00 lb	13.11%
No. 4 invert sugar	0.50 lb	6.56%
caramel	0.13 lb	1.64%
Strisselspalt 120 mins	0.50 oz		
Fuggles 60 mins	0.50 oz		
Fuggles 30 mins	0.25 oz		
OG	1033		
FG	1009		
ABV	3.18		
Apparent attenuation	72.73%		
IBU	16		
SRM	40		
Mash at	151° F		
Sparge at	170° F		
Boil time	120 minutes		
pitching temp	61° F		
Yeast	Wyeast 1099 Whitbread Ale		

1918 Courage X Ale (November)

The end of 1918 was a particularly dark time for British brewing. Or, rather, British drinkers. The breweries were doing just fine, operating much more profitably than before the war.

At least you weren't going to be bothered by a hangover after drinking this version of X Ale. At just 2.25% ABV, it's barely stronger than shandy.

The recipe has been tinkered with since the beginning of the year. Both the black and crystal malt content has been boosted considerably. For two reasons. First, to compensate for the fall in gravity. Second, to offset the replacement of No. 3 invert by glucose. At this point brewers were extremely limited in the types of sugar they were allowed to purchase.

The hopping is quite heavy – 1 lb per barrel, 11 lbs per quarter of malt – but it needs to be, given their age. About a third were Poperinge hops from 1914, the remainder English hops from 1915. I've almost halved the quantity to take this into account.

Happily for drinkers, the gravity of X Ale increased again in 1919. But it wasn't until the autumn of that year that it rose above 1030°.

1918 Courage X Ale (November)		
pale malt	3.00 lb	66.67%
black malt	0.25 lb	5.56%
crystal malt 60 L	0.75 lb	16.67%
glucose	0.50 lb	11.11%
Strisselspalt 120 mins	0.33 oz	
Fuggles 60 mins	1.00 oz	
OG	1021	
FG	1004	
ABV	2.25	
Apparent attenuation	80.95%	
IBU	12	
SRM	14	
Mash at	152° F	
Sparge at	165° F	
Boil time	90 minutes	
pitching temp	61° F	
Yeast	Wyeast 1099 Whitbread Ale	

1919 Courage Stout

When this beer was brewed in the July 1919, things were beginning to look up for drinkers.

A few months earlier, in May, average permitted gravity had been increased to 1044°. Which is why Courage was able to raise the gravity of their Stout. By this point their Horsleydown brewery was only producing two beers: X Ale and Stout.

The malt part of the grist remains the classic London combination of pale, brown and black. And in pretty much identical proportions of each as in 1918. The sugar has changed, however, now being described as "Cuban" which must mean some sort of cane sugar.

As was the case at most breweries in this period around the end of the war, the hops were pretty old. A 50-50 split of Californian and English, both from the 1915 harvest. To take that into account, I've reduced the quantity by 25%.

The mash was a bit more complicated than indicated in the recipe below. There was an initial 90-minute mash at 144° F, followed by an underlet which increased the temperature to 158° for a further 90 minutes.

1919 Courage Stout		
pale malt	7.50 lb	68.18%
brown malt	1.00 lb	9.09%
black malt	1.25 lb	11.36%
cane sugar	1.00 lb	9.09%
caramel	0.25 lb	2.27%
Cluster 90 mins	1.00 oz	
Fuggles 30 mins	1.00 oz	
OG	1048.5	
FG	1011	
ABV	4.96	
Apparent attenuation	77.32%	
IBU	30	
SRM	44	
Mash at	151° F	
Sparge at	165° F	
Boil time	90 minutes	
pitching temp	61° F	
Yeast	Wyeast 1099 Whitbread Ale	

1919 Courage X Ale

By late 1919 many beers were starting to acquire something like their interwar form. At least in terms of gravity.

Though the OG remains 15 points lower than it was pre-war. This version could get you pissed, unlike the late 1918 X Ale. I wonder if the alcohol content was a shock after years of watery crap?

With more raw materials becoming available, the grist has reverted to being much the same as in 1914. Except now it includes flaked maize and a tiny amount of "Cuban" sugar.

The hops are two-thirds English from the 1917 crop and one third Californian from 1915. I've considerably reduced the latter to account for their age.

As with the Stout above, a sort of step mash was employed, starting at 147° for 90 minutes, followed by an underlet and another 90 minutes at 156° F.

1919 Courage X Ale		
pale malt	5.50 lb	61.76%
black malt	0.125 lb	1.40%
crystal malt 60 L	1.25 lb	14.04%
flaked maize	0.75 lb	8.42%
No. 3 invert sugar	1.25 lb	14.04%
cane sugar	0.03 lb	0.34%
Cluster 90 mins	0.50 oz	
Fuggles 60 mins	0.75 oz	
Fuggles 30 mins	0.50 oz	
OG	1040	
FG	1007.5	
ABV	4.30	
Apparent attenuation	81.25%	
IBU		
SRM		
Mash at	151° F	
Sparge at	165° F	
Boil time	90 minutes	
pitching temp	63° F	
Yeast	Wyeast 1099 Whitbread Ale	

1920 Courage X Ale

Just because the war was over and things were returning to normality doesn't mean that gravities continued to rise. Some beers, like Courage X, got weaker again.

It's odd, because in 1919 they seemed to be plumping for a gravity typical of the 1920's London X Ale, something in the low 1040°s. Then, in 1920, they dropped the gravity to that of an interwar 4d Ale. Not sure why they did that. Though they did introduce a new Mild Ale in the mid-1920s with an OG of 1043°, the classic 6d strength.

Some changes have been made to the grist, too. The black malt and "Cuban" sugar have been dropped. The removal of the former must have had an effect on the colour of the finished beer, especially as the OG has dropped, too.

The hops are a third each of Saaz, English and Californian. The first two from 1917, the latter from 1916. Quite a few foreign hops appeared after the war's end, including ones which had been grown while the conflict was still raging, like the Saaz here. I'm guessing that the almost total shutdown of brewing in Central Europe at the end of the war had led to a glut of hops.

If you want to go all authentic on the mash, start at 148° F for 90 minutes then raise the temperature to 158° F for another 90.

1920 Courage X Ale		
pale malt	4.75 lb	65.52%
crystal malt 60 L	1.25 lb	17.24%
flaked maize	0.50 lb	6.90%
No. 3 invert sugar	0.75 lb	10.34%
Cluster 90 mins	0.50 oz	
Fuggles 60 mins	0.50 oz	
Saaz 30 mins	0.50 oz	
OG	1033	
FG	1005.5	
ABV	3.64	
Apparent attenuation	83.33%	
IBU	23	
SRM	12	
Mash at	152° F	
Sparge at	162° F	
Boil time	90 minutes	
pitching temp	63° F	
Yeast	Wyeast 1099 Whitbread Ale	

1920 Courage Porter

The rise in gravity of Courage Stout in 1920 created space for a Porter again. It duly returned, though at a much lower gravity than in 1914.

In terms of grist, it's very similar to the Porter brewed in 1918 just before it was discontinued. The ingredients are identical and the proportions quite similar. It is a very traditional looking London Porter/Stout grist.

Again there are wartime hops from the enemy, this time in the form of 1917 Alsace hops. The rest are a combination of 1917 English and 1916 Californian. I've reduce the quantities accordingly.

I'm intrigued by the difference in the mashing scheme between X Ale and Porter. In this case, there was no underlet and a single mashing temperature of 148° F.

1920 Courage Porter		
pale malt	4.50 lb	65.45%
brown malt	0.75 lb	10.91%
black malt	1.00 lb	14.55%
No. 4 invert sugar	0.50 lb	7.27%
caramel	0.125 lb	1.82%
Cluster 90 mins	0.50 oz	
Strisselspalt 60 mins	0.75 oz	
Fuggles 30 mins	0.75 oz	
OG	1030	
FG	1007.5	
ABV	2.98	
Apparent attenuation	75.00%	
IBU	29	
SRM	42	
Mash at	148° F	
Sparge at	164° F	
Boil time	90 minutes	
pitching temp	61° F	
Yeast	Wyeast 1099 Whitbread Ale	

1920 Courage Double Stout

It wasn't just Courage X Ale that fell in gravity between 1919 and 1920. Exactly the same happened with their Stout.

I understand why. It wasn't about direct restrictions on gravity, but about price. In April 1920, the tax per standard barrel (36 gallons at 1055°) increased from 80s to 100s, effectively adding 1d to the price per pint. It's important to remember that there were still price controls at this point. By dropping the OG of their Stout below 1045°, it kept it in the 7d per pint category. Courage must have guessed that their customers didn't have enough money to pay more for their beer.

How ironic that they changed the name back to Double Stout at the same time as they reduced its OG.

For comments on the recipe see the Porter above which was parti-gyled with this Stout.

1920 Courage Double Stout		
pale malt	7.00 lb	69.14%
brown malt	1.00 lb	9.88%
black malt	1.25 lb	12.35%
No. 4 invert sugar	0.75 lb	7.41%
caramel	0.125 lb	1.23%
Cluster 90 mins	0.75 oz	
Strisselspalt 60 mins	1.00 oz	
Fuggles 30 mins	1.00 oz	
OG	1044	
FG	1012	
ABV	4.23	
Apparent attenuation	72.73%	
IBU	37	
SRM	45	
Mash at	148° F	
Sparge at	164° F	
Boil time	90 minutes	
pitching temp	62° F	
Yeast	Wyeast 1099 Whitbread Ale	

1920 Courage SA

After a couple of year's absence, a Strong Ale or Burton made a return to Horsleydown at the start of 1920. Though not under the same name, at least in the brewhouse.

It was at a much lower gravity than the 1073° of 1917 KK. Which was logical enough. At a time of price controls, in made no economic sense. Whatever its strength, the maximum price you could charge for a beer over 1054° was 9d per pint at this point (December 1920). A beer of 1073° was economic suicide.

While before the was Courage brewed their Burton single-gyle, SA was parti-gyled with X Ale. Leading inescapably to this effectively being a strong Mild. The only difference being that SA was dry hopped.

The hops are Saaz and English from 1917 and Californian from 1916, plus Saaz dry hops from 1919. Using them as dry hops shows how highly UK brewers rated Saaz.

1920 Courage SA		
pale malt	7.75 lb	65.96%
crystal malt 60 L	2.25 lb	19.15%
flaked maize	0.75 lb	6.38%
No. 3 invert sugar	1.00 lb	8.51%
Cluster 90 mins	0.75 oz	
Fuggles 60 mins	0.75 oz	
Saaz 30 mins	0.75 oz	
Saaz dry hops	0.50 oz	
OG	1053.5	
FG	1014	
ABV	5.23	
Apparent attenuation	73.83%	
IBU	30	
SRM	16	
Mash at	152° F	
Sparge at	163° F	
Boil time	90 minutes	
pitching temp	63° F	
Yeast	Wyeast 1099 Whitbread Ale	

Crowley

A brewery in Alton, Hampshire. Originally established by Janes Baverstock in 1763, it was bought by the Crowley family in 1823. Despite being sold to the Burrell family in 1871, but continued to trade under the Crowley name. It became a limited company in 1901. When it was purchased by Watney in 1947, it had just shy of 250 tied houses. It closed in 1970.

Alton was a popular location for breweries, due to its well water, which resembled that of Burton. This is reflected in the large range of Pale Ales brewed by Crowley.

At the start of the war, Crowley brewed quite a lot of beers, but not in a very wide range of styles:

Crowley beers in 1914							
Beer	Style	OG	FG	ABV	App. Atten-uation	lbs hops/ qtr	hops lb/brl
AK	Pale Ale	1047.1	1011.1	4.76	76.47%	6.25	1.10
B	Pale Ale	1038.8	1007.2	4.18	81.43%	7.17	1.01
BB	Pale Ale	1045.7	1009.4	4.80	79.39%	9.82	1.64
BBB	Pale Ale	1054.0	1011.6	5.61	78.46%	10.75	2.11
L	Pale Ale	1052.6	1014.4	5.06	72.63%	6.25	1.24
Porter	Porter	1049.9	1016.6	4.40	66.67%	5.63	1.05
Stout	Stout	1067.9	1026.0	5.53	61.63%	5.63	1.43
Source: Brewing record held at Hampshire Archives and Local Studies, document number 37M86-2.							

1914 Crowley AK

As far as beer ranges go, Crowley's is pretty confusing. Making AK a welcome, understandable sight.

The OG is right where I would expect a pre-war AK to be: somewhere in the mid-1040°s. I keep finding new AK's from this period. But the war was not kind to them. As they were often a brewery's weakest Pale Ale, they disappeared as strengths fell and what had been posher beers took their gravity slot.

The recipe, which consists of just pale malt and No. 3 invert sugar, is almost Whitbread-like in its simplicity. Though it is odd to see No. 3 in a Bitter. The colour is a little on the dark side, but not crazily so. I've other brews which use No. 2 instead of No. 3. It all depends on what AK was being parti-gyled with. This one was brewed with L, others with B. It's the L parti-gyles that have the No. 3.

The hops are English from 1912 and 1913 plus Oregon from 1913. Given the age of some of the hops, I've reduced the quantity.

1914 Crowley AK		
pale malt	10.00 lb	93.02%
No. 3 invert sugar	0.75 lb	6.98%
Cluster 120 mins	0.75 oz	
Fuggles 90 mins	0.50 oz	
Goldings 30 mins	0.50 oz	
Goldings dry hops	0.25 oz	
OG	1047	
FG	1011	
ABV	4.76	
Apparent attenuation	76.60%	
IBU	28	
SRM	8	
Mash at	148° F	
Sparge at	160° F	
Boil time	120 minutes	
pitching temp	60° F	
Yeast	Wyeast 1275 Thames Valley ale	

1914 Crowley L

I would have had L down as a Pale Ale but apparently it was their Mild Ale. Unfortunately, a price list I've seen from 1910 doesn't include it for some reason.

As it was parti-gyled with the AK above, everything mentioned about that recipe applies here, too.

1914 Crowley L		
pale malt	11.00 lb	91.67%
No. 3 invert sugar	1.00 lb	8.33%
Cluster 120 mins	0.75 oz	
Fuggles 90 mins	0.75 oz	
Goldings 30 mins	0.50 oz	
Goldings dry hops	0.50 oz	
OG	1053	
FG	1014	
ABV	5.16	
Apparent attenuation	73.58%	
IBU	30	
SRM	9	
Mash at	149° F	
Sparge at	160° F	
Boil time	120 minutes	
pitching temp	59° F	
Yeast	Wyeast 1275 Thames Valley ale	

1914 Crowley B

By 1914 standard Crowley B was a very low-gravity Pale Ale. It was unusual to see one with a gravity below 1040° in England.

It can't have been a very popular beer, as it was always parti-gyled with AK in relatively small quantities: 35-40 barrels. For comparison, their other Pale Ales were brewed in batches of 150-175 barrels.

There's not much to say about the recipe: a single malt and a single type of sugar. Not much complication in the hops, either: English from 1912 and 1913, Oregon from 1913.

1914 Crowley B		
pale malt	8.00 lb	91.43%
No. 2 invert sugar	0.75 lb	8.57%
Cluster 150 mins	0.50 oz	
Fuggles 90 mins	0.50 oz	
Fuggles 60 mins	0.50 oz	
Fuggles 30 mins	0.50 oz	
Goldings dry hops	0.25 oz	
OG	1039	
FG	1007	
ABV	4.23	
Apparent attenuation	82.05%	
IBU	31	
SRM	8	
Mash at	150° F	
Sparge at	160° F	
Boil time	120 minutes	
pitching temp	59.5° F	
Yeast	Wyeast 1275 Thames Valley ale	

1914 Crowley BB

Here's an oddity: a single-gyle Crowley beer.

Superficially, it looks very their AK. The OG's are very similar, as are the recipes. Except BB has No. 2 invert rather than No. 3. Though there is a big difference in the hopping. While AK had around 6 pounds of hops per quarter of malt. That accounts for the big difference in calculated IBUs, 48 here as opposed to 28 in AK.

A high degree of attenuation pushes the ABV to close to 5%. Which in just a couple of years would have made it a pretty strong Bitter. In 1914, it was on the weak side even for an Ordinary Bitter.

1914 Crowley BB		
pale malt	9.75 lb	92.86%
No. 2 invert sugar	0.75 lb	7.14%
Cluster 150 mins	0.75 oz	
Fuggles 90 mins	1.00 oz	
Fuggles 60 mins	0.75 oz	
Fuggles 30 mins	0.75 oz	
Goldings dry hops	0.25 oz	
OG	1046	
FG	1009	
ABV	4.89	
Apparent attenuation	80.43%	
IBU	48	
SRM	8	
Mash at	151° F	
Sparge at	160° F	
Boil time	150 minutes	
pitching temp	59° F	
Yeast	Wyeast 1275 Thames Valley ale	

1914 Crowley BBB

Strongest among Crowley's Pale Ales was BBB, though it still wasn't at the level of a Burton-brewed example.

Like all their beers, there's nothing at all complicated about the grist, which is just pale malt and sugar. There's not even any hidden complexity as there's just one pale malt. And English one. It really is a dead simple recipe.

The hopping isn't exactly complicated, either, just 1913 English and Oregon. The additions, as usual, are pure guesswork. Feel free to fiddle with them.

Having seen a price list, I would have guessed that B, BB and BBB were all parti-gyled together. But they weren't. BB and BBB were always brewed single-gyle. This allowed them to have a different level of hopping for each. B had 7 lbs per quarter, BB 10 lbs and BBB 11 lbs. This is reflected in the much higher IBU rating of BBB.

1914 Crowley BBB		
pale malt	11.50 lb	93.88%
No. 2 invert sugar	0.75 lb	6.12%
Cluster 120 mins	1.25 oz	
Fuggles 90 mins	1.25 oz	
Fuggles 60 mins	1.00 oz	
Fuggles 30 mins	1.00 oz	
Goldings dry hops	0.50 oz	
OG	1054	
FG	1012	
ABV	5.56	
Apparent attenuation	77.78%	
IBU	63	
SRM	7	
Mash at	153° F	
Sparge at	160° F	
Boil time	120 minutes	
pitching temp	59° F	
Yeast	Wyeast 1275 Thames Valley ale	

1914 Crowley Porter

Unusually for a provincial brewery, Crowley still produced a Porter in 1914.

At 1050°, it's a similar strength to London Porter. Though the grist is quite different. For a start there's no brown malt, which a London Porter would always include. No black malt, either, instead there's chocolate malt. It's a very early date to see this type of malt. Though Whitbread started using it in the 1920s.

The presence of a small amount of oats mean they must have been selling some of the brew as Oatmeal Stout. There's not much of it, despite it being considerably more than London brewers bothered with.

Then there's lots of sugar: around 14% of the grist in total. The original had three sugars, in addition to the caramel, 10 cwt cane, 2 cwt candy and 1 cwt CDW. I've rolled the last two together as candy.

As with most of Crowley's beers, the hops are a combination of 1912 and 1913 English with 1913 Oregon.

1914 Crowley Porter		
pale malt	7.00 lb	75.68%
chocolate malt	0.75 lb	8.11%
flaked oats	0.25 lb	2.70%
cane sugar	0.75 lb	8.11%
candy sugar	0.25 lb	2.70%
caramel 500 SRM	0.25 lb	2.70%
Cluster 120 mins	1.00 oz	
Fuggles 60 mins	1.00 oz	
OG	1050	
FG	1017	
ABV	4.37	
Apparent attenuation	66.00%	
IBU	46	
SRM	35	
Mash at	155° F	
Sparge at	176° F	
Boil time	120 minutes	
pitching temp	59° F	
Yeast	Wyeast 1275 Thames Valley ale	

1914 Crowley Stout

Parti-gyled with Porter was Stout. While it would have been on the weak side in London, it's about in line with other provincial English Stouts.

Obviously, the grist is identical to the Porter, them having been brewed together.

1914 Crowley Stout			
pale malt		10.75 lb	74.19%
chocolate malt		1.00 lb	6.90%
flaked oats		0.33 lb	2.28%
cane sugar		1.75 lb	12.08%
candy sugar		0.33 lb	2.28%
caramel 500 SRM		0.33 lb	2.28%
Cluster 120 mins		1.25 oz	
Fuggles 60 mins		1.50 oz	
OG		1068	
FG		1026	
ABV		5.56	
Apparent attenuation		61.76%	
IBU		44	
SRM		38	
Mash at		155° F	
Sparge at		176° F	
Boil time		120 minutes	
pitching temp		58° F	
Yeast	Wyeast 1275 Thames Valley ale		

1916 Crowley AK

A trend in the middle war years was for the more popular beers to have their gravities reduced, while posher beers were mostly unaffected. That's clear in the case of Crowley AK, where the gravity dropped four points between 1914 and 1916. Things were only going to get worse.

The big change to the recipe is the addition of CDM – caramelised dextro-maltose. That's the caramel that you can see in the recipe. There's also a quantity of a sugar called laevuline, for which I've substituted more No. 3 invert.

The hops in this example were all pretty old, English from the 1914 harvest, Oregon from 1912. In the later war years more and more ancient hops appeared, presumably emergency stocks that were being raided.

1916 Crowley AK		
pale malt	8.50 lb	88.31%
No. 3 invert sugar	1.00 lb	10.39%
caramel 500 SRM	0.13 lb	1.30%
Cluster 120 mins	0.25 oz	
Fuggles 120 mins	0.50 oz	
Goldings 30 mins	1.00 oz	
Goldings dry hops	0.25 oz	
OG	1043	
FG	1011	
ABV	4.23	
Apparent attenuation	74.42%	
IBU	24	
SRM	13	
Mash at	149º F	
Sparge at	160º F	
Boil time	120 minutes	
pitching temp	59.75º F	
Yeast	Wyeast 1275 Thames Valley ale	

1916 Crowley AK F

I've no idea what the "F" stands for here. Nor why Crowley produced two versions of AK with gravities just a couple of points apart.

The big difference between this beer and straight AK is the lack of the sugar CDM. Otherwise the recipes are identical. The difference might be explained by the fact that this example was parti-gyled with B.

The hops were exactly the same as in the AK above. Older hops were typical as the war progressed. Especially after 1917 when the crop of UK hops was drastically reduced when farmers were compelled to grub up some of their hop bines to make way for food production.

1916 Crowley AK F		
pale malt	8.50 lb	91.89%
No. 3 invert sugar	0.75 lb	8.11%
Cluster 120 mins	0.25 oz	
Fuggles 120 mins	0.50 oz	
Goldings 30 mins	1.00 oz	
Goldings dry hops	0.25 oz	
OG	1041.5	
FG	1009.5	
ABV	4.23	
Apparent attenuation	77.11%	
IBU	24	
SRM	8	
Mash at	150° F	
Sparge at	160° F	
Boil time	120 minutes	
pitching temp	59.5° F	
Yeast	Wyeast 1275 Thames Valley ale	

1916 Crowley L

Crowley's rather enigmatic L, which I'm not sure whether it was really a Mild Ale or a Pale Ale, continued to be one of the mainstays of their range. Often it was parti-gyled with the weaker AK. As was this, though not with the AK above.

The grist consists of just three elements: pale malt, No. 3 invert sugar and laevuline. For the latter I've simply substituted more No. 3. Laevulose is an old name for fructose, so possibly that's what laevuline is, or something similar. If you like, replace a quarter of a pound of the No. 3 invert sugar.

The hops were the same as the two beers above: 1914 English and 1912 Oregon.

1916 Crowley L		
pale malt	9.50 lb	90.48%
No. 3 invert sugar	1.00 lb	9.52%
Cluster 120 mins	0.25 oz	
Fuggles 120 mins	0.50 oz	
Goldings 30 mins	1.00 oz	
OG	1047	
FG	1012	
ABV	4.63	
Apparent attenuation	74.47%	
IBU	23	
SRM	9	
Mash at	149° F	
Sparge at	160° F	
Boil time	120 minutes	
pitching temp	60° F	
Yeast	Wyeast 1275 Thames Valley ale	

1916 Crowley B

Not a huge amount as changed with B since the start of the war, other than 1.5 points being shaved off the OG.

The grist remains just pale malt and invert sugar, though the latter has changed from No. 2 to No. 3. That's probably on account of this beer having been parti-gyled with the L above.

The hopping has been reduced, too. Down from 7 lbs per quarter of malt (1 lb per barrel) to 6 lbs per quarter (0.84 lbs per barrel). That's reflected in the (calculated) IBU count, which has dropped from 31 to 21.

The hops are the same as for all the other beers so far this year.

1916 Crowley B		
pale malt	7.75 lb	91.18%
No. 3 invert sugar	0.75 lb	8.82%
Cluster 120 mins	0.25 lb	
Fuggles 120 mins	0.25 oz	
Fuggles 60 mins	0.50 oz	
Fuggles 30 mins	0.50 oz	
Goldings dry hops	0.25 oz	
OG	1037.5	
FG	1009.5	
ABV	3.70	
Apparent attenuation	74.67%	
IBU	21	
SRM	8	
Mash at	150° F	
Sparge at	160° F	
Boil time	120 minutes	
pitching temp	63.25° F	
Yeast	Wyeast 1275 Thames Valley ale	

1916 Crowley BB

The next Pale Ale up strength-wise has also fallen in gravity since 1914. This time by three points.

The only change to the grist is the addition of some laevuline to supplement the No. 2 invert. If you like, you can swap 20% of the invert for fructose.

The hopping rate has fallen here, too. Down from 10 lbs per quarter of malt (1.64 lbs per barrel) to 8 lbs per quarter (1.33 lbs per barrel). I'm not sure why that might have been, other than that hops were be3coming more difficult to find.

For a little variety, the hops here were all English, two different types from 1914. Which isn't quite as old as it might sound as this beer was brewed on 1st February.

1916 Crowley BB		
pale malt	8.75 lb	92.11%
No. 2 invert sugar	0.75 lb	7.89%
Fuggles 120 mins	1.25 oz	
Goldings 30 mins	1.50 oz	
Goldings dry hops	0.50 oz	
OG	1043	
FG	1010	
ABV	4.37	
Apparent attenuation	76.74%	
IBU	35	
SRM	8	
Mash at	151° F	
Sparge at	160° F	
Boil time	120 minutes	
pitching temp	59.75° F	
Yeast	Wyeast 1275 Thames Valley ale	

1916 Crowley BBB

Crowley's top-level Pale Ale, BBB, has also lost three gravity points since the start of the war, but remains a powerful beer.

It was parti-gyled with the BB above, so its recipe comments apply. With one addition. The hopping rate has fallen even more, as the 1914 version was hopped at 10.75 lbs per quarter of malt, while this one has only 8 lbs per quarter.

That's knocked the (calculated) IBUs down from 63 to 39. Surely drinkers must have noticed the change? I can imagine you might not spot the small change in OG, but that's a big drop in the bitterness level.

1916 Crowley BBB		
pale malt	10.76 lb	93.48%
No. 2 invert sugar	0.75 lb	6.52%
Fuggles 120 mins	1.50 oz	
Goldings 30 mins	1.75 oz	
Goldings dry hops	0.50 oz	
OG	1051	
FG	1014	
ABV	4.89	
Apparent attenuation	72.55%	
IBU	39	
SRM	8	
Mash at	151° F	
Sparge at	160° F	
Boil time	120 minutes	
pitching temp	58.75° F	
Yeast	Wyeast 1275 Thames Valley ale	

1916 Crowley Porter

A couple of years into the war, not that much has changed with Crowley Porter. Other than a drop of a point and a half in the gravity.

The presence of oats is a giveaway that some of the Stout that it was parti-gyled with was marketed as Oatmeal Stout. The percentage of oats is quite high – actually enough to have an impact on the finished beer. Unlike in many London Oatmeal Stouts.

The malts remain a simple – for a black beer – combination of pale and chocolate malt. There have been some changes to the sugars, with candy and CDW being dropped.

The hops are English from the 1914 crop plus Oregon from 1913. Barely any newer than those in the version from 2 years earlier, which contained hops from the 1912 and 1913 season. The age of the hops used and the reduction in the proportion of US hops have halved the (calculated) IBUs compared to 1914.

1916 Crowley Porter		
pale malt	6.50 lb	65.00%
chocolate malt	0.75 lb	7.50%
oats	0.75 lb	7.50%
cane sugar	1.75 lb	17.50%
caramel 500 SRM	0.25 lb	2.50%
Cluster 135 mins	0.25 lb	
Fuggles 135 mins	0.50 oz	
Goldings 30 mins	0.75 oz	
OG	1048.5	
FG	1015	
ABV	4.43	
Apparent attenuation	69.07%	
IBU	23	
SRM	30	
Mash at	150° F	
Sparge at	170° F	
Boil time	135 minutes	
pitching temp	58.5° F	
Yeast	Wyeast 1275 Thames Valley ale	

1916 Crowley Stout

The other element of the oats parti-gyle was Crowley's Stout. Another beer that had seen its gravity drop by a modest three points since the start of the war.

Like the Porter, there's been a considerable drop in the bitterness in the two years of war. Loss of access to high-alpha acid American hops must have caused brewers headaches, especially when UK hops were also becoming difficult to source.

They seem to have got by for a while by using up old stocks of US hops, imported before the war. In this case, the Oregon hops were from 1913. Its noticeable that the longer the war lasted, the older the hops – especially foreign ones – that were used.

1916 Crowley Stout			
pale malt		9.25 lb	65.70%
chocolate malt		1.00 lb	7.10%
oats		1.00 lb	7.10%
cane sugar		2.50 lb	17.76%
caramel 500 SRM		0.33 lb	2.34%
Cluster 135 mins		0.25 oz	
Fuggles 135 mins		0.75 oz	
Goldings 30 mins		1.00 oz	
Goldings dry hops		0.50 oz	
OG		1065	
FG		1022	
ABV		5.69	
Apparent attenuation		66.15%	
IBU		26	
SRM		37	
Mash at		150° F	
Sparge at		170° F	
Boil time		135 minutes	
pitching temp		58.25° F	
Yeast	Wyeast 1275 Thames Valley ale		

1917 Crowley L

April 1917 was when the serious problems for the UK brewing industry kicked in. As the UK government reacted to disruption of food imports by the German U-boat campaign that had kicked off at the start of the year by restricting brewers access to raw materials and slashing the amount of beer that they were allowed to brew.

That's evident in this beer, which was brewed in May. The OG is eight points lower than just a couple of months earlier. Though the recipe remains much the same, consisting of pale malt, No. 3 invert and laevuline. Though the percentage of total sugar has declined slightly.

The level of hopping is around the same. Mode up of English from 1914 and 1916, plus Oregon from 1912. It's one year later, yet the Oregon hops are from one year earlier. See what I mean about the foreign hops getting older and older as the war progressed?

1917 Crowley L		
pale malt	8.00 lb	91.43%
No. 3 invert sugar	0.75 lb	8.57%
Cluster 120 mins	0.33 oz	
Fuggles 90 mins	0.75 oz	
Goldings 30 mins	0.50 oz	
OG	1039	
FG	1009	
ABV	3.97	
Apparent attenuation	76.92%	
IBU	24	
SRM	8	
Mash at	149° F	
Sparge at	160° F	
Boil time	120 minutes	
pitching temp	59.5° F	
Yeast	Wyeast 1275 Thames Valley ale	

1917 Crowley AK

The restrictions of spring 1917 began to form a real existential threat to many AKs. As their gravity was forced down towards oblivion.

Crowley's AK has lost a full ten gravity points over the course of just a few months, forcing it down to a very watery 1033°. Starting off relatively weak even before the war, successive gravity drops left many AKs inviably low strength. It wasn't uncommon for what had been a full-strength Pale Ale before the war to end up claiming the Light Bitter slot previously occupied by AK.

See the L above for recipe notes, as these two beers were parti-gyled together.

1917 Crowley AK		
pale malt	7.00 lb	93.33%
No. 3 invert sugar	0.50 lb	6.67%
Cluster 120 mins	0.25 oz	
Fuggles 90 mins	0.67 oz	
Goldings 30 mins	0.50 oz	
OG	1033	
FG	1006.5	
ABV	3.51	
Apparent attenuation	80.30%	
IBU	22	
SRM	6	
Mash at	149° F	
Sparge at	160° F	
Boil time	120 minutes	
pitching temp	60° F	
Yeast	Wyeast 1275 Thames Valley ale	

1917 Crowley BB

Posher Pale Ale BB hasn't fared so badly as AK or L in terms of a gravity hit, dropping just three points since 1916. Though at this point it was Crowley's strongest Pale Ale, BBB having been discontinued.

The bitterness has also stood up well, the IBUs even rising a little according to my calculation.

Once again, the grist changes have all been in the sugars, with some of the No. 2 invert and laevuline being replaced by CDM, which I've listed as caramel in my recipe.

The hops are relatively fresh for this stage of the war – three types of English hops, all from the 1916 harvest. English hops from later than the 1916 crop were relatively rare as the government forced growers to root up a large percentage of their hop bines in 1917 to make way for food production.

1917 Crowley BB		
pale malt	8.00 lb	90.14%
No. 2 invert sugar	0.75 lb	8.45%
caramel 500 SRM	0.125 lb	1.41%
Fuggles 150 mins	1.50 oz	
Goldings 30 mins	1.50 oz	
Goldings dry hops	0.50 oz	
OG	1040	
FG	1008	
ABV	4.23	
Apparent attenuation	80.00%	
IBU	39	
SRM	12	
Mash at	149° F	
Sparge at	160° F	
Boil time	150 minutes	
pitching temp	58.5° F	
Yeast	Wyeast 1275 Thames Valley ale	

1917 Crowley Porter

Another beer whose gravity was continuing to stand up relatively well was the Porter, down 5.5 points.

Though that may be because Crowley were no longer brewing much Stout. In earlier years, their Porter and Stout were always brewed as parti-gyles, but in 1917 there were many single-gyle brews of Porter. I've seen various claims that Porter was often sold as Stout in the later war years. Maybe that's what was going on here.

As with the other beers, the main change in the grist is a reduction in the sugar. The malt content has risen from 73% to 90%. I'm sure purely as a result of sugar being diverted to food production. That was the name of the game in 1917. Every possible food resource was exploited as U-boats began to strangle imports.

That this wasn't as classy a beer as BB is reflected in the hops, which are generally older: English from 1914 and 1916, Oregon from 1912.

1917 Crowley Porter			
pale malt		7.75 lb	81.58%
chocolate malt		0.75 lb	7.89%
cane sugar		0.75 lb	7.89%
caramel 500 SRM		0.25 lb	2.63%
Cluster 135 mins		0.33 oz	
Fuggles 135 mins		0.75 oz	
Goldings 30 mins		0.67 oz	
OG		1043	
FG		1011	
ABV		4.23	
Apparent attenuation		74.42%	
IBU		29	
SRM		30	
Mash at		150° F	
Sparge at		170° F	
Boil time		135 minutes	
pitching temp		59° F	
Yeast	Wyeast 1275 Thames Valley ale		

1917 Crowley Stout

Though they were mostly churning out single-gyle brews of Porter, there was till the occasional parti-gyle with Stout.

The gravity was holding up very well. Not many beers were brewed with an OG of over 1060° after spring 1917. With a limitation on output based on standard barrels, the more strong beer you brewed, the less of everything else you could make. Which doubtless explains their Stout only being brewed occasionally.

Though not parti-gyled with the Porter above, the two do share very similar grists. Which consist of pale and chocolate malt, cane sugar and caramel. Crowley were very early in their use of chocolate malt to colour their black beers. It's rare to see before the 1920s.

The hope were identical to the Porter above.

1917 Crowley Stout		
pale malt	10.75 lb	79.63%
chocolate malt	1.00 lb	7.41%
cane sugar	1.25 lb	9.26%
caramel 500 SRM	0.50 lb	3.70%
Cluster 120 mins	0.50 oz	
Fuggles 120 mins	1.00 oz	
Goldings 30 mins	1.00 oz	
OG	1061	
FG	1020.5	
ABV	5.36	
Apparent attenuation	66.39%	
IBU	36	
SRM	40	
Mash at	149° F	
Sparge at	170° F	
Boil time	120 minutes	
pitching temp	58.5° F	
Yeast	Wyeast 1275 Thames Valley ale	

1918 Crowley AK

Like many other breweries, Crowley drastically pruned their beer range in 1917. In 1918, they only brewed three different beers. The vast majority was AK, with only occasional brews of BBB and Stout.

The gravity has dropped another 6 points, but an extremely high degree of attenuation leaves the finished beer over 3% ABV. This was the lowest the OG of Crowley AK fell.

The grist has been hugely simplified. It genuinely contains just a single element: one type of English pale malt. You can't get any simpler than that. You might think: "Oh, that's because they couldn't get any sugar." But that would be wrong.

Because they were still using sugar. Just not in their standard beers, but in these other weird concoctions. There were things called AH and BH in the brewing record. These were made from sugars boiled with a few hops. They had very low gravities – around 1015° - and were barely fermented, leaving an ABV under 0.5%. I've no idea what they did with them. My best guess is that they were blended with their "real" beers.

Some pretty ancient hops were used: English (1914 and 1916), Oregon (1912 and 1914).

1918 Crowley AK		
pale malt	6.50 lb	100.00%
Cluster 90 mins	0.25 oz	
Fuggles 60 mins	0.33 oz	
Goldings 30 mins	0.50 oz	
OG	1027.5	
FG	1003	
ABV	3.24	
Apparent attenuation	89.09%	
IBU	17	
SRM	4	
Mash at	150° F	
Sparge at	165° F	
Boil time	90 minutes	
pitching temp	59.5° F	
Yeast	Wyeast 1275 Thames Valley ale	

1918 Crowley BBB

When Crowley shuffled their beer range pack in 1917, they dropped Pale Ales L and BB, but revived BBB.

It wasn't as strong as it had been in 1914, nor even in 1916, but, at 1047°, it was about as strong as draught beer got in 1918.

The recipe literally couldn't be any simpler. There's just a single type of English malt and a single type of English hops (from the 1917 harvest). It looks like an early 19th-century beer. Really bizarre to see a beer like this being brewed in the 20th century.

Crowley were clearly making at effort with BBB. Their other two beers of the time, AK and Stout, both contained some pretty ancient hops. While BBB got ones that were reasonably fresh.

1918 Crowley BBB		
pale malt	11.00 lb	100.00%
Goldings 150 mins	1.25 oz	
Goldings 90 mins	1.25 oz	
Goldings 30 mins	1.25 oz	
Goldings dry hops	0.50 oz	
OG	1047	
FG	1011.5	
ABV	4.70	
Apparent attenuation	75.53%	
IBU	52	
SRM	4	
Mash at	152° F	
Sparge at	165° F	
Boil time	150 minutes	
pitching temp	60° F	
Yeast	Wyeast 1275 Thames Valley ale	

1918 Crowley Stout

The trend towards simplification continued with Crowley Stout. Though not quite to such extremes.

In that there's one more than one element to the grist. A massive three ingredients, in fact. There is wonderfully elegant simplicity to Crowley's beers at this point. Three beers, all very different in character, brewed from very simple recipes. It makes their pre-war efforts look needlessly complicated.

There's a surprisingly deep colour considering there's only one dark malt, chocolate. Though that is present in quite a large quantity. What's listed as caramel in the recipe below was CDM – Caramelised Dextro-Maltose. Pretty sure you won't find that in your local homebrew shop and caramel seems like a good substitute.

The hops were getting on the old side, with none from the most recent season, 1917. This is typical of 1917 onwards. For the record, they were English (1914, 1916) and Oregon (1914).

Crowley only brewed Stout occasionally. For the very good reason of that's all they were allowed to. Because of its OG, which was well over the required average of 1030°. With AK at 1027.7°, Crowley needed to brew 11 barrels of it to be able to brew 1 barrel of Stout.

1918 Crowley Stout		
pale malt	11.75 lb	89.52%
chocolate malt	1.25 lb	9.52%
caramel 500 SRM	0.125 lb	0.95%
Cluster 145 mins	0.50 oz	
Fuggles 60 mins	0.67 oz	
Goldings 30 mins	1.00 oz	
OG	1055.5	
FG	1012	
ABV	5.75	
Apparent attenuation	78.38%	
IBU	33	
SRM	38	
Mash at	150° F	
Sparge at	165° F	
Boil time	145 minutes	
pitching temp	59° F	
Yeast	Wyeast 1275 Thames Valley ale	

1919 Crowley AK

With brewing restrictions starting to ease, AKs gravity began to rise again. Though there were still price controls in place. In May 1919, when this beer was brewed, a beer of 1036° retailed for a maximum of 6d per pint in the public bar.

The recipe hasn't got any more complicated, mind. There's still just a single type of English pale malt.

The hops are starting to get pretty ancient. Obviously, Crowley was raiding its emergency supplies for some very old American hops. I've no idea if they had been stored cold because, unlike many other brewers, Crowley didn't bother noting if hops had been kept in a cold store. Because of their age, I've massively reduced the quantity.

For the record, the hops were: English (1914, 1916) and Oregon (1912).

1919 Crowley AK		
pale malt	8.25 lb	100.00%
Cluster 75 mins	0.33 oz	
Fuggles 60 mins	0.50 oz	
Goldings 30 mins	0.67 oz	
OG	1036	
FG	1007	
ABV	3.84	
Apparent attenuation	80.56%	
IBU	22	
SRM	2.5	
Mash at	150° F	
Sparge at	165° F	
Boil time	75 minutes	
pitching temp	59.5° F	
Yeast	Wyeast 1275 Thames Valley ale	

1919 Crowley BBB

Crowley's tactics with their beer range are interesting. And different to most of their rivals

In order to hit average gravity targets, but still be able to brew some beer at a reasonable strength, many brewers brewed considerable quantities of beer well under 1030°, as low as 1011° in some cases. But, rather than brewing tiny quantities of much stronger beer, brewed reasonable quantities of beer in the mid 1030°s. Whitbread is a good example of this approach.

Crowley churned out masses and masses of AK just a few points under the required average. Supplemented by very small amounts of Stout and BBB, which were at near pre-war strength. I'm not sure which was the more profitable strategy.

When this was brewed in February 1919, it was in the top price band – anything over 1050° - which meant it retailed for 8d per pint in the public bar. And worth every penny, I'm sure. If you could find it. The amounts made are so small, it can't have been a common sight.

The hops – which are much fresher than those used in their AK – are a sure sign this was a classy beer. They're all English, from the 1916, 1917 and 1918 harvests.

1919 Crowley BBB		
pale malt	12.50 lb	96.15%
No. 3 invert sugar	0.50 lb	3.85%
Goldings 90 mins	1.25 oz	
Goldings 60 mins	1.50 oz	
Goldings 30 mins	1.50 oz	
Goldings dry hops	0.50 oz	
OG	1055.5	
FG	1015	
ABV	5.36	
Apparent attenuation	72.97%	
IBU	52	
SRM	7.5	
Mash at	150° F	
Sparge at	165° F	
Boil time	90 minutes	
pitching temp	59.5° F	
Yeast	Wyeast 1275 Thames Valley ale	

1919 Crowley Stout

It's fascinating that Crowley chose to abandon their Porter and concentrate solely of their Stout. And one that was genuinely "stout".

Most London brewers did the opposite, sticking with Porter and dropping Stout. Though, by all accounts, that Porter was often sold as Stout. With a gravity as high as Crowley Stout's, there was no way that it could be brewed in very large quantities. It's not that much weaker than the pre-war version.

An increase in the rate of attenuation – not sure why that might have happened – leaves this version with a higher ABV than that from 1914. I can't imagine that was true of hardly any other beer.

The only change to the grist since 1918 is the replacement of CDM by No. 3 invert sugar.

It being a Stout, though, there wasn't the need to waste good hops on it. Which Crowley didn't, using the same ancient ones as in AK: English (1914, 1916) and Oregon (1912).

1919 Crowley Stout		
pale malt	11.75 lb	83.93%
chocolate malt	1.50 lb	10.71%
No. 3 invert sugar	0.75 lb	5.36%
Cluster 75 mins	0.75 oz	
Fuggles 60 mins	1.00 oz	
Goldings 30 mins	1.00 oz	
OG	1061	
FG	1016.5	
ABV	5.89	
Apparent attenuation	98.28%	
IBU	38	
SRM	41	
Mash at	150° F	
Sparge at	165° F	
Boil time	75 minutes	
pitching temp	58.5° F	
Yeast	Wyeast 1275 Thames Valley ale	

Drybrough

One of the larger Edinburgh breweries, Drybrough wasn't particularly large by English standards. Founded 1750, moved to Duddingston in 1895. When bought by Watney in 1965 it had almost 450 tied houses, which is a lot for a Scottish brewery.

It was located in Duddingston, a village on the edge of Edinburgh that was home to more breweries than houses. It eventually fell prey to Watney. Not a great fate for any brewery. It was sold on to Allied Breweries in 1987 and closed almost immediately.

Drybrough brewed a dazzling array of beers before WW I. Many of which, unfortunately, it's not possible to work out the details of due to undocumented gyling. It's very frustrating

Drybrough beers 1913 - 1915							
Beer	Style	OG	FG	ABV	App. Attenuation	lbs hops/ qtr	hops lb/brl
42/- m	Mild						
48/- m	Mild						
60/- m	Mild						
80/- m	Mild						
100/- m	Mild	1060	1020	5.29	66.67%	4.59	1.14
Pl	IPA	1045	1013	4.23	71.11%	4.98	0.94
Pl 42/-	IPA	1034	1012	2.91	64.71%	4.98	0.71
Pl 48/-	IPA	1040	1016	3.18	60.00%	4.59	0.76
Pl 60/-	IPA	1052	1018	4.50	65.38%	4.59	0.99
XP	IPA	1044	1014	3.97	68.18%	5.89	1.11
XX	Stout						
XXX	Stout	1087	1030	7.54	65.52%	4.68	1.96
Sources: Drybrough brewing records held at the Scottish Brewing Archive, document numbers D/6/1/1/2 and D/6/1/1/3.							

After the war, the number of beers Drybrough brewed was drastically reduced:

Drybrough beers in 1920							
Beer	Style	OG	FG	ABV	App. Attenuation	lbs hops/ qtr	hops lb/brl
60/- Mild	Mild	1040	1013	3.57	67.50%	5.85	1.00
60/-	Pale Ale	1038	1015	3.04	60.53%	4.80	0.77
70/-	Pale Ale	1045	1015	3.97	66.67%	4.80	0.91
80/-	Pale Ale	1054	1021	4.37	61.11%	4.80	1.10
XX	Stout	1033	1019	1.85	42.42%		0.60
BS	Stout	1074	1025	6.48	66.22%	3.82	1.16
Source: Drybrough brewing record held at the Scottish Brewing Archive, document number D/6/1/1/3.							

Almost all the Shilling Mild Ales have disappeared and the number of Pale Ales has been reduced from five to three. The 60/-, 70/- and 80/- look remarkably similar to the post-WW II beers bearing those names, just with OGs about seven point higher.

A philosophical question: what style of beer was PI? The name implies it was an IPA. However in 1920 the names of all Drybrough's Pale Ales were changed from PI to PA. PA presumably standing for Pale Ale. There was no change in the character of the beers. So were they IPA's or Pale Ales? It's this sort of shit that has me seriously considering just using Pale Ale as the style for any Pale Ale or IPA. There is no way of differentiating the two styles, other than what the brewer called them.

1913 Drybrough PI

By the eve of WW I, Scottish brewers had already gone over to mostly brewing Pale Ale variations. The war would only exacerbate this trend and virtually killed off Mild Ale north of the border.

Drybrough's biggest-seller was a beer simply called PI. With a gravity of just 1044° it would have counted as a Light Bitter in England. But there had been a divergence in average gravity between England and Scotland. In 1913, average OG in England was 1051.52°, in Scotland just 1047.85°.[37]

Scottish recipes tended to be quite simple, with nothing other than base malt. Which is the case here, though there were different types of pale malt: Smyrna, Hungarian, Balkan, Bohemian and Scotch. The latter making up just four of the 43 quarters of malt. The UK soon wouldn't be importing barley from any of those regions, as they were all in territory controlled by the Central Powers.

1913 Drybrough PI		
pale malt	7.25 lb	77.05%
flaked maize	0.33 lb	3.51%
flaked rice	0.75 lb	7.97%
No. 1 invert sugar	0.33 lb	3.51%
No. 2 invert sugar	0.75 lb	7.97%
Fuggles 120 min	0.50 oz	
Fuggles 60 min	0.50 oz	
Goldings 30 min	0.50 oz	
Goldings dry hop	0.50 oz	
OG	1044	
FG	1013	
ABV	4.10	
Apparent attenuation	70.45%	
IBU	19	
SRM	6	
Mash at	150° F	
Sparge at	170° F	
Boil time	90 minutes	
pitching temp	60° F	
Yeast	WLP028 Edinburgh Ale	

---

[37] Brewers' Almanack 1928, page 110.

1913 Drybrough Pl 60/-

Top of Drybrough's range of Pale Ales was Pl 60/-. How ironic that, 40 years later, 60/- was usually a Scottish brewery's weakest pale Ale. The 20th century wasn't kind to beers it OG terms.

Looking at the OG of this beer and the Pl 48/- that follows, it becomes clear that the beer simply called Pl could also have been called Pl 54/-. That is, a beer costing 1/- per gallon. Which in London would have implied an OG of around 1050°. Barclay Perkins and Whitbread's X Ales, also 1/- per gallon beers, had gravities of 1052° and 1054°.

The most expensive Pale Ales in London were considerably stronger than Pl 60/-. Using Barclay Perkins and Whitbread again as examples, their classiest Pale Ales had gravities of 1062° and 1061°. Pl 60/- was only a couple of gravity points higher than the weakest Pale Ales of Barclay Perkins and Whitbread.

In this beer – and all the other Pale Ales of this year – the hops were 20% Altmark from 1912, the rest English from 1911 and 1912. I'm not really sure what type of hops they might have been. If you have a good guess, feel free to swap out some of the 120 minute Fuggle addition.

1913 Drybrough Pl 60/-		
pale malt	8.50 lb	75.56%
flaked maize	0.50 lb	4.44%
flaked rice	0.75 lb	6.67%
No. 1 invert sugar	0.50 lb	4.44%
No. 2 invert sugar	1.00 lb	8.89%
Fuggles 120 min	0.75 oz	
Fuggles 60 min	0.50 oz	
Goldings 30 min	0.50 oz	
Goldings dry hop	0.50 oz	
OG	1052	
FG	1016	
ABV	4.76	
Apparent attenuation	69.23%	
IBU	21	
SRM	7	
Mash at	150° F	
Sparge at	170° F	
Boil time	120 minutes	
pitching temp	60° F	
Yeast	WLP028 Edinburgh Ale	

1913 Drybrough Pl 48/-

Though not quite as popular as PI or PI 60/-, PI 48/- was still produced in considerable quantities. Though in England you would have struggled to find a Pale Ale this week before WW I.

The recipe, obviously, is just the same as the preceding two Pale Ales. No surprise there, as they were all parti-gyled together in various combinations. Drybrough didn't ever brew any of its Pale Ales single-gyle at this point.

All the Pale Ales contained a tiny amount of dextrose. If you'd like to go for total authenticity, the amount to add to this recipe is about two-thirds of an ounce. You can probably guess why I didn't bother including it in the recipe.

1913 Drybrough Pl 48/-		
pale malt	6.25 lb	78.13%
flaked maize	0.25 lb	3.13%
flaked rice	0.50 lb	6.25%
No. 1 invert sugar	0.33 lb	4.13%
No. 2 invert sugar	0.67 lb	8.38%
Fuggles 120 min	0.50 oz	
Fuggles 60 min	0.50 oz	
Goldings 30 min	0.25 oz	
Goldings dry hop	0.50 oz	
OG	1038	
FG	1011	
ABV	3.57	
Apparent attenuation	71.05%	
IBU	17	
SRM	6	
Mash at	149° F	
Sparge at	170° F	
Boil time	120 minutes	
pitching temp	60° F	
Yeast	WLP028 Edinburgh Ale	

1913 Drybrough Pl 42/-

At the budget end of Drybrough's Pale Ales was Pl 42/-. As you would expect, it was a few gravity points weaker than Pl 48/-.

You wouldn't have found a Pale Ale as weak as this in England. Though out in the country there were Mild Ales with similar gravities. For example, Adnams X Ale. Though, based on the very low level of hopping, Pl 42/- could easily have passed for a Light Mild.

The grist and hops are identical to the other Pale Ales above.

1913 Drybrough Pl 42/-		
pale malt	6.00 lb	80.00%
flaked maize	0.25 lb	3.33%
flaked rice	0.50 lb	6.67%
No. 1 invert sugar	0.25 lb	3.33%
No. 2 invert sugar	0.50 lb	6.67%
Fuggles 120 min	0.50 oz	
Fuggles 60 min	0.25 oz	
Goldings 30 min	0.25 oz	
Goldings dry hop	0.50 oz	
OG	1034	
FG	1012	
ABV	2.91	
Apparent attenuation	64.71%	
IBU	14	
SRM	5	
Mash at	148° F	
Sparge at	170° F	
Boil time	90 minutes	
pitching temp	60° F	
Yeast	WLP028 Edinburgh Ale	

1913 Drybrough XP

This beer is identical to PI, except for the dry hopping, which is much heavier. And the copper hopping, which is a bit heavier. Though the latter also applied to the PI it was partigyled with.

What was XP? It's an oddly common name for a Pale Ale in Scotland. William Younger's version was one of their most popular beers. Why would Drybrough brew a beer that was so similar to one of their other Pale Ales, PI?

The best explanation I can think of is that it was intended for a different market. Though it doesn't look like a beer destined to be exported outside the UK. The gravity is too low for that. And, even though it's more heavily hopped than Drybrough's other Pale Ales, the hopping still looks far too light for a true export beer. Maybe it was intended for the English market.

It's indicative of the low level of hopping in Drybrough's Pale Ales that even XP has fewer IBUs than either Barclay Perkins of Whitbread X Ale.

1913 Drybrough XP		
pale malt	7.25 lb	77.05%
flaked maize	0.33 lb	3.51%
flaked rice	0.75 lb	7.97%
No. 1 invert sugar	0.33 lb	3.51%
No. 2 invert sugar	0.75 lb	7.97%
Fuggles 120 min	0.75 oz	
Fuggles 60 min	0.75 oz	
Goldings 30 min	0.75 oz	
Goldings dry hop	1.25 oz	
OG	1044	
FG	1014	
ABV	3.97	
Apparent attenuation	68.18%	
IBU	29	
SRM	6	
Mash at	150° F	
Sparge at	170° F	
Boil time	120 minutes	
pitching temp	60° F	
Yeast	WLP028 Edinburgh Ale	

1915 Drybrough 100/- Mild

Drybrough's records are a nightmare when it comes to anything other than Pale Ales. The root of the problem is that they parti-gyle multiple beers together, but miss out some important pieces of information. Such as the starting gravities.

Which means, although I know Drybrough produced a wide range of Shilling Ales, from 42/- to 160/-, I can't produce recipes for most of them without a huge amount of guesswork. With the occasional exception. Like this beer.

I'm not sure what in particular makes this beer a Mild Ale rather than a Pale Ale. It was parti-gyled with PI, thus had exactly the same ingredients and hopping rate. The only difference is the dry-hopping. 100/- Mild had none, while PI had 4 oz. per barrel.

For the record, the hops were Californian (1913), English (1912, 1913 and 1914). I've reduced the amounts a little to account for the age of the hops.

1915 Drybrough 100/- Mild		
pale malt	10.50 lb	81.84%
flaked maize	1.00 lb	7.79%
No. 1 invert sugar	0.33 lb	2.57%
No. 2 invert sugar	0.50 lb	3.90%
No. 3 invert sugar	0.50 lb	3.90%
Cluster 120 mins	0.50 oz	
Fuggles 120 min	0.25 oz	
Goldings 60 min	0.75 oz	
Goldings 30 min	0.75 oz	
OG	1060	
FG	1020	
ABV	5.29	
Apparent attenuation	66.67%	
IBU	30	
SRM	9	
Mash at	148° F	
Sparge at	175° F	
Boil time	120 minutes	
pitching temp	59.5° F	
Yeast	WLP028 Edinburgh Ale	

1915 Drybrough XXX Stout

Drybrough Stouts are a similar problem to their Mild Ales: they're parti-gyled but there's no details of the gyle blending. It's very frustrating. But in a few cases I was able to sort of work it out. I'm not sure that it's 100% correct, but it's at least somewhere close.

This beer is the result of a particularly complex and incomprehensible parti-gyle that also included 36/- B (I think that B stands for Bottling), 48/- and 80/- Mild plus PI 36/-. Sadly, it's not possible to work out the gravities of any of these beers.

How were they able to parti-gyle pale beers with a Stout? Simple: all the caramel went onto one of the worts. It's a trick I've seen other Scottish breweries use. How Stout-like the finished beer was is open to debate. There's zero roasted malt and all the colour comes from sugar, in the form of No. 4 invert and caramel. The result is a very dark, but not roasty Stout.

The hops were identical to the 100/- Mild above, that is: Californian (1913), English (1912, 1913 and 1914)

1915 Drybrough XXX Stout		
pale malt	12.25 lb	64.47%
flaked maize	2.25 lb	11.84%
No. 1 invert sugar	0.75 lb	3.95%
No. 2 invert sugar	0.75 lb	3.95%
No. 4 invert sugar	1.25 lb	6.58%
caramel 500 SRM	1.75 lb	9.21%
Cluster 120 mins	0.75 oz	
Fuggles 120 min	0.50 oz	
Fuggles 60 min	1.25 oz	
Goldings 30 min	1.25 oz	
OG	1087	
FG	1030	
ABV	7.54	
Apparent attenuation	65.52%	
IBU	40	
SRM	55	
Mash at	148° F	
Sparge at	170° F	
Boil time	120 minutes	
pitching temp	60° F	
Yeast	WLP028 Edinburgh Ale	

1917 Drybrough Pl

1917 was the year when things started to get tough for UK brewing. And that's reflected in this version of Pl, which is eight gravity points weaker than the one from 1913.

The grist hasn't changed a great deal. The flaked maize has been dropped, probably because it was unavailable. And caramel has been added, presumably to maintain the beer's colour despite the drop in gravity.

The hops are a real mixture, comprising of Poperinge (1914), New Zealand (1915) and English hops (1914, 1916). I've no idea what variety the New Zealand hops might have been and have just lumped them in as Fuggles.

Despite the low level of hopping, the finished beer might well have had some hop character due to the relatively heavy dry hopping. Interestingly, all Drybrough's Pale Ales, whatever their gravity, all received 4 oz. of dry hops per barrel.

1917 Drybrough Pl		
pale malt	5.75 lb	76.46%
flaked maize	0.75 lb	9.97%
No. 1 invert sugar	0.50 lb	6.65%
No. 2 invert sugar	0.50 lb	6.65%
caramel 500 SRM	0.02 lb	0.27%
Strisselspalt 120 mins	0.25 oz	
Fuggles 120 min	0.25 oz	
Fuggles 60 min	0.25 oz	
Goldings 30 min	0.33 oz	
Goldings dry hops	0.50 oz	
OG	1036	
FG	1012	
ABV	3.18	
Apparent attenuation	66.67%	
IBU	14	
SRM	6	
Mash at	148° F	
Sparge at	170° F	
Boil time	120 minutes	
pitching temp	61° F	
Yeast	WLP028 Edinburgh Ale	

1917 Drybrough PI 60/-

The stronger PI 60/- has also shed eight gravity points since 1913. Making it essentially the same as the PI from that year.

There's little more to add as this example was parti-gyled with the PI above. All the remarks on that beer's recipe also apply here.

1917 Drybrough PI 60/-		
pale malt	7.50 lb	78.78%
flaked maize	1.00 lb	10.50%
No. 1 invert sugar	0.50 lb	5.25%
No. 2 invert sugar	0.50 lb	5.25%
caramel 500 SRM	0.02 lb	0.21%
Strisselspalt 120 mins	0.25 oz	
Fuggles 120 min	0.33 oz	
Fuggles 60 min	0.33 oz	
Goldings 30 min	0.33 oz	
Goldings dry hops	0.50 oz	
OG	1044	
FG	1017	
ABV	3.57	
Apparent attenuation	61.36%	
IBU	16	
SRM	6.5	
Mash at	148° F	
Sparge at	170° F	
Boil time	120 minutes	
pitching temp	61° F	
Yeast	WLP028 Edinburgh Ale	

1917 Drybrough PI 42/-

In the four years since 1913, Drybrough PI 42/- hasn't fallen in gravity quite as much as the two Pale Ales we've already seen. In this case the drop was just four gravity points. Though, starting at just 1034°, it didn't have as far it could go.

Though it wasn't parti-gyled with the preceding Ale Ales, the recipe is very similar. The only difference being slightly lower amount of both sugars.

The hops are exactly the same. Though there aren't a great deal of them leaving a paltry 12 (calculated) IBUs.

1917 Drybrough PI 42/-		
pale malt	5.50 lb	83.46%
flaked maize	0.50 lb	7.59%
No. 1 invert sugar	0.25 lb	3.79%
No. 2 invert sugar	0.33 lb	5.01%
caramel 500 SRM	0.01 lb	0.15%
Strisselspalt 120 mins	0.125 oz	
Fuggles 120 min	0.25 oz	
Fuggles 60 min	0.25 oz	
Goldings 30 min	0.25 oz	
Goldings dry hops	0.50 oz	
OG	1030	
FG	1009	
ABV	2.78	
Apparent attenuation	70.00%	
IBU	12	
SRM	5	
Mash at	148° F	
Sparge at	170° F	
Boil time	120 minutes	
pitching temp	61° F	
Yeast	WLP028 Edinburgh Ale	

Mini Book Series volume XXXII: Armistice!

1917 Drybrough Pl 48/-

If you're wondering why Pl 48/- has a lower OG than Pl 42/-, there's a simple explanation. The latter was brewed in February while the former was brewed in August. The situation with regard to the supply of brewing materials had worsened in the intervening six months. The gravity is 11 points lower than in 1913.

There have been further tweaks to the recipe, with the quantity of No. 1 invert sugar being greatly reduced.

The hops are very slightly different: Poperinge (1916), New Zealand (1915) and English hops (1915, 1916). Though the quantity remains very small. If you compare Drybrough's Pale Ales to those from London breweries you'll see that they are far less bitter.

1917 Drybrough Pl 48/-		
pale malt	4.75 lb	82.25%
flaked maize	0.50 lb	8.66%
No. 1 invert sugar	0.06 lb	1.04%
No. 2 invert sugar	0.33 lb	5.71%
white sugar	0.125 lb	2.16%
caramel 500 SRM	0.01 lb	0.17%
Strisselspalt 120 mins	0.125 oz	
Fuggles 120 min	0.25 oz	
Fuggles 60 min	0.25 oz	
Goldings 30 min	0.25 oz	
Goldings dry hops	0.50 oz	
OG	1027	
FG	1010	
ABV	2.25	
Apparent attenuation	62.96%	
IBU	12.5	
SRM	4	
Mash at	150° F	
Sparge at	165° F	
Boil time	120 minutes	
pitching temp	61° F	
Yeast	WLP028 Edinburgh Ale	

1917 Drybrough 80/- Mild

Out of the dozens of entries for Mild Ales in Drybrough's records, there are only a handful that I can do anything with. It's very frustrating, as I can see that they had a wide range of Mild Ales, but can't produce recipes for them. Or even work out what their OG was.

Very occasionally, the clouds part and there's enough information for me to have a reasonable stab at a recipe. Though, unlike most of those I produce, I can't be certain that it's 100% accurate.

Unsurprisingly, since it was parti-gyled with PI, the grist is identical to Drybrough's Pale Ales. Including the hopping rate. Which begs the question: what exactly makes this a Mild Ale and how is it different from their Pale Ales? There's only one difference that I can see: dry hopping. Unlike their Pale Ales, Drybrough didn't dry hop their Mild Ales.

Of course, Drybrough might have coloured up their Mild Ales post fermentation. Then again, they probably did the same with their Pale Ales. And Mild Ales were by no means universally dark in 1917. Few Milds were the dark brown colour that we associate with the style today. They were either pale or semi-dark.

The hops in the original were Poperinge from 1916 and a couple of different types of English ones from 1915 and 1916.

1917 Drybrough 80/- Mild		
pale malt	7.50 lb	85.42%
flaked maize	0.50 lb	5.69%
No. 1 invert sugar	0.25 lb	2.85%
No. 2 invert sugar	0.25 lb	2.85%
white sugar	0.25 lb	2.85%
caramel 500 SRM	0.03 lb	0.34%
Strisselspalt 120 mins	0.25 oz	
Fuggles 120 min	0.25 oz	
Fuggles 60 min	0.25 oz	
Goldings 30 min	0.25 oz	
OG	1040	
FG	1014	
ABV	3.44	
Apparent attenuation	65.00%	
IBU	13	
SRM	6	
Mash at	148° F	
Sparge at	170° F	
Boil time	120 minutes	
pitching temp	61° F	
Yeast	WLP028 Edinburgh Ale	

1917 Drybrough 60/- Mild

There's not much to say about Drybrough 60/- Mild that I haven't already said about 80/- Mild. The two were parti-gyled together and hence have identical recipes.

At just 2.5% ABV, 60/- Mild is pretty watery. When it was brewed, in November 917, drinkers were getting used to this type of very weak beer. They weren't impressed, but were happy to get beer at all. Though, to be fair, in Scotland beers not much stronger than this had existed before the start of the war.

1917 Drybrough 60/- Mild		
pale malt	5.50 lb	86.00%
flaked maize	0.50 lb	7.82%
No. 1 sugar	0.125 lb	1.95%
No. 2 sugar	0.125 lb	1.95%
white sugar	0.125 lb	1.95%
caramel 500 SRM	0.02 lb	0.31%
Strisselspalt 120 mins	0.125 oz	
Fuggles 120 min	0.125 oz	
Fuggles 60 min	0.25 oz	
Goldings 30 min	0.25 oz	
OG	1029	
FG	1010	
ABV	2.51	
Apparent attenuation	65.52%	
IBU	10	
SRM	4.5	
Mash at	148° F	
Sparge at	170° F	
Boil time	120 minutes	
pitching temp	61° F	
Yeast	WLP028 Edinburgh Ale	

1917 Drybrough XXX Stout

There's been quite a drop in the gravity of XXX Stout. Though that could just be me misinterpreting the brewing records. They aren't exactly clear when it comes to anything other than Drybrough's Pale Ales.

The grist isn't very Stout-like: pale malt, sugar and loads of caramel. I can see its big advantage, mind: it makes it possible to parti-gyle Stout and Pale Ale. Simply by being careful about where you threw all that caramel. The idea being to get most of it into the Stout.

The recipe is quite different from in 1915. The No. 1 and No. 4 inverts sugars are gone, as is the flaked maize. Which by this point in the war seems to have been unavailable.

The hops were Poperinge from 1916 and English from 1915 and 1916.

Bittersweet is probably how this tasted. There's a fair amount of hop bitterness, but the FG is very high, there's no roasted malt, but lots of sugar.

1917 Drybrough XXX Stout		
pale malt	6.25 lb	71.51%
No. 2 invert sugar	0.33 lb	3.78%
No. 3 invert sugar	0.33 lb	3.78%
cane sugar	0.33 lb	3.78%
caramel 500 SRM	1.50 lb	17.16%
Strisselspalt 120 mins	0.33 oz	
Fuggles 90 min	0.67 oz	
Fuggles 60 min	0.67 oz	
Goldings 30 min	0.50 oz	
OG	1046	
FG	1021	
ABV	3.31	
Apparent attenuation	54.35%	
IBU	27	
SRM	39	
Mash at	147° F	
Sparge at	170° F	
Boil time	120 minutes	
pitching temp	61° F	
Yeast	WLP028 Edinburgh Ale	

1918 Drybrough PI

The longer the war lasted, the more it simplified Drybrough's range of beers. Both in terms of the number of different beers brewed and in the ingredients employed. For most of 1918, Drybrough only brewed three beers: PI, PI 48/- and XX Stout. Very occasionally a stronger Pale Ale, PI X, was brewed.

Looking specifically at PI, there's been a further cut in its gravity, now down to a mere 1030°. With all a brewery's beers have to average out to 1030°, there were limited opportunities to brew anything stronger.

The recipe has become way simpler. With flaked maize being dropped, there are no longer any adjuncts. The No. 1 invert sugar has also gone. I can't imagine either of these changes was voluntary.

There were three types of hops: Poperinge from 1916 and two types of English hops, both from 1916.

1918 Drybrough PI			
pale malt	6.00 lb	91.19%
No. 2 invert sugar	0.33 lb	5.02%
white sugar	0.25 lb	3.80%
Strisselspalt 90 min	0.50 oz	
Fuggles 60 min	0.50 oz	
Goldings 30 min	0.25 oz	
Goldings dry hops	0.50 oz	
OG	1030	
FG	1009	
ABV	2.78	
Apparent attenuation	70.00%	
IBU	17	
SRM	4	
Mash at	147° F	
Sparge at	170° F	
Boil time	90 minutes	
pitching temp	62° F	
Yeast	WLP028 Edinburgh Ale	

1918 Drybrough Pl 48/-

Though brewed continuously throughout the war, Pl 48/- was very much the junior partner to Pl. While the latter was brewed in batches of 250-275 barrels, the former was in batches of just 25-60 barrels.

This particular Pl 48/- was parti-gyled with the Pl above.

I suspect that this beer was coloured up with some sort of caramel post-fermentation. The colour is very pale. And there are entries in the brewing log where they're making something called "color" from caramel. They must have been using it somewhere.

Later in the 20th century, I know for certain that Scottish brewers coloured up their Pale Ales to different shades for different markets. Sometimes very dark – like Dark Mild. They'd probably already started this by WW I. Which means you can probably darken this with caramel to any shade you fancy and there still be a chance it's authentic.

1918 Drybrough Pl 48/-		
pale malt	4.75 lb	90.48%
No. 2 invert sugar	0.25 lb	4.76%
white sugar	0.25 lb	4.76%
Strisselspalt 90 min	0.33 oz	
Fuggles 60 min	0.33 oz	
Goldings 30 min	0.25 oz	
Goldings dry hops	0.50 oz	
OG	1024	
FG	1007	
ABV	2.25	
Apparent attenuation	70.83%	
IBU	13	
SRM	3	
Mash at	147° F	
Sparge at	170° F	
Boil time	90 minutes	
pitching temp	62° F	
Yeast	WLP028 Edinburgh Ale	

1918 Drybrough Pl X

Drinkers must have been so happy when this beer was introduced in 1918. Finally a beer with a bit of poke again. This particular example was brewed just a couple of weeks before the Armistice.

It must have been a bit of a shock for drinkers used to beer of 3% ABV or less. Because the higher gravity, combined with a higher than usual degree of attenuation, results in an ABV of over 4%. It must have had people dancing in the streets.

There's not much to the recipe, just pale malt and sugar. Though the No. 3 invert is a substitution for a proprietary sugar Called D.C.M. No real idea what that was like so feel frr to substitute some other sugar. Such as more No. 2 invert, for example.

Though more heavily hopped than Drybrough's other Pale Ales, is still not exactly bursting with bitterness. The hops are a little on the old side, Poperinge from 1916 and English from 1915 and 1916.

1918 Drybrough Pl X		
pale malt	7.25 lb	86.57%
No. 2 invert sugar	1.00 lb	11.94%
No. 3 invert sugar	0.125 lb	1.49%
Strisselspalt 90 min	0.67 oz	
Fuggles 60 min	0.67 oz	
Goldings 30 min	0.33 oz	
Goldings dry hops	0.75 oz	
OG	1040	
FG	1009	
ABV	4.10	
Apparent attenuation	77.50%	
IBU	21	
SRM	7	
Mash at	148° F	
Sparge at	170° F	
Boil time	90 minutes	
pitching temp	60° F	
Yeast	WLP028 Edinburgh Ale	

1918 Drybrough XX Stout

Drybrough continued to produce occasional brews of Stout right through the war years. Though the quantities were pretty small: this beer was brewed in a batch of just 57 barrels.

XXX Stout seems to have been discontinued towards the end of 1917, presumably because it was no longer practical to brew a stronger Stout. XX Stout, on the other hand, continued to be brewed throughout the war years.

Once again, there's not a trace of coloured malt in the grist, with the colour all coming from the No. 4 invert sugar and caramel.

The hops were a combination of English and Poperinge, all from the 1916 crop.

1918 Drybrough XX Stout		
pale malt	6.75 lb	73.05%
No. 2 invert sugar	0.33 lb	3.57%
No. 4 invert sugar	0.33 lb	3.57%
cane sugar	0.33 lb	3.57%
caramel 500 SRM	1.50 lb	16.23%
Strisselspalt 90 min	0.67 oz	
Fuggles 60 min	0.67 oz	
Goldings 30 min	0.33 oz	
OG	1039	
FG	1018	
ABV	2.78	
Apparent attenuation	53.85%	
IBU	21	
SRM	41	
Mash at	148° F	
Sparge at	179° F	
Boil time	90 minutes	
pitching temp	62° F	
Yeast	WLP028 Edinburgh Ale	

1919 Drybrough Pl 48/-

Drybrough's weakest Pale Ale had only a slightly lower OG than in 1918. Though, at just 1024°, it was pathetically low. But this wasn't its nadir: a couple of months earlier it had been a truly pathetic 1021° and just 1.85% ABV. Not a beer you could have a lot of fun with.

Not that this slightly stronger version was going to have you rolling in the aisles. Not unless you had a double whisky with every pint.

Surprisingly, the grist is quite different from those of the other Pale Ales. There's no flaked maize, but there is glucose. And instead of No. 3 invert sugar, there's No. 2 invert.

The hops were Poperinge, and two types of English, all from the 1916 harvest. Note that all Drybrough's Pale Ales were dry hopped at the same rate, no matter what the strength of the beer.

1919 Drybrough Pl 48/-		
pale malt	4.50 lb	90.00%
No. 2 invert sugar	0.25 lb	5.00%
glucose	0.25 lb	5.00%
Strisselspalt 75 min	0.33 oz	
Fuggles 60 min	0.33 oz	
Goldings 30 min	0.25 oz	
Goldings dry hops	0.50 oz	
OG	1023	
FG	1007	
ABV	2.12	
Apparent attenuation	69.57%	
IBU	12.5	
SRM	3	
Mash at	148° F	
Sparge at	170° F	
Boil time	75 minutes	
pitching temp	61° F	
Yeast	WLP028 Edinburgh Ale	

1919 Drybrough Pl

The year after the Armistice, Drybrough were still knocking out a range of mostly Pale Ales, as they had done before the war started. Though the range had been reduced considerably in OG over the course of the war.

The gravity of Pl remained 1030°, as it had been a year earlier. But that doesn't mean everything has remained the same. There have been changes to the grist, specifically in the sugar. Gone are the white sugar and No. 2 invert, replaced by No. 3 invert. While flaked maize has returned after a year or so's absence.

The hops are getting to be on the old side, but not nearly as ancient as at some other breweries. They are all English, from the 1916 and 1917 harvests.

1919 Drybrough Pl		
pale malt	5.75 lb	87.39%
flaked maize	0.33 lb	5.02%
No. 3 invert sugar	0.50 lb	7.60%
Fuggles 90 min	0.50 oz	
Fuggles 60 min	0.25 oz	
Goldings 30 min	0.25 oz	
Goldings dry hops	0.50 oz	
OG	1030	
FG	1009	
ABV	2.78	
Apparent attenuation	70.00%	
IBU	14	
SRM	6	
Mash at	148° F	
Sparge at	170° F	
Boil time	90 minutes	
pitching temp	60° F	
Yeast	WLP028 Edinburgh Ale	

1919 Drybrough Pl 54/-

This may look like a new beer, as nothing in Drybrough's range was specifically called PI 54/- until late 1919. Though what had simply been called PI previous, was effectively PI 54/- as it slotted exactly mid-way in terms of gravity between PI 48/- and PI 60/-.

The gravity is a few points higher than the PI above, reflected in the improvement in the situation between July, when PI was brewed, and October when this hit the mash tun.

The grist is near-identical to the PI above, just the proportion of pale malt has been reduced a little. The hops are a little fresher, too, being all English from the 1917 harvest. Given that even before the war some of the hops Drybrough used weren't from the most recent crop, it's almost back to normal.

1919 Drybrough Pl 54/-		
pale malt	6.50 lb	88.68%
flaked maize	0.33 lb	4.50%
No. 3 invert sugar	0.50 lb	6.82%
Fuggles 105 min	0.50 oz	
Fuggles 60 min	0.50 oz	
Goldings 30 min	0.25 oz	
Goldings dry hops	0.50 oz	
OG	1033	
FG	1010	
ABV	3.04	
Apparent attenuation	69.70%	
IBU	17	
SRM	6	
Mash at	148° F	
Sparge at	170° F	
Boil time	105 minutes	
pitching temp	60° F	
Yeast	WLP028 Edinburgh Ale	

1919 Drybrough Pl 60/-

Before the war Pl 60/- had been Drybrough's strongest Pale Ale, with a gravity of 1052°. Not super-strong by London or Burton standards, but still respectable.

Early in 1917, the gravity was still 1044°. But Pl 60/- didn't survive the April 1917 cull, which saw so many beers dropped by brewers across the country. Many never to return. Pl 60/- was luckier, reappearing in the summer of 1919, after an absence of around two and a half years.

The gravity may have been a relatively feeble 1036°, but at least it was back.

This example was parti-gyled with the Pl above. See that for recipe comments.

1919 Drybrough Pl 60/-		
pale malt	6.50 lb	83.87%
flaked maize	0.50 lb	6.45%
No. 2 invert sugar	0.75 lb	9.68%
Fuggles 90 min	0.50 oz	
Fuggles 60 min	0.50 oz	
Goldings 30 min	0.25 oz	
Goldings dry hops	0.50 oz	
OG	1036	
FG	1009	
ABV	3.57	
Apparent attenuation	75.00%	
IBU	17	
SRM	7.5	
Mash at	148° F	
Sparge at	170° F	
Boil time	90 minutes	
pitching temp	60° F	
Yeast	WLP028 Edinburgh Ale	

1919 Drybrough PI 60/- X

You could argue that the war has improved Drybrough's beers. The malt percentage has increased and the adjuncts are down to just 5%. Of course, that wasn't exactly a voluntary choice, but one dictated by circumstances.

A few months after the reintroduction of PI 60/-. Drybrough brought out a new, even stronger Pale Ale, PI 60/- X. At 1046°, it was just a couple of gravity points stronger than PI had been before the war, but still half a dozen points shy of pre-war PI 60/-.

The recipe, unsurprisingly, is essentially the same as PI 60/-. It was parti-gyled with it, after all. Though not with the example of PI above.

The hops were all English from the 1917 harvest. Getting on a bit in age, but not outrageously so.

1919 Drybrough PI 60/- X			
pale malt		9.00 lb	87.80%
flaked maize		0.50 lb	4.88%
No. 3 invert sugar		0.75 lb	7.32%
Fuggles 105 min		0.67 oz	
Fuggles 60 min		0.67 oz	
Goldings 30 min		0.33 oz	
Goldings dry hops		0.25 oz	
OG		1046	
FG		1015	
ABV		4.10	
Apparent attenuation		67.39%	
IBU		21	
SRM		8	
Mash at		148° F	
Sparge at		170° F	
Boil time		105 minutes	
pitching temp		61° F	
Yeast		WLP028 Edinburgh Ale	

1919 Drybrough XX Stout

Despite the war being over, there's still no dark malt in Drybrough's Stout. Though there wasn't any at the start, either, to be fair.

Scottish Stout can be a very strange affair, especially in the 20th century. Scottish Stout already began to diverge from the English version in the second half of the 19th century. Some brewers, such as William Younger, brewed some Stout along English lines, but I suspect they were for consumption outside Scotland. Domestic version became sweeter and sweeter. And, because some breweries parti-gyled them with Pale Ale, had some pretty odd recipes.

I assume that the demand for Stout just wasn't big enough to justify brewing it single-gyle. It's typical of what happens when a beer style is becoming marginalised.

The base of this recipe – Pale malt, flaked maize and No. 3 invert sugar – is the same as for Drybrough's Pale Ales. The extra ingredient is a whole load of caramel, which was added to just one of the coppers so it didn't get into the Pale Ale as well.

The hops were all English from 1916 and 1917.

1919 Drybrough XX Stout		
pale malt	7.25 lb	69.05%
flaked maize	1.00 lb	9.52%
No. 3 invert sugar	0.50 lb	4.76%
caramel 500 SRM	1.75 lb	16.67%
Fuggles 90 min	0.67 oz	
Fuggles 60 min	0.67 oz	
Goldings 30 min	0.33 oz	
OG	1042	
FG	1019	
ABV	3.04	
Apparent attenuation	54.76%	
IBU	22	
SRM	43	
Mash at	148° F	
Sparge at	170° F	
Boil time	90 minutes	
pitching temp	61° F	
Yeast	WLP028 Edinburgh Ale	

1920 Drybrough Pl 48/-

Even a couple of years into the Peace, Drybrough was still producing a very watery Pale Ale. One legacy of the war was a new breed of low-gravity Pale Ales in Scotland. Ones corresponding to England's 4d Mild Ales.

The gravity had at least increased by a few points, up from a low of a meagre 1020° in November 1918. Though it remained pretty much a temperance drink at just 2.5% ABV.

Drybrough seems to have settled on a recipe for their Pale Ales: pale malt, flaked maize and No. 3 invert. Which they stuck with right through 1920.

A sure sign of the improving situation with regard to war materials is the presence of some relatively fresh foreign hops, presumably imported after the end of the war. They are: Californian (1918), English (1917) and Burgundy (1917).

1920 Drybrough Pl 48/-		
pale malt	5.25 lb	86.35%
flaked maize	0.33 lb	5.43%
No. 3 invert sugar	0.50 lb	8.22%
Cluster 105 min	0.33 oz	
Strisselspalt 60 min	0.33 oz	
Goldings 30 min	0.33 oz	
Goldings dry hops	0.50 oz	
OG	1027	
FG	1008	
ABV	2.51	
Apparent attenuation	70.37%	
IBU	16	
SRM	16	
Mash at	148° F	
Sparge at	170° F	
Boil time	90 minutes	
pitching temp	61° F	
Yeast	WLP028 Edinburgh Ale	

1920 Drybrough Pl 54/-

In the immediate post-war years, Pl 54/- remained one of Drybrough's most popular beers. As it had been under the guise of simply Pl before the war.

But, with its strength much reduced since 1914, its popularity was fading and it was being overtaken by Pl 60/- as drinkers' favourite. By the 1930s, 60/-, as it was then called, accounted for over 80% of Drybrough's output.

54/- disappeared for a while in the 1920s, but reappeared when times got hard in the 1930s. When it was Drybrough's second best-selling beer after 60/-. A long way after. Its sales were only about 10% of 60/-'s. Rather surprisingly, 54/- managed to struggle through WW II, before finally leaving the brewing stage for good in the early 1950s. A victim of rising living standards.

The recipe is the same as for all their other Pale Ales. Obviously, as they were all parti-gyled together in various combinations.

1920 Drybrough Pl 54/-		
pale malt	6.50 lb	88.68%
flaked maize	0.33 lb	4.50%
No. 3 invert sugar	0.50 lb	6.82%
Cluster 105 min	0.50 oz	
Strisselspalt 60 min	0.50 oz	
Goldings 30 min	0.33 oz	
Goldings dry hops	0.50 oz	
OG	1033	
FG	1010	
ABV	3.04	
Apparent attenuation	69.70%	
IBU	22	
SRM	6	
Mash at	148° F	
Sparge at	170° F	
Boil time	105 minutes	
pitching temp	60° F	
Yeast	WLP028 Edinburgh Ale	

1920 Drybrough Pl 60/-

Whatever names they gave them, Drybrough basically produced a range of lowish-gravity Pale Ales both before, during and after WW I.

Top of the range for most of that period was PI 60/-. Having started the war at over 1050°, it was a mere shadow of its former self by 1920. Though it was clearly beloved by drinkers, judging by the quantities of it that Drybrough brewed.

But 60/-'s days as top dog were numbered. As we'll see when we look at the next beer.

1920 Drybrough Pl 60/-		
pale malt	7.25 lb	84.40%
flaked maize	0.67 lb	7.80%
No. 3 invert sugar	0.67 lb	7.80%
Cluster 105 min	0.75 oz	
Strisselspalt 60 min	0.75 oz	
Goldings 30 min	0.50 oz	
Goldings dry hops	0.50 oz	
OG	1039	
FG	1012	
ABV	3.57	
Apparent attenuation	69.23%	
IBU	32	
SRM	7	
Mash at	148° F	
Sparge at	170° F	
Boil time	105 minutes	
pitching temp	60° F	
Yeast	WLP028 Edinburgh Ale	

1920 Drybrough Special 8d PA

Now here's an unusual beer. A Full-strength (pretty much) Pale Ale. It's odd because it's stronger than any Pale Ale Drybrough produced immediately before WW I.

It's also the beer that pushed poor old PI 60/- off its top spot. I suppose after all those years of watery beer there was a hankering, among some drinkers at least, for something a little stronger.

Even without the 8d in the name, I would have immediately spotted it as an 8d beer. The gravity is a dead giveaway: 1055°. The 8d band was anything over 1054°. Obviously, you wouldn't want to make your beer too strong. No matter how much over 1054° it was, you couldn't charge more than 8d per pint for it.

That simple rule had an enormous impact on British beer of the interwar period. Even though all price controls were abolished in 1921. The concept of 4d, 5d, 6d, 7d and 8d classes of beer had been established and breweries mostly stuck to it until the disruption of another war brought the construct crashing down.

Renamed 80/- later in 1920, it continued to be brewed until WW II, though mostly at the lower gravity of 1050°.

1920 Drybrough Special 8d PA		
pale malt	10.50 lb	84.00%
flaked maize	1.00 lb	8.00%
No. 3 invert sugar	1.00 lb	8.00%
Cluster 105 min	1.00 oz	
Strisselspalt 60 min	1.00 oz	
Goldings 30 min	0.75 oz	
Goldings dry hops	0.50 oz	
OG	1055	
FG	1018	
ABV	4.89	
Apparent attenuation	67.27%	
IBU	38	
SRM	9	
Mash at	148° F	
Sparge at	170° F	
Boil time	105 minutes	
pitching temp	60° F	
Yeast	WLP028 Edinburgh Ale	

1920 Drybrough BS XXX

The biggest change at Drybrough after the war's end was how they brewed Stout. As they stopped parti-gyling it with Pale Ale and started using some dark malts. A real revolution. What must drinkers have thought?

There's a whole load of roasted malt: 16% of the grist. When before there was none at all. That must have been very noticeable.

Though, given the strength of this Stout, I wouldn't have been complaining. Not only is the OG high, the attenuation is decent, too. Creating a beer of over 7% ABV. Though that OG has got me wondering: was this an export beer? Because price controls were still in effect, making a beer this strong economic suicide. At least if it were sold inside the UK.

It also has the classic Guinness Foreign Extra Stout OG. If I were to guess, I'd say this was meant for exactly the same markets as Guinness FES – so the Caribbean and the Far East. Could be wrong, mind.

1920 Drybrough BS XXX		
pale malt	9.75 lb	56.52%
black malt	1.00 lb	5.80%
amber malt	1.75 lb	10.14%
crystal malt 60 L	1.75 lb	10.14%
No. 3 invert sugar	2.25 lb	13.04%
caramel 200 SRM	0.75 lb	4.35%
Cluster 120 min	0.50 oz	
Strisselspalt 120 min	0.50 oz	
Fuggles 60 min	1.00 oz	
Goldings 30 min	1.00 oz	
OG	1074	
FG	1019	
ABV	7.28	
Apparent attenuation	74.32%	
IBU	34	
SRM	50	
Mash at	150° F	
Sparge at	170° F	
Boil time	120 minutes	
pitching temp	62.5° F	
Yeast	WLP028 Edinburgh Ale	

Fullers

Of all the breweries covered, only Adnams and Fullers remain open today. Located next to the Thames in Chiswick, it's the only London brewery to predate WW II.

At the time of WW I, Fullers was a relatively medium-sized brewery, with brew lengths of 200 – 450 barrels. While large firms such as Whitbread or Barclay Perkins had batch sizes of up to 1,200 barrels.

They brewed a full range of the beers typical in London: Mild, Porter, Stout, Burton and two Pale Ales. Surprisingly, they came out of the war with more beers: two Milds, Porter, Stout, Burton and three Pale Ales.

And here they are:

Fullers beers in 1914							
Beer	Style	OG	FG	ABV	App. Attenuation	lbs hops/ qtr	hops lb/brl
X	Mild	1050.7	1011.6	5.17	77.05%	5.44	2.38
AK	Pale Ale	1044.3	1009.1	4.65	79.38%	7.33	1.34
PA	Pale Ale	1054.2	1012.2	5.56	77.52%	8.14	1.98
P	Porter	1045.5	1012.5	4.37	72.59%	6.74	1.38
BS	Stout	1066.4	1020.8	6.03	68.70%	6.74	2.01
BO	Strong Ale	1071.4	1015.5	7.40	78.29%	9.50	3.04
Source: Fullers brewing record held at the brewery.							

And here is their atypically larger selection after the war:

Fullers beers in 1920							
Beer	Style	OG	FG	ABV	App. Attenuation	lbs hops/ qtr	hops lb/brl
X	Mild	1030.6	1006.4	3.21	79.20%	6.74	0.90
XX	Mild	1041.2	1009.4	4.20	77.12%	6.98	1.20
AK	Pale Ale	1030.6	1007.5	3.06	75.59%	9.80	1.21
XK	Pale Ale	1036.8	1006.6	3.98	81.91%	8.82	1.29
PA	Pale Ale	1055.0	1015.2	5.26	72.31%	9.80	2.17
P	Porter	1034.6	1009.7	3.29	71.96%	7.10	1.14
BS	Stout	1054.8	1019.4	4.68	64.61%	7.60	1.83
BO	Strong Ale	1063.6	1018.3	6.00	71.27%	6.92	1.87
Source: Fullers brewing record held at the brewery.							

Note that the hopping rate per quarter of malt – which is effectively the rate independent of the gravity of the beer – increased for Mild and porter and Stout.

1914 Fullers X Ale

As with other London brewers, by 1914 Fullers brewed a single Mild Ale at the outbreak of war.

There may have only been the one Mild, but X Ale was still Fullers biggest seller, the beer the common man would be drinking in the public bar. And it was still quite a powerful beer, weighing in at over 5% ABV. At least for the moment.

It's another relatively simple beer: a single malt, flaked maize and some sugar. Though the pale malt was a mix of English, Danish, Indian and Oregon. At least the barley it was made from It was all malted in the UK. The glucose is listed as amber glucose so would have added some colour.

The hops are Mid-Kent (1913), Poperinge (1913) and Cobbs (1913, 1914). Cobbs, a type of Canterbury whitebine are still grown, but aren't usually sold under that name. They're one of a group of related varieties which are usually marketed as Goldings.

Those hops only made up 50% of those used. The other 50% were from a brew of PA earlier that day. Which makes it difficult to work out the hopping. The quantities in the recipe are just my best guess.

The real mashing scheme was mash of an hour with an initial heat of 148° F, raised to 154° F after 30 minutes by an underlet. Left to stand for a further 2 hours.

1914 Fullers X Ale			
pale malt		8.00 lb	76.19%
flaked maize		0.75 lb	7.14%
No. 3 invert sugar		1.25 lb	11.90%
glucose		0.50 lb	4.76%
Strisselspalt 120 mins		1.00 oz	
Fuggles 90 mins		1.00 oz	
Goldings 30 mins		1.00 oz	
OG		1051	
FG		1012	
ABV		5.16	
Apparent attenuation		76.47%	
IBU		33	
SRM		10	
Mash at		148° F	
Sparge at		168° F	
Boil time		120 minutes	
pitching temp		60° F	
Yeast	Wyeast 1968 London ESB		

1914 Fullers PA

In the 1890s, Fullers brewed a total of five Pale Ales, but by 1914 that was down to two: PA and the weaker AK.

PA underwent many changes over the years and was eventually discontinued as a cask beer, before making a comeback under the name Chiswick Bitter.

The grist isn't that dissimilar from X Ale's, the principal one being the use of No. 2 invert sugar rather than No. 3. Though the proportion of flaked maize is much smaller in PA. The total sugar content is about the same, but with more glucose and less invert.

A combination of pale malt, flaked maize and sugar was typical of pre-war Pale Ales. The proportions of which would vary, depending on how classy it was and what the brewer was aiming for. Some liked to have their beers as pale as possible and so would use a high percentage of sugar. Counter to what might be expected, it was often the most expensive version that contained the highest percentage of sugar.

Mid-Kent (1913), Cobbs (1913, 1914) and Oregon (1913) are the hops, about half of which were reused in the X Ale above.

The real mashing scheme was mash of an hour with an initial heat of 143° F, raised to 152° F after 25 minutes by an underlet. Left to stand for a further hour and 35 minutes.

1914 Fullers PA		
pale malt	9.00 lb	79.93%
flaked maize	0.25 lb	2.22%
No. 2 invert sugar	1.00 lb	11.10%
glucose	1.00 lb	6.66%
caramel 500 SRM	0.01 lb	0.09%
Cluster 105 mins	0.50 oz	
Fuggles 105 mins	0.75 oz	
Goldings 60 mins	1.25 oz	
Goldings 30 mins	1.25 oz	
Goldings dry hops	0.50 oz	
OG	1054	
FG	1012	
ABV	5.56	
Apparent attenuation	77.78%	
IBU	50	
SRM	8	
Mash at	152° F	
Sparge at	168° F	
Boil time	105 minutes	
pitching temp	59.5° F	
Yeast	Wyeast 1968 London ESB	

Mini Book Series volume XXXII: Armistice!

1914 Fullers AK

Going into the war, Fullers AK had a classic gravity in the mid-1040°s. Though, obviously, that wasn't going to last.

The grist is very similar to that of PA, only there's a bit more flaked maize and a bit less sugar. Not really that significant of a difference. The pale malt was made from English, Chilean and Oregon barley.

The hops are Mid-Kent (1913), Poperinge (1913), Cobbs (1913, 1914), Oregon (1913). Though as the quantities of Poperinge and Oregon were pretty small (20 lbs of each out of a total of 270 lbs) I've combined them as Cluster.

The real mashing scheme was mash of an hour with an initial heat of 143° F, raised to 149° F after 25 minutes by an underlet. Left to stand for a further hour and 35 minutes.

1914 Fullers AK		
pale malt	8.00 lb	81.43%
flaked maize	0.50 lb	5.25%
No. 2 invert sugar	0.50 lb	7.88%
glucose	0.50 lb	5.25%
caramel 500 SRM	0.02 lb	0.18%
Cluster 90 mins	0.375 oz	
Fuggles 90 mins	0.75 oz	
Goldings 60 mins	0.75 oz	
Goldings 30 mins	0.75 oz	
Goldings dry hops	0.75 oz	
OG	1044	
FG	1009	
ABV	4.63	
Apparent attenuation	79.55%	
IBU	33	
SRM	6	
Mash at	149° F	
Sparge at	168° F	
Boil time	90 minutes	
pitching temp	60.5° F	
Yeast	Wyeast 1968 London ESB	

1914 Fullers Porter

As a London brewer, Porter was still an important part of Fuller's beer portfolio. In the capital, draught Porter was remained very much a mainstream beer.

Fuller's version was rather weaker than those from larger London brewers, such as Whitbread and Courage. Their gravities were above 1050°.

But, just like at larger brewers, a combination of pale, brown and black malt formed the backbone of the grist. In addition, there's quite a large amount of sugar and a ridiculously small amount of oatmeal. Presumably its presence is to allow some of the Stout parti-gyled with this Porter to be legally sold as Oatmeal Stout.

What's down as No. 4 invert in the recipe is my substitution for something called Sp. Dx. Just my best guess.

As was usual before the war, the hops are a mix of English and foreign: Mid-Kent (1913), Poperinge (1913), Hallertau (1912), Cobbs (1913, 1914).

The real mashing scheme was mash of an hour with an initial heat of 140° F, raised to 148° F after 20 minutes by an underlet. Left to stand for a further 2 hours.

1914 Fullers Porter		
pale malt	5.25 lb	53.08%
brown malt	1.00 lb	10.62%
black malt	0.33 lb	3.50%
flaked maize	0.25 lb	2.65%
oatmeal	0.09 lb	0.96%
caramel 500 SRM	0.33 lb	5.31%
glucose	1.00 lb	10.62%
No. 4 invert sugar	1.25 lb	13.27%
Strisselspalt 90 mins	1.25 oz	
Fuggles 90 mins	0.50 oz	
Goldings 30 mins	0.75 oz	
OG	1045.5	
FG	1012.5	
ABV	4.37	
Apparent attenuation	72.53%	
IBU	29	
SRM	41	
Mash at	148° F	
Sparge at	170° F	
Boil time	90 minutes	
pitching temp	59° F	
Yeast	Wyeast 1968 London ESB	

1914 Fullers BS

Parti-gyled with the Porter above was this Stout. The BS probably stands for Brown Stout, the earliest name for what is now known simply as Stout.

There's not much to say about this that isn't above in the Porter description. As with the Porter, it's rather weaker than most Stouts from the larger London breweries. It's also the only Stout Fullers brewed, while the larger outfits generally brewed at least two or three. BS seems to have been discontinued in the early 1930's. Their Porter continued in production into the 1950's, though it was marketed as Nourishing Stout.

Almost forgot to mention. Fullers did something very London with the black malt: some went in the mash tun, some in the copper. For this beer, one of the two quarters, so 50%. Barclay Perkins did the same. I assume that it was to extract as much colour as possible. Try the same, if you're after total authenticity.

1914 Fullers BS		
pale malt	7.75 lb	55.54%
brown malt	1.50 lb	10.75%
black malt	0.50 lb	3.58%
flaked maize	0.33 lb	2.36%
oatmeal	0.13 lb	0.90%
caramel 500 SRM	0.50 lb	3.58%
glucose	1.50 lb	10.75%
No. 4 invert sugar	1.75 lb	12.54%
Strisselspalt 90 mins	1.75 oz	
Fuggles 60 mins	0.75 oz	
Goldings 30 mins	1.00 oz	
OG	1066	
FG	1021	
ABV	5.95	
Apparent attenuation	68.18%	
IBU	41	
SRM	38	
Mash at	148° F	
Sparge at	170° F	
Boil time	90 minutes	
pitching temp	59° F	
Yeast	Wyeast 1968 London ESB	

1914 Fullers BO

The unfortunately named BO – it probably stands for Burton Old – was the strongest beer Fullers produced.

In terms of strength, BO is very similar to the draught Burton Ale produced elsewhere in London, which were usually in the low 1070°'s. It remained a part of Fullers core range until after WW II.

The grist is rather simpler than most of their other beers. It's just pale malt, sugar and flaked maize. And there are no irritating proprietary sugars, just No. 3 invert and glucose. Really, just those sugars, I've not substituted anything.

The most unusual feature is the very long boil, presumably to concentrate the wort. The hops were Poperinge (1913), Oregon (1913), Cobbs (1914) and Mid-Kent (1914). The dry hops are a guess as Fullers didn't record them in their records. I've based my guess on what happened at Barclay Perkins, whose Burton Ales were very heavily dry-hopped.

The real mashing scheme was mash of an hour with an initial heat of 145° F, raised to 150° F after 30 minutes by an underlet. Left to stand for a further 2 hours.

1915 Fullers BO		
pale malt	13.25 lb	84.56%
flaked maize	1.00 lb	6.38%
No. 3 invert sugar	0.67 lb	4.28%
glucose	0.67 lb	4.28%
caramel 500 SRM	0.08 lb	0.51%
Strisselspalt 165 mins	0.50 oz	
Cluster 165 mins	0.50 oz	
Fuggles 90 mins	1.75 oz	
Goldings 30 mins	3.50 oz	
Goldings dry hops	0.75 oz	
OG	1072	
FG	1020.5	
ABV	6.81	
Apparent attenuation	71.53%	
IBU	106	
SRM	11	
Mash at	150° F	
Sparge at	168° F	
Boil time	165 minutes	
pitching temp	60° F	
Yeast	Wyeast 1968 London ESB	

1916 Fullers X Ale

We're a couple of years into the war and already there's starting to be a notable drop in gravity. Especially among Fullers more popular beers, of which X Ale was one.

Though the recipe, at least for the time being, is pretty much unchanged. It contains the same ingredients in much the same proportions.

The hops are Cobbs (1914, 1915), Mid-Kent (1915) and spent hops from a previous brew of AK. The latter have been recorded as just a third of their real weight in the brewing record. Presumably to take into account that they'd already been used.

As with all Fullers beers X Ale was fermented using the dropping system. It started off in a tall, narrow cylindrical vessel and after around 12 hours was dropped to a shallow, square vessel where fermentation was completed.

The real mashing scheme was mash of an hour with an initial heat of 145° F, raised to 149° F after 30 minutes by an underlet. Left to stand for a further 2 hours.

1916 Fullers X Ale		
pale malt	7.75 lb	76.73%
flaked maize	1.25 lb	12.38%
No. 3 invert sugar	0.50 lb	4.95%
glucose	0.50 lb	4.95%
caramel 500 SRM	0.10 lb	0.99%
Fuggles 120 mins	0.75 oz	
Fuggles 90 mins	0.75 oz	
Goldings 30 mins	0.75 oz	
OG	1047	
FG	1011	
ABV	4.76	
Apparent attenuation	76.60%	
IBU	29	
SRM	10	
Mash at	149° F	
Sparge at	168° F	
Boil time	120 minutes	
pitching temp	60° F	
Yeast	Wyeast 1968 London ESB	

1916 Fullers AK

There's only been a minimal change in the gravity of AK since the start of the war, just a single point.

Not much has happened with the grist, either. The proportion of sugar and flaked maize has fallen a little, with a corresponding increase in the base malt.

The hops are slightly different, being all English: Cobbs (1914, 1915) and Mid-Kent (1915). The change presumably wasn't voluntary, but due to the unavailability of imports.

The real mashing scheme was mash of an hour with an initial heat of 151° F, raised to 155° F after 25 minutes by an underlet. Left to stand for a further 1 hour and 35 minutes.

1916 Fullers AK		
pale malt	7.75 lb	83.73%
flaked maize	0.50 lb	5.40%
No. 2 invert sugar	0.50 lb	5.40%
glucose	0.50 lb	5.40%
Caramel 500 SRM	0.006 lb	0.06%
Fuggles 90 mins	0.75 oz	
Goldings 60 mins	1.25 oz	
Goldings 30 mins	1.25 oz	
Goldings dry hops	0.25 oz	
OG	1043	
FG	1009	
ABV	4.50	
Apparent attenuation	79.07%	
IBU	42	
SRM	5	
Mash at	155° F	
Sparge at	168° F	
Boil time	90 minutes	
pitching temp	60° F	
Yeast	Wyeast 1968 London ESB	

1916 Fullers PA

Like with AK, the effect of the war on the gravity of PA has been slight: a drop of just two points. Drinkers didn't realise just how lucky they'd been up until now.

There's been a little juggling of the proportions in the grist, but nothing massive. There's a bit more flaked maize and a bit less No. 2 invert.

The hops are Cobbs (1914, 1915) and Mid-Kent (1915). All English, obviously. The dry hops are just my guess. Everyone dry-hopped their Pale Ales and a beer of this strength usually had at least the equivalent of a half ounce per five imperial gallons.

The real mashing scheme was mash of an hour with an initial heat of 145° F, raised to 152° F after 25 minutes by an underlet. Left to stand for a further 1 hour and 35 minutes.

1916 Fullers PA		
pale malt	9.50 lb	84.38%
flaked maize	0.50 lb	4.44%
No. 2 invert sugar	0.50 lb	4.44%
glucose	0.75 lb	6.66%
caramel 500 SRM	0.009 lb	0.08%
Fuggles 90 mins	1.25 oz	
Goldings 60 mins	1.50 oz	
Goldings 30 mins	1.50 oz	
Goldings dry hops	0.50 oz	
OG	1052	
FG	1011	
ABV	5.42	
Apparent attenuation	78.85%	
IBU	52	
SRM	6	
Mash at	152° F	
Sparge at	168° F	
Boil time	90 minutes	
pitching temp	60° F	
Yeast	Wyeast 1968 London ESB	

1916 Fullers Porter

The war has so far not had much impact on Fullers Porter, other than a single point being shaved off its gravity.

One notable change to the grist is the dropping of glucose. While the black malt percentage has more than doubled and the amount of brown malt increased a little. The Sp. DX I've once again replaced with No. 4 invert sugar. There's still a token amount of oatmeal, though I can't imagine anyone could have detected its presence.

As in all the other Fullers beers, all the foreign hops have disappeared, leaving just English ones: Cobbs (1914, 1915), and Mid-Kent (1915).

The real mashing scheme was mash of an hour with an initial heat of 145° F, raised to 148° F after 20 minutes by an underlet. Left to stand for a further 2 hours.

1916 Fullers Porter		
pale malt	5.75 lb	56.76%
brown malt	1.25 lb	12.34%
black malt	1.00 lb	9.87%
flaked maize	0.50 lb	4.94%
oatmeal	0.05 lb	0.49%
caramel 500 SRM	0.33 lb	3.26%
No. 4 invert sugar	1.25 lb	12.34%
Fuggles 90 mins	0.75 oz	
Goldings 60 mins	1.00 oz	
Goldings 30 mins	1.00 oz	
OG	1044.5	
FG	1010.5	
ABV	4.50	
Apparent attenuation	76.40%	
IBU	35	
SRM	49	
Mash at	148° F	
Sparge at	170° F	
Boil time	90 minutes	
pitching temp	60° F	
Yeast	Wyeast 1968 London ESB	

1916 Fullers BS

Other than having a small gravity reduction of three points, BS remains basically the same.

Though, of course, all the recipe notes from the Porter above that it was parti-gyled with apply.

It's the last you'll be seeing of Fullers Brown Stout for a while. It was dropped in the spring of 1917 and didn't reappear again until late 1919. Brewing a strong beer like Stout just wasn't possible when brewing restrictions really began to bite.

1916 Fullers BS		
pale malt	8.00 lb	54.91%
brown malt	2.00 lb	13.73%
black malt	1.25 lb	8.58%
flaked maize	0.75 lb	5.15%
oatmeal	0.07 lb	0.48%
caramel 500 SRM	0.50 lb	3.43%
No. 4 invert sugar	2.00 lb	13.73%
Fuggles 90 mins	1.00 oz	
Goldings 60 mins	1.50 oz	
Goldings 30 mins	1.50 oz	
OG	1063	
FG	1021	
ABV	5.56	
Apparent attenuation	66.67%	
IBU	44	
SRM	63	
Mash at	149° F	
Sparge at	170° F	
Boil time	90 minutes	
pitching temp	60° F	
Yeast	Wyeast 1968 London ESB	

1917 Fullers X Ale

About exactly three years into the war, August 1917, and the changes are really starting to pick up pace.

The most obvious at first glance is a large reduction in the OG, down from 1047° to just 1035°. But there have been ever bigger changes to the grist.

The flaked maize and all the sugars have disappeared, replaced by just a little black malt. The changes have been so monumental and in such a short space of time that drinkers must have noticed. And probably weren't very happy. The removal of all the sugar and the big drop in strength would have made it appear thin and watery.

The hops, unsurprisingly, continue to be 100% English: Cobbs (1915, 1916), Mid-Kent (1916). Unlike some other brewers, who had emergency stocks of old foreign hops that they used in the later war years, Fullers appear to have had nothing held back.

The real mashing scheme was mash of an hour with an initial heat of 146° F, raised to 149° F after 30 minutes by an underlet. Left to stand for a further 2 hours.

1917 Fullers X Ale		
pale malt	8.00 lb	96.97%
black malt	0.25 lb	3.03%
Fuggles 120 mins	0.50 oz	
Goldings 60 mins	0.75 oz	
Goldings 30 mins	0.75 oz	
OG	1035	
FG	1007	
ABV	3.70	
Apparent attenuation	80.00%	
IBU	28	
SRM	12	
Mash at	149° F	
Sparge at	168° F	
Boil time	120 minutes	
pitching temp	62° F	
Yeast	Wyeast 1968 London ESB	

1917 Fullers AK

In the middle of 1917 Fuller's beers became ludicrously simple, pared back to pure malt or near as dammit pure malt. Like their AK.

There's a tiny amount of caramel colouring, but otherwise the grist is 100% pale malt. As an enthusiastic user of both sugar and flaked maize for decades, I can't imagine this was a voluntary decision of Fuller's part. It does make for some interesting beers, though.

The hops, just like in their X Ale, were all English. In fact they were exactly the same hops. All their beers at this point contained the same three types: Cobbs (1915, 1916) and Mid-Kent (1916).

The real mashing scheme was mash of an hour with an initial heat of 148° F, raised to 151° F after 25 minutes by an underlet. Left to stand for a further 1 hour and 35 minutes.

1917 Fullers AK		
pale malt	8.25 lb	99.95%
caramel 500 SRM	0.004 lb	0.05%
Fuggles 90 mins	0.75 oz	
Goldings 60 mins	1.00 oz	
Goldings 30 mins	1.00 oz	
Goldings dry hops	0.25 oz	
OG	1035	
FG	1006	
ABV	3.84	
Apparent attenuation	82.86%	
IBU	37	
SRM	4	
Mash at	151° F	
Sparge at	168° F	
Boil time	90 minutes	
pitching temp	60° F	
Yeast	Wyeast 1968 London ESB	

1917 Fullers PA

Parti-gyled with the AK above was this PA. A beer that seemed to be surviving the war well.

The biggest surprise is the strength: just three points below the pre-war level. It would have been expensive, but at least it packed some punch. How long would this last? Not very much. Amazingly, Fullers continued to brew PA at this strength right up until April 1918. At which point it became infeasible.

The quantities brewed had been severely reduced. While pre-war batches had been 200 barrels plus, by late 1917 that was down to 50 – 80 barrels. Better than nothing, though, I suppose. If you had the money to afford it.

1917 Fullers PA		
pale malt	11.75 lb	99.96%
caramel 500 SRM	0.005 lb	0.04%
Fuggles 90 mins	1.00 oz	
Goldings 60 mins	1.75 oz	
Goldings 30 mins	1.75 oz	
Goldings dry hops	0.50 oz	
OG	1051	
FG	1008	
ABV	5.69	
Apparent attenuation	84.31%	
IBU	55	
SRM	5	
Mash at	148° F	
Sparge at	168° F	
Boil time	90 minutes	
pitching temp	60° F	
Yeast	Wyeast 1968 London ESB	

1917 Fullers Porter

By the time this Porter was brewed in August 1917, it was the only Black Beer Fullers brewed. Brown Stout having been discontinued earlier in the year.

From what I've read, it's possible that this Porter was sold in some pubs as Stout. WW I seriously eroded the distinction between the two types. Something that would prove fatal to Porter after war's end.

As always, a combination of pale, brown and black malt is at the heart of the grist. The biggest change since 1916 is a big reduction in the percentage of sugar, down from 13% to around 2.5%. The amount of the three malts have all increased to compensate. The flaked maize has also disappeared.

The hops are the same as in all their other beers: Cobbs (1915, 1916) and Mid-Kent (1916).

There's been a big fall in gravity, too, down from 1044.5° to 1036°. It still had quite a way to fall before hitting rock bottom.

The real mashing scheme was mash of an hour with an initial heat of 146° F, raised to 149° F after 20 minutes by an underlet. Left to stand for a further 2 hours.

1917 Fullers Porter		
pale malt	5.50 lb	66.67%
brown malt	1.25 lb	15.15%
black malt	1.00 lb	12.12%
No. 4 invert sugar	0.125 lb	1.52%
brown sugar	0.125 lb	1.52%
caramel 500 SRM	0.25 lb	3.03%
Fuggles 120 mins	0.50 oz	
Goldings 60 mins	1.00 oz	
Goldings 30 mins	1.00 oz	
OG	1036	
FG	1008	
ABV	3.70	
Apparent attenuation	77.78%	
IBU	34	
SRM	37	
Mash at	149° F	
Sparge at	170° F	
Boil time	120 minutes	
pitching temp	61° F	
Yeast	Wyeast 1968 London ESB	

1918 Fullers X Ale

Unlike many other brewers, Fullers didn't drop their X Ale and introduce a Government Ale to replace it. They just kept on brewing X Ale, but with ever more swingeing gravity cuts.

Once again, there have been considerable alterations to the recipe since the previous year. Gone is the black malt and back again is No. 3 invert sugar. Plus rather a lot of glucose. The latter being the sugar the government preferred brewers to use. Though, to be fair, Fullers had used glucose pre-war. The overall result is a much paler beer. I can't help wondering if caramel was added at racking time.

I'm not sure what the point of the oat husks is. I can't imagine they added anything in terms of extract.

The hops remain all English: Cobbs (1916) and Mid-Kent (1916). No surprise that there are none from 1917, as the hop harvest was very small that year after growers were ordered by the government to replace half their bines with other crops.

The real mashing scheme was mash of an hour with an initial heat of 149° F, raised to 151° F after 30 minutes by an underlet. Left to stand for a further 2 hours.

1918 Fullers X Ale		
pale malt	4.00 lb	71.68%
oat husks	0.25 lb	4.48%
No. 3 invert sugar	0.33 lb	5.91%
glucose	1.00 lb	17.92%
Fuggles 90 mins	0.50 oz	
Goldings 60 mins	0.50 oz	
Goldings 30 mins	0.50 oz	
OG	1027	
FG	1005.5	
ABV	2.84	
Apparent attenuation	79.63%	
IBU	22	
SRM	5	
Mash at	151° F	
Sparge at	168° F	
Boil time	90 minutes	
pitching temp	61° F	
Yeast	Wyeast 1968 London ESB	

1918 Fullers AK

It wasn't just X Ale that had its gravity slashed. The same fate befell Fullers AK.

Not really surprising as on 1st April 1918, a few weeks before this beer was brewed, average gravity was cut to 1030°. It was logical that big-selling beers would need to have a gravity lower than that.

There have been more adjustments to the recipe, too. Back are No. 2 invert sugar and glucose, leaving the grist quite similar to the 1916 version, save for the absence of flaked maize.

The hops are exactly the same two types as in X Ale: Cobbs (1916) and Mid-Kent (1916).

The real mashing scheme was mash of an hour with an initial heat of 150° F, raised to 152° F after 25 minutes by an underlet. Left to stand for a further 1 hour and 35 minutes.

1918 Fullers AK		
pale malt	4.25 lb	77.20%
No. 2 invert sugar	1.00 lb	18.17%
glucose	0.25 lb	4.54%
caramel 500 SRM	0.005 lb	0.09%
Fuggles 90 mins	0.75 oz	
Goldings 60 mins	0.75 oz	
Goldings 30 mins	0.75 oz	
Goldings dry hops	0.25 oz	
OG	1026	
FG	1005.5	
ABV	2.71	
Apparent attenuation	78.85%	
IBU	33	
SRM	6	
Mash at	152° F	
Sparge at	168° F	
Boil time	90 minutes	
pitching temp	60° F	
Yeast	Wyeast 1968 London ESB	

1918 Fullers PA

Parti-gyled with the previous AK was this PA. The only one of Fullers beers in 1918 that might actually get you pissed.

This is the reason all their other beers were under 1030°. To brew a beer of this strength and still average out to 1030°, they had to brew quite a lot of beer well below 1030°.

It's a shock that Fullers brewed their top-class Pale Ale all through the war. Most breweries dropped their flagship Bitters to concentrate on churning out large quantities of lower strength ones. Of course, the only reason they could continue to turn out some beer of this strength was that Fullers had two other beers – AK and X Ale – with gravities below 1030°.

It's interesting to trace the arc of PA's gravity. In 1914 it was 1054°, about the same as today's ESB. At this point, it had an OG closer to London Pride. By 1946, it was 1035° - about the same as Chiswick Bitter.

1918 Fullers PA		
pale malt	6.25 lb	77.27%
No. 2 invert sugar	1.50 lb	18.55%
glucose	0.33 lb	4.08%
caramel 500 SRM	0.01 lb	0.10%
Fuggles 90 mins	1.00 oz	
Goldings 60 mins	1.00 oz	
Goldings 30 mins	1.00 oz	
Goldings dry hops	0.50 oz	
OG	1039	
FG	1009	
ABV	3.97	
Apparent attenuation	76.92%	
IBU	40	
SRM	8	
Mash at	152° F	
Sparge at	168° F	
Boil time	90 minutes	
pitching temp	60° F	
Yeast	Wyeast 1968 London ESB	

1918 Fullers Porter

Porter was another of Fullers beers that had to sacrifice its own gravity to leave PA at a decent strength.

There's been some more fiddling with the grist, mostly a big increase in the percentage of sugar from 2.5% to 18%. The greatest part of that sugar being glucose. The increase in sugar has inevitably caused a fall in the percentage of malt, particularly the base malt.

Talking of sugar, the No. 4 invert is my substitution for something called Sp. Dark, and brown sugar my interpretation of "Manilla". I could be way off the mark on both counts.

At this point, Fullers used the same hops in all of their beer: Cobbs (1916) and Mid-Kent (1916). It makes my life easy.

The real mashing scheme was mash of an hour with an initial heat of 148° F, raised to 150° F after 20 minutes by an underlet. Left to stand for a further 2 hours.

1918 Fullers Porter		
pale malt	3.50 lb	57.14%
brown malt	0.75 lb	12.24%
black malt	0.50 lb	8.16%
No. 4 invert sugar	0.125 lb	2.04%
brown sugar	0.25 lb	4.08%
glucose	0.67 lb	10.94%
caramel 500 SRM	0.33 lb	5.39%
Fuggles 120 mins	0.50 oz	
Goldings 60 mins	0.50 oz	
Goldings 30 mins	0.50 oz	
OG	1027.5	
FG	1007	
ABV	2.71	
Apparent attenuation	74.55%	
IBU	22	
SRM	28	
Mash at	150° F	
Sparge at	168° F	
Boil time	120 minutes	
pitching temp	60° F	
Yeast	Wyeast 1968 London ESB	

1919 Fullers X Ale

We're now getting on for a tear after war's end, August 1914. And, while things are improving in terms of beer strength, it's still nowhere near back to normal.

On the bright side, most beers now were actually capable of getting you intoxicated, if you were determined enough. At just about 3% ABV, you'd have need to knock back a bucket or two of X Ale to feel much effect.

With the return of flaked maize, the grist is staring to get back to where it was in 1914. The only difference being the lack of No. 3 invert. Instead there's rather more glucose and a touch of caramel. The colour is pale than in 1914, but that could just be down to me not selecting a dark enough caramel.

After using exclusively English hops for a couple of years, foreign hops have reappeared in the form of very old Belgian ones. The full hop charge was: Poperinge (1914), English (1914, 1917 and 1918). I've seen a lot of quite old Belgian and US hops used at several breweries just after the end of the war. Must have been a lot of them knocking about.

The real mashing scheme was mash of an hour with an initial heat of 146° F, raised to 149° F after 30 minutes by an underlet. Left to stand for a further 2.25 hours.

1919 Fullers X Ale		
pale malt	4.50 lb	71.49%
flaked maize	0.67 lb	10.64%
glucose	1.00 lb	15.89%
caramel 500 SRM	0.13 lb	1.99%
Strisselspalt 90 mins	0.50 oz	
Fuggles 60 mins	0.50 oz	
Goldings 30 mins	0.75 oz	
OG	1030.5	
FG	1008	
ABV	2.98	
Apparent attenuation	73.77%	
IBU	23	
SRM	8	
Mash at	149° F	
Sparge at	168° F	
Boil time	90 minutes	
pitching temp	60.5° F	
Yeast	Wyeast 1968 London ESB	

1919 Fullers XX Ale

A sign of improving beer times was the appearance at Fullers of a couple of new beers, one being a stronger Mild Ale, XX.

XX survived the interwar period and WW II, but disappeared in 1946. Between the wars it had the typical gravity of a 6d Mild Ale, 1043°. In the same period Barclay Perkins also brewed a 6d Mild with the same gravity.

It's a big improvement on the Mild Ales brewed in the later war years, but the gravity is still way short of the 1051° of Fullers pre-war X Ale.

As this was parti-gyled with X Ale, see the previous recipe for details of the grist and hopping.

1919 Fullers XX Ale		
pale malt	6.00 lb	71.64%
flaked maize	0.75 lb	8.96%
glucose	1.50 lb	17.91%
caramel 500 SRM	0.125 lb	1.49%
Strisselspalt 90 mins	0.67 oz	
Fuggles 60 mins	0.67 oz	
Goldings 30 mins	1.00 oz	
OG	1041	
FG	1012	
ABV	3.84	
Apparent attenuation	70.73%	
IBU	28	
SRM	8	
Mash at	149° F	
Sparge at	168° F	
Boil time	90 minutes	
pitching temp	61° F	
Yeast	Wyeast 1968 London ESB	

1919 Fullers BS

After an absence of more than two years, Brown Stout returned in November 1919. But it wasn't fated to be around for that much longer. It was killed off by the 1931 emergency budget.

It wasn't as strong as either the 1914 or 1916 versions, however. It's no coincidence the gravity is 1055°. When it was brewed the 8d per pint category started at 1054°. There was no economic sense in brewing anything much over 1054°, as you could still only sell for a maximum of 8d per pint.

There have been yet more changes to the grist, once again mostly concerning sugar. Gone is the glucose and Sp. Dark, replaced by something simply described as "Peruvian". I'm assuming it's a form of raw cane sugar. Flaked maize has reappeared, replacing some of the malt.

The hops were an odd mixture of English and foreign, new and old Poperinge: (1914), Sussex (1914) and English (1918).

The real mashing scheme was mash of an hour with an initial heat of 148° F, raised to 152° F after 20 minutes by an underlet. Left to stand for a further 2 hours.

1919 Fullers BS		
pale malt	5.75 lb	48.94%
brown malt	1.25 lb	10.64%
black malt	1.00 lb	8.51%
flaked maize	1.25 lb	10.64%
brown sugar	2.00 lb	17.02%
caramel 500 SRM	0.50 lb	4.26%
Strisselspalt 90 mins	0.75 oz	
Fuggles 60 mins	0.75 oz	
Goldings 30 mins	1.25 oz	
OG	1055	
FG	1022	
ABV	4.37	
Apparent attenuation	60.00%	
IBU	30	
SRM	41	
Mash at	152° F	
Sparge at	170° F	
Boil time	90 minutes	
pitching temp	62° F	
Yeast	Wyeast 1968 London ESB	

1919 Fullers Porter

If you can remember that far back, in 1914 Fullers Porter was, at 1045.5°, quite weak for a London example. Well. The war didn't do it any favours.

In 1918, the most difficult year for British brewing, its gravity hit a low of 1027.5°. The end of the war helped it recover a little. In the summer of 1919, it crawled back over 1030°. Though, in this example, that's let down by a poor degree of attenuation. Which wasn't always the case. Some others finished at 1010-1012°.

The gravity might have yoyoed, but the grist has remained quite constant, at least in terms of its main elements. These were pale, brown and black malt. Accompanied by flaked maize, most of the time. Then various sugars, which varied a bit.

In this case, the sugars are Peruvian and a couple of types of caramel. Which I've taken to be brown sugar and, well, caramel. Though, obviously, the shade of it is just my best guess.

The hops were Poperinge (1914), Sussex (1914) and unspecified English (1918).

1919 Fullers Porter		
pale malt	3.50 lb	47.75%
brown malt	0.75 lb	10.23%
black malt	0.50 lb	6.82%
flaked maize	0.75 lb	10.23%
brown sugar	1.50 lb	20.46%
caramel 500 SRM	0.33 lb	4.50%
Strisselspalt 90 mins	0.50 oz	
Fuggles 60 mins	0.50 oz	
Goldings 30 mins	1.00 oz	
OG	1035	
FG	1014	
ABV	2.78	
Apparent attenuation	60.00%	
IBU	25	
SRM	27	
Mash at	152° F	
Sparge at	170° F	
Boil time	90 minutes	
pitching temp	62° F	
Yeast	Wyeast 1968 London ESB	

1919 Fullers AK

The easing of wartime restrictions is also evident in AK, whose gravity has increased by 4.5 points since the previous year.

Though that still left it at just a shade over 3% ABV. Which was about two-thirds of what it had been in 1914. That's quite a fall. And one which would eventually lead to its downfall. For, while there was a market for this type of low-gravity beer, once things had got back to relative normality in the 1920s, it was a limited one. It was the same story with 4d Mild Ale.

The recipe has undergone one change: half of the No. 2 invert has been replaced by flaked maize. Fullers had been enthusiastic users of this adjunct pre-war and I'm certain only dropped it because it was unavailable. Once maize was being imported again, it returned to their recipes.

There are just two types of hops: Poperinge from the 1914 crop and English from 1918. In a ratio of 40 to 60. Which is quite a high percentage of fresh hops.

The mashing scheme was typical of Fuller: mash of an hour with an initial heat of 147° F, raised to 151° F after 25 minutes by an underlet. Left to stand for a further 1 hour and 50 minutes.

1919 Fullers AK		
pale malt	5.00 lb	76.80%
flaked maize	0.50 lb	7.68%
No. 2 invert sugar	0.50 lb	7.68%
glucose	0.50 lb	7.68%
caramel 500 SRM	0.01 lb	0.15%
Strisselspalt 90 mins	0.50 oz	
Goldings 60 mins	0.75 oz	
Goldings 30 mins	0.75 oz	
Goldings dry hops	0.25 oz	
OG	1030.5	
FG	1007	
ABV	3.11	
Apparent attenuation	77.05%	
IBU	27	
SRM	5	
Mash at	151° F	
Sparge at	168° F	
Boil time	90 minutes	
pitching temp	60° F	
Yeast	Wyeast 1968 London ESB	

1919 Fullers XK

The second new beer to appear in 1919 was XK, a new mid-strength Bitter. Though it wasn't 100% new as Fullers had already brewed a beer with the same brewhouse name in the late 19th century.

Clearly Fullers saw a demand for something stronger than the now watery AK, but more affordable than full-strength PA. Very unusually, Fullers emerged from the war with an expanded range of Pale Ales, going from two in 1914 to three in 1919. Mostly it was the other way around.

Surprisingly, though popular, XK was never quite produced in quantities as large as PA. In the interwar years, Fullers brewed about 60 to 40 PA to XK. Only PA made it through WWW II, with XK falling along with AK in 1941.

This example was parti-gyled with the AK above.

1919 Fullers XK		
pale malt	5.50 lb	74.83%
flaked maize	0.50 lb	6.80%
No. 2 invert sugar	0.67 lb	9.12%
glucose	0.67 lb	9.12%
caramel 500 SRM	0.01 lb	0.14%
Strisselspalt 90 mins	0.75 oz	
Goldings 60 mins	1.00 oz	
Goldings 30 mins	1.00 oz	
Goldings dry hops	0.25 oz	
OG	1034	
FG	1010	
ABV	3.18	
Apparent attenuation	70.59%	
IBU	36	
SRM	5	
Mash at	151° F	
Sparge at	168° F	
Boil time	90 minutes	
pitching temp	61° F	
Yeast	Wyeast 1968 London ESB	

1919 Fullers PA

The third element of the Pale Ale parti-gyle was PA, the strongest of the bunch. And, ultimately, the longest-lived of all three. You could argue that it's still around today (at least occasionally) as Chiswick Bitter is a direct descendant.

Though this version was a very different beast. Amazingly, PA was back to its 1914 strength. I can't stress enough how much of a rarity this was. Fullers was able to do that because of some very specific characteristics of this beer.

In particular, the gravity it had in 1914: 1054°. Which was very handy. When this version was brewed in August 1914, 1054° was the minimum OG for the top price control band. Making it a very attractive gravity to brew to. While Barclay Perkins would have struggled to restore their PA to its pre-war strength, as that was an uneconomic 1062°.

1919 Fullers PA		
pale malt	8.50 lb	73.78%
flaked maize	1.00 lb	8.68%
No. 2 invert sugar	1.00 lb	8.68%
glucose	1.00 lb	8.68%
caramel 500 SRM	0.02 lb	0.17%
Strisselspalt 90 mins	1.00 oz	
Goldings 60 mins	1.50 oz	
Goldings 30 mins	1.50 oz	
Goldings dry hops	0.50 oz	
OG	1054	
FG	1013	
ABV	5.42	
Apparent attenuation	75.93%	
IBU	46	
SRM	7	
Mash at	151° F	
Sparge at	168° F	
Boil time	90 minutes	
pitching temp	61° F	
Yeast	Wyeast 1968 London ESB	

1925 Fullers X Ale

We're jumping forward a few years now to the mid-1920s to get an impression of what Fullers beer range looked like when things had become stable again.

X Ale remained Fullers most popular beer and they churned it out in large quantities – between 300 and 500 barrels per batch. A larger size than any of their other beers. Not really much of a surprise, as Mild was easily biggest selling type of beer at the time.

The grist was quite simple: pale malt, flaked maize, glucose and caramel. Rather odd grist for a Mild, where you would expect to find No. 3 invert and probably crystal malt, too. But Fullers generally shied away from coloured malts, other than in Porter and Stout. They seem to have picked up the use of glucose during the war and stuck with it. Right up until the 1960s.

One weird ingredient is oat husks. For this batch size, it contained the equivalent of approximately 0.33 lb of oat husks. No idea what the point of that was. I can't imagine that added either flavour or fermentable material.

The hops were Pacific from 1922, and English from 1923 and 1924.

The real mashing scheme was mash of an hour with an initial heat of 146° F, raised to 150° F after 25 minutes by an underlet. Left to stand for a further 2.25 hours.

1925 Fullers X Ale		
pale malt	6.50 lb	77.61%
flaked maize	1.25 lb	14.93%
glucose	0.50 lb	5.97%
caramel 500 SRM	0.125 lb	1.49%
Cluster 90 mins	0.33 oz	
Fuggles 60 mins	0.75 oz	
Goldings 30 mins	1.00 oz	
OG	1036	
FG	1010	
ABV	3.44	
Apparent attenuation	72.22%	
IBU	27	
SRM	8	
Mash at	150° F	
Sparge at	168° F	
Boil time	90 minutes	
pitching temp	62° F	
Yeast	Wyeast 1968 London ESB	

1925 Fullers BO

When Fullers started brewing Burton again after WW I there was one big difference. Rather than being brewed single-gyle it was parti-gyled with Mild. This example being parti-gyled with the X Ale above.

Presumably this was because of the quantity they brewed. Before the war they brewed BO in batches of around 150 barrels. In this brew there were just 80 barrels, along with 550 of X Ale. Brewing less than 100 barrels just wouldn't have been viable on the kit they had.

As far as I can tell, BO was reincarnated late in 1920, initially with a gravity a few points higher than here. The gravity fell a little further in the 1930s, settling at around 1055° after the disastrous 1931 emergency budget. WW II reduced the gravity even further to 1039° by 1946.

1925 Fullers BO		
pale malt	11.25 lb	80.70%
flaked maize	2.00 lb	14.35%
glucose	0.50 lb	3.59%
caramel 500 SRM	0.19 lb	1.36%
Cluster 90 mins	0.50 oz	
Fuggles 60 mins	1.25 oz	
Goldings 30 mins	1.75 oz	
Goldings dry hops	0.50 oz	
OG	1061.5	
FG	1019	
ABV	5.62	
Apparent attenuation	69.11%	
IBU	40	
SRM	11	
Mash at	150° F	
Sparge at	168° F	
Boil time	90 minutes	
pitching temp	60° F	
Yeast	Wyeast 1968 London ESB	

1925 Fullers XX Ale

XX Ale was brewed in far smaller quantities than the weaker X Ale. Unsurprisingly, then, it was parti-gyled with it. This particular batch was just 43 barrels, along with 522 barrels of X Ale.

The gravity has increased a little since 1919, rising by 4.5 points. That's still a good bit short of what X Ale had been in 1914.

XX - what would have been classified as Best Mild – hung around for quite a long while. It was still a reasonable gravity in 1939: 1042.5°. Also managing to struggle through the war at 1035°, before finally succumbing in early 1946.

The real mashing scheme was mash of an hour with an initial heat of 145° F, raised to 149° F after 25 minutes by an underlet. Left to stand for a further 2.25 hours.

1925 Fullers XX Ale		
pale malt	8.25 lb	79.33%
flaked maize	1.50 lb	14.42%
glucose	0.50 lb	4.81%
caramel 500 SRM	0.15 lb	1.44%
Cluster 90 mins	0.50 oz	
Fuggles 60 mins	1.25 oz	
Goldings 30 mins	1.25 oz	
OG	1045.5	
FG	1014	
ABV	4.17	
Apparent attenuation	69.23%	
IBU	40	
SRM	9	
Mash at	149° F	
Sparge at	168° F	
Boil time	90 minutes	
pitching temp	62° F	
Yeast	Wyeast 1968 London ESB	

1925 Fullers XK

Introduced in 1919, XK was Fuller's new mid-strength Bitter. By 1925 the gravity had increased by a fair bit, from 1034° to 1040.5°. Though, surprisingly, it was brewed in smaller quantities than the full-strength PA.

There have been some changes to the grist since 1919. In a good way, really. The percentage of pale malt has increased, while the proportion of No. 2 invert sugars and glucose has declined considerably. The flaked maize is the one element to have remained fairly constant.

The hops are a mixed bag in terms of age. There are old Pacific hops from 1922. While the English ones are somewhat fresher, being from the 1923 and 1924 harvests. Though the Pacific hops only made up 18% of the total.

1925 Fullers XK		
pale malt	8.00 lb	87.48%
flaked maize	0.75 lb	8.20%
No. 2 invert sugar	0.25 lb	2.73%
glucose	0.125 lb	1.37%
caramel 500 SRM	0.020 lb	0.22%
Cluster 90 mins	0.50 oz	
Fuggles 60 mins	1.25 oz	
Goldings 30 mins	1.25 oz	
Goldings dry hops	0.25 oz	
OG	1040.5	
FG	1011	
ABV	3.90	
Apparent attenuation	72.84%	
IBU	43	
SRM	5	
Mash at	150° F	
Sparge at	168° F	
Boil time	90 minutes	
pitching temp	60.5° F	
Yeast	Wyeast 1968 London ESB	

1925 Fullers AK

When you see the quantities that were brewed of AK, you wonder why Fullers bothered. This batch, parti-gyled with the XK above and PA below, was just 9 barrels. It can't have been sold in more than a couple of pubs.

What's incredible, is that Fullers AK managed to limp on into the 1940s with miniscule sales. Batches from the 1940s were mostly just two barrels. That implies no more than one or two pubs sold it. I wonder which ones. Why did they keep brewing it? Unless it was the head brewer's favourite tipple.

The real mashing scheme was mash of an hour with an initial heat of 145° F, raised to 150° F after 25 minutes by an underlet. Left to stand for a further 110 minutes.

1925 Fullers AK		
pale malt	6.50 lb	89.47%
flaked maize	0.50 lb	6.88%
No. 2 invert sugar	0.125 lb	1.72%
glucose	0.125 lb	1.72%
caramel 500 SRM	0.015 lb	0.21%
Cluster 90 mins	0.25 oz	
Fuggles 60 mins	1.00 oz	
Goldings 30 mins	1.00 oz	
Goldings dry hops	0.25 oz	
OG	1032	
FG	1007	
ABV	3.31	
Apparent attenuation	78.13%	
IBU	33	
SRM	4	
Mash at	150° F	
Sparge at	168° F	
Boil time	90 minutes	
pitching temp	60° F	
Yeast	Wyeast 1968 London ESB	

1925 Fullers PA

The finally element of Fullers Pale Ale parti-gyle remained PA. Which also remained at its pre-WW I strength.

It's heartening to see the quantities that were brewed. In this brew, there were 341 barrels of PA, 150 barrels of XK and just 9 barrels of AK. PA was only outsold by X Ale. Why did such a strong Bitter sell so well? At Barclay Perkins, whose PA and XLK had roughly equivalent gravities to Fullers PA and XK, the weaker Bitter outsold the stronger one by three or four times to one. Maybe Fullers drinkers were just better off.

1925 Fullers PA		
pale malt	10.50 lb	88.20%
flaked maize	1.00 lb	8.40%
No. 2 invert sugar	0.25 lb	2.10%
glucose	0.125 lb	1.05%
caramel 500 SRM	0.030 lb	0.25%
Cluster 90 mins	0.75 oz	
Fuggles 60 mins	1.75 oz	
Goldings 30 mins	1.95 oz	
Goldings dry hops	0.50 oz	
OG	1054	
FG	1015	
ABV	5.16	
Apparent attenuation	72.22%	
IBU	56	
SRM	6	
Mash at	150° F	
Sparge at	168° F	
Boil time	90 minutes	
pitching temp	60° F	
Yeast	Wyeast 1968 London ESB	

1925 Fullers Porter

Fullers Porter was a bit beefier than most interwar Porters, which were usually around 1036°, or even weaker. Most brewers in London had Porters in the 5d per pint class, while Fuller's was a 6d beer.

Which may explain why it survived right through until WW II and beyond. Though at some point it stopped being draught Porter and was transformed into Nourishing Stout, a bottled beer. Though the brewhouse name remained P for many years after this change.

The grist is unusual for London, in that it contains no brown malt. That was dropped sometime in the early 1920s. Most London brewers remained faithful to brown malt until the bitter end.

The real mashing scheme was mash of an hour with an initial heat of 145° F, raised to 149° F after 25 minutes by an underlet. Left to stand for a further 2 hours.

1925 Fullers Porter		
pale malt	5.50 lb	60.01%
black malt	0.75 lb	8.18%
flaked maize	0.75 lb	8.18%
oatmeal	0.06 lb	0.65%
No. 4 invert sugar	1.78 lb	19.37%
caramel 500 SRM	0.33 lb	3.60%
Cluster 90 mins	0.50 oz	
Fuggles 60 mins	1.25 oz	
Goldings 30 mins	1.25 oz	
OG	1041.5	
FG	1015.5	
ABV	3.44	
Apparent attenuation	62.65%	
IBU	41	
SRM	47	
Mash at	149° F	
Sparge at	170° F	
Boil time	90 minutes	
pitching temp	61.5° F	
Yeast	Wyeast 1968 London ESB	

1925 Fullers BS

Parti-gyled with Porter, BS was another of Fuller's low-volume beers. This batch was a mere 35 barrels.

I'm surprised that they weren't brewing more, as Stout remained a popular draught beer in London between the wars. Perhaps it was because their Porter was stronger than most. It looks as if a lot of pre-war Porter drinkers switched to Stout in the 1920's. It was, after all, much like pre-war Porter had been in terms of strength.

The reappearance of oatmeal in the grist is a sure sign that some was being marketed as Oatmeal Stout. For some reason the oats were dropped after 1917. Was that because they were unobtainable, or just because they couldn't be bothered to mess around with Oatmeal Stout?

Surprisingly, BS was dropped in the early 1930s. A surprise, because Stout was still extremely popular in London.

1925 Fullers BS		
pale malt	7.50 lb	59.67%
black malt	1.00 lb	7.96%
flaked maize	1.00 lb	7.96%
oatmeal	0.07 lb	0.56%
No. 4 invert sugar	2.50 lb	19.89%
caramel 500 SRM	0.50 lb	3.98%
Cluster 90 mins	0.75 oz	
Fuggles 60 mins	1.75 oz	
Goldings 30 mins	1.75 oz	
OG	1057	
FG	1022	
ABV	4.63	
Apparent attenuation	61.40%	
IBU	52	
SRM	60	
Mash at	149° F	
Sparge at	170° F	
Boil time	90 minutes	
pitching temp	61.5° F	
Yeast	Wyeast 1968 London ESB	

Kidd

Kidd was a smallish brewery just outside London in Dartford, Kent. One for which some brewing records have been preserved, due to being taken over by Courage in 1937. It was pretty small, owning just 65 tied houses.

Based on their brew length of around 150 barrels, I estimate their annual production was between 40,000 and 50,000 barrels. To put that into perspective, in 1917 Whitbread brewed 578,502 barrels.[38] And they weren't even the largest brewery in London.

These are the Kidd beers, unfortunately not from 1914. Though not a huge amount changed between 1914 and March 1917. The gravities were probably a couple of points higher for all the beers at the start of the war.

Kidd beers in early 1917									
Date	Year	Beer	Style	OG	FG	ABV	App. Attenuation	lbs hops/ qtr	hops lb/brl
19th Mar	1917	X	Mild	1044.3	1013.9	4.03	68.75%	8.00	1.52
16th Feb	1917	SXXX	Mild	1052.6	1018.0	4.58	65.79%	8.98	2.07
15th Mar	1917	BB	Pale Ale	1038.2	1011.1	3.59	71.01%	14.08	2.30
20th Mar	1917	Porter	Porter	1044.9	1015.0	3.96	66.67%	8.00	1.67
6th Feb	1917	Stout	Stout	1062.6	1018.8	5.79	69.91%	9.00	2.28
23rd Mar	1917	XXXX	Strong Ale	1069.8	1023.3	6.16	66.67%	15.00	4.65
Source: Kidd brewing record held at the London Metropolitan Archives, document number ACC/305/16/013.									

Kidd brewed a range of six beers in early 1917, most likely fewer than they had been making at the start of the war. As the war progressed breweries gradually discontinued less popular beers and ones with high gravities. By the time the war ended, many were just brewing four or five beers.

By the end of the war Kidd's set of beers had been similarly reduced to just four:

Kidd beers in 1920							
Beer	Style	OG	FG	ABV	App. Attenuation	lbs hops/ qtr	hops lb/brl
X	Mild	1027.7	1006.1	2.86	78.00%	10.00	1.15
Stock PA	Pale Ale	1046.5	1013.9	4.32	70.24%	8.00	1.64
Stout	Stout	1047.6	1013.9	4.47	70.93%	8.22	1.71
XXX	Strong Ale	1056.0	1019.4	4.84	65.35%	9.05	2.20
Source: Kidd brewing record held at the London Metropolitan Archives, document number ACC/305/16/013.							

---

[38] Whitbread brewing records held at the London Metropolitan Archives, document numbers LMA/4453/D/01/082 and LMA/4453/D/09/111.

1917 Kidd BB

Kidd was a small brewery in Dartford, Kent, just outside London. It was bought and closed by Courage in 1937.

BB probably stands for Best Bitter, though by this stage of the war "best" was a much devalued term. In fact it looks remarkably like a post WW II Ordinary Bitter.

There's not much to the grist, just pale malt, some sugar and the merest hint of malt extract. As I've mentioned many times before, crystal malt in Bitter is really quite a recent thing. Pretty much unknown before WW I and not common until after WW II.

I know a little more about the hops in this case. Half were Kent, the other half Farnhams. As the latter hops aren't generally available nowadays, I've replaced them with the very similar Goldings. All the hops were from the 1916 crop and, as this beer was brewed at the start of February, they were pretty fresh. It results in quite a bitter beer for something of such relatively low gravity.

This was one of the final brews of BB, on 1st February 1917. It was discontinued at the end of March. Like many other brewers, Kidd completely rejigged their beer ranges on April 1st 1917.

1917 Kidd BB		
pale malt	6.00 lb	78.69%
No. 3 invert sugar	1.50 lb	19.67%
malt extract	0.125 lb	1.64%
Fuggles 135 mins	1.75 oz	
Goldings 30 mins	1.75 oz	
Goldings dry hops	0.75 oz	
OG	1038	
FG	1010	
ABV	3.70	
Apparent attenuation	73.68%	
IBU	46	
SRM	11	
Mash at	150° F	
Sparge at	165° F	
Boil time	135 minutes	
pitching temp	59° F	
Yeast	Wyeast 1099 Whitbread Ale	

1917 Kidd X

Kidd had a couple of Mild Ales in 1917, X being the one they produced the most of. In fact, this was probably the most popular beer of their range.

I'm including a series of recipe for Kidd because it's a good example of a small, southern brewery. If I just stuck with the large London breweries it would give a very false impression of the overall picture. For, although they produced a large quantity of beer, they weren't typical of brewers across the whole country.

If you compare Kidd X to the 1916 Courage X Ale a few pages back, you'll see that they have quite similar gravities (1042° and 1045°, respectively). The Kidd Mild is slightly more heavily hopped: 29 calculated IBUs as opposed to 26. All the Kidd beers contain lots of hops, more so even than London brewers, who were renowned for producing bitter beer.

The grist has many of the elements you would expect: English and Californian pale malt, crystal malt and No. 3 invert sugar. Not so usual is the malt extract. There's also no flaked maize, though that's probably due to the war. It all had to be imported, which starting to be a problem. I'm surprised that they still had California malt as supplies of that were also interrupted.

The sugar is listed at 2 cwt. of No. 3 invert and 7 cwt. of something called Budgett. I've interpreted that as more No. 3, though it could be something totally different.

The hops are described Sussex, Farnham and Kent, which I've interpreted as Fuggles and Goldings. I've reduced the hopping as some of the hops are from the 1914 crop.

1917 Kidd X		
pale malt	4.75 lb	59.38%
crystal malt 60 L	1.00 lb	12.50%
No. 3 invert sugar	2.00 lb	25.00%
cane sugar	0.125 lb	1.56%
malt extract	0.125 lb	1.56%
Fuggles 135 mins	0.75 oz	
Fuggles 60 mins	0.75 oz	
Goldings 30 mins	0.75 oz	
OG	1042	
FG	1011	
ABV	4.10	
Apparent attenuation	73.81%	
IBU	29	
SRM	16	
Mash at	152° F	
Sparge at	165° F	
Boil time	135 minutes	
pitching temp	59° F	
Yeast	Wyeast 1099 Whitbread Ale	

1917 Kidd SXXX

This is a beer that originally had me confused. I assumed that it was some sort of Burton Ale.

But when I looked more closely at the hopping rate, I realised that it was really a strong Mild. At least that's what I think at the moment. I might change my mind.

The big difference with the other Mild Ale, X, is the type of sugar. X has No. 3 invert and Budgett, SXXX has No. 1 invert alone. The percentage of sugar in the grist is far lower than in X. Probably an indication that this was a fancier beer. Unlike X, there's no crystal malt. That, combined with the use of No. 1 rather than No. 3 invert makes this a paler beer than X.

The hops are listed as Farnham and Kent, which, as usual, I've interpreted as Goldings and Fuggles, respectively. They were all from the 1916 crop so I haven't reduced the quantity. That all the hops were fresh is another indication that this was a posh beer.

1917 Kidd SXXX		
pale malt	9.00 lb	82.76%
No. 1 invert sugar	1.50 lb	13.79%
cane sugar	0.25 lb	2.30%
malt extract	0.125 lb	1.15%
Fuggles 150 mins	2.25 oz	
Goldings 30 mins	2.25 oz	
Goldings dry hops	0.75 oz	
OG	1053	
FG	1018	
ABV	4.63	
Apparent attenuation	66.04%	
IBU	55	
SRM	6	
Mash at	153° F	
Sparge at	165° F	
Boil time	150 minutes	
pitching temp	59° F	
Yeast	Wyeast 1099 Whitbread Ale	

1917 Kidd XXXX

Obviously, Kidd did brew a Strong Ale. Something along the lines of a London Burton Ale. XXXX was roughly the equivalent of a KK.

The unique feature of XXXX's grist is the use of both No. 1 and No. 3 invert sugar. The latter, along with the caramel colouring, leave the finished beer quite dark. Not quite as dark as Dark Mild, but on the way there.

If you're wondering about the small amount of cane sugar in these recipes, it wasn't added in the copper as you would expect. Instead it seems to have been added during fermentation, in this case on the second day. I'm not really sure what the purpose of this was.

Another thing I should probably mention is that Kidd used the dropping system of fermentation. That's where the fermentation starts in tall, narrow open cylinders and after a while is dropped to much shallower, square fermenters. The purpose being to remove yeast. This beer was dropped 36 hours into the fermentation, as were most other beers.

The hops were evenly split between 1916 Kents and 1916 Farnhams, which, as usual, I've taken to be Fuggles and Goldings, respectively. There's an awful lot of them. It's also quite heavily dry hopped, though the type of hops isn't mentioned in the brewing record.

1917 Kidd XXXX		
pale malt	10.75 lb	77.20%
no. 1 sugar	2.00 lb	14.36%
no. 3 sugar	0.75 lb	5.39%
caramel 2000 SRM	0.05 lb	0.36%
cane sugar	0.125 lb	0.90%
malt extract	0.25 lb	1.80%
Fuggles 150 mins	5.00 oz	
Goldings 30 mins	5.00 oz	
Goldings dry hops	0.75 oz	
OG	1070	
FG	1023	
ABV	6.22	
Apparent attenuation	67.14%	
IBU	109	
SRM	16	
Mash at	154° F	
Sparge at	165° F	
Boil time	150 minutes	
pitching temp	59° F	
Yeast	Wyeast 1099 Whitbread Ale	

1917 Kidd Porter

I've published dozens of Porter recipes from the big London brewers, but rarely ones from smaller provincial breweries.

Having said that, this Porter isn't hugely different from London ones. Perhaps not so odd, given that Kidd's Dartford location was just outside the capital. The gravity looks a bit low, but by February 1917, when this was brewed, strengths had begun to fall. Pre-war, London Porter was around 1050°.

The standard pale, brown and black malt combination is there. As well as crystal malt and oats. Which leads me to believe that this was also sold as Oatmeal Stout. The No. 2 invert is a guess. In the original it's something called "Budgett". With all the dark malts and some caramel for good measure, it's unsurprisingly a pretty damn black beer.

The hops were Sussex and Farnham, which I've interpreted as Fuggles and Goldings, respectively. That should get you somewhere in the zone, though other English hop combinations are available. It's fairly heavily hopped, giving calculated IBUs of over 30.

The recipe also contained 2lbs of "Spanish juice", which I suppose is a type of liquorice. That was for 145 barrels and works out to 0.03 oz for a brew of this size (5 Imperial, 5 US gallons, 23 litres).

1917 Kidd Porter		
pale malt	5.75 lb	58.97%
brown malt	0.50 lb	5.13%
black malt	0.50 lb	5.13%
crystal malt	0.50 lb	5.13%
oats	0.50 lb	5.13%
No. 2 invert sugar	1.50 lb	15.38%
caramel 1000 SRM	0.50 lb	5.13%
Fuggles 135 mins	0.75 oz	
Fuggles 60 mins	0.75 oz	
Goldings 30 mins	1.00 oz	
OG	1042	
FG	1010	
ABV	4.23	
Apparent attenuation	76.19%	
IBU	32	
SRM	53	
Mash at	152° F	
Sparge at	165° F	
Boil time	135 minutes	
pitching temp	59° F	
Yeast	Wyeast 1099 Whitbread Ale	

1917 Kidd Stout

Though they didn't parti-gyle them together, Kidd still had the same basic recipe that they used for their Porter and Stout.

Which doesn't leave me much to say about the grist. Everything I said about the porter also applies here. Except that the Stout contains no oats.

There is a difference in the hopping. Porter had 2/3rd 1914 Sussex and one third 1916 Farnhams. Stout was 50-50 1916 Kents and 1916 Farnhams. Again, all fresh hops is a sign that this was a posher beer.

Like the Porter, the Stout recipe also contained "Spanish juice", this time one pound. It works out to 0.03 oz for a brew of this size (5 Imperial, 5 US gallons, 23 litres).

1917 Kidd Stout		
pale malt	8.50 lb	58.62%
brown malt	1.00 lb	6.90%
black malt	1.00 lb	6.90%
crystal malt 60 L	1.00 lb	6.90%
caramel 1000 SRM	1.00 lb	6.90%
No. 2 invert sugar	1.75 lb	12.07%
malt extract	0.25 lb	1.72%
Fuggles 120 mins	2.50 oz	
Goldings 30 mins	2.50 oz	
OG	1063	
FG	1019	
ABV	5.82	
Apparent attenuation	69.84%	
IBU	56	
SRM	44	
Mash at	148° F	
Sparge at	165° F	
Boil time	120 minutes	
pitching temp	59° F	
Yeast	Wyeast 1099 Whitbread Ale	

1917 Kidd GA X (13th July)

On 1st July 1917 a new restriction on brewing was introduced. Half a brewery's output had to have a gravity of no more than 1036°. This was the first direct restriction on beer strength.

Flick back a couple of pages and you'll see that in early 1917 Kidd's X Ale had an OG of 1042°. Judging by the number of entries in their brewing book, it was their most popular beer. Which made it pretty much inevitable that they'd need to drop the gravity below 1036°.

The grist hasn't changed a great deal: less sugar and more base malt. Plus the addition of caramel. The main sugar dose was half No. 3 invert, half Budgett. I've just interpreted it as all No. 3.

Despite the drop in gravity, the hopping rate has remained generally similar. Resulting in a hoppier beer. Which is the main difference between this and a modern Mild. The hops were quite a mixed bunch, both in terms of age and origin: Sussex (1914, 1915), Farnham (1916) and Kent (1916).

1917 Kidd GA X (13th July)		
pale malt	5.00 lb	68.78%
crystal malt 60L	1.00 lb	13.76%
No. 3 invert sugar	1.00 lb	13.76%
cane sugar	0.125 lb	1.72%
malt extract	0.125 lb	1.72%
caramel 2000 SRM	0.02 lb	0.28%
Fuggles 150 mins	1.00 oz	
Fuggles 60 mins	0.75 oz	
Goldings 30 mins	0.75 oz	
OG	1034	
FG	1009	
ABV	3.31	
Apparent attenuation	73.53%	
IBU	35	
SRM	14	
Mash at	151° F	
Sparge at	165° F	
Boil time	135 minutes	
pitching temp	58° F	
Yeast	Wyeast 1099 Whitbread Ale	

1917 Kidd LPA (24th August)

In the middle of 1917, Kidd completely revamped their beer range. X Ale was replaced by GA and BB, their Bitter, was displaced by LPA.

I'm not quite sure why they changed the name, because it's not greatly different from BB, at least not in terms of OG, being just a point or so lower. Which is slightly odd, as it leaves it just over 1036°, the level that 50% of their production could not exceed. On closer inspection, I noticed that there's a Excise section on the brewing record. Which gives the declared gravity: 1036.

The recipe, on the other hand, has changed. Out goes the No. 3 invert sugar, replaced by glucose. There's also an addition of caramel colouring, presumably to make up for the colour lost with the removal of No. 3 from the grist.

The hops have been simplified to just Kent with the dropping of Farnhams. The changes aren't enormous and were most likely prompted by supply difficulties. Interestingly, the pale malt remained half English, half Californian.

1917 Kidd LPA (24th August)		
pale malt	4.50 lb	66.57%
glucose	1.75 lb	25.89%
cane sugar	0.25 lb	3.70%
malt extract	0.25 lb	3.70%
caramel 2000 SRM	0.01 lb	0.15%
Fuggles 135 mins	1.50 oz	
Goldings 30 mins	1.50 oz	
Goldings dry hops	0.50 oz	
OG	1037	
FG	1010	
ABV	3.57	
Apparent attenuation	72.97%	
IBU	40	
SRM	5	
Mash at	152° F	
Sparge at	165° F	
Boil time	135 minutes	
pitching temp	58.5° F	
Yeast	Wyeast 1099 Whitbread Ale	

1917 Kidd Porter (24th July)

The changes in the Beer Orders at the beginning of July 1917 had an impact on all Kidd's beers. Quite a simple change, really. They all had their gravities cut. Unsurprisingly, to 1036° or less.

Other than the drop in strength, not much changed with Kidd's Porter. There's a slight change in the hopping, which went from Kent and Sussex to just Sussex. Fairly old ones, too, as they were from the 1914 and 1915 harvest.

The grist retains the classic pale, brown, black malt backbone. The oats are clearly a token amount, presumably so some could be sold as Oatmeal Stout. There's also a tiny amount of Spanish juice: 1 pound for 75 barrels. Which works out to 0.03 oz. for a batch of this size.

But this wasn't where it ended. 1918 was an even tougher year for brewers with increasingly draconian restrictions.

1917 Kidd Porter (24th July)		
pale malt	4.75 lb	62.91%
brown malt	0.33 lb	4.37%
black malt	0.33 lb	4.37%
crystal malt	0.33 lb	4.37%
oats	0.06 lb	0.79%
No. 2 invert sugar	1.25 lb	16.56%
caramel 2000 SRM	0.50 lb	6.62%
Fuggles 135 mins	1.25 oz	
Fuggles 30 mins	1.25 oz	
OG	1035	
FG	1009	
ABV	3.44	
Apparent attenuation	74.29%	
IBU	32	
SRM	37	
Mash at	150° F	
Sparge at	165° F	
Boil time	135 minutes	
pitching temp	60.25° F	
Yeast	Wyeast 1099 Whitbread Ale	

1918 Kidd DA

Brewers got up to some weird shit during WW I. Especially when it came to extremely low-gravity beer.

Brewers were restricted both with regards to how much they could brew, and its strength. For them the Holy Grail was higher gravity beer, on which there were no price controls and was consequently more profitable.

This beer was originally brewed 5th April 1918, just a few days after new harsh regulations were introduce on 1st April:

> "average gravity of all beer brewed shall not exceed 1030° for great Britain and 1045° for Ireland, and that no beer shall be brewed below 1010°: and prices fixed at 4d. per pint below 1030°, and 5d. per pint for 1030° to 1034°."
> "The Brewers' Almanack 1928" pages 100 - 101.

The goal was to brew enough beer below 1030° so that you could brew some above 1034°. This set of regulations were the first to specify a minimum OG for beer. That they bothered to set a limit as low as 1010° implies that brewers had been making weaker beers, incredible as that might sound.

The 145 barrels Kidd brewed of DA meant that they could brew 145 barrels of beer at 1045°, or a larger quantity at, say, 1036°.

Whitbread brewed a version of their GA that was even weaker than this, just 1011°. But that was a very weak parti-gyle of conventionally-brewed GA. Whereas Kidd DA I wouldn't really count as a beer as it contains no malt, being brewed from just sugar and hops.

It's a bit of a weird devil. It's hardly fermented, which I guess was deliberate to leave some body. They achieved the low attenuation, I believe, by keeping the fermentation cool. It was pitched at 59° and the temperature dropped a little to 58.5° F. Believe it or not, it fermented for 5 days. It was also massively underpitched. Kidd usually pitched 70-80 lbs of yeast for a brew of this size. DA received just 12 lbs.

I suspect that DA wasn't sold straight but blended with an actual beer. Unfortunately, there's no way of telling from the brewing record what happened with this "beer".

1918 Kidd DA			
glucose	2.00 lb	91.95%	
cane sugar	0.13 lb	5.75%	
caramel 2000 SRM	0.05 lb	2.30%	
Fuggles 30 mins	1.25 oz		
Goldings dry hops	0.01 oz		
OG	1015		
FG	1012		
ABV	0.40		
Apparent attenuation	20.00%		
IBU	15		
SRM	9		
Mash at	n/a		
Sparge at	n/a		
Boil time	30 minutes		
pitching temp	59° F		
Yeast	Wyeast 1099 Whitbread Ale		

1918 Kidd XXXX (16th Jan)

It's always a surprise to find late WW I with a decent gravity. A pleasant surprise. All the sub-1035° beers can get a bit boring.

Though they don't show up very often. I've only got a couple of examples of XXXX, but loads of X, GA and Porter. It's clear that these stronger beers were being brewed in very small quantities. They can't have been very easy to find and would have been pricey. But money wasn't as much a problem as supply. The war had pushed up wages and many workers had plenty of disposable cash.

The grist has been simplified since the 1917 example. Out go No. 1 invert and cane sugars. The sugar content has remained at around, but now it's all in the form of No. 3 invert. The hops have also been simplified, from Farnham and Kent to just Farnham. Odd that, despite the brewery being located in Kent, the hops are from Surrey.

All the hops were from the 1917 season, accordingly I've left the amount unadjusted. Which is why it comes out at over 100 calculated IBUs.

Almost forgot to tell you what this is: a Burton Ale. Quite likely sold on draught. Perfect for a cold January evening.

1918 Kidd XXXX (16th Jan)		
pale malt	11.00 lb	78.24%
no. 3 sugar	2.75 lb	19.56%
caramel 2000 SRM	0.06 lb	0.43%
malt extract	0.25 lb	1.78%
Goldings 150 mins	5.00 oz	
Goldings 60 mins	2.50 oz	
Goldings 30 mins	2.50 oz	
Goldings dry hops	1.00 oz	
OG	1070	
FG	1029	
ABV	5.42	
Apparent attenuation	58.57%	
IBU	116	
SRM	22	
Mash at	154° F	
Sparge at	165° F	
Boil time	150 minutes	
pitching temp	60° F	
Yeast	Wyeast 1099 Whitbread Ale	

1918 Kidd GA (12th April)

Surprisingly, Kidd GA has only shed one gravity point since the summer of 1917. Lucky drinkers.

There not much altered in the grist either, which remains pale malt, crystal malt and sugar. The pale malt, as in 1917, is a mix of English and Californian. The difference being that there's only about half as much of the latter compared to 1917. Doubtless this was because of supply problems.

There's no No.3 invert in the recipe, all the sugar being something called Budgett. I've substituted No. 3 invert.

The hops are older than in 1916, when half the hops were from the latest crop. They are Sussex from 1914 and Farnham from 1915.

1918 Kidd GA (12th April)			
pale malt		4.75 lb	68.59%
crystal malt 60 L		1.00 lb	14.44%
No. 3 invert sugar		1.00 lb	14.44%
malt extract		0.125 lb	1.81%
caramel 2000 SRM		0.05 lb	0.72%
Fuggles 135 mins		0.75 oz	
Fuggles 60 mins		0.75 oz	
Goldings 30 mins		0.50 oz	
OG		1033	
FG		1008	
ABV		3.31	
Apparent attenuation		75.76%	
IBU		28	
SRM		17	
Mash at		150° F	
Sparge at		165° F	
Boil time		135 minutes	
pitching temp		60° F	
Yeast	Wyeast 1099 Whitbread Ale		

1918 Kidd Porter (17th April)

Porter isn't much down in gravity either, having just lost two points compared to the previous summer.

The recipe is much unchanged, other than the dropping of oats. That makes sense. The 1917 version was parti-gyled with Stout and I presume that they sold some as Oatmeal Stout. Whereas this was brewed single-gyle.

Once again there were 2 lbs of "Spanish juice", which equates to about 0.2 oz for a 6 US gallon batch.

This must have been one of the last batches of Porter. Because from May on, Kidd only brewed one Black Beer: Stout. I'm not sure if Porter ever made a comeback, as I don't have Kidd's records for the 1920s. They definitely weren't brewing it in the 1930s, though.

1918 Kidd Porter (17th April)		
pale malt	5.25 lb	74.10%
brown malt	0.33 lb	4.66%
black malt	0.33 lb	4.66%
crystal malt 60 L	0.33 lb	4.66%
cane sugar	0.125 lb	1.76%
No. 2 invert sugar	0.67 lb	9.46%
caramel 2000 SRM	0.05 lb	0.71%
Goldings 135 mins	1.25 oz	
Goldings 60 mins	1.00 oz	
OG	1033	
FG	1010	
ABV	3.04	
Apparent attenuation	69.70%	
IBU	36	
SRM	37	
Mash at	150° F	
Sparge at	165° F	
Boil time	135 minutes	
pitching temp	60° F	
Yeast	Wyeast 1099 Whitbread Ale	

1918 Kidd Stout

After disappearing, I think, in April 1917, Kidd Stout made a sudden comeback in May 1918. Presumably at the same time as the Porter disappeared.

Which makes it look more like a renaming exercise than a true revival. The strength certainly isn't very Stout-like. Though it is 2 points higher than the last iteration of Porter.

The grist is much the same as that Porter's. Save for dropping the cane sugar and doubling the No. 2 invert sugar at the expense of the base malt. It remains a complex malt bill, with a reasonable amount of roast. As usual, the No. 2 invert is my substitute for something simply listed as "Budgett".

The hops were pretty old: all Kent from 1915. Obviously, I've slashed the hopping rate in the recipe to allow for that.

1918 Kidd Stout		
pale malt	5.00 lb	63.94%
brown malt	0.33 lb	4.22%
black malt	0.33 lb	4.22%
crystal malt 60 L	0.33 lb	4.22%
No. 2 invert sugar	1.33 lb	17.01%
caramel 2000 SRM	0.50 lb	6.39%
Fuggles 120 mins	1.25 oz	
Fuggles 60 mins	1.25 oz	
OG	1035	
FG	1010	
ABV	3.31	
Apparent attenuation	71.43%	
IBU	36	
SRM	37	
Mash at	153° F	
Sparge at	165° F	
Boil time	120 minutes	
pitching temp	59° F	
Yeast	Wyeast 1099 Whitbread Ale	

1918 Kidd PB (16th April)

In April 1918, Kidd introduced a new, low-gravity Bitter called PB. It's an obvious child of the restrictions introduced at the start of the month.

The average gravity of all a brewery's beers could not exceed 1030°. Which meant, if you wanted to produce anything above that figure, you also had to brew stuff below it. Hence a beer like PB. It's the Pale Ale equivalent of a GA Mild.

April 1917 and April 1918 were the graveyard of many beers. Drastic changes to the orders governing brewing came into effect on both dates. Prompting brewers to massively overhaul their range of beers. Mostly discontinuing unviable or marginal beers, sometimes also introducing new ones. As is the case here.

The recipe is quite different from Kidd's other Pale Ales. Containing, as it does, crystal malt and a sugar called "Budgett", for which I've substituted No. 2 invert. The hops were all Farnhams from the 1915 harvest.

1918 Kidd PB (16th April)		
pale malt	4.25 lb	74.89%
crystal malt 60 L	0.75 lb	13.22%
caramel 2000 SRM	0.05 lb	0.88%
No. 2 invert sugar	0.50 lb	8.81%
malt extract	0.13 lb	2.20%
Goldings 135 mins	1.25 oz	
Goldings 60 mins	1.00 oz	
OG	1026	
FG	1006	
ABV	2.65	
Apparent attenuation	76.92%	
IBU	40	
SRM	14	
Mash at	149° F	
Sparge at	165° F	
Boil time	135 minutes	
pitching temp	60° F	
Yeast	Wyeast 1099 Whitbread Ale	

1918 Kidd XX PB (30th April)

With PB, Kidd didn't just introduce one new beer. Effectively it was two, as there was a stronger variant called XX PB.

And when I say stronger, I really mean stronger. XX PB wasn't far short of having double the gravity of plain old PB. Though, with a brewery's beers needing to average 1030°, you'd need to brew 4 barrels of PB to be able to brew 1 barrel of XX PB.

The grist is very similar to PB, except that there's more "Budgett" (No. 2 invert sugar is my substitution). The malt extract was thrown into all Kidd's beers, presumably for extra enzymes. It was a very popular practice during the 20th century. Though none of the large breweries seem to have adopted it.

The hops, as for PB, were all 1915 Farnhams.

1918 Kidd XX PB (30th April)		
pale malt	6.75 lb	69.02%
crystal malt 60 L	1.25 lb	12.78%
No. 2 invert sugar	1.25 lb	12.78%
cane sugar	0.25 lb	2.56%
caramel 2000 SRM	0.03 lb	0.31%
malt extract	0.25 lb	2.56%
Goldings 135 mins	1.75 oz	
Goldings 60 mins	1.00 oz	
OG	1047	
FG	1012	
ABV	4.63	
Apparent attenuation	74.47%	
IBU	42	
SRM	16	
Mash at	149° F	
Sparge at	165° F	
Boil time	135 minutes	
pitching temp	60° F	
Yeast	Wyeast 1099 Whitbread Ale	

1918 Kidd LPA

It's frustrating only having Kidd's brewing records from January 1917. It means I can't be sure whether LPA predated April 1917 or not. My guess is not, but I can't be sure.

The recipe has changed a lot since the previous year. Out are the glucose and cane sugar, in No. 3 invert sugar. Overall, there's quite a lot less sugar and more base malt.

The hops are much fresher than in their other beers: 1917 Farnhams. Implying that this was a classy beer.

1918 Kidd LPA		
pale malt	6.50 lb	82.33%
No. 3 invert sugar	1.25 lb	15.83%
malt extract	0.13 lb	1.58%
caramel 2000 SRM	0.02 lb	0.25%
Goldings 105 mins	1.50 oz	
Goldings 60 mins	1.50 oz	
Goldings dry hops	0.50 oz	
OG	1037	
FG	1009.5	
ABV	3.64	
Apparent attenuation	74.32%	
IBU	40	
SRM	12	
Mash at	150° F	
Sparge at	165° F	
Boil time	105 minutes	
pitching temp	59° F	
Yeast	Wyeast 1099 Whitbread Ale	

1919 Kidd X

Either late in in 1918 or early 1919, Kidd changed the name of their Mild back from GA to X Ale. No idea why. Perhaps it was after the government forbade breweries selling beer under the name "Government Ale".

Though the new X Ale was a good bit weaker than GA – 1027° in place of 1033°. The ABV is, naturally, also lower, 2.71% as opposed to 3.31%. As a drinker, I wouldn't have been happy.

The main changes to the recipe since 1918 are connected with the sugars. This version contains more sugar in total and some different types. The quantity of No. 3 invert has been reduced and "Budgett" added.

None of the hops were fresh and some were pretty ancient: Kent (1912), Farnham (1916).

1919 Kidd X		
pale malt	3.75 lb	63.99%
crystal malt 60 L	0.50 lb	12.25%
No. 3 invert sugar	0.33 lb	6.03%
No. 2 invert sugar	0.67 lb	12.25%
cane sugar	0.125 lb	2.29%
caramel 2000 SRM	0.05 lb	0.91%
malt extract	0.125 lb	2.29%
Fuggles 120 mins	0.50 oz	
Goldings 60 mins	1.00 oz	
OG	1027.5	
FG	1007	
ABV	2.71	
Apparent attenuation	74.55%	
IBU	23	
SRM	14	
Mash at	153° F	
Sparge at	165° F	
Boil time	120 minutes	
pitching temp	60° F	
Yeast	Wyeast 1099 Whitbread Ale	

1919 Kidd XXX

It's a sign that circumstances were improving that Kidd resurrected their Strong Ale, though under the name of XXX rather than XXXX.

That's very honest of them, as XXX was a good bit weaker than XXXX had been: a full 20 points lower. I'm pretty sure this is the equivalent of a London Burton Ale. Which implies that it was principally a draught beer. Though, based on the OG and when it was brewed, this falls into the 7d per pint class, while Burton was usually in the 8d class.

The recipe is much what you would expect from a Burton: pale malt, crystal malt and sugar. The result is a dark brown beer, which is what Burton was expected to be at this point.

The hops aren't very fresh: Worcester (1912), Farnham (1916).

1919 Kidd XXX		
pale malt	7.50 lb	69.57%
crystal malt 60 L	1.50 lb	13.91%
No. 3 invert sugar	1.50 lb	13.91%
caramel	0.03 lb	0.28%
malt extract	0.25 lb	2.32%
Fuggles 120 mins	1.50 oz	
Goldings 60 mins	1.50 oz	
OG	1050	
FG	1018	
ABV	4.23	
Apparent attenuation	64.00%	
IBU	42	
SRM	19	
Mash at	151° F	
Sparge at	165° F	
Boil time	120 minutes	
pitching temp	60.5° F	
Yeast	Wyeast 1099 Whitbread Ale	

1919 Kidd Stout

Another year on and Kidd Stout is starting to bear some resemblance to a Stout again, in terms of gravity.

Though it's still far short of the 1069° OG the beer had in early 1917. In all likelihood, Kidd never brewed a Stout as strong as that again.

The recipe is much the same as in 1918, both in terms of the elements and their quantities. The backbone being the classic pale, brown, black malt combination. The recipe contains a small amount of liquorice ("Spanish juice"), around 0.04 oz for a homebrew batch. It's a pretty tiny amount.

The hops were all old-ish: 1916 Kent.

1919 Kidd Stout		
pale malt	6.00 lb	58.54%
brown malt	0.50 lb	4.88%
black malt	0.50 lb	4.88%
crystal malt 60 L	0.50 lb	4.88%
No. 2 invert sugar	2.00 lb	19.51%
caramel 2000 SRM	0.75 lb	7.32%
Fuggles 120 mins	1.25 oz	
Fuggles 60 mins	1.25 oz	
OG	1045	
FG	1014	
ABV	4.10	
Apparent attenuation	68.89%	
IBU	34	
SRM	50	
Mash at	153° F	
Sparge at	165° F	
Boil time	120 minutes	
pitching temp	60° F	
Yeast	Wyeast 1099 Whitbread Ale	

1919 Kidd PA

The effects of the war on brewing didn't come to an immediate halt the moment the Armistice was signed in November 1918. It took until the early 1920's before everything stabilised and the pattern of interwar beer was set.

Before the war kicked off, beers called Pale Ale were usually full-strength. Stock Pale Ales, with an OG 1060-1065°, which would have been matured for months before sale. WW I pretty much killed off that style of Pale Ale, except for in Burton. This beer looks more like a post-WW II Best Bitter.

Again, it's just pale malt, sugar and a tiny bit of malt extract. Half the malt was from Californian barley, the rest from English barley. One of the things that most upset British brewers was the interruption in the supply of Californian barley. They liked it because of its high diastatic power, amongst other attributes. Which was handy for brewers using a high percentage of adjuncts. Though clearly that isn't the case here.

The hopping is pretty heavy, this time 100% Farnhams. I've substituted Goldings again. Odd that a Kent brewer was using hops from another county. Farnham is in Surrey. It comes in at over 50 calculated IBUs.

1919 Kidd PA		
pale malt	6.50 lb	77.47%
no. 3 sugar	1.25 lb	14.90%
Caramel 2000 SRM	0.02 lb	0.18%
glucose	0.50 lb	5.96%
malt extract	0.125 lb	1.49%
Goldings 120 mins	2.00 oz	
Goldings 30 mins	2.00 oz	
Goldings dry hops	0.50 oz	
OG	1042	
FG	1014	
ABV	3.70	
Apparent attenuation	66.67%	
IBU	54	
SRM	15	
Mash at	151° F	
Sparge at	165° F	
Boil time	120 minutes	
pitching temp	60° F	
Yeast	Wyeast 1099 Whitbread Ale	

1920 Kidd X

Not much has changed with Kidd X since 1919. Except for the odd little tweak.

The gravity remains pretty low, having increased by just half a point. Leaving it still a watery affair, just about saved by enough attenuation to leave it just a whisker under 3% ABV. Which is about the minimum level of alcohol for a serious beer.

The main change to the grist has been the replacement of some of the base malt by flaked maize. This wasn't uncommon at this point, when maize became available again and brewers returned to pre-war practices. Some of the No. 3 invert has also been replaced by more Budgett (No.2 invert is my substitution).

None of the hops were particularly fresh, being Kent (1914, 1918) and Farnham (1916).

1920 Kidd X		
pale malt	3.25 lb	58.09%
crystal malt 60 L	0.67 lb	11.97%
flaked maize	0.50 lb	8.94%
No. 3 invert sugar	0.25 lb	4.47%
No. 2 invert sugar	0.75 lb	13.40%
caramel 2000 SRM	0.05 lb	0.89%
malt extract	0.125 lb	2.23%
Fuggles 120 mins	0.75 oz	
Goldings 60 mins	0.75 oz	
OG	1028	
FG	1006	
ABV	2.91	
Apparent attenuation	78.57%	
IBU	24	
SRM	15	
Mash at	154° F	
Sparge at	165° F	
Boil time	120 minutes	
pitching temp	61° F	
Yeast	Wyeast 1099 Whitbread Ale	

1920 Kidd XXX

A small increase in the OG – from 1050° to 1056° - has seen XXX move up into the 8d per pint class. Exactly where you'd expect a Burton Ale to be.

As with X Ale, the big news for the grist is the return of flaked maize. Though in this case it's replacing crystal rather than pale malt. The percentage of base malt actually increasing. According to my brewing software, the colour is a little paler than in 1919, but that could just be due to me having the hue of the caramel wrong.

The rate of attenuation remains quite low, leaving me to wonder whether XXX got a few weeks of secondary conditioning before sale. That would almost certainly have been the case with the stronger XXXX pre-war.

The hops are at least fresh. Probably as fresh as would be used in normal times. Kent (1918, 1919); Alsace (1919) dry hops. Had Alsace already been returned top France by this point? I'm not sure.

1920 Kidd XXX		
pale malt	10.00 lb	81.23%
flaked maize	0.75 lb	6.09%
No. 3 invert sugar	1.25 lb	10.15%
caramel 2000 SRM	0.06 lb	0.49%
malt extract	0.25 lb	2.03%
Fuggles 120 mins	2.25 oz	
Fuggles 60 mins	2.25 oz	
Strisselspalt dry hops	1.00 oz	
OG	1056	
FG	1019.5	
ABV	4.83	
Apparent attenuation	65.18%	
IBU	59	
SRM	16	
Mash at	151° F	
Sparge at	165° F	
Boil time	120 minutes	
pitching temp	61° F	
Yeast	Wyeast 1099 Whitbread Ale	

1920 Kidd Stout

The gravity of Kidd Stout continues to rise. Yippee. It's now solidly in the 7d per pint class.

The recipe is largely unchanged. True, the percentage of black malt has increased at the expense of the brown. But that's about it. And there's a little more sugar, replacing some of the base malt. All fairly small changes. Tweaking rather than a radical recipe overhaul.

The hops are getting fresher, though still not exactly new: Kent (1914, 1919), Farnham (1916). At least some were from the most recent season.

1920 Kidd Stout		
pale malt	7.00 lb	64.64%
brown malt	0.67 lb	6.19%
black malt	0.33 lb	3.05%
crystal malt 60 L	0.33 lb	3.05%
No. 2 invert sugar	1.75 lb	16.16%
caramel 2000 SRM	0.75 lb	6.93%
Fuggles 120 mins	1.25 oz	
Goldings 60 mins	1.00 oz	
OG	1047.5	
FG	1014	
ABV	4.43	
Apparent attenuation	70.53%	
IBU	30	
SRM	51	
Mash at	153° F	
Sparge at	176° F	
Boil time	120 minutes	
pitching temp	61° F	
Yeast	Wyeast 1099 Whitbread Ale	

1920 Kidd Stock PA

The last couple of entries in the brewing book have "Stock" written in red next to "PA". Which would imply that the beer was going to undergo a secondary conditioning.

Though it looks a little on the weak side to be up to that. Despite the OG having bounced up by 5 points. But if it didn't mean anything, why would they go to the trouble of writing "Stock" on the record. Sadly, there's no mention on the brewing record of what happened after racking, nor where it was racked to.

Flaked maize has again made an entry, displacing some of the No. 3 invert and pale malt. The percentage of glucose has increased, too.

The hops are a combination of English and foreign hops. Of ages that that would have been normal in pre-war years. Kent (1919), Farnham (1916) and Oregon (1918); Alsace (1919) dry hops.

1920 Kidd Stock PA		
pale malt	6.75 lb	70.64%
flaked maize	0.67 lb	7.01%
No. 3 invert sugar	1.00 lb	10.47%
glucose	1.00 lb	10.47%
malt extract	0.125 lb	1.31%
caramel 2000 SRM	0.01 lb	0.10%
Cluster 120 mins	1.00 oz	
Fuggles 90 mins	1.00 oz	
Goldings 30 mins	1.00 oz	
Strisselspalt dry hops	0.50 oz	
OG	1047	
FG	1014	
ABV	4.37	
Apparent attenuation	70.21%	
IBU	46	
SRM	13	
Mash at	155° F	
Sparge at	165° F	
Boil time	120 minutes	
pitching temp	60° F	
Yeast	Wyeast 1099 Whitbread Ale	

Noakes

Noakes was one of the smaller London breweries, located in Bermondsey, just south of London Bridge station. Very close to the railway-arch breweries that make up the Bermondsey Beer Mile today.

Noakes' Black Eagle brewery was pretty old, dating back to the 1690's. Though it never seems to have got very big.[39]

In October 1917 they were fined for having brewed too much beer in the previous quarter. Namely 5,116 barrels rather than the 4,775 barrels allowed. Which means they must have been brewing around 20,000 standard barrels a year at the time. After April 1917, beer output was restricted to about a third of the 1914 level, making their pre-war output around 60,000 standard barrels.[40] Their output in bulk barrels would have been only slightly more than the standard barrel number.

Map of the 1890's showing the Noakes brewery

When they were bought by Courage in 1930, they owned 120 pubs. Which seems a lot if they were only brewing 60,000 barrels.

---

[39] "London Brewed" by Mike Brown, The Brewery History Society, 2015, page 55.
[40] "London Brewed" by Mike Brown, The Brewery History Society, 2015, page 55.

1915 Noakes LBA

Just a year into the war, British beers hadn't changed that much, at least not in terms of strength.

LBA looks very much like the type of beer that was often called AK. A Light Bitter. As the name, which I'm sure was Light Bitter Ale, implies. In modern parlance, an Ordinary Bitter. Quite light in alcohol and body, but still quite bitter.

There's not much to the grist, just pale malt and sugar with tiny amount of rice. I'm not really sure what the sugar type is. In the ingredient list, it's down as No. 1 invert. In another part where it details the sugar additions to the copper, it's called No. 3. No. 1 makes more sense, so I've gone with that.

Some of the hops are from the 1915 crop, but most are from 1914. I've knocked the quantities down a little accordingly. I've no idea of where they were from, other than that they were all English. My guess would be from Kent, as that wasn't far away. But the brewery was very close to the Southwark hop market so they could have been from anywhere.

In addition to the 30 cwts. of No.1 invert sugar in the copper, there's 15 cwts. of No. 3 which are described as "heading", presumably meaning it was used for priming. This sugar raises the effective OG by 10 points, to 1055°.

1915 Noakes LBA		
pale malt	6.00 lb	61.16%
flaked rice	0.06 lb	0.61%
No. 1 invert sugar	2.50 lb	25.48%
No. 3 invert sugar	1.25 lb	12.74%
Fuggles 120 mins	1.25 oz	
Goldings 90 mins	1.25 oz	
Goldings 30 mins	1.25 oz	
Goldings dry hops	1.00 oz	
OG	1055	
FG	1015	
ABV	5.29	
Apparent attenuation	72.73%	
IBU	50	
SRM	7	
Mash at	153° F	
Sparge at	170° F	
Boil time	120 minutes	
pitching temp	61° F	
Yeast	Wyeast 1099 Whitbread Ale	

1915 Noakes Porter

Comparing Noakes Porter with those from the larger London breweries is interesting.

It's noticeably weaker: just 1039° when the big brewers' versions were over 1050°. Though in terms of ingredients, it's not that dissimilar.

There are no fewer than five malts in the grist, with amber and crystal malt in addition to the standard pale, brown and black. In all, coloured malts make up more than 30% of the grist. The No. 4 invert sugar is a substitute for CDM - Caramelized Dextro-Maltose.

The hops are a 50-50 split between Californian and English. Cluster and Fuggles seem like a safe bet.

1915 Noakes Porter		
pale malt	4.50 lb	50.00%
brown malt	0.50 lb	5.56%
black malt	1.00 lb	11.11%
amber malt	1.00 lb	11.11%
crystal malt 60 L	0.50 lb	5.56%
No. 3 invert sugar	1.00 lb	11.11%
No. 4 invert sugar	0.50 lb	5.56%
Cluster 90 mins	0.50 oz	
Fuggles 30 mins	0.50 oz	
OG	1039	
FG	1010	
ABV	3.84	
Apparent attenuation	74.36%	
IBU	39	
SRM	16	
Mash at	152° F	
Sparge at	165° F	
Boil time	90 minutes	
pitching temp	61° F	
Yeast	Wyeast 1099 Whitbread Ale	

1915 Noakes Double Stout

After seeing the relatively low gravity of Noakes Porter, I was surprised to see that their Stout was fairly standard strength for London.

As it was parti-gyled with the Porter, all the comments about that recipe apply here.

One of the things I love about Noakes' records is the level of detail. Especially when it comes to cost. So I know that the parti-gyle of 252 barrels of Porter and 62.5 barrels of Double Stout cost £416 13s. 6d., of which £265 7s. 2d. was duty. Fascinating, eh?

The large percentage of coloured malts leave this an extremely dark beer.

1915 Noakes Double Stout		
pale malt	8.50 lb	52.31%
brown malt	0.75 lb	4.62%
black malt	1.75 lb	10.77%
amber malt	1.75 lb	10.77%
crystal malt 60 L	1.00 lb	6.15%
No. 3 invert sugar	1.75 lb	10.77%
No. 4 invert sugar	0.75 lb	4.62%
Cluster 90 mins	1.00 oz	
Fuggles 30 mins	1.00 oz	
OG	1075	
FG	1024	
ABV	6.75	
Apparent attenuation	68.00%	
IBU	26	
SRM	56	
Mash at	152° F	
Sparge at	165° F	
Boil time	90 minutes	
pitching temp	62° F	
Yeast	Wyeast 1099 Whitbread Ale	

1915 Noakes XXX

XXX looks very much like the draught Burton Ale from Noakes. While KK was the more common brew house name, some breweries did use X designations for such beers.

The gravity is pretty decent, being higher than Whitbread KK and almost the same as their 2KKK.

Compared to some London breweries, the grist is quite complicated, containing three malts and two types of sugar. Once again, the No.4 invert sugar is a substitute for CDM.

The hops – and there are plenty of them – were all English, but that's where the information ends. I've just made an educated guess and gone for a combination of Fuggles and Goldings.

The brewing record helpfully tells me that XX cost £2 11s 3d per barrel; to brew. That included about £1 10s tax per barrel. That's just over 2d. per pint.

1915 Noakes XXX		
pale malt	12.75 lb	78.46%
crystal malt 60 L	0.75 lb	4.62%
black malt	0.25 lb	1.54%
No. 1 invert sugar	2.25 lb	13.85%
No. 4 invert sugar	0.25 lb	1.54%
Fuggles 90 mins	3.00 oz	
Goldings 60 mins	3.00 oz	
Goldings 30 mins	3.00 oz	
Goldings dry hops	1.00 oz	
OG	1077	
FG	1030	
ABV	6.22	
Apparent attenuation	61.04%	
IBU	92	
SRM	21	
Mash at	151° F	
Sparge at	165° F	
Boil time	90 minutes	
pitching temp	56.5° F	
Yeast	Wyeast 1099 Whitbread Ale	

Tetley

In a region that traditionally had few commercial brewers, Tetley, based in Leeds, was one of the larger operators in Yorkshire. Very successful for many years, even after becoming part of Allied Breweries in the early 1960s. They wouldn't fare so well when that became Carlsberg Tetley and the brewery closed for good in 2001.

When the war started Tetley brewed quite a lot of different beers. Mostly Mild Ales. But unusually, in addition to a Stout, they also brewed a Porter. Which was very uncommon outside the London area.

This was Tetley's range in 1916. I assume it's quite close to that of 1914.

Tetley Beers in 1916							
Beer	Style	OG	FG	ABV	App. Atten-uation	lbs hops/ qtr	hops lb/brl
X	Mild	1033.5	1010.5	3.04	68.60%	3.39	0.47
X Pale	Mild	1032.4	1012.2	2.68	62.39%	4.66	0.59
X1	Mild	1043.8	1010.0	4.47	77.22%	3.39	0.61
X1 Pale	Mild	1042.9	1011.9	4.10	72.26%	1.47	0.78
X2	Mild	1053.7	1010.8	5.68	79.90%	5.76	1.18
X2 Pale	Mild	1052.9	1013.9	5.17	73.82%	4.66	0.96
X3	Mild	1063.4	1012.2	6.78	80.79%	7.60	1.86
XX	Mild	1072.6	1013.9	7.77	80.92%	7.60	2.13
K	Pale Ale	1043.8	1012.2	4.18	72.15%	6.65	1.11
PA	Pale Ale	1059.0	1011.6	6.27	80.28%	12.26	2.36
P	Porter	1048.2	1018.6	3.92	61.49%	4.72	0.97
S	Stout	1064.8	1030.7	4.51	52.56%	4.72	1.31
Source: Tetley brewing record held at the West Yorkshire Archives, document number WYL756/53/ACC1903.							

Quite a lot of different Mild Ales in there. Which, as a Tetley Mild fanatic, it's nice to see.

The war chopped their range in half, being particularly cruel to the non-Mild Ales:

Tetley Beers in 1920							
Beer	Style	OG	FG	ABV	App. Atten-uation	lbs hops/ qtr	hops lb/brl
F	Mild	1033.8	1009.1	3.26	72.95%	3.82	0.54
X	Mild	1031.3	1012.2	2.53	61.06%	1.54	0.19
X1	Mild	1041.8	1011.1	4.07	73.51%	3.82	0.67
X2	Mild	1053.7	1014.7	5.17	72.68%	5.70	1.21
K	Pale Ale	1049.3	1010.0	5.20	79.78%	6.76	1.26
Source: Tetley brewing record held at the West Yorkshire Archives, document number WYL756/54/ACC1903.							

The gravities of the various Milds have hardly changed at all. They've simply dropped the two strongest versions. While the remaining Bitter has even increased in strength, presumably as a compromise between the strengths of the two pre-war examples,

It's very odd that Tetley completely stopped brewing Stout. Pretty much every brewery made at least one, right through until the 1950s. They must have got it from somewhere as there must have been plenty of Stout drinkers in their pubs. Maybe they all drank Guinness.

1916 Tetley X

Tetley produced a dazzling array of Mild Ales – five, in total, in 1916. And weakest of the bunch was plain old X.

Sadly, Tetley's brewing records from the first couple of war years haven't been preserved. So I don't know for sure how strong X was in 1914. But, based on what I've seen from other breweries, the gravity had probably only fallen a few points by 1916. Plus I know that, in 1904, X had an OG of 1039°. My guess is that it kicked off the war around 1035-1036°.

The grist is an odd one, with the two base malts not even quite making up 50% of the total. The largest single ingredients were the grits. William Younger is the only other brewery I've come across that used a similar percentage of grits.

The descriptions in the brewing record of the sugars are: 3360 lbs "D Brazilian", 490 lbs "CSPF" and 112 lbs "Clowes". The "Brazilian" I'm guessing is some type of brown sugar. No idea about the others. I've plumped for No. 3 invert.

The hops were Worcester (1914), Sonoma (1913) and Burgundy (1914).

1916 Tetley X		
pale malt	1.50 lb	24.00%
mild malt	1.50 lb	24.00%
grits	1.75 lb	28.00%
brown sugar	1.25 lb	20.00%
No. 3 invert sugar	0.25 lb	4.00%
Cluster 115 min	0.33 oz	
Strisselspalt 30 min	0.25 oz	
Fuggles 30 min	0.125 oz	
OG	1032	
FG	1011	
ABV	2.78	
Apparent attenuation	65.63%	
IBU	12	
SRM	5	
Mash at	148° F	
Sparge at	165° F	
Boil time	115 minutes	
pitching temp	64° F	
Yeast	Wyeast 1469 West Yorkshire Ale	

1916 Tetley X1

Next Mild up in strength was what I'm referring to as X1. Though that wasn't really the brew house name. That was an X with a horizontal line through the middle.

It had more like a normal strength for a base-level provincial Mild Ale. Though, by London standards, it looks a little on the watery side.

I won't go into the recipe in detail since this example of X1 was parti-gyled with the X above. Interestingly, though the OG of X1 was 10 points higher than X, there's only 1 point difference in the FG.

1916 Tetley X1		
pale malt	2.00 lb	24.01%
mild malt	2.00 lb	24.01%
grits	2.50 lb	30.01%
brown sugar	1.50 lb	18.01%
No. 3 invert sugar	0.33 lb	3.96%
Cluster 115 min	0.50 oz	
Strisselspalt 30 min	0.25 oz	
Fuggles 30 min	0.25 oz	
OG	1042.5	
FG	1012	
ABV	4.03	
Apparent attenuation	71.76%	
IBU	16	
SRM	6	
Mash at	148° F	
Sparge at	165° F	
Boil time	115 minutes	
pitching temp	64° F	
Yeast	Wyeast 1469 West Yorkshire Ale	

1916 Tetley X2

The grist of the next Mild up was different from its two weaker siblings we've seen above in one important aspect: it contained no grits.

It wasn't just a war thing, as the same had also been true in 1904. Only the two weakest Milds contained grits. Implying that its inclusion was on cost grounds, X and X1 being Tetley's two cheapest beers.

The hops were different from the cheaper Milds, too. Worcester (1914), English (1913) and California (1914). Still nothing less than two years old, though. You can really tell from brewing records how hop supplies became stretched around the middle of the war. More and more old hops were used.

1916 Tetley X2		
pale malt	5.00 lb	44.44%
mild malt	5.00 lb	44.44%
brown sugar	1.25 lb	11.11%
Cluster 130 min	0.75 oz	
Fuggles 60 min	0.75 oz	
Fuggles 30 min	0.50 oz	
OG	1054	
FG	1011	
ABV	5.69	
Apparent attenuation	79.63%	
IBU	31	
SRM	5	
Mash at	150° F	
Sparge at	165° F	
Boil time	130 minutes	
pitching temp	62° F	
Yeast	Wyeast 1469 West Yorkshire Ale	

1916 Tetley X3

Tetley had a ridiculously large range of Mild Ales. Especially for the 20th century. I wonder where they sold then all? I can't imagine many pubs wanting three or four Milds at once. What was the intended market for a Mild of this strength?

The recipe is exactly the same as X2. At least in terms of the grist. The hopping rate is higher here, 7.5 lbs per quarter (336 lbs) of malt as opposed to 5.75 lbs for XX. But, other that strength, there isn't a huge difference in recipes across the whole Tetley range of Milds.

The hops weren't any newer than in their other beers: Worcester (1914), English (1913) and California (1914).

1916 Tetley X3		
pale malt	5.50 lb	44.00%
mild malt	5.50 lb	44.00%
brown sugar	1.50 lb	12.00%
Cluster 130 min	1.00 oz	
Fuggles 60 min	1.00 oz	
Fuggles 30 min	1.00 oz	
OG	1059	
FG	1011.5	
ABV	6.28	
Apparent attenuation	80.51%	
IBU	44	
SRM	6	
Mash at	151° F	
Sparge at	165° F	
Boil time	130 minutes	
pitching temp	62° F	
Yeast	Wyeast 1469 West Yorkshire Ale	

1916 Tetley XX

By WW I there were few Milds of this strength left. Before 1860, Milds of 10% ABV had been, if not common, at least around. But as the 19th century progressed, the stronger Milds slowly died out.

For example, the big London brewers brewed X, XX, XXX and XXXX in the 1830s. By the 1890s most only retained the weakest, X Ale. Though even those were still well over 5% ABV.

As this was parti-gyled with the X3 above, look there for more recipe details.

1916 Tetley XX		
pale malt	6.50 lb	44.07%
mild malt	6.50 lb	44.07%
brown sugar	1.75 lb	11.86%
Cluster 130 min	1.25 oz	
Fuggles 60 min	1.25 oz	
Fuggles 30 min	1.00 oz	
OG	1070	
FG	1018	
ABV	6.88	
Apparent attenuation	74.29%	
IBU	48	
SRM	7	
Mash at	151° F	
Sparge at	165° F	
Boil time	130 minutes	
pitching temp	62° F	
Yeast	Wyeast 1469 West Yorkshire Ale	

1916 Tetley PA

Unusually for a Yorkshire brewery, Tetley was big on Pale Ale. They had brewed one since at least 1848, which is a very early date indeed. Few breweries outside classic Pale Ale towns such as Burton and Edinburgh brewed the style at that time.

Which isn't to say that Pale Ale was the bulk of their production. It wasn't. Various Mild Ales were. But it was obviously a speciality, as they advertised it heavily. Though in the adverts it wasn't called Pale Ale but East India Pale Ale.

Other than the gravity being a touch low, Tetley PA very much resembles a pre-1880 Pale Ale. The grist is extremely simple, consisting of just pale malt and sugar. The type of sugar isn't clear, and I've guessed No. 1 invert. That they usually wanted to keep the colour as pale as possible in this type of beer is my line of reasoning.

The hops were Kent form the 1913 and 1914 crop, both kept in a cold store.

1916 Tetley PA		
pale malt	11.00 lb	88.00%
No. 1 invert sugar	1.50 lb	12.00%
Fuggles 120 min	2.25 oz	
Goldings 30 min	2.25 oz	
Goldings dry hops	0.50 oz	
OG	1057	
FG	1009	
ABV	6.35	
Apparent attenuation	84.21%	
IBU	51	
SRM	6.5	
Mash at	150° F	
Sparge at	165° F	
Boil time	120 minutes	
pitching temp	62° F	
Yeast	Wyeast 1469 West Yorkshire Ale	

1916 Tetley K

It took me quite a while of pondering before I finally decided that K was a Pale Ale. A light Pale Ale.

There are no obvious giveaways. Like it being parti-gyled with a beer called PA. The hopping rate isn't all that high, either: 6.75 lbs per quarter of malt, which is lower than that of the stronger Milds, X3 and XX. And way lower than PA's rate of 19.75 lbs per quarter.

The grist doesn't help, as it contains mild malt. Not usually a sign of a Pale Ale. And not present in Tetley's PA. Both contain the same sugar, which I think is listed as RC(3). I've just guessed No. 1 invert.

I don't find it so strange that K is quite different in many ways from PA. That's often the case with breweries that started out brewing a Stock Pale Ale and only later introduced a Light Pale Ale. They didn't just produce a watered down Stock Pale Ale as a Light pale would be conditioned very differently.

The hops are exactly the same as those in PA, cold-stored Kent from 1913 and 1914.

1916 Tetley K			
pale malt		4.00 lb	76.19%
mild malt		3.75 lb	71.43%
No. 1 invert sugar		1.50 lb	28.57%
Fuggles 120 min		1.00 oz	
Goldings 30 min		1.00 oz	
Goldings dry hops		0.25 oz	
OG		1044	
FG		1009	
ABV		4.63	
Apparent attenuation		79.55%	
IBU		25	
SRM		6	
Mash at		150° F	
Sparge at		165° F	
Boil time		120 minutes	
pitching temp		61° F	
Yeast	Wyeast 1469 West Yorkshire Ale		

1916 Tetley Porter

By the start of WW I, though Stout remained popular, ordinary draught Porter was did in most of the country. Tetley was one of a very small number of breweries in the North of England that still produced one. Only in London was Porter still a mainstream beer.

Speaking of which, Tetley's Porter looks very similar to London versions, both in terms of strength and ingredients. Particularly in the use of both brown and black malt. In much of the UK brewers dropped brown malt from their Porter and Stout in the second half of the 19th century, going over to a simpler grist of just pale and black malt.

I'm not totally sure what the sugars in the original were, with 490 lbs being described as "D Brazilian" and 40 lbs as "Clowes". I've guessed that the former was some sort of raw cane sugar.

The hops were Worcester from 1914, Sonoma from 1913 and Burgundy from 1914. I've interpreted those as Fuggles, Cluster and Strisselspalt, respectively. From the middle of the war on, more and more old hops were used. Though one or two year old hops weren't uncommon pre-war, it was unusual to find beers with no hops less than two years old.

1916 Tetley Porter		
mild malt	5.00 lb	48.78%
pale malt	1.50 lb	14.63%
brown malt	1.25 lb	12.20%
black malt	1.00 lb	9.76%
brown sugar	1.50 lb	14.63%
Cluster 120 min	1.00 oz	
Strisselspalt 60 min	0.50 oz	
Fuggles 30 min	0.50 oz	
OG	1048	
FG	1018.5	
ABV	3.90	
Apparent attenuation	61.46%	
IBU	32	
SRM	32	
Mash at	150° F	
Sparge at	165° F	
Boil time	120 minutes	
pitching temp	61° F	
Yeast	Wyeast 1469 West Yorkshire Ale	

1916 Tetley Stout

Parti-gyled with the Porter above was this Stout. A reasonably powerful beer. And with the same London-like grist.

What struck me first about this Stout was the low degree of attenuation. Which makes me think that it might have been vatted. If not that, at least given some sort of secondary conditioning, either in casks or tank. So feel free to ferment it out further.

1916 Tetley Stout		
mild malt	7.00 lb	50.00%
pale malt	2.25 lb	16.07%
brown malt	1.50 lb	10.71%
black malt	1.25 lb	8.93%
brown sugar	2.00 lb	14.29%
Cluster 120 min	1.25 oz	
Strisselspalt 60 min	0.67 oz	
Fuggles 30 min	0.67 oz	
OG	1065	
FG	1030.5	
ABV	4.56	
Apparent attenuation	53.08%	
IBU	37	
SRM	38	
Mash at	150° F	
Sparge at	165° F	
Boil time	120 minutes	
pitching temp	61° F	
Yeast	Wyeast 1469 West Yorkshire Ale	

1919 Tetley X

I'm very surprised that X managed to survive the war. It wasn't very strong to start with, being only 1032° in 1916, when gravities had only dropped the odd point or two.

Yet here it is in 1919, alive and kicking and only a touch more watery than in 1916. Not sure for how much longer. As it isn't in their 1931 brewing records.

The recipe isn't that much different from in 1917, the highlight change being the replacement of No. 3 invert sugar by chocolate malt. Which leaves the colour of this version a little darker. The percentage of grits remains very high.

The hops weren't too ancient: Sussex (1916, 1917) and Pacific (1918).

1919 Tetley X		
mild malt	2.50 lb	40.82%
pale malt	1.25 lb	20.41%
chocolate malt	0.125 lb	2.04%
grits	1.50 lb	24.49%
brown sugar	0.75 lb	12.24%
Cluster 140 min	0.33 oz	
Fuggles 60 min	0.33 oz	
Fuggles 30 min	0.33 oz	
OG	1029.5	
FG	1012	
ABV	2.32	
Apparent attenuation	59.32%	
IBU	17	
SRM	8	
Mash at	148° F	
Sparge at	165° F	
Boil time	120 minutes	
pitching temp	64° F	
Yeast	Wyeast 1469 West Yorkshire Ale	

1919 Tetley F

I'm guessing that F stands for "Family Ale" as I know Tetley had a beer called that. Both from seeing old labels and seeing it in the shops in the 1970s.

"Family" in this sense merely means a beer intended to be drunk at home. In the 20th century it almost exclusively referred to a low-gravity bottled beer. Sometimes, as in this case for what was effectively a Mild Ale, but also for other styles, such as Pale Ale or Stout.

In this case, it's just a slightly stronger version of X. This example was parti-gyled with the X above. It survived much longer than X, not being killed off until the early years of WW II.

1919 Tetley F		
mild malt	2.50 lb	36.36%
pale malt	1.50 lb	21.82%
chocolate Malt	0.125 lb	1.82%
grits	1.75 lb	25.45%
brown sugar	1.00 lb	14.55%
Cluster 140 min	0.50 oz	
Fuggles 60 min	0.33 oz	
Fuggles 30 min	0.33 oz	
OG	1033.5	
FG	1013	
ABV	2.71	
Apparent attenuation	61.19%	
IBU	20	
SRM	8	
Mash at	148° F	
Sparge at	165° F	
Boil time	120 minutes	
pitching temp	64° F	
Yeast	Wyeast 1469 West Yorkshire Ale	

1919 Tetley X1

Just a couple of gravity points weaker than in 1916, X1 was a decent strength Mild.

As with X, they've substituted chocolate malt for No. 3 invert sugar. Possibly that was an enforced change in the later war years when many types of sugar became difficult to obtain. There are fewer grits than in X, but it's still more than 15% of the total grist.

The hops are slightly different types from X, but of the same age: Kent (1916), Sussex (1917) and Pacific (1918).

1919 Tetley X1		
mild malt	3.00 lb	36.36%
pale malt	2.50 lb	30.30%
chocolate malt	0.25 lb	3.03%
grits	1.25 lb	15.15%
brown sugar	1.25 lb	15.15%
Cluster 140 min	0.67 oz	
Fuggles 60 min	0.50 oz	
Fuggles 30 min	0.50 oz	
OG	1040	
FG	1008	
ABV	4.23	
Apparent attenuation	80.00%	
IBU	27	
SRM	12	
Mash at	152° F	
Sparge at	165° F	
Boil time	140 minutes	
pitching temp	64° F	
Yeast	Wyeast 1469 West Yorkshire Ale	

1919 Tetley X2

Tetley were still producing an impressive four Milds in 1919. True, they'd dropped the two strongest, X3 and XX, but they had also introduced a new one, F.

After 1917, Milds over 1050° were virtually unknown. It's really odd that X2 should have survived. Where was it sold? I'm assuming it was a draught beer. And who drank it? I'd love to imagine punters shovelling it down on a Friday night in the cardigan Arms. But that probably wasn't the case.

The recipe is the same as X1. The two were parti-gyled together on occasion, but not here. This X2 was brewed single-gyle.

1919 Tetley X2		
mild malt	3.75 lb	34.09%
pale malt	4.00 lb	36.36%
chocolate Malt	0.25 lb	2.27%
grits	1.50 lb	13.64%
brown sugar	1.50 lb	13.64%
Cluster 140 min	0.75 oz	
Fuggles 60 min	0.75 oz	
Fuggles 30 min	0.75 oz	
OG	1052	
FG	1021.5	
ABV	4.03	
Apparent attenuation	58.65%	
IBU	32	
SRM	12.5	
Mash at	148° F	
Sparge at	165° F	
Boil time	130 minutes	
pitching temp	64° F	
Yeast	Wyeast 1469 West Yorkshire Ale	

1919 Tetley K

The gravity of K has really bounced back. To 4.5 points higher than in 1916. It may seem odd, but there's a simple explanation: the stronger PA was discontinued somewhere towards the arse end of the war.

This version of K has a gravity between that of the old K and PA. It's clearly a compromise beer. One intended to plug the gap of the two previous Pale Ales. It's a shame PA was discontinued as they had been brewing it since at least the 1840s. Making it a very early provincial English Pale Ale.

There's not much to the recipe: pale malt, mild malt and a sugar described as "Glebe". I've guessed No.1 invert. No idea how accurate a guess that is. Feel free to make a guess of your own.

The hops were slightly newer than for the Milds: Worcester (1917 cold store), Kent (1917).

1919 Tetley K		
mild malt	4.00 lb	38.10%
pale malt	5.25 lb	50.00%
No. 1 invert sugar	1.25 lb	11.90%
Fuggles 100 min	1.25 oz	
Fuggles 30 min	1.25 oz	
Goldings dry hops	0.25 oz	
OG	1048.5	
FG	1011	
ABV	4.96	
Apparent attenuation	77.32%	
IBU	29	
SRM	5	
Mash at	149° F	
Sparge at	165° F	
Boil time	100 minutes	
pitching temp	61° F	
Yeast	Wyeast 1469 West Yorkshire Ale	

Mini Book Series volume XXXII: Armistice!

Truman (Burton)

Truman bought a brewery in Burton in 1873 for the express purpose of brewing Pale Ales, which were very much in fashion. The brewery made a wide range of Burton Ales, not just Pale Ale. There was almost no overlap in products with the original Truman brewery in Brick Lane, which concentrated on Porter and London Ales.

The brewery had been built in 1860 by the Philips brothers. Truman never managed to run it at full all the years they owned. It finally closed in 1971.

Here's what they were brewing in Burton in 1914:

Truman's Burton-brewed beers in 1914									
Beer	Style	OG	FG	ABV	App. Atten-uation	lbs hops/ qtr	hops lb/brl	boil time (hours)	boil time (hours)	Pitch temp
P2	Pale Ale	1056.8	1009.4	6.27	83.41%	8.77	2.00	2	2	56°
P3	Pale Ale	1049.9	1008.3	5.50	83.33%	8.79		2	2	56.5°
3	Ale	1091.4	1021.6	9.23	76.36%	6.87		2	2	55°
5	Ale	1074.8	1016.6	7.70	77.78%	5.67	1.76	2	2	56°
6	Mild	1061.8	1012.2	6.56	80.27%	6.54		2	2	56°
7	Mild	1056.0	1011.1	5.94	80.20%	7.37	1.69	2	2	56.5°
8	Mild	1047.9	1010.0	5.02	79.19%	7.57		2	2	57.5°
8K	Ale	1047.1	1011.6	4.69	75.29%	6.67	1.23	1.5	1.5	58°
A	Ale	1041.8	1008.9	4.36	78.81%	7.20		1.5	1.5	58°
Source: Truman brewing records held at the London metropolitan archives										

Unfortunately, I missed a couple. Most notably No. 1. It's easily done. There were only a couple of brews each year.

You'll notice that the attenuation is greater than at some other breweries. There's a simple explanation. I'm pretty sure it really is the racking gravity that's given in the logs.

1917 was a cataclysmic year. The German U-boat campaign was at its peak and Britain was down to just a few week's supply of grain. Knowing the background makes the draconian restrictions on brewing imposed in April of that year more understandable. Output was limited to 10 million standard barrels per annum. That was about a third of the pre-war level.

The effect was dramatic. Breweries slashed both their product range and the gravity or their remaining beers.

Truman's Burton brewery discontinued all of its beers. The three Pale Ales (P1, P2 and P3) and its number Burton Ales (1 to 9). Hardly any ever returned. P1 was the first to be revived, in early 1919. P2 came back a little later. Most numbered Ales disappeared forever. For two years (march 1917 to March 1919) Truman's Pale Ale brewery produced no Pale Ale whatsoever.

The table below demonstrates this perfectly.

Truman's Burton-brewed beers 1914 - 1921

Month	P1	P2	P3	1	3	4	5
Sep 1914		1056.8	1049.9		1091.4		1074.8
Apr 1915	1063.7	1056.8	1047.1				1069.3
May 1915					1085.9		1069.3
Oct 1915			1047.1				
Jul 1916		1052.6	1044.6	1097			1061.8
Oct 1916						1069.5	
Mar 1917		1048.9	1041.8	1088.6		1057.9	1060.7
Mar 1919	1050.4						
Sep 1919	1055.4						
Jul 1921	1054.6						

Source: Truman brewing records held at the London metropolitan archives

Truman's Burton-brewed beers 1914 - 1921

Month	6	7	8	8K	9	A
Sep 1914	1061.8	1056	1047.9	1047.1		1041.8
Apr 1915	1061.8	1056	1047.9	1047.1		1041.8
May 1915		1053.7				
Oct 1915					1041.8	
Jul 1916	1055.4	1049.9	1044.6	1044.6	1038.7	
Oct 1916		1049.9	1044.6			1038.8
Mar 1917	1053.7	1047.6	1039.9	1042.1		1032.7
Mar 1919						
Sep 1919						
Jul 1921						

Source: Truman brewing records held at the London metropolitan archives

In their place, five new Ales were brewed, though two, S1 and XM, only very occasionally.

Truman's Burton-brewed beers 1917 - 1921

Month	S1	X	XM	XX	XXX
Apr 1917	1099.7	1035.7			1047.6
Jun 1917		1032.6		1037.7	1044.0
Jul 1917		1031.6		1036.8	1042.4
Oct 1917				1035.7	1041.6
Mar 1918	1072			1036.6	1043.5
Apr 1918		1025.2			
Sep 1918		1022.4	1026.3	1029.9	
Dec 1918		1022.4		1029.4	1034.3
Mar 1919	1072	1023.5		1029.9	1042.7
Sep 1919				1033.8	1047.4
Jan 1921				1033.8	1047.4

Source: Truman brewing records held at the London metropolitan archives

XX and XXX continued to be brewed, at 1033.8 and 1047.4 respectively, throughout the 1920's.

Truman's strongest Pale Ale, P1, suffered a relatively minor drop in gravity across the war. 14% as opposed to an average for all beer of about 25%. It fell from 1064° in 1914 to 1055° in 1921, which is where it remained for the rest of the 1920's.

1914 Truman P2

At their Burton brewery, Truman produced several Pale Ales at different strengths. P2 was the middle one.

It has a typical Edwardian stripped-down recipe, basically just pale malt with a tiny amount of maize and sugar. I've no idea what the sugar is, but No. invert is the one used most often in Pale Ales. 21 of the 27 quarters of malt were of Truman's own manufacture. In the 19th century, Burton Pale Ale brewers liked to make their own malt as they wanted a very high quality and a very pale colour.

The hops were a mixture of Pacific and English. I've gone with Cluster, Fuggles and Goldings. Though, as this was a relatively classy beer, the English hops may have all been something similar to Goldings.

P2 may have been brewed as a semi-Stock Pale Ale and aged a couple of months in trade casks before sale.

1914 Truman P2			
pale malt		9.25 lb	336.36%
flaked maize		1.25 lb	45.45%
No. 1 invert sugar		1.50 lb	54.55%
Cluster 120 mins		0.50 oz	
Fuggles 120 mins		0.75 oz	
Goldings 60 mins		1.25 oz	
Goldings 30 mins		1.25 oz	
Goldings dry hops		0.50 oz	
OG		1057	
FG		1009	
ABV		6.35	
Apparent attenuation		84.21%	
IBU		51	
SRM		6.2	
Mash at		151° F	
Sparge at		170° F	
Boil time		120 minutes	
pitching temp		56° F	
Yeast	Wyeast 1028 London Ale (Worthington White Shield)		

1914 Truman P3

Parti-gyled with P2, P3 was the weakest of Truman's Pale Ales. From Burton, at least. They brewed a cheap and cheerful Pale Ale, XLK, at their brewery on Brick Lane.

Obviously, the recipe is essentially the same. Just a little less of everything. It's a good example of the beauty of parti-gyling. From two worts, one 1089° of and one of 1028°, Truman was able to brew Pale Ales of 1057° and 1050°.

When I first looked at Victorian price lists, I was amazed at how many different beers even tiny breweries were producing. Four or five Mild, three Pale Ales, a couple of Strong Ales, a Porter and three Stouts. I now realise that, in most cases, there were probably only three or four basic recipes, with everything parti-gyled together.

I'm not sure about ageing with this one. It could have been semi-Stock. But it could also have been a strong Running Beer, in which case it wouldn't have been matured for more than a couple of weeks.

1914 Truman P3		
pale malt	8.25 lb	76.74%
flaked maize	1.00 lb	9.30%
No. 1 invert sugar	1.50 lb	13.95%
Cluster 120 mins	0.25 oz	
Fuggles 120 mins	0.75 oz	
Goldings 60 mins	1.00 oz	
Goldings 30 mins	1.00 oz	
Goldings dry hops	0.50 oz	
OG	1050	
FG	1008	
ABV	5.56	
Apparent attenuation	84.00%	
IBU	41	
SRM	6	
Mash at	151° F	
Sparge at	170° F	
Boil time	120 minutes	
pitching temp	56.5° F	
Yeast	Wyeast 1028 London Ale (Worthington White Shield)	

1914 Truman A

Truman's Burton brewery produced a dazzling array of Burton Ales. The higher numbers Burton Ale, the lower numbers Mild Ales. At the very bottom end of the gravity scale was A, the weakest Mild Ale.

For a pre-WW I beer, it's pretty watery, being barely more than 4% ABV. Though it is reasonably heavily hopped for such a light beer.

It has a typical Truman Burton Ale grist that combines pale and high-dried malt with sugar and flaked maize. The type of sugar isn't specified so I've guessed No. 2 invert.

1914 Truman A		
pale malt	6.50 lb	520.00%
high dried malt	1.50 lb	120.00%
flaked maize	0.75 lb	60.00%
No. 2 invert sugar	0.50 lb	40.00%
Cluster 120 mins	0.25 oz	
Fuggles 120 mins	0.50 oz	
Goldings 60 mins	0.75 oz	
Goldings 30 mins	0.50 oz	
OG	1042	
FG	1011	
ABV	4.10	
Apparent attenuation	73.81%	
IBU	29	
SRM	6	
Mash at	155° F	
Sparge at	170° F	
Boil time	120 minutes	
pitching temp	55.5° F	
Yeast	Wyeast 1028 London Ale (Worthington White Shield)	

1914 Truman No. 8K

Truman's Burton brewery had two ranges of beers: Burton Pale Ales and Burton Ales. The latter went from No. 1 right through to No. 8, in declining order of strength. 8K was the weakest of all.

From No. 5 or No. 6 down they were considered Mild Ales. Still Burton Ales, just ones that were sold young. I'm assuming mostly on draught, though I have seen labels for No. 6, so that must have been bottled.

In terms of recipe, it's much like all their Burton Ales. Consisting of pale malt, high dried malt, flaked maize and sugar. I'm still not quite sure what the closest modern equivalent is to high dried malt. Probably something like pale Munich malt. It's a shame that no-one seems to make the real thing any more.

The hops were Pacific from 1912 and three types of English ones from 1913. All had been kept in a cold store.

1914 Truman No. 8K		
pale malt	7.25 lb	69.05%
high dried malt	1.75 lb	16.67%
flaked maize	1.00 lb	9.52%
No. 2 invert sugar	0.50 lb	4.76%
Cluster 120 mins	0.25 oz	
Fuggles 120 mins	0.50 oz	
Goldings 60 mins	0.75 oz	
Goldings 30 mins	0.75 oz	
OG	1047	
FG	1011	
ABV	4.76	
Apparent attenuation	76.60%	
IBU	30	
SRM	6	
Mash at	155° F	
Sparge at	170° F	
Boil time	120 minutes	
pitching temp	55.5° F	
Yeast	Wyeast 1028 London Ale (Worthington White Shield)	

1914 Truman No. 8

Ever so slightly stronger than 8K was No. 8. Not sure why they needed two such similar beers.

The only real difference between the two is that No. 8 is slightly more heavily hopped than 8K. Which seems counterintuitive, as K normally denotes a keeping beer, which would usually be more heavily hopped. That's not the case here. In any case, Truman's Burton brewery used an "S" (for "Stock") rather than K to signify keeping versions.

The grist and hops are the same as 8K.

1914 Truman No. 8		
pale malt	6.25 lb	58.14%
high dried malt	3.25 lb	30.23%
flaked maize	0.75 lb	6.98%
No. 2 invert sugar	0.50 lb	4.65%
Cluster 120 mins	0.25 oz	
Fuggles 120 mins	0.75 oz	
Goldings 60 mins	0.75 oz	
Goldings 30 mins	0.75 oz	
OG	1048	
FG	1010	
ABV	5.03	
Apparent attenuation	79.17%	
IBU	34	
SRM	7	
Mash at	153° F	
Sparge at	170° F	
Boil time	120 minutes	
pitching temp	57.5° F	
Yeast	Wyeast 1028 London Ale (Worthington White Shield)	

1914 Truman No. 7

Moving one more notch up the strength scale, we get to No. 7. It's about the same strength as the strongest London X Ale.

No. 7, like all Truman's numbered Burton Ales, was discontinued in April 1917. Just when real restrictions on brewing were being introduced.

It did sort of return after the war. A Mild Ale called 7 was produced during 1930s, but tracing its history backwards, I can see that in 1921 it was called 7d. With 7d being the price. Going back a little further to 1919, it was called 6d, the change in name having been prompted by an increase in tax which raised the price of beer by 1d per pint. So, even though both were Burton Mild Ales, there's no direct connection between the old No. 7 and post-war 7d or 7.

Like all Truman's Burton Mild Ales, No. 7 is quite heavily hopped for the style. It was probably a Burton thing. They contained 6.5-7 lbs per quarter of malt, while London Mild Ales, which were themselves quite heavily hopped, contained 5-5.5 lbs per quarter.

1914 Truman No. 7		
pale malt	7.50 lb	58.82%
high dried malt	3.75 lb	29.41%
flaked maize	1.00 lb	7.84%
No. 2 invert sugar	0.50 lb	3.92%
Cluster 120 mins	0.25 oz	
Fuggles 120 mins	1.00 oz	
Goldings 60 mins	1.00 oz	
Goldings 30 mins	1.00 oz	
OG	1056	
FG	1009	
ABV	6.22	
Apparent attenuation	83.93%	
IBU	42	
SRM	8	
Mash at	153° F	
Sparge at	170° F	
Boil time	120 minutes	
pitching temp	56.5° F	
Yeast	Wyeast 1028 London Ale (Worthington White Shield)	

1914 Truman No. 6

Most of Truman's numbered Burton Ales didn't make it through the war. But No. 6, a Mild Burton Ale, did and was widely available as a bottled beer. Though obviously at a much reduced gravity.

At over 6.5% ABV, No. 6 was strong for a Mild Ale, even by pre-WW I standards. The high degree of attenuation only accentuates its strength. It's also pretty heavily hopped, at 6.6 lbs per quarter of malt. That's more than most provincial Pale Ales.

It's very pale for a Mild Ale of this period. Though that colour shouldn't be taken as gospel. It might well have been darkened with either caramel or primings at racking time.

1914 Truman No. 6		
pale malt	8.00 lb	58.18%
high dried malt	3.75 lb	27.27%
flaked maize	1.00 lb	7.27%
No. 2 invert sugar	1.00 lb	7.27%
Cluster 120 mins	0.25 oz	
Fuggles 120 mins	1.00 oz	
Goldings 60 mins	1.00 oz	
Goldings 30 mins	1.00 oz	
OG	1062	
FG	1012	
ABV	6.61	
Apparent attenuation	80.65%	
IBU	40	
SRM	9	
Mash at	150° F	
Sparge at	170° F	
Boil time	120 minutes	
pitching temp	56° F	
Yeast	Wyeast 1028 London Ale (Worthington White Shield)	

1914 Truman No. 5

The middle beers in Truman's numbered Burton Ales have always a been a bit of a puzzle for me, stylistically speaking.

Nos. 1, 2 and 3 are obviously Strong Ales. No. 4 probably, too, as it was brewed in both Runner and Stock versions. The latter indicating a beer that was aged before sale. But what of No. 5? It's rather on the strong side for a Mild Ale. But was it strong enough to count as a strong Burton Ale? I've no idea.

The recipe is the same as all their other Burton Ales. Not surprising, really, as they were parti-gyled together in various combinations.

1914 Truman No. 5		
pale malt	9.00 lb	54.55%
high dried malt	4.75 lb	28.79%
flaked maize	1.50 lb	9.09%
No. 2 invert sugar	1.25 lb	7.58%
Cluster 120 mins	0.50 oz	
Fuggles 120 mins	1.25 oz	
Goldings 60 mins	1.25 oz	
Goldings 30 mins	1.25 oz	
OG	1075	
FG	1018	
ABV	7.54	
Apparent attenuation	76.00%	
IBU	49	
SRM	11	
Mash at	150° F	
Sparge at	170° F	
Boil time	120 minutes	
pitching temp	55.5° F	
Yeast	Wyeast 1028 London Ale (Worthington White Shield)	

1914 Truman No. 3

I do know for certain that Truman No. 3 wasn't a Mild Ale. Old Ale is, I guess, what it was sold as. Not that the distinction has much impact on the recipe.

Though it was parti-gyled with the No. 5 above. The more I look at old brewing records, the more the hard and fast differences between beer styles evaporate before me. Many breweries used very similar – or even identical – recipes for most of their beers. I'm thinking here of Scotland in particular. Strictly-defined beer styles didn't seem to exist in the real world. Only in the heads of modern style Nazis.

My guess is that No. 3 was aged for a while before sale so I would expect the FG at time of consumption to be lower than the one given below, which was the racking gravity.

1914 Truman No. 3		
pale malt	11.00 lb	54.32%
high dried malt	6.00 lb	29.63%
flaked maize	1.75 lb	8.64%
No. 2 invert sugar	1.50 lb	7.41%
Cluster 120 mins	0.50 oz	
Fuggles 120 mins	1.50 oz	
Goldings 60 mins	1.50 oz	
Goldings 30 mins	1.50 oz	
OG	1091	
FG	1022	
ABV	9.13	
Apparent attenuation	75.82%	
IBU	52	
SRM	12	
Mash at	150° F	
Sparge at	170° F	
Boil time	120 minutes	
pitching temp	56.5° F	
Yeast	Wyeast 1028 London Ale (Worthington White Shield)	

Mini Book Series volume XXXII: Armistice!

1915 Truman No. 4

At least I know for a fact that No. 4 was considered a Strong Ale. That's because Truman made both Running and Stock versions.

This example was parti-gyled with that most indeterminate of beers, No. 5. As the gravity of this No. 4 is lower than that of 1914 No. 5, it seems certain that Truman's gravities had fallen a little since the start of the war. Which is confirmed by the fact that the accompanying No. 5 had an OG of 1067°, 8 points lower than the year before. I'd guess that No. 4 started the war with an OG of around 1080°.

There's been a change in the hopping since 1914. Gone are the Pacific hops. Here there are just two types of English hops, both from 1914 and both kept in a cold store.

The sugar used seems to have change, too. In earlier records there's nothing to indicate what type of sugar it might have been. Here there's a note next to the sugar entry that read "2 G". I've taken that to mean two quarters of glucose. As I can't think of another sugar that can be abbreviated to "G" and I've seen other brewers start using glucose during the war. Probably for supply reasons.

1915 Truman No. 4		
pale malt	6.75 lb	44.26%
high dried malt	6.25 lb	40.98%
flaked maize	1.25 lb	8.20%
No. 2 invert sugar	0.50 lb	3.28%
glucose	0.50 lb	3.28%
Fuggles 120 mins	1.25 oz	
Fuggles 60 mins	1.25 oz	
Goldings 30 mins	1.25 oz	
OG	1073	
FG	1022	
ABV	6.75	
Apparent attenuation	69.86%	
IBU	40	
SRM	9.5	
Mash at	150° F	
Sparge at	170° F	
Boil time	120 minutes	
pitching temp	57° F	
Yeast	Wyeast 1028 London Ale (Worthington White Shield)	

1915 Truman P1

As you would expect of a brewery based in Burton, Truman produced top-class Pale Ales. And pick of the bunch was P1.

At 1064°, it had the classis Burton IPA gravity. The ABV might look a bit low at a little under 6%, though it was almost certainly stronger when sold. As this was a Stock Pale Ale that would have undergone a secondary conditioning of 6 to 12 months. AT the end of that time, the FG would have been considerably lower.

They didn't go in for fancy grists at Truman's Burton brewery. I doubt they had any coloured malts on the premises, as all their Porter and Stouts were brewed in London. Though the pale malt is a mix of Indian, Smyrna and English. I'm not sure what the sugar was. It could easily have been No, 1 invert, which would leave the finish beer a little paler.

Most of the hops were English from the 1914 crop, though they were a few described as Pacific from 1912. The varieties are just my guesses.

1915 Truman P1		
pale malt	11.00 lb	80.00%
flaked maize	1.50 lb	10.91%
No. 2 invert sugar	1.25 lb	9.09%
Cluster 120 mins	0.25 oz	
Goldings 90 mins	1.50 oz	
Goldings 60 mins	1.50 oz	
Goldings 30 mins	1.75 oz	
Goldings dry hops	0.50 oz	
OG	1064	
FG	1020	
ABV	5.82	
Apparent attenuation	68.75%	
IBU	61	
SRM	8	
Mash at	152° F	
Sparge at	170° F	
Boil time	120 minutes	
pitching temp	57° F	
Yeast	Wyeast 1028 London Ale (Worthington White Shield)	

1916 Truman No. 1 Barley Wine

Things weren't yet so bad in 1916 that brewers couldn't bash out the odd batch of very strong beer. And they didn't come much stronger than Truman No. 1.

It's a beer very much along the lines of the original Barley Wine, Bass No. 1. Which I'm sure was the intention. And it proved a worthy rival, especially in London. Truman No. 1 was a real survivor, lasting until at least the late 1960s. And still retained its strength, being 1105° in 1964.

I assume that this is the Stock version, that is the one that was aged for a year or so before being blended with a Running version and bottled.

The recipe has one notable difference from Truman's other Burton Ales: there's no sugar. Which is a surprise in a beer of this strength. But I guess the extended ageing would have lightened the body a good bit. Speaking of which, the real FG, after ageing, would have been a good bit lower than the one ion the recipe below. That's the racking gravity after primary fermentation.

1916 Truman No. 1 Barley Wine		
pale malt	14.50 lb	64.44%
high dried malt	5.25 lb	23.33%
flaked maize	2.75 lb	12.22%
Cluster 120 mins	0.67 oz	
Fuggles 120 mins	2.00 oz	
Fuggles 90 mins	2.00 oz	
Goldings 30 mins	2.00 oz	
Goldings dry hops	1.00 oz	
OG	1097	
FG	1033	
ABV	8.47	
Apparent attenuation	65.98%	
IBU	66	
SRM	9	
Mash at	149° F	
Sparge at	170° F	
Boil time	120 minutes	
pitching temp	57° F	
Yeast	Wyeast 1028 London Ale (Worthington White Shield)	

1917 Truman P2

By early 1917, P1, Truman's strongest Pale Ale had been dropped. P2 and P3, however, were still going strong. At least for the moment.

So far, P2 hadn't fared too badly, only having lost three gravity points. It was still a pretty hefty Pale Ale, about as strong as the strongest draught Bitters would be in the 1920s.

The big difference with the numbered Burton Ales is the absence of high dried malt. Understandable, as a Pale Ale like this was meant to be as pale as possible.

The hops were all English, from the 1914 and 1915 crops, both kept in cold store, and the 1916 crop.

1917 Truman P2		
pale malt	10.50 lb	85.71%
flaked maize	1.50 lb	12.24%
glucose	0.25 lb	2.04%
Fuggles 120 min	1.00 oz	
Fuggles 90 min	1.00 oz	
Goldings 30 min	0.75 oz	
Goldings dry hops	0.50 oz	
OG	1054	
FG	1014	
ABV	5.29	
Apparent attenuation	74.07%	
IBU	34	
SRM	8	
Mash at	151° F	
Sparge at	170° F	
Boil time	120 minutes	
pitching temp	59° F	
Yeast	Wyeast 1028 London Ale (Worthington White Shield)	

1917 Truman P3

Brewed only five days after the P2 above, there's already been a recipe change for this P2/P3 parti-gyle.

The glucose is gone, leaving an extremely simple grist of just pale malt and flaked maize. Though there was pale malt made from both English and Oregon barley. Most of which – 19 of the 31 quarters – had been malted by Truman themselves.

Making their own pale malt was typical of Burton breweries, which need the highest quality and palest malt for their Pale Ales.

The hops have also changed slightly from the P2, being English from the 1915 and 1916 crops, the former having been in a cold store.

1917 Truman P3		
pale malt	8.50 lb	87.18%
flaked maize	1.25 lb	12.82%
Fuggles 120 min	1.00 oz	
Fuggles 90 min	0.75 oz	
Goldings 30 min	0.75 oz	
Goldings dry hops	0.50 oz	
OG	1042	
FG	1009	
ABV	4.37	
Apparent attenuation	78.57%	
IBU	37	
SRM	8	
Mash at	150° F	
Sparge at	170° F	
Boil time	120 minutes	
pitching temp	60° F	
Yeast	Wyeast 1028 London Ale (Worthington White Shield)	

1917 Truman A

Three years of war haven't been kind to Truman's bottom of the range Mild, the beautifully simply-named A.

There is a tale to be spun around A. Relating to one of my favourite obsessions AK. While Mild Ales usually went through a range of X's, some did go one step down in terms of strength. And that beer was often called A. So when breweries brought out a light Pale Ale of a similar gravity, calling it AK was pretty obvious. A for the strength K (for Keeping) to indicate that it was a Pale Ale and not a Mild Ale.

The gravity has dropped nine points since 1914. I can't say that worse was about to happen, because this was the last ever batch of A. Rest in peace.

The grist remains the classic Truman Burton Ale combination of pale and high dried malt, flaked maize and sugar. Nothing new there.

All English hops, 1914 and 1915 from cold store, 1916 fresh.

1917 Truman A		
pale malt	3.00 lb	41.38%
high dried malt	3.00 lb	41.38%
flaked maize	1.00 lb	13.79%
glucose	0.25 lb	3.45%
Fuggles 105 min	0.75 oz	
Fuggles 90 min	0.50 oz	
Goldings 30 min	0.50 oz	
OG	1033	
FG	1008	
ABV	3.31	
Apparent attenuation	75.76%	
IBU	25	
SRM	5	
Mash at	150° F	
Sparge at	170° F	
Boil time	105 minutes	
pitching temp	62° F	
Yeast	Wyeast 1028 London Ale (Worthington White Shield)	

1917 Truman No. 8

Brewed just a day after the A above, the grist of No. 8 is quite different. Simpler.

The high dried malt and glucose are gone. I'm not sure why, because they're back in the next brew. Let's just call it a mystery. The hops are identical to A, however.

This was just about No. 8's last hurrah. Brewed on the 15th March, there were only two further brews before it departed for the beery netherworld.

1917 Truman No. 8		
pale malt	8.25 lb	84.62%
flaked maize	1.50 lb	15.38%
Fuggles 105 min	0.75 oz	
Fuggles 90 min	0.75 oz	
Goldings 30 min	0.50 oz	
OG	1043	
FG	1009	
ABV	4.50	
Apparent attenuation	79.07%	
IBU	27	
SRM	4	
Mash at	150° F	
Sparge at	170° F	
Boil time	105 minutes	
pitching temp	61° F	
Yeast	Wyeast 1028 London Ale (Worthington White Shield)	

1917 Truman No. 7

Brewed in March, these beers were the final throes of Truman's pre-war range of Mild Ales. The next month they'd be on the bonfire or beer styles.

It's not a great deal stronger than No. 8. And has an identical recipe, obviously, as the two were parti-gyled. I'm not surprised that Truman used the war as an excuse to overhaul their beer range. They had lots of very similar Milds.

Though I'm not sure they really simplified them that much, if you look at what replaced the numbered ones. Which you will do if you read a few pages further.

1917 Truman No. 7		
pale malt	4.50 lb	41.55%
high dried malt	4.50 lb	41.55%
flaked maize	1.50 lb	13.85%
glucose	0.33 lb	3.05%
Fuggles 105 min	1.00 oz	
Fuggles 90 min	0.75 oz	
Goldings 30 min	0.75 oz	
OG	1049	
FG	1011	
ABV	5.03	
Apparent attenuation	77.55%	
IBU	31	
SRM	8	
Mash at	150° F	
Sparge at	170° F	
Boil time	105 minutes	
pitching temp	59.5° F	
Yeast	Wyeast 1028 London Ale (Worthington White Shield)	

1917 Truman No. 5

The gravity of No. 5 has taken quite a hit since 1914, having dropped 14 gravity points.

The recipe has changed a bit since 1914. The sugar has been changed to glucose from something unspecified. And a little black malt has been added. Perhaps to compensate for the proportion of high dried malt falling.

The hops were English from 1914 and 1915 which had been kept in a cold store and from 1916 which hadn't.

1917 Truman No. 5		
pale malt	6.00 lb	43.32%
high dried malt	5.50 lb	39.71%
black malt	0.10 lb	0.72%
flaked maize	1.75 lb	12.64%
glucose	0.50 lb	3.61%
Fuggles 120 min	1.00 oz	
Fuggles 90 min	1.00 oz	
Goldings 30 min	1.00 oz	
OG	1061	
FG	1017	
ABV	5.82	
Apparent attenuation	72.13%	
IBU	35	
SRM	11	
Mash at	150° F	
Sparge at	170° F	
Boil time	120 minutes	
pitching temp	60.5° F	
Yeast	Wyeast 1028 London Ale (Worthington White Shield)	

1917 Truman No. 4

No. 4 hasn't fared much better, shedding 15 gravity points since 1915. Definitely a big enough change in strength for drinkers to notice.

There's been a small change to the grist, with a small quantity of black malt being added. My guess is that this was to compensate for the drop in gravity and keep the colour of the finished beer about the same.

Though it isn't specified, this looks like the Running version of No. 4. The Stock version, as you'll see in a few pages, was much more heavily hopped.

1917 Truman No. 4		
pale malt	5.75 lb	43.89%
high dried malt	5.00 lb	38.17%
black malt	0.10 lb	0.76%
flaked maize	1.75 lb	13.36%
glucose	0.50 lb	3.82%
Fuggles 120 min	1.00 oz	
Fuggles 90 min	1.00 oz	
Goldings 30 min	1.00 oz	
OG	1058	
FG	1017	
ABV	5.42	
Apparent attenuation	70.69%	
IBU	36	
SRM	11	
Mash at	150° F	
Sparge at	170° F	
Boil time	120 minutes	
pitching temp	58.5° F	
Yeast	Wyeast 1028 London Ale (Worthington White Shield)	

1917 Truman No. 1 Barley Wine

Though it doesn't specifically say so on the brewing record, I'm sure that this is the Running version of No. 1.

There are a couple of giveaways. One is the OG, which is lower than the 1100° of the Stock version. The other is the level of hopping. As you'll see in the following recipe, the Stock version was much more heavily hopped.

Though this still isn't exactly a puny, lightly-hopped beer, at over 7% ABV and 51 (calculated) IBUs. Not that anyone would have ever tasted it, other than inside the brewery. Neither the Running nor the Stock versions of No. 1 were ever available in their pure form. Only a blend of the two was sold.

Other than the tiny amount of black malt, the recipe is much the same as Truman's other Burton Ales.

The hops were English from 1914 and 1915 kept in a cold store and 1916 fresh.

1917 Truman No. 1 Barley Wine			
pale malt		8.50 lb	42.75%
high dried malt		7.50 lb	37.72%
black malt		0.125 lb	0.63%
flaked maize		2.76 lb	13.88%
glucose		1.00 lb	5.03%
Fuggles 120 min		1.75 oz	
Fuggles 90 min		1.50 oz	
Goldings 30 min		1.50 oz	
OG		1089	
FG		1034	
ABV		7.28	
Apparent attenuation		61.80%	
IBU		51	
SRM		13	
Mash at		150° F	
Sparge at		170° F	
Boil time		120 minutes	
pitching temp		56.5° F	
Yeast	Wyeast 1028 London Ale (Worthington White Shield)		

1917 Truman Stock No. 1 Barley Wine

The Stock version of No. 1 is the second part of the blend needed to create Truman No. 1 Barley Wine.

The recipe is quite similar to the Running version, save for the absence of flaked maize. And, obviously, much heavier hopping. As a beer that would need to survive a year of maturation, the hops were needed to keep it sound. Obviously, their effect would have faded by the time the beer was consumed.

The hops were Pacific from the 1915 crop, kept in a cold store and English from 1916.

Truman don't mention dry hopping in their brewing records. I've just made an educated guess that a beer like No. 1 would have been dry-hopped in the maturation vessel. Whether that be trade casks, vats or tanks.

1917 Truman Stock No. 1 Barley Wine		
pale malt	13.50 lb	59.67%
high dried malt	8.00 lb	35.36%
black malt	0.125 lb	0.55%
No. 1 invert sugar	0.33 lb	1.46%
glucose	0.67 lb	2.96%
Cluster 120 min	3.00 oz	
Fuggles 90 min	5.00 oz	
Goldings 30 min	5.00 oz	
Goldings dry hops	1.00 oz	
OG	1100	
FG	1029	
ABV	9.39	
Apparent attenuation	71.00%	
IBU	132	
SRM	14	
Mash at	150° F	
Sparge at	170° F	
Boil time	120 minutes	
pitching temp	55° F	
Yeast	Wyeast 1028 London Ale (Worthington White Shield)	

1917 Truman X

The introduction of harsh restrictions on 1st April 1917 caused breweries to rejig their beer range, but nowhere as drastically as at Truman.

Truman's Burton brewery discontinued all of their beers and introduced several totally new ones. I wonder what drinkers though? Out went all the Pale Ales and Burton Ales, replaced by a series of Mild Ales. Which, breaking from tradition weren't numbered but instead had X designations. X was, unsurprisingly, the weakest of the bunch.

Though there is a great deal of continuity in the recipe, which is much like that of the numbered Burton Ales: pale and high dried malt, flaked maize and glucose. It was more a rebranding exercise than a total reformulation.

The hops were all English, from the 1915 and 1916, the former having been kept in a cold store.

As with the previous Mild Ales, X is pretty bitter for the style. Considerably more bitter than for example, Drybrough's Pale Ales.

1917 Truman X		
pale malt	5.00 lb	59.70%
high dried malt	2.25 lb	26.87%
flaked maize	1.00 lb	11.94%
glucose	0.125 lb	1.49%
Fuggles 120 min	0.75 oz	
Fuggles 90 min	0.75 oz	
Goldings 30 min	0.75 oz	
OG	1036	
FG	1007	
ABV	3.84	
Apparent attenuation	80.56%	
IBU	31	
SRM	5	
Mash at	150° F	
Sparge at	170° F	
Boil time	120 minutes	
pitching temp	60.5° F	
Yeast	Wyeast 1028 London Ale (Worthington White Shield)	

1917 Truman XX

Logically enough, XX is the next up strength-wise in Truman's new range of Mild Ales.

I can't really see the point of XX, to be honest. It's a mere two gravity points stronger than X. Why have two beers of such a similar strength?

The recipe is a bit different from the XX above, in that there's no glucose. Which might have been an enforced change due to supply problems.

The hops were English from 1915 and 1916, most having been kept in a cold store.

1917 Truman XX		
pale malt	5.00 lb	58.82%
high dried malt	2.50 lb	29.41%
flaked maize	1.00 lb	11.76%
Fuggles 120 min	0.75 oz	
Fuggles 90 min	0.75 oz	
Goldings 30 min	0.75 oz	
OG	1038	
FG	1007	
ABV	4.10	
Apparent attenuation	81.58%	
IBU	31	
SRM	5	
Mash at	150° F	
Sparge at	170° F	
Boil time	120 minutes	
pitching temp	59.5° F	
Yeast	Wyeast 1028 London Ale (Worthington White Shield)	

1917 Truman XXX

The strongest of Truman's new Milds, XXX, had a pretty decent gravity. Though the days of Milds of this strength were numbered.

This example was parti-gyled with the X above. Look there for comments on the recipe.

The heavy hopping leaves this up there with Best Bitter in terms of bitterness.

1917 Truman XXX		
pale malt	6.25 lb	56.82%
high dried malt	3.00 lb	27.27%
flaked maize	1.50 lb	13.64%
glucose	0.25 lb	2.27%
Fuggles 120 min	1.00 oz	
Fuggles 90 min	1.00 oz	
Goldings 30 min	1.00 oz	
OG	1048	
FG	1009.5	
ABV	5.09	
Apparent attenuation	80.21%	
IBU	38	
SRM	6	
Mash at	150° F	
Sparge at	170° F	
Boil time	120 minutes	
pitching temp	59° F	
Yeast	Wyeast 1028 London Ale (Worthington White Shield)	

1918 Truman X

There's been quite a change in X since 1917. And not for the better. The gravity has fallen to a stupidly low level. Less than two-thirds pf the level of a year earlier.

The glucose has gone and in comes a little black malt. Presumably at attempt to salvage the colour. Such a big drop in OG would have lightened the colour considerably. The flaked maize is also gone, probably because there was simply none to be bought.

The hops are all English, from the 1916 and 1917 crop, all kept in a cold store.

X disappeared in 1920, probably because it was just too watery. But a beer with the same name suddenly popped up in 1939 and made it through until at least 1953.

1918 Truman X		
pale malt	3.25 lb	61.21%
high dried malt	2.00 lb	37.66%
black malt	0.06 lb	1.13%
Fuggles 90 mins	0.75 oz	
Fuggles 60 mins	0.75 oz	
Goldings 30 mins	0.50 oz	
OG	1022.5	
FG	1004.5	
ABV	2.38	
Apparent attenuation	80.00%	
IBU	29	
SRM	6.5	
Mash at	150° F	
Sparge at	170° F	
Boil time	105 minutes	
pitching temp	60° F	
Yeast	Wyeast 1028 London Ale (Worthington White Shield)	

1918 Truman XXX W

I'm not sure why Truman bothered with two Milds with gravities of no more than 1025°. Nor why one should confusingly be called XXX. And where the hell did XX come in? Three different Mild, each is a few different versions. It's crazy complicated.

XXX W was the weakest of the three XXX variations. I'm guessing the "W" stands for 'weak'.

The grist is virtually all malt, in contrast with the version from a year earlier. Most of the extra

The hops are all English from 1916, kept in a cold store.

1918 Truman XXX W		
pale malt	3.50 lb	59.57%
high dried malt	2.25 lb	38.30%
No. 2 invert sugar	0.125 lb	2.13%
Fuggles 90 mins	0.50 oz	
Fuggles 60 mins	0.50 oz	
Goldings 30 mins	0.25 oz	
OG	1025	
FG	1005.5	
ABV	2.58	
Apparent attenuation	78.00%	
IBU	18	
SRM	5	
Mash at	149° F	
Sparge at	170° F	
Boil time	90 minutes	
pitching temp	61.25° F	
Yeast	Wyeast 1028 London Ale (Worthington White Shield)	

1918 Truman XXX

Middle of the three versions of XXX, you'd suppose this was the "normal" version. Yet, in reality, it was a blend of XXX W and XXX S. I told you it was weird.

It's a bit weird to blend post-fermentation when the beers were already parti-gyled. From three different worts, with gravities of 1078°, 1041° and 1036°. Plus water. They could just as easily blended this pre-fermentation, too. The only reason I can think of is that they wanted a stronger wort than 1035° for reasons of yeast health.

1918 Truman XXX		
pale malt	5.00 lb	61.54%
high dried malt	3.00 lb	36.92%
No. 2 invert sugar	0.125 lb	1.54%
Fuggles 90 mins	0.50 oz	
Fuggles 60 mins	0.50 oz	
Goldings 30 mins	0.50 oz	
OG	1035	
FG	1006	
ABV	3.84	
Apparent attenuation	82.86%	
IBU	20	
SRM	6	
Mash at	149° F	
Sparge at	170° F	
Boil time	120 minutes	
pitching temp	61° F	
Yeast	Wyeast 1028 London Ale (Worthington White Shield)	

1918 Truman XXX S

The strongest version of XXX was a decent strength. With a high degree of attenuation taking it over 4.5% ABV.

It's also reasonably bitter for a Mild Ale. Though the (calculated) IBUs are lower than in the 1917 version.

The recipe is identical to XXX W above, with which it was parti-gyled.

1918 Truman XXX S		
pale malt	5.50 lb	57.89%
high dried malt	3.75 lb	39.47%
No. 2 invert sugar	0.25 lb	2.63%
Fuggles 90 mins	1.00 oz	
Fuggles 60 mins	0.75 oz	
Goldings 30 mins	0.75 oz	
OG	1041	
FG	1006.5	
ABV	4.56	
Apparent attenuation	84.15%	
IBU	32	
SRM	7	
Mash at	149° F	
Sparge at	170° F	
Boil time	90 minutes	
pitching temp	59.5° F	
Yeast	Wyeast 1028 London Ale (Worthington White Shield)	

1918 Truman S4

Despite the restrictions on gravity, Truman still managed to brew a small quantity of Strong Burton Ale. Admittedly, this mas brewed in March, just before the biggest cuts in gravity kicked in.

Admittedly, it was the weakest of the set, No. 4. But in 1918 anything over 1040° was strong. While this is brewed to pretty much the pre-war strength.

The S prefix indicates that this is a Stock version, which explains the heavy hopping. It would need that to survive the long secondary conditioning. I assume that the extended storage it would undergo is also the reason for the high OG. The running version brewed in 1917 was just 1058°.

The recipe is the usual Truman mix of pale and high dried malt, plus flaked maize and sugar. Pretty dull, eh?

Surprisingly, No. 4 did survive WW II, the Running and Stock versions both being brewed right up until WW II.

1918 Truman S4		
pale malt	7.25 lb	45.31%
high dried malt	6.00 lb	37.50%
flaked maize	1.75 lb	10.94%
No. 2 invert sugar	1.00 lb	6.25%
Cluster 120 mins	3.00 oz	
Fuggles 90 mins	1.75 oz	
Goldings 30 mins	1.75 oz	
Goldings dry hops	1.00 oz	
OG	1072	
FG	1022	
ABV	6.61	
Apparent attenuation	69.44%	
IBU	91	
SRM	10	
Mash at	151° F	
Sparge at	170° F	
Boil time	120 minutes	
pitching temp	57.5° F	
Yeast	Wyeast 1028 London Ale (Worthington White Shield)	

1919 Truman P1

Truman seem to have discontinued all their Pale Ales in April 1917. I assume that they replaced them with XLK, a lower-gravity Bitter, brewed in their London brewery. It wasn't until after the end of the was, in the spring of 1919, that they brewed

As you would expect, the revived version was a good bit weaker than the pre-war version. Though it still weighed in at a decent 5% ABV. Which I'm sure drinkers appreciated.

The one big difference in the grist as compared to 1915 is sugar in place of flaked maize. I've guessed No. 2 invert, but it could have been anything. All I know for certain is that is was sugar.

Some of the hops were from the most recent crop, but others were pretty damn old: Pacific (1911), English (1915, 1916 CS, 1918). In normal times a top-class beer like P1 would never have contained 8-year old hops.

P1 had a pretty good run, surviving even the closure of Truman's Burton brewery. In its latter days it was a keg Bitter called Ben Truman.

1919 Truman P1		
pale malt	8.00 lb	69.57%
high dried malt	3.00 lb	26.09%
No. 2 invert sugar	0.50 lb	4.35%
Cluster 90 mins	0.50 oz	
Fuggles 90 mins	1.00 oz	
Goldings 30 mins	1.00 oz	
Goldings dry hops	0.50 oz	
OG	1050.5	
FG	1012.5	
ABV	5.03	
Apparent attenuation	75.25%	
IBU	33	
SRM	7	
Mash at	150° F	
Sparge at	170° F	
Boil time	90 minutes	
pitching temp	60.5° F	
Yeast	Wyeast 1028 London Ale (Worthington White Shield)	

1919 Truman S4

Somehow Truman S4 managed to go through the war at just about the same strength. Even in that most difficult year, 1918.

Though, given the rules in force, they couldn't have brewed very much of it. Despite having several beers with gravities below 1030°.

The grist has seen flaked maize dropped and a tiny black malt added. As with all Truman's beers, the base remains a combination of pale and high dried malt.

The hops are noticeably better than for their other, weaker beers. They're all English from the 1918 harvest. So basically as fresh as was possible, given this beer was brewed in March.

1919 Truman S4		
pale malt	8.25 lb	51.16%
high dried malt	6.75 lb	41.86%
black malt	0.125 lb	0.78%
No. 2 invert sugar	1.00 lb	6.20%
Goldings 120 mins	3.75 oz	
Goldings 30 mins	3.75 oz	
Goldings dry hops	1.00 oz	
OG	1072	
FG	1020.5	
ABV	6.81	
Apparent attenuation	71.53%	
IBU	84	
SRM	14	
Mash at	151° F	
Sparge at	170° F	
Boil time	120 minutes	
pitching temp	57.5° F	
Yeast	Wyeast 1028 London Ale (Worthington White Shield)	

Mini Book Series volume XXXII: Armistice!

1919 Truman XXX S

The easing of government restrictions has allowed Truman to boost the gravity of the strong version of XXX to something like a pre-war X Ale.

They even brewed a reasonable amount of it: 214 barrels in this batch. Though I'm pretty sure that some of that was blended with XXX W to produce XXX. It's really weird some of the stuff that went on in the later years of WW I. I think mostly because brewers were afraid of what might happen to their yeast if they brewed everything at a low gravity.

I've ignored the tiny amount of 1911 Pacific hops – 40 lbs of a total of 540 lbs. The rest were all English from the 1915, 1916 and 1918 harvests, the latter two having been kept in a cold store.

1919 Truman XXX S		
pale malt	7.25 lb	62.13%
high dried malt	2.50 lb	21.42%
flaked maize	1.25 lb	10.71%
No. 2 invert sugar	0.67 lb	5.74%
Fuggles 90 mins	0.75 oz	
Fuggles 60 mins	0.75 oz	
Goldings 30 mins	0.75 oz	
OG	1052	
FG	1012.5	
ABV	5.23	
Apparent attenuation	75.96%	
IBU	27	
SRM	6	
Mash at	150° F	
Sparge at	170° F	
Boil time	90 minutes	
pitching temp	57.5° F	
Yeast	Wyeast 1028 London Ale (Worthington White Shield)	

1919 Truman XXX W

The gravity of the weaker version of XXX had also increased, in this case up by 10.5 points. A big improvement on the pathetically watery version of the previous year.

As on all their brewing records, Truman didn't bother to note exactly what type of sugar was being employed. No. 2 invert is my best guess.

The recipe details are identical to the XXX S above, with which this was parti-gyled.

1919 Truman XXX W		
pale malt	4.75 lb	59.38%
high dried malt	1.75 lb	21.88%
flaked maize	1.00 lb	12.50%
No. 2 invert sugar	0.50 lb	6.25%
Fuggles 90 mins	0.50 oz	
Fuggles 60 mins	0.50 oz	
Goldings 30 mins	0.50 oz	
OG	1035.5	
FG	1008	
ABV	3.64	
Apparent attenuation	77.46%	
IBU	20	
SRM	6	
Mash at	150° F	
Sparge at	170° F	
Boil time	90 minutes	
pitching temp	59° F	
Yeast	Wyeast 1028 London Ale (Worthington White Shield)	

1919 Truman XXX

This beer wasn't brewed, as such, but made from a blend of XXX S and XXX W post fermentation.

The blend looks remarkably like a 1920s 6d/7d Ale. The type of classier Mild that had an OG 1040-1045°. This type was one of the staple London beers after WW I, though most breweries also brewed a weaker Mild.

1919 Truman XXX		
pale malt	6.00 lb	63.16%
high dried malt	2.00 lb	21.05%
flaked maize	1.00 lb	10.53%
No. 2 invert sugar	0.50 lb	5.26%
Fuggles 90 mins	0.67 oz	
Fuggles 60 mins	0.67 oz	
Goldings 30 mins	0.67 oz	
OG	1044	
FG	1010.5	
ABV	4.43	
Apparent attenuation	76.14%	
IBU	25	
SRM	6	
Mash at	150° F	
Sparge at	170° F	
Boil time	90 minutes	
pitching temp	58° F	
Yeast	Wyeast 1028 London Ale (Worthington White Shield)	

1919 Truman XX

Next down in Truman's rather confusing range of Mild Ales was, logically enough, XX. With its OG of around 1030°, it looks much like a post-war 4d Ale. A type of cheap Mild Ale that was brewed in quite modest quantities.

The recipe is much like the XXX Ale above, save that XX includes a tiny amount of black malt, presumably simply for colour.

The hops are identical to XXX. Again with a tiny quantity of 1911 Pacific: 34 lbs out of 450 lbs.

1919 Truman XX		
pale malt	3.75 lb	55.23%
high dried malt	2.00 lb	29.46%
flaked maize	0.67 lb	9.87%
black malt	0.04 lb	0.59%
No. 2 invert sugar	0.33 lb	4.86%
Fuggles 90 mins	0.33 oz	
Fuggles 60 mins	0.33 oz	
Goldings 30 mins	0.33 oz	
OG	1030	
FG	1006	
ABV	3.18	
Apparent attenuation	80.00%	
IBU	14	
SRM	7	
Mash at	151° F	
Sparge at	170° F	
Boil time	90 minutes	
pitching temp	60° F	
Yeast	Wyeast 1028 London Ale (Worthington White Shield)	

1919 Truman 6d

As if they didn't already brew enough different Milds, Truman introduced a new one in 1919, 6d Ale. I'm not sure why, as it's very similar to a couple of their other beers.

Unsurprisingly, the recipe is very like Truman's other Milds: pale and high dried malt, flaked maize and a poorly-described sugar.

The hops are the same, too, with once again a very small quantity of old Pacific hops.

1919 Truman 6d		
pale malt	5.00 lb	55.56%
high dried malt	2.50 lb	27.78%
flaked maize	1.00 lb	11.11%
No. 2 invert sugar	0.50 lb	5.56%
Fuggles 90 mins	0.75 oz	
Fuggles 60 mins	0.50 oz	
Goldings 30 mins	0.50 oz	
OG	1040	
FG	1007	
ABV	4.37	
Apparent attenuation	82.50%	
IBU	23	
SRM	6.5	
Mash at	150° F	
Sparge at	170° F	
Boil time	90 minutes	
pitching temp	59° F	
Yeast	Wyeast 1028 London Ale (Worthington White Shield)	

1919 Truman X

Despite the easing of the situation, Truman continued to brew a very watery Mild, X, which was barely stronger than it had been the previous year.

Beers this weak weren't brewed much past war's end. There were watery Milds, but not quite this watery. Mostly they had gravities of at least 1027°

The recipe is identical to the XX above, with which it was parti-gyled.

1919 Truman X		
pale malt	3.00 lb	55.97%
high dried malt	1.50 lb	27.99%
flaked maize	0.50 lb	9.33%
black malt	0.03 lb	0.56%
No. 2 invert sugar	0.33 lb	6.16%
Fuggles 90 mins	0.25 oz	
Fuggles 60 mins	0.25 oz	
Goldings 30 mins	0.25 oz	
OG	1024	
FG	1005	
ABV	2.51	
Apparent attenuation	79.17%	
IBU	11	
SRM	6	
Mash at	151° F	
Sparge at	170° F	
Boil time	90 minutes	
pitching temp	60.5° F	
Yeast	Wyeast 1028 London Ale (Worthington White Shield)	

Truman (London)

Located in the Easy End of London, Truman had a very long history, having been established in 1666, just after the Great Fire of London. It was of the large Porter breweries in the 18th century and in the 18th century continued to be one of the largest breweries in the world. Though un the second half of the century it was overtaken by the likes of Guinness, Bass and Watney.

After a takeover battle between Grand Metropolitan Hotels and Watney, it was purchased by the former in 1971. The competition for Truman was intense because it was the last large, independent brewing company in the UK. Grand Metropolitan later bought Watney as well and merged it with Truman in 1974. Truman ceased brewing in 1989.

1916 Truman (London) X

In the summer of 1916, when this particular X Ale was brewed, nothing much had changed since the outbreak of war, other than the odd point or two being knocked off the OG of some beers.

Other than that, beers were much the same as they had always been. Truman's X Ale, at around 1050°, was fairly typical of a standard London Mild. AS was its grist of pale and crystal malt, flaked maize and sugar.

Unfortunately, all I know about the sugar is the name of the manufacturer: Fowler. I've guessed No. 3 invert as the most likely candidate. But it could just as easily have been No. 2 invert or something similar.

The period immediately before WW I is when Mild started to darken. But few had yet hit the dark brown that we would associate with Dark Mild today. They were more in the twilight zone between pale and dark, around 10-12 SRM. Darker enough to be distinguishable from Bitter, but not properly dark.

The hops weren't too old, Kent from 1914 and 1915, the former having been kept in a cold store, and Pacific from 1915. There are lots of them, too, as is reflected in the high (calculated) IBUs.

1916 Truman (London) X		
pale malt	7.75 lb	75.61%
crystal malt 60 L	0.25 lb	2.44%
flaked maize	1.00 lb	9.76%
No. 3 invert sugar	1.25 lb	12.20%
Cluster 90 mins	1.25 oz	
Fuggles 60 mins	2.00 oz	
Fuggles 30 mins	2.00 oz	
OG	1048.5	
FG	1014	
ABV	4.56	
Apparent attenuation	71.13%	
IBU	68	
SRM	11	
Mash at	150° F	
Sparge at	175° F	
Boil time	90 minutes	
pitching temp	60.5° F	
Yeast	Wyeast 1099 Whitbread Ale	

1916 Truman (London) LK

The Ale side of Truman's London operation was pretty dull. They only produced two beers: X Ale, a Mild, and LK, an Ordinary Bitter. There were other beers brewed in London, but they were on the Porter side.

The classier Bitters were sourced from Truman's Burton brewery. It's a strange setup Truman had. Just two Ales in London but a dozen or so in Burton, including several Mild Ales. I'm puzzled as to where all of these different beers were sold.

There's nothing complicated about LK. The grist is just pale malt, though there were five different kinds, three English, one Canadian and one Indian. The sugar is again just described as "Fowler". This time I've guessed No. 2 invert.

There's not a great deal of difference between the hopping rate of LK and X. I'm surprised by how little difference there often was between Bitter and Mild. I've assumed that LK was dry hopped. Bitters pretty well universally were. The copper hops are the same as in X Ale.

Parti-gyled with this was a slightly weaker version at 1040°. Which also seems to have been called LK. How confusing. Perhaps it was a bottling version. They were usually weaker than the draught version during WW I.

1916 Truman (London) LK		
pale malt	8.50 lb	87.18%
No. 2 invert sugar	1.25 lb	12.82%
Cluster 90 mins	1.75 oz	
Fuggles 60 mins	1.75 oz	
Fuggles 30 mins	1.75 oz	
Fuggles dry hops	0.25 oz	
OG	1044.5	
FG	1013	
ABV	4.17	
Apparent attenuation	70.79%	
IBU	76	
SRM	7	
Mash at	150° F	
Sparge at	168° F	
Boil time	90 minutes	
pitching temp	60.5° F	
Yeast	Wyeast 1099 Whitbread Ale	

1917 Truman (London) X

I'm surprised at how little X Ale has changed since the previous year. Especially the gravity, as this example was brewed in May, after the introduction of harsh new regulation on 1st April.

The specifications may have remained the same, but the recipe hasn't. Glucose has been added to the recipe, as has another sugar described as "B. Invert". I've again gone with No. 3, though that's purely a guess.

The FGs on all these Truman London recipes are guesses. There's no fermentation record on the brewing log as Truman had a separate "Square Book" for that.

The hops have changed, too. Now being something called C. F. and Sussex, both from the 1916 crop. I assume that the F stands for Farnhams. Not sure about what the C means. The hopping is again very heavy for a Mild Ale.

1917 Truman (London) X		
pale malt	9.00 lb	83.72%
crystal malt 60 L	0.33 lb	3.07%
flaked maize	0.67 lb	6.23%
glucose	0.25 lb	2.33%
No. 3 invert sugar	0.50 lb	4.65%
Fuggles 90 mins	2.00 oz	
Goldings 60 mins	1.75 oz	
Goldings 30 mins	1.75 oz	
OG	1048.5	
FG	1014	
ABV	4.56	
Apparent attenuation	71.13%	
IBU	69	
SRM	8	
Mash at	149° F	
Sparge at	175° F	
Boil time	90 minutes	
pitching temp	61° F	
Yeast	Wyeast 1099 Whitbread Ale	

1917 Truman (London) LK (May)

Remember me saying it was hard to figure out what the difference between Bitter and Mild was sometimes? Well here's a confusing one: this LK was parti-gyled with the X Ale above.

The only difference between the two is that, rather surprisingly, LK is the weaker of the two. I'm struggling to see what makes this a Bitter and X Ale a Mild. Possibly it's the dry-hopping. At some Scottish breweries at this time the only difference between beers called Mild and Pale Ale was that the latter were dry hopped.

I've assumed that was the case here. It would be pretty weird if Truman hadn't dry hopped a Bitter. There might well even have been more dry hops. Barclay Perkins XLK, which was an equivalent beer contained 0.5 oz of dry hops in a batch this size.

1917 Truman (London) LK (May)		
pale malt	7.75 lb	86.54%
crystal malt 60 L	0.25 lb	2.79%
flaked maize	0.50 lb	5.58%
glucose	0.125 lb	1.40%
No. 3 invert sugar	0.33 lb	3.69%
Fuggles 90 mins	1.50 oz	
Goldings 60 mins	1.50 oz	
Goldings 30 mins	1.50 oz	
Goldings dry hops	0.25 oz	
OG	1040	
FG	1012	
ABV	3.70	
Apparent attenuation	70.00%	
IBU	60	
SRM	7	
Mash at	149° F	
Sparge at	175° F	
Boil time	90 minutes	
pitching temp	61° F	
Yeast	Wyeast 1099 Whitbread Ale	

1917 Truman Government Ale

I was dead pleased to discover that one of the two Truman's brewing books Derek Prentice has in his office at the Wimbledon Brewery covers almost all of WW I.

It certainly has the most interesting period, i.e. 1917 and 1918, when brewers didn't to become inventive. This beer was brewed in July 1917, when the first set of heavy restrictions on brewing were just starting to bite. And when gravities began to plunge fearlessly from the roof.

It's basically a weakened version of their Mild, X Ale. That was still a respectable 1048.5° right up until June 1917, not much lower than the pre-war gravity of 1052.5°. This version of GA was the first step on the road to gravity Armageddon. A couple of years later and it would be firmly encamped in non-intoxicating territory.

There are a couple of significant differences between this recipe and X Ale. Almost certainly the result of restrictions or shortages. Out were flaked maize and liquid glucose, replaced by more pale malt. Ironic, in a way, that wartime problems improved the recipe.

It's a pretty simple recipe, containing just three ingredients: pale malt, crystal malt and sugar. All it says for the sugar is "Fowler", which I know was a producer of invert sugar. So I've guessed no. invert. There are half a dozen types of pale malt made from barley from different countries. So feel free to throw in some US six row if you fancy.

The hops are specified as Pacifics and CF. Pretty obvious that the first is Cluster, but I've no idea about the other. Pretty sure that they're English. Fuggles seems a safe bet, but you could also use Goldings. This being a Mild, my money would be on Fuggles.

For once, the BeerSmith calculated colour matches the original exactly. Not sure what that tells me.

1917 Truman GA		
pale malt	7.00 lb	86.63%
crystal malt 80 L	0.33 lb	4.08%
No. 2 invert sugar	0.75 lb	9.28%
Cluster 90 min	1.00 oz	
Fuggles 90 mins	0.50 oz	
Fuggles 60 mins	1.50 oz	
Fuggles 30 mins	1.50 oz	
OG	1036	
FG	1009	
ABV	3.57	
Apparent attenuation	75.00%	
IBU	65	
SRM	8	
Mash at	149° F	
Sparge at	175° F	
Boil time	90 minutes	
pitching temp	60.5° F	
Yeast	Wyeast 1099 Whitbread ale	

1917 Truman (London) LK (August)

A couple more months into 1917 and there have been more changes to LK. For a start, the gravity has dropped another four points.

The grist is a bit different, too. Gone is the flaked and glucose. What remains is pale and crystal malt plus B. Invert. I've substituted No. 3 invert sugar for the latter. This looks more like the Mild recipe from earlier in the year, with the inclusion of crystal malt.

The hops are CF from 1916 and Pacific from 1915.

1917 Truman (London) LK (August)		
pale malt	6.75 lb	87.10%
crystal malt 60 L	0.33 lb	4.26%
No. 3 invert sugar	0.67 lb	8.65%
Cluster 90 mins	1.50 oz	
Fuggles 60 mins	1.50 oz	
Fuggles 30 mins	1.50 oz	
Fuggles dry hops	0.25 oz	
OG	1036	
FG	1010	
ABV	3.44	
Apparent attenuation	72.22%	
IBU	70	
SRM	8.5	
Mash at	149° F	
Sparge at	175° F	
Boil time	90 minutes	
pitching temp	60.5° F	
Yeast	Wyeast 1099 Whitbread Ale	

1918 Truman (London) LK

The restrictions on brewing were relaxed slightly in the autumn of 1917 and that's reflected in the slight increased gravity of LK.

Not that it was going to last. Even more draconian measures came into effect in April 1918. Happy times they were not for drinkers. At least this version of LK is reasonably intoxicating.

By this point Truman had discontinued all the Pale Ales from their Burton brewery. LK was the only Bitter they were producing. It must have taken quite some getting used to for drinkers whose usual tipple was one of the strong Burton Bitters.

The grist is much like the previous recipe, except that flaked maize has returned. As before, I've substituted No, 3 invert sugar for what's described as "B. Invert" in the brewing record.

The hops are Kent form the 1915 and 1916 crop, the former having been kept in a cold store, plus Pacific from 1915.

1918 Truman (London) LK		
pale malt	7.25 lb	87.03%
crystal malt 60 L	0.25 lb	3.00%
flaked maize	0.50 lb	6.00%
No. 3 invert sugar	0.33 lb	3.96%
Cluster 90 mins	0.75 oz	
Fuggles 60 mins	1.00 oz	
Fuggles 30 mins	1.00 oz	
Fuggles dry hops	0.25 oz	
OG	1037.5	
FG	1011	
ABV	3.51	
Apparent attenuation	70.67%	
IBU	40	
SRM	7	
Mash at	148° F	
Sparge at	168° F	
Boil time	90 minutes	
pitching temp	62.5° F	
Yeast	Wyeast 1099 Whitbread Ale	

1918 Truman (London) Government Ale

The gravity of GA, on the other hand, has fallen a few points since the previous year.

The grist has changed, too. Most notably through the addition of caramel, I'm guessing to offset the effect on the colour of the falling gravity. Flaked maize seems to come and go in Truman's recipes of this period. Possibly because they couldn't always get hold of it. The No. 3 invert is my substitution for a sugar described simply as "Fowler".

The hops were identical to the LK above. This is much more lightly hopped than the Truman Milds from earlier in the war.

1918 Truman (London) GA		
pale malt	6.25 lb	81.97%
crystal malt 60 L	0.33 lb	4.33%
flaked maize	0.67 lb	8.79%
No. 3 invert sugar	0.25 lb	3.28%
caramel 500 SRM	0.125 lb	1.64%
Cluster 90 mins	0.50 oz	
Fuggles 60 mins	0.75 oz	
Fuggles 30 mins	0.75 oz	
OG	1033	
FG	1009	
ABV	3.18	
Apparent attenuation	72.73%	
IBU	30	
SRM	10	
Mash at	149° F	
Sparge at	175° F	
Boil time	90 minutes	
pitching temp	62° F	
Yeast	Wyeast 1099 Whitbread Ale	

1918 Truman (London) X

Surprisingly, as late as January 1918 Truman was still brewing some X Ale at just about full strength.

At least that's what it looks like they were doing. But in later 1917, though they were brewing the strong version of X Ale, they were watering it down after primary fermentation to an effective OG of 1043°. I suspect they were still doing the same in 1918, just that it isn't noted down on the brewing records.

All the recipe details are the same as the Government Ale above, with which this beer was parti-gyled.

1918 Truman (London) X		
pale malt	8.75 lb	81.36%
crystal malt 60 L	0.50 lb	4.65%
flaked maize	1.00 lb	9.30%
No. 3 invert sugar	0.33 lb	3.07%
caramel 500 SRM	0.175 lb	1.63%
Cluster 90 mins	0.75 oz	
Fuggles 60 mins	1.00 oz	
Fuggles 30 mins	1.00 oz	
OG	1047	
FG	1014	
ABV	4.37	
Apparent attenuation	70.21%	
IBU	38	
SRM	13	
Mash at	149° F	
Sparge at	175° F	
Boil time	90 minutes	
pitching temp	62° F	
Yeast	Wyeast 1099 Whitbread Ale	

Whitbread

Another one of the big Porter brewers, Whitbread was located on Chiswell Street in the City of London. From 1742 to 1976, when it closed. Quite a few bits of the brewery remain and are used as a conference centre. Quite nice Georgian architecture.

Ales

Since the 1830s Whitbread had brewed Ales and by the time WW I erupted, they brewed eight different ones: a Mild, four Pale Ales and three Burton Ales, This is what happened to them during the war:

Whitbread Ales 1914 - 1919								
	X	FA	IPA	PA	2PA	KK	2KK	KKK
Aug 1914	1055.12	1048.48	1049.86	1061.11	1053.21	1072.71	1077.98	1081.99
Jan 1916	1050.97	1045.43	1047.09	1056.54	1048.06			1069.58
July 1916	1047.92		1046.26	1051.91				
Mar 1917	1045.48		1046.76	1050.28				1069.97
May 1917	1044.49	1045.84	1047.12	1045.29				
July 1917		1033.41	1045.62	1045.29				
Oct 1917		1035.32	1039.03	1047.59				
Jun 1918		1032.69	1032.69	1035.07				
Oct 1918		1032.41	1032.41	1035.21				
Dec 1918		1032.41	1032.41					
Feb 1919		1032.13	1032.13	1041.02				
Mar 1919		1032.41	1032.41	1036.12				
Source: Whitbread brewing records held at the London metropolitan archives								

Known as PA or Pale Ale within the brewery, Bitter was, as today, part of the standard pub draught range. The style was increasing in popularity and in London was already beginning to rival Mild. In 1881, PA was just 5% of Whitbread's Ale output. By 1891, it was up to 10%; by 1901 23%; by 1910 23%. However, most of this wasn't the strong PA, but the weaker 2PA and FA, which were around 1050° in 1914.

In 1914 standard PA had a gravity in the range 1055-1060° and was hopped at 1.75 to 2.5 pounds per barrel, 9 to 12 pounds per quarter of malt. The alcohol content was fairly modest for the gravity, as it was usually only 65-70% attenuated, giving it about 5.5% ABV.

Of all the major styles, Bitter suffered least from wartime gravity cuts. It wouldn't fare so well in WW II.

A table in the section on Pale Ale above shows the changes in Whitbread PA during the war years.

Porter and Stout

The table shows Whitbread's Ale and Porter output for the years 1902 to 1926. Very interesting reading it makes. Not exactly what I had expected.

Whitbread Ale and Porter output 1902 – 1926					
	Ale		Porter		total
Year	barrels	%	barrels	%	
1902	502,200	67.06%	246,628	32.94%	748,828
1903	511,092	65.69%	266,940	34.31%	778,032
1904	507,966	64.52%	279,337	35.48%	787,303
1905	503,748	63.29%	292,192	36.71%	795,940
1906	522,869	63.84%	296,156	36.16%	819,025
1907	528,984	63.29%	306,786	36.71%	835,770
1908	497,805	61.48%	311,891	38.52%	809,696
1909	496,975	61.10%	316,355	38.90%	813,330
1910	459,662	57.36%	341,673	42.64%	801,335
1911	505,889	59.19%	348,841	40.81%	854,730
1912	564,047	60.65%	365,978	39.35%	930,025
1913	494,149	57.99%	358,021	42.01%	852,170
1914	485,167	57.26%	362,105	42.74%	847,272
1915	423,543	58.55%	299,881	41.45%	723,424
1916	394,208	53.16%	347,384	46.84%	741,592
1917	286,662	51.06%	274,788	48.94%	561,450
1918	285,033	72.91%	105,902	27.09%	390,935
1919	426,099	79.59%	109,273	20.41%	535,372
1920	479,024	68.32%	222,114	31.68%	701,138
1921	423,722	65.10%	227,160	34.90%	650,882
1922	370,237	66.72%	184,693	33.28%	554,930
1923	314,657	65.72%	164,147	34.28%	478,804
1924	366,482	68.02%	172,341	31.98%	538,823
1925	349,232	68.52%	160,453	31.48%	509,685
1926	325,848	66.75%	162,329	33.25%	488,177
Source: Whitbread archive document number LMA/4453/D/02/16 **Note:** Year ending July					

Starting at about a third of total output in 1902, the percentage of Porter and Stout increased steadily before WW I. By 1914, it was almost 43%. It peaked just shy of 50% in 1917. There was a big change in 1918, when its share almost halved. 1919 was even worse, at just over 20%. Post-war it soon got back to over 30%, about the same level as in 1902.

This is a breakdown of the Porter figures for the specific beers:

Whitbread Porter and Stout output by type 1902 – 1920								
	P	C	CS	S	SS	SSS	Extra S	total	% Porter
1902	79,512	34,848	74,832	3,945	43,412	10,439		246,988	32.19%
1903	77,266	33,664	90,843	3,582	50,173	11,410		266,938	28.95%
1904	79,673	29,757	101,169	3,298	53,104	12,334		279,335	28.52%
1905	84,251	23,818	115,553	3,285	38,957	13,236	13,090	292,190	28.83%
1906	77,943	19,023	129,501	3,311	34,490	16,345	15,540	296,153	26.32%
1907	77,140	12,053	146,007	1,370	34,648	15,184	20,381	306,783	25.14%
1908	75,092	8,241	157,975	1,085	33,722	14,104	21,671	311,890	24.08%
1909	72,493	5,393	169,243	912	30,998	13,308	24,006	316,353	22.92%
1910	106,224		171,746	789	26,494	10,062	26,356	341,671	31.09%
1911	92,915		189,638	670	25,156	10,780	29,320	348,479	26.66%
1912	87,376		210,033	508	24,927	10,468	32,665	365,977	23.87%
1913	77,068		205,971	419	26,975	10,731	36,855	358,019	21.53%
1914	72,113		211,492	416	25,381	10,567	42,134	362,103	19.92%
1915	69,237		183,419	678	22,471	8,217	15,857	299,879	23.09%
1916	75,853		222,046	550	26,534	7,135	15,265	347,383	21.84%
1917	60,951		171,817	340	22,019	7,497	12,101	274,725	22.19%
1918	36,421		61,956			7,524		105,901	34.39%
1919	38,455		65,484		4,021		1,312	109,272	35.19%
1920	21,597		133,406		44,707		22,404	222,114	9.72%
Source: Whitbread archive document number LMA/4453/D/02/16 Note: Year ending July									

Porter output was around 70,000 barrels for most years up until 1918, when it slumped to just 36,000 barrels. Its share of Whitbread's Porter and Stout production fell from 25-30% to under 10%. So although as a whole Porter and Stout recovered to around their pre-war levels, a much higher proportion was in the form of Stout.

So what are my conclusions? Porter and Stout production did decline more than Ale in the last war years. But by the early 1920's was pretty much back to its pre-war level. However post-war the proportion that was Porter was much smaller than it had ever been before. 1918 seems to have been the pivotal year. Whitbread Porter sales never again exceeded 40,000 barrels a year.

Was a shortage of brown and black malt the reason for the drop in Porter and Stout production 1918-1920? I don't think so. The proportion of those malts used remained fairly constant. The fall in Porter brewing coincides with the appearance of brown malt in Mild grists. It seems that because they were brewing less Porter and Stout, there was spare roasted malts available for use in other beers.

1914 Whitbread P

Whitbread had been one of the largest London Porter breweries in the 18th and 19h centuries. Porter remained an important product for them on the eve of WW I.

In the year ending July 1914, they brewed 123,085 barrels of Porter out of a total of 900,636 barrels. Only X Ale, London Stout and IPA were brewed in larger quantities, though only around 400 barrels of IPA were brewed.[41]

It was always brewed in a parti-gyle with London Stout, though often there were often only a couple of gravity point between the two.

1914 Whitbread P		
pale malt	8.25 lb	68.52%
brown malt	1.50 lb	12.46%
black malt	1.25 lb	10.38%
oats	0.04 lb	0.33%
No. 3 invert sugar	1.00 lb	8.31%
Fuggles 105 mins	0.75 oz	
Fuggles 90 mins	0.75 oz	
Goldings 30 mins	0.75 oz	
OG	1052	
FG	1013	
ABV	5.16	
Apparent attenuation	75.00%	
IBU	28	
SRM	39	
Mash at	153° F	
Sparge at	168° F	
Boil time	105 minutes	
pitching temp	61° F	
Yeast	Wyeast 1099 Whitbread Ale	

---

[41] Whitbread brewing record held at the London Metropolitan Archives, document number LMA/4453/D/09/108.

1914 Whitbread LS

Like all the old London Porter breweries, Whitbread brewed a range of Stouts. Some Stouter than others.

Their London Stout wasn't the stoutest by any means. It was barely stronger than their Porter, just 2 or 3 gravity points. The two were often parti-gyled together.

The presence of that tiny quantity of oats speaks volumes. They must have been selling some of this beer as Oatmeal Stout. London brewers were notorious for throwing in miniscule quantities of oats into a Porter/Stout parti-gyle so they could market some as the then trendy Oatmeal Stout. Did anyone drinking the Porter parti-gyled with this realise it was an Oatmeal Porter? I doubt it, given the quantities.

Other than the token oats, the grist is a classic London combination of pale, brown and black malt. Plus some invert sugar. The high percentage of roasted malts results in a pretty darn black beer. And, despite me reducing the hopping rate for more than half of the hops coming from the 1912 season, it's still pretty bitter.

Talking of the hops, they're a flush of the Kents: Kent, East Kent and Mid Kent. The malt was, unusually, all from English barley. Hutchison (½ + ½) and Thetford, if you're interested.

It was a monster brew, 530 barrels of Porter and 814 of LS. With more than three quarters of a ton of hops.

1914 Whitbread LS		
pale malt	9.00 lb	68.97%
brown malt	1.75 lb	13.41%
black malt	1.25 lb	9.58%
oats	0.05 lb	0.38%
No. 3 invert sugar	1.00 lb	7.66%
Fuggles 105 mins	0.75 oz	
Fuggles 90 mins	0.75 oz	
Goldings 30 mins	0.75 oz	
OG	1056	
FG	1016	
ABV	5.29	
Apparent attenuation	71.43%	
IBU	28	
SRM	40	
Mash at	153° F	
Sparge at	168° F	
Boil time	105 minutes	
pitching temp	61° F	
Yeast	Wyeast 1099 Whitbread Ale	

1914 Whitbread ES

Extra Stout was one of Whitbread's weaker Stouts. And, unlike their other Black Beers, was always brewed single-gyle. I say always, it was only brewed once before WW I. Though it did reappear in the early 1920's.

But you can see that it's a classier beer than London Stout from the composition of its grist. Specifically in the presence of amber malt. While the classic London Porter/Stout grist was pale, brown and black malt, the classier versions often included a big dose of amber malt.

London Stouts remained true to their origin as Beers and always had a very healthy dosing of hops. What strikes me about Whitbread is their use of exclusively English hops. Which was pretty rare before the war kicked off. This beer being brewed just a few weeks before the apocalypse on the 17th July.

I just noticed that some of the base malt is from Earp, a Newark maltster. My secondary school was on a street named in his honour, Earp Avenue. There's so much brewing and malting related stuff I never noticed as a kid.

The hops in the original were East Kent and Mid Kent from the 1912 and 1913 seasons.

1914 Whitbread ES		
pale malt	8.25 lb	56.90%
brown malt	1.25 lb	8.62%
black malt	1.00 lb	6.90%
amber malt	2.25 lb	15.52%
No. 3 invert sugar	1.75 lb	12.07%
Fuggles 115 mins	1.50 oz	
Goldings 90 mins	1.50 oz	
Goldings 30 mins	1.50 oz	
OG	1067	
FG	1020	
ABV	6.22	
Apparent attenuation	70.15%	
IBU	53	
SRM	37	
Mash at	150° F	
Sparge at	170° F	
Boil time	115 minutes	
pitching temp	57° F	
Yeast	Wyeast 1099 Whitbread Ale	

1914 Whitbread Export Stout

Like Extra Stout, Export Stout was always brewed single-gyle. Which wasn't so strange, given the hopping. It was brewed in tiny quantities: just 1,022 barrels in the year ending July 1914.[42]

There are couple of signs that this was a posh beer. There's a large amount of amber malt in the grist and all the hops were East Kent. Also, the base malt isn't plain pale malt but PA (Pale Ale) malt, which was the highest quality. The percentage of roasted malts, at well over 30%, is extremely high. Unsurprisingly, the beer is very dark in colour.

As was usual with export beers, it was more heavily hopped than domestic beers, with 13 lbs per quarter of malt. In contrast, Porter and Stout were hopped at just 5 lbs per quarter and SS and SSS at 8lbs. I've reduced the hipping rate a little because some of the hops were from the 1912 season.

The original may well have been vatted before leaving the brewery. Unfortunately, there's no way of knowing that for sure.

1914 Whitbread Export Stout		
pale malt	7.50 lb	50.00%
brown malt	1.50 lb	10.00%
black malt	1.00 lb	6.67%
amber malt	2.50 lb	16.67%
No. 3 invert sugar	2.50 lb	16.67%
Goldings 115 mins	2.75 oz	
Goldings 90 mins	2.75 oz	
Goldings 30 mins	2.75 oz	
OG	1071	
FG	1018	
ABV	7.01	
Apparent attenuation	74.65%	
IBU	96	
SRM	40	
Mash at	157° F	
Sparge at	170° F	
Boil time	115 minutes	
pitching temp	57° F	
Yeast	Wyeast 1099 Whitbread Ale	

---

[42] Whitbread brewing record held at the London Metropolitan Archives, document number LMA/4453/D/09/108.

1914 Whitbread SS

Double Stout was one of Whitbread's oldest products. It turns up in their earliest brewing record to survive, from 1805.

Its strength had remained remarkably constant over the years, essentially unchanged between 1837 and 1914. In the 19th century, it wasn't a huge seller, between 10,000 and 15,000 barrels a year were brewed annually between 1874 and 1900. It gained popularity in the 20th century, with 40,000 to 50,000 barrels a year being brewed in the decade before WWI. It was always parti-gyled with SSS.

The grist is very similar to Export Stout's, including a large percentage of amber malt. Roasted malts make up more than 35% of the grist.

The hops are described as MK, EK and DK. No idea what the latter stands for. Obviously, they're from somewhere in Kent, but I can't for the life of me work out what the "D" means. You'll note that Whitbread liked to use exclusively English hops. Even more specific than that: all Kent hops. This was unusual before WW I when large quantities of hops were imported. AS some of the hops for this brew were from the 1912 harvest, I've reduced the hopping a little.

1914 Whitbread SS		
pale malt	9.25 lb	51.39%
brown malt	2.25 lb	12.50%
black malt	1.00 lb	5.56%
amber malt	3.25 lb	18.06%
No. 3 invert sugar	2.25 lb	12.50%
Fuggles 115 mins	2.00 oz	
Goldings 90 mins	2.00 oz	
Goldings 30 mins	2.00 oz	
OG	1082	
FG	1020	
ABV	8.20	
Apparent attenuation	75.61%	
IBU	65	
SRM	42	
Mash at	155° F	
Sparge at	170° F	
Boil time	115 minutes	
pitching temp	57° F	
Yeast	Wyeast 1099 Whitbread Ale	

1914 Whitbread SSS

Triple Stout was another long-standing Whitbread product. It seems to have first been brewed in the 1930's, though there were some years in the 1840's 1850's and 1870's when none was brewed. After 1867, it was brewed continuously.

Surprisingly, in the 1870's and 1880's, more SSS was brewed than SS, between 15,000 and 18,000 barrels, so still not a huge amount. It was overtaken by SS in the 1880's. In the decade before WW I, 10,000 to 12,000 barrels were brewed annually.

As this beer was parti-gyled with the SS above, all the comments on ingredients there count for this, too.

A Stout of this strength would certainly have been aged before sale, probably by vatting. My guess would be that it would have had a minimum of 12 months in oak.

1914 Whitbread SSS		
pale malt	10.50 lb	51.85%
brown malt	2.50 lb	12.35%
black malt	1.25 lb	6.17%
amber malt	3.50 lb	17.28%
No. 3 invert sugar	2.50 lb	12.35%
Fuggles 115 mins	2.25 oz	
Goldings 90 mins	2.25 oz	
Goldings 30 mins	2.25 oz	
OG	1095	
FG	1027	
ABV	9.00	
Apparent attenuation	71.58%	
IBU	69	
SRM	47	
Mash at	155° F	
Sparge at	170° F	
Boil time	115 minutes	
pitching temp	57° F	
Yeast	Wyeast 1099 Whitbread Ale	

1914 Whitbread X

When war erupted, X Ale was Whitbread's biggest seller, with 274,247 barrels brewed in the year ending July 1914. That was about 30% of their total output.[43]

Like most of the large London breweries, Whitbread brewed a single Mild before the war. It's odd that they only made one example of the most popular style. The war would change that.

The recipe isn't quite as simple as it looks as it contained four different types of pale malt. Mostly English, but 17% was malt from Indian-grown barley. The type of sugar isn't specified in the brewing record. I've guessed No. 3 invert. A reasonable guess, as for some other brews of X earlier in the year specifically say No. 3.

The hops are listed a Pacific and two types of MK. I've reduced the hopping rate as these were all from the 1913 harvest (this beer was brewed in October).

1914 Whitbread X		
pale malt	9.00 lb	80.00%
No. 3 invert sugar	2.25 lb	20.00%
Cluster 115 mins	0.50 oz	
Fuggles 90 mins	0.50 oz	
Fuggles 60 mins	0.75 oz	
Fuggles 30 mins	0.75 oz	
OG	1055	
FG	1017	
ABV	5.03	
Apparent attenuation	69.09%	
IBU	32	
SRM	14	
Mash at	156° F	
Sparge at	168° F	
Boil time	115 minutes	
pitching temp	60° F	
Yeast	Wyeast 1099 Whitbread Ale	

---

[43] Whitbread brewing record held at the London Metropolitan Archives, document number LMA/4453/D/01/079.

1914 Whitbread IPA

Before the war, IPA was Whitbread's biggest selling Pale Ale, 123,509 barrels being brewed in the year ending July 1914.[44]

First brewed in 1900, it was Whitbread's joint weakest Pale Ale, along with Family Ale. After WW I it was only available in bottled form. It may have been available on draught before the war, but I have no evidence about that. Whitbread was unusual it bottling a large percentage of its beer. 1n 1914, 49.38% was draught, 50.45% bottled.[45] Most breweries were 80-90% draught at the time.

Like all Whitbread's Ales, it has a very simple recipe of just base malt and sugar. The malt is of just two types, 27% Smyrna, i.e. from the Middle East and 73% Earp. Which I know came from my home town of Newark.

The hops are all East Kent, from the 1912 and 1913 crop (this beer was brewed 6th October), but most had been in a cold store. So I've only reduced the hopping a little.

What makes a beer an IPA? Whitbread's Pale Ale, which they'd brewed since 1st November 1865[46], had an OG 0f 1061° in 1914, a good bit higher than the IPA. But IPA was more heavily hopped, 12 lbs per quarter of malt compared to 9 lbs. That's the same level of hopping as their Burton Ales, KK and KKK.

1914 Whitbread IPA		
pale malt	8.50 lb	82.93%
No. 1 invert sugar	1.75 lb	17.07%
Goldings 110 mins	1.50 oz	
Goldings 60 mins	1.50 oz	
Goldings 30 mins	1.50 oz	
Goldings dry hops	0.50 oz	
OG	1050	
FG	1015	
ABV	4.63	
Apparent attenuation	70.00%	
IBU	59	
SRM	6	
Mash at	158° F	
Sparge at	165° F	
Boil time	110 minutes	
pitching temp	58.5° F	
Yeast	Wyeast 1099 Whitbread Ale	

---

[44] Whitbread brewing record held at the London Metropolitan Archives, document number LMA/4453/D/01/079.
[45] Whitbread document number LMA/4453/D/02/16 held at the London Metropolitan Archives.
[46] Whitbread brewing record held at the London Metropolitan Archives, document number LMA/4453/D/01/030.

1914 Whitbread Family Ale

I've always loved the name Family Ale. I remember Tetley's, which was a sort of bottled Dark Mild.

The name is meant to convey the idea that it's a beer for drinking at home with the family. I know that Whitbread's was sold in bottled form, though I'm not sure if it was exclusively available in that format. It was one of Whitbread's earliest Pale Ales, first being brewed in 1873.

FA is a very similar strength to Whitbread's IPA, just one point weaker. It's not quite as heavily hopped, 10 lbs per quarter of malt to IPA's 12 lbs. But it's more heavily hopped than the stronger PA and 2PA.

The grist is very simple: pale malt and No. 1 invert sugar. Smyrna malt made up 28% of the grist, the other 72% being PA malt from Earp in Newark.

The hops were all East Kent, so most likely Goldings or something similar. They were from the 1912 and 1913 crop, but around half had been in a cold stroe so I haven't knocked the quantity down too much.

1914 Whitbread FA		
pale malt	7.75 lb	79.49%
No. 1 invert sugar	2.00 lb	20.51%
Goldings 90 mins	1.25 oz	
Goldings 60 mins	1.25 oz	
Goldings 30 mins	1.25 oz	
Goldings dry hops	0.25 oz	
OG	1049	
FG	1015	
ABV	4.50	
Apparent attenuation	69.39%	
IBU	49	
SRM	6	
Mash at	158° F	
Sparge at	160° F	
Boil time	90 minutes	
pitching temp	58.5° F	
Yeast	Wyeast 1099 Whitbread Ale	

1914 Whitbread 2PA

Whitbread brewed a confusing array of very similar Pale Ales in 1914. I'm not sure what the point of such similar beers was.

Introduced in 188 as a weaker version of their Pale Ale, it soon outstripped it in terms of sales. In the year ending in July 1914, Whitbread brewed 6,311 barrels of PA and 36,234 barrels of 2PA.

29% of the pale malt was Smyrna, the rest Earp PA. The hops were all East Kent from the 1912 and 1913 crop.

1914 Whitbread 2PA		
pale malt	8.50 lb	79.07%
No. 1 invert sugar	2.25 lb	20.93%
Goldings 105 mins	1.25 oz	
Goldings 60 mins	1.25 oz	
Goldings 30 mins	1.25 oz	
Goldings dry hops	0.25 oz	
OG	1053	
FG	1018	
ABV	4.63	
Apparent attenuation	66.04%	
IBU	48	
SRM	7	
Mash at	156° F	
Sparge at	165° F	
Boil time	105 minutes	
pitching temp	57° F	
Yeast	Wyeast 1099 Whitbread Ale	

1914 Whitbread PA

PA was the first Pale Ale that Whitbread brewed, starting on November 1st, 1865. It was one of Whitbread's longest-lived products, still being brewed at Chiswell Street when the brewery closed 1976. In fact, it was the very last brew there.[47] Though the final versions had an OG not much morethan half of this, 1036°.[48]

This beer was parti-gyled with the 2PA above. Everything I said about that beer applies here as well.

In strength, this is similar to Burton Pale Ales, which usually had an OG in the 1060°-1065° range.

1914 Whitbread PA		
pale malt	10.00 lb	80.00%
No. 1 invert sugar	2.50 lb	20.00%
Goldings 105 mins	1.50 oz	
Goldings 60 mins	1.50 oz	
Goldings 30 mins	1.50 oz	
Goldings dry hops	0.50 oz	
OG	1061	
FG	1021	
ABV	5.29	
Apparent attenuation	65.57%	
IBU	54	
SRM	8	
Mash at	156° F	
Sparge at	165° F	
Boil time	105 minutes	
pitching temp	58.5° F	
Yeast	Wyeast 1099 Whitbread Ale	

---

[47] "London Brewed" by Mike Brown, The Brewery History Society, 2015, page 10.
[48] Whitbread brewing record held at the London Metropolitan Archives, document number LMA/4453/D/09/141.

1914 Whitbread KK

KK was Whitbread's standard draught Burton Ale. They'd brewed it since at least 1844, which wasn't long after they first started brewing Ales.

It's hard to believe that beers this strong were standard draughts before WW I. The ABV would have been higher at time of sale as I've given the racking gravity. KK would have been aged at least a couple of months, possibly more. By this time, I think in trade cask rather than vats.

You're probably seeing a theme in these Whitbread Ale grists. They're all just base malt and invert sugar. With no crystal malt anywhere to be seen.

The malt is 31% Smyrna, 50% PA (Pale Ale) malt and 19% SA (Stock Ale) malt. The latter is a base malt kilned in way that produces a less fermentable malt. Presumably to leave more material to slowly ferment during maturation.

The hops are all described as East Kent and Mid Kent, which I've interpreted as Goldings and Fuggles, respectively. All from the 1913 season.

1914 Whitbread KK		
pale malt	13.75 lb	85.00%
No. 3 invert sugar	1.5 lb	15.00%
Fuggles 105 mins	2.25 oz	
Goldings 60 mins	2.25 oz	
Goldings 30 mins	2.25 oz	
Goldings dry hops	0.50 oz	
OG	1071	
FG	1027	
ABV	5.82	
Apparent attenuation	61.97%	
IBU	74	
SRM	12	
Mash at	158° F	
Sparge at	180° F	
Boil time	105 minutes	
pitching temp	60° F	
Yeast	Wyeast 1099 Whitbread Ale	

1914 Whitbread 2KKK

In 1888, Whitbread introduced 2KK, a new Stock Ale that fitted, gravity-wise, between their existing KK and KKK.

I'm not sure why they did this. Maybe there was a demand for something slightly weaker – and cheaper – that their exiting KKK. In the run-up to WW I, Whitbread 2,000 – 3,000 barrels of 2KKK. Which was about double the amount of KKK and half the amount of KK. That's not a huge amount. All three Stock Ales combined only amounted to a little over 1% of their total output. I'm surprised that they breed three different variations when the total sales were so small.

As this would have been aged, the FG when sold would have been lower than shown below.

1914 Whitbread 2KK		
pale malt	15 lb	84.62%
No. 3 invert sugar	1.75 lb	15.38%
Fuggles 105 mins	2.50 oz	
Goldings 60 mins	2.50 oz	
Goldings 30 mins	2.50 oz	
Goldings dry hops	0.50 oz	
OG	1078	
FG	1026	
ABV	6.88	
Apparent attenuation	66.67%	
IBU	78	
SRM	13	
Mash at	158° F	
Sparge at	180° F	
Boil time	105 minutes	
pitching temp	60° F	
Yeast	Wyeast 1099 Whitbread Ale	

1914 Whitbread KKK

This completes the full range of Whitbread's beers in 1914. There are fourteen in total: 1 Porter, 5 Stouts, 1 Mild, 4 Pale Ales and 3 Stock Ales. We'll see later how many of them made it through the war alive.

1914 Whitbread KKK		
pale malt	16.00 lb	90.14%
No. 3 invert sugar	1.75 lb	9.86%
Fuggles 105 mins	2.75 oz	
Goldings 60 mins	2.75 oz	
Goldings 30 mins	2.75 oz	
Goldings dry hops	0.75 oz	
OG	1082	
FG	1028	
ABV	7.14	
Apparent attenuation	65.85%	
IBU	83	
SRM	13	
Mash at	158° F	
Sparge at	180° F	
Boil time	105 minutes	
pitching temp	60° F	
Yeast	Wyeast 1099 Whitbread Ale	

1916 Whitbread X

Half way through the war and not a lot about Whitbread X Ale has changed. The relative calm wouldn't last much longer.

The gravity is down four points at 1051°. Though that still looks very strong for a Mild to modern eyes. The only change to the recipe is that the proportion of sugar has decreased. The hops are a little on the old side, being Mid-Kents from the 1914 harvest (this beer was brewed in January 1916).

The rate of attenuation has increased considerably since 1914, from 69% to 80%. Were Whitbread trying to compensate for the fall in gravity?

Not much more to be said, other than: enjoy strong Mild while it's still around.

1916 Whitbread X		
pale malt	10.50 lb	93.33%
No. 3 invert sugar	0.75 lb	6.67%
Fuggles 105 mins	0.75 oz	
Fuggles 60 mins	0.75 oz	
Fuggles 30 mins	0.75 oz	
OG	1051	
FG	1010	
ABV	5.42	
Apparent attenuation	80.39%	
IBU	32	
SRM	8	
Mash at	156° F	
Sparge at	168° F	
Boil time	105 minutes	
pitching temp	60° F	
Yeast	Wyeast 1099 Whitbread Ale	

1916 Whitbread IPA

The story with IPA is similar to X, with minimal changes having occurred since the outbreak of war.

The OG has fallen by three points and again there's been a shift in the proportions of malt and sugar. Though this time in the favour of sugar. I've no idea why that might have been.

1916 Whitbread IPA		
pale malt	7.50 lb	78.95%
No. 2 invert sugar	2.00 lb	21.05%
Goldings 90 mins	1.50 oz	
Goldings 60 mins	1.50 oz	
Goldings 30 mins	1.50 oz	
Goldings dry hops	0.50 oz	
OG	1047	
FG	1015	
ABV	4.23	
Apparent attenuation	68.09%	
IBU	60	
SRM	6	
Mash at	152° F	
Sparge at	168° F	
Boil time	105 minutes	
pitching temp	60° F	
Yeast	Wyeast 1099 Whitbread Ale	

1916 Whitbread PA

Just like X Ale and IPA, PA hadn't changed a huge amount since the start of the war.

The gravity has dropped four points, but it's still an impressive 1057°. Don't be fooled by the apparent poor degree of attenuation as I'm sure that this was brewed as a Stock Ale. A long, slow secondary fermentation would have boosted the attenuation to at least 75-80%.

The recipe is near-identical to that of 1914, the only change being a slightly smaller percentage of invert sugar. I'm not sure about the sugar, as Whitbread couldn't be arsed to note down the type in the brewing record. Pretty sure it was either No. 1 or No. 2. Take your pick.

It's hopped at just about exactly the same rate per barrel as IPA, despite the latter being significantly weaker. The hops were all East Kent from the 1914 season, but as around half had been in a cold store, I've not reduced the quantities by much. This was also brewed in January 1916.

1916 Whitbread PA		
pale malt	9.75 lb	82.98%
No. 2 invert sugar	2.00 lb	17.02%
Goldings 90 mins	1.50 oz	
Goldings 60 mins	1.50 oz	
Goldings 30 mins	1.50 oz	
Goldings dry hops	0.50 oz	
OG	1057	
FG	1020	
ABV	4.89	
Apparent attenuation	64.91%	
IBU	56	
SRM	7	
Mash at	151° F	
Sparge at	165° F	
Boil time	90 minutes	
pitching temp	60° F	
Yeast	Wyeast 1099 Whitbread Ale	

1916 Whitbread KKK

Nothing much had happened at Whitbread in early 1916. Their beers had changed little since the outbreak of hostilities.

KKK is proof of that. Unlike most of Whitbread's other beers, the OG is unchanged at 1082°. The hopping ng is near-identical, too. The only real change since 1914 is in the sugar, the proportion of which has doubled. As I've assumed that it's No. 3 invert, the colour of the finished beer is a good bit darker.

Sadly, KKK wasn't around much longer, disappearing in 1917, never to return.

1916 Whitbread KKK		
pale malt	13.00 lb	78.79%
No. 3 invert sugar	3.50 lb	21.21%
Goldings 90 mins	2.75 oz	
Goldings 60 mins	2.75 oz	
Goldings 30 mins	2.75 oz	
Goldings dry hops	0.75 oz	
OG	1082	
FG	1028	
ABV	7.14	
Apparent attenuation	65.85%	
IBU	86	
SRM	19	
Mash at	148° F	
Sparge at	180° F	
Boil time	105 minutes	
pitching temp	60° F	
Yeast	Wyeast 1099 Whitbread Ale	

1917 Whitbread P

Whitbread's Porter retained a decent gravity for a surprisingly long time, still being around 1050° until April 1918.

Unusually, this brew was single-gyle. Whitbread mostly parti-gyled a Stout of some description with their Porter. And that's probably why it lacks the oats in the 1914 recipe. When they wanted to sell some of the parti-gyled Stout as Oatmeal Stout, the Porter ended up with oats in it. Though the quantity was so small, I'm sure no-one noticed.

I love the simplicity of Whitbread's brews, just malt and a single sugar. The grist is the classic London combination of pale, brown and black, with a bit of sugar. No. 3 is a guess, but, I think, a reasonable one.

The hops were EK from the 1915 and 1916 seasons, and MK from 1916.

1917 Whitbread Porter		
pale malt	8.00 lb	68.09%
brown malt	1.50 lb	12.77%
black malt	1.25 lb	10.64%
No. 3 invert sugar	1.00 lb	8.51%
Fuggles 90 mins	1.00 oz	
Goldings 60 mins	1.00 oz	
Goldings 30 mins	0.75 oz	
OG	1051	
FG	1011	
ABV	5.29	
Apparent attenuation	78.43%	
IBU	34	
SRM	39	
Mash at	150° F	
Sparge at	160° F	
Boil time	90 minutes	
pitching temp	61.5° F	
Yeast	Wyeast 1099 Whitbread Ale	

1917 Whitbread X

The first restrictions on gravity were introduced 1st July 1917, just four days before this beer was brewed. It would prove to be one of the last brews of X Ale before it was replaced by Government Ale. It wouldn't reappear until 1920.

There's already been quite a cut to the gravity, which has fallen from 1055° in 1914 and 1051° in early 1916. Though 1044° looks high-gravity compared to its replacement GA.

The recipe is another of Whitbread's exercises in simplicity, just pale malt, invert sugar and East Kent hops. About half of the latter were from the 1916 crop, the rest from the 1915 crop. I've reduced the quantity of hops to take account of the age of some of them.

1917 Whitbread X		
pale malt	7.75 lb	81.58%
No. 3 invert sugar	1.75 lb	18.42%
Fuggles 105 mins	0.75 oz	
Fuggles 60 mins	0.75 oz	
Fuggles 30 mins	0.75 oz	
OG	1044	
FG	1008	
ABV	4.76	
Apparent attenuation	81.82%	
IBU	33	
SRM	12	
Mash at	148° F	
Sparge at	168° F	
Boil time	105 minutes	
pitching temp	61° F	
Yeast	Wyeast 1099 Whitbread Ale	

1917 Whitbread GA

Brewed just two weeks after the X Ale above, this GA is a good demonstration of brewing restrictions starting to bite.

The OG has been reduced to just 1034°. That level of gravity is no coincidence as the rules introduced on 1st July 1917 stipulated that half a brewery's output should be at a gravity of less than 1036°. With X Ale being one of Whitbread's biggest sellers:

Whitbread's biggest selling beers 1914 - 1919						
Year	X	MA	IPA	P	LS	Total
1914	274,247		123,509	123,085	198,806	900,636
1915	243,730		106,630	65,216	208,733	762,438
1916	221,046		97,101	80,298	244,889	777,127
1917	162,353		71,807	8,493	241,280	578,502
1918	2,476	187,565	66,534	7,136	95,882	413,112
1919		304,135	103,545	21,602	89,165	565,624
Sources: Whitbread brewing records held at the London Metropolitan Archives, document numbers LMA/4453/D/01/079, LMA/4453/D/01/080, LMA/4453/D/01/081, LMA/4453/D/01/082, LMA/4453/D/01/083, LMA/4453/D/01/084, LMA_4453_D_09_108, LMA_4453_D_09_109, LMA_4453_D_09_110, LMA_4453_D_09_111 and LMA_4453_D_09_112.						

MA is the name Whitbread later adopted for GA.

Here's that same information in percentages:

Whitbread's biggest selling beers 1914 - 1919						
Year	X	MA	IPA	P	LS	Total
1914	30.45%		13.71%	13.67%	22.07%	79.90%
1915	31.97%		13.99%	8.55%	27.38%	81.88%
1916	28.44%		12.49%	10.33%	31.51%	82.78%
1917	28.06%		12.41%	1.47%	41.71%	83.65%
1918	0.60%	45.40%	16.11%	1.73%	23.21%	87.04%
1919	0.00%	53.77%	18.31%	3.82%	15.76%	91.66%
Sources: Whitbread brewing records held at the London Metropolitan Archives, document numbers LMA/4453/D/01/079, LMA/4453/D/01/080, LMA/4453/D/01/081, LMA/4453/D/01/082, LMA/4453/D/01/083, LMA/4453/D/01/084, LMA_4453_D_09_108, LMA_4453_D_09_109, LMA_4453_D_09_110, LMA_4453_D_09_111 and LMA_4453_D_09_112.						

It makes clear where Whitbread needed to reduce gravities to hit government-stipulated targets.

The grist had changed a little, with the proportion of invert sugar being doubled. Looking at the numbers BeerSmith spits out, it looks like that was to keep the colour about the same.

The hopping, however, is exactly the same as for the X Ale from two weeks earlier. Despite

GA having a considerably lower OG. Meaning the hopping rate per quarter of malt increased from 6.6 lbs to 8.5 lbs. Which boosts the (calculated) IBUs a bit.

1917 Whitbread GA		
pale malt	5.25 lb	77.78%
No. 3 invert sugar	1.50 lb	22.22%
Fuggles 105 mins	0.75 oz	
Fuggles 60 mins	0.75 oz	
Fuggles 30 mins	0.75 oz	
OG	1034	
FG	1005	
ABV	3.84	
Apparent attenuation	85.29%	
IBU	36	
SRM	11	
Mash at	148° F	
Sparge at	168° F	
Boil time	105 minutes	
pitching temp	61° F	
Yeast	Wyeast 1099 Whitbread Ale	

1918 Whitbread MA (strong)

By June 1918, things were really bad. A couple of months earlier, in April, average gravity had been set at just 1030°.

This caused brewers all sorts of problems. Foremost being: how could they still brew a reasonable amount of beer outside the price-controlled categories? Whitbread came up with a novel solution brewing three different versions of MA, (Mild Ale) which replaced GA in late 1917. (Though they were essentially the same beer, just under a different name.)

This is the strongest version.

The big change to the grist is the addition of brown malt. I'm guessing that's there to make up for the loss of colour caused by the drop. The colour has remained very constant at 11 – 12 SRM across various recipe and gravity changes. The colour suddenly becoming paler would be a sure sign to drinkers of a reduction in strength.

Even though I've reduced the hopping a lot – especially the 1913 Pacifics I've interpreted as Cluster – it's still turned out quite hoppy. Perhaps that was also deliberate to mask other changes.

1918 Whitbread MA (strong)		
pale malt	6.75 lb	79.41%
brown malt	0.75 lb	8.82%
No. 3 invert sugar	1.00 lb	11.76%
Cluster 105 mins	1.00 oz	
Fuggles 60 mins	0.75 oz	
Goldings 30 mins	0.75 oz	
OG	1038	
FG	1005	
ABV	4.37	
Apparent attenuation	86.84%	
IBU	40	
SRM	11	
Mash at	148° F	
Sparge at	168° F	
Boil time	105 minutes	
pitching temp	61° F	
Yeast	Wyeast 1099 Whitbread Ale	

1918 Whitbread MA (straight)

The June brew of MA this beer was part of was split just about exactly evenly three ways between the strong, straight and weak versions.

The parti-gyles are pretty weird looking. Usually every beer in a parti-gyle would receive some of each wort. Even the weakest beer would contain some first wort and the strongest beer some of the weakest wort. But In this parti-gyle, this was only true of one beer, MA (straight).

This middle-strength version was a blend of 110 barrels of the first wort (1063°), 220 barrels of second wort (1026°) and 200 barrels of water. The strong version contained 324 barrels of first wort and 211 barrels of water. This isn't how you would normally parti-gyle but was forced on Whitbread by the need to produce a large volume of low-gravity beer.

By fermenting it out a long way, they almost made this intoxicating. Well, if you knocked back a dozen or so pints. Though the chances are you wouldn't have been able to find that much beer in 1918.

1918 Whitbread MA (straight)		
pale malt	3.75 lb	75.00%
brown malt	0.50 lb	10.00%
No. 3 invert sugar	0.75 lb	15.00%
Cluster 105 mins	0.75 oz	
Fuggles 60 mins	0.50 oz	
Goldings 30 mins	0.50 oz	
OG	1024	
FG	1003	
ABV	2.78	
Apparent attenuation	87.50%	
IBU	32	
SRM	9	
Mash at	148° F	
Sparge at	168° F	
Boil time	105 minutes	
pitching temp	65° F	
Yeast	Wyeast 1099 Whitbread Ale	

1918 Whitbread MA (weak)

Weak really does mean weak in this case. It's the lowest-gravity beer I've ever come across.

How it was parti-gyled is unusual, too. 232 barrels of the second wort (1026°) were blended with 293 barrels of water. That has me wondering: was this beer ever sold straight or was used it to blend post-fermentation? All second wort would make a pretty watery beer, even without all the additional water.

I don't expect anyone to try to brew this beer. I've included it for the sake of completeness and to demonstrate the true horror of WW I beer.

1918 Whitbread MA (weak)		
pale malt	1.75 lb	75.11%
brown malt	0.25 lb	10.73%
No. 3 invert sugar	0.33 lb	14.16%
Cluster 105 mins	0.33 oz	
Fuggles 60 mins	0.25 oz	
Goldings 30 mins	0.25 oz	
OG	1011.5	
FG	1004	
ABV	0.99	
Apparent attenuation	65.22%	
IBU	16	
SRM	5	
Mash at	148° F	
Sparge at	168° F	
Boil time	105 minutes	
pitching temp	68° F	
Yeast	Wyeast 1099 Whitbread Ale	

1918 Whitbread IPA

There's been a big change in the strength of Whitbread IPA since 1916, with the OG falling from a pre-war-like 1047° to 1033°.

Though the beer remains much the same in terms of recipe. Just pale malt and invert sugar. Was it really No. 1 invert? I'm really not sure. It's not specific in this particular brewing record, but a brew of IPA a few months later does say No. 1. However, with recipes changing as much as they did during WW I, it's uncertain if this can be extrapolated back.

The hops were quite old – 1915 and 1916 East Kents – but had been kept in a cold store. Accordingly, I've only reduced the hopping a little.

1918 Whitbread IPA		
pale malt	6.75 lb	93.10%
No. 1 invert sugar	0.50 lb	6.90%
Goldings 90 mins	1.00 oz	
Goldings 60 mins	1.00 oz	
Goldings 30 mins	1.00 oz	
Goldings dry hops	0.50 oz	
OG	1033	
FG	1008	
ABV	3.31	
Apparent attenuation	75.76%	
IBU	43	
SRM	4	
Mash at	154° F	
Sparge at	165° F	
Boil time	90 minutes	
pitching temp	62° F	
Yeast	Wyeast 1099 Whitbread Ale	

1918 Whitbread PA

The war years were very tough on Whitbread Pale Ale.

It started the war at a very decent 1061°, but by mid-1918 was down to just 1035°, barely any stronger than their IPA. But in terms of the recipe, not much has altered. It's another gem of simplicity: base malt and invert sugar.

It was slightly more complicated than that in reality. 74 of the 104 quarters of malt were PA malt – the top grade of pale malt – the other 30 quarters, pale malt made from Californian barley.

As with their IPA, the hops were a little on the old side, 1915 and 1916 East Kents. But had also been stored cold. So I've only made a small adjustment to the quantity.

1918 Whitbread PA		
pale malt	7.25 lb	96.67%
No. 1 invert sugar	0.25 lb	3.33%
Goldings 90 mins	1.00 oz	
Goldings 60 mins	1.00 oz	
Goldings 30 mins	0.75 oz	
Goldings dry hops	0.50 oz	
OG	1035	
FG	1007	
ABV	3.70	
Apparent attenuation	80.00%	
IBU	40	
SRM	4	
Mash at	154° F	
Sparge at	165° F	
Boil time	120 minutes	
pitching temp	62° F	
Yeast	Wyeast 1099 Whitbread Ale	

1918 Whitbread P

Brewed in April, this was exactly when the gravity of Whitbread's Porter came under real attack. A few weeks earlier it's OG had been 1048°.

The percentage of dark malts in the grist has increased, from around 30% to 43%. Perhaps it was to keep the colour sufficiently dark. Or even to boost the body. I'm sure there must have been a good reason. They didn't make significant changes for nothing.

The hopping, on the other hand, has remained near identical, at least in its level. The hops themselves have changed, with around half being Pacific hops from 1913. The rest were Mid-Kents from 1916 and 1915. The latter having been kept in a cold store. Obviously, with some hops almost five years old, I've reduced the hopping rate in the recipe.

1918 Whitbread Porter		
pale malt	4.75 lb	55.88%
brown malt	1.50 lb	17.65%
black malt	1.00 lb	11.76%
No. 3 invert sugar	1.25 lb	14.71%
Cluster 105 mins	0.75 oz	
Fuggles 60 mins	0.75 oz	
Fuggles 30 mins	0.75 oz	
OG	1039	
FG	1011	
ABV	3.70	
Apparent attenuation	71.79%	
IBU	36	
SRM	35	
Mash at	145° F	
Sparge at	168° F	
Boil time	105 minutes	
pitching temp	62° F	
Yeast	Wyeast 1099 Whitbread Ale	

1918 Whitbread Imperial Stout

Whitbread tinkered with their range of beers during the war. Mostly dropping beers. But there was one new arrival, Imperial.

Imperial was a replacement for Whitbread's two strong Stouts, SS and SSS. This beer, brewed in March 1918, was one of the last brews, with only four coming after it. It was the end of really strong Stouts at Whitbread.

The grist has the same components as all Whitbread's Black Beers: pale, brown and black malt plus No. 3 invert sugar. The proportion of roasted malts is slightly smaller than in London Stout, but not drastically so.

The hops used are exactly the same as in their Porter: Mid-Kent (1915 Cold Store, 1916) and Pacific (1913). Not that surprising as this beer was parti-gyled with Porter. Given the age of the hops, I've reduced the quantity in the recipe by quite a lot.

1918 Whitbread Imperial Stout		
pale malt	10.75 lb	65.43%
brown malt	2.50 lb	15.22%
black malt	1.43 lb	8.70%
No. 3 invert sugar	1.75 lb	10.65%
Cluster 105 mins	1.50 oz	
Fuggles 60 mins	1.50 oz	
Fuggles 30 mins	1.50 oz	
OG	1073	
FG	1028	
ABV	5.95	
Apparent attenuation	61.64%	
IBU	57	
SRM	47	
Mash at	146° F	
Sparge at	170° F	
Boil time	105 minutes	
pitching temp	57° F	
Yeast	Wyeast 1099 Whitbread Ale	

1918 Whitbread LS

LS – London Stout – was a relatively newcomer to Whitbread's range, first being brewed in 1910.

It was immediately popular, with almost 200,000 barrels of it brewed in that first year. The war didn't dim its popularity and the 200,000 barrel level was maintained until 1918 when only 99,000 barrels were produced. Post-war, it never returned to its earlier success, never exceeding 100,000 barrels in the 1920's.

I suspect that it was brewed for markets outside London. Especially as it seems to have replaced CS (Country Stout). That would explain its relatively low gravity for a Stout, usually just one or two points higher than their Porter.

In March 1918, when the original was brewed, LS was Whitbread's only Stout. SS and SSS had been dropped in 1917, replaced by a new beer called Imperial. That didn't last very long, disappearing in April 1918 when brewing such a strong beer became impossible.

1918 Whitbread London Stout		
pale malt	6.50 lb	65.00%
brown malt	1.50 lb	15.00%
black malt	1.00 lb	10.00%
No. 3 invert sugar	1.00 lb	10.00%
Cluster 105 mins	1.00 oz	
Fuggles 60 mins	0.75 oz	
Goldings 30 mins	0.75 oz	
OG	1043	
FG	1011	
ABV	4.23	
Apparent attenuation	74.42%	
IBU	42	
SRM	35	
Mash at	146° F	
Sparge at	168° F	
Boil time	90 minutes	
pitching temp	61.5° F	
Yeast	Wyeast 1099 Whitbread Ale	

1919 Whitbread MA

By 1919, Whitbread's post-war range of beer was starting to crystallise. Weakest of the bunch being MA.

A low-gravity Mild Ale that developed out of wartime GA, MA (after 1924 under the name LA) hung around for the whole of the interwar period, finally disappearing in 1940 when the gravity of their X Ale dropped to a similar level.

MA was brewed in huge quantities in the final war years: 187,565 barrels in 1918 and 304,135 barrels in 1919. After that, production fell off sharply and after 1927 Whitbread never brewed more than 12,000 barrels a year. Mostly it was fewer than 10,000 barrels. A drop in the ocean compared to Whitbread's total production of around half a million barrels.

The only complication in the original's grist are four different types of pale malt, all English, except for one from Chilean barley.

The hops are a slightly odd bunch. There are Mid-Kent from 1917 and 1918, plus Oregon from 1917 and 1911. So nothing from the two most recent crops (the original was brewed in November 1919). Very old American hops turn up just after the end of the war in more than one brewery. Presumably hops that had been kept back for emergencies and needed to be used up.

1919 Whitbread MA		
pale malt	4.75 lb	86.36%
No. 3 invert sugar	0.75 lb	13.64%
Cluster 90 mins	0.75 oz	
Fuggles 60 mins	0.50 oz	
Goldings 30 mins	0.50 oz	
OG	1026	
FG	1004	
ABV	2.91	
Apparent attenuation	84.62%	
IBU	31	
SRM	7	
Mash at	145° F	
Sparge at	168° F	
Boil time	90 minutes	
pitching temp	64° F	
Yeast	Wyeast 1099 Whitbread Ale	

1919 Whitbread X

As before the war, Whitbread's principal Mild post-war was X Ale. More than 100,000 barrels was brewed a year in the 1920's, rising to over 200,000 barrels in the late 1930s.

X Ale has the typical 1920's full-strength Mild gravity of 1043°. It remained there until 1931, when its gravity was slashed to the mid-1030°s.

As it was parti-gyled with MA, all the comments about the recipe of that beer apply here, too.

1919 Whitbread X		
pale malt	8.25 lb	89.19%
No. 3 invert sugar	1.00 lb	10.81%
Cluster 90 mins	1.25 oz	
Fuggles 60 mins	0.75 oz	
Goldings 30 mins	0.75 oz	
OG	1043	
FG	1010	
ABV	4.37	
Apparent attenuation	76.74%	
IBU	44	
SRM	9	
Mash at	145° F	
Sparge at	168° F	
Boil time	90 minutes	
pitching temp	61° F	
Yeast	Wyeast 1099 Whitbread Ale	

1919 Whitbread IPA

IPA was another beer than would become one of Whitbread's mainstays in the interwar period. Most years well over 100,000 barrels were brewed.

As an exclusively bottled product, it filled the Light Ale niche that was becoming increasingly important as drinkers turned away from draught beer.

Whitbread did seem to differentiate between IPA and Pale Ale when it came to hopping. Despite being considerably weaker, IPA contained more hops per barrel than PA. So that sort of fits in with IPA theory. Though I'm sure style Nazis would dismiss this beer as being far too weak for an IPA.

The only malt excitement comes from there being both pale and PA malt and some malt from Chilean barley. Topped off with a bit of invert sugar.

The hops wear a combination of 1917 and 1918 East Kent, 1918 Mid-Kent and 1917 Oregon. In contrast to the Milds, there are hops from fairly recent seasons.

1919 Whitbread IPA		
pale malt	6.50 lb	81.25%
No. 1 invert sugar	1.50 lb	18.75%
Cluster 90 mins	0.75 oz	
Fuggles 60 mins	1.00 oz	
Goldings 30 mins	1.00 oz	
Goldings 15 mins	1.00 oz	
Goldings dry hops	0.50 oz	
OG	1036	
FG	1009	
ABV	3.57	
Apparent attenuation	75.00%	
IBU	49	
SRM	5	
Mash at	150° F	
Sparge at	165° F	
Boil time	90 minutes	
pitching temp	62° F	
Yeast	Wyeast 1099 Whitbread Ale	

1919 Whitbread PA

One of the biggest beneficiaries of more liberal gravity rules was Whitbread PA. It's gravity increased by 13 points between June 1918 and November 1919. And 1048° was the gravity it would stick with right up until WW II.

Like IPA, it has a grist of pale malt and sugar. Some of the pale malt being from Californian barley and some the higher quality pale ale malt.

Though it contained fewer hops than IPA, they were, on average, higher-quality ones. Two-thirds East Kent from 1918 and the remainder 1917 Oregon.

1919 Whitbread PA		
pale malt	9.00 lb	87.80%
No. 1 invert sugar	1.25 lb	12.20%
Cluster 90 mins	1.25 oz	
Goldings 60 mins	1.25 oz	
Goldings 30 mins	1.25 oz	
Goldings dry hops	0.50 oz	
OG	1048	
FG	1013	
ABV	4.63	
Apparent attenuation	72.92%	
IBU	56	
SRM	6	
Mash at	150° F	
Sparge at	165° F	
Boil time	90 minutes	
pitching temp	62° F	
Yeast	Wyeast 1099 Whitbread Ale	

1919 Whitbread P

Brewed six months after the Armistice, the gravity of this Whitbread Porter had risen a little form the previous year.

Which makes sense, because about a month earlier average gravity had been raised to 1044°, Meaning Whitbread could basically brew as much of this beer as they wanted. The percentage of coloured malt has fallen from 28% in 1914 to 24%. The proportion of sugar is also slightly lower.

The hops are a bit weird in this one. On the face of it, the hopping appears to be heavier than usual. However, half the hops were "Pacific" from 1910. Ancient, in other words. The remaining half is made up of East Kent from 1917. If they had all been fresh hops, that would have made 3.75 ozs. for a batch of this size.

Unexpectedly, this is as strong as Whitbread Porter got after the war. In 1920 it had a gravity of 1041° and in 1921 just 1028°.

Though I notice that while this is called P in the brewing record, according to the weekly totals at the back of the book there was no Porter brewed after February, only London Stout. It's weird, there are brewing records for both LS and P and they seem to have been at the same gravity. The distinction between Porter and Stout was more blurred than ever towards the end of the war.

It was brewed as a 7d beer, the gravity band for which was 1042° - 1049°. It made economic sense to brew at the bottom end of the gravity range for a price class.

1919 Whitbread Porter		
pale malt	6.00 lb	63.16%
brown malt	1.25 lb	13.16%
black malt	1.00 lb	10.53%
No. 3 invert sugar	1.25 lb	13.16%
Cluster 105 mins	0.75 oz	
Goldings 60 mins	0.75 oz	
Goldings 30 mins	0.75 oz	
OG	1043	
FG	1011	
ABV	4.23	
Apparent attenuation	74.42%	
IBU	38	
SRM	35	
Mash at	145° F	
Sparge at	168° F	
Boil time	90 minutes	
pitching temp	61.5° F	
Yeast	Wyeast 1099 Whitbread Ale	

1919 Whitbread S

Parti-gyled with the Porter above was a new Stout called simply S. This brew, on 23rd May was the second ever. It wasn't that long-lived, being discontinued in 1931.

It was an 8d. per pint beer, the class that was anything over 1050°. As with the Porter, it's gravity was just above the minimum for that price.

At the front of the brewing book there's a table of S for export and this gyle appears in it. Though the quantity given is 160 barrels, while there are 690 barrels of S in the actual brewing record. I assume they took part of the batch for export, possibly giving it a different secondary conditioning.

Unusually, in 1919 all Whitbread's bottled beers were still bottle-conditioned. Most breweries by this point had chilled and filtered bottled beers, apart from specialities like Burton Pale Ale and strong Stouts.

1919 Whitbread S		
pale malt	7.25 lb	61.70%
brown malt	1.75 lb	14.89%
black malt	1.25 lb	10.64%
No. 3 invert sugar	1.50 lb	12.77%
Cluster 105 mins	1.00 oz	
Goldings 60 mins	1.00 oz	
Goldings 30 mins	0.75 oz	
OG	1053	
FG	1014	
ABV	5.16	
Apparent attenuation	73.58%	
IBU	44	
SRM	41	
Mash at	145° F	
Sparge at	168° F	
Boil time	90 minutes	
pitching temp	61.5° F	
Yeast	Wyeast 1099 Whitbread Ale	

1921 Whitbread P

Sometimes it's dead handy to have more than one set of figures. It can prevent dreadful mistakes.

This is particularly true in the case of 1920's Porter. In the brewing records of Whitbread and Barclay Perkins, the OG as brewed of their Porters were under 1030°. But when I look at the same beers in the Whitbread Gravity Book (which is based on samples purchased in pubs) the OG is considerably higher, at around 1034°.

There are two possible explanations. The beers could have been primed with a high-gravity sugar solution (around 1150°) at racking time, which would have increased the effective OG. Or they could have been blended with a stronger Stout. I'm pretty sure the first wasn't the case at Barclay Perkins, because their records detail the primings and there are none in TT. As Whitbread didn't bother detailing primings, I've no idea what they did.

Which all means to say: the OG of the beer below should be higher, 1034°. Still pretty feeble compared to 1914, but at least intoxicating.

There has been one change to the grist: oats. For the simple reason that this was parti-gyled with London Stout, some of which was sold as Oatmeal Stout. Though the quantity of oats involved is miniscule. Before the war there were usual oats in Whitbread's Porter/Stout parti-gyles, but that stopped in 1915, when I suppose they discontinued Oatmeal Stout. Oats don't appear again until December 1919.

The hopping is very unusual: all Oregon hops. It was rare to have a beer with only American hops. There were usually always some English hops. About half were from the 1916 crop of "ND" which I assume stands for "no date". The rest were evenly split between the 1917 and 1919 harvest. As the newest hops were a couple of years old, I've drastically reduced the quantity in the recipe.

1921 Whitbread Porter		
pale malt	3.50 lb	58.14%
brown malt	0.75 lb	12.46%
black malt	0.75 lb	12.46%
oats	0.02 lb	0.33%
No. 3 invert sugar	1.00 lb	16.61%
Cluster 150 min	0.50 oz	
Cluster 90 min	0.25 oz	
Cluster 30 min	0.25 oz	
OG	1028	
FG	1008	
ABV	2.65	
Apparent attenuation	71.43%	
IBU	20	
SRM	28	
Mash at	144° F	
Sparge at	168° F	
Boil time	150 minutes	
pitching temp	64° F	
Yeast	Wyeast 1099 Whitbread Ale	

1921 Whitbread LS

This is the other half of the Porter parti-gyle, London Stout. And London Oatmeal Stout, though it's identical to the vanilla London Stout.

London Stout was Whitbread's draught Stout all through the interwar period. From 1922 to 1931, it had a gravity of around 1055°. After the disastrous tax increase in 1931, the OG fell to 1045°, where it stayed until WW II.

1921 Whitbread LS		
pale malt	6.00 lb	58.25%
brown malt	1.25 lb	12.14%
black malt	1.25 lb	12.14%
oats	0.30 lb	2.91%
No. 3 invert sugar	1.50 lb	14.56%
Cluster 150 min	0.75 oz	
Cluster 90 min	0.50 oz	
Cluster 30 min	0.50 oz	
OG	1046	
FG	1012	
ABV	4.50	
Apparent attenuation	73.91%	
IBU	30	
SRM	40	
Mash at	144° F	
Sparge at	168° F	
Boil time	150 minutes	
pitching temp	61.5° F	
Yeast	Wyeast 1099 Whitbread Ale	

1921 Whitbread KK

It took quite a while for Whitbread to bring back a Burton Ale. In 1918, 1919 and 1920 they brewed none at all.

Surprisingly, they brewed much more Burton after the war than they did before it. In 1914, they only brewed 12,000 barrels of all three Burtons combined. In the 1920s, they made 40,000 – 50,000 barrels a year of just KK. Though, by then, it was their only Burton.

The Whitbread is typical Whitbread: just base malt and sugar. They really did like to keep things simple. Though the base was a blend of English pale ale malt, and English and Californian pale malt.

The hops were East Kent (1919), Mid-Kent (1918, 1919), Oregon (1919) and Bohemian (1919). So not the newest of hops and none from the most recent crop.

1921 Whitbread KK		
pale malt	10.75 lb	91.49%
No. 3 invert sugar	1.00 lb	8.51%
Cluster 105 mins	1.00 oz	
Fuggles 90 mins	1.00 oz	
Goldings 30 mins	0.50 oz	
Saaz 30 mins	0.50 oz	
Goldings dry hops	0.50 oz	
OG	1054	
FG	1016	
ABV	5.03	
Apparent attenuation	70.37%	
IBU	42	
SRM	9	
Mash at	149° F	
Sparge at	170° F	
Boil time	105 minutes	
pitching temp	61° F	
Yeast	Wyeast 1099 Whitbread Ale	

William Younger

According to the brewery, it was founded in Leith in 1749. However Martyn Cornell has fairly definitively proved this to be incorrect, the real founding date being somewhat later. The brewery moved to Edinburgh in 1778 to premises at the bottom end of the Royal Mile, close to Holyrood Palace. Its site is currently occupied by the Scottish parliament. In 1933, it merged with William McEwan, forming Scottish Breweries. A merger with Newcastle Breweries in 1860 created Scottish & Newcastle Breweries.

A second site, the Holyrood Brewery was built to supplement its existing Abbey Brewery. Holyrood was specifically built to brew Pale Ales and was equipped with Burton union sets.

William Younger beers 1913/1914							
Beer	Style	OG	FG	ABV	App. Atten-uation	lbs hops/ qtr	hops lb/brl
H 60/-	Ale	1044	1013	4.10	70.45%	4.00	0.67
60/-	Ale	1047	1023	3.18	51.06%	3.04	0.28
80/-	Ale	1056	1027	3.84	51.79%	3.60	0.75
100/-	Ale	1066	1032	4.50	51.52%	3.60	0.89
160/-	Ale	1097	1038	7.81	60.82%	5.33	2.83
XX - X	Mild	1055	1017	5.03	69.09%	4.07	0.88
XX	Mild	1055	1018	4.89	67.27%	4.07	0.87
XXK	Mild	1056	1016	5.29	71.43%	4.07	0.81
XXX	Mild	1065	1021.5	5.75	66.92%	4.55	1.15
XXXX	Stock Ale	1070	1024	6.09	65.71%	9.72	2.71
XXXX Sc	Stock Ale	1070	1023	6.22	67.14%	9.35	2.64
1	Strong Ale	1097	1037	7.94	61.86%	10.28	7.40
2 Sc	Strong Ale	1076	1025	6.75	67.11%	9.35	2.86
3	Strong Ale	1065	1021.5	5.75	66.92%	4.55	1.15
3a	Strong Ale	1072	1025	6.22	65.28%	5.48	1.22
3 Sc	Strong Ale	1065	1022	5.69	66.15%	4.55	1.20
3 btg	Strong Ale	1070	1022	6.35	68.57%	5.48	1.78
LDA	Pale Ale	1037	1012	3.31	67.57%	3.33	0.49
P	Pale Ale	1045	1014	4.10	68.89%	4.12	0.69
XP	Pale Ale	1048	1014	4.50	70.83%	4.57	0.85
XXP	Pale Ale	1057	1017	5.29	70.18%	5.64	1.18
LAE	Pale Ale	1045	1013	4.23	71.11%	10.00	1.77
SLE	Pale Ale	1055	1014	5.42	74.55%	10.36	2.20
MM	Pale Ale	1048	1015	4.37	68.75%	3.91	0.70
S1	Stout	1065	1031	4.50	52.31%	2.00	0.54
S2	Stout	1059	1029	3.97	50.85%	1.88	0.45
DBS	Stout	1065	1022	5.69	66.15%	10.65	2.63
MBS	Stout	1065	1020	5.95	69.23%	3.50	0.74
Sources: William Younger brewing records held at the Scottish Brewing Archive, document numbers WY/6/1/3/46 and WY/6/1/2/58.							

They were very atypical of Scottish breweries, mostly eschewing parti-gyling and brewing a huge range of beers when most of their rivals only made a handful. It's an insanely large number of different beers that they brewed.

I've never come across a brewery that brewed so many beers.

It was only slightly less mad after the war:

| \multicolumn{8}{|l|}{William Younger beers 1921/1922} |
Beer	Style	OG	FG	ABV	App. Atten-uation	lbs hops/ qtr	hops lb/brl
120/-	Ale	1082	1028	7.14	65.85%	6.58	2.49
160/- B	Ale	1082	1023	7.81	71.95%	6.58	2.49
200/- B	Ale	1092	1032	7.94	65.22%	9.14	3.30
XX	Mild	1044	1012	4.23	72.73%	3.91	0.65
XXX	Mild	1044	1012	4.23	72.73%	4.09	0.68
LAE	Pale Ale	1047	1013	4.50	72.34%	9.57	1.76
LE	Pale Ale	1042	1011	4.10	73.81%	9.52	1.50
SE	Pale Ale	1057	1015	5.56	73.68%	9.23	2.00
SLE	Pale Ale	1052	1015	4.89	71.15%	9.60	1.94
XXPS	Pale Ale	1060	1017	5.69	71.67%	5.00	1.18
1	Strong Ale	1082	1028	7.14	65.85%	7.37	2.52
2 Btg	Strong Ale	1072	1022	6.61	69.44%	8.53	2.75
3	Strong Ale	1060	1017	5.69	71.67%	5.00	1.18
Btg DBS	Stout	1060	1019	5.42	68.33%	10.65	2.63
DBS	Stout	1060	1025	4.63	58.33%	3.89	0.92
MBS	Stout	1055	1017.5	4.96	68.18%	9.00	1.94
XXS	Stout	1050	1020	3.97	60.00%	3.89	0.77
\multicolumn{8}{	l	}{Sources: William Younger brewing records held at the Scottish Brewing Archive, document numbers WY/6/1/3/46 and WY/6/1/2/58.}

And I think there are a couple missing. Pretty sure they still brewed XP at the time.

1913 William Younger XXP

William Younger had been early to the Pale Ale game and even built a new brewery specifically to brew the style.

Their initial brews were quite similar to Burton versions. In 1858 XXP had an OG of 1059° and was hopped at a massive 21 lbs per quarter, 5 lbs per barrel. The gravity was lopped back a little and the hopping rate a lot over the next 60 years. This 1913 version was hopped at 5.85 lbs per quarter, 1.25 per barrel. Which is quite a change.

The grist is typical of this period William Younger beers: simply pale malt and a huge amount of grits. I know. It looks terrible. But the beers couldn't have been that bad, given how successful the brewery was. The pale malt was a combination of Oregon, Indian and Scottish.

I've reduced the hopping rate quite a bit, as almost 50% were from the 1910 crop. They're listed as Kent and Pacific, which I've interpreted as Fuggles and Cluster, respectively. There's no mention of the variety used as dry hops and I've guessed Goldings. It probably is an English variety, but it could equally be Fuggles.

The finished beer was almost certainly darker than indicated below. Knowing how Scottish brewers operated, it was most likely coloured up at racking time to a variety of different shades for different markets.

1913 William Younger XXP		
pale malt	7.00 lb	53.85%
grits	6.00 lb	46.15%
Cluster 120 mins	1.00 oz	
Cluster 90 mins	0.50 oz	
Fuggles 60 mins	0.50 oz	
Goldings dry hops	0.50 oz	
OG	1056	
FG	1017	
ABV	5.16	
Apparent attenuation	69.64%	
IBU	36	
SRM	4	
Mash at	150° F	
Sparge at	160° F	
Boil time	120 minutes	
pitching temp	59° F	
Yeast	WLP028 Edinburgh Ale	

1913 William Younger XP

One class down from XXP was XP. Very similar, just a bit weaker.

XP and XXP had been brewed right from the start of William Younger's Pale Ale adventure. And, just like XXP, the gravity and hopping had been reduced. Fifty years earlier, XP had an OG of 1054° and was hopped at almost 15 lbs per quarter, 4.5 lbs per barrel. This version had barely more hops per quarter than the old one had per barrel: 4.57 lbs. per barrel it was just 0.85 lbs, fewer than a London X Ale.

The ingredients are the same as for XXP. A combination of Oregon, Indian and Scottish malt plus grits, with Kent and Pacific hops. William Youngers were very enthusiastic users of grits, which appeared in all their beers.

1913 William Younger XP		
pale malt	6.25 lb	54.35%
grits	5.25 lb	45.65%
Cluster 120 mins	0.50 oz	
Cluster 90 mins	0.50 oz	
Fuggles 60 mins	0.25 oz	
Goldings dry hops	0.50 oz	
OG	1048	
FG	1014	
ABV	4.50	
Apparent attenuation	70.83%	
IBU	24	
SRM	3	
Mash at	150° F	
Sparge at	160° F	
Boil time	120 minutes	
pitching temp	59° F	
Yeast	WLP028 Edinburgh Ale	

1913 William Younger P

William Younger was a funny brewery. They had lots of very similar beers that they all brewed single-gyle.

This beer is only ever so slightly weaker than XP and a bit more lightly-hopped. I'm not sure why you would bother making two such similar beers. The ingredients are identical to XP and XXP, though this time there's a slightly higher percentage of grits.

1913 William Younger P		
pale malt	5.50 lb	53.66%
grits	4.75 lb	46.34%
Cluster 120 mins	0.50 oz	
Cluster 90 mins	0.25 oz	
Fuggles 60 mins	0.25 oz	
Goldings dry hops	0.50 oz	
OG	1045	
FG	1014	
ABV	4.10	
Apparent attenuation	68.89%	
IBU	20	
SRM	3	
Mash at	150° F	
Sparge at	160° F	
Boil time	120 minutes	
pitching temp	60° F	
Yeast	WLP028 Edinburgh Ale	

1913 William Younger MM

There are some very confusing beers in William Younger's brewing records. Like this enigmatically-named MM.

I assume, without being 100% certain, that this was a Pale Ale. Mostly because it was brewed in the Holyrood Brewery, which had been built to brew Pale Ales. But also because I can't think what the hell else it could. As for what MM stands for and what the beer was marketed as, I haven't a clue.

It seems to have first been brewed just before the start of the war. But not to have hung around for long. I can't find it in Younger's post-war records so it must have been another casualty of the conflict.

It's extremely lightly-hopped for a beer of this gravity. Coupled with all those grits, it must have been pretty light and pretty bland.

1913 William Younger MM		
pale malt	5.75 lb	53.49%
grits	5.00 lb	46.51%
Cluster 120 mins	0.50 oz	
Cluster 90 mins	0.25 oz	
Fuggles 60 mins	0.25 oz	
Goldings dry hops	0.33 oz	
OG	1047	
FG	1013	
ABV	4.50	
Apparent attenuation	72.34%	
IBU	19	
SRM	3	
Mash at	150° F	
Sparge at	160° F	
Boil time	120 minutes	
pitching temp	60° F	
Yeast	WLP028 Edinburgh Ale	

1914 William Younger Export

I am, at least, pretty sure what this beer was marketed as: Export. Though whether it ever saw the inside of a ship is another matter.

Given the level of hopping, which is very high at 11 lbs per quarter, it's a possibility. That's double the rate of XXP, a beer of a very similar gravity. This beer has the level of hopping I would expect to find in a strong pre-war Pale Ale. While Younger's standard range of P, XP and XXP were particularly lightly hopped.

The grist is essentially the same as all their other Pale Ales: pale malt and a shitload of grits. The pale malt was a mix of Oregon, Indian and Scottish. The hops were mostly Pacifics, from the 1911 and 1912 crops, plus some Kent hops from 1912. The dry hopping is extremely heavy.

What would it have tasted like? Given the decent rate of attenuation and all those grits, my guess would be surprisingly light with a very firm bitterness.

1914 William Younger Export		
pale malt	7.00 lb	56.00%
grits	5.50 lb	44.00%
Cluster 150 mins	1.50 oz	
Cluster 90 mins	1.50 oz	
Fuggles 60 mins	1.50 oz	
Goldings dry hops	1.25 oz	
OG	1054	
FG	1015	
ABV	5.16	
Apparent attenuation	72.22%	
IBU	81	
SRM	4	
Mash at	150° F	
Sparge at	160° F	
Boil time	150 minutes	
pitching temp	59° F	
Yeast	WLP028 Edinburgh Ale	

1914 William Younger LAE

Here's another of William Younger's enigmatic beers. What does LAE stand for? I've not really much of a clue. Light Ale Export? Probably not.

Though the E might well designate export as this is another relatively heavily hopped beer. From looking at Younger's standard range of draught Pale Ales, it looks like Scottish drinkers already expected less bitter beers than those south of the border,

The grist is the same as all their Pale Ales: just pale malt and grits. Younger were unusual not just in their use of grits, but also the quantities they employed. Usually over 40% of the grist. Which, I must admit, makes the recipe look a bit crap.

The hops are the same as in Export: Pacifics from 1911 and 1912, coupled with Kents from 1912.

1914 William Younger LAE		
pale malt	6.00 lb	54.55%
grits	5.00 lb	45.45%
Cluster 150 mins	1.25 oz	
Cluster 90 mins	1.00 oz	
Fuggles 60 mins	1.00 oz	
Goldings dry hops	1.00 oz	
OG	1048	
FG	1013	
ABV	4.63	
Apparent attenuation	72.92%	
IBU	62	
SRM	3	
Mash at	150° F	
Sparge at	160° F	
Boil time	150 minutes	
pitching temp	59° F	
Yeast	WLP028 Edinburgh Ale	

1914 William Younger SLE

As I've already mentioned, William Younger brewed a number of confusingly similar beers. SLE and Ext being good examples.

The grists are pretty much identical: 56% pale malt, 44% grits. The hopping rate is nearly identical – Ext had a smidgen more. The types of hops are the same: Kent (1912), Pacific (1911, 1912). And there's only one point between their OGs. What was the point in having two such similar beers? I've no idea.

SLE didn't have a particularly long life, first appearing in the 1890's and disappearing again in the 1930's. I'm inclined to believe that it may have been a beer genuinely intended for export as the OG in the 1922 was only a little lower at 1052°.

The grist may look quite boring but it contains five types of pale malt: Oregon, India, Smyrna, Cheviot and Danube. That's quite a spread of barley sources.

1914 William Younger SLE		
pale malt	7.25 lb	56.86%
grits	5.50 lb	43.14%
Cluster 150 mins	1.50 oz	
Cluster 90 mins	1.50 oz	
Fuggles 60 mins	1.50 oz	
Goldings dry hops	1.00 oz	
OG	1055	
FG	1014	
ABV	5.42	
Apparent attenuation	74.55%	
IBU	81	
SRM	4	
Mash at	150° F	
Sparge at	160° F	
Boil time	150 minutes	
pitching temp	59° F	
Yeast	WLP028 Edinburgh Ale	

1913 William Younger LDA

Weakest of Younger's baffling large range of Pale Ales was LDA, which I assume stands for Light Dinner Ale.

To me, that name implies a bottled beer. And that it was racked into hogsheads, half hogshead and quarter hogsheads seems to confirm that. Those are the barrel sizes that were usually sent to bottlers. A draught beer was mostly racked into barrels and kilderkins.

$1037°$ is a really weedy gravity for before WW I. Something you wouldn't have seen in London. Especially in a Pale Ale.

The recipe, like all Younger's other Pale Ales, is simply pale malt and loads of grits.

1913 William Younger LDA		
pale malt	4.50 lb	52.94%
grits	4.00 lb	47.06%
Cluster 120 min	0.33 oz	
Cluster 60 min	0.25 oz	
Fuggles 30 min	0.25 oz	
Goldings dry hops	0.33 oz	
OG	1037	
FG	1012	
ABV	3.31	
Apparent attenuation	67.57%	
IBU	16	
SRM	3	
Mash at	150° F	
Sparge at	160° F	
Boil time	120 minutes	
pitching temp	61° F	
Yeast	WLP028 Edinburgh Ale	

1913 William Younger H 60/-

While many Scottish breweries had discontinued, or drastically reduced their number of traditional Shilling Ales, William Younger still produced a wide range of such beers.

The weakest of the bunch was H 60/-. Don't ask me what the H stands for. I've absolutely no idea. As for style, the weaker Shilling Ales roughly approximated to English Mild Ales. Though the level of hopping is lower than London Mild Ales.

Before you ask, this has no connection with the 60/- sold after WW II. That was a type of low-gravity Pale Ale.

The grist is classic William Younger: pale malt and grits. The pale malt was made a mix of foreign and Scottish and foreign barley, which was pretty typical. Brewers rarely used a single type of base malt.

The hops are listed as Kent and Pacific, which I've interpreted as Fuggles and Cluster, respectively. As some were from the 1910 crop, I've reduced the level of hopping.

1913 William Younger H 60/-		
pale malt	5.25 lb	52.50%
grits	4.75 lb	47.50%
Cluster 120 min	0.50 oz	
Cluster 60 min	0.33 oz	
Fuggles 30 min	0.25 oz	
Goldings dry hops	0.33 oz	
OG	1044	
FG	1012	
ABV	4.23	
Apparent attenuation	72.73%	
IBU	20	
SRM	3	
Mash at	150° F	
Sparge at	160° F	
Boil time	120 minutes	
pitching temp	60° F	
Yeast	WLP028 Edinburgh Ale	

1913 William Younger 60/-

60/- without the H is slightly different. Both in strength and the recipe.

There's still the foreign and Scottish pale malt and a load of grits, but in addition there's also something just described as syrup. I've made a guess and plumped for glucose. Feel free to substitute any other syrup you fancy.

Another difference is that this beer wasn't dry-hopped. Not sure what the reason for that might have been. Possibly because this beer was for bottling. Some breweries only dry-hopped beers that were meant to be sold on draught.

There was also 4 gallons of colour added. Presumably that's a very dark caramel solution, which I assume darkened the colour quite a bit. So for full authenticity, add caramel to get to 15 – 20 SRM.

1913 William Younger 60/-		
pale malt	5.75 lb	53.49%
grits	4.75 lb	44.19%
glucose	0.25 lb	2.33%
Cluster 105 min	0.50 oz	
Cluster 60 min	0.25 oz	
Fuggles 30 min	0.25 oz	
OG	1047	
FG	1022	
ABV	3.31	
Apparent attenuation	53.19%	
IBU	13	
SRM	3	
Mash at	150° F	
Sparge at	160° F	
Boil time	105 minutes	
pitching temp	60° F	
Yeast	WLP028 Edinburgh Ale	

1913 William Younger 80/-

The next Shilling Ale, in terms of strength, was, predictably, 80/-. This has absolutely no connection with modern 80/-, which is a type of Pale Ale. The older type of Shilling Ale, to which this beer belongs, were Mild Ales.

This is really just a big brother of 60/-. Literally, really, as the two were parti-gyled together. As with 60/-, there were 4 gallons of colour added. I imagine that the real colour was quite a bit darker, probably 15 – 20 SRM.

1913 William Younger 80/-		
pale malt	6.75 lb	52.94%
grits	5.50 lb	43.14%
glucose	0.50 lb	3.92%
Cluster 105 min	0.50 oz	
Cluster 60 min	0.50 oz	
Fuggles 30 min	0.25 oz	
OG	1056	
FG	1026	
ABV	3.97	
Apparent attenuation	53.57%	
IBU	21	
SRM	4	
Mash at	150° F	
Sparge at	160° F	
Boil time	105 minutes	
pitching temp	59.5° F	
Yeast	WLP028 Edinburgh Ale	

1913 William Younger 100/-

Stepping up through the Shilling Ales, the next is 100/-.

No shock to discover that it's a slightly beefier version of the 80/-. With exactly the same three elements in the grist: pale malt, grits and glucose. You may have noticed a slight element of repetition in Younger's recipes. Both in terms of ingredients and gravities. It still baffles why they had so many different beers, many very similar.

Stylistically, it looks like a strong Mild. Which I suppose is what it was.

1913 William Younger 100/-		
pale malt	7.75 lb	51.67%
grits	6.50 lb	43.33%
glucose	0.75 lb	5.00%
Cluster 135 min	0.50 oz	
Cluster 60 min	0.50 oz	
Fuggles 30 min	0.50 oz	
OG	1066	
FG	1032	
ABV	4.50	
Apparent attenuation	51.52%	
IBU	28	
SRM	4	
Mash at	150° F	
Sparge at	160° F	
Boil time	135 minutes	
pitching temp	59° F	
Yeast	WLP028 Edinburgh Ale	

1914 William Younger 160/-

The beers of William Younger can be very confusing. Like the parallel sets of Strong Ales: Shilling Ales and Numbered Ales. What was the point of having a double set?

On the surface, none at all. But I suspect it's to do with the nature of Younger's business. Which wasn't restricted to Scotland. Far from it. Their beer was available all over the globe. It makes sense to have beers of a similar type, but different character for various markets.

Somewhere, they preferred their beer sweeter. Or at least less bitter. Those with a taste for bitterness would have plumped for Younger's numbered Strong Ales. Their No. 1 is the same strength as 160/-, but twice as bitter. Flip forward a few pages and you'll see.

The ingredients are the same as normal. It's hard to find much to discuss about Younger's recipes.

1914 William Younger 160/-		
pale malt	11.25 lb	52.33%
grits	9.25 lb	43.02%
No.3 invert sugar	0.50 lb	2.33%
glucose	0.50 lb	2.33%
Cluster 135 min	2.00 oz	
Cluster 60 min	1.75 oz	
Fuggles 30 min	1.25 oz	
Goldings dry hops	0.50 oz	
OG	1097	
FG	1037	
ABV	8.07	
Apparent attenuation	61.62%	
IBU	66	
SRM	8	
Mash at	150° F	
Sparge at	160° F	
Boil time	135 minutes	
pitching temp	58° F	
Yeast	WLP028 Edinburgh Ale	

1913 William Younger XX K

This is another what-the-hell-style-is-this beer. The K would imply a Keeping or Stock Ale. But the hopping and gravity aren't right. Looks more like a Mild to me.

It does look quite like a London X Ale of the period. Take a look at the 1914 Whitbread X Ale a few pages back. It's very similar to this, except a little darker. Though I wouldn't pay too much attention to the colour. It's quite possible that XX K was coloured darker at racking time.

No. 3 invert is once again my substitution for something described as "DM".

1913 William Younger XX K		
pale malt	7.00 lb	55.64%
grits	5.25 lb	41.73%
No. 3 invert	0.33 lb	2.62%
Cluster 120 min	0.50 oz	
Cluster 60 min	0.50 oz	
Fuggles 30 min	0.50 oz	
Goldings dry hops	0.25 oz	
OG	1056	
FG	1016	
ABV	5.29	
Apparent attenuation	71.43%	
IBU	24	
SRM	6	
Mash at	151° F	
Sparge at	160° F	
Boil time	120 minutes	
pitching temp	59° F	
Yeast	WLP028 Edinburgh Ale	

1913 William Younger XXXX

I usually class Younger XXXX as a Stock Ale, though I'm not sure that's what the brewery itself considered it. It doesn't really matter.

X's usually signify Mild Ale, but a quick look at the hopping dispels that idea. Also, there were few Mild Ales of such a high gravity at the time.

The grist is much the same as pretty much every other William Younger beer. Except for the small amount of sugar. It's listed as "DM" for which No.3 invert is my best guess.

As "6 gallons of colour" were added, I assume that the real finished colour of the beer was in the range 15 – 20 SRM.

At 10lbs per quarter (336 lbs) of malt, this is very heavily hopped. Which is reflected in the (calculated) bitterness of 79 IBUs. That's even after reducing the quantities a little to take account of the hops age, as some of the Cluster were from 1910 and the rest of the hops wer from the 1912 harvest.

1913 William Younger XXXX		
pale malt	8.75 lb	55.56%
grits	6.50 lb	41.27%
No. 3 invert	0.50 lb	3.17%
Cluster 150 min	2.00 oz	
Cluster 60 min	2.00 oz	
Fuggles 30 min	1.25 oz	
Goldings dry hops	1.00 oz	
OG	1070	
FG	1024	
ABV	6.09	
Apparent attenuation	65.71%	
IBU	84	
SRM	7	
Mash at	153° F	
Sparge at	160° F	
Boil time	150 minutes	
pitching temp	59° F	
Yeast	WLP028 Edinburgh Ale	

1913 William Younger No. 1

Here's a beer for those who think the Scots used virtually no hops. A crazily hopped Strong Scotch Ale. Or whatever you want to call it.

No.1 is a classic Strong Ale in the Burton style. A beer along the lines of Bass No. 1 or Truman No. 1. Hence the heavy hopping. William Younger had a range of numbered Strong Ales that were clearly Burton-inspired. Surely no coincidence that sons of the Younger family served apprenticeships at Evershed in Burton.

Though the introduction of these new-fangled numbered thingies didn't mean Younger stopped brewing the older Scottish style strong Shilling Ales. The two types were clearly aimed at different drinkers. 160/- (look back a few pages for details) was for those who liked a sweeter beer. No. 1 was for the others.

Billed as Strong Ale in Scotland and Scotch Ale in England, No. 1 was one of Younger's flagship products. One that hung around a long time. I think it was only in the 1970s that it finally passed away.

Younger's recipes all contain much the same elements. Just in different proportions and quantities. No. 1 is no exception. It just has more of everything than the other beers. Especially.

1913 William Younger No. 1		
pale malt	11.75 lb	54.65%
grits	8.75 lb	40.70%
No. 3 invert	0.50 lb	2.33%
Glucose	0.50 lb	2.33%
Cluster 150 min	3.25 oz	
Cluster 60 min	3.25 oz	
Fuggles 30 min	2.25 oz	
Goldings dry hops	1.00 oz	
OG	1096	
FG	1033	
ABV	8.33	
Apparent attenuation	65.63%	
IBU	130	
SRM	8	
Mash at	153° F	
Sparge at	160° F	
Boil time	150 minutes	
pitching temp	57° F	
Yeast	WLP028 Edinburgh Ale	

1914 William Younger No. 2 Sc

Unsurprisingly, the second-strongest of Younger's numbered Ales was No. 2.

Remember my theory about the Shilling Ales being for the local market and the numbered Ales for export? This beer scuppers that. As the "Sc" suffix obviously stands for Scotland.

No. 2 wasn't brewed as frequently as No. 1 or No, 3. Pretty rarely, really. It seems to have more in common with No. 1 than No. 3. Both include glucose. And the hopping rate, while not quite as high as No. 1, is much higher than No. 3. Those rates are, in lbs of hops per quarter (336 lbs) of malt: No. 1 10.83 lbs, No. 2 9.35 lbs, No. 3 4.24 lbs.

1914 William Younger No. 2 Sc		
pale malt	9.50 lb	54.57%
grits	7.25 lb	41.64%
No. 3 invert sugar	0.33 lb	1.90%
Glucose	0.33 lb	1.90%
Cluster 90 min	2.00 oz	
Cluster 60 min	2.00 oz	
Fuggles 30 min	1.25 oz	
Goldings dry hops	1.00 oz	
OG	1076	
FG	1025	
ABV	6.75	
Apparent attenuation	67.11%	
IBU	80	
SRM	7	
Mash at	152° F	
Sparge at	160° F	
Boil time	150 minutes	
pitching temp	58° F	
Yeast	WLP028 Edinburgh Ale	

1913 William Younger No. 3

No. 3 Scotch Ale was one of Younger's most long-lived products. Brewed from the 1850s to, well, virtually the present day, off and on.

Taking a quick look on RateBeer, it looks like 2012 is the last time it was brewed. Unbelievably, they have it classified as a Bitter. Surely the dark brown colour would have tipped them off that they've got the style wrong.

No. 3 was available both on draught and bottled. In Younger's London outlets, it substituted for Burton, to which it is quite similar, though quite a lot less bitter.

The recipe is much the same as many of their other beers: pale malt and a shitload of grits. Plus a tiny dash of sugar. So little sugar, you wonder why they bothered. Later versions were definitely dark brown in colour. This one may well have been coloured at racking time.

1913 William Younger No. 3		
pale malt	8.25 lb	55.93%
grits	6.25 lb	42.37%
No. 3 invert sugar	0.25 lb	1.69%
Cluster 90 min	0.75 oz	
Cluster 60 min	0.75 oz	
Fuggles 30 min	0.50 oz	
Goldings dry hops	0.33 oz	
OG	1065	
FG	1021.5	
ABV	5.75	
Apparent attenuation	66.92%	
IBU	31	
SRM	6	
Mash at	152° F	
Sparge at	160° F	
Boil time	120 minutes	
pitching temp	59° F	
Yeast	WLP028 Edinburgh Ale	

1913 William Younger S1

Younger had two separate lines of Stout. I used to wonder why, but know I think I've cracked it: they were intended for different markets.

In Scotland, Stout started to turn sweet towards the end of the 19th century. Through a combination of poor attenuation and very light hopping, a style of think, sweet Stout was developing. But William Younger also had an extensive trade both in England and further afield. Markets where the taste was for more traditional type Stouts.

My guess is that S1 and S2, which you'll see next, were Stouts destined for the local market, while DBS and MBS were for elsewhere.

It comes as a shock to see all the malts and sugars in S1, after spending some time with Younger's other beers, where the grists are mostly just pale malt and grits. Other than the latter, it's not a million miles away from a provincial English Stout grist.

No. 3 invert is my guess for something described simply as "DM" in the brewing record. I could be wrong, but it does only seem to appear in dark beers.

The hops are a challenge with some of Younger's beers, because they had a habit of using spent hops. Which was the case here. Though there were unused ones, too. For the spent hops,
I've reduced the alpha acid to 1%. As you can see, it's not exactly a hoppy beer.

1913 William Younger S1		
pale malt	6.25 lb	41.67%
black malt	1.00 lb	6.67%
crystal malt	1.00 lb	6.67%
grits	4.75 lb	31.67%
No. 3 invert sugar	0.50 lb	3.33%
glucose	1.00 lb	6.67%
caramel 500 SRM	0.50 lb	3.33%
Cluster 120 min spent	0.75 oz	
Cluster 90 min	0.50 oz	
Cluster 60 min	0.25 oz	
Fuggles 30 min	0.25 oz	
OG	1068	
FG	1031	
ABV	4.89	
Apparent attenuation	54.41%	
IBU	17	
SRM	41	
Mash at	150° F	
Sparge at	160° F	
Boil time	120 minutes	
pitching temp	59.5° F	
Yeast	WLP028 Edinburgh Ale	

1913 William Younger S2

The younger brother of S1 was S2. The two were often parti-gyled together.

Essentially, S2 is the same beer as S1, just weaker. It, too, contains spent hops, which I've accounted for in the same way.

The combination of minimal hopping and high FG must have left a pretty heavy tasting, sweet beer, despite the OG not being that enormous.

1913 William Younger S2		
pale malt	5.50 lb	41.51%
crystal malt 60 L	1.00 lb	7.55%
roast barley	1.00 lb	7.55%
grits	4.25 lb	32.08%
caramel 500 SRM	0.50 lb	3.77%
glucose	0.50 lb	3.77%
No. 3 invert sugar	0.50 lb	3.77%
Cluster 120 min spent	0.75 oz	
Cluster 90 min	0.25 oz	
Cluster 60 min	0.25 oz	
Fuggles 30 min	0.25 oz	
OG	1059	
FG	1026	
ABV	4.37	
Apparent attenuation	55.93%	
IBU	13	
SRM	47	
Mash at	150° F	
Sparge at	160° F	
Boil time	120 minutes	
pitching temp	60° F	
Yeast	WLP028 Edinburgh Ale	

1913 William Younger MBS

MBS is a strange beast. It seems to straddle Younger's two types of Stouts.

It has a reasonable degree of attenuation, but still uses some spent hops. The hopping rate is about double that of S1 and S2, however. Leaving the beer with a reasonable level of bitterness.

The grist is much the same as S1 and S2, except there's no glucose. Not such a huge difference. Younger also seemed to swap around between black malt and roast barley. Or maybe that's just down to scruffy handwriting and it's really all roast barley.

The types of hops are exactly the same as for all their other beers: Kent (1912), Pacific (1910 and 1912).

1913 William Younger MBS		
pale malt	7.25 lb	50.00%
crystal malt 60 L	0.75 lb	5.17%
black malt	0.75 lb	5.17%
grits	4.75 lb	32.76%
No. 3 invert sugar	0.50 lb	3.45%
caramel 500 SRM	0.50 lb	3.45%
Cluster 120 min spent	1.00 oz	
Cluster 90 min	0.50 oz	
Cluster 60 min	0.50 oz	
Fuggles 30 min	0.25 oz	
Goldings dry hops	0.75 oz	
OG	1065	
FG	1020	
ABV	5.95	
Apparent attenuation	69.23%	
IBU	24	
SRM	36	
Mash at	152° F	
Sparge at	160° F	
Boil time	150 minutes	
pitching temp	60° F	
Yeast	WLP028 Edinburgh Ale	

1913 William Younger DBS

DBS remained Younger's flagship Stout, as it had been since at least the 1850s. They were still brewing it in the 1940s.

The grist is pretty much identical to MBS, though there is roast barley in place of black malt. All William Younger's Stouts, for that matter, had very similar grists. It does make you wonder what the point of brewing so many different ones was.

Where DBS differs radically from Younger's other Stouts is in the hopping. Which is way heavier. The hopping rates, in lbs per quarter (336 lbs) of malt, were:

S1 and S2	1.88 lbs
MBS	3.5 lbs
DBS	5.88 lbs

Another difference with their other Stouts is what happened at racking. DBS was filled into butts, which implies that it was being aged before sale. Because no-one delivered that large a cask to a pub. The other Stouts were mostly racked into hogshead and half hogsheads, implying that they were meant to be bottled.

This looks very like a London Stout, save for the lack of brown malt. The specs are very similar to 1914 Whitbread ES.

1913 William Younger DBS		
pale malt	6.00 lb	42.86%
black malt	0.75 lb	5.36%
crystal malt 60 L	0.75 lb	5.36%
grits	4.75 lb	33.93%
No. 3 invert sugar	1.25 lb	8.93%
caramel 500 SRM	0.50 lb	3.57%
Cluster 150 min	2.00 oz	
Cluster 60 min	1.75 oz	
Fuggles 30 min	1.25 oz	
Goldings dry hops	1.00 oz	
OG	1068	
FG	1022	
ABV	6.09	
Apparent attenuation	67.65%	
IBU	48	
SRM	48	
Mash at	152° F	
Sparge at	160° F	
Boil time	150 minutes	
pitching temp	59.5° F	
Yeast	WLP028 Edinburgh Ale	

1917 William Younger P

Three years into the war, there's starting to be a noticeable impact on William Younger's beers.

P, their bottom-of-the-range Pale Ale, has lost 7 gravity points. Yet, oddly, the rate of hopping has risen from 0.69 to 0.92 lbs per barrel. Was the hopping rate increased to mask the fall in gravity? Or were they trying to compensate for the age of the hops?

The hops were Kent (1915) and Pacific (1914). Given that this beer was brewed in September, that means the hops were two and three years old. Breweries had little option but to use older hops, given the huge reduction in the UK crop and the virtual impossibility of importing them.

The grist remains the same as before the war: pale malt and loads of grits. Let's see if Younger's supply of the latter lasts through the war.

1917 William Younger P		
pale malt	4.75 lb	54.29%
grits	4.00 lb	45.71%
Cluster 120 mins	0.50 oz	
Cluster 90 mins	0.50 oz	
Fuggles 60 mins	0.50 oz	
Goldings dry hops	0.50 oz	
OG	1038	
FG	1013	
ABV	3.31	
Apparent attenuation	65.79%	
IBU	24	
SRM	3	
Mash at	150° F	
Sparge at	160° F	
Boil time	120 minutes	
pitching temp	59° F	
Yeast	WLP028 Edinburgh Ale	

1917 William Younger XP

The war has been kinder to XP than P. It's only shed two gravity points over three years of war.

A with P, the hopping rate has increased slightly, from 4.5 lbs per quarter (336 lbs) to 5 lbs. Which is reflected in a slight increase in the (calculated) IBUs, from 24 to 27. Though that's still pretty low for a Pale Ale of this strength.

XP was another old Younger product, having been brewed since at least 1851. Sadly, it wasn't going to make it out of WW I alive.

1917 William Younger XP		
pale malt	5.75 lb	54.76%
grits	4.75 lb	45.24%
Cluster 120 mins	0.50 oz	
Cluster 90 mins	0.50 oz	
Fuggles 30 mins	0.50 oz	
Goldings dry hops	0.50 oz	
OG	1046	
FG	1013	
ABV	4.37	
Apparent attenuation	71.74%	
IBU	27	
SRM	3	
Mash at	151° F	
Sparge at	160° F	
Boil time	90 minutes	
pitching temp	59.5° F	
Yeast	WLP028 Edinburgh Ale	

1917 William Younger XXP

Like XP, XXP has only seen a 2 degree drop in gravity. Lucky XXP.

Talking of long-lived beers, XXP was around from the early 1850s and lasted long enough for me to have drunk it. What was it called? I remember: Younger's Scotch. Or McEwan's 70/-. It was sold under both names.

In terms of the recipe, it's no change. Pale malt, grits. Kent and Pacific hops. All very dull. But still worth documenting. As I'm doing.

1917 William Younger XXP		
pale malt	7.25 lb	55.77%
grits	5.75 lb	44.23%
Cluster 120 mins	0.75 oz	
Cluster 90 mins	0.75 oz	
Fuggles 30 mins	0.75 oz	
Goldings dry hops	0.67 oz	
OG	1054	
FG	1015	
ABV	5.16	
Apparent attenuation	72.22%	
IBU	37	
SRM	4	
Mash at	151° F	
Sparge at	160° F	
Boil time	90 minutes	
pitching temp	58.5° F	
Yeast	WLP028 Edinburgh Ale	

1917 William Younger LAE

While I may not know what the hell LAE stood for, I can see how it's changed since 1914. Not very much, is the answer.

The gravity has dropped three points, which isn't such a big deal. The hopping is a little lighter, too.

The grist is identical to that of 1914 LAE: 19 quarters of pale malt and 16 quarters of grits. Come to think of it, that's much the same grist that Younger used for most of their beers.

The hops are around the same age as in 1914, either two or three seasons old. Which isn't exactly very fresh. They are: Kent (1915) and Pacific (1914, 1915). That's also very similar to the ones used in 1914.

1917 William Younger LAE		
pale malt	5.50 lb	53.66%
grits	4.75 lb	46.34%
Cluster 150 mins	1.00 oz	
Cluster 90 mins	1.00 oz	
Fuggles 30 mins	1.00 oz	
Goldings dry hops	1.00 oz	
OG	1045	
FG	1012	
ABV	4.37	
Apparent attenuation	73.33%	
IBU	54	
SRM	3	
Mash at	154° F	
Sparge at	160° F	
Boil time	150 minutes	
pitching temp	59° F	
Yeast	WLP028 Edinburgh Ale	

1917 William Younger Export

Export has fared slightly better than LAE, having lost just two points off its gravity since 1914. Which, percentage-wise, is an even smaller change.

It remains a powerful Pale Ale by modern UK standards, clocking in just shy of 5% ABV. Few would be drinking beers as strong as this in the coming couple of years.

The grist remains 45% grits, 55% pale malt. As all Younger's beers, pretty much. That must be getting close to the maximum percentage of grits that's practical, without adding extra enzymes.

The hops are a little fresher than in LAE, being all from 1915. The types are the same, however, Kent and Pacific.

1917 William Younger Export		
pale malt	6.50 lb	54.17%
grits	5.50 lb	45.83%
Cluster 120 mins	1.25 oz	
Cluster 90 mins	1.25 oz	
Fuggles 30 mins	1.25 oz	
Goldings dry hops	1.00 oz	
OG	1052	
FG	1015	
ABV	4.89	
Apparent attenuation	71.15%	
IBU	63	
SRM	4	
Mash at	154° F	
Sparge at	160° F	
Boil time	150 minutes	
pitching temp	59° F	
Yeast	WLP028 Edinburgh Ale	

1917 William Younger H 60/-

Younger continued to brew a rather confusingly large range of beers in 1917. Most of them rather similar.

H 60/- has fared rather badly compared to their other beers in terms of gravity. It's dropped 7 points, or around 17%. While Export's gravity had dropped a bit under 4%. That's quite a difference. Implying that it was a cheap beer. They were the ones that tended to suffer most from gravity cuts. Those and the really big sellers.

I can't tell you much about the grist, which, as most of the rest of their beers is 55% pale malt and 45% grits. Younger certainly loved them some grits.

The hops are Kent (1915) and Pacific (1914). Another sign that this is a budget beer.

1917 William Younger H 60/-		
pale malt	4.75 lb	55.88%
grits	3.75 lb	44.12%
Cluster 120 mins	0.50 oz	
Cluster 90 mins	0.50 oz	
Fuggles 30 mins	0.25 oz	
Goldings dry hops	0.33 oz	
OG	1037	
FG	1012	
ABV	3.31	
Apparent attenuation	67.57%	
IBU	22	
SRM	3	
Mash at	150° F	
Sparge at	160° F	
Boil time	120 minutes	
pitching temp	59° F	
Yeast	WLP028 Edinburgh Ale	

1917 William Younger 60/-

The other 60/- variant hasn't been hit so much in its gravity. It's fallen just three points since 1913.

There has been a significant change in the recipe, though. Grits are down to 32% of the grist. Quite a big change from the 45% Younger usually used. Don't read too much into the difference between this beer and the preceding H 60/-. That was brewed six weeks earlier and there had clearly been a change in the supply situation around the beginning of October 1917. All their beers from then contained a lot fewer grits.

The hops haven't got any newer, being Kent (1915) and Pacific (1915). At least none were older than three years.

It's hopped at exactly the same rate per barrel as H 60/-, despite being a good bit stronger.

1917 William Younger 60/-		
pale malt	7.00 lb	68.29%
grits	3.25 lb	31.71%
Cluster 120 mins	0.50 oz	
Cluster 90 mins	0.50 oz	
Fuggles 30 mins	0.25 oz	
Goldings dry hops	0.50 oz	
OG	1044	
FG	1019	
ABV	3.31	
Apparent attenuation	56.82%	
IBU	21	
SRM	3.5	
Mash at	150° F	
Sparge at	160° F	
Boil time	120 minutes	
pitching temp	61° F	
Yeast	WLP028 Edinburgh Ale	

1917 William Younger Mild

A new beer has appeared since 1914, something simply called Mild.

Mild was becoming a bit of a rarity in Scotland by WW I. Its place increasingly being taken by low-gravity, lightly-hopped Pale Ales. In the 1920s, it almost completely disappeared, save at William Younger. I suspect they only brewed it for their pubs in England, where Mild was still a must have.

It's very similar to 60/-, except for one thing: the hopping. Mild has around 50% more hops. Which you can see from the much higher (calculated) IBUs. Weirdly, that's higher than in XP or XXP, two Pale ales of equal or greater strength. The ABV is also higher because of a greater degree of attenuation.

The hops were 1915 Kent and 1915 Pacific, as in all their other beers.

1917 William Younger Mild		
pale malt	6.75 lb	65.85%
grits	3.50 lb	34.15%
Cluster 120 mins	0.75 oz	
Cluster 90 mins	0.75 oz	
Fuggles 30 mins	0.50 oz	
Goldings dry hops	0.50 oz	
OG	1044	
FG	1011	
ABV	4.37	
Apparent attenuation	75.00%	
IBU	38	
SRM	3.5	
Mash at	151° F	
Sparge at	160° F	
Boil time	120 minutes	
pitching temp	61° F	
Yeast	WLP028 Edinburgh Ale	

1917 William Younger S1

The war has had an obvious impact, reducing the gravity of S1 by 13 points. That's below the OG of S2 in 1914. Which might explain why S2 seems to have disappeared.

The grist has also changed, with amber malt being added. Otherwise it's much the same. Though the percentage of grits, which is under 30%, is quite low for this period Younger recipes.

There are no spent hops in this version. Which makes my life easier. The hops used are quite old, 1915 Kent and 1915 Pacific. As this beer was brewed in October, that makes them 2 years old.

There were 14 lbs of liquorice in the original, which works out to about a third of an ounce for a batch this size.

1917 William Younger S1		
pale malt	6.50 lb	49.06%
amber malt	1.00 lb	7.55%
crystal malt 60 L	1.00 lb	7.55%
grits	3.50 lb	26.42%
roast barley	1.00 lb	7.55%
caramel 1000 SRM	0.25 lb	1.89%
Cluster 120 mins	0.50 oz	
Cluster 90 mins	0.33 oz	
Fuggles 30 mins	0.33 oz	
OG	1055	
FG	1020	
ABV	4.63	
Apparent attenuation	63.64%	
IBU	20	
SRM	34	
Mash at	150° F	
Sparge at	160° F	
Boil time	120 minutes	
pitching temp	60° F	
Yeast	WLP028 Edinburgh Ale	

1917 William Younger S3

Younger still brewed a weaker sweet Stout than S1. Not S2, but S3. Doubtless because of its lower gravity.

And S2 doesn't seem to have totally disappeared. Because the racking record for this brew mentions S1, S2 and S3. I assume that S1 was a blend of the other two.

The grist is the same as S1, based around pale and amber malt and roast barley, plus caramel. There are spent hops in this batch, from a brew of LAE earlier in the day. I've assumed just 1% alpha acid for the spent hops. Maybe I'm being too generous.

The attenuation is quite a bit higher than for pre-war S1 and S2. Perhaps to keep it vaguely intoxicating. Had the rate of attenuation been, like for those beers, around 54%, the ABV would have been just 3.2%.

1917 William Younger S3		
pale malt	6.25 lb	59.52%
amber malt	0.75 lb	7.14%
grits	2.50 lb	23.81%
roast barley	0.75 lb	7.14%
caramel 1000 SRM	0.25 lb	2.38%
spent Cluster 120 mins	0.75 oz	
Cluster 120 mins	0.25 oz	
Cluster 90 mins	0.25 oz	
Fuggles 30 mins	0.25 oz	
OG	1044	
FG	1015.5	
ABV	3.77	
Apparent attenuation	64.77%	
IBU	16	
SRM	29	
Mash at	150° F	
Sparge at	160° F	
Boil time	120 minutes	
pitching temp	61° F	
Yeast	WLP028 Edinburgh Ale	

Mini Book Series volume XXXII: Armistice!

1917 William Younger No. 1

For October 1917, this was an incredibly strong beer. Most beers over 1050° perished in the April 1917 apocalypse.

That said, the gravity has still fallen by 15 points. But some of that has been offset by an increase in the rate of attenuation. It's less than 1% ABV weaker than the 1813 version.

The recipe has been considerably simplified, trimmed down to just pale malt and grits. I assume supply problems were the cause of that. While not as crazily hopped as the pre-war version, it still comes out to over 80 (calculated) IBUs.

The hops were the same combination of Pacific and Kent as all Younger's other beers.

1917 William Younger No. 1		
pale malt	13.75 lb	73.33%
grits	5.00 lb	26.67%
Cluster 150 mins	2.00 oz	
Cluster 60 mins	2.00 oz	
Fuggles 30 mins	2.00 oz	
Goldings dry hops	1.00 oz	
OG	1081	
FG	1023.5	
ABV	7.61	
Apparent attenuation	70.99%	
IBU	84	
SRM	5.5	
Mash at	153° F	
Sparge at	160° F	
Boil time	150 minutes	
pitching temp	59° F	
Yeast	WLP028 Edinburgh Ale	

1918 William Younger 5B

I was puzzling for a while about the name of this beer – which has appeared out of nowhere – then I twigged. It stands for 5d Bitter.

5d per pint was one of the price-controlled categories when this was brewed in January 1916. It was defined as a beer with a gravity 1036-1042°. Hang on, I hear you say. How can this be a 5d beer if its OG is 1044°. Simple, they mixed in water at racking time. 15 barrels in 183 barrels of beer. Which knocks the effective OG down to 1040.7°.

The grist is just pale malt and grits. Not even all that many grits by William Younger's standards: less than 10% of the total.

The hopping is quite light and the hops quite old. Namely: Kent (1915 and 1916), Pacific (1915). Hence the very low (calculated) IBU count.

1918 William Younger 5B		
pale malt	8.25 lb	80.49%
grits	2.00 lb	19.51%
Cluster 120 mins	0.50 oz	
Fuggles 30 mins	0.75 oz	
Goldings dry hops	0.33 oz	
OG	1044	
FG	1013	
ABV	4.10	
Apparent attenuation	70.45%	
IBU	19	
SRM	4	
Mash at	151° F	
Sparge at	160° F	
Boil time	120 minutes	
pitching temp	60.5° F	
Yeast	WLP028 Edinburgh Ale	

1918 William Younger XXP

How come XXP has suddenly increased in strength? It's all to do with how Younger brewed in the later war years. They brewed at high gravities, then watered down at racking time. They continued to do this right through the 1920s. Not sure why. Perhaps it was for yeast health.

XXP received – I think, because it is a bit confusing in the brewing record – 34 barrels of water to 134 barrels of beer) at racking time. Which would have reduced the effective OG to about 1048°. For full authenticity, brew to this strength then water down after primary fermentation.

The recipe is, boringly, exactly the same as 5B.

1918 William Younger XXP		
pale malt	11.50 lb	80.70%
grits	2.75 lb	19.30%
Cluster 120 mins	0.75 oz	
Fuggles 30 mins	1.00 oz	
Goldings dry hops	0.50 oz	
OG	1060	
FG	1020	
ABV	5.29	
Apparent attenuation	66.67%	
IBU	24	
SRM	5	
Mash at	151° F	
Sparge at	160° F	
Boil time	120 minutes	
pitching temp	59.5° F	
Yeast	WLP028 Edinburgh Ale	

1918 William Younger Export

The gravity of Export is unchanged since 1917. At least as it was brewed.

And that's how it stayed. There's no mention of added water so I have to assume that Export reached drinkers unfiddled with. Perhaps that's it's because it really was destined for export. Small quantities of beer were exported during the war. And William Younger had been a big exporter before the war.

The level of hopping – much higher than in Younger's other Pale Ales – is another clue that it might be a genuine export beer. Or it was a Stock Pale Ale that was meant to undergo a secondary conditioning. Hang on, it was all racked into butts. A sure sign that it was going to be aged.

Stock Pale Ales, once the only type of Pale Ale, were becoming increasingly rare. Only the real specialists in Burton and Edinburgh persisted with the style between the wars. Even fewer after WW II. Iyt died out in the 1950s.

1918 William Younger Export		
pale malt	9.00 lb	75.00%
grits	3.00 lb	25.00%
Cluster 150 mins	1.50 oz	
Fuggles 30 mins	2.00 oz	
Goldings dry hops	1.00 oz	
OG	1052	
FG	1015	
ABV	4.89	
Apparent attenuation	71.15%	
IBU	51	
SRM	4	
Mash at	154° F	
Sparge at	160° F	
Boil time	150 minutes	
pitching temp	59° F	
Yeast	WLP028 Edinburgh Ale	

1918 William Younger S1

Surprisingly, S1 has only lost a single gravity point since 1917. But that's doubtless because it was brewed in January 1918. The apocalypse only arrived in April.

The grist remains much the same as in the previous year. But there has been a big change in one area: the hopping. It was very high before, now it's ludicrously low. Just a quarter of what it had been. No big shock then that the (calculated) IBUs are incredibly low.

The few hops were Kent (1915, 1916) and Pacific (1915), Not only bugger all hops, also pretty old ones.

This beer must have tasted weird. Minimal hopping, quite a high FG but also quite a lot of roast barley. Sweet and roasty, I suppose.

1918 William Younger S1		
pale malt	8.25 lb	63.07%
crystal malt 60 L	1.00 lb	7.65%
grits	2.50 lb	19.11%
roast barley	1.00 lb	7.65%
caramel 1000 SRM	0.33 lb	2.52%
Cluster 150 mins	0.25 oz	
Fuggles 30 mins	0.125 oz	
OG	1054	
FG	1019	
ABV	4.63	
Apparent attenuation	64.81%	
IBU	7	
SRM	36	
Mash at	150° F	
Sparge at	160° F	
Boil time	120 minutes	
pitching temp	60.5° F	
Yeast	WLP028 Edinburgh Ale	

1918 William Younger 5S

It took a while to twig what "5S" meant. Then it dropped: 5d Stout. They're talking in price categories again.

According to the rule in force when this beer was brewed in January 1918, a 5d beer (one that retailed for 5d per pint in a public bar) had an OG between 1036° and 1042°. Making this 5S too strong for the category.

My immediate thought, was that they'd probably watered it down at racking time. But they didn't. Well, they did add 1 barrel to the 64 barrels that were brewed. But that's not going to change the gravity much.

Grist-wise, it's identical to the S1 above, with which it was parti-gyled.

1918 William Younger 5S		
pale malt	6.75 lb	64.29%
crystal malt 60 L	0.75 lb	7.14%
grits	2.00 lb	19.05%
roast barley	0.75 lb	7.14%
caramel 1000 SRM	0.25 lb	2.38%
Cluster 150 mins	0.125 oz	
Fuggles 30 mins	0.125 oz	
OG	1044	
FG	1022	
ABV	2.91	
Apparent attenuation	50.00%	
IBU	4	
SRM	30	
Mash at	150° F	
Sparge at	160° F	
Boil time	120 minutes	
pitching temp	61° F	
Yeast	WLP028 Edinburgh Ale	

1918 William Younger 5M

I'm going to go out on a limb here and guess that 5M means a 5d Mild.

You may wonder what makes this a Mild. I don't blame you. I suppose it is more lightly hopped that their Pale Ales. Though they themselves contain fewer hops than London Mild. What you expected from a type of beer must have depended on where in the country you lived.

The grist is the same old Younger pale malt/grits combination, though with rather fewer of the latter than in earlier years. Not very exciting. There's a good chance that is was primed with caramel at racking time, at least for some markets. Though few Milds were really dark at this point. Rarely more than 12-15 SRM at most.

The hops were Kent (1915, 1916) and Pacific (1915).

1918 William Younger 5M		
pale malt	8.25 lb	84.62%
grits	1.50 lb	15.38%
Cluster 150 mins	0.50 oz	
Fuggles 30 mins	0.50 oz	
Goldings dry hops	0.25 oz	
OG	1042	
FG	1010	
ABV	4.23	
Apparent attenuation	76.19%	
IBU	16	
SRM	4	
Mash at	151° F	
Sparge at	160° F	
Boil time	120 minutes	
pitching temp	61° F	
Yeast	WLP028 Edinburgh Ale	

IV Appendix

Food Control Orders

Beer

THE INTOXICATING LIQUOR (OUTPUT AND DELIVERY) ORDER, 1917. DATED MARCH 29, 1917.

1917. No. 270.

Whereas the Food Controller is empowered by Regulation 2F of the Defence of the Realm Regulations to make orders regulating, or- giving directions with respect to the production, manufacture, treatment, use, consumption, transport, storage, distribution, supply, sale or purchase of, or other dealing in, or measures to be taken in relation to, any article (including orders as to maximum or minimum price) where it appears to him necessary or expedient to make any such order for the purpose of encouraging or maintaining the food supply of the country: And whereas it appears to the Food Controller to be -expedient, for the purpose of encouraging and maintaining the food supply of the country, to extend the existing restrictions on the output, delivery, and distribution of beer and other intoxicating liquor in manner appearing in this Order, Now, therefore, in pursuance of his powers under the said regulations and all other powers enabling him in that behalf, the Food Controller hereby orders, as follows:

I. Beer.

1. (1) A brewer for sale shall not brew at his brewery in any quarter more than the maximum barrelage for the quarter[49] as determined under this Order.

(2) The maximum barrelage shall be determined for the purposes of this Order in the same manner as under the Output of Beer (Restriction) Acts, 19.16, except that

> (a) in ascertaining the standard barrelage under subsection (2) of Section two of the Output of Beer (Restriction) Act, 1916, 66 per cent, shall be substituted as the amount of reduction where 15 per "cent, is under that provision the amount of reduction, and 72 per cent, shall be substituted as the amount of reduction where 30 per cent, is under that provision the amount of reduction ; and

> (b) ten million barrels shall be substituted for twenty-six million barrels as the rate of the total output of beer in the United Kingdom under the proviso to subsection (2) of Section two of that Act; and

> (c) in determining the maximum barrelage for the quarter commencing on the first day of April, 1917, or any subsequent quarter, any surplus barrelage

---

[49] MAXIMUM BARRELAGE FOR QUARTER COMMENCING OCTOBER IST, 1917. For that quarter the maximum barrelage is increased by the Intoxicating Liquor (Output and Delivery) Order, No. 3, p. 78.
A similar increase in the maximum barrelage for the past quarter, i.e., that commencing July 1st, 1917, was made by the Intoxicating Liquor (Output and Delivery) Order, No. 2 (St. R. & 0., 1917, No. 700), which was in identical terms with Order No. 3, except as to dates and except that the "original gravity" referred to in Clauses 3 (a) and 6 (c) thereof was 1036° instead of 1042°.

accrued in respect of any quarter previous to that commencing on the first day of April, 1917, shall not be taken into account.

(3) Where it appears to the Commissioners of Customs and Excise (hereinafter referred to as the Commissioners) that, owing to the transfer of licensed premises from one brewery to another or for the purpose of meeting any change in the amount of beer required to meet the supply of any localities, it is expedient to transfer barrelage from one brewer to another, the Commissioners may by order make the necessary transfer, and the maximum
barrelages of the respective brewers shall be increased or decreased accordingly.

(4) The rights of brewers under subsection (3) of Section 2 of the Output of Beer (Restriction) Act, 1916, shall be suspended while this Order is in force.

(5) If the Food Controller, at the request of the Army Council, grants a special certificate to any brewer authorising him to brew beer in excess of the limits prescribed by this Order, on the ground that the addition is required for the use of military canteens, the amount of beer which that brewer is entitled to brew shall thereupon be increased by the number of barrels stated in the certificate; and this Order shall apply accordingly.

2.- (1) The same provision shall be applicable in relation to the effect of this Order on contracts as is applicable in relation to the effect of the Output of Beer (Restriction) Act, 1916, on contracts under Section 4 of that Act.

(2) Licence holders, and persons having the same rights as licence holders under Section 5 of the Output of Beer (Restriction) Act, 1916, as amended by any subsequent Act, shall have the same rights, and brewers shall be under the same obligations, in connection with the output of beer as limited by this Order as under the said Section 5, except that the percentage of reduction in the number of standard barrels which a licence holder is entitled to obtain under that section and the reduction from the amount stated in the certificate for the purpose of ascertaining the reduction and transfer of maximum barrelage shall be increased so as to be 66 per cent, instead of 15 per cent.

(3) Any brewer who has not given to a licence holder any particulars or certificate which the licence holder is entitled to obtain from him under Section 5 of the Output of Beer (Restriction) Act, 1916, shall give the particulars or certificate to the licence holder within fourteen days after a request in writing therefor is made by the licence holder.

(4) A brewer shall give to a licence holder a copy of any certificate which has been obtained from him for the purpose of Section 5 of the Output of Beer (Restriction) Act, 1916, within fourteen days after a request in writing for the copy is made to him by the licence holder showing that the certificate originally obtained is either lost or for some other reason not available for use by the licence holder.

(5) Where beer has been supplied to a licence holder through a person recognised by the brewer as his agent

(a) the agent shall be under the same obligation to give particulars and certificates of the beer as if he was the brewer; and

(b) the beer shall be deemed to be beer supplied by the brewer to the licence holder and not by the brewer to the agent.

3. Expressions to which a special meaning is attached by the Output of Beer (Restriction) Act, 1916, have (unless the context otherwise requires) the same meaning when used in this Part of this Order.

"Food Supply Manual October 1917", pages 71-74

THE INTOXICATING LIQUOR (OUTPUT AND DELIVERY) ORDER, 1917, DATED MARCH 29, 1917, AS AMENDED BY THE INTOXICATING LIQUOR (OUTPUT AND DELIVERY) ORDER No. 4, 1917.

1917. No. 270 as amended by No. 1213.

Whereas the Food Controller is empowered by Regulation 2F of the Defence of the Realm Regulations to make orders regulating, or giving directions with respect to the production, manufacture, treatment, use, consumption, transport, storage, distribution, supply, sale or purchase of, or other dealing in, or measures to be taken in relation to, any article (including orders as to maximum or minimum price) where it appears to him necessary or expedient to make any such order for the purpose of encouraging or maintaining the food supply of the country : And whereas it appears to the Food Controller to be expedient, for the purpose of encouraging and maintaining the food supply of the country, to extend the existing restrictions on the output, delivery, and distribution of beer and other intoxicating liquor, in manner appearing in this Order, Now, therefore, in pursuance of his powers under the said regulations and all other powers enabling him in that behalf, the Food Controller hereby orders, as follows:

1. Beer.

1.

(1) A brewer for sale shall not brew at his brewery in any quarter more than the maximum barrelage for the quarter as determined under this Order.

(2) The maximum barrelage shall be determined for the purposes of this Order in the same manner as under the Output of Beer (Restriction) Acts, 1916, except that

(a) in ascertaining the standard barrelage under subsection (2) of Section two of the Output of Beer (Restriction) Act, 1916, 66 per cent, shall be substituted as the amount of reduction where 15 per cent, is under that provision the amount of reduction, and 72 per cent, shall be substituted as the amount of reduction where 30 per cent, is under that provision the amount of reduction; and

(b) ten million barrels shall be substituted for twenty-six million barrels as the rate of the total output of beer in the United Kingdom under the proviso to subsection (2) of Section two of that Act; and

(c) in determining the maximum barrelage for the quarter commencing on the first day of April, 1917, or any subsequent quarter, any surplus barrelage accrued in respect of any quarter previous to that commencing on the first day of April, 1917, shall not be taken
into account.

(3) Where it appears to the Commissioners of Customs and Excise (hereinafter referred to as the Commissioners) that, owing to the transfer of licensed premises from one brewery to another or for the purpose of meeting any change in the amount of beer required to meet the supply of any localities, it is expedient to transfer barrelag6 from one brewer to another, the Commissioners may by order make the necessary transfer, and the maximum
barrelages of the respective brewers shall be increased or decreased accordingly.

(4) The rights of brewers under subsection (3) of Section 2 of the Output of Beer (Restriction) Act, 1916, shall be suspended while this Order is in force.

(5) If the Food Controller , at the request of the Array Council, grants a special certificate to any brewer authorising him to brew beer in excess of the limits prescribed by this Order, on the ground that the addition is required for the use of military canteens, the amount of beer which that brewer is entitled to brew shall thereupon be increased by the number of barrels stated in the certificate; and this Order shall apply accordingly.

2.

(1) The same provision shall be applicable in relation to the effect of this Order on contracts as is applicable in relation to the effect of the Output of Beer (Restriction) Act, 1916, on contracts under Section 4 of that Act.

(2) Licence holders, and persons having the same rights as licence holders under Section 5 of the Output of Beer (Restriction) Act, 1916, as amended by any subsequent Act, shall have the same rights, and brewers shall be under the same obligations, in connection with the output of beer as limited by this Order as under the said Section 5, except that the percentage of reduction in the number of standard barrels which a licence holder is entitled to obtain under that section and the reduction from the amount stated in the certificate for the purpose of ascertaining the reduction and transfer of maximum barrelage shall be increased so as to be 66 per cent, instead of 15 per cent.

(3) Any brewer who has not given to a licence holder any particulars or certificate which the licence holder is entitled to obtain from him under Section 5 of the Output of Beer (Restriction) Act, 1916, shall give the particulars or certificate to the licence holder within fourteen days after a request in writing therefore is made by the licence holder.

(4) A brewer shall give to a licence holder a copy of any certificate which has been obtained from him for the purpose of Section 5 of the Output of Beer (Restriction) Act, 1916, within fourteen days after a request in writing for the copy is made to him by the licence holder showing that the certificate originally obtained is either lost or for some other reason not available for use by the licence holder.

(5) Where beer has been supplied to a licence holder through a person recognised by the brewer as his agent

(a) the agent shall be under the same obligation to give particulars and certificates of the beer as if he was the brewer; and

(b) the beer shall be deemed to be beer supplied by the brewer to the licence holder and not by the brewer to the agent.

3. Expressions to which a special meaning is attached by the Output of Beer (Restriction) Act, 1916, have (unless the context.otherwise requires) the same meaning when used in this Part of this Order.

"Food Supply Manual April 1918", pages 154-157.

THE INTOXICATING LIQUOR (OUTPUT AND DELIVERY) ORDER No. 3, 1917. DATED OCTOBER 15, 1917.

1917. No. 1059:

In exercise of the powers conferred upon him by the Defence of the Realm Regulations, and of all other powers enabling him in that behalf, the Food Controller hereby orders as follows:

1. During the quarter commencing on the 1st October, 1917 (hereinafter referred to as the current quarter) the maximum barrelage[50] which a brewer for sale is authorised to brew under the Intoxicating Liquor (Output and Delivery) Order, 1917 (hereinafter referred to as the principal Order) shall be increased.

(a) By twenty per cent, if he gives such notice and .complies with such conditions as are hereinafter mentioned and such increase is, in this Order, referred to as the twenty per cent, increase ; and

(b) By such further amount, if any, as in his case may be authorised by licence of the Food Controller if he complies with the conditions subject to which such a licence is granted, and the increase authorised by such licence is

---

[50] INCREASE OF MAXIMUM BARRELAGE. A similar increase in the maximum barrelage for the past quarter, i.e., that commencing July 1st, 1917, was made by the Intoxicating Liquor (Output and Delivery) Order No. 2 (St. R. & O., 1917, No. 700), which was in identical terms with the present Order No. 3 except as to dates and except that the "original gravity" referred to in Clauses 3 (a) and 6 (c) of this Order (No. 3) was in the (No. 2) Order 1036° instead of 1042°.

hereinafter called the licensed increase: Provided that the aggregate amount of the licensed increases shall not exceed such an amount as with the aggregate amount of the twenty percent, increases will increase the aggregate barrelage to be brewed by all brewers for sale in the current quarter by more than thirty-three and one-third per cent.

2. A brewer for sale shall be authorised to brew in the current quarter the twenty per cent, increase if he gives notice to the Commissioners of Customs and Excise (hereinafter referred to as the Commissioners) on or before the 20th October, 1917, that he accepts and will comply with the conditions subject to which the twenty per cent, increase is authorised by this Order, and such brewer is hereinafter referred to as an accepting brewer.

3. The conditions subject to which the twenty per cent, increase is authorised are the following :

>   (a) One-half of the total amount of beer brewed by the accepting -brewer in the current quarter (exclusive of the licensed increase) shall be brewed and delivered out of his brewery at a gravity not exceeding an original gravity of 1042° :
>
>   (b) The remaining half of the beer brewed (exclusive of the licensed increase) shall be brewed at an average original gravity not exceeding the average original gravity of the total beer brewed at his brewery during the quarter commencing on the 1st October, 1916:
>
>   (c) In the month of October not more than one-third and in the months of October and November not more than two-thirds of the total amount of beer which the brewer is entitled to brew during the current quarter (exclusive of the licensed increase) shall be delivered out of his brewery :

And it shall be the duty of every accepting brewer to comply with such conditions.

4. The additional barrelage authorised to be brewed by this Order and by licences under this Order shall not be taken into account in reckoning the ten million barrels referred to in sub-section (2) of Clause 1 of the principal Order. Principal Order.

5. The same provision shall be applicable in relation to the Contracts, effect of this Order on contracts as is applicable in relation to the effect of the Output of Beer (Restriction) Act, 1916, on contracts under Section 4 of that Act.

6. The following provisions shall apply with respect to certificates available for the current quarter granted or to be granted to a licence holder:

>   (a) Except under the authority of the Food Controller a certificate granted by an accepting brewer shall not during the current quarter be used to transfer barrelage to a person who is not an accepting brewer.
>
>   (b) The number of standard barrels which a licence holder may obtain from an accepting brewer under a certificate shall be increased by 20 per cent.

(c) An accepting brewer who has undertaken to supply the licence holder with beer under a certificate shall not supply more than one-half of such beer at a gravity exceeding an original gravity of 1042°.

(d) This clause shall apply to persons having the same rights as licence holders in the same way as it applies to licence holders.

7. If any question shall arise under this Order as to the average Gravity of original gravity of beer such question shall be determined by the beer Commissioners.

8. Every accepting brewer shall keep such records as to gravity Records, and amount of beer brewed and delivered and other matters as are requisite to determine whether or not the provisions of this Order are being complied with, and all such records and documents
connected therewith shall at all times be open to the inspection of the Food Controller and of the Commissioners.

9.

(a) No account shall be taken of any surplus barrelage accrued since the 1st April, 1917, for the purpose of computing the increase permitted by Clause 1 of this Order.

(b) In the case of a brewer who was an accepting brewer within the meaning of the Intoxicating Liquor (Output and Delivery) Order (No. 2), 1917[51] such surplus barrelage may except in such cases as the Food Controller otherwise directs, only be brewed subject to the conditions applicable under conditions (a) and (b) of clause 3 of this Order to the beer therein referred to.

10. Infringements of this Order are summary offences against the Defence of the Realm Regulations.

11. This Order may be cited as the Intoxicating Liquor (Output and Delivery) Order No. 3, 1917, and should be read as one with the principal Order.

"Food Supply Manual October 1917", pages 78-80

---

[51] "ACCEPTING BREWER WITHIN THE MEANING OF ORDER (No. 2)," i.e., a brewer for sale who gave notice to the Commissioners of Customs and Excise on or before the 21st July, 1917, that he accepted and would comply with the three following conditions :
1. One-half of the total amount of beer brewed by the accepting brewer in the quarter commencing on the 1st July, 1917 (exclusive of the licensed increase) shall be brewed and delivered out of his brewery at a gravity not exceeding an original gravity of 1036° :
2. The remaining half of the beer brewed (exclusive of the licensed increase) shall be brewed at an average original gravity not exceeding the average original gravity of the total beer brewed at his brewery during the quarter commencing on the 1st July, 1916 :
3 In the month of July not more than one-third and in the months of July and August not more than two-thirds of the total amount of beer which the brewer is entitled to brew during the quarter commencing on the 1st July, 1917 (exclusive of the licensed increase)
shall be delivered out of his brewery :

THE BEER (PRICES AND DESCRIPTION) ORDER, 1917. DATED OCTOBER 15, 1917.

1917. No. 1058.

In exercise of the powers conferred upon him by the Defence of the Realm Regulations and of all other powers enabling him in that behalf, the Food Controller hereby orders that except under the authority of the Food Controller the following regulations shall be observed by all persons concerned:

1. A person shall not on or after the 28th October, 1917, sell or offer to sell any beer of the gravities hereinafter mentioned in any part of any licensed premises having a public bar or public bars unless

   (a) such beer at the time of such sale or offer for sale is on sale by imperial measure in the public bar or public bars of the licensed premises ; and also

   (b) such beer when sold by imperial measure in the public bar or public bars is sold at prices not exceeding the maximum prices provided by this Order.

2. Where beer is sold by imperial measure in a public bar, the maximum price for beer of an original gravity less than $1036°$ shall be at the rate of 4d. per imperial pint, and for beer of an original gravity not exceeding $1042°$ and not less than $1036°$ shall be at the rate of 5d. per imperial pint.

3.

   (a) Where beer is delivered after the 18th October, 1917, in a barrel or cask

   (i) the brewer or dealer disposing of such beer shall state on the invoice, if such be the fact, that the original gravity of the beer exceeds $1042°$ and, in any other case, the maximum price at which the beer in each such barrel or cask may under this Order be sold in the public bar of licensed premises ; and

   (ii) the brewer shall also before permitting delivery out of his brewery plainly and durably mark on the head of any barrel or cask containing beer of an original gravity less than $1036°$ the mark "4d." and on any barrel or cask containing beer of an original gravity not exceeding $1042°$ and not less than $1036°$ the mark "5d." the figures to be not less than two inches long.

   (b) No dealer in or retailer of beer shall alter or deface such mark or permit such mark to be altered or defaced, or dilute or permit to be diluted the beer in any barrel or cask.

4. A person authorised in that behalf by the Food Controller, or a Food Committee to procure for analysis samples of beer on sale in any licensed premises shall have all

the powers of procuring samples conferred by the Sale of Food and Drugs Acts, and a person selling beer by retail shall, on tender of the price for the quantity which he shall reasonably require for the purpose of analysis, sell the same to him accordingly.

5. In any proceedings in respect of an infringement of this Order the production of the certificate of the principal chemist of the Government Laboratories or of an analyst appointed under the Sale of Food and Drugs Acts, shall be sufficient evidence of the facts therein stated unless the defendant require that the person who made the analysis be called as a witness.
The certificate of the principal chemist or of the analyst shall, so far as circumstances permit be in the form required by the Sale of Food and Drugs Acts.

6. If in any proceedings against a retailer of beer in respect of an infringement of this Order, it is proved that an offence has been committed but the person charged with the offence proves :

> (a) that he purchased the beer, in respect of which the offence was committed, from a person who sold the beer as or for beer which might lawfully be sold in a public bar at the price charged ;
>
> (b) that he had no reason to believe at the time of sale that the gravity of the beer was not such as permitted of it being sold at the price charged or that the provisions of Clause 3 (b) of this .Order had not been duly observed ; and
>
> (c) that he has given due notice to the prosecutor that he intended to rely on the provisions of this clause: such person shall be entitled to be discharged from the
> prosecution.

7. Where the Food Controller is of opinion that the price payable under any contract subsisting at the date of this Order for the sale of beer of a gravity not exceeding an original gravity of 1042° is such that the beer cannot at the prices permitted by this Order be sold or supplied by retail in a public bar at a reasonable profit, he may, if he thinks fit, cancel such contract or may modify the terms thereof in such manner as shall appear to him to be just.

8. A person shall not on the occasion of a sale of any beer of an original gravity less than 1036° or in any advertisement, circular or placard relating to any such beer describe the same as "Government Ale" or "Government Beer" or use any other form of words calculated to lead to the belief that such beer is brewed under the authority, or pursuant to the directions of His Majesty's Government, or any Government Department.

9. Except in Clause 8 the expression "Beer" shall not include "Bottled Beer."

10. In this Order :-
The "Food Committee " means in respect of any area in Great Britain the Food Control Committee established for the area pursuant to the Food Control Committees (Constitution) Order, 1917 and in respect of Ireland the Food Control Committee appointed for Ireland by the Food Controller.

"Beer" includes ale, porter, spruce beer, black beer and any other description of beer.
"Public Bar" means :-

 (a) where there is only one bar on the licensed premises such bar ;

 (b) where there is more than one bar on the licensed premises, all such bars except that bar or those bars if any, where prior to the 1st October, 1917, beer has customarily been sold at a higher rate than the rate charged for the like beer in some other bar on such premises ; and

 (c) any place where beer is sold for consumption off the premises.

"Licensed Premises" shall not include any registered club, canteen, theatre, music hall, passenger vessel, railway restaurant car, or any buffet at a railway station, but subject as aforesaid shall include any premises where the sale of intoxicating liquor is carried on under a license.

11 . Infringements of this Order are summary offences against the Defence of the Realm Regulations.

12. This Order may be cited as the Beer (Prices and Description) Order, 1917.

"Food Supply Manual October 1917", pages 80-83

THE INTOXICATING LIQUOR (OUTPUT AND DELIVERY) ORDER No. 5, 1917. DATED DECEMBER 24, 1917.

1917. No. 1337.

In exercise of the powers conferred upon him by the Defence of the Realm Regulations, and of all other powers enabling him in that behalf, the Food Controller hereby orders as follows:

1. During the quarter commencing on the 1st January, 1918 (hereinafter referred to as the current quarter) the maximum barrelage which a brewer for sale is authorised to brew under the Intoxicating Liquor (Output and Delivery) Order, 1917 (hereinafter referred to as the principal Order)(b) shall be increased.

 (a) By twenty per cent, if he gives such notice and complies with such conditions as are hereinafter mentioned and such increase is, in this Order, referred to as the twenty per cent, increase ; and

 (b) By such further amount, if any, as in his case may be authorised by licence of the Food Controller if he complies with the conditions subject to which such a licence is granted, and the increase authorised by such licence is hereinafter called the licensed increase :

Provided that the aggregate amount of the licensed increases shall not exceed such an amount as with the aggregate amount of the twenty per cent, increases will increase the aggregate barrelage to be brewed by all brewers for sale in the current quarter by more than thirty-three and one-third per cent.

2. A brewer for sale shall be authorised to brew in the current quarter the twenty per cent, increase if he gives notice to the Commissioners of Customs and Excise (hereinafter referred to as the Commissioners) (c) on or before the 26th January, 1918, that ne accepts and will comply with the conditions subject to which the twenty per cent, increase is authorised by this Order, and such brewer is hereinafter referred to as an accepting brewer.

3. The conditions subject to which the twenty per cent, increase is authorised are the following:

> (a) One-half of the total amount of beer brewed by the accepting brewer in the current quarter (exclusive of the licensed increase) shall be brewed and delivered out of his brewery at a gravity not exceeding an original gravity of 1042^{o52} :
>
> (b) The remaining half of the beer brewed (exclusive of the licensed increase) shall be brewed at an average original gravity not exceeding the average original gravity of the total beer brewed at his brewery during the quarter commencing on the 1st January, 1917 :
>
> (c) In the month of January not more than one-third and in the months of January and February not more than two-thirds of the total amount of beer which the brewer is entitled to brew during the current quarter (exclusive of the licensed increase) shall be delivered out of his brewery :

And it shall be the duty of every accepting brewer to comply with such conditions.

4. The additional barrelage authorised to be brewed by this Order and by licences under this Order shall not be taken into account in reckoning the ten million barrels referred to in sub- section (2) of Clause 1 of the principal Order.

5. The same provision shall be applicable in relation to the effect of this Order on contracts as is applicable in relation to the effect of the Output of Beer (Restriction) Act, 1916, on contracts under Section 4 of that Act.

6. The following provisions shall apply with respect to certificates available for the current quarter granted or to be granted to a licence holder :

> (a) Except under the authority of the Food Controller a certificate granted by an accepting brewer shall not during the current quarter be used to transfer barrelage to a person who is not an accepting brewer.

---

[52] GRAVITY OF BEER. The Intoxicating Liquor (Output and Delivery) Order, 1918 (p. 171), provides that no beer shall be brewed at a gravity below 1010 or above an average of 1030 in Ireland and 1045 elsewhere in United Kingdom.

(b) The number of standard barrels which a licence holder may obtain from an accepting brewer under a certificate shall be increased by 20 per cent.

(c) An accepting brewer who has undertaken to supply the licence holder with beer under a certificate shall not supply more than one-half of such beer at a gravity exceeding an original gravity of 1042°.

(d) This clause shall apply to persons having the same rights as licence holders in the same way as it applies to licence holders.

7. If any question shall arise under this Order as to the average original gravity of beer such question shall be determined by the Commissioners.

8. Every accepting brewer shall keep such records as to gravity and amount of beer brewed and delivered and other matters as are requisite to determine whether or not the provisions of this Order are being complied with, and all such records and documents
connected therewith shall at all times be open to the inspection of the Food Controller and of the Commissioners.

9.

(a) No account shall be taken of any surplus barrelage accrued since the 1st April, 1917, for the purpose of computing the increase permitted by Clause 1 of this Order.

(b) In the case of a brewer who was an accepting brewer within the meaning of the Intoxicating Liquor (Output and Delivery) Order (No. 2), 1917 or the Intoxicating Liquor (Output and Delivery) Order, No. 3, 1917,[53] such surplus barrelage may except in such cases as the Food Controller otherwise directs, only be brewed subject to the conditions applicable under conditions (a) and (b) of clause 3 of this Order to the beer therein referred to.

10. Infringements of this Order are summary offences against the Defence of the Realm Regulations.

11. This Order may be cited as the Intoxicating Liquor (Output and Delivery) Order No. 3, 1917, and should be read as one with the principal Order.

---

[53] "ACCEPTING BREWER WITHIN THE MEANING OP ORDERS (No. 2) or (No. 3)/' i.e., a brewer for sale who gave notice to the Commissioners of Customs and Excise on or before the 21st July, 1917, that he accepted and would comply with the three following conditions :

1. One- half of the total amount of beer brewed by the accepting brewer in the quarter commencing on the 1st July, 1917 (exclusive of the licensed increase) shall be brewed and delivered out of his brewery at. a gravity not exceeding an original gravity of 1036° :
2. The remaining half of the beer brewed (exclusive of the licensed increase) shall be brewed at an average original gravity not exceeding the average original gravity of the total beer brewed at his brewery during the quarter commencing on the 1st July, 1916 :
3. In the month of July not more than one-third and in the months of July and August not more than two-thirds of the total amount of beer which the brewer is entitled to brew during the quarter commencing on the 1st July, 1917 (exclusive of the licensed increase)
shall be delivered out of his brewery :

Mini Book Series volume XXXII: Armistice!

"Food Supply Manual April 1918", pages 162-164.

THE BEER (PRICES AND DESCRIPTION) ORDER, 1918. DATED MARCH 19, 1918.

1918. No. 343.

In exercise of the powers conferred upon him by the Defence of the Realm Regulations and all other powers enabling him in that behalf, the Food Controller hereby orders that except under the authority of the Food Controller, the following regulations shall be observed by all persons concerned :

1. A person shall not on or after the 1st April, 1918, sell or offer to sell any beer of the gravities mentioned in Clause 3, or any beverage containing any beer of such gravities, in any part of any licensed premises having a public bar or public bars unless

(a) such beer at the time of such sale or offer for sale is on sale by imperial measure in the public bar or public bars of the licensed premises ; and also

(b) such beer when sold by imperial measure in the public bar or public bars is sold at prices not exceeding the maximum prices provided by this Order.

2. A person shall not on or after the 1st April, 1918, sell or offer to sell any beverage containing any beer of the gravities mentioned in Clause 3 in any public bar of any licensed premises unless beer of such gravity is on sale in that public bar.

3. Where beer is sold by imperial measure in a public bar, the maximum price for beer of an original gravity less than 1030° shall be at the rate of 4d. per imperial pint, and for beer of an original gravity not exceeding 1034° and not less than 1030° shall be at the rate of 5d. per imperial pint.

4.

(a) Where beer is delivered on or after the 1st April, 1918, in a barrel or cask

(i) the brewer or dealer disposing of such beer shall state on the invoice, if such be the fact, that the original gravity of the beer exceeds 1034 and, in any other case, the maximum price at which the beer in each such barrel or cask may under this Order be sold in the public bar of licensed premises; and

(ii) the brewer shall also before permitting delivery out of his brewery plainly and durably mark on the head of any barrel or cask containing beer of an original gravity less than 1030° the mark "4d." and on any barrel or cask containing beer of an original gravity not exceeding 1034° and not less than 1030° the mark "5d.," the figures to be not less than two inches long.

(b) No dealer in or retailer of beer shall alter or deface such mark or permit such mark to be altered or defaced, or dilute or permit to be diluted the beer in any barrel or cask.

5. A person authorised in that behalf by the Food Controller or a Food Committee to procure for analysis samples of beer on sale in any licensed premises shall have all the powers of procuring samples conferred by the Sale of Food and Drugs Acts, and a person selling beer by retail shall, on tender of the price for the quantity which he shall reasonably require for the purpose of analysis, sell the same to him accordingly.

6. In any proceedings in respect of an infringement of this Order the production of the certificate of the principal chemist of the Government Laboratories or of an analyst appointed under the Sale of Food and Drugs Acts, (a) shall be sufficient evidence of the facts therein stated unless the defendant require that the person who made the analysis be called as a witness. The certificate of the principal chemist or of the analyst shall, so far as circumstances permit, be in the form required by the Sale of Food and Drugs Acts.

7. If in any proceedings against a retailer of beer in respect of an infringement of this Order, it is proved that an offence has been committed but the person charged with the offence proves

(a) that he purchased the beer, in respect of which the offence was committed, from a person who sold the beer as or for beer which might lawfully be sold in a public bar at the price charged;

(b) that he had no reason to believe at the time of sale that the gravity of the beer was not such as permitted of it being- sold at the price charged or that the provisions of Clause 4 (b) of this Order had not been duly observed; and

(c) that he has given due notice to the prosecutor that he intended to rely on the provisions of this Clause; such person shall be entitled to be discharged from the
prosecution.

8. Where the Food Controller is of opinion that the price payable under any contract subsisting at the date of this Order for the sale of beer of a gravity not exceeding an original gravity of $1034°$ is such that the beer cannot at the prices permitted by this Order be sold or supplied by retail in a public bar at a reasonable profit, he may, if he thinks fit, cancel such contract or may modify the terms thereof in such manner as shall appear
to him to be just.

9. A person shall not, when selling any beer of an original gravity less than $1030°$, or in any advertisement, circular, or placard relating to any such beer, describe the same as "Government Ale" or "Government Beer" or use any other form of words calculated to lead to the belief that such beer is brewed under the authority, or pursuant to the directions of His Majesty's Government, or any Government Department.

10. Where on or after the 1st April, 1918, Beer in respect of which a maximum price is fixed by this Order, is on sale in any part of the licensed premises other than a Public Bar the licensee of such premises shall cause to be conspicuously exhibited in such part of the premises a notice to the effect that Beer is on sale in the Public Bar or Public Bars at the prices permitted by this Order.

11. Except in Clause 9 the expression "Beer" shall not include Bottled Beer.

12. In this Order:-
"Food Committee" means in respect of any area in Great Britain the Food Control Committee established for the area pursuant to the Food Control Committee (Constitution) Order, 1917, and in respect of Ireland the Food Control Committee appointed for Ireland by the Food Controller.
"Beer" includes ale, porter, spruce beer, black beer and any other description of beer.
"Public Bar" means -

> (a) where there is only one bar on the licensed premises such bar ;
>
> (b) where there is more than one bar on the licensed premises, all such bars except that bar or those bars, if any, where prior to the 1st October, 1917, beer has customarily been sold at a higher rate than the rate charged for the like beer in some other bar on such premises; and
>
> (c) any place where beer is sold under a retail off-licence. "Licensed Premises" shall not include any registered club, canteen, theatre, music-hall, passenger vessel, railway restaurant car, or any buffet at a railway station, but subject as aforesaid shall include any premises where the sale of intoxicating liquor is carried on under a licence.

13. Infringements of this Order are summary offences against the Defence of the Realm Regulations.

14. The Beer (Prices and Description) Order, 1917, is hereby revoked as on the 1st April, 1918, but without prejudice to any proceedings in respect of any contravention thereof.

15. This Order may be cited as the Beer (Prices and Description) Order, 1918.

"Food Supply Manual April 1918", pages 168-171

THE INTOXICATING LIQUOR (OUTPUT AND DELIVERY) ORDER, 1918. DATED MARCH 19, 1918.
1918. No. 339.

In exercise of the powers conferred upon him by the Defence of the Realm Regulations and of all other powers enabling him in that behalf, the Food Controller hereby orders that except under the authority of the Food Controller, the following regulations shall be observed by all persons concerned:

1. A Brewer for Sale shall not in any quarter brew any beer at his brewery at an original gravity below 1010°.

2.
(a) A Brewer for Sale shall not in any quarter brew beer at his brewery except at such original gravities as secure that the average original gravity of all the beer brewed by him at that brewery during such quarter (other than beer brewed under any license granted by or under the authority of the Food Controller, specially stating the gravity at which the beer to be brewed thereunder is to be brewed) does not exceed in the case of a brewery situate in Ireland 1045°, or in the case of a brewery situate elsewhere in the United Kingdom 1030°.

(b) Where provision has been made to the satisfaction of the Commissioners of Customs and Excise for the dilution with water of beer after brewing, and the dilution is carried out under conditions approved by the Commissioners, the diluted beer shall for the purpose of the foregoing sub-clause be deemed to have been brewed at such original gravity as the Commissioners may determine.

3. The same provision shall be applicable in relation to the effect of this Order on contracts as is applicable in relation to the effect of the Output of Beer (Restriction) Act, 1916, on contracts under Section 4 of that Act.

4. Where the title of a Certificate under the Intoxicating Liquor (Output and Delivery) Order, 1917, arises in respect of Beer which was brewed in Great Britain, such Certificate shall not on or after 1st April, 1918, be available for increasing the Barrelage of a Brewer in respect of any Brewery situate in Ireland ; and where the title to such a certificate arises in respect of beer which was brewed in Ireland, such certificate shall not after the same date be available for increasing the barrelage of a brewer in respect of any brewery situate in Great Britain.

5. If any question shall arise under this Order as to the average original gravity of beer, such question shall be determined by the Commissioners.

6. Infringements of this Order are summary offences against the Defence of the Realm Regulations.

7.
(a) This Order may be cited as the Intoxicating Liquor (Output and Delivery) Order, 1918, and shall be read as one with the Intoxicating Liquor (Output and Delivery) Order, 1917.
(b) This Order shall come into force on the 1st April, 1918.

"Food Supply Manual April 1918", pages 168-171

Malt

THE BREWERS (MALT PURCHASES) ORDER, 1917. DATED FEBRUARY 3, 1917.

1917. No. 132.

In exercise of the powers conferred upon him by Regulation 2F of the Defence of the Realm Regulations, and of all other powers enabling him in that behalf, the Food Controller hereby orders as follows :

1. Except under the authority of the Food Controller no maltster or dealer in malt shall on or after the 10th February, 1917, agree to sell any malt to any brewer for sale or make
delivery to any brewer for sale of any malt other than malt deliverable under contracts made before that date.

2. Except under the authority of the Food Controller no brewer for sale shall on or after the 10th February, 1917, agree to buy any malt or to take delivery of any malt other than malt deliverable under contracts made before that date.

3. Except under the authority of the Food Controller no brewer for sale shall manufacture any malt from any barley agreed to be bought on or after the 10th February, 1917.

4. For the purposes of this Order:-

The expression "brewer for sale" shall mean any person who brews beer for the use of any other person at anyplace other than the premises of the person for whose use the beer shall be brewed and any person licensed to deal in or retail beer who brews beer.

The expression "beer" includes ale, porter, spruce beer, black beer and any other description of beer. The expression "malt" shall mean malt suitable for use in the brewing of beer.

5. Any person acting in contravention of this Order is guilty Penalty. of a summary offence against the Defence of the Realm Regulations.

6. This Order may be cited as the Brewers (Malt Purchases) Title of Order, 1917.

"Food Supply Manual October 1917", pages 68-69

THE MALT (RESTRICTION) ORDER, 1917. DATED FEBRUARY 20, 1917.

1917. No. 159.

In exercise of the powers conferred upon him by Regulation 2F of the Defence of the Realm Regulations, and of all other powers enabling him in that behalf, the Food Controller hereby orders as follows :-

> 1. Except under the authority of the Food Controller no Prohibition person shall manufacture from barley or any other cereals any of Malting, malt suitable for use in the brewing of beer.
>
> 2. This Order shall not apply to barley or other cereals steeped at the date of this Order.
>
> 3. For the purposes of this Order, the expression "beer" shall include ale, porter, spruce beer, black beer and any other description of beer.
>
> 4. If any person acts in contravention of this Order or aids or abets any other person in doing anything. in contravention of this Order, that person is guilty of a summary offence against the Defence of the Realm Regulations, and if such person is a company every director and officer of the company is also guilty of a summary offence against those regulations unless he proves that the contravention took place without his knowledge or
> consent.
>
> 5. This Order may be cited as the Malt (Restriction), 1917.

"Food Supply Manual October 1917", page 69

THE WHEAT, BARLEY AXD OATS (PRICES) ORDER, 1917, DATED APRIL 16, 1917, RELATING TO GRAIN HARVESTED IN 1916.

1917. No. 363.

In exercise of the powers conferred upon him by Regulation 2F of the Defence of the Realm Regulations, and of all other powers enabling him in that behalf, the Food Controller hereby orders as follows :

> 1. Except under the authority of the Food Controller no wheat, barley (other than kiln dried barley) or oats harvested in the United Kingdom in the year 1916 may be sold at prices exceeding prices at the following rates :
>   Wheat 78s. - per quarter of 480 lbs.
>   Barley 66s.- per quarter of 400 lbs.
>   Oats 55s. - per quarter of 312 lbs.
>
> 2. The buyer shall be entitled to require the grain to be placed on rail or (at the option of the seller) to be delivered to the buyer's premises, and no additional charge may be

made in respect thereof.

3. Except in so far as the Food Controller may in any particular case otherwise determine, the following provision shall have effect in the case of any contract subsisting at the date of this Order for the sale of any of the grains mentioned where the contract price exceeds the permitted maximum price : -
The contract shall stand so far as concerns any such grain which has been paid for or has been delivered or which under the contract is to be delivered within one month from the date of such contract, but otherwise shall be avoided.

4. No person shall sell or buy or offer to sell or buy any of the grain mentioned at a price exceeding the permitted maximum price or in connection with a sale or proposed sale of any such grain enter or offer to enter into any fictitious or artificial transaction or make any unreasonable charge.

5. If any person acts in contravention of this Order or aids or abets any other person in doing anything in contravention of the Order, that person is guilty of a summary offence against the Defence of the Realm Regulations, and if such person is a company every director and officer of the company is also guilty of a summary offence against those regulations unless he proves that the contravention took place without his knowledge or consent.

6. This Order may be cited as the Wheat, Barley and Oats (Prices) Order, 1917.

"Food Supply Manual October 1917", page 37

THE BARLEY (REQUISITION) ORDER, 1917. DATED APRIL 16, 1917.

1917. No. 364.

In exercise of the powers conferred upon him by Regulations 2p and 2a of the Defence of the Realm Regulations, and of all other powers enabling him in that behalf, the Food Controller hereby orders as follows :

1. All persons owning or having power to sell or dispose of any barley (other than home grown barley which has not been kiln dried) shall place such barley at the disposal of the Food Controller and shall deliver the same to him or such persons as may be named by him in such quantities and at such time as the Food Controller may from time to time require.

2. Pending any direction no person shall remove or otherwise dispose of any such barley (whether in pursuance of a contract existing at the date of this Order or not) and all persons concerned shall take such steps as may be reasonably necessary to maintain the same in good condition.

3. All persons owning or having power to sell or dispose of such barley shall on or before the 30th April, 1917, furnish to the Food Controller, Grosvenor House, Upper Grosvenor Street, London, W.I, a statement on forms to be obtained from the Food

Controller, giving particulars of all such barley in their possession or under their control at the date of this Order, and of all their existing contracts if any for the sale of such barley.

4. The Food Controller will subsequently communicate to the owners of barley taken over by him the prices which he will be prepared to pay for the same.

5. The arbitrator to determine in default of agreement the compensation to be paid for barley requisitioned under this Order shall be appointed by the Lord Chief Justice of England

6. This Order shall not apply

>(a) to persons who do not own more than 25 qrs. (448 lbs. Per quarter) of barley at the date of the Order ;

>(b) to barley in the hands of or held to the order of flour millers at the date of this Order ;

>(c) to barley agreed to be sold to the Royal Commission on the Wheat Supply.

7. If any person acts in contravention of this Order or aids or abets any other person in doing anything in contravention of this Order, that person is guilty of a summary offence against the Defence of the Realm Regulations, and if such person is a company every director and officer of the company is also guilty of a summary offence against those regulations unless he proves that the contravention took place without his knowledge or
consent.

8. This Order may be cited as the Barley (Requisition) Order, 1917.

"Food Supply Manual October 1917", page 38

THE MALT (RESTRICTION ON SHIPPING) ORDER, 1917. DATED MARCH 21, 1917.

1917. No. 259.

In exercise of the powers conferred upon him by Regulation 2F of the Defence of the Realm Regulations, and of all other powers enabling him in that behalf, the Food Controller hereby orders as follows :

1. Except under the authority of the Food Controller no person shall export, ship or consign any malt,

>(a) from Ireland to any destination in any part of Great Britain, the Channel Islands or the Isle of Man; or

(b) from any part of Great Britain to any destination in Ireland, the Channel Islands or the Isle of Man.

2. If any person acts in contravention of this Order or aids or abets any other person, in doing anything in contravention of this Order, that person is guilty of a summary offence against the Defence of the Realm Regulations, and if such person is a company every director and officer of the company is also guilty of a summary offence against those regulations unless he proves that the contravention took place without his knowledge or consent.

3.

(a) This Order may be cited as the Malt (Restriction on Shipping) Order, 1917.

(b) This Order shall come into force on the 26th March, 1917.

"Food Supply Manual April 1918", pages 153-154

THE MALT (RESTRICTION) No. 2 ORDER, 1917. DATED APRIL 12, 1917.

1917. No. 345.

In exercise of the powers conferred upon him by Regulation 2F of the Defence of the Realm Regulations, and of all other powers enabling him in that behalf, the Food Controller hereby orders as follows :-

1.

(a) Except under the authority of the Food Controller no person shall after the date of this Order manufacture any malt from any cereals.

(b) This article shall not apply to cereals in course of being manufactured into malt at the date of this Order.

2. No person shall after the date of this Order agree to sell any malt or after the 14th April, 1917, make delivery of any malt except under and in accordance with the terms of a licence issued by the Food Controller, or except to a brewer for sale in manner permitted by the Brewers' (Malt Purchases) Order 1917.

3.

(a) Except under the authority of the Food Controller no person shall after the 14th April, 1917, use any malt for any purpose.

(b) This article shall not apply to a brewer for sale so far as is necessary for enabling him to brew the maximum barrelage permitted to him under the Intoxicating Liquor (Output and Delivery) Order, 1917.

4. If any person acts in contravention of this Order or aids or abets any other person,

in doing anything in contravention of this Order, that person is guilty of a summary offence against the Defence of the Realm Regulations, *and if such person is a company every director and officer of the company is also guilty of a summary offence against those regulations unless he proves that the contravention took place without his knowledge or*
consent.

5. This Order may be cited as the Malt (Restriction) No. 2 Order, 1917.

"Food Supply Manual October 1917", pages 70-71

THE BARLEY (RESTRICTION) ORDER, 1917. DATED AUGUST 15, 1917.

1917. No. 821.

In exercise of the powers conferred upon him by Regulation 2F of the Defence of the Realm Regulations and of all other powers enabling him in that behalf, the Food Controller hereby orders that except under the authority of the Food Controller the following regulations shall be observed by all persons concerned :

1.

(a) No person shall on or after the 1st September, 1917, use any Barley except for the purpose of seed or except in the process of manufacturing flour.

(b) This clause shall not apply to tailings or screenings or Barley which has been so damaged as to be unfit for milling.

2.

(a) No person shall on or after the 1st September, 1917, use any Barley Flour, except in the manufacture of articles suitable for human food or use any article containing any Barley Flour except as human food.

(b) This clause shall not apply to Barley Flour which on the 1st September, 1917, had been so treated as to be unsuitable for the purpose of human food, or to any Barley Flour or any article containing Barley Flour which is or may become unfit for such purpose.

3. No person shall damage or permit to be damaged on or after 1st September, 1917, treat or permit to be treated any Barley or Barley Flour or any article containing Barley Flour so as to render the same less fit for the purpose for which under this Order it is reserved.

4. Any person authorised by the Food Controller and any Local Authority empowered to enforce the provisions of this Order, may take samples of any Barley or Barley Flour, or other article which he has reason to suspect is being used, treated or damaged in contravention of this Order.

5. If any question shall arise whether any Barley is so damaged to be unfit for milling

or whether any Barley Flour or article containing Barley Flour is unfit for the purpose of human food such question may be referred to and determined by any person authorised in that behalf by the Food Controller or in England and Wales and Scotland by a Local Authority empowered to enforce this Order as to Barley or Barley Flour or any such article within the district of such Local Authority.

6. Infringements of this Order are summary offences against the Defence of the Realm Regulations.

7. After the 31st August, 1917, the Maize, Barley and Oats (Restriction) Order, 1917, (a) shall cease to be in force so far as the same relates to Barley but without prejudice to any proceedings in respect of any previous contravention thereof.

8. This Order may be cited as the Barley (Restriction) Order, 1917.

"Food Supply Manual October 1917", pages 52-52

THE MALT (RESTRICTION) ORDER, 1918. DATED FEBRUARY 26, 1918.

1918. No. 225.

In exercise of the powers conferred upon him by the Defence of the Realm Regulations and of all other powers enabling him in that behalf, the Food Controller hereby orders that except under the authority of the Food Controller the following regulations shall be observed by all persons concerned:

1. Except under and in accordance with the terms of a licence issued by the Food Controller no person shall on or after the 1st March, 1918, manufacture any Malt or Malt Extract other than Malt or Malt Extract in process of manufacture on the 28th February, 1918.

2. Except under and in accordance with the terms of a licence issued by the Food Controller no person shall on or after 1st March, 1918, sell or buy or make or take delivery of or use any Malt or Malt Extract for any purpose.

This Clause shall not apply to :

(a) The use of Malt or Malt Extract by a Brewer for Sale so far as is necessary to enable him to brew the maximum barrelage permitted to him under the Orders of the Food Controller for the time being in force relating to the brewing of beer, and the further
barrelage, if any, permitted to him under any licence granted by the Food Controller ; or

(b) the delivery to a brewer for sale under contracts existing at the date of this Order of such quantities of Malt or Malt Extract as together with his existing stocks, are requisite to enable him in the ordinary course to brew such maximum and further barrelage up to and including 30th June, 1918; or

(c) the purchase of Malt or Malt Extract from a person licenced by the Food Controller to sell Malt or Malt Extract or the use of Malt or Malt Extract by a baker for the purpose of making bread.

3. Where Malt is supplied to a Brewer for Sale by any person under Clause 2 of this Order, that person shall be entitled to rely on a statement in writing signed by or on behalf of the brewer for sale as to the lawfulness of the proposed supply.

4. For the purposes of this Order:
The expression "Malt, or Malt Extract," shall include all such Malt, Malt Extract or substitutes for Malt as are manufactured by the steeping, roasting or treatment of any cereal.

5. The Brewers (Malt Purchases) Order, 1917, The Malt (Restriction) Older, 1917,and the Malt (Restriction) No. 2 Order 1917, are revoked as from the 1st March, 1918 but without prejudice to any proceedings in respect of any infringement thereof.

6. Infringements of this Order are summary offences against the Defence of the Realm Regulations.

7. This Order may be cited as the Malt (Restriction) Order, 1918.

"Food Supply Manual April 1918", pages 167-168

Hops

THE HOPS (RESTRICTION) ORDER, 1917, DATED AUGUST 31, 1917, AS AMENDED BY THE HOPS (RESTRICTION) ORDER No. 2, 1917, DATED SEPTEMBERS, 1917.

1917, No. 914 as amended by No. 925.

In exercise of the powers conferred upon him by the Defence of the Realm Regulations and of all other powers enabling him in that behalf, the Food Controller after consultation with the Board of Agriculture and Fisheries hereby orders as follows :

1. No person shall without a permit issued under the authority of the Food Controller either on his own behalf, or on the behalf of any other person, buy or sell or agree or offer to buy or sell any Hops whether imported or home grown. A person shall not without a permit issued under the authority of the Food Controller make delivery of any hops contracted to be sold by him before the 4th September, 1917.

2. Infringements of this Order are summary offences against Penalty, the Defence of the Realm Regulations.

3.
    (a) This Order may be cited as the Hops (Restriction) Order, 1917.

    (b) This Order shall come into force on the 1st September, 1917.

"Food Supply Manual April 1918", page 161.

Sugar

THE BREWERS SUGAR ORDER, 1917. DATED FEBRUARY 8, 1917. 1917. No. 90.

In exercise of the powers conferred upon him by Regulation 2F of the Defence of the Realm Regulations and of all other powers enabling him in that behalf, the Food Controller hereby orders as follows :

1. (a) Except under the authority of the Food Controller all brewers sugar in a ship arrived or to arrive, or on quay shall be delivered into a warehouse, and no brewers sugar shall be delivered from any warehouse.

(b) This article shall not apply to

(i) British West India Grocery Crystallised Sugar or British West India Muscovado Sugar or British West India Grocery Syrup Sugar;

(ii) any brewers sugar which has been or shall be sold to any brewer or to any manufacturer of brewers sugar to be used for the purpose of their respective trades;

(iii) any brewers sugar which has been or shall be imported under any licence issued by the Royal Commission on the Sugar Supply the terms whereof provide that such sugar shall be sold only to brewers or brewers sugar manufacturers.

2. Except under the authority of the Food Controller no brewers sugar shall be sold by retail at a price exceeding the current retail price for granulated sugar.

3. For the purpose of this Order the expression "brewers sugar" shall mean sugar which when tested by the polariscope indicates a polarisation not exceeding 89 degrees.

4. Any person acting in contravention of this Order is guilty of a summary offence against the Defence of the Realm Regulations.

5. This Order may be cited as the Brewers Sugar Order, 1917.

"Food Supply Manual April 1918", page 477

THE SUGAR (BREWERS RESTRICTION) ORDER, 1917, DATED NOVEMBER 19, 1917, AS AMENDED BY THE SUGAR (BREWERS RESTRICTION) ORDER No. 2, 1917, DATED DECEMBER 21, 1917.
1917 No. 1185, as amended by No. 1312.

In exercise of the powers conferred upon him by the Defence of the Realm Regulations and of all other powers enabling him in that behalf, the Food Controller hereby orders that, except under the authority of the Food Controller, the following regulations shall be observed by all persons concerned:

1. A brewer for sale may, subject to the limitation as to quantity hereinafter contained, use in the brewing of beer:

   (a) Solid Glucose;

   (b) Invert of Low Grade Cane Sugar of a polarisation not exceeding 89 from which not less than 40 per cent, of its weight in the form of Crystal Sugar or Grocery Syrup or Grocery Honey Sugar has been extracted ;

   (c) Any caramelised products of Solid Glucose or of such Invert of Low Grade Cane Sugar as is hereinbefore described ; and

   (d) Mixtures of Solid Glucose and the Invert and caramelized products hereinbefore mentioned or of any of them. But, except that a brewer for sale may use in the brewing of beer any sugar which at the date of this Order he had in stock or which was in course of transit to his brewery from any manufacturer in the United Kingdom, he shall not use any sugar other than sugar of the kinds hereinbefore specifically mentioned.

2. A brewer for sale shall not during any of the periods hereinafter referred to use in the brewing of beer more sugar than the amount prescribed for use in that period.

3. The prescribed amount shall be ascertained by reference to the total amount of sugar used in the year 1915 for the purpose of brewing beer by the brewer for sale or, in the case where there has been a transfer of the brewing business from a brewer for sale in or since the year 1915, by such brewer for sale and his predecessors in that business.

The prescribed amount shall for each period mentioned in the first column of the subjoined table be the percentage of such total amount shown in the second column thereof.

Period for which percentages are applicable.	Percentage of 1915 Sugar which may be used.
1st January, 1918, to 31st March, 1918	10
1st January, 1918, to 30th June, 1918	20
1st January, 1918, to 30th September, 1918	30
1st January, 1918, to 31st December, 1918	40

4. (a) A person shall not supply to a brewer for sale for the purposes of his brewery any sugar of a kind not permitted under this Order to be used in the brewing of beer, and a brewer for sale shall not take delivery of any such sugar.
(b) Until the contrary be proved, sugar supplied to a brewer for sale shall be deemed to be supplied for the purposes of his brewery.

5. In this Order:
The expression "Sugar" includes every description of sugar, whether cane sugar, or invert, or glucose, or other saccharine substance or extract or syrup, and partially or fully caramelized products of the above or any mixture of them.
The expressions "brewer for sale" and "beer" have the same meaning as in the Customs and Inland Revenue Act, 1885. 6. Infringements of this Order are summary Offences against the Defence of the Realm Regulations.

7. As from the 1st October, 1917, the Sugar (Restriction) Order, 1917, as amended, shall cease to apply to brewers for sale in relation to the brewing of beer, but without prejudice to any proceedings in respect of any previous contraventions thereof.

8. This Order may be cited as the Sugar (Brewers Restriction) Order, 1917.

"Food Supply Manual April 1918", pages 493-494.

LICENSING ACT 1921.

11 & 12 Geo. V. Ch. 42. Aug. 17 1921.
Past I.—-Conditions or Sale &c. of Intoxicating Liquor.

1. Permitted Hours on week-days.—(I) The hours during which intoxicating liquor may be sold or supplied on week-days in any licensed premises or club, lor consumption either on or off the premises, shall be as follows, that is to say: eight hours, beginning not earlier than 11 in the morning and ending not later than 10 at night, with a break of at least two hours after 12 (noon):

> Provided that—
>
> (a) in the application of this provision to the metropolis "nine" shall be substituted for "eight," and "11 at night" shall be substituted for " 10 at night" ; and
>
> (b) The licensing justices for any licensing district outside the metropolis may by order, if satisfied that the special requirements of the district render it desirable, make, as respects their district, either or both of the following directions—
>
> (i) that this provision shall have effect as though "eight and a half" were substituted for "eight" and "10.30 at night" were substituted for "10 at night" ; or
>
> (ii) that this provision shall have effect as though some hour specified in the order earlier than 11, but not earlier than 9 in the morning were substituted for "11 in the morning."

(2) Subject to the foregoing provisions, the permitted hours on week-days shall be such as may be fixed, in the case of licensed premises by order of the licensing justices of the licensing district, and La the case of a club in accordance with the rules of the club:

> Provided that, pending any decision under this sub-section, the permitted hours on week-days shall be—
>
> (a) in the metropolis, the hours between 11.30 in the morning and 3 in the afternoon, and between 6.30 in the afternoon and 11 at night: and
>
> (b) elsewhere, the hours between 11.30 in the morning and 3 in the afternoon, and between 6.30 in the afternoon and 10 at night.

2. Permitted hours on Sundays.—(1) The hours during which intoxicating liquor may be sold or supplied on Sundays, Christmas Day, and Good Friday in any licensed premises or club, for consumption either on or off the premises, shall he as follows, that is to say, five hours, of which not more than two shall be between 12 (noon) and 3 in the afternoon, and not more than three between 6 and 10 in the evening:

Provided that in Wales and Monmouthshire there shall be no permitted hours for licensed premises on Sundays, or on Christmas Day when it falls on a Sunday

(2) Subject to the foregoing provisions the permitted hours on Sundays shall be such as may be fixed, in the case of licensed premises by order of the licensing justices of the licensing

district, and in the case of a club in accordance with the rules of the club:

Provided that, pending any decision under this sub-section, the permitted hours on Sundays, Christmas Day, and Good Friday shall be the hours between 12.30 and 2.30 in the afternoon, and the hours between 7 and 10 in the evening.
Brewers' Almanack 1922, pages 64 - 65.

Licensing Act 1988

Modification of permitted hours

(1) In section 60(1)(a) of the principal Act (permitted hours in licensed premises on weekdays)—

    (a) for the words "half past ten" there shall be substituted the word "eleven"; and

    (b) the words "with a break of two and a half hours beginning at three in the afternoon" shall be omitted.

(2) In section 60(1)(b) of the principal Act (permitted hours in licensed premises on Sundays etc.), for the words "five hours beginning at two" there shall be substituted the words "four hours beginning at three".

(3) In subsection (4) of that section (power of licensing justices to modify the permitted hours for their district within specified limits), for the words from "within" to the end there shall be substituted the words "so that the permitted hours begin at a time earlier than eleven, but not earlier than ten, in the morning".

(4) In subsection (6) of that section (premises licensed for the sale of intoxicating liquor for consumption off the premises), the words "half past" shall be omitted.

(5) In section 62 of that Act (permitted hours in clubs), the following subsection shall be substituted for subsection (1)—

    "(1) The permitted hours in premises in respect of which a club is registered shall be—

        (a) on weekdays, other than Christmas Day or Good Friday, the general licensing hours; and

        (b) on Sundays, Christmas Day and Good Friday, the hours fixed by or under the rules of the club in accordance with the following conditions—

            (i) the hours fixed shall not be longer than five and a half hours and shall not begin earlier than twelve noon nor end later than half past ten in the evening;

            (ii) there shall be a break in the afternoon of not less than two hours which shall include the hours from three to five; and

(iii) there shall not be more than three and a half hours after five."

(6) In section 76(2) of that Act (permitted hours on weekdays where special hours certificate in force) for the words from "be the periods" to "evening and" there shall be substituted the words "extend until".

Weights and measures

Not everyone went to school in pre-metric days as I did. So an overview of Imperial measure is in order.

Weight

16 oz (ounces) = 1 lb (pound)
112 lbs = 1 cwt (hundredweight)

1 lb = 0.4535 kilograms

Volume

8 gallons = 1 bushel
8 bushels = 1 quarter
1 quarter malt = 336 lbs

1 bushel = 36.369 litres

Liquid

20 fl. oz (fluid ounce) = 1 pint
8 pints = 1 gallon
4.5 gallons = 1 pin
9 gallons = 1 firkin
18 gallons = 1 kilderkin
36 gallons = 1 barrel
54 gallons = 1 hogshead
108 gallons = 1 butt
216 gallons = 1 tun

1 pint = .568 litre
1 barrel = 163.584 litres

Money

12d (pence) = 1s (shilling)
20s = 1 pound

Temperature

Fahrenheit to Celsius			
°F	°C	°F	°C
50	10	150	65.6
51	10.6	151	66.1
52	11.1	152	66.7
53	11.7	153	67.2
54	12.2	154	67.8
55	12.8	155	68.3
56	13.3	156	68.9
57	13.9	157	69.4
58	14.4	158	70.0
59	15.0	159	70.6
60	15.6	160	71.1
61	16.1	161	71.7
62	16.7	162	72.2
63	17.2	163	72.8
64	17.8	164	73.3
65	18.3	165	73.9
66	18.9	166	74.4
67	19.4	167	75.0
68	20.0	168	75.6
69	20.6	169	76.1
70	21.1	170	76.7
71	21.7	171	77.2
72	22.2	172	77.8
73	22.8	173	78.3
74	23.3	174	78.9
75	23.9	175	79.4
76	24.4	176	80.0

Index
100/-, 7, 11, 81, 82, 147,
 321, 328, 329, 527,
 540
120/-, 528
160/-, 11, 147, 328, 527,
 528, 541, 544
18th century, 181, 264,
 475
19th century, 69, 72, 105,
 114, 116, 121, 135,
 141, 147, 162, 181,
 184, 264, 346, 377,
 425, 428, 438, 492,
 547
20th century, 41, 66, 114,
 135, 142, 149, 181,
 283, 316, 324, 338,
 346, 404, 424, 431,
 492
40/-, 92
4d Ale, 83, 182, 204,
 290, 472
54/-, 8, 92, 121, 324, 343,
 348
60/-, 7, 8, 11, 12, 73, 74,
 81, 82, 86, 87, 92, 97,
 103, 104, 112, 113,
 147, 321, 324, 325,
 331, 335, 343, 344,
 345, 348, 349, 350,
 527, 537, 538, 539,
 541, 556, 557, 558
70/-, 103, 321, 553
80/-, 7, 11, 73, 81, 82,
 103, 112, 147, 321,
 329, 334, 335, 350,
 527, 539, 540
90/-, 103, 104, 115
Abbey Brewery, 527
Aitchison, 104
Aitken, 104
AK, 5, 6, 7, 8, 90, 91, 96,
 97, 99, 100, 224, 231,
 232, 239, 240, 242,
 243, 248, 294, 295,
 296, 297, 298, 302,
 303, 304, 311, 312,
 315, 316, 317, 318,
 319, 320, 352, 354,
 355, 359, 360, 361,
 365, 366, 369, 370,
 376, 377, 383, 384,
 415, 452
Ale, 4, 5, 8, 11, 16, 17,
 18, 20, 28, 29, 33, 37,
 38, 41, 58, 59, 69, 70,
 71, 72, 73, 74, 75, 77,
 78, 79, 80, 81, 82, 83,
 84, 85, 86, 88, 89, 90,
 91, 92, 93, 94, 95, 96,
 99, 100, 101, 102, 103,
 104, 105, 108, 111,
 112, 113, 127, 138,
 139, 140, 141, 142,
 143, 144, 146, 147,
 148, 149, 150, 157,
 158, 159, 160, 161,
 165, 166, 167, 168,
 170, 171, 172, 180,
 181, 182, 184, 185,
 186, 187, 188, 190,
 191, 192, 193, 194,
 195, 196, 197, 198,
 199, 200, 201, 202,
 203, 204, 205, 206,
 207, 208, 209, 210,
 211, 212, 213, 214,
 215, 216, 218, 219,
 220, 221, 222, 223,
 224, 225, 227, 228,
 234, 235, 242, 243,
 244, 247, 248, 249,
 252, 262, 264, 265,
 268, 269, 270, 271,
 272, 273, 274, 275,
 276, 277, 278, 279,
 280, 281, 282, 283,
 284, 285, 286, 287,
 288, 289, 290, 291,
 292, 293, 294, 295,
 296, 297, 304, 306,
 307, 311, 312, 321,
 322, 323, 324, 325,
 326, 327, 328, 329,
 330, 331, 332, 333,
 334, 335, 336, 337,
 338, 339, 340, 341,
 342, 343, 344, 345,
 346, 347, 348, 349,
 350, 351, 352, 353,
 354, 358, 359, 364,
 365, 368, 369, 370,
 372, 373, 376, 378,
 379, 380, 381, 384,
 387, 388, 389, 390,
 391, 392, 393, 394,
 395, 396, 398, 399,
 400, 401, 402, 403,
 404, 405, 406, 407,
 408, 409, 410, 411,
 412, 413, 415, 416,
 417, 418, 419, 421,
 422, 423, 424, 425,
 426, 427, 428, 429,
 430, 431, 432, 433,
 434, 435, 437, 438,
 439, 440, 441, 442,
 443, 444, 445, 446,
 447, 448, 449, 450,
 451, 452, 453, 454,
 455, 456, 457, 458,
 459, 460, 461, 462,
 463, 464, 465, 466,
 467, 468, 469, 470,
 471, 472, 473, 474,
 476, 477, 478, 479,
 480, 481, 482, 483,
 484, 485, 486, 487,
 488, 489, 490, 491,
 492, 493, 494, 495,
 496, 497, 498, 499,
 500, 501, 502, 503,
 504, 505, 506, 507,
 508, 509, 510, 511,
 512, 513, 514, 515,
 516, 517, 518, 519,
 520, 521, 522, 523,
 524, 525, 526, 527,
 528, 529, 530, 531,
 532, 533, 534, 535,
 536, 537, 538, 539,
 540, 541, 542, 543,
 544, 545, 546, 547,
 548, 549, 550, 551,
 552, 553, 554, 555,
 556, 557, 558, 559,
 560, 561, 562, 563,

Mini Book Series volume XXXII: Armistice!

564, 565, 566, 567, 577, 582
Alloa, 114, 120
Allsopp, 15, 105, 113, 131, 152, 153
amber malt, 85, 124, 126, 130, 135, 153, 163, 164, 169, 173, 177, 184, 189, 190, 196, 197, 200, 201, 202, 203, 204, 205, 209, 210, 215, 218, 219, 220, 221, 222, 223, 229, 230, 238, 245, 253, 259, 263, 351, 416, 417, 490, 491, 492, 493, 559, 560
American hops, 178, 225, 309, 318, 518, 524
Amsterdam, 2, 13, 55
Australia, 64, 65, 66
Austria, 3, 48, 54, 55, 64, 76, 111, 151, 189
Austria-Hungary, 48, 64
Austrian, 54, 163
Ballantine, 70
Ballingall, 104, 136, 151
Bamberg, 52
Barclay Perkins, 5, 17, 20, 21, 73, 83, 84, 89, 90, 99, 100, 114, 116, 118, 120, 129, 138, 140, 141, 151, 153, 156, 181, 182, 183, 184, 185, 186, 187, 188, 189, 190, 191, 192, 193, 194, 195, 196, 197, 198, 199, 200, 201, 202, 203, 204, 205, 206, 207, 208, 209, 210, 211, 212, 213, 214, 215, 216, 217, 218, 219, 220, 221, 222, 223, 265, 267, 324, 327, 352, 357, 358, 373, 378, 384, 479, 524
barley, 16, 17, 20, 22, 31, 32, 49, 50, 54, 55, 56, 62, 99, 152, 161, 166,

172, 203, 204, 219, 220, 221, 222, 223, 231, 274, 278, 323, 353, 355, 409, 451, 480, 489, 494, 514, 518, 520, 521, 535, 537, 548, 549, 550, 559, 560, 565, 566, 585, 586, 587, 588
Bass, 71, 104, 105, 113, 131, 138, 144, 145, 146, 151, 152, 181, 449, 475, 544
Bavaria, 50, 51, 52, 53
Bavarian, 18, 51, 52, 53, 55, 71, 151, 184
Beamish, 136
Beamish & Crawford, 136
Beasley, 89, 129
beer tax, 34, 35
Belgium, 3, 18, 48, 49, 64, 65, 66, 111, 113, 275
Berliner, 50
Bernard, 103, 104, 115, 136, 150
Best Mild, 89, 159, 381
Best Stout, 183, 220
Bitter, 6, 70, 86, 88, 93, 95, 99, 100, 101, 102, 108, 114, 152, 161, 172, 175, 176, 178, 179, 185, 193, 194, 201, 205, 224, 225, 228, 232, 233, 247, 248, 251, 252, 257, 258, 270, 271, 283, 295, 298, 311, 323, 354, 370, 377, 378, 382, 384, 388, 395, 403, 409, 415, 419, 461, 467, 476, 477, 479, 482, 485, 546, 562
black malt, 17, 75, 117, 126, 130, 134, 135, 139, 145, 162, 203, 217, 218, 219, 223, 230, 238, 245, 253,

259, 263, 265, 266, 268, 269, 270, 272, 273, 274, 275, 276, 277, 280, 281, 282, 283, 284, 285, 286, 287, 288, 289, 290, 291, 292, 300, 351, 356, 357, 362, 363, 364, 367, 368, 371, 374, 375, 385, 386, 392, 393, 396, 401, 402, 408, 412, 416, 417, 418, 428, 429, 455, 456, 457, 458, 462, 468, 472, 474, 487, 488, 489, 490, 491, 492, 493, 506, 515, 516, 517, 522, 523, 524, 525, 547, 549, 550
Blair, 103
Bock, 54, 238
Bohemia, 66, 76, 260
Bohemian, 18, 76, 108, 163, 227, 231, 323, 526
Bohemian hops, 18, 76, 227
bottled beer, 27, 56, 59, 60, 61, 62, 89, 103, 113, 138, 186, 199, 212, 273, 385, 431, 444, 523, 536
bottom-fermenting, 52, 60, 152
British beer, 13, 49, 53, 54, 59, 64, 65, 69, 71, 144, 149, 180, 350, 415
British Lager, 152
Brown Ale, 3, 88, 89
brown malt, 17, 117, 124, 130, 135, 162, 164, 169, 200, 203, 204, 218, 219, 220, 221, 222, 223, 266, 268, 272, 273, 274, 276, 277, 280, 281, 284, 285, 286, 288, 291, 292, 300, 356, 357,

362, 363, 367, 371, 374, 375, 385, 392, 393, 396, 401, 402, 408, 412, 416, 417, 428, 429, 487, 488, 489, 490, 491, 492, 493, 506, 510, 511, 512, 515, 516, 517, 522, 523, 524, 525, 550
Brown Stout, 123, 162, 163, 183, 220, 357, 363, 367, 374
Budweiser, 153
Burton, 4, 9, 22, 62, 69, 70, 71, 85, 90, 91, 105, 108, 113, 114, 115, 138, 139, 140, 141, 142, 143, 144, 145, 146, 147, 149, 151, 152, 172, 188, 193, 195, 208, 215, 216, 222, 264, 268, 271, 282, 293, 294, 299, 344, 352, 358, 380, 390, 391, 399, 407, 409, 411, 418, 426, 435, 436, 438, 439, 440, 441, 442, 443, 444, 445, 448, 449, 450, 451, 452, 457, 459, 466, 467, 475, 477, 482, 485, 495, 498, 499, 523, 526, 527, 529, 544, 546, 564
Burton Ale, 4, 70, 138, 139, 140, 141, 142, 143, 144, 149, 188, 195, 208, 216, 222, 264, 268, 271, 358, 390, 391, 399, 407, 411, 418, 435, 440, 441, 443, 444, 445, 449, 450, 452, 457, 459, 466, 485, 495, 499, 526
Calder, 136
Californian, 16, 17, 76, 99, 110, 111, 153, 156,

166, 172, 225, 227, 228, 229, 231, 232, 235, 236, 237, 239, 241, 242, 243, 245, 246, 247, 248, 249, 252, 253, 256, 259, 276, 278, 282, 288, 289, 290, 291, 293, 328, 329, 347, 389, 395, 400, 409, 416, 514, 521, 526
Canada, 64, 65
Cannon, 84, 100, 114, 118, 141
caramel, 20, 75, 86, 98, 99, 112, 117, 126, 131, 134, 135, 139, 145, 158, 159, 165, 167, 170, 171, 174, 175, 177, 178, 179, 180, 184, 188, 190, 195, 196, 197, 200, 203, 204, 208, 209, 210, 211, 212, 213, 215, 216, 217, 219, 223, 230, 238, 245, 253, 259, 263, 266,268, 276, 277, 280, 281, 284, 285, 286, 288, 291, 292, 300, 301, 302, 308, 309, 312, 313, 314, 317, 329, 330, 331, 332, 333, 334, 335, 336, 338, 340, 346, 351, 354, 355, 356, 357, 358, 359, 361, 362, 363, 365, 366, 367, 368, 369, 370, 371, 372, 373, 374, 375, 376, 377, 378, 379, 380, 381, 382, 383, 384, 385, 386, 391, 392, 393, 394, 395, 396, 398, 399, 400, 401, 402, 403, 404, 405, 406, 407, 408, 410, 411, 412, 413, 444, 483, 484, 538, 547, 548, 549, 550, 559,

560, 565, 566, 567
cask, 59, 61, 199, 216, 225, 231, 354, 499, 550, 576, 581
Castle Brewery, 102
Charrington, 84, 89, 100, 129, 141
Chiswell Street, 485, 498
City of London, 84, 89, 100, 118, 141, 485
Cluster, 156, 158, 159, 161, 162, 164, 165, 166, 167, 168, 169, 170, 171, 172, 173, 174, 175, 176, 177, 178, 179, 180, 188, 195, 208, 209, 210, 211, 212, 213, 215, 218, 219, 220, 221, 222, 226, 227, 228, 230, 231, 232, 233, 234, 235, 237, 238, 239, 240, 241, 242,243, 244, 246, 247, 248, 249, 250, 251, 252, 253, 254, 256, 257, 258, 260, 261, 262, 263, 271, 276, 277, 278, 282, 288, 289, 290, 291, 292, 293, 295, 296, 297, 298, 299, 300, 301, 302, 303, 304, 305, 308, 309, 310, 311, 313, 314, 315, 317, 318, 320, 328, 329, 347, 348, 349, 350, 351, 354, 355, 358, 379, 380, 381, 382, 383, 384, 385, 386, 413, 416, 417, 421, 422, 423, 424, 425, 428, 429, 430, 431, 432, 433, 438, 439, 440, 441, 442, 443, 444, 445, 446, 448, 449, 458, 466, 467, 476, 477, 480, 481, 482, 483, 484, 494, 510, 511, 512,

515, 516, 517, 518,
519, 520, 521, 522,
523, 524, 525, 526,
529, 530, 531, 532,
533, 534, 535, 536,
537, 538, 539, 540,
541, 542, 543, 544,
545, 546, 547, 548,
549, 550, 551, 552,
553, 554, 555, 556,
557, 558, 559, 560,
561, 562, 563, 564,
565, 566, 567
Combe, 89
Country, 48, 65, 66, 517
Courage, 6, 7, 73, 74, 75,
76, 77, 79, 83, 84, 100,
116, 117, 118, 120,
122, 124, 128, 129,
138, 139, 140, 141,
181, 182, 264, 265,
266, 267, 268, 269,
270, 271, 272, 273,
274, 275, 276, 277,
278, 279, 280, 281,
282, 283, 284, 285,
286, 287, 288, 289,
290, 291, 292, 293,
356, 387, 388, 389,
414
crystal malt, 16, 18, 75,
78, 82, 85, 130, 135,
139, 142, 159, 165,
167, 170, 171, 174,
175, 178, 180, 188,
195, 196, 197, 200,
208, 209, 210, 215,
216, 220, 221, 223,
265, 270, 275, 279,
283, 287, 289, 290,
293, 351, 379, 388,
389, 390, 392, 393,
394, 396, 400, 401,
402, 403, 404, 406,
407, 408, 410, 412,
416, 417, 418, 476,
478, 479, 480, 481,
482, 483, 484, 499,
547, 548, 549, 550,
559, 565, 566

Czechoslovakia, 64, 66
D.O.R.A., 42
Dalkeith, 150
Dark Mild, 86, 184, 338,
391, 476, 496
decoction, 153, 189
Denmark, 3, 48, 56, 57,
58, 59, 60, 63, 64, 65,
152, 153, 189
Derek Prentice, 480
Deuchar, 104
Double Stout, 4, 6, 7, 9,
120, 122, 123, 124,
131, 133, 163, 164,
169, 173, 175, 177,
229, 265, 267, 268,
273, 277, 281, 285,
286, 292, 417, 492
draught Porter, 356, 385,
428
draught Stout, 118, 220,
525
Dry Stout, 173
Drybrough, 7, 8, 82, 83,
92, 97, 98, 112, 121,
126, 127, 134, 135,
136, 321, 322, 323,
324, 325, 326, 327,
328, 329, 330, 331,
332, 333, 334, 335,
336, 337, 338, 339,
340, 341, 342, 343,
344, 345, 346, 347,
348, 349, 350, 351,
459
Duddingston, 321
Dundee, 39, 151
Duty, 25, 26, 36, 47
Earp, 490, 495, 496, 497
Edinburgh, 71, 80, 114,
151, 321, 323, 324,
325, 326, 327, 328,
329, 330, 331, 332,
333, 334, 335, 336,
337, 338, 339, 340,
341, 342, 343, 344,
345, 346, 347, 348,
349, 350, 351, 426,
527, 529, 530, 531,
532, 533, 534, 535,

536, 537, 538, 539,
540, 541, 542, 543,
544, 545, 546, 547,
548, 549, 550, 551,
552, 553, 554, 555,
556, 557, 558, 559,
560, 561, 562, 563,
564, 565, 566, 567
Edinburgh Ale, 323, 324,
325, 326, 327, 328,
329, 330, 331, 332,
333, 334, 335, 336,
337, 338, 339, 340,
341, 342, 343, 344,
345, 346, 347, 348,
349, 350, 351, 529,
530, 531, 532, 533,
534, 535, 536, 537,
538, 539, 540, 541,
542, 543, 544, 545,
546, 547, 548, 549,
550,551, 552, 553,
554, 555, 556, 557,
558, 559, 560, 561,
562, 563, 564, 565,
566, 567
Edwardian, 42, 271, 438
England, 15, 24, 38, 43,
47, 71, 77, 80, 84, 86,
91, 92, 95, 101, 108,
113, 122, 127, 130,
131, 133, 134, 143,
149, 150, 162, 181,
297, 323, 325, 326,
347, 428, 544, 547,
558, 588, 591
English Mild, 73, 82, 537
ES, 10, 58, 119, 129, 488,
489, 490, 491, 550
Export, 5, 10, 11, 12, 54,
57, 93, 115, 128, 131,
223, 491, 492, 533,
534, 555, 556, 564
Extra Stout, 69, 71, 93,
127, 128, 131, 136,
137, 490, 491
flaked barley, 22
flaked oats, 300, 301
Food Control, 12, 17, 25,
26, 30, 31, 32, 51, 124,

569, 570, 571, 572,
573, 574, 575, 576,
577, 578, 579, 580,
581, 582, 583, 584,
585, 586, 587, 588,
589, 590, 591, 592,
593, 594, 595
Food Controller, 25, 26,
30, 31, 32, 51, 569,
570, 571, 572, 573,
574, 575, 576, 577,
578, 579, 580, 581,
582, 583, 584, 585,
586, 587, 588, 589,
590, 591, 592, 593,
594, 595
Foreign Extra Stout, 127,
128, 137, 351
Fowler, 149, 150, 476,
477, 480, 483
France, 3, 18, 23, 48, 49,
64, 65, 66, 67, 411
Free Mash Tun Act, 19
Fuggle, 324
Fuggles, 156, 158, 161,
164, 165, 166, 167,
168, 169, 170, 171,
172, 173, 174, 175,
176, 177, 178, 179,
180, 184, 185, 186,
187, 188, 189, 190,
191, 192, 193, 194,
195, 196, 197, 198,
199, 200, 201, 202,
203, 204, 205, 206,
207, 208, 209, 210,
211, 212, 213,
214, 215, 216, 218,
219, 220, 221, 222,
223, 226, 227, 228,
230, 231, 232, 233,
234, 235, 236, 237,
238, 239, 240, 241,
242, 243, 244, 245,
246, 247, 248, 249,
250, 251, 252, 253,
254, 255, 256, 257,
258, 259, 260, 261,
262, 270, 271, 272,
273, 274, 275, 276,

277, 278, 279, 280,
281, 282, 283, 284,
285, 286, 287, 288,
289, 290, 291, 292,
293, 295, 296, 297,
298, 299, 300, 301,
302, 303, 304, 305,
306, 307, 308, 309,
310, 311, 312, 313,
314, 315, 317, 318,
320, 323, 324, 325,
326, 327, 328, 329,
330, 331, 332, 333,
334, 335, 336, 337,
338, 339, 340, 341,
342, 343, 344, 345,
346, 351, 353, 354,
355, 356, 357, 358,
359, 360, 361, 362,
363, 364, 365, 366,
367, 368, 369, 370,
371, 372, 373, 374,
375, 379, 380, 381,
382, 383, 384, 385,
386, 388, 389, 390,
391, 392, 393, 394,
395, 396, 398, 400,
402, 406, 407, 408,
410, 411, 412, 413,
415, 416, 417, 418,
421, 422, 423, 424,
425, 426, 427, 428,
429, 430, 431, 432,
433, 434, 438, 439,
440, 441, 442, 443,
444, 445, 446, 447,
449, 450, 451, 452,
453, 454, 455, 456,
457, 458, 459, 460,
461, 462, 463, 464,
465, 466, 467, 469,
470, 471, 472, 473,
474, 476, 477, 478,
479, 480, 481, 482,
483, 484, 488, 489,
490, 492, 493, 494,
499, 500, 501, 502,
506, 507, 509, 510,
511, 512, 515, 516,
517, 518, 519, 520,

526, 529, 530, 531,
532, 533, 534, 535,
536, 537, 538, 539,
540, 541, 542, 543,
544, 545, 546, 547,
548, 549, 550, 551,
552, 553, 554, 555,
556, 557, 558, 559,
560, 561, 562, 563,
564, 565, 566, 567
Fuller, 13, 70, 90, 116,
118, 120, 138, 140,
215, 356, 365, 376,
382, 385, 386
Germany, 3, 48, 49, 50,
51, 52, 53, 54, 61, 62,
63, 64, 65, 66, 76, 111,
151, 178, 189, 209
Glasgow, 23, 71, 151
glucose, 21, 75, 78, 95,
96, 98, 99, 131, 142,
145, 148, 185, 186,
191, 193, 194, 268,
287, 341, 353, 354,
355, 356, 357, 358,
359, 360, 361, 362,
368, 369, 370, 371,
372, 373, 374, 376,
377, 378, 379, 380,
381, 382, 383, 384,
395, 398, 405, 409,
413, 447, 450, 451,
452, 453, 454, 455,
456, 457, 458, 459,
460, 461, 462, 478,
479, 480, 481, 538,
539, 540, 541, 545,
547, 548, 549, 596
Gold Label, 146
Goldings, 108, 156, 158,
159, 161, 162, 164,
165, 166, 173, 177,
179, 180, 184, 185,
186, 187, 188, 191,
193, 194, 195, 198,
200, 201, 202, 205,
214, 215, 216, 223,
227, 242, 243, 260,
261, 262, 270, 274,
282, 295, 296, 297,

Mini Book Series volume XXXII: Armistice!

298, 299, 302, 303,
304, 305, 306,
307, 308, 309, 310,
311, 312, 313, 314,
315, 316, 317, 318,
319, 320, 323, 324,
325, 326, 327, 328,
329, 330, 331, 332,
333, 334, 335, 336,
337, 338, 339, 340,
341, 342, 343, 344,
345, 346, 347, 348,
349, 350, 351, 353,
354, 355, 356, 357,
358, 359, 360, 361,
362, 363, 364, 365,
366, 367, 368, 369,
370, 371, 372, 373,
374, 375, 376, 377,
378, 379, 380, 381,
382, 383, 384, 385,
386, 388, 389, 390,
391, 392, 393, 394,
395, 398, 399, 400,
401, 403, 404, 405,
406, 407, 409, 410,
412, 413, 415, 418,
426, 427, 434, 438,
439, 440, 441, 442,
443, 444, 445, 446,
447, 448, 449, 450,
451, 452, 453, 454,
455, 456, 457, 458,
459, 460, 461, 462,
463, 464, 465, 466,
467, 468, 469, 470,
471, 472, 473, 474,
478, 479, 480, 488,
489, 490, 491, 492,
493, 495, 496, 497,
498, 499, 500, 501,
503, 504, 505, 506,
510, 511, 512, 513,
514, 517, 518, 519,
520, 521, 522, 523,
526, 529, 530, 531,
532, 533, 534, 535,
536, 537, 541, 542,
543, 544, 545, 546,
549, 550, 551, 552,

553, 554, 555, 556,
557, 558, 561, 562,
563, 564, 567
Gordon & Blair, 103
Gourvish, 33, 101
Government Ale, 3, 10,
  28, 29, 73, 83, 197,
  200, 210, 368, 406,
  480, 483, 484, 507,
  577, 582
Guinness, 69, 71, 92,
  127, 136, 137, 152,
  181, 222, 351, 420,
  475
Guinness Extra Stout, 69,
  71, 93, 127
Guinness Foreign Extra
  Stout, 351
Guinness Porter, 69, 71
Hallertau, 76, 184, 270,
  272, 273, 274, 356
Hoare, 84, 100, 118, 129,
  141
Holland, 2, 3, 62, 63,
  152, 153, 189
Holyrood, 92, 527, 532
Holyrood Brewery, 527,
  532
Home Brewed, 144
hops, 18, 19, 20, 35, 49,
  64, 65, 66, 72, 73, 74,
  75, 76, 77, 79, 81, 82,
  83, 85, 90, 91, 92, 94,
  96, 97, 98, 100, 106,
  107, 108, 109, 110,
  111, 112, 116, 117,
  118, 120, 121, 122,
  123, 125, 127, 129,
  130, 134, 138, 139,
  140, 142, 143, 145,
  147, 148, 153, 156,
  157, 158, 159, 161,
  163, 164, 165, 166,
  167, 168, 170, 171,
  172, 173, 174, 175,
  176, 177, 178, 179,
  180, 181, 182, 184,
  185, 186, 187, 188,
  189, 190, 191, 193,
  194, 195, 196, 198,

200, 201, 203, 205,
208, 209, 210, 211,
214, 215, 216, 217,
218, 219, 220, 221,
222, 223, 224, 225,
226, 227, 228, 229,
231, 232, 233, 234,
235, 236, 237, 239,
240, 241, 242, 243,
244, 245, 246, 247,
248, 249, 250, 251,
252, 253, 254, 255,
256, 257, 258, 259,
260, 261, 262, 263,
264, 266, 267, 268,
269, 270, 271, 274,
275, 276, 278, 279,
280, 282, 283, 284,
285, 287, 288, 289,
290, 291, 293, 294,
295, 296, 297, 298,
299, 300, 302, 303,
304, 305, 306, 307,
308, 309, 310, 312,
313, 315, 316, 317,
318, 319, 320, 321,
324, 326, 328, 329,
330, 331, 332, 333,
334, 336, 337, 338,
339, 340, 341, 342,
343, 344, 345, 346,
347, 348, 349, 350,
352, 353, 354, 355,
356, 358, 359, 360,
361, 362, 364, 365,
366, 367, 368, 369,
370, 371, 372, 374,
375, 376, 377, 378,
379, 380, 382, 383,
384, 387, 388, 389,
390, 391, 392, 393,
394, 395, 397, 398,
399, 400, 402, 403,
404, 405, 406, 407,
408, 409, 410, 411,
412, 413, 415, 416,
418, 419, 421, 423,
424, 426, 427, 428,
430, 432, 434, 435,
438, 439, 441, 442,

Mini Book Series volume XXXII: Armistice!

447, 448, 449, 450,
451, 452, 453, 455,
457, 458, 459, 460,
462, 463, 466, 467,
468, 469, 472, 473,
476, 477, 478, 479,
480, 481, 482, 483,
489, 490, 491, 492,
494, 495, 496, 497,
498, 499, 500, 501,
502, 503, 504, 505,
506, 507, 513, 514,
515, 516, 518, 520,
521, 522, 524, 526,
527, 528, 529, 530,
531, 532, 533, 534,
535, 536, 537, 541,
542, 543, 544, 545,
546, 547, 548, 549,
550, 551, 552, 553,
554, 555, 556, 557,
558, 559, 560, 561,
562, 563, 564, 565,
567, 593
Imperial Stout, 6, 11, 70,
120, 122, 131, 136,
265, 267, 271, 273,
274, 277, 516
India, 21, 64, 65, 114,
426, 535, 594
India Pale Ale, 426
invert sugar, 20, 21, 75,
95, 112, 117, 142, 145,
161, 162, 164, 165,
166, 167, 168, 169,
170, 171, 172, 173,
174, 175, 176, 177,
179, 180, 184, 185,
186, 187, 188, 190,
191, 192, 193, 194,
195, 196, 197, 198,
199, 200, 201, 202,
203, 204, 205, 206,
207, 208, 209, 210,
211, 212, 213, 214,
215, 216, 218, 219,
221, 223, 226, 227,
228, 230, 231, 232,
233, 234, 235, 236,
237, 238, 239, 240,
241, 242, 243, 244,
245, 246, 247, 248,
249, 250, 251, 252,
253, 254, 255, 256,
257, 258, 259, 260,
261, 262, 263, 270,
271, 272, 273, 274,
275, 276, 277, 278,
279, 280, 281, 282,
283, 284, 285, 286,
289, 290, 291, 292,
293, 295, 296, 297,
298, 299, 302, 303,
304, 305, 306, 307,
310, 311, 312, 319,
320, 323, 324, 325,
326, 327, 328, 329,
330, 331, 332, 333,
334, 336, 337, 338,
339, 340, 341, 342,
343, 344, 345, 346,
347, 348, 349, 350,
351, 353, 354, 355,
356, 357, 358, 359,
360, 361, 362, 363,
367, 368, 369, 370,
371, 376, 377, 378,
382, 383, 384, 385,
386, 388, 389, 390,
391, 392, 393, 394,
395, 396, 400, 401,
402, 403, 404, 405,
406, 407, 408, 410,
411, 412, 413, 415,
416, 417, 418, 421,
422, 426, 427, 430,
432, 434, 438, 439,
440, 441, 442, 443,
444, 445, 446, 447,
448, 458, 463, 464,
465, 466, 467, 468,
469, 470, 471, 472,
473, 474, 476, 477,
478, 479, 480, 481,
482, 483, 484, 488,
489, 490, 491, 492,
493, 494, 495, 496,
497, 498, 499, 500,
501, 502, 503, 504,
505, 506, 507, 508,
509, 510, 511, 512,
513, 514, 515, 516,
517, 518, 519, 520,
521, 522, 523, 524,
525, 526, 541, 545,
546, 547, 548, 549,
550
IPA, 4, 10, 11, 58, 90, 91,
93, 100, 105, 106, 107,
108, 109, 111, 112,
113, 114, 115, 144,
172, 179, 224, 233,
321, 322, 448, 485,
488, 495, 496, 503,
504, 508, 513, 514,
520, 521
Ireland, 15, 26, 28, 31,
71, 92, 121, 122, 127,
136, 137, 397, 577,
579, 583, 584, 588
Irish Stout, 222
Jeffrey, 104, 149, 150
K Ales, 138
Keeping, 452, 542
keg, 467
KK, 5, 6, 11, 58, 69, 71,
138, 140, 141, 181,
182, 188, 195, 208,
215, 216, 268, 269,
278, 282, 293, 391,
418, 485, 495, 499,
500, 526
KKK, 11, 58, 138, 140,
181, 182, 216, 485,
495, 500, 501, 505
KKKK, 138, 271
Kräusen, 222
Lager, 4, 5, 57, 60, 62,
63, 70, 71, 151, 152,
153, 154, 181, 189
Leeds, 39, 41, 199, 419
Leith, 527
Light Ale, 69, 71, 199,
520, 534
Light Bitter, 88, 96, 101,
161, 311, 323, 415
Light Mild, 326
Lloyd George, 23, 24, 36
London, 10, 17, 20, 21,
23, 24, 25, 35, 36, 37,

608

38, 41, 42, 43, 44, 45,
46, 58, 60, 69, 70, 71,
72, 73, 74, 75, 76, 77,
78, 80, 81, 83, 84, 85,
86, 88, 89, 90, 91, 93,
94, 95, 99, 100, 101,
102, 103, 105, 106,
107, 108, 111, 112,
113, 114, 115, 116,
117, 118, 119, 120,
121, 122, 123, 125,
127, 128, 129, 130,
131, 132, 133, 134,
135, 136, 137, 138,
139, 140, 141, 143,
144, 145, 146, 149,
150, 151, 152, 153,
157, 158, 162, 163,
167, 178, 179, 181,
182, 183, 184, 187,
188, 189, 193, 219,
220, 225, 226, 227,
228, 230, 231, 232,
233, 234, 235, 236,
237, 238, 239, 240,
241, 242, 243, 244,
245, 246, 247, 248,
249, 250, 251, 252,
253, 254, 255, 256,
257, 258, 259, 260,
261, 262, 263, 264,
265, 266, 267, 268,
269, 270, 271, 272,
274, 283, 288, 290,
291, 300, 301, 308,
320, 324, 333, 344,
352, 353, 354, 355,
356, 357, 358, 359,
360, 361, 362, 363,
364, 365, 366, 367,
368, 369, 370, 371,
372, 373, 374, 375,
376, 377, 378, 379,
380, 381, 382, 383,
384, 385, 386, 387,
388, 389, 391, 392,
407, 414, 416, 417,
418, 419, 422, 425,
428, 429, 435, 436,
438, 439, 440, 441,
442, 443, 444, 445,
446, 447, 448, 449,
450, 451, 452, 453,
454, 455, 456, 457,
458, 459, 460, 461,
462, 463, 464, 465,
466, 467, 468, 469,
470, 471, 472, 473,
474, 475, 476, 477,
478, 479, 481, 482,
483, 484, 485, 488,
489, 490, 491, 494,
495, 498, 506, 508,
516, 517, 522, 524,
525, 530, 536, 537,
542, 546, 550, 567,
587
London Metropolitan
 Archive, 17, 20, 21,
 58, 60, 73, 74, 75, 76,
 83, 84, 85, 86, 89, 90,
 91, 93, 94, 95, 100,
 101, 102, 103, 106,
 107, 108, 113, 114,
 115, 116, 117, 118,
 119, 120, 122, 127,
 129, 130, 131, 132,
 133, 134, 136, 137,
 138, 139, 140, 141,
 144, 145, 146, 149,
 150, 153, 181, 182,
 233, 264, 265, 266,
 267, 268, 269, 387,
 488, 491, 494, 495,
 498, 508
London Porter, 116, 118,
 120, 121, 125, 162,
 291, 300, 392, 488,
 489, 490
London Stout, 120, 128,
 129, 135, 219, 263,
 488, 489, 490, 516,
 517, 522, 524, 525,
 550
Löwenbräu, 54
MA, 11, 58, 73, 83, 84,
 87, 210, 508, 510, 511,
 512, 518, 519
Mackay, 87, 104
Mackeson, 120
Maclay, 73, 92, 120, 121,
 147
Maize, 22, 591
malt, 16, 17, 20, 30, 31,
 49, 52, 62, 153, 266,
 268, 269, 485, 487,
 585, 586, 588, 589,
 600
Malt, 3, 12, 16, 30, 31,
 51, 86, 120, 124, 133,
 173, 431, 433, 585,
 586, 589, 590, 591,
 592
maltose, 302
Mann, 84, 88, 89, 100,
 118, 129, 141, 146
Martyn Cornell, 527
Märzen, 54
Mauritius, 21, 124, 177
McEwan, 103, 104, 115,
 136, 149, 150, 527,
 553
Midlands, 131
Mild, 1, 3, 7, 12, 16, 20,
 22, 23, 25, 33, 35, 37,
 38, 58, 59, 60, 70, 72,
 73, 74, 77, 78, 79, 80,
 81, 82, 83, 84, 85, 86,
 87, 89, 95, 99, 109,
 116, 138, 141, 143,
 152, 157, 158, 159,
 160, 162, 163, 167,
 168, 169, 175, 178,
 180, 181, 182, 184,
 187, 197, 201, 203,
 205, 209, 210, 215,
 222, 224, 225, 227,
 228, 232, 235, 236,
 237, 244, 247, 249,
 260, 261, 262, 264,
 265, 270, 271, 275,
 283, 290, 293, 296,
 304, 321, 323, 326,
 328, 329, 334, 335,
 338, 347, 352, 353,
 373, 376, 379, 380,
 381, 387, 389, 390,
 391, 394, 403, 406,
 419, 421, 422, 423,
 424, 426, 431, 432,

435, 439, 440, 441, 443, 444, 445, 446, 452, 454, 459, 460, 463, 465, 471, 472, 474, 476, 477, 478, 479, 480, 481, 485, 487, 494, 496, 501, 502, 510, 518, 519, 527, 528, 537, 539, 540, 542, 543, 558, 567
Mild Ale, 3, 16, 20, 59, 70, 72, 73, 74, 77, 79, 80, 81, 82, 83, 84, 85, 86, 95, 138, 141, 143, 157, 158, 162, 167, 168, 180, 184, 197, 201, 203, 209, 210, 215, 222, 225, 228, 235, 244, 247, 249, 270, 271, 290, 296, 304, 321, 323, 326, 328, 329, 334, 347, 353, 373, 376, 389, 390, 419, 421, 422, 424, 426, 431, 440, 441, 443, 444, 445, 446, 452, 454, 459, 460, 465, 472, 477, 478, 510, 518, 537, 539, 543
mild malt, 17, 96, 124, 130, 142, 153, 158, 159, 162, 163, 164, 165, 167, 169, 170, 171, 172, 173, 174, 175, 176, 177, 178, 180, 188, 191, 192, 194, 195, 198, 205, 206, 207, 208, 210, 211, 215, 216, 217, 218, 219, 220, 221, 222, 223, 421, 422, 423, 424, 425, 427, 428, 429, 430, 431, 432, 433, 434
Mitchell & Butler, 131
Münchner, 153
Munich, 50, 52, 53, 57, 60, 71, 151, 153, 229,
441
Murphy, 121, 136
Murray, 87, 103, 104, 149, 150
Napoleonic Wars, 35
New Zealand, 64, 65, 330, 333
No.1 invert, 415, 434
No.2 invert, 410
No.3 invert, 259, 270, 400, 541, 543
Oatmeal Stout, 20, 116, 120, 131, 132, 133, 217, 300, 308, 356, 386, 392, 396, 401, 489, 506, 524, 525
oats, 22, 116, 120, 132, 217, 218, 300, 301, 308, 309, 386, 392, 393, 396, 401, 488, 489, 506, 524, 525, 586
Old Ale, 4, 83, 138, 141, 142, 143, 144, 157, 165, 180, 446
PA, 4, 5, 8, 9, 11, 17, 20, 33, 58, 90, 91, 92, 93, 94, 95, 96, 100, 102, 103, 104, 105, 106, 107, 114, 157, 166, 172, 175, 176, 179, 181, 182, 187, 194, 211, 214, 217, 224, 232, 233, 322, 350, 352, 353, 354, 355, 361, 366, 370, 371, 377, 378, 382, 383, 384, 387, 409, 413, 419, 426, 427, 434, 485, 491, 496, 497, 498, 499, 504, 514, 520, 521
PA malt, 17, 95, 107, 194, 214, 217, 496, 514, 520
Pale Ale, 4, 16, 18, 37, 38, 58, 69, 70, 71, 74, 80, 86, 90, 91, 92, 93, 94, 95, 96, 97, 99, 100, 101, 102, 103, 104,
105, 108, 111, 112, 113, 127, 134, 144, 149, 157, 161, 166, 172, 181, 182, 187, 191, 193, 194, 199, 202, 205, 211, 214, 222, 223, 224, 231, 232, 233, 242, 243, 248, 252, 264, 270, 271, 294, 295, 296, 297, 299, 304, 306, 307, 311, 312, 316, 321, 322, 323, 324, 325, 326, 327, 328, 330, 332, 333, 334, 336, 337, 338, 339, 341, 342, 344, 345, 346, 347, 348, 349, 350, 351, 352, 354, 361, 370, 377, 378, 384, 387, 403, 409, 419, 426, 427, 431, 434, 435, 437, 438, 439, 441, 444, 448, 450, 451, 452, 459, 467, 479, 482, 485, 491, 495, 496, 497, 498, 499, 501, 514, 520, 523, 527, 528, 529, 530, 532, 533, 534, 536, 537, 539, 551, 552, 555, 558, 564, 567
pale malt, 16, 17, 75, 78, 80, 82, 85, 95, 96, 98, 99, 107, 110, 112, 113, 117, 124, 126, 130, 135, 139, 142, 145, 148, 153, 158, 159, 161, 162, 163, 164, 165, 166, 167, 168, 169, 170, 171, 172, 173, 174, 175, 176, 177, 178, 179, 180, 184, 185, 186, 187, 188, 189, 190, 191, 192, 193, 194, 195, 196, 197, 198, 199, 200, 201, 202, 203, 204, 205, 206, 207,

Mini Book Series volume XXXII: Armistice!

208, 209, 210, 211,
212, 213, 214, 215,
217, 218, 222, 223,
225, 226, 227, 228,
229, 230, 231, 232,
233, 234, 235, 236,
237, 238, 239, 240,
241, 242, 243, 244,
245, 246, 247, 248,
249, 250, 251, 252,
253, 254, 255, 256,
257, 258, 259, 260,
261, 262, 263, 265,
266, 268, 269, 270,
271, 272, 273, 274,
275, 276, 277, 278,
279, 280, 281, 282,
283, 284, 285, 286,
287, 288, 289, 290,
291, 292, 293, 295,
296, 297, 298, 299,
300, 301, 302, 303,
304, 305, 306, 307,
308, 309, 310, 311,
312, 313, 314, 315,
316, 317, 318, 319,
320, 323, 324, 325,
326, 327, 328, 329,
330, 331, 332, 333,
334, 335, 336, 337,
338, 339, 340, 341,
342, 343, 344, 345,
346, 347, 348, 349,
350, 351, 353, 354,
355, 356, 357, 358,
359, 360, 361, 362,
363, 364, 365, 366,
367, 368, 369, 370,
371, 372, 373, 374,
375, 376, 377, 378,
379, 380, 381, 382,
383, 384, 385, 386,
388, 389, 390, 391,
392, 393, 394, 395,
396, 399, 400, 401,
402, 403, 404, 405,
406, 407, 408, 409,
410, 411, 412, 413,
415, 416, 417, 418,
421, 422, 423, 424,
425, 426, 427, 428,
429, 430, 431, 432,
433, 434, 438, 439,
440, 441, 442, 443,
444, 445, 446, 447,
448, 449, 450, 451,
452, 453, 454, 455,
456, 457, 458, 459,
460, 461, 462, 463,
464, 465, 466, 467,
468, 469, 470, 471,
472, 473, 474, 476,
477, 478, 479, 480,
481, 482, 483, 484,
488, 489, 490, 491,
492, 493, 494, 495,
496, 497, 498, 499,
500, 501, 502, 503,
504, 505, 506, 507,
509, 510, 511, 512,
513, 514, 515, 516,
517, 518, 519, 520,
521, 522, 523, 524,
525, 526, 529, 530,
531, 532, 533, 534,
535, 536, 537, 538,
539, 540, 541, 542,
543, 544, 545, 546,
547, 548, 549, 550,
551, 552, 553, 554,
555, 556, 557, 558,
559, 560, 561, 562,
563, 564, 565, 566,
567, 600
parti-gyle, 22, 81, 82, 99,
102, 117, 127, 132,
134, 139, 159, 160,
186, 192, 196, 199,
202, 204, 210, 212,
213, 215, 265, 267,
272, 273, 274, 277,
281, 284, 286, 292,
293, 295, 296, 297,
299, 303, 304, 305,
307, 308, 309, 311,
313, 314, 325, 327,
328, 329, 331, 332,
334, 335, 336, 338,
344, 345, 346, 348,
356, 363, 373, 377,
378, 380, 381, 383,
384, 393, 397, 401,
417, 422, 425, 427,
431, 433, 439, 445,
446, 447, 451, 454,
461, 464, 465, 470,
474, 479, 484, 488,
489, 492, 493, 498,
506, 511, 512, 516,
519, 524, 525, 539,
548, 566
parti-gyled, 81, 82, 99,
102, 117, 134, 139,
159, 186, 192, 196,
199, 202, 204, 210,
212, 215, 265, 267,
272, 273, 274, 281,
284, 286, 292, 293,
295, 296, 297, 299,
303, 304, 305, 307,
308, 311, 314, 325,
327, 328, 329, 331,
332, 334, 335, 338,
344, 345, 346, 348,
356, 363, 373, 377,
380, 381, 383, 401,
417, 422, 425, 427,
431, 433, 439, 445,
446, 447, 454, 461,
464, 465, 470, 474,
479, 484, 489, 492,
493, 498, 506, 512,
516, 519, 524, 539,
548, 566
parti-gyling, 83, 140,
160, 163, 351, 439,
527
Peter Mathias, 181
Pilsener, 57, 59, 60, 61,
63, 153
Pilsner Urquell, 55
police, 43, 44, 46, 55
Porter, 4, 6, 7, 8, 9, 16,
20, 25, 33, 38, 58, 69,
70, 71, 88, 95, 116,
117, 118, 119, 120,
123, 125, 128, 132,
137, 162, 163, 181,
182, 183, 203, 220,
222, 224, 229, 264,

611

265, 266, 267, 271,
272, 273, 274, 276,
277, 280, 281, 284,
286, 291, 292, 294,
300, 301, 308, 309,
313, 314, 320, 352,
356, 357, 362, 363,
367, 371, 375, 379,
385, 386, 387, 392,
393, 396, 399, 401,
402, 416, 417, 419,
428, 429, 435, 439,
448, 475, 477, 485,
486, 487, 488, 489,
490, 491, 501, 506,
515, 516, 517, 522,
523, 524, 525
Prussian, 50
Reinheitsgebot, 49
rice, 22, 50, 63, 185, 323,
324, 325, 326, 327,
415, 439
roast barley, 203, 204,
219, 220, 221, 222,
223, 274, 548, 549,
550, 559, 560, 565,
566
roast malt, 219
Royal Mile, 527
Runner, 116, 445
Running, 179, 439, 447,
449, 456, 457, 458,
466
Russian Stout, 181, 219
S, 5, 10, 11, 35, 44, 119,
120, 121, 123, 124,
129, 130, 131, 173,
217, 218, 220, 222,
278, 351, 386, 419,
442, 464, 465, 466,
469, 470, 471, 476,
487, 489, 517, 523,
525, 566
SA malt, 17, 188, 195,
208, 209, 216, 217,
219
Saaz, 76, 111, 164, 180,
214, 216, 218, 223,
227, 231, 260, 261,
262, 263, 290, 293,
526
Schenkbier, 54
Scotch Ale, 4, 99, 147,
148, 149, 150, 544,
546
Scotland, 15, 22, 23, 24,
71, 73, 74, 80, 86, 90,
91, 92, 97, 99, 102,
111, 114, 126, 134,
149, 150, 151, 323,
327, 335, 346, 347,
446, 541, 544, 545,
547, 558, 591
Scottish Mild, 73, 87
Shilling Ales, 147, 328,
537, 540, 541, 544,
545
Single Stout, 70, 229
Southwark, 415
SS, 10, 58, 120, 121, 229,
267, 487, 491, 492,
493, 516, 517
SSS, 10, 58, 120, 267,
487, 491, 492, 493,
516, 517
Steel Coulson, 103
Stingo, 144
Stock Ale, 58, 69, 90,
105, 138, 166, 172,
181, 188, 499, 500,
501, 504, 527, 542,
543
Stout, 4, 5, 6, 7, 8, 9, 10,
16, 20, 33, 37, 38, 57,
58, 61, 69, 70, 71, 88,
93, 116, 117, 118, 119,
120, 121, 122, 123,
124, 125, 126, 127,
128, 129, 130, 131,
132, 133, 134, 135,
136, 137, 140, 148,
152, 157, 162, 163,
164, 169, 172, 173,
175, 177, 178, 181,
182, 183, 203, 208,
217, 219, 220, 222,
224, 228, 229, 230,
232, 234, 238, 244,
245, 253, 255, 259,
263, 265, 267, 268,
271, 273, 274, 277,
281, 284, 285, 286,
288, 289, 291, 292,
294, 300, 301, 308,
309, 313, 314, 315,
316, 317, 319, 320,
321, 329, 336, 337,
340, 346, 351, 352,
356, 357, 363, 367,
374, 379, 385, 386,
387, 392, 393, 396,
401, 402, 408, 412,
417, 419, 420, 428,
429, 431, 485, 486,
487, 488, 489, 490,
491, 492, 493, 506,
516, 517, 522, 523,
524, 525, 527, 528,
547, 550, 560, 566
Strong Ale, 4, 17, 33,
102, 138, 142, 144,
147, 149, 150, 180,
182, 224, 234, 243,
262, 268, 269, 293,
352, 387, 391, 407,
439, 445, 447, 527,
528, 541, 544
sugar, 16, 19, 20, 21, 49,
63, 75, 78, 80, 82, 83,
85, 95, 96, 98, 99, 107,
110, 112, 113, 117,
124, 126, 131, 135,
139, 142, 145, 148,
156, 158, 159, 161,
162, 164, 165, 166,
167, 168, 169, 170,
171, 172, 173, 174,
175, 176, 177, 178,
179, 180, 184, 185,
186, 187, 188, 190,
191, 192, 193, 194,
195, 196, 197, 198,
199, 200, 201, 202,
203, 204, 205, 206,
207, 208, 209, 210,
211, 212, 213, 214,
215, 216, 217, 218,
219, 220, 221, 223,
225, 226, 227, 228,
229, 230, 231, 232,

233, 234, 235, 236,
237, 238, 239, 240,
241, 242, 243, 244,
245, 246, 247, 248,
249, 250, 251, 252,
253, 254, 255, 256,
257, 258, 259, 260,
261, 262, 263, 265,
266, 268, 269, 270,
271, 272, 273, 274,
275, 276, 277, 278,
279, 280, 281, 282,
283, 284, 285, 286,
287, 288, 289, 290,
291, 292, 293, 295,
296, 297, 298, 299,
300, 301, 302, 303,
304, 305, 306, 307,
308, 309, 310, 311,
312, 313, 314, 315,
319, 320, 323, 324,
325, 326, 327, 328,
329, 330, 331, 332,
333, 334, 335, 336,
337, 338, 339, 340,
341, 342, 343, 344,
345, 346, 347, 348,
349, 350, 351, 353,
354, 355, 356, 357,
358, 359, 360, 361,
362, 363, 364, 365,
367, 368, 369, 370,
371, 374, 375, 376,
377, 378, 382, 383,
384, 385, 386, 388,
389, 390, 391, 392,
393, 394, 395, 396,
397, 398, 399, 400,
401, 402, 403, 404,
405, 406, 407, 408,
409, 410, 411, 412,
413, 415, 416, 417,
418, 421, 422, 423,
424, 425, 426, 427,
428, 429, 430, 431,
432, 433, 434, 438,
439, 440, 441, 442,
443, 444, 445, 446,
447, 448, 449, 452,
455, 458, 463, 464,
465, 466, 467, 468,
469, 470, 471, 472,
473, 474, 476, 477,
478, 479, 480, 481,
482, 483, 484, 488,
489, 490, 491, 492,
493, 494, 495, 496,
497, 498, 499, 500,
501, 502, 503, 504,
505, 506, 507, 508,
509, 510, 511, 512,
513, 514, 515, 516,
517, 518, 519, 520,
521, 522, 523, 524,
525, 526, 541, 543,
545, 546, 547, 548,
549, 550, 594, 595,
596
taxation, 54, 138
Tennent, 71, 103, 104,
 136, 149, 151, 153
Tetley, 9, 91, 116, 121,
 144, 236, 419, 420,
 421, 422, 423, 424,
 425, 426, 427, 428,
 429, 430, 431, 432,
 433, 434, 496
Thomas Usher, 73, 80,
 81, 82, 87, 92, 102,
 103, 104, 113, 115,
 121, 132, 134, 135,
 136, 146, 147, 149,
 150
top-fermenting, 52, 61
Triple Stout, 493
Truman, 9, 10, 22, 33, 73,
 84, 85, 86, 89, 90, 91,
 100, 105, 116, 118,
 129, 131, 133, 134,
 141, 144, 145, 146,
 193, 268, 435, 436,
 437, 438, 439, 440,
 441, 442, 443, 444,
 445, 446, 447, 448,
 449, 450, 451, 452,
 453, 454, 455, 456,
 457, 458, 459, 460,
 461, 462, 463, 464,
 465, 466, 467, 468,
 469, 470, 471, 472,
473, 474, 475, 476,
 477, 478, 479, 480,
 481, 482, 483, 484,
 544
TT, 116, 118, 181, 182,
 183, 524
Twelve Guinea Ale, 150
underlet, 288, 289, 291,
 353, 354, 355, 356,
 358, 359, 360, 361,
 362, 364, 365, 367,
 368, 369, 371, 372,
 374, 376, 379, 381,
 383, 385
underletting, 153
United Kingdom, 15, 19,
 21, 569, 571, 579, 584,
 586, 595
United States, 62
USA, 18, 22, 64, 66, 70,
 153, 275
Usher, 73, 80, 81, 82, 87,
 92, 102, 103, 104, 113,
 115, 121, 132, 134,
 135, 136, 146, 147,
 149, 150
Victorian, 439
Vienna, 55
Vollbier, 54
Wahl & Henius, 70, 105
Wales, 38, 47, 591, 597
Warwicks &
 Richardsons, 72, 91,
 121
Watney, 5, 84, 89, 100,
 118, 129, 141, 193,
 294, 321, 475
Wee Heavy, 150
Weissbier, 52
Wenlock, 84, 100, 118,
 129, 141
West Indies, 21
wheat, 55, 586
Whitbread, 10, 11, 20,
 33, 39, 40, 57, 58, 60,
 62, 73, 83, 84, 86, 89,
 90, 93, 94, 95, 100,
 101, 102, 103, 105,
 106, 107, 108, 109,
 113, 114, 115, 116,

118, 119, 120, 127, 129, 130, 131, 132, 133, 134, 136, 137, 138, 140, 141, 144, 146, 149, 150, 151, 162, 184, 185, 186, 187, 188, 190, 191, 192, 193, 194, 195, 196, 197, 198, 199, 200, 201, 202, 203, 204, 205, 206, 207, 208, 209, 210, 211, 212, 213, 214, 215, 216, 218, 219, 220, 221, 222, 223, 229, 233, 265, 267, 270, 271, 272, 273, 274, 275, 276, 277, 278, 279, 280, 281, 282, 283, 284, 285, 286, 287, 288, 289, 290, 291, 292, 293, 295, 300, 319, 324, 327, 352, 356, 387, 388, 389, 390, 391, 392, 393, 394, 395, 396, 397, 398, 399, 400, 401, 402, 403, 404, 405, 406, 407, 408, 409, 410, 411, 412, 413, 415, 416, 417, 418, 435, 476, 477, 478, 479, 480, 481, 482, 483, 484, 485, 486, 487, 488, 489, 490, 491, 492, 493, 494, 495, 496, 497, 498, 499, 500, 501, 502, 503, 504, 505, 506, 507, 508, 509, 510, 511, 512, 513, 514, 515, 516, 517, 518, 519, 520, 521, 522, 523, 524, 525, 526, 542, 550
Whitbread Gravity Book, 33, 129, 524
William Younger, 11, 12, 22, 73, 92, 102, 111, 121, 134, 135, 147, 148, 150, 327, 346, 421, 527, 528, 529, 530, 531, 532, 533, 534, 535, 536, 537, 538, 539, 540, 541, 542, 543, 544, 545, 546, 547, 548, 549, 550, 551, 552, 553, 554, 555, 556, 557, 558, 559, 560, 561, 562, 563, 564, 565, 566, 567
WW I, 3, 4, 15, 16, 17, 19, 22, 32, 34, 35, 36, 37, 38, 39, 42, 48, 49, 54, 56, 58, 62, 64, 65, 66, 67, 70, 72, 73, 74, 77, 80, 83, 84, 85, 86, 87, 88, 89, 90, 91, 92, 93, 95, 97, 99, 100, 101, 102, 103, 104, 105, 108, 113, 114, 115, 116, 118, 120, 121, 122, 126, 128, 129, 130, 131, 132, 133, 134, 135, 136, 137, 138, 140, 141, 143, 144, 145, 147, 148, 149, 150, 151, 153, 159, 160, 161, 162, 180, 181, 182, 184, 186, 209, 210, 225, 227, 228, 231, 250, 254, 271, 283, 285, 321, 323, 325, 338, 348, 349, 350, 352, 358, 367, 373, 380, 384, 385, 388, 397, 399, 409, 425, 428, 431, 440, 444, 466, 469, 471, 476, 477, 480, 485, 486, 488, 490, 492, 493, 495, 499, 500, 512, 513, 521, 525, 536, 537, 552, 558, 564
WW II, 22, 34, 70, 74, 86, 137, 148, 209, 210, 254, 321, 348, 350, 352, 358, 373, 380, 385, 388, 409, 431, 466, 485, 521, 525, 537, 564
X, 4, 5, 6, 7, 8, 9, 10, 11, 22, 36, 37, 38, 58, 69, 72, 73, 74, 75, 76, 77, 78, 79, 83, 84, 86, 139, 157, 158, 159, 160, 161, 165, 167, 178, 180, 181, 182, 184, 190, 196, 197, 200, 203, 204, 205, 209, 210, 215, 225, 227, 264, 265, 270, 275, 276, 279, 283, 287, 288, 289, 290, 291, 292, 293, 324, 326, 327, 337, 339, 345, 352, 353, 354, 359, 364, 365, 368, 369, 370, 372, 373, 379, 380, 381, 384, 387, 389, 390, 394, 395, 399, 406, 410, 411, 418, 419, 421, 422, 423, 425, 430, 431, 432, 436, 443, 452, 459, 460, 461, 462, 469, 474, 476, 477, 478, 479, 480, 484, 485, 488, 494, 502, 503, 504, 507, 508, 518, 519, 527, 530, 542, 543
X Ale, 4, 5, 6, 7, 8, 38, 69, 72, 73, 74, 75, 77, 78, 83, 84, 139, 158, 159, 161, 165, 167, 180, 184, 190, 196, 197, 200, 203, 204, 205, 209, 210, 215, 225, 227, 264, 265, 270, 275, 276, 279, 283, 287, 288, 289, 290, 291, 292, 293, 324, 326, 327, 353, 354, 359, 364, 365, 368, 369, 370, 372, 373, 379, 380, 381, 384, 389, 394, 395,

406, 411, 425, 443,
469, 476, 477, 478,
479, 480, 484, 488,
494, 502, 504, 507,
508, 518, 519, 530,
542
XK, 8, 100, 352, 377,
382, 383, 384
XLK, 5, 90, 99, 100, 181,
182, 185, 186, 187,
191, 192, 193, 198,
199, 201, 202, 205,
206, 207, 211, 212,
213, 384, 439, 467,
479
XP, 7, 11, 12, 92, 105,
321, 327, 527, 528,
530, 531, 533, 552,
553, 558
XX, 4, 6, 8, 9, 10, 11, 22,
72, 73, 77, 78, 79, 80,
81, 82, 83, 85, 86, 126,
127, 138, 157, 159,
160, 167, 168, 170,
171, 174, 175, 176,
178, 179, 180, 184,
209, 224, 244, 247,
250, 251, 256, 257,
260, 261, 262, 268,
269, 271, 278, 321,
337, 340, 346, 352,
373, 381, 404, 418,
419, 424, 425, 427,
433, 436, 460, 463,
472, 474, 527, 528,
542
XXK, 73, 527
XXP, 11, 12, 92, 105,
527, 529, 530, 531,
533, 553, 558, 563
XXX, 5, 6, 7, 8, 9, 10, 22,
72, 73, 78, 83, 85, 91,
121, 140, 184, 224,
225, 226, 228, 235,
244, 246, 247, 321,
329, 336, 340, 351,
387, 407, 411, 418,
425, 436, 461, 463,
464, 465, 469, 470,
471, 472, 527, 528
XXXX, 4, 5, 9, 11, 72,
86, 144, 157, 160, 170,
171, 178, 180, 184,
387, 391, 399, 407,
411, 425, 527, 543
XXXXX, 72
Yorkshire, 39, 91, 116,
121, 419, 421, 422,
423, 424, 425, 426,
427, 428, 429, 430,
431, 432, 433, 434
Young, 86
Younger, 22, 73, 87, 92,
102, 103, 104, 105,
111, 113, 115, 121,
134, 135, 136, 146,
147, 148, 149, 150,
327, 346, 421, 527,
528, 529, 530, 531,
532, 533, 534, 535,
536, 537, 538, 539,
540, 541, 542, 543,
544, 545, 546, 547,
548, 549, 550, 551,
552, 553, 554, 555,
556, 557, 558, 559,
560, 561, 562, 563,
564, 565, 566, 567

www.ingramcontent.com/pod-product-compliance
Lightning Source LLC
Chambersburg PA
CBHW050131240426
43673CB00043B/1630